Eccentric Existence
Volume 1

Eccentric Existence:
A Theological Anthropology

Volume 1

David H. Kelsey

WESTMINSTER
JOHN KNOX PRESS
LOUISVILLE · KENTUCKY

© 2009 David H. Kelsey

First edition
Published by Westminster John Knox Press
Louisville, Kentucky

09 10 11 12 13 14 15 16 17 18 — 10 9 8 7 6 5 4 3 2 1

Book design by Drew Stevens
Cover design by Lisa Buckley

Library of Congress Cataloging-in-Publication Data

Kelsey, David H.
  Eccentric existence : a theological anthropology / David H. Kelsey.
    p. cm.
  Includes bibliographical references and index.
  ISBN 978-0-664-22052-5 (v. 1 : alk. paper) 1. Theological anthropology—Christianity. I.
Title.
  BT701.3.K46 2009
  233'.5—dc22

                                                                    2009006572

PRINTED IN THE UNITED STATES OF AMERICA

∞ The paper used in this publication meets the minimum requirements of the American National Standard for Information Sciences—Permanence of Paper for Printed Library Materials, ANSI Z39.48–1992.

Westminster John Knox Press advocates the responsible use of our natural resources. The text paper of this book is made from at least 30% post-consumer waste.

For Julie
sine qua non

Contents

Part Two
Consummated: Living on Borrowed Time

VOLUME 2

Part Three
Reconciled: Living by Another's Death

Codas

Acknowledgments

Theological anthropology has been on my mind most of my life as an academic theologian. After several false starts, this project in this form has been in process for a very long time. Partly that is because work on it has been interrupted periodically while I researched and wrote three other books. Mostly, however, it is because it seemed appropriate to proportion each of its three constituent parts on a large enough scale to do it justice, with the result that the whole is very long. Readers need to understand at the outset that, although each of its three parts (leaving aside its introductions and codas) can be read on its own, the three do constitute an interconnected, interdependent, and mutually reinforcing whole. The sense of the proposals made throughout this project, and the force of the arguments supporting them, rest equally on the three parts.

Roughly the first half of this project was drafted during a year's leave from Yale Divinity School funded by a grant from the Eli Lilly Endowment. I am deeply grateful for the warm support and encouragement of this project given by two successive vice presidents for religion at the Endowment, Dr. Robert Lynn and Dr. Craig Dykstra.

In the course of this long period I have accumulated personal and intellectual debts to more patient and perceptive readers than I shall be able to remember by name. Some acts of extraordinary supererogation must be thanked explicitly, however. Three times over a period of about eight years the annual doctoral seminar in theology—which includes all theology faculty in the Department of Religious Studies, Yale University, all theology doctoral students in "course of study," and often several doctoral students in philosophy of religion and religious ethics—read sections of the manuscript that were available at the time. The text is significantly clearer, the argument tighter, and the issues more nuanced because of their careful, probing, and friendly but firm discussion of what I had written. Subsequently I have profited from written and oral questioning of chapters 2A and 3A by Professor Christopher Beeley, of the introductions and parts 1 and 2 by Professors Fred Simmons and Edward Waggoner, and of part 3 (especially chapters 19A and B) by Professor Edwin vanDriel. I thank them all warmly, comfortable in the certainty that no one will charge them with whatever errors, confusions, or obscurities I exhibit in this project despite their best efforts to protect me from myself.

This theological meditation on what and who we are as God's human creatures, and how we ought to be oriented to our lived worlds, is dedicated to my wife, Julie Kelsey, without whose continuous encouraging enthusiasm for this project it would not have been written, and without whose continual expressions of impatience to have it done and out of the house it would never have been finished!

About Introductions

A book of theology really ought to have two types of introduction. The first should explain what the project of the book is, what questions it seeks to answer, and what its most important background assumptions are. It should give the reader a general orientation to what the author is up to. The second, more technical, introduction should be for readers who are interested in where the author stands on relevant methodological issues in academic theology. The first type of introduction is important and ought to be interesting. The second is as unavoidable as it is (often) tedious. I have provided both here, clearly distinguished and labeled, respectively, chapters 1A, 2A, and 3A and chapters 1B, 2B, and 3B. Indeed, through-out this book I aim to segregate the more technical, in-house-academic-theology discussions to "B" chapters that will follow up my constructive theological proposals in "A" chapters. They will be readily distinguishable because they are printed in different-sized typefaces.

Nearly all the wisdom we possess, that is to say, true and sound wisdom, consists of two parts: the knowledge of God and of ourselves. But, while joined by many bonds, which one precedes and which brings forth the other is not easy to discern.

JOHN CALVIN

CHAPTER **1 A**

The Questions

You are entitled to know at the outset whether a book addresses questions you—or anyone else—really ask. That is especially true of a book of theology that, as Paul Tillich insisted, is supposed to address questions that are of "ultimate concern" to their readers. The subject of this three-part project as a whole is what ancient Greeks called *anthropos*, human being.

But that doesn't yet tell you what its questions are. Whether the questions discussed here are of ultimate concern is another matter, but Gertrude Stein had it right. Framing the question correctly lies at the heart of the matter. Literary legend has it that when the American avant-garde writer lay on her deathbed and had been in apparent coma for several days, she suddenly sat bolt upright and called out to her companion Alice B. Toklas.

"Alice, Alice, what is the answer?"

Ever imperturbable, Miss Toklas, who had been nursing her through her final illness, answered in her most soothing tone, "I don't know, Gertrude. I don't know what the answer is."

"Well then," Stein demanded sternly, "what is the question?"

And with that, she lay back and died.

Questions raised at the point of death about what it is to be human clearly have some claim to be of ultimate concern. However, questions like "What is human being?" and "What is human nature?" are too broad to be discussed easily. In the literature of anthropological reflection they tend to be divided into three subordinate types of question. Call them the "what," the "how," and the "who" questions:

1. *What* are we? Is there a human essence? Is there a set of attributes exhibited by all human persons no matter how different their location by race, gender, ethnicity, culture, and history? Is there a set of attributes

that are singly necessary and collectively sufficient for any individual who exhibits them to count as a "human being"? If so, what is it? This set of questions is best understood as a set of metaphysical questions.

2. *How* ought we to be? What ought to be our fundamental orientation in life: our most basic dispositions, attitudes, and policies; our defining emotions, passions, and feelings if we are to be authentically human? This set of questions is best understood as a set of existential-historical questions. These are not in the first instance a set of moral questions, such as "How should we behave?" Rather they are the question at the core of existentialist philosophical and literary traditions, namely, "How should we be related to ourselves in our decisions moment by moment?" and "How should we be 'set' into the larger history of which we are a part?"

3. *Who* am I and who are we? What constitutes my peculiar, unsubstitutable personal identity? And what constitutes our common identity as just this community and no other? These are psychological, sociological, and historical as well as religious questions.

These what, how, and who questions are formal classes of anthropological questions. The questions that most secular and religious anthropologies actually address arguably belong to one or the other of these three sets of questions. Not all views of human being address all three of these questions. Dividing the anthropological question into the what, how, and who questions implies no view about whether they are all equally important questions or how they are related to one another. It merely provides a useful taxonomy of questions addressed by many if not most anthropologies of all sorts.

We are fascinated by what, how, and who questions about ourselves, and rightly so. They arise not only when death is faced but also, I shall suggest, at the point of a new birth. Indeed, they arise just as insistently in the midst of the humdrum practices of everyday life. These questions rightly fascinate us because the way we live our lives is deeply shaped by our explicit or implicit answers to them.

Who's Asking?
True as it may be, all that I've written above is almost uselessly abstract. The what, how, and who questions do not just float in pure form in an intellectual vacuum. Indeed, fascinating as they are, such abstract questions are rarely discussed. They are always asked, and have answers proposed, by particular people who are concretely located in some particular society with its traditions of thought and practice. In Delwin Brown's graceful phrase (1994), such traditions constitute the "boundaries of their habitation." Logically possible questions that are identical in the abstract, like, "What is it to be human being?" or "Who am I?" or "How ought I to be?" are often framed in significantly different ways when they are actually asked and answered by people with different concrete social and cultural

locations. So, to discover whether this project addresses questions that really interest you, you need to know not only what the abstract questions are, but also who's asking.

This project is addressed to two types of people who ask anthropological questions in ways framed by the boundaries of their respective habitations. It addresses those who identify themselves with Christian communities and their traditions of thought and practice. It tries to frame its questions in ways that are shaped by those traditions, and it seeks to give reasons for adopting its proposals that are grounded in those traditions. That, broadly speaking, is what is meant by calling the project an exercise in Christian theological anthropology. In doing these things, the project also addresses those people who are for any reason interested in what Christians propose as answers to anthropological questions, and why they say such things. Such folk have their own locations in various traditions of practices and thought that form the boundaries of their habitations.

So far as I can see, there is no common-denominator location comprising both types of audience as a single "we," no actual generic "us" that asks generic anthropological questions. Anthropological questions are asked from some "where." Indeed, they are asked from many "wheres." They are not the peculiar property of Christian communities, whose questions are also addressed from some "where." But that "where" need not be identical to the one in which the question was framed in the first place. There is no reason that it is impossible in principle for persons—say, Christians—to frame and to address from the resources of their own traditions questions that are also asked by others in ways framed by their traditions. While I explicitly raise and address anthropological questions in ways that are shaped by particularly Christian traditions of practices and thought, I seek to do so in a fashion that invites those who do not identify with those traditions to entertain the same questions and address them from their own location.

How Tradition-Particularism Shapes the Questions

Framing anthropological questions in ways shaped by just one tradition does not make the project simpler to execute. It is not as though the decision to confine the discussion to the particularities of only Christian traditions makes the task easier.

Traditions are patterns of thought and practice that are handed on (*traditio*, Latin for "delivery;" *tradere*, "to deliver") from one person to another in community, from one generation to the next. They are enormously complex tangles of concepts, beliefs, and practices of all kinds that make up communities' cultures, and they are inherently ambiguous, constituted at once by dynamics that make for relative communal stability and order across time and by dynamics that make for conflict.

Recent culture theory stresses that cultures are constituted by ceaseless negotiation to create and sustain individual and collective identities.

Consequently, cultures are marked by cracks and seams, contradictions and stark breaks. They are marked in that way inherently, and not simply as pathologies. For their part, traditions are seen as the cultures' strategies to negotiate order and chaos. As theological commentators on culture theory (D. Brown 1994; Tanner 1997) have pointed out in quite different ways, for Christian theologians this approach underscores that to construe Christian faith as a tradition entails stressing its internal conflictual seams and stark breaks quite as much as its ordering "inner logic." Better then, perhaps, to speak of Christian *traditions* than of *the* Christian tradition.

On the other side, societies are given continuity and identifiable shapes by their traditions handed on across time. Their traditions help make them recognizable as "this" society and its culture in contradistinction to "those" societies and their cultures. The determinate shape that traditions give to a society's common life is not necessarily either static or rigid. The patterns of practices and thought that are handed on are more appropriately likened to the rules of a generative grammar or an informal logic. They are rules that govern how to act, think, speak, or even express yourself nonverbally. Rather than telling us what we must do or say, the grammar-like patterns that constitute traditions are what make it possible for us to say or do anything; to think; to express ourselves; even to feel; above all, to disagree. Traditions are inherently traditions of disagreement and argument (MacIntyre 1981).

Any effort, such as this one, both to frame the major anthropological questions and to propose answers in ways particularly shaped by Christian traditions of thought and practice must seek to instantiate the traditions' relevant informal "logic" or "generative grammar" while also acknowledging and forthrightly engaging key cracks, seams, and contradictions in the traditions. Generalizations about *the* Christian point of view on anthropological questions that abstract from the particularities of the traditions' own ambiguities will not do, even if they facilitate intertradition conversations. Christian particularism merely complexifies the task.

Background beliefs are parts of the traditions of thought and practice that compose the common life of living communities, in this case, communities of Christian faith. Two broad types of beliefs are background to any anthropology. We ask anthropological questions against the background of beliefs about the character of the *proximate contexts* of our lives, the physical and social worlds in which we live. We also ask them against the background of beliefs about the *ultimate context* in which we live, the context that is most fundamental and decisive regarding what, how, and who we are. We who ask anthropological questions always ask them in a conceptual context provided by such background beliefs. Thus, background beliefs that are part of given traditions deeply shape the way persons who share those traditions formulate their questions and argue in support of them.

Beliefs about our proximate and ultimate contexts are deep parts of our personal identities. They are not changed easily or lightly, and people differ enormously about them. Jews, Christians, and Muslims trust the reality of God and God actively relating to us to be our ultimate context. The respective understandings of God and the ways in which God relates to us shape the way these faiths see their proximate contexts. By contrast, those who take our proximate physical and social contexts to be the only contexts we have do not lack a view of our ultimate context. Their understandings of our proximate context simply *are* their understanding of our ultimate context.

Differences in background beliefs, especially differences about the character of our ultimate context, cannot simply be bracketed in the course of exploring anthropological questions—say, in the interest of neutralizing tensions among religious traditions or between secular and religious points of view. Undoubtedly, a great many areas of convergence and overlap exist among these diverse sets of background beliefs, which is what makes possible significant agreements and disagreements among those who hold them and whose personal identities are shaped by them. Nonetheless, taking note of these personal-identity-forming differences in background beliefs serves to underscore that there is no generic "we" asking generic anthropological questions. Even if it were possible to frame and address the what, how, and who questions in abstraction from any background beliefs, those questions would not quite be the actual questions that any actual "we's" are asking, for the latter always do so in ways shaped by their background beliefs.

In Christian traditions of thought and practice, background beliefs about our ultimate context are particularly complex. God is understood to relate to us in three complexly interrelated but distinct ways: to create us, to draw us to eschatological consummation, and, when we have alienated ourselves from God, to reconcile us. In most Christian traditions, the God who relates in these ways is understood in a Trinitarian way. Correlatively, our proximate contexts are understood, not just as "nature" and "culture," but as creation; not merely as time to be made meaningful, but as promising and promissory history; not only as an arena of moral responsibility and moral struggle, but as a realm of reconciliation. In face of the cracks, seams, and contradictions among so complex an array of its beliefs, it will not do to abstract from this array a generalized reference to "God acting" as the single salient theological background belief. Focusing anthropological remarks in a Christian-specific way complexifies the task of theological anthropology by requiring it to frame its questions and argue its proposals in ways that are shaped by this complex set of background Christian beliefs about our ultimate and proximate contexts. Questions addressed by this project are framed in this manner.

Why Christian Particularism?

Of course, not all of the background beliefs that help shape Christians' anthropological questions arise exclusive from traditions of thought and practices that constitute Christian communities. The boundaries of Christians' habitations are multiple. Their personal and communal identities are shaped by and negotiated within more than one tradition. Christian communities and their members are always set in the context of larger host cultures. The traditions of practices and thought that make up the common lives of Christian communities are always in some degree of overlap and some degree of tension with the traditions of thought and practices that compose the common life of their host cultures. Rooted in the traditions of practices and thought of their host cultures are beliefs that shape the personal identities of the members of Christian communities as deeply as do beliefs rooted in the traditions of thought and practices that constitute the common life of their Christian faith communities.

For example, as a North American white male Presbyterian, my anthropological questions and proposals are framed by background beliefs about our ultimate and proximate contexts that are rooted in traditions of Christian thought and practice that originate in New Testament and patristic writings and are shaped by religious reformations in Geneva and Scotland, by movements of religious revival in eighteenth- and nineteenth-century America, and by earlier and later phases of the Enlightenment. At the same time, as a North American Presbyterian, my anthropological questions and proposals cannot escape being shaped by background beliefs about our proximate physical and social contexts that are rooted in traditions of thought and practices I unavoidably share with most other middle-class, well-educated males in a late-capitalist, consumerist society.

Obviously, one consequence of their locations in more than one tradition is that Christians' beliefs about their proximate physical, social, and cultural contexts tend to overlap extensively with beliefs about the same matters held by neighbors in their host culture who do not share their beliefs about the ultimate context of life. In addition, it may turn out on inspection that there are areas of overlap in beliefs about the ultimate context of life. That is why, for all of its being framed from the outset in Christian-tradition-specific ways, the internal logic of a Christian theological anthropology requires it to be open to conversation with and learning from atheological wisdom about what it is to be human.

A Christian theological anthropology might, then, be spoken in a different voice. It might be articulated as an exercise in intertraditional conversation. While affirming its specifically Christian roots, a theological anthropology might be constructed as a conversation with anthropological wisdom, not only from other religious traditions, but also from several relevant sciences. Perhaps it might be thought of as an exercise in conceptual bridge-building.

Indeed, I once set out to do just that. Christian theological anthropology intrigued me because it is the point at which Christian and secular thought most easily and immediately engage each other in the service of practices that make up Christian life and also practices within the common life of a pluralistic culture. By way of its anthropological concepts, theological ethics engages and appropriates arguments from secular ethics and information from secular analyses of morally problematic social situations. By way of its anthropological concepts, Christian pastoral care engages and appropriates secular psychological theory. And by way of its anthropological ideas, Christian theology has had the deepest, if anonymous, impact on modern culture. Anthropology seemed the most exciting theological topic because it is the topic at which theology most directly bears on practical matters. The best way to articulate it, I thought, would be as a dialogue with strategically selected secular conversation partners.

The reason I eventually abandoned that project may also be a reason that commends this project to readers who do not identify themselves with Christian traditions. Simply put, a bridge requires two abutments, and I was clearer about the content of the abutment consisting of the anthropological wisdom of certain atheological conversation partners than I was about the content of the abutment consisting of specifically Christian anthropological wisdom. The historical evidence seemed to be that Christians in every age have largely appropriated the best anthropological wisdom of their host culture. Their theological anthropologies mostly came from the other abutment, but they were selective about what they appropriated, and the ways in which they used what they appropriated bent it conceptually. However, it was not at all clear to me what the principles of selection were and where the conceptual gravity came from that bent what was borrowed. I realized that before I could undertake the bridge-building project, I needed to formulate the theological end of the bridge. My question became, "Does Christian faith bring with it any convictions about human being that are so rock bottom for it that they are, so to speak, nonnegotiable in intellectual exchange with anthropologies shaped by other traditions?"

Anyone who is interested in Christians' answers to common anthropological questions probably has the same question. In particular, anyone who does not identify with Christian traditions of thought and practice and is interested in an intertradition discussion of anthropological questions ought to have the same question. Before venturing very far out onto the bridge from the side of his or her own traditions, that person ought to want to know where the Christians are coming from. That is exactly what a Christianly particularist anthropology such as this one tries to provide.

The Root Question

I suggest that the claims about human beings that are nonnegotiable for Christian faith are claims about how God relates to human beings. These claims are as follows: (a) God actively relates to human beings to create them, (b) to draw them to eschatological consummation, and (c) to reconcile them when they are alienated from God.

These claims describe human beings' ultimate context, and they deeply shape descriptions of human beings' proximate contexts. Christian anthropology's remarks about human beings take them in their ultimate and proximate contexts. Hence such anthropological remarks are nonnegotiable to the extent that they are implied by Christian beliefs about our ultimate and proximate backgrounds.

Theological anthropology's background beliefs about our ultimate and proximate contexts do not generate all of the content of a theological anthropology. However, they do provide the criteria of selection regulating what anthropological wisdom is borrowed from Christian communities' current host cultures. They also generate the conceptual pressures under which that borrowed wisdom is conceptually bent as it is used in Christian theological anthropology.

In the famous opening to *Institutes of the Christian Religion*, quoted as the epigraph to this chapter, John Calvin points out: "Nearly all the wisdom we possess, that is to say, true and sound wisdom, consists of two parts: the knowledge of God and of ourselves. But, while joined by many bonds, which one precedes and which brings forth the other is not easy to discern." Calvin subsequently elected to begin with questions about knowledge of God. Although I do not follow Calvin by focusing first on questions about knowledge of God, I do propose to follow Calvin's example by subordinating claims about humankind to claims about God. Although our questions are anthropological, we should frame the questions and the proposed answers in terms governed by a doctrine of God.

Accordingly, the root question to which this Christian theological anthropology proposes answers is this: *What is implied about human being by the claim that God actively relates to us to create us, to draw us to eschatologiocal consummation, and to reconcile us when we have become estranged from God?* Correlatively, the three perennial anthropological questions, "What are we?" "Who are we?" and "How ought we to be?" should be reframed in ways shaped by Christian background beliefs about our ultimate and proximate contexts.

These background beliefs that help frame the questions asked, as well as the answers proposed, by Christian theological anthropology are rooted in the common life of Christian communities whose traditions are conflictual. For Christians the ultimate context of life is God and God's ways of relating to us, as Christians understand these matters. And the way Christians understand these matters is shaped in some way by their beliefs about Jesus Christ and God's relation to him. That is ultimately what qualifies theological answers proposed to anthropological questions as authentically Christian theological anthropology. At the same time, the phrases "as Christians understand these matters" and "in some way" are placeholders for seams and stark breaks within and between Christian communities generated by ongoing arguments and conflicts through which Christians negotiate their individual and communal identities. They disagree precisely on how to understand God's ways of relating to us, how to understand God's relation to Jesus, and in what ways the latter should shape the former. To insist on framing anthropological questions and proposals theocentrically is not a move that makes theological anthropology easy by giving it a pre-formed "basis" and a consensus conceptual scheme. Quite to the contrary, theological anthropology merely identifies a set of continuing arguments that it must engage.

The Tone of Voice and Structure of the Project

I consider this entire project in theological anthropology to be in the mode of making theological proposals so that it repeatedly has the form: Here is an important theological question; try looking at it this way. In that fashion, this project seeks to promote and provoke further exploration of the issues and further discussion, rather than assert conversation-stopper pronouncements of what Christians must say on a given topic.

I also consider the project to be in the hypothetical mode, in this fashion:

1. Assume with me that there are communities that describe themselves in self-involving ways as communities whose common life and whose members' individual lives seek to be formed as appropriate responses to the ways God relates to all else. I propose that we characterize the communities' common life as consisting of sets of social practices whose enactments express appropriate responses to God's ways of relating to all else, that enactments of those practices constitute some of the members' "existential hows," and that the practices themselves shape the communities' identity and the members' individual identities.

2. Assume with me further that some such communities include in their self-involving self-descriptions that the ways in which God relates to all else are mediated to them in part through the ways in which they live with the writings of canonical Christian Holy Scripture in the practices that constitute their common life of response to God and that shape their collective and individual identities.

3. Assume with me that some such communities also include in their self-involving self-descriptions that they hold themselves accountable to be self-critical about whether they are indeed responding appropriately in their current contexts to the ways in which God relates to them (judgment begins at home), that self-critique is a rational endeavor, and that it

is responsible in particular to the accounts given in canonical Christian Holy Scripture of the ways in which God relates to all else, as norms of what count as "appropriate" responses.

Note that the practice of self-critical examination of the appropriateness of the communities' other practices as "appropriate" responses to the ways God relates to all else itself has two levels. The practice of primary theology is usually ad hoc critique of current concrete enactments of communal practices that employs received conceptualizations and formulations (creeds, confessions, and traditional locutions) as criteria. The practice of secondary theology (the second level of the practice of theology) is enacted when the adequacy or appropriateness of the received conceptualizations and formulations themselves come into question. I think of *Eccentric Existence* as a set of remarks regarding three types of anthropological questions (the "what?" "who?" and "how to be oriented to proximate contexts?" questions) that are made as enactments of the communal practice of secondary theology. A major hypothesis is that there are now a lot of reasons to reexamine the adequacy of received theological anthropological formulations used in current primary theology.

The intersection of the rationally self-critical character of secondary theology, the three ways in which God relates to all else as narrated in canonical Christian Holy Scripture, and the three types of perennial anthropological questions generate a structure for *Eccentric Existence* that has four sections:

Introductions (chaps. 1A and B, 2A and B, 3A and B). These address questions about the nature of this kind of theological project, questions about how the Bible is read and used in this project, and questions about how the God who relates to humankind is to be understood (answer: in a Trinitarian way).

Part 1. Living on Borrowed Breath (chaps. 4A and B, 5A and B, 6–8, 9A and B, 10, 11). These explore the anthropological implications of the theological claim that God relates to all else creatively.

Part 2. Living on Borrowed Time (chaps. 12A and B, 13, 14, 15A and B, 16, 17). These explore the anthropological implications of the theological claim that God relates to all else to draw it to eschatological consummation.

Part 3. Living by Another's Death (chaps. 18, 19A and B, 20A and B, 21A and B, 22–25). These explore the anthropological implications of the theological claim that God relates to all else when it is estranged to reconcile it to God.*

Each of these three parts has the same structure:
— An account of human beings' ultimate context entailed by the way in which God relates that is under consideration.

* Part 3 appears in vol. 2 of this book.

— An account of human beings' proximate contexts (i.e., lived worlds) entailed by the way in which God relates that is under consideration.
— An address to the anthropological "What?" question.
— An address to the anthropological "How?" question.
— An address to the anthropological "Who?" question.
— Exploration of ways in which human "existential hows" may be distorted and human flourishing compromised (i.e., "sins in the plural") and how such distortion is possible.
— Exploration of ways in which human personal identities (who they are) may be in bondage to living deaths and their flourishing obscured (i.e., "sin in the singular").

Codas (Coda: Introductions A & B; Coda). These exhibit how the three parts hold together as a systematically unsystematic whole in which they are related to one another in a triple helix as facets of the way in which human beings are imagers of the image of God, Jesus Christ.

Existence is not a system.
SØREN KIERKEGAARD

CHAPTER **1B**

What Kind of Project Is This?

There are a number of questions about the craft of theology that are appropriate to ask of any project like the one announced in the previous chapter. Implicit in what I said in chapter 1A are judgments about how to go about developing a Christian theological anthropology. They are broadly methodological judgments about the sort of enterprise this theological anthropology is, what it has to go on, what it has to go by, and how it relates to other projects of roughly the same kind. At least in today's methodologically hyper-self-conscious world of technical academic theology, they are controversial judgments. The task of this chapter (along with chaps. 2B and 3B) is to identify and explain some of this project's methodological commitments.

The identification of some of the key methodological commitments of this project is largely retrospective. We should probably be skeptical of efforts to formulate the correct theological method in the abstract, prior to any effort to formulate and commend particular material theological proposals, as though a theological method could serve as an instructions booklet about how to assemble your very own Christian theological conceptual structure. The craft of developing theological proposals, it seems to me, is too much of an art form to be regulated in that way. The intellectual and imaginative challenges peculiar to different theological topics are so diverse that any set of methodological rules purporting to cover them all would have to be so general as to be useless. The general categories conventionally used to identify supposedly contrasting overall theological methods (e.g., liberal/conservative, neo-orthodox/liberal, postliberal/revisionist, narrative/correlational) seem to me to be utterly unilluminating and unhelpful. In any case, this project on anthropology in particular has not been worked out in accordance with an a priori method specifying the proper way in which to go about it.

Nevertheless, it is possible after the fact to identify contestable choices about procedure, mostly made implicitly in the course of developing material theological proposals about anthropology in particular. With no interest in claiming their methodological superiority regarding the craft of theology in general, I am concerned here to identify and, where appropriate, warrant their appropriateness in Christian theological anthropology.

Theology as Ecclesial Practice

There are several kinds of inquiry that are rightly called "theology," although the word is used in slightly different senses in regard to each. The project of which this anthropology is a subsection is best understood this way: this kind of theology is one of several practices that make up the common life of some self-identified communities of Christian faith.

"Communities of Christian faith" is a term of art for Christian churches. I adopt it because, at least in North America, the denotation of "Christian church" is usually assumed to be either institutions called "denominations" or familiar local social and cultural institutional phenomena called "congregations" or "parishes." That conventional denotation of the word "church" is not theologically mistaken. "Communities of Christian faith" are churches, and they are necessarily social and cultural institutions with extended histories. They are historically contingent. The shape of their practices and their languages, social and cultural values, and patterns of thought are relative to their social and cultural contexts even when they stand in tension with their contexts as countercultural communities.

However, by itself that denotation is one-sided. It obscures features of the church that can only be expressed appropriately in theocentric terms and are hardly identifiable empirically. The key Christian theological name for church, frequently used in the New Testament, has been "ecclesia." In secular Greek, the *ek kletoi* were those citizens of a city who were "called out," summoned together in an assembly by a herald for some civic purpose. However, almost all of the nearly one hundred uses of *ekklesia* in the Greek translation of the Hebrew Bible (the Septuagint) serve to translate *kehal* (community) in the phrase *kehal Yahweh* (the community of God). The shift from "called to assemble" to "community" is crucially important. "Communities of Christian faith" do not understand themselves to be constituted by a purpose for which they have assembled, or have been assembled, although it is the case that, having been constituted by God, they understand themselves to be sent in mission in and for the world. Rather, they understand themselves to be constituted by God relating to them to gather them as the "community of God." (For a good brief discussion of these matters, see Kung 1967, 81–87.) More exactly, they understand themselves to be gathered by God as "communities of God" precisely in their historical contingency and social and cultural relativism, neither despite such contingency and relativity nor to the end of escaping such contingency and relativity. Communities of Christian faith must be understood in theocentric terms.

I characterize the communities I have in mind as "self-identified" communities of Christian faith to avoid the vacuity of a vicious circle created by my arbitrarily stipulating what count as "churches." Instead, I assume that it is a matter of empirical fact that these communities exist in a variety of societies worldwide, and hence embedded in the cultures of those societies, and identify themselves as "Christian." In important respects they are social and cultural phenomena and proper subjects for social-scientific investigation. Whether, and in what sense, any one of them is also, in some normative sense, "really" or "authentically" or "validly" a community of specifically "Christian" faith is quite another question. It is a theological question. As these remarks on theological anthropology are developed, they will include a few proposals by me of some (but by no means all) theological standards that positive answers to that question ought to satisfy. However, at this point all that is required is to posit that there exist human communities that identify themselves as "communities of Christian faith."

I adopt the phrase "communities of Christian faith" because "Christian" and "faith" are theological terms that are central to explicating the theocentricity of the self-identification of the communities in question. For convenience, I shall also call these communities "ecclesial communities." To characterize the kind of theological project represented by this theological anthropology as "one of several practices that make up the common life of self-identified communities of Christian faith" is to characterize it as part of a project we may call "ecclesial theology." As I hope to make clear and keep clear, this does not mean that "ecclesial theology" is theology about communities of faith or about the personal faith of members of such communities. Its subject matter is neither churches' nor persons' piety. The subject matter of ecclesial theology is God, and all else as related to by God and as related to God.

I suggested that we characterize the common life of such communities as comprising a large number of interrelated practices. "Practice" is a term I use often in the following chapters in ways that follow at some distance Alasdair MacIntyre's analysis in *After Virtue* (1981, 175–283). By a practice I mean *any form of socially established human interactivity that is conceptually formed, is complex and internally coherent, is subject to standards of excellence that partly define it, and is done to some end but does not necessarily have a product.* Any such practice is enacted in the context of a host society, its culture, and its history. Hence any such practice is historically contingent, deeply shaped by and relative to some society and its culture.

In the next few sections of this chapter, I explore and develop my characterization of the kind of project this is in terms of key phrases in this summary account of practices.

Communal Practices and Communal Identity

I characterized the kind of project this is as "one of several practices that make up the common life of some self-identified communities of Christian faith." I take it to be descriptively accurate to say that some, but not all, communities that identify themselves as "communities of Christian faith" describe their communal identity—that is, who they are as a community—in a way that typically makes three points. That communal identity-description has the following general form: who we are—that is, our communal identity—can be described in the following manner:

1. We are a community of response—that is, a community whose common life comprises a set of practices that seek to be appropriate responses to the ways in which God relates to all that is not God as that relating is explicitly

or implicitly narrated, commented on, celebrated, longed for, alluded to, or assumed in various ways in various parts of canonical Holy Scripture.

2. Our communal identity—that is, who we are—is formed in us: evoked, sustained, deepened, re-formed, and deepened again, as God works in and through the ways in which we self-involvingly live with canonical Holy Scripture in the practices that compose our common life.

3. Moreover, we are a community whose responses in various practices to the ways in which God relates to all that is not God are defined more particularly by the christocentric way in which we understand who God is. We understand Who we are responding to, how that One relates to us, and how our identities are formed through our efforts to respond appropriately, in terms of the peculiar way in which God relates concretely to humankind in the life, ministry, death, and resurrection appearances of Jesus Christ, as that is narrated and commented on in canonical Holy Scripture and is understood in the larger context of the way God relates to humankind through the covenant relationship God has with the children of Israel as that is narrated and commented on in Holy Scripture.

Here a distinction between two questions is crucially important: (1) In what ways does God relate to all that is not God? (2) Who is that God? These are the fundamental questions in Christian theology. The first of the three points made above in the general form of these communities' communal-identity description assumes that God relates to all that is not God in several ways that are narrated in Holy Scripture. The third point assumes that in all of the ways in which God relates, God is consistently self-same. It assumes that God is, as it were, faithful to God's own character. And it acknowledges that it understands God's self-same character, God's identity, in terms of Holy Scripture's accounts of who Jesus is—that is, in terms of Scripture's narrative identity descriptions of Jesus Christ. This third point is the one that makes the community's practices specifically Christian communal practices. Hence it is a tautology that theology, as one of the practices comprising the common life of communities of Christian faith, is Christian theology and that this anthropological project is an exercise in Christian theology.

This anthropological project is part of a practice of theology that is one of the practices comprising the common life of self-identified communities of Christian faith whose descriptions of their own communal identities make these three points.

Practices, Concepts, and Beliefs

Practices are not only socially established but also conceptually formed. Obviously, they are conceptually formed in the sense that they meet the definition of "practice" given above. If a form of human activity is not socially established, or is not interactive; is either not complex or is not internally coherent; or lacks an end or has no standards of excellence, it simply is not a practice.

Beyond that, however, each kind of practice is also conceptually formed in its own way, in part by the end of that specific kind of practice, and in part by its peculiar standards of excellence. Furthermore, if a practice's end is itself complex, the practice may be conceptually formed by only one or a few aspects of that end in a way that distinguishes it from other, related practices that are differentiated from it by being conceptually formed by another or other aspects of the same complex end.

The practices that constitute the common life of ecclesial communities share certain formal and substantive standards of excellence that partly give them definition—that is, form them conceptually as, precisely, the set of practices that comprise the common life of ecclesial communities (discussed later). The substantive standards of excellence identify, among other things, conceptual standards that measure the relative excellence of enactments of the practices.

In addition, such practices share the overall end of aiming to be appropriate responses to the ways in which God relates to all that is not God as that relating is explicitly or implicitly narrated, commented on, celebrated, longed for, alluded to, or assumed in various ways in various parts of Holy Scripture. Given that God does relate to all that is not God in several irreducibly different ways, that end is internally complex. Specifications of those differences must be based on differences among the ways in which God's relating to all that is not God are narrated, commented on, celebrated, longed for, alluded to, or assumed in various ways in various parts of Holy Scripture if it is to just those ways of relating that the practices seek to be appropriate responses.

Notwithstanding the complexity of their common end and the consequent conceptual differences among these responsive practices, it is also the case that, if "who God is" who relates in several ways is understood in terms of the peculiar way in which God relates concretely to humankind in the life, ministry, death, and resurrection appearances of Jesus Christ, as that is narrated and commented on in Holy Scripture, and is understood in the larger context of the way God relates to humankind through the covenant relationship God has with the children of Israel as that is narrated and commented on in Holy Scripture, then all of these responsive practices have in common a conceptual shaping that is based on the ways in which God's relating to all that is not God in, with, and under the person of Jesus as narrated in Holy Scripture. More specifically, they are shaped christologically by concepts of Jesus' relation to God and God's relation to Jesus.

The practices that constitute the common life of ecclesial communities are not only conceptually formed. They also imply, or involve explicit affirmation of, beliefs about God, about God's ways of relating to all that is not God, including God's way of relating in the person of Jesus, and about all else in relation to God. The beliefs are formulated in terms provided by the concepts that form and define the practices. As we shall note in the next section, some are practices of worship oriented to God that consist of certain ways of explicitly affirming such beliefs, often in ritualized liturgical forms. Others are mixed practices oriented both to God and to fellow human beings, such as proclamatory and educational practices, which consist of explicit affirmation of such beliefs. Other mixed practices, oriented both to God and to fellow human beings, only imply such beliefs inasmuch as they are practices that construe fellow human beings as caught up in the same ways in which God, understood in terms of the person of Jesus, relates to all that is not God as are those who enact the practices. For example, ecclesial practices of reconciliation, charity, and correction of injustice are the specific and definite practices they are in large part because they assume that those for and with whom they are enacted share with the enactors of the practices the status of being created by God, drawn to eschatological consummation by God, and reconciled to God by God. Still other mixed practices that only imply certain beliefs are oriented to God and to nonhuman and human fellow creatures. Beliefs about creation, eschatological consummation, and reconciliation, beliefs about God and God relating in these ways to all that is not God are implicit in such practices. They, in turn, imply beliefs about human beings as creatures, destined for eschatological consummation, and reconciled though estranged.

Anthropologically speaking, the decision to frame this account of the common life of communities of Christian faith in terms of this concept of practices is hardly innocent. It permits an account of the relations among public bodily action (as in, "en-act-ments of practices"), concepts and beliefs, and the entire range of human capacities—physical, mental, and affective—that avoids anthropological assumptions of alternative conceptualities that are, I suggest, inherently problematic for Christian theological anthropology. In particular, it avoids simply assuming three problematic sets of anthropological assumptions in the framing of theological anthropology: that concepts and beliefs (in this case, theological concepts and beliefs) are related to human action in the way theory is applied in practice (think of the transition from pure theory to practical application in engineering); that (theological) concepts and theory are related to human action as rationalizations and ideology are related to praxis that is in fact to be explained exhaustively in other ways (say by unconscious motives or material—largely economic—causes); and that (theological) beliefs and concepts and actions are two kinds of parallel, objective, outward, more or less creative "expressions" of theologically important subjective states that are inward, private, passive, and preconceptual. Just why these assumptions are problematic for Christian theological anthropology is a complex story that it will take much of the rest of this project to tell.

Public Practices, the Common Life of Communities of Christian Faith, and Primary Theology

Practices in general, including the practice of theology, are inherently public. As socially established, they are not privately devised. They are already in the societies into which human agents are born or with which they come to identify themselves, including ecclesial communities. Practices are part of human agents' inherited social and cultural capital.

To be socially established, practices need to be acknowledged, agreed upon, and enacted by some society of human agents in their interactions with one another. Acknowledgment of a practice, and agreement about what the practice is, requires a communicative network among human agents. Communication requires a medium. Although they usually include a spoken, if not a written, language, the media of communication need not be linguistic and in any case may include other forms of communication as well, such as bodily gestures, facial expressions, dance, visual images, music, masks, special clothing, and so on. In short, the communication required by the social establishment of practices itself requires the matrix of a society's culture. Hence practices are inherently public in the sense that they require the public of a communally shared social and cultural space.

This sense of "public" must not be overgeneralized. The public realm does not need, not even in principle, to include all human agents whatsoever as possible enactors of practices in order for those practices to count as public. Absolute universality of participation is not essential to the idea of the public. Nor is egalitarianism. In no public constituted by communally shared social and cultural space are all human agents who are part of that society necessarily entitled to enact all of its public practices. In the cultures of many societies, like that of eighteenth-century New England, it is socially (publicly) established that some practices central to the health and life of the society, like voting and holding office, may only be enacted by a subset of the members of that society—say, only by white male property owners. The practices of voting and holding office are nonetheless public. Nor is transparency to non-enactors of practices—that is, transparency to "outsiders"—essential to the idea of the "public." Some communities separate themselves from other communities so thoroughly that they count as secret societies. The space constituted by their shared society and its culture wholly excludes those who live only in the space constituted by their larger host society and its culture. Nonetheless, practices enacted in secret are public practices relative to those who do share the same social and cultural space.

Because practices are inherently public, the concept of practice is particularly appropriate to use in characterization of the makeup of the common life of ecclesial communities. That life is a public life lived in public worlds, some of whose citizens are not members of ecclesial communities. That life is misrepresented when it is theologically characterized in conceptual schemes that construe it as at bottom a type of subjective or intersubjective inwardness, an interiority to which its subjects have privileged cognitive access so that it is an intrinsically private domain.

What makes these practices a set comprising the common life of ecclesial communities is the fact that they share a single end: to respond appropriately to the distinctive ways in which God relates to all that is not God.

Some of the practices constituted by the common life of ecclesial communities are oriented to God. They are, after all, practices that seek to be appropriate responses to God's ways of relating to all that is not God. Examples are characteristically Christian practices of praise, adoration, worship, prayer, confession, repentance, and gratitude.

Some are mixed practices oriented in one way to fellow human beings and in another way to God. They are mixed in this way because they are practices that seek to be appropriate responses to God, who does not relate to each human being in isolation but rather relates to each human being as she or he is part of the interrelated web of beings constituting all that is not God. Therefore, response to the ways in which God relates is appropriate to the extent that some of its practices reflect the fact that God relates to the ones enacting the response only as they are related to fellow human beings to whom God also relates. Examples are practices of reconciliation, moral guidance, obedience, discipleship, education, pastoral care, healing, charity, relief of suffering, correction of injustices, overcoming of oppression, and ordering and governing the communities' common life.

Others are mixed practices oriented in one way to nonhuman creatures and in another way to God. They are mixed in this way because they are practices that seek to be appropriate responses to God, who relates to each human being as she or he is part of the interrelated web of nonhuman beings constituting all that is not God. Therefore, response to the ways in which God relates is appropriate to the extent that some of its practices reflect the fact that God relates to the ones enacting the response only as they relate to nonhuman creatures. Examples are practices of thanksgiving for harvests, table blessings, blessing of the animals, stewardship of the earth and the creatures that live on it, and environmental responsibility.

There is a self-critical dimension to every one of these practices. In the course of the common life of ecclesial communities, disagreements arise about three matters: Are the communities' practices as received in fact appropriate responses to the ways in which God relates to all that is not God? That is, do these practices in fact achieve their overall end? Second, do current concrete enactments of those practices best meet their own standards of excellence? Third, what is the most perspicuous way to formulate both the practices' end and their standards of excellence? Out of such disagreements come reforms of the communities' practices of worship, preaching, teaching, methods of pastoral care, ways of addressing the injustice and oppression society visits on fellow human beings, and environmental responsibility. Consequently, the set of practices comprising the common life of ecclesial communities must also include practices of exploring and negotiating, and sometimes resolving, such disagreements.

To repeat: The end to which all of these practices are enacted, along with their self-critical edge—that is, the end or *telos* of the common life of ecclesial communities—is to respond appropriately to the distinctive ways in which God relates to all that is not God.

I propose to call this self-critical dimension of every practice in the set that comprises the common life of ecclesial communities "primary theology." In it those who are interacting in any given ecclesial practice consider whether their enactment is in fact appropriate in that place and time as a response to the particularities of God's ways of relating to all that is not God. In this dimension of each practice, members of ecclesial communities engage in ongoing exchanges. Proposals and counterproposals are made about the adequacy of the communities' enactments of the practices that constitute their common life: their adequacy both to the practices' standards of excellence and to their end. Primary theology is, then, a communicative practice. It is like a conversation that is inherently open to disagreements and conflicts. It involves conceptual clarification and assessments of the intelligibility of things said about received practices. It involves drawing relevant distinctions, imagining fresh ways in which to interpret received practices. It involves making and assessing arguments for and against proposals about such matters. It is an informal, non-technical, often un-selfconscious engagement in the practice of theology. The judgments of community members without formal training whose personal identities are, so to speak, that of native speakers well grounded in the communities' received practices are likely to be especially perceptive and weighty. Self-identified ecclesial communities engage in this practice all the time. Primary theology is not the preserve of scholars having the appropriate specializations.

This project in theological anthropology is not an enactment of the practice of primary theology.

Secondary Theology and Its End

However, this project is an enactment of part of a practice of theology that grows out of, depends on, and is inseparable from the practice of primary theology. In the course of primary theological discussion, disagreement may shift to a second level of questions. Discussion of the issues raised at this second level constitutes not so much an aspect of the other practices as an additional practice in its own right. I propose to call this practice of ecclesial theology "secondary theology." It is one in the set of practices that makes up the common life of ecclesial communities.

After clarification of what constitutes the second level of theological disagreements within the common life of ecclesial communities and specifies its end, I shall comment on why the practice of secondary theology arises out of primary theology and note several of its general features.

The standards that must be met by proposals and counterproposals advanced in the course of primary theological arguments are formulated in received—that is, "traditional"—ways. Such formulations are conventionally called the communities' "doctrines." They consist of received or traditional claims about God and the ways in which God relates to all that is not God, and claims about all else in relation to God. The issue in debate may shift from questions about the appropriateness of particular types of enactment of a practice as response to the particularities of God's active relating (the basic question addressed in primary theology) to questions about the meaning, pertinence, or adequacy of the formulations of the standards—that is, the doctrines, the claims about God, and all else in relation to God—to which appeal has been made in the course of primary theologizing.

That shift in question gives rise, in turn, to efforts to propose new and more adequate theological formulations of the communities' claims about God and all else in relation to God. This is the overall end to which secondary ecclesial theology is enacted.

The need for more adequate theological formulations may be generated in two ways. First, it may be generated in part by the integrity of the communities' communal identity. That is, it may be generated by the community's effort to be faithful to its own commitments to respond appropriately to the ways in which God relates. Part of such faithfulness is a mandate for constant critical assessment of the perspicuity, coherence, and compelling power of received formulations of the theological claims.

In large part, however, the need for more adequate formulations is generated by the inherent historicity and relativity of the practices that compose the common life of such communities. We have noted that the ecclesial communities whose common life consists in these practices are located in host societies and their cultures. Often the concepts used in accounts of God's ways of relating to all that is not God, and the concepts that inform and define the practices, are themselves borrowed from or shaped by those cultures. As those host societies and their cultures change over time, the community's received doctrines, which use those concepts, although intelligible in earlier periods or in other societies, become misleading or unintelligible. Another part of such cultural change may take the form of new historical knowledge of the cultural contexts in which authoritative Scriptures and theological formulations were written that require changes in how those Scriptures or theological formulations should be interpreted, and thereby change their bearing on the theological claims they were once thought to authorize. Or such cultural change may take the form of new knowledge of aspects of "all that is not God" that is inconsistent with received theological claims about how God relates to it. More adequate formulations are required. Whatever its cause, this shift to a second level of question gives rise to a second, distinguishable but related practice of theology. We call it the practice of "secondary theology."

This second level of theological practice proposes fresh formulations of the standards to which all participants in primary theology appeal to warrant their own points of view on whatever issue is the subject of controversy concerning a communal practice. Because this practice of secondary theology aims to propose new formulations in the light of cultural changes and new knowledge, it usually requires of those who engage in it specialized background in various forms of new knowledge and research into historical and cultural changes, and it is often conducted in a more formal, technical, explicit, and intellectually rigorous way than are enactments of the practice of primary theology. As an ongoing conversation about how best to formulate the standards employed in primary theology when assessing the merits of conflicting proposals, secondary theology is an interlocking set of ongoing arguments among members of ecclesial communities, both contemporaries and predecessors.

Secondary theology is inherently an analytically descriptive, critical, and revisionary practice. Going beyond description of what the traditional claims have been, it analyzes how in the past they have been used in the communities' common life, how they have been understood to be related to one another conceptually and logically, what implications have been thought to be rightly inferred from them and what apparently possible implications blocked, and why. Secondary theology analyzes critically why the traditional formulations of some such claims have become problematic. It is inescapably a revisionary practice in that it proposes revisions of traditional formulations of some of the claims about God and all else in relation to God that serve as the standards to which disagreements in primary theology appeal. At their most radical, proposals of such revisions may take the form of proposing that certain traditional claims be entirely abandoned and the proposal of substitute new claims that are deemed to be well-warranted theologically.

Although in the modern world the practice of secondary theology has come to be housed institutionally in the academy, it is misleading to characterize the practice of this theology as "academic theology." Its institutional location most certainly forms it in many ways, for the better as well as for the worse. But it should not define the kind of practice it is (for a fuller development of this remark see Kelsey 1992). It is not, for example, "academic" in the sense that its product is a body of pure theory whose concrete applicability to human life and its problems must be worked out subsequently in some nonacademic, practical, applied theory context. The practice of secondary theology is not enacted on the supposition that its product (theory) will subsequently generate new practices. To the contrary, its enactment supposes that it is itself, as a practice, rooted in the self-critical dimension (primary theology) of already ongoing practices constituting the common life of ecclesial communities. So too, although the purpose of the academy may be defined as the production of new and documented knowledge, secondary theology is not defined as a practice whose end is to produce a type of document. Theological writings emerge as a product from the practice; but they are not the end of the practice and do not define it. Rather, the barbarism "doing theology" is literally correct. Christian theology, whether primary or secondary, is an activity that consists of enactments of a practice that is socially established by ecclesial communities as part of their common life.

The proposals promoted by this anthropological project are part of a practice of secondary theology, which gives the project certain general features. The proposals it promotes are analytical and critical, offered to the end of developing more adequate, and hence revisionary, formulations of some of the received or traditional standards—that is, the doctrines to which all parties to disagreements about anthropological issues appeal in the course of doing primary theology.

This analysis of the end of the practice of secondary theology brings out another general feature of the project: its tone of voice. This project doubtless has similarities to the kind of theology whose technical name is "dogmatic" theology, although it should become clear as the chapter proceeds that it does not meet the definition of that kind of theology. However this project must not adopt the dogmatic tone of voice that is frequently and unfairly attributed to dogmatics. The overall end or purpose of this project is to commend proposals to ecclesial communities about how best to formulate their claims about what and who human beings are and how they ought to be existentially set into and oriented toward their lived worlds. It commends those proposals by giving reasons for adopting them, offering arguments on their behalf. The arguments do not rest on premises thought to be self-evident or indubitable. Rather, the arguments are addressed to ecclesial communities and mostly rest on premises that are assumed to be shared by members of such communities. Hence the proposals, the arguments advanced in their support, and, indeed, the very practice of secondary theology, are epistemically fallible. Consequently, the tone of voice in which a theological project like this one commends its proposals is more hypothetical than assertory, as though to say, "*If* you in fact believe such and such about God, God's ways of relating to all that is not God, and all else in relation to God, *then* should you not in all consistency adopt the following proposals about how to formulate your claims about what and who human beings are and how they ought to be."

Secondary Theology and Its Standards of Excellence

Like all practices, the ecclesial practice of secondary theology is subject to several different standards of excellence that partly define it. They partly define it in that some of these standards define enactments of this practice as specifically Christian and ecclesial secondary theology. We can distinguish between formal and substantial standards of excellence. I simply identify them here. Some of them are discussed at greater length elsewhere in this project.

Because the practice of secondary theology is a communicative practice in which proposals are made and reasons given why they ought to be adopted, it is subject to well-known formal standards of excellence to which all forms of reasoned reflection are subject. Formal standards of excellence are necessary, although not sufficient, conditions for effective communication and good arguments. Satisfying formal standards does not establish the truth of any proposal, theological or otherwise. However, it does make it maximally possible to understand the proposals whose truth needs to be assessed. To propose a fresh formulation of a doctrinal standard is to engage in a communicative practice that is subject to standards of excellence, such as the conceptual clarity of its proposals, internal consistency, and consistency with related proposals. To give reasons that a proposal ought to be adopted is to engage in an argument-making practice that is subject to standards of excellence that require transparency of the structure of arguments, whether informal or formal; giving good reasons for the proposal being defended, as "good" reasons are defined by the subject matter and field of inquiry; and, insofar as the arguments can be formalized, formally valid argument.

Practices like secondary theology that incorporate arguments in a number of very different argument-making practices (e.g., history, literary criticism, philology, and metaphysics) are subject to one more formal standard of excellence. When they incorporate an argument from another kind of argument-making practice, the standards of what counts as a good argument must be those of the practice from which the argument is appropriated and not necessarily the standards of what counts as a good argument in secondary theology. For example, when a proposal in secondary theology is defended as a historical proposal (say, "Jesus of Nazareth was crucified by the Romans"), the arguments advanced in support of the proposal must count as good arguments in the practice of history (e.g., arguments based on what counts as good evidence in the practice of history). Simply meeting the standards of excellence to which the practice of secondary theology is subject is not sufficient (say, e.g., that Christianly recognized authorities, such as Scripture and tradition, testify that Jesus was crucified and that the Roman authorities were responsible). The fact that the argument plays a role in an enactment of the practice of secondary theology does not excuse the argument from having to meet the standards of excellence to which the practice of history is subject. To continue with the example: What in fact count as good arguments in, respectively, the practice of history and the practice of secondary theology are defined by the two practices' respective substantive standards of excellence, not merely by their formal standards. But the requirement that, say, a historical argument mounted in the course of a theological argument must meet the substantive standards of excellence of the practice of history, and not the substantive standards of excellence of the practice of secondary theology, is itself a formal standard of excellence to which the practice of secondary theology is subject.

In addition to formal standards of excellence, the practice of secondary theology is subject to four substantive standards of excellence. It is either explicitly or implicitly subjected to these four by the nature of the communal identity of the communities of Christian faith as outlined in the three-point general form of the communities' self-description of their communal identity given earlier in this chapter. Recall that, as one of the practices that make up the common life of ecclesial communities, a central responsibility of the practice of secondary theology is to assess the adequacy of the formulations of received, traditional standards for the adequacy of the communities' practices to which debates in primary theology appeal and, if necessary, to propose revised or entirely new formulations. The proposals aim to shape the communities' practices so that under current circumstances they are more faithful to the communities' identity. Enactments of the practice of secondary theology, then, are subject to standards of excellence defined by the communities' description of their own communal identities.

Explicit in the three-point general form of the communities' description of their communal identity are two such substantive standards of excellence. The first is that proposals about who the God is who relates to all else in ways to which the community responds in its common life must comport with the person of Jesus. I develop this point at greater length in chapters 2A and 3A and in part 3. The second is that proposals about the ways in which God relates to all that is not God must comport with Holy Scripture's accounts of the ways in which God relates. I repeatedly develop this point at greater length in each part of this project.

Implicit in the three-point general form of the communities' description of their communal identity are two further substantive standards of excellence. One is that theological proposals on any topic must either be shown to comport with relevant theological formulations in the communities' theological traditions or be shown to be preferable to them. This standard assumes that enactments of secondary theology must take the contents of the theological traditions very seriously as formulations from which important insights may be learned, but not taken uncritically. This standard is developed further in the next section of this chapter.

The fourth substantive standard of excellence to which enactments of the practice of secondary theology are subject is that they provide analyses of the relation between received—that is, traditional—theological formulations and relevant features of the current culture of the ecclesial community's host society that show in what ways and why the former are inadequate in that cultural context. This standard is developed in a bit more detail in the final section of this chapter.

Practices and Tradition

Because they are temporally extended and have histories, the practices that constitute the common life of communities of Christian faith have the character of "traditions." *Traditio* means both the action of "handing over," "traditioning" (Lat.: *tradere*; Gk.: *paradosis*), and what it is that is handed over: "the tradition."

Tradition-as-action is inherent in each of the practices that make up the common life of communities of Christian faith. As responses to the good news—that is, the gospel—of the ways in which God relates to all that is not God, ecclesial practices explicitly or implicitly hand over that good news in two ways: by celebrating ways in which God concretely relates to all else and by holding themselves accountable to the concrete ways in which God relates as the standards of the appropriateness of practices as a response.

Consequently, tradition as action shares the ambiguity and fallibility of all the practices that constitute the community's common life. It can go wrong. The Greek word stem for "hand over," as it is used in the New Testament, can mean both the faithful handing over of the good news of the way God relates to estranged humankind to reconcile them in the life, ministry, death, and resurrection appearances of Jesus, and the treacherous handing over by Judas of Jesus to the authorities for his arrest, trial, and crucifixion.

Tradition-as-what-is-handed-over in enactments of ecclesial practices can name a variety of kinds of things: particular practices; orally transmitted beliefs; Christian Scripture; theological formulations; writings by especially respected Christian thinkers; memories of especially revered persons, transmitted orally or in writing; sacred places, such as pilgrimage sites; and sacred objects, such as icons.

However, not everything that is handed over is equally significant to the practice of theology. The aspect of tradition-as-what-is-handed-over that is important to the practice of theology is the aspect that is directly concerned with the concepts and beliefs that give definition to the responsive practices that are the common life of communities of Christian faith and shape its common identity, and do so insofar as they are theological concepts and beliefs in the narrow sense—that is, they address the questions about who God is, the ways in which God relates to all that is not God, and how to understand all else in relation to God. Following conventional usage, it may be called the specifically "theological tradition."

In itself, this theological tradition is, of course, a very large and mixed collection. It includes formulations of the rule of faith that begin to appear from influential Christian writers like Irenaeus in the mid-second century onward; checklists of beliefs that distinguish faithful interpretation of Scripture from misinterpretation, especially gnostic "heresies"; creeds adopted by ecumenical councils—for example, the Nicene Creed—and broadly used in the communities' liturgies; creeds widely used in communities' liturgies whose origin is not clearly conciliar—for example, the Apostles' Creed; theological formulas adopted by ecumenical councils, designed to distinguish acceptable theological proposals from unacceptable proposals on controversial theological issues— for example, the Chalcedonian formula regarding the relation between the two natures of Christ; and writings of widely respected and influential Christian thinkers, conventionally called the "fathers." I suggest that for all of the differences in genre among these formulations, they may all be seen as attempting to articulate how canonical Holy Scripture ought best to be interpreted insofar as it bears on one aspect or another of one or more of the following questions: "In what ways does God relate to all that is not God?" "Who is God?" and "How should we understand all else in relation to God?"

This theological tradition is the aspect of tradition-as-what-is-handed-over that is important for primary theology because it provides the conventional, received theological formulations that serve as the theological standards to which appeal is made in arguments for and against proposals advanced in primary theology. Practiced in the service of primary theology, part of the task of secondary theology is to propose more adequate formulations of the standards to which primary theology is subject. Hence the theological tradition is important for the practice of secondary theology because it provides the received theological standards whose very formulation is just what is at issue in disagreements in secondary theology. One of the central responsibilities of the practice of secondary theology is to discern what insights into Holy Scripture's renderings of the ways God relates, who God is, and its visions of all else as related to God were at issue for those who devised the formulations in the theological tradition, to discern which formulations of those insights are still valid, which need to be discarded, what modifications or substitutes would be improvements, and why. Thus, the contents of the theological tradition, part of that-which-is-handed-over, are to be taken very seriously by enactments of secondary theology as formulations from which important insights may be learned, but not taken uncritically or as unreformable, much less infallible.

The phrase "the theological tradition" may misleadingly suggest that there is something called "*the* theological tradition" or even "*the* Christian tradition." It does not require extensive observation of the current practices of ecclesial communities or of the history of their practices to know that, descriptively speaking, communities of Christian faith do not all engage in one self-same *traditio*. Expressions such as "the Christian tradition" or "the Tradition" or "the Great Tradition" may name useful ideal types or theoretical constructs. But if *traditio* occurs as an aspect of concrete enactments of the particular practices of actual communities of Christian faith, such expressions name no single reality actually resident in those practices. As we have seen, all such practices have a single end in common: to respond appropriately to various aspects of the ways in which God freely relates to all that is not God. As we have also seen, however, in their concrete reality, these practices are very diverse because they are historically contingent and socially and culturally relative. In consequence, some practices of some communities of Christian faith are not only different from, but appear to be at least inconsistent with, some practices of other such communities. Correlatively, the theological traditions that are aspects of those practices also are not only different but sometimes apparently inconsistent.

This is not surprising, even though, assessed against the communities' self-descriptions of their communal identities, it may count as a scandal. Because they are aspects of the array of practices that constitute the common life of communities of Christian faith, it can be fruitful to study ecclesial traditions on analogy with study of cultures and cultural traditions construed as complexes of practices in the manner, for example, of George Lindbeck's "cultural-linguistic" construal of Christian doctrines (1984). However, it is also the case, as recent theories of culture have tended to stress, that cultural traditions themselves are inherently conflictual, marked by breaks and seams (see D. Brown 1994 and Tanner 1997 for exploration of the theological implications of this trend in theorization of culture). Concrete enactments of the practices that compose the common life of communities of Christian faith may all be said to count as Christian if they exhibit family resemblances, but not if they must exhibit a uniformity grounded in a single self-same "tradition" that can admit, at most, only minor variations. Correlatively, the theological traditions that are aspects of the practices of different ecclesial communities may count as Christian if they exhibit family resemblances. It is difficult, however, to see how they can be shown to exhibit a uniformity grounded in a single self-same theological tradition that admits only of minor variations. Family resemblances can embrace notoriously intense family quarrels.

Desiderata for a Secondary Theology Anthropology

The history of Christian theological anthropology yields, I suggest, a number of features that would be desirable to find in contemporary anthropological proposals. Call them *desiderata* for any contemporary theological anthropology.

In order to bring out why they are desirable, it will be useful to distinguish among three questions that, singly or in combination, guide most projects of secondary theology. The questions are:

1. What is the logic of the *beliefs* that inform the practices composing the common life of communities of Christian faith?
2. What is the logic of *coming to belief* or of coming to faith in God so that one joins with companions in enacting the practices that compose the common life of ecclesial communities?
3. What is the logic of the *life of Christian believing* or the life of Christian faith?

These three questions may not exhaust the list of questions that guide projects of secondary theology. Each of them has deep roots in the history of Christian theology, and most important for this project, one or more of them have guided major projects of theological anthropology in the modern period. They are all perfectly valid questions to guide such projects. However, it is a methodological thesis of this project that it is a mistake to confuse or to conflate a project of secondary theology, like this one, guided and structured by its address to the first question, with projects of secondary theology that are guided and structured by their address to either or both of the second and third questions.

Part of what determines the kind of project this theological anthropology represents is that, like premodern secondary theology, it addresses only the first of these questions. Consequently, I only explore the first question in this chapter, taking premodern theological anthropology as the classical example of secondary theology focused by this question. I return to the question about the logic of coming to faith in chapter 2B, where I argue the thesis that the question of the logic of beliefs ought not to be conflated or confused with the question about the logic of coming to belief or to faith or with the question about the logic of the life of belief or the life of faith.

"Logic" in the question *What is the logic of the beliefs of communities of Christian faith?* refers to the formal logical relations among the claims that are made, explicitly and implicitly, in the course of enacting the practices that constitute the common life of communities of Christian faith. Sometimes the formal patterns of the relations among these beliefs is likened to their grammar rather than to their logic. I take it that in this context the two metaphors are largely interchangeable.

When a project of secondary theology, such as this project in theological anthropology, is guided by this question, its task is more than simply to give a descriptive account of the content of Christian beliefs. Obviously, it must do that also. Such a project assumes that members of ecclesial communities explicitly and implicitly make claims about God, God's relations to all else, and all else in relation to God, in the course of enacting the practices that constitute their common life. It further assumes that they believe the claims they make are true. The claims are their beliefs, and the logic of their relations to one another can be explored only if the beliefs themselves are articulated.

However, answers proposed to the question of the "logic" of these beliefs go beyond description of the beliefs to ask what the beliefs imply, what they do not imply that they might appear to imply, and what blocks those apparent implications—that is, why some apparent implications do not follow. They ask how these claims may be related to claims that are well-warranted by practices of inquiry, such as the natural and social sciences, that lie outside the practices constituting the communities' common life. They ask whether received—that is, traditional—formulations of those beliefs can be readily understood in the current cultural context or are widely misunderstood, if not found to be incomprehensible. They ask what theological considerations warrant communities' acceptance of proposals of fresh—that is, revisionary—articulations of such beliefs. They then venture some such proposals.

Projects in secondary theology that explore the logic of Christian beliefs have conventionally called particular theological topics (such as the nature of God, creation, the person and identity of Jesus Christ, the meaning of Jesus' life and death, sin, grace, the church, etc.) *loci* or "places" about which a variety of theological proposals can and have been made and around which theological disagreements cluster. The question about the logic of Christian beliefs is in large part a question about how these *loci* are formally related to one another.

Premodern discussions of topics in theological anthropology provide an especially clear example of this. What is instructive, I suggest, is the particular *loci* in which anthropological questions were typically located in premodern or classical theological writings, from the "fathers" through the Middle Ages to the sixteenth-century Reformation and Counter-Reformation. Anthropological questions did not constitute a *locus* of their own in premodern secondary theology. Anthropological questions were scattered among discussions of various ways in which God relates to all that is not God, and especially to human beings. Consequently, anthropological proposals were made as answers to questions that were raised by proposals made, in the first instance, about God.

That placement of anthropological proposals reflects the judgment that there is a rough logical hierarchy among Christian theological *loci*. Beliefs about God and the ways in which God relates to all that is not God are logically more basic than many other beliefs, including anthropological beliefs. Hence anthropological proposals made as part of a project exploring the logic of Christian beliefs were structured as secondary beliefs implied by, derived from, and conceptually dependent on more basic beliefs about God and God's ways of relating to all that is not God.

Consequently such anthropological proposals, even when they were controversial in their day and opposed to one another, had in common that their internal logic was theocentric. God's relation to human beings and human beings' relation to God was structurally essential to such proposals, and not a topic to be raised after (conceptually "after") the anthropological proposals had been framed in a way that bracketed the God-relation. I argue in this project that such theocentricity is a major *desideratum* in theological anthropology.

In premodern theology, anthropological questions were mostly scattered among four *loci*: doctrines of God relating creatively to all else, relating to save or redeem "fallen" creatures, relating to draw creatures to eschatological consummation, and making Godself known.

1. The principal theological context in which anthropological proposals are made in premodern Christian thought is the *locus* "creation." That is, their context is a doctrine of creation that focuses on universal features of creatureliness as such, the general features that natural kinds of beings have by virtue of God relating to them creatively. Consequently, the internal logic of anthropological proposals answering this question in this doctrinal context is inherently theocentric: God's creative relation to human beings and their relation to God is conceptually essential to them.

More precisely, backed by the creation stories in Genesis 1 and 2, both the question, "What are human beings?" and proposed theological answers are framed in a comparative and contrastive way: "In what ways are human beings like other creatures and in what ways are they distinguished from and superior to all other creatures?"

Proposals in answer to this question are articulated in one or another of competing versions of the technical philosophical conceptual pair "body/rational soul." Although there is conceptual room for a good bit of disagreement about just what "body" and "soul" mean and how they are related to each other, the terms are used to make the same fundamental theocentric points about human being.

On one hand, as *bodied*, human beings are like all physical lives in being radically dependent for their reality on God's creative relating to them ("creaturely"); are integral to the larger creaturely context of the physical cosmos as a whole, which is essentially good; are inherently temporal beings, which both entails that they are changeable physically and provides them, unlike other physical lives, the opportunity of freedom of action and the possibility of moral change for better or worse ("mutable"); are subject to definite limits of vitality and power ("finitude"); are, like some but not all physical lives, inherently social creatures whose social relations have a God-given hierarchical structure in which males are socially superior to females, free persons superior to slaves, adults superior to children, hereditary ruling families superior to the ruled, those with the resources required by the leisure for a life of contemplation or a life of civic action superior to those who must earn their living, and so on; and, like all physical lives, inherently have an end or *telos* for whose actualization they are created ("teleological" beings).

On the other hand, as *ensouled*, human beings are distinct from and superior to all other physical lives in having capacities to know and to love other creatures and God (are "rational souls"), so that the end for which they were created is to rule over other creatures in this life ("dominion") and, certainly in the next life but perhaps beginning now, to enjoy an unending intimacy of communion with God of which no other physical life is capable ("eschatological consummation in communion with God").

In short, premodern theological proposals answering the question "What is human being?" generally understand human beings as part of the larger creaturely context of a good physical cosmos, rationally self-directing, finitely free, *public agents* responsible for actualizing the two-sided purpose for which they were created: stewardship of the well-being of other creatures and intimate communion with God.

In two respects the comparative and contrastive terms in which premodern Christian anthropologies are framed are very profoundly problematic. For one thing, by construing the question "What is human being?" as the question "What distinguishes human being from, and makes it superior to, all other creatures?" such anthropologies tend to be anthropocentric in regard to the value of other creatures. Their internal logic entails a construal of the value of human being in relation to all other creatures in a highly problematic fashion. The doctrines of creation that conceptually house these anthropologies assume that, by God's creative act, creatures, while all good, fall on a continuum of degrees of value that not only culminates in but derives from the inestimable value of human beings for whose well-being they were created and who, in turn, are the stewards of other creatures' well-being. Such "value anthropocentrism" is problematic because it can yield no theological resistance to the conflation of human stewardship with human self-interested exploitation and devastation of fellow creatures.

A second way in which premodern Christian anthropologies are problematically framed in comparative and contrastive terms concerns the difference and relation between "rational soul" and "body." Although these two concepts may be understood in a variety of ways, generally each is defined by contrast to the other. Because the doctrines of creation that conceptually house these anthropologies, warranted by Genesis 1–3, locate the "image of God" that grounds human beings' inestimable value chiefly in the human soul's unique rational and volitional capacities, the internal logic of these premodern anthropologies is that the rational soul is inherently more valuable than the body. "Rational soul" in understood by contrast to "body" to the body's disadvantage. Because the body has its own needs and goals, and offers attractively pleasurable ways in which to realize them, it threatens to distract the rational soul from its proper double *telos* so that it fails properly to relate to fellow creatures and to God. Despite premodern Christian anthropologies' vigorous affirmation of the goodness of all creation including the human body, the familiar critique seems accurate that their internal logic entails suspicion, fear, and disparagement of the body. At very least, the contradiction between affirmation of the body's goodness and disparagement of it is theologically problematic.

Because it generates both a problematic value anthropocentrism and a problematic denigration of human physicality, the basic method of identifying what human being is by comparing and contrasting it with other kinds of creaturely being, which is constant throughout premodern Christian anthropology, must itself be considered problematic.

Accordingly, while *desiderata* for a contemporary theological anthropology include a conceptuality in which to frame its proposals that stresses that human creatures are bodily public agents, it is also a *desideratum* that they include a method for identifying what human beings are that does not rely on invidious comparison and contrast either with other, allegedly lesser creatures, or between human creatures' "physical" and "mental" capacities.

2. A second doctrinal context in which premodern anthropological proposals are made is the *locus* "salvation" or "redemption." Theological proposals about the nature of God's relating to save human beings are inseparable from proposals about what it is from which they need to be saved. In premodern theology what human beings need to be saved from are sin and evil, which are the consequence of humankind's fall. The anthropological question that is generated by theological proposals about the fall and how God saves human beings from its consequences is, "How can 'fallen' human creatures still be considered to be 'human' creatures?" Because the doctrinal context in which this question is located concerns a way in which God relates to human beings, the question itself and anthropological proposals answering it are both framed theocentrically.

Until the sixteenth-century Reformation, proposals answering this question trade on a common philosophical distinction in the ancient world between a substance and the dynamics of its operations. The substances in question are individual instances of what God creates as human being—that is, individual human beings. The operations are the actions they do on the basis of what they are—that is, actions exercising the powers that are essential to what they are. The predicament into which human creatures fall does not alter what they are by God's creative relating to them. The predicament itself is a deep-rooted distortion of their operations, in particular, a distortion of the ways in which they exercise their volitional and cognitive powers. It is a distortion so profound that they are incapable of correcting it without God's transforming grace.

Prior to the Reformation most Christian anthropological proposals about how the dynamics of human operations can be so distorted rely on some philosophical psychology that offers analysis of what goes wrong in immoral human beings and how to correct it. There is conceptual space for theological proposals about the nature of human beings' distortions in "fallenness" to be formulated in quite different ways. However, there are four themes that they all seem to share. First is the assumption that human action in general is teleological—that is, purposive, oriented to and defined by a goal that is seen as good. Here "good" just means "desired," "the goal that is sought." Second, from the Christian anthropological claim that human beings are created with the *telos* of communion with God, who is their true good, it is inferred that it is essential to what human beings are that they have an in-built desire for just that communion as their greatest good. In Western Christian theology, the classic expression of this thesis is Augustine's frequently quoted line, "You have made us for yourself, and our hearts are restless until they rest in you." This desire may be characterized as a love for God that is inherent in what human being is. Third, it is held that human beings' exercise of their distinctive cognitive and volitional capacities—that is, the dynamics of their operations—can be strengthened by disciplined training and practice that patterns the dynamics of those operations. The technical name for such patterns is *habitus*. Finally, it is agreed that such *habitus* are good when they strengthen human beings' capacities in ways that so orient them toward God that they realize their desire for communion with God, and they are evil when they orient them away from God so that they cannot realize that desire. The former *habitus* are theological virtues; the latter are vices. What happens in human beings' fall is not that they cease in any way to be "what" they are—that is, creaturely human substances with an in-built desire for God—but that they themselves are oriented away from God so that they cannot realize their true good: communion with God. That in turn distorts all their teleologically defined operations—their actions ordered to finite, creaturely goals—because they take the creaturely relative goods they seek to be the absolute good itself—God—rather than goods sought in the service of one's relationship to God. Furthermore, they are unable to reorient themselves properly by themselves. God's grace is required for so profound a transformation of human beings' fundamental orientation in this life. The conceptual apparatus employed in most premodern anthropology before the sixteenth century left ample room for deep disagreements about how to formulate the relation between God's grace and human creatures' agency. The upshot of this general line of analysis is that in human beings' fallen condition, what they are remains unchanged but is concretely enacted in its operations as a diseased and distorted version of itself.

Framed by the substance/operations distinction and by these four commonly held convictions about the dynamics of human operations, premodern theological proposals answering the question how human beings, profoundly distorted in their fallenness, can nonetheless remain what they are created to be have been found problematic in three different types of ways.

One type of problem is relative to modern culture. Two examples of it are especially important. The first example is that, to many modern critics, theological anthropological proposals formulated in the categories "substance" and "operation" do not yield descriptions of human beings that sound like descriptions of genuinely *personal* beings. "Substance" and "operations" are categories that were originally formulated in the context of premodern systematic explanatory theories regarding questions moderns consider the province of biology, chemistry, and physics. Modern explanatory theories in those fields are deemed systematically to bracket out all that distinguishes the personal from the impersonal, and so do premodern explanatory theories. It is problematic, the objection goes, to formulate anthropological proposals using the family of concepts to which substance and operations are systematically central, because they inappropriately objectivize genuinely personal, subjective reality.

It is only fair to note that it remains an open question how powerful this culturally relative objection really is. It is unclear that the features held to be definitive of personal reality cannot be adequately expressed and analyzed using, in appropriately nuanced fashion, the family of terms gathered about "substance" and "operations." Obviously, everything depends on such use being "appropriately nuanced." Given the conceptual incommensurability of modern theories of matter and material entities and ancient theories of material entities as "formed matter," and the incommensurability of modern theories of "event causality" and premodern theories of "substance causality," it is clear that terms like "substance" and "cause" would need to be used in ways purged of their classical hylomorphic (matter/form) connotations if they are going to be used in ways adequate to personal reality. However, the history of words does not define their meanings in current use, and the history in ancient science of the family of terms that cluster around "substance" and "operations" is not necessarily relevant to the question of their appropriateness in current discussion of personal being.

Objections from the opposite direction raise a second example of a modern culture–relative problem found in theological anthropological proposals framed in terms of "substance" and "operations." To the extent that their premise is the claim that human beings are universally created with a desire for communion with God as their absolute good, such claims seem to rely on armchair psychology. To many modern critics, such universal claims sound like empirical claims. The critics want to know what empirical psychological studies have established their truth. This type of objection finds the theological claim of a universal human desire for God problematic from the opposite direction from the first type of objection, not because it is too objectifying of human subjects, but because it is insufficiently objective in making a universal empirical claim. To continue making such a claim in the modern context requires further clarification of the logical status of universal claims about human desire for God— that is, clarification of whether they have the status of empirical claims or that of some other type of claim.

A second, theological, type of problem is found in premodern theological proposals about how human beings can remain what they are created to be even though they are profoundly distorted in their fallenness, when the proposals are framed in terms of the substance/operations distinction. The reformers Martin Luther and John Calvin find such proposals problematic because of the way they frame theological accounts of God relating to humankind to save it from the consequences of its fallenness. The Reformers retain both the general outline of the premodern account of God relating to create humankind and its anthropological implications. Their primary theological concern is to reformulate a theological account of God relating freely to save fallen human beings in a way that keeps it crystal clear that, as the New Testament tells the story, human beings neither earn that salvation nor exact it from God by the righteousness of their own actions.

That does not imply they rejected the claim that human beings are, by God's creative act, agents in public physical and social space. To the contrary, it is precisely *as* public agents who are called to stewardship of fellow creatures and universally desire communion with God as their absolute good that fallen human beings need to be saved. When Calvin, for example, addresses the principal anthropological question, "What is human being?" he does so in the conventional way as part of his account, in book 1 of the *Institutes* (1960, 1.15) of God relating to create all else, and he frames his anthropological proposal by using the conventional body/soul pair of categories.

However, when Calvin turns to the anthropological question about how fallen human beings still remain what they are created to be, he seems not to frame his proposed answers in terms of human creaturely substance and its operations. Arguably, he finds it problematic to do so because, when the claims are conceived in those terms, their conceptual grammar entails that in being saved human beings must cooperate with God—that is, do works on which their salvation depends. On that conceptual scheme, if human beings do not operate, even if it is a cooperating, they are not actually there to be saved. But in the Reformer's view, that contradicts the way in which, according to canonical Holy Scripture, God relates to save fallen humankind.

Although Calvin expresses himself inconsistently, it is arguable that he adopts as an alternative a broadly relational conceptuality in which to frame theological proposals addressing the question of how human beings, profoundly distorted in their fallenness, can nonetheless remain what they are created to be. In such an anthropology, human agents' reality does not consist in a substance somehow behind and underlying human operations, but rather human beings have their reality *in* their operations. Calvin takes up this question in book 2 of the *Institutes*, where he discusses the fall and what the predicament is from which human beings need to be saved and how God accomplishes that in Jesus Christ (esp. 2.1, 2, 4, 12, 16, 17), and in book 3, where he discusses how God brings that salvation to bear on the lives of human beings across time, "regenerating" them by the work of the Holy Spirit (esp. 3.1–3, 7–14, 19). In the context of those soteriological *loci*, he seems to adopt a relational anthropology (for quite different relationalist anthropology interpretations of Calvin, see Torrance 1952 and Engel 1988). Relationalist accounts of human being face serious conceptual problems (Harris 1998; Hartt 1957). It is not clear that, at least to date, anthropological proposals that adopt "relationalist" conceptual schemes in anthropology have addressed those problems satisfactorily.

A third, historical type of problem is found in premodern theological proposals about how human beings can remain what they are even though they are profoundly distorted in their fallenness. Premodern anthropological proposals, both those located in the *locus* "creation" and those located in the *locus* "salvation," including the Reformers' proposals, assume that Adam and Eve were historical figures created *ex nihilo* as fully actualized adult human beings, perfect specimens in every way, and that the fall was a disaster in their personal lives whose consequences include the necessity of hard labor for physical survival, social injustice and oppression, disease, pain in childbirth, and death of the body. In particular, premodern theological accounts of the predicament from which human beings need to be saved make those assumptions. The problem, of course, is that modern historical study of the origins of humankind make incredible the assumption that there ever was a period when human beings' physical survival did not require hard labor, child bearing was not painful, and people did not face death. The narrative of a calamity of those proportions befalling humankind lacks any historical evidence. The notion of there being an individual or a pair who began the species *Homo sapiens* as fully actualized human beings *ex nihilo*, without living antecedents, is unintelligible in the context of an evolutionary view of the origin of every living species. It is no longer believable that a unique fall ever happened or that it happened to anyone like Adam and Eve. The theological question this raises is whether Christian beliefs about God relating to save humankind and beliefs about what is so wrong with human beings as to require the divine saving act to which the Gospels testify are logically dependent on claims that Adam and Eve are historical figures and the fall is a unique historical event (for an influential nineteenth-century American defense of the position that the two are logically inseparable, see Hodge 1872, 33–42, 75–92). If they are dependent on those historical claims, and the claims are false, does that entail that premodern theological proposals about sin and salvation must be radically reformulated or else wholly abandoned? In particular, must anthropological proposals be abandoned that seek to show how human beings can still be what they are created to be despite their distortion in the fall? Any argument for positive answers to these questions needs to show that the logic of Christian beliefs about sin and salvation is independent of the historicity of Adam, Eve, and the fall.

Accordingly, while *desiderata* for a contemporary theological anthropology may include a conceptuality in which to frame its proposals that stresses that human creatures are bodily public agents, it is also a *desideratum* that such a conceptuality describes human beings in a way that (1) is recognizable to contemporary readers as an account of genuinely "personal" beings, (2) makes clear how its conceptuality is like and unlike that of the dominant mode of scientific study of "persons"—that is, psychology—(3) is a conceptuality that can be employed to make clear the theological claim that creaturely human agents can neither earn or exact their salvation from God, and (4) is a conceptuality that makes it clear that theological anthropological proposals do not logically depend on the historicity of Adam, Eve, and the fall.

3. A third doctrinal context in which premodern anthropological proposals are made is the *locus* "eschatological consummation." Premodern proposals about God's drawing human beings to eschatological consummation are framed in a rhetoric of the glorification of human creatures, their transformation into immortal beings who, in their perfect communion with God, not only are oriented toward God but can no longer turn away from God. Theological proposals about the way God relates to draw human beings to their eschatological consummation in communion with God presuppose proposals about what human beings are by virtue of God relating to them creatively. It is creatures as creatures, and without ceasing to be creatures, who are drawn to eschatological consummation. The anthropological question that is generated by the tension between the claim that in eschatological consummation human beings remain what they were created to be and yet are glorified is, "What about human being makes it possible for the *same* human bodied agents who have died to be raised subsequently for eschatological communion with God?" The question is not

"How does God raise the dead?" but "What is the raised human being?" Here too, because the doctrinal context in which this question is located concerns a way in which God relates to human beings, both the question itself and the anthropological proposals answering it are framed theocentrically.

Anthropological proposals answering this question against the background of anthropological proposals about what human creatures are created to be are framed in terms of the body/rational soul distinction. Lodged in the context of an account of God relating to draw human beings to their eschatological consummation, however, they divide the question about the continuity between pre-death and resurrected human beings into proposals about the soul and proposals about the body.

On one side, what makes it possible for the one who is resurrected to be the same as the one who lived and died is her or his rational soul. This point depends on reciprocally contrastive definitions of "rational soul" and "body." Living physical bodies can die because physical bodies are made of matter that is a composite of parts that can come a-part, and, in bodies dynamically integrated as a life, can dis-integrate in death. In short, it is subject to "corruption." By contrast, "rational souls" are the "principle" of the life of living bodies. They are simple, have no parts into which to disintegrate, and therefore cannot die. By virtue of God's creative relating to them, rational souls are immortal. Strictly speaking, souls do not die; bodies die. However, in eschatological consummation, rational souls, even souls that once were oriented away from God—that is, were fallen so that their operations were thoroughly distorted—are glorified in that they not only become properly oriented toward God, but become incapable of turning away from God. That is, the *telos* for which they are created is fully actualized. The immortal rational soul is what makes the risen human being the same as the one who died, at least in the sense of "numerically identical with."

On the other side, human bodies are essential to what human being is by virtue of God's creative relating to them. Although a human being's soul is the basis of the numerical identity of a raised human being with the one who died, it is not, as eschatologically consummated, fully the same person apart from its body. Warranted by Paul's discussion of the general resurrection in 1 Corinthians 15:35–57, premodern anthropology insists that eschatological consummation of human beings entails the resurrection of the body.

In the context of any version of the body/rational soul conceptual pair, however, the very same text creates conceptual puzzles. Paul distinguishes between, on the one hand, a physical body, characterized as "perishable," "sown" (i.e., buried?) in "dishonor" and in "weakness," "of dust," "mortal," and on the other hand a "spiritual body" characterized as "imperishable," raised in "glory" and in "power," and "of heaven." Paul claims that in the resurrection "we" will be changed from the first to the second (1 Cor. 15:42b–53). He seems to suggest that the paradigm for the transformation the risen body undergoes is the transformation Jesus' body undergoes in his own resurrection (1 Cor. 15:45–49). Although both are "imperishable," "spirit" and "spiritual" are not to be conflated with "soul" or "soulish." Paul is not taken to say that at the resurrection a physical body turns into a soul. Rather, it *somehow* remains the self-same body that had died (it is the resurrection of the body), but in a radically transformed state, perhaps an analogy with the transformation of Jesus' body in his resurrection, although recognizable as the one who had lived and died.

That "somehow" leaves a great deal of conceptual room in premodern theological anthropology for alternative and conflicting proposals about what constitutes the identity, not between a risen human creaturely agent and one who had died, but between that agent's perishable physical body that died and the risen imperishable spiritual body. Such proposals range from the thesis that the risen body is reconstituted by reassembling the "dust"—that is, the matter—into which it had disintegrated following death but now as a body that cannot disintegrate, to the thesis that the risen body is formed by the same form that unified into a living whole the matter of the body that had died, giving definition to its uniquely individual life (for overviews of such proposals in patristic literature, see Daley 1991; and in the Middle Ages, Bynum 1995).

Such premodern theological proposals answering the question about what makes it possible for the same human bodied agents who died subsequently to be raised for eschatological communion with God are problematic in two broad ways.

One broad way in which they are problematic embraces a set of objections raised by modern scientific understanding of the physical world, organic and inorganic. Here again, problems are raised by the apparent incommensurability of the theoretical frameworks in which premodern and modern cultures describe and explain inorganic and organic matter, the nature of life, and what happens in death. Life exhibiting complex mental capacities is no longer understood to be a function of a single metaphysical principle—that is, a rational soul that is both distinguishable from and separable from a living body. This modern understanding of life is part of the origin of by now standard objections to anthropological reliance on body-soul dualisms. It is also the basis of the huge literature of vigorous scientific and philosophical debates about the relation between mind and brain or mind and body and about the nature of consciousness.

However, the problems facing anthropological proposals conceptually housed in and framed by theological claims about God relating to draw all else to eschatological consummation go much deeper. The basis of objections to such anthropological proposals is not that resurrection is demonstrably impossible. It is, after all, very difficult to prove in the abstract that any coherently describable event is impossible. The more basic question is whether theological claims about resurrection, and therewith proposals about the anthropological implications of resurrection, can be formulated in intelligible and internally coherent ways that are consonant with modern concepts of matter, the physical, organic life, consciousness, and mind.

A second broad way in which such anthropological proposals are problematic embraces a set of theological objections largely raised by modern biblical scholarship. It is objected that biblical eschatological texts invoke distinctions quite different from those expressed by the "body/rational soul" conceptual pair and are distorted when interpreted in terms of that pair and the family of anthropological concepts that gather around them in premodern theology. In particular, the view of death in the texts of canonical Holy Scripture is, on the whole, that human creatures as such die. The objection follows that use of any conceptual scheme that distinguishes, as premodern anthropology regularly does, between a human being's mortal body, which dies, and immortal soul, in order to elucidate an anthropology of death and resurrection, systematically distorts the scriptural anthropological claims they profess to honor. More important, perhaps, modern biblical scholarship has shown that hope in God's drawing creation to a long-promised eschatological consummation is fundamental and pervasive in the theologies of most New Testament texts. Such hope does not focus primarily on the ultimate fate of individual human beings, but on the cosmos, history as a whole, the structure of the present social and cultural context of human life, and the mission in "this world" of communities of Christian faith. The theological objection is that premodern anthropological proposals located in and framed by accounts of God drawing all else to eschatological consummation consist of a set of heterogeneous claims about a clutch of loosely related "last things" (*eschata*), like one's own resurrection and personal salvation or damnation at judgment day, that are framed in an individualistic fashion that does not comport with most scriptural accounts of God drawing all else to eschatological consummation. Finally, it is objected that premodern anthropological proposals framed by eschatological beliefs tend to fail to take into account the peculiar rhetoric of New Testament stories of God drawing creation to eschatological consummation. It is a rhetoric in which language is used at the outermost border of what can be said. The objection urges that it is doubtful that such rhetoric can be appropriately interpreted as making truth claims about resurrected human beings from which additional truth claims can be inferred and further conclusions drawn about the metaphysical identity and structure of bodily risen human beings.

Accordingly, *desiderata* for a contemporary theological anthropology also include explicit attention to how the way in which its proposals are conceptualized comports with two quite different types of discourse, modern and biblical. It needs to be shown how the way in which theological anthropological proposals are conceptualized comports with the way in which modern scientific interpretations of human being are conceptualized. It also needs to be shown how the way in which theological anthropological proposals are conceptualized comports with canonical Christian Holy Scripture's narratives of God drawing all else, including human creatures, to eschatological consummation. Reasons for acknowledging the authority of canonical Holy Scripture in ecclesial secondary theology in regard to theological proposals about ways in which God relates to all that is not God were given earlier in this chapter. They do not entail any privileging of the historically relative, culturally conditioned conceptualities in which those narratives are articulated. Calvin famously taught that in the divinely inspired biblical texts, God "accommodates himself" to the mind-set of their original hearers and readers. Charles Hodge, as vigorous a defender as one could hope to find of the view that the divinely inspired, inerrant biblical texts have the logical force of assertion, teaching doctrine, held that the texts reveal all kinds of culturally conditioned beliefs that their human writers held (and we believe to be false, e.g., that the sun revolves around the earth) but did not teach them in their biblical writings (Hodge 1857, 668, 669; 1872, 165). The *desideratum* here is not that it be shown how the conceptuality of contemporary anthropological proposals comports with the conceptuality in which biblical eschatological texts is articulated, but how it comports with the narrative logic of canonical accounts of how God relates to all that is not God. In particular, it is desirable that, negatively, anthropological proposals avoid individualistic formulations that do not comport with canonical accounts of the way God relates to draw creation to eschatological consummation.

4. The fourth major doctrinal context in which premodern anthropological proposals are made is discussion of "revelation." In that context, theological proposals are made about how best to understand the claim that God relates to human beings to disclose God's will regarding some particular situation, God's moral commands, some event that is going to happen in the future, God's disposition toward and purposes for creatures, God's promises, or even "God Godself."

In premodern theology proposals about revelation are made in each of the three *loci* we have considered so far, and in each a different anthropological question arises.

In regard to God relating creatively, proposals about God relating to reveal something raise the question, "How can finite human creatures with their limited cognitive capacities know the infinite God?" In premodern theology, anthropological proposals answering that question take the form of explicating the "image of God" in which, according to Genesis 1:27, God created Adam. If "only like knows like" (note the epistemological assumption), then it must be in virtue of the likeness to God by which human beings are in God's "image" that finite human beings can know the infinite God. The "image of God" accounts for the human capacity to receive God's revelation, and it may in addition ground a human capacity to discover truths about God from close study of creation. However, it only makes possible very limited knowledge of God, who is humanly incomprehensible.

Given the variety of technical meanings that "soul" and "body" can have and the variety of ways in which their relation to each other may be understood, there is conceptual room in premodern secondary theology for different explanations of the "image." Despite their variety, however, anthropological proposals about the image of God all share the view that the image is to be located somehow more in human beings' rational souls than in their bodies. Moreover, they all presuppose a hierarchical relation between body and rational soul in which a human being's rational soul is more "God-like" than is the body.

In regard to God relating to save fallen human creatures, proposals about God relating to reveal something raise the question, "If human beings are so profoundly distorted that God must relate in the radical way of Incarnation to save them, how can such 'fallen' creatures know God?" In premodern theology, anthropological proposals answering that question generally take the form of an account of the Holy Spirit bringing the operations of fallen human beings to conform increasingly to the pattern of Jesus Christ's life and of his relationship with the One he called "Father" so that the distortions of those operations are healed (the root meaning of "save") and the image of God restored so that it becomes possible again to know God.

In regard to God relating to draw creation to eschatological consummation, proposals about God relating to reveal something raise the question, "How can human creatures who are ontologically radically dependent on God come to know God in the intimate way of eschatological communion while truly remaining creatures?" In premodern theology, anthropological proposals answering that question tend to trade on the proposal that, by virtue of God's creative relating, what human beings are includes both rational soul with cognitive capacities and the *telos* of eschatological consummation in intimate communion with God. Exercise of the rational soul's cognitive capacities in intimate communion with God is what human beings were created for. Eschatological realization of intimate communion with God is not a violation of what human beings are by God's creative relating; rather, it is the final actualization of what they are. Their participation in communion with God, and the knowledge of God they have in that communion, remain specifically human communing and knowing. They remain what they are. But, fully conformed by the power of the Holy Spirit to Jesus Christ in his communion with the One he calls "Father," their capacities for knowledge and love are eschatologically transformed. In that transformation their creaturely powers are not just healed from the effects of sin, but enhanced. Such enhancement does not entail that they cease having limits. They remain finite creaturely powers, and God remains beyond human powers to comprehend God. But eschatologically enhanced, those powers are capable of knowing and loving God more deeply, not only more deeply than they could as fallen, but more deeply than they could as created.

[handwritten marginal note: Thus the communion seems to be one of Spirit]

The fact that the anthropological questions that arise in the context of premodern proposals about God relating to reveal are scattered in this way among secondary theology discussions of the ways in which the three other ways in which God relates to all else (i.e., to create, to save, and to draw to eschatological consummation) are revelatory raises an important point about the place of the topic of revelation in the logic of Christian beliefs. It does not seem to be logically basic in the way the *loci* creation, salvation or redemption, and eschatology are basic. It seems plausible to conclude that in premodern theology revelation it is not so much a *locus* in its own right as an aspect of each of the other three, a revelatory aspect of God relating to all else, respectively, to create it, to save it, and to consummate it eschatologically. In that case, theological proposals to answer anthropological questions raised in a secondary theology discussion of the topic of revelation are shaped by their location in the larger theological context of a discussion of creation, or salvation, or eschatological consummation.

Accordingly, what is found to be problematic in premodern proposals answering anthropological questions raised in discussions of revelation are variations of what is found to be problematic in the anthropological proposals answering questions raised in the three previous subsections.

This section of the chapter has further specified the kind of project this is by identifying a question that guides it: what is the logic of Christian beliefs? The chapter has exhibited some of the implications of this question for this project. Taking premodern Christian theological anthropology as the paradigmatic instance of doing theology in a way guided by that question, we have at once outlined some analyses of the way a few specifically anthropological beliefs are logically related to each other and to more basic Christian beliefs about ways in which God relates to all that is not God, with special attention to what in premodern anthropological proposals is especially problematic in the early twenty-first-century cultural context, and generated a budget of *desiderata* for contemporary theological anthropological proposals guided by the question about the logic of Christian beliefs.

The *desiderata* fall into roughly three groups: thematic, systematic, and conceptual. Thematically, they include an insistence that anthropological proposals be materially theocentric and that what is privileged about human beings is that they are bodily public agents in community. Systematically, it is desirable that it be kept clear that anthropological proposals have a secondary, dependent status, logically derivative from more basic Christian theological claims about ways God relates to all that is not God; that it be kept clear that human beings in no way earn or exact that relationship with God; that anthropological proposals be formulated in ways that avoid reliance on invidious comparison and contrast either with other creatures or between various aspects of human beings themselves; and that they be formulated in ways that are logically independent of the historicity of Adam, Eve, and the fall. Conceptually, it is desirable that contemporary anthropological proposals be formulated in ways in which human beings are recognizably personal, but also in ways that make clear how theological anthropological claims are and are not like modern psychological accounts of human being, and more broadly are formulated in ways that show how they comport conceptually with scriptural and modern scientific discourses about human being. Part of the kind of project this anthropology is, is its attempt to satisfy these *desiderata*.

Secondary Theology as "Faith Seeking Understanding"

If "understanding" and "faith" may be construed in the ways they have been thus far in this chapter, the kind of project in secondary theology represented by this anthropology can be characterized as "faith seeking understanding." The phrase is Anselm of Canterbury's description of his own theological projects—for example, in *Cur Deus Homo*, *Proslogium*, and *Monologium*—and this anthropological project could be called "Anselmian" only in a very loose and extended use of the term, given the ways in which "understanding" and "faith" are used here. Consider each of them in turn.

In this anthropological project addressed to the question "What is the logic of Christian beliefs?" "seeking understanding" does not consist, as it arguably does for Anselm, of seeking the internal rationale that, once grasped, makes Christian beliefs impossible to doubt or to deny. Rather, "seeking understanding" is construed here as the project of exhibiting the intelligibility of practices that compose the common life of communities of Christian faith by identifying the ways in which they are conceptually formed, the "end" to which they are enacted, their "standards of excellence," and how they hang together—that is, the patterns of their relationships with one another—all in order to assess critically whether the community's enactments of the practices are adequate. Such a project must itself be self-critical. That is, it must include critical assessment of whether received and proposed ways of conceptualizing each of the above are adequate in regard to the ways in which they are conceptually formed, their end, their standards of excellence, the relationships among the practices they form, and how they comport with other beliefs that are important but not inherent in the practices that make up the common life of ecclesial communities.

For its part, the faith for which understanding is sought is not construed in this project as the name of a set of beliefs that are affirmed and taught by communities of Christian faith—that is, dogmas (as in "the faith of the church"). Nor is it construed, as it is in much modern and contemporary theology understood to be in the Anselmian mode, as the name of an existential condition (as in "faith as subjectivity at its most intense" or "faith as ultimate concern"). Rather "faith" is used to name a complex of conceptually formed practices that make up much of the common life of communities of Christian faith, practices that deeply define the communal identities and the personal identities of the communities' members who enact the practices.

I suggest that construing "understanding" and "faith" in these ways goes a long way toward framing anthropological proposals in ways that can realize several of the *desiderata* for a contemporary theological anthropology identified in the critical overview of classical Christian anthropologies in the previous section of this chapter. Therefore, it is important to deflect possible misinterpretations by noting what this proposal does *not* do.

Construing "understanding" and "faith" in this way, for example, is a move to avoid systematically interiorizing them by defining them exclusively in privatizing categories, while at the same time it avoids de-subjectivizing or objectivizing them. My understanding something said or done is not an interior and private mental process that I subsequently describe and report by saying or writing, in effect, "I am understanding it." Rather, understanding human behavior and speech involves at least two human beings. On my side it is more closely related to "being able" (to address the problem, to follow the instructions, to respond relevantly to the comment, etc.) than it is to a private interior process. And on the other person's side, my understanding is established by their being satisfied that I am able to (address the problem, follow the instructions, respond relevantly to the comment, etc.). However, because "understanding" is closer to being able (i.e., to a capacity) than it is to a private mental process, it does not follow that it can be objectivized through an exhaustively reductionist explanation by a life science or behaviorist psychological analysis. Coming to understand some things said and done can be existentially shaping, forming a human being's personal identity. It is not bodies, but whole human beings who understand.

Parallel consequences follow when faith is construed as enactment of practices that constitute the common life of communities of Christian faith. Given that these practices are conceptually formed, they involve both acting and believing. They are not the practices of systematically elusive souls, spirits, subjectivities (not even intersubjectivities), minds, or interiorities. Rather, their enactments are at least partly conscious and intentional human action, in which bodied human beings interact with one another in public spaces, both the public space constituted by the immediate community itself, and public spaces constituted by their larger host societies. Nonetheless, enactments of such practices cannot be adequately analyzed exhaustively in objectivizing ways by the social and behavioral sciences. Learning to enact the practices regularly and self-critically with others often shapes deeply and decisively the personal identities of the human beings who participate in them, including their conscious and unconscious subjectivities. If "heart" is used, as it most often is in canonical Christian Holy Scripture, to stand for the whole of a human being and not for the affections only, we may say that these practices shape and give form to the heart. Construed this way, "faith" embraces at once a lived life and identity-shaping beliefs, what classically have been distinguished and all too often separated as "will," "heart," and "mind."

Construing "understanding" and "faith" in this way is also a move to avoid individualizing faith. The complex of practices that constitute faith are socially established human interactivities. These practices define the communities' corporate or communal identity. They also decisively shape the personal identities of the members of the community who enact them. Of course, the human activity that enacts practices is inherently the activity of individual human beings, and many of them may be enacted in isolation from others in the community. However, doing so is parasitic on participation in communal enactments of those practices. The relation between shaping communal identity and shaping personal identities is dialectical; each requires the other to be itself. Nonetheless, as socially established, these practices are antecedent to any one individual who enters the community by birth or otherwise. The community is not an association of those who have come antecedently to participate individually in the same practices and find it helpful to continue enacting them in concert. It is not an association of persons of faith where "faith" is understood individualistically.

At the same time this proposal is not a move that necessarily communalizes faith in such a way that personal identity is wholly absorbed in communal identity. Nor does it necessarily entail that human beings whose personal identities are decisively shaped by participation in the communal practices of a community of Christian faith come to have, if not identical personal identities, identities whose differences are so marginal that they are virtually interchangeable. That, of course, is a logical possibility. Tragically, it is not news that this possibility has often been actualized in disastrous ways in highly authoritarian communities, Christian and otherwise, both religious and secular. However, it is not logically or psychologically necessary that this danger be actualized.

Whether or not this danger is actualized depends in large part on the specific character of the practices that constitute the common life of a community. It especially depends on two things: whether the community's socially established practices are so formed as to respect the array of concrete particularities that mark one human being as different from another, and whether the practices as socially established are so formed as to be constantly self-critical regarding how well enactments of the practices meet the standards of excellence that partly define them, and whether they are in fact consonant with their end (which is not necessarily a product). I hold that properly Christian practices exhibit those two qualities. They could function to dissolve personal identities into a communal identity only on pain of radical failure both to be directed to their proper end and to meet their own standards of excellence.

Nor does the way this proposal construes understanding and faith entail that the practices that comprise the common life of ecclesial communities are identically the same in all genuine or true communities of Christian faith. It is obvious from the history of Christianity that they are not. Construal of faith as a set of practices allows plenty of conceptual space for acknowledgment of disagreements and conflicts about the practices that constitute the common life of communities of Christian faith, both between different communities and within each of them. The practices that constitute the common life of communities of Christian faith and define their communal identities give them a certain unity, but they do not necessarily require uniformity of practice in order for the communities to count as communities of Christian faith.

The way this proposal construes "understanding" and "faith" is also a move to avoid dehistoricizing faith. Faith construed as a set of practices, and the communities of Christian faith whose common life they comprise, are always located in concrete social and cultural contexts at particular times and places in history. Communities of Christian faith are always communities of human beings who live in larger host societies and their cultures and whose identities are shaped by those cultures. The practices that constitute the common life of such communities have developed and changed over time, shaped by practices, iconography, gestures, music, rhetorical forms, beliefs, technical terms, and concepts borrowed from their host societies and their cultures. They are inescapably historically relative to those cultures. At the same time, these practices have thus far proven to have integrity of their own and, with that, a certain amount of power to shape their host society and its culture as well. It is not as though these practices are socially reconstructed *de novo* with every minor or major change in their host societies' cultures. While it is certainly true that efforts to specify in the abstract what constitutes the self-sameness of a community's identity, or a human being's personal identity, across historical and cultural change regularly prove inadequate, it is equally true that such self-sameness cannot simply be reduced to a chronicle cataloging the causal connections between what it was at one moment, period, or epoch in the past and what it became in the subsequent moment, period, or epoch.

Finally, the way this proposal construes "understanding" and "faith" is a move to avoid undue systematization of the logic of Christian beliefs, and the logic of anthropological beliefs in particular. The assumption, which Anselm seems to make concerning beliefs about God in his description of theology as "faith seeking understanding," that Christian beliefs (i.e., the "faith") have an internal rationale that, once grasped (i.e., "understood"), makes it impossible to doubt or to deny them, implies that the logic of the beliefs is systematic such that they form a logical system. In contrast, the practices that constitute the common life of communities of Christian faith do not appear to be systematic, and the effort to understand them ought not to begin by simply assuming that they have some deep underlying systematic rationale. Furthermore, the personal lives they shape existentially do not themselves appear to be systems. Kierkegaard's maxim, "Existence is not a system," ought to be taken seriously, at least as a warning not to begin exploration of the logic of Christian anthropological beliefs by simply assuming that human existence is some kind of system. An account of the logic of Christian anthropological beliefs aiming to exhibit them as a "system" may turn out itself to be a systematically distorted account of human being. Focusing on the apparently unsystematic, conceptually shaped practices that constitute the common life of ecclesial communities as the faith that is to be understood serves, I propose, to make this a project in systematically unsystematic secondary theology.

CHAPTER **2A**

The One with Whom We Have to Do

If the root question for Christian anthropology is "What is implied about human personhood by the claim that God actively relates to us?" then obviously the next question is "Who or what is God?" If the ultimate context in which we must be understood is God relating to us, how is God best understood? And, most important for our purposes, what does that understanding of God imply about how we should characterize the way in which God relates to us?

Classically, Christian understandings of God are Trinitarian. By a "Trinitarian understanding" of God, I mean any understanding of God that is accountable to the Nicene Creed as summarized in the more recently conventional formula: God is one substance in three persons. The claim that classical Christian understandings of God are Trinitarian is a descriptive historical claim. I shall proceed as though it were also a normative claim, but I shall not attempt to defend its normative status here. That is the task of another book, as yet unwritten by me.

My aim in this project is to think through the agenda of theological anthropology in a way shaped from beginning to end by the triunity of the God with whom we have to do. By this move I locate theological anthropology in the larger theological context of a revival of interest among theologians in the topic of the Trinity (e.g., Jenson 1982, 1984, 1997; Johnson 1994; Jungel 1976; LaCugna 1991; Moltmann 1981; Pannenberg 1991; cf. Barth 1936, 1957; Rahner 1970; Welch 1952). This revival has the character of a conversation among thinkers whose disagreements about the Trinity emerge in a larger context of shared convictions. It has generated contrasting, indeed conflicting, doctrines of the Trinity. However, rather than defend any particular Trinitarian understanding of God, I want in this chapter to bring out aspects of Trinitarian understandings of God that have important implications for theological anthropology.

46

Perhaps the best way to do this lies in telling a story about the process of discovering Trinitarian ways to understand God that moves through five moments, each with major anthropological implications. This story also provides the warrant for speaking in the plural of Trinitarian understandings of God rather than *the* doctrine of the Trinity.

The story that follows (1) begins with reflection on the threefold way in which canonical Christian Scripture leads us to speak of God's relating to us and how that is related to a triadic formula of divine names used in Christian practices ("Father," "Son," "Holy Spirit"); (2) moves away from the threefoldness of God's active relating to us to focus on God's relation to Jesus in just one of the ways in which God relates to us; (3) formulates creedally the implications for understanding God of that one way in which God relates to humankind; (4) moves then from God's active relating to all-that-is-not-God to reflection on how God is intrinsically self-relating; and (5) returns finally to the original topic, reflection on the threefold way in which God relates to all-that-is-not-God, reconceiving it more complexly.

Doxology and Personal Identity

It is important to Christian theological anthropology that Christian reflection on how to talk about God begins as it originally began, with the way God is named and addressed in Christian practices. In their cultural contexts, these practices deeply shaped early Christians' personal identities, both individual and communal. Contemporary Christians continue to engage in these practices in ways that, for better and worse in quite different cultural contexts, shape their identities as well. Particularly important for our topic is the fact that, early and late, practices of prayer and corporate worship, instruction and education, and all manner of blessing of important turning points in persons' lives such as births, meals, marriages, burials, and especially baptism, are concluded "in the name of the Father, the Son, and the Holy Spirit" (see, e.g., Matt. 28:19; 2 Cor. 13:13). This formula acknowledges God actively relating to human persons in, through, and under these practices that shape their personal identities. The formula is not yet, properly speaking, a Trinitarian formula, let alone a brief Trinitarian creed. It is rather a triadic doxological formula whose use is warranted by slight New Testament precedent (cf. Kelly 1958, part 2). The formula is used in talk to God and on behalf of God, not in talk about God.

Then as now, this triadic doxological phrase gives a specifically Christian description of God's identity by reference to three sets of stories about God: stories about God as the source of all reality other than God, God as "Father of us all"; stories about God as reconciler of alienated humankind in Jesus Christ; and stories about God bringing us to consummation in eschatological life in the Holy Spirit.

An important feature of these uses of the triadic expression is that they are self-involving. That is, the way they are used not only acknowledges that the people who worship and pray, who are being blessed or baptized, are located within the ultimate context of God's active relating to them. More than that, use of the triadic formula explicitly places those people and their histories in the context of longer stories telling of God's threefold way of relating to them. To use the formula is to say that, among other things, what and who we are and how we ought to be is constituted by God relating to us in this threefold way. Thus, the triadic formula serves to give an identity description, not only of God, but also of its users.

Such self-involving use of the triadic formula in conjunction with scriptural stories of God's three ways of relating to us raises the question of how to understand God's singularity in this threefoldness. Posed this way, the challenge appeared to be to synthesize the threefold identity description of God into a single coherent account of God. As we shall see, such synthesizing is not, in fact, what happened historically.

What is important to note here is that the process of reflection on who God is, which was provoked by the threefoldness of the doxological formula, has been anthropologically significant from the beginning because it arose in identity-shaping Christian practices, and no matter how abstruse the speculations it has generated subsequently, it has remained rooted in that context thereafter.

The Economy of Salvation and Trinity

The next moment in the story of theological reflection's movement to properly Trinitarian understandings of God involved a shift of focus. Focus shifted from the full range of the threefold way in which God is said to relate to us to just one of the ways in which God relates to us: God redemptively relating to us in Jesus Christ. The shift was driven by the terms used to frame an early-fourth-century controversy sparked by a long series of conflicts, largely over the interpretation of Origen, that came to a head in a controversy, already under way by AD 321, between Arius, a priest of Alexandria, and his bishops, first Alexander and then Alexander's successor as bishop, Athanasius (for dating based on documentary remains, see the survey in R. Williams 1987, 48–91).

As I noted earlier, Christian reflection about God began with puzzlement about how to reconcile God's singularity with the threefoldness of God's active relating to all-that-is-not-God. Since the late second century, Christian writers had called God's ways of relating actively to the cosmos the "divine economy." The secular meaning of "economy" (Gk. *oikonomia*) was that of administering or managing a household. Christian writers used the term to designate God's way of ordering God's household, the entire cosmos. God manages all-that-is-not-God in creating it, in drawing it to an eschatological consummation, and in reconciling it when it is estranged and distorted in sin. The divine economy in this broad sense was the original framework within which Christians reflected on how best to characterize God.

The shift of focus involved narrowing the theological meaning of "divine economy." "Economy" continues to be used for all God's relations with the created order. However, "economy" tended in the context of the controversy centered on Arius to be understood as a synonym for God's saving act in Jesus Christ, the economy of reconciliation. This shift was driven by fourth-century Christian thinkers' preoccupation with controversies about how best to describe the particular relation between God and the Word of God incarnate in Jesus Christ.

The great fixed point in the controversies was the Christian gospel, the good news that "in Christ God was reconciling the world" to God (2 Cor. 5:19). God's reconciling act was narrated in the church's four canonical Gospels. They tell the story of God accomplishing this reconciliation in the ministry, crucifixion, and resurrection of Jesus Christ, a story told by the church as continuous with Old Testament accounts of God's saving history with Israel. There are three principal characters in each of the four tellings of this story: Jesus, who is also called "Son" and "Word"; the one whom Jesus calls "Father"; and the "Holy Spirit." However, it was also evident to early Christian thinkers that the four Gospels tell their apparently common story in ways that yield puzzlingly different pictures of the identities of these three principal characters. The Gospels do this by telling their generally common story with differences in detail and narrative sequence, thematic emphasis, and dominant image. The controversies turned on questions about how best to fit the Gospels' several identity descriptions of "Son," "Father," and "Holy Spirit" together coherently within the one story of the divine economy of reconciliation.

Thus, the controversies debated contrasting proposals about how best to understand the relations between the "Son" and the "Father" within the economy of reconciliation. That is, the controversies turned on how best to analyze the story of the divine economy so as most accurately to characterize God's relation to the Word or Son and the Word or Son's relation to God within that story. That was, of course, perfectly reasonable to do. The controversies were about how best to interpret the Gospels' several narratives, and they, in turn, all present themselves as stories about Jesus, who is variously called "Son" and "Word" of God.

In the course of their controversy, Bishop Alexander and Arius each enlisted the support of bishops in other cities to his own side. There were exchanges of letters and a flurry of essays as well as formal confessional statements defending and attacking each side. The theological issues driving the conflict were entangled with political and economic issues. The emperor feared that division in the church threatened unity in the empire. The controversy was also tangled with long-standing political conflicts in Egypt. At one point it embroiled Bishop Athanasius in charges that he was responsible also for an Egyptian economic crisis brought on by a threat to cut export of grain on which much of the empire depended. The whole tale would be darkly comic were it not so reprehensible, apparently on all sides. It takes a very strong doctrine of the Holy Spirit to construe the hand of God working through all of this to bring the Christian community to clearer understanding of God (see Pettersen 1995, 1–19; R. Williams 1987, 29–48).

By imperial edict the emperor called an ecumenical council in AD 325 to meet at Nicaea to resolve the controversy. The "resolution" consisted of the adoption by the vast majority of bishops of a creed summarizing in brief verbal formulas what was supposed thereafter to be common understanding of the relation between the Father and the Son. It did not end the controversy, but it did provide a textual focus—that is, a semantic and syntactic focus—for another five decades or more of controversies.

Perhaps the theologically most important spokesperson supporting the Nicene formulation in the years following the council was Athanasius, who did not succeed Alexander as bishop of Alexandria until three years after the council. Athanasius described the writers whom he opposed as followers of Arius. However, that is misleading. They resisted various formulations of Nicaea, or the implications and interpretations offered by Athanasius, but they did not necessarily agree with Arius either. There was no Arian sect, nor was Arius the titular head of a coherent theological "school." Athanasius's opponents were not necessarily even anti-Nicene; several professed to accept the Nicene formulas, but to interpret them in a different way than Athanasius. Better, perhaps, to call them simply un-Nicene. In order to show the consequences of the controversy on which Nicaea focused for anthropology as well as for understanding God, it will be useful to outline the core issues as each side perceived them and the internal logic driving each side's proposed resolution of the issues, using Athanasius and Arius as prototypes of each side.

Athanasius and Arius presented themselves as biblical theologians and can be read as primarily engaged in a hermeneutical dispute (see Kannengeisser 1991, 1–40; R. Williams 1987, 106–16). What is at stake is the authenticity of Christian practices of interpreting Scripture in preaching, celebration of sacraments, and teaching. The crucial question to ask about each such act of interpretation is this: "Does it really tell the stories that define the identities of Christian persons and communities, or does it, however unintentionally, tell some other story that defines some other identity?" Scriptural interpreters then, as in every generation, used conceptual equipment available to them in the culture they shared with non-Christians. In effect, each side to the controversy held that the extrabiblical concepts that the other side employed in telling the story of reconciliation, while adequate perhaps to certain features of the common story, were so inadequate to other features of the story that they deformed it into something Christianly unrecognizable.

What they shared needs to be stressed. They shared some theological convictions which functioned as common background beliefs that provided the context in which their disagreements could be formulated. Both sides agreed that the God who reconciles humankind in Jesus Christ is identical with the "Father" God who creates humankind and all-else-that-is-not-God from nothing (*ex nihilo*) by a free and sovereign act rather than by emanation. Hence they agreed that there is in some sense a disjunction in being, rather than a continuum of being, between Creator and creation. Both agreed that the "Father" God who creates alone exercises *monarchia* (Gk. *monos* = one; *arche* = first principle; that is, God alone is the first principle of the cosmos), managing the cosmos without resistance from other ultimate principles. Hence they agree that, without violation of the distinction between Creator and creatures, God, in exercising *monarchia*, is in some way causally related to, and thus in some way involved with, creatures. Both agree that God is rational, utterly free, active, and alive. Both agree that such a reality cannot be comprehended by human minds, who must, therefore, finally acknowledge that God in Godself is ineffable. Both sides affirmed that in some sense Jesus is the divine Logos or Word incarnate and is the Savior of the world. Both wanted to stress that the Savior truly shared human suffering. Both sides further agreed that, as "Son of God who has assumed human flesh" and as "Word of God become flesh," Jesus is genuinely other than God the Father. "Logos" and "Father" are not merely two different modes in which one divine reality somehow beyond the two of them manifested itself for certain periods of history. The church had rejected that view ("modalism") by the end of the third century. Both sides affirmed that the relation between Logos and God was in some way filial, like that between a father and a son, as well as mental or psychological, like the relation between an intellect and its wisdom or its ideas.

The question dividing Athanasius and Arius could only be posed against the background of these shared background beliefs about the relations between Son and Father. They share these and other views in large part because they both were products of theological education in the Origenist theological conventions traditional in the Alexandrian church. Their shared theological legacy turned out to be both internally inconsistent and, at key points, fatally vague. The inconsistencies might, perhaps, have been brought to focus by any one of a number of issues. In the event, the question that divided them was: should we say that the Logos or Son stands on the Creator's side of the ontological distinction between Creator and creation, or on the creatures' side? The vagueness of terms key to their shared theological conventions permitted each of them to claim that his answer to the focal question was required by the commonly received Alexandrian tradition.

Arius saw himself as a spokesman for mainstream Christianity and was, in his context, a theological conservative. It seemed obvious to him that the Son must be located on the creatures' side of the ontological distinction. Part of the story that renders the Son's unsubstitutable personal identity must be, Arius contended, "He was created by the Father." Were the Son on the Creator's side of the ontological distinction between Creator and creatures, then either the real distinction between Son and Father is undercut, and they are two names for the same reality, or there are two ultimate principles, two gods exercising one *monarchia*.

Both sides agreed that neither of these conclusions was Christianly acceptable. The first makes the Gospels' story of God's saving work unintelligible, for the stories quite clearly distinguish Son from Father and speak of the Son as sent by the Father and of the Son being obedient to the Father. The dynamics that drive the Gospels' narratives are undercut if the Son is not really other than the Father. And if the real difference between the two is preserved on the Creator's side of the Creator-creature distinction as simply two distinct divine beings, then it looks as though the singularity of God's *monarchia* is undercut.

Central to the logic of Arius's position (as also to Athanasius's position) was his theological premise that God is radically free in creating. Creaturely reality is a gift as freely given by God as is the gift of salvation of creatures from sin and death. The conceptual conventions that were available to Arius (and to Athanasius) in which to articulate this point largely come from Platonic, Neoplatonic, and Neopythagorean cosmological traditions, as developed in the early third century, according to which the ultimate principle (*arche*) that rationally explains the structure and changes of the cosmos must be singular ("the one"; *monos*), self-subsistent, spiritual (i.e., nonmaterial), unchanging, and unchangeable (see R. Williams 1987, part 2, for an overview of the relevant history of philosophy). If it cannot change, no relationship and no change in relationship can make any difference to it. The nature of such an unconditioned One is strictly incomprehensible to human minds that can only comprehend things-in-relationship-to-other-things, order-in-multiplicity. As the ground of order and change in the cosmos, the One affects the cosmos simply by being actually itself, an unchanging and unchangeable changer. It inherently radiates reality and order; the cosmos of multiplicity and change emanates from its unchanging singularity. However, given its pure spirituality and radical singularity, the ultimate principle cannot be directly related to a material and multiple cosmos. Its relation to a material and changing cosmos must be mediated by some reality other than both of them, but in some way like each of them. Hence the first emanation from the One is the Logos, which at once refracts the singular mind of the One, reflecting it in a unified multiplicity of divine Ideas or Forms, and is the principle that grounds the unity-in-multiplicity of the ever-changing material cosmos. The Logos mediates between the One and the cosmos.

This is not to say that Arius (or Athanasius, for that matter) was essentially a philosopher. It is to say that Arius and Athanasius as well were products of the intellectual culture of their time. How could they not be? Arius sought to explicate the biblical account of God and God's ways of relating to all that is not God. He did so using a fund of concepts made available by that culture. In the process he modified some (but perhaps not enough) of them.

For example, like all orthodox Christians of his time, Arius rejected the thesis that it is simply "natural"—inherent in the very nature of the ultimate cosmological principle—for God actually to "radiate" reality and order. God has a natural capacity to create, but it must be enacted by a specific, punctiliar decision to create. Given that modification of the philosophical themes they appropriated, the received conceptual conventions appear to serve nicely to explicate biblical accounts of the Father and the Word and their relationship. New Testament and liturgical references to the Father may be interpreted in ways guided by the logic of use of "the One." The Father is purely spiritual, utterly singular, incomprehensible, and unchanged by any relation. The received conventions thus admirably underscore the radical freedom of the Father's punctiliar acts of creating and saving. New Testament and liturgical references to the Word of God or to the Son of God may be interpreted in ways guided by the logic of uses of "Logos." The Word is the intermediary through whom the Father creates and affects the creation. The crux of the story of reconciliation is that it is precisely through this same Logos that the Father works to save sinful humankind. The received Alexandrian conventions about the relation between the Logos and the One admirably stressed both the Word's genuine otherness to the Father and its closeness in being to the Father.

The internal logic of the received conventions moved interpretation of biblical accounts of the relationship between Father and Word in a particular direction, however. There is necessarily a certain hierarchy: as the One is prior in being to Logos, so is Father prior to Word or Son. Scripture characterizes this relationship as "begetting." The Word is the "only-begotten Son." Arius could see only two possible interpretations of "begetting." Following received conventions, it might be interpreted as "emanate," but that is to start down a line of cosmological thought ruled out by the doctrine of creation from nothing. Or it might be interpreted as "created."

Biblical filial metaphors were exegetically troubling to Arius. Rowan Williams (1987) shows how Arius uses the metaphor "Word of God," interpreted in ways guided by received philosophical cosmological conventions, to govern exegesis of the New Testament filial expressions "Son of God" and "only-begotten Son of God." More than a century before, Origen had complicated Arius's conceptual difficulties by introducing into Alexandrian Christian discourse the observation that concepts of Father and Son are defined in terms of each other. No "Father" unless a "Son";

no "Son" unless a "Father." So if the Father is eternal, the Son must be also. Origen proposed that the Father's "begetting" (or "generating") the Son must be an eternal relation. Nonetheless, it is a hierarchical relation. Fathers are in some way prior to their sons. Although the idea of "eternally creating" is awkward, Arius agreed with Origen to the extent that the Father's bringing the Son into being as a subsistent individual distinct from the Father is done "before all ages." Nonetheless, the Son is not timelessly self-subsistent. There is a way in which the Father is prior to the Son, an interval before the Father begets him. For Arius, the Son as "Word of God" is the one of whom Scripture says, "The LORD created me at the beginning of his work" (Prov. 8:22). The Word is thus on the creatures' side of the unchangeable Creator/changeable creature disjunction. This makes it admirably clear that it is entirely conceivable how the Word could suffer on the cross, because as a creature he is capable of it, whereas God as Father, fully divine in the proper sense of the term, could not suffer.

For Arius, the Son has a higher status in being than the rest of creation. He is inheritor of all the gifts and glories God can give him. Still, the Son belongs on the creaturely side of the Creator-creature distinction. In Arius's view, if the Son is not said to be on the creatures' side of the ontological distinction between Creator and creation, the Gospels' stories of our salvation would be rendered unrecognizable. The Savior would not subsist as something genuinely other than the Father; could have no relation, filial or otherwise, to the Father; and could not participate in human suffering. Arius arguably had some traditional Christian thought and terminological usage on his side.

For his part, it seemed to Athanasius, in his writings following the Council of Nicaea, that Arius undercut the Gospels' stories of our salvation in his own fashion, however unintentionally, and turned them into some other story. In particular, as Athanasius saw it, Arius's explication used terms that contradict the heart of the story of our reconciliation to God. Salvation is a reuniting of creatures with God from whom they have been alienated. It comes about, as Athanasius read the Gospel narratives, by God taking our alienated and sinful reality on Godself so that we, in turn, may be made holy by being united with God's reality. Reconciliation cannot be accomplished by God's employing a third party, a creaturely instrument as mediator. But that is precisely the thrust of Arius's way of telling the story of God's saving act. Rather, it must be God Godself who comes among us to share our fallen life so that we may come to participate in God's life. Hence, the Son must be said to be on the Creator's side, not the creature's side, of the ontological distinction between Creator and creature. Left at that, such a conclusion raises the objection that, if the distinction between the Father and the Son is on the Creator's side of the Creator/creature distinction, then the *monarchia* is divided between two distinct divine beings and monotheism has given way to polytheism. Precisely in order to rule out that inference, Athanasius insists it must also be affirmed that, if the Son is indeed fully divine, he is of one substance (Gk. *homoousios*) with the Father. The distinction between them is not in respect to divinity. Though they are both fully divine, they are not two "gods."

Hence, contrary to Arius's objection, Athanasius contended that locating the real distinction between Father and Son on God's side of the Creator-creation distinction does not necessarily imply that "Father" and "Son" are two names or two modes of one underlying divine reality or that they name two gods. Athanasius's exegesis of New Testament metaphors for the Savior's status and relation to the Father tends to respect their diversity more than Arius's exegesis did (R. Williams 1987, 107–15). In Athanasius's exegesis, the logic inherent in the image "Logos" or "Word of God" does not rule how other metaphors, such as "only begotten Son" and "God's own Son," are to be interpreted. In particular, Proverbs 8:22, where Wisdom says that "the LORD created me at the beginning of his work," was denied the hermeneutical primacy Arius assigned it in interpreting just how the Word is related to the Father.

Perhaps it is not too much to say that in effect Athanasius's exegesis ended up reversing the way in which Arius related the biblical images "Word" and "Son" to each other. Where for Arius the metaphor "Word," and perhaps a certain philosophical understanding of the Word's relation to the One of which it is the Word, controlled interpretation of the metaphor "begotten Son," Athanasius comes to interpret "Logos" or "Word" in light of the force of the metaphors "begotten Son" and "God's own Son."

To explicate his point, Athanasius invoked a novel distinction between "creating" and "begetting." No clear distinction between the two notions had previously been developed in ordinary Christian usage. The point of the distinction is roughly this: in ordinary begetting, like begets like; for example, horses beget horses and dogs beget dogs. Begetter and begotten are related to each other as genuinely other than each other, but in their otherness they are nonetheless one kind of reality. For Athanasius the only features of this analogy that are relevant to Father/Son relation are its being a relation of derivation marked by genuine otherness in identity of kind.

Creating, he pointed out, is quite different. A person may create a poem, a wooden house, or a sword of steel. Creator and created are related to each other as genuinely other than each other, and in their otherness they are not necessarily any one kind of reality. This is all the more the case when the creating is creation *from nothing*. A major point of the claim that God creates all else "from nothing" is that in their mutual otherness Creator and creation are not embraced by any common kind of reality; their otherness is that of an ontological distinction, a disjunction in being. Athanasius was pointing out that "creating" and "begetting" are metaphors for two quite different types of relationship that are possible between two terms that are genuinely different from each other. If the biblical phrases "only begotten

Son" and "God's own Son" are privileged as the most apt metaphors for the Son's relation to the Father, then it is appropriate to characterize that relation more abstractly as a relation of derivation, at once a relation of genuine otherness, analogous to the way offspring are other than their parent, and genuine identity in kind of being, analogous to the identity in kind of being between a parent and that parent's "own" offspring.

Hence, contrary to Arius's contention, the Son can consistently be said to be on the Creator's side of the Creator/creature distinction and nonetheless be genuinely different from the Father. The reality of the distinction between them does not have to derive from the Father's having created the Son, as Arius had supposed. The relation between Father and Son does not have to be understood as an instance of the general creator-creature relation. It can instead be understood as a quite different and unique relation expressed by metaphorical use of "begetting."

Here Athanasius was building on part of the Alexandrian legacy from Origen that Arius shared. The real distinction between the Father and the Son, while both are understood to be on the Creator side of the Creator/creature distinction, can be derived from the Father's eternally begetting the Son. "Eternally" was a crucially important modifier in the formula "eternally begotten." On one side it served to deny Arius's thesis that while the Word was created "before all ages" and as the precondition of creation of the cosmos, nonetheless there is an ontological "interval" between the Father and the Son. Arius's formulation suggested that the Father's punctiliar decision to create the cosmos was the occasion for the creation of the Word also. The Word as a subsistent being comes into being only on the occasion of and as the condition of creation of the cosmos. Athanasius's formulation served to separate in principle the Father's begetting the Son from the Father's creating through the Son. The former would obtain even if, contrary to fact, the latter did not. On the other side, it served to remind us that, used in relation to God, the analogy drawn to animal begetting of young is stretched to the breaking point. None of the ordinary features of animal begetting are relevant other than genuine otherness in identity of kind of reality. In particular, any notion of a temporally extended process of begetting is excluded.

Conversely, if the Son is eternally begotten of the Father, not created out of nothing by the Father, then he is of the same substance (*homoousios*) as the Father (Gk. *homo* = same; *ousios* = substance). This was a relatively novel use of the term *homoousios*. Second- and early-third-century Christian writers had tended to reject *homoousios* as a term describing the Son's relation to the Father for at least two reasons. Valentinian gnostics had used the term to characterize the relation to God of all rational spirits, including the Logos. They were all somehow "pieces" of the same divine substance. That was unacceptable because it implied that God's substance could be divided and, since only matter can be divided, it suggests that

God's substance is material and not purely spiritual. Further, to say that the Word was of the same substance as the Father implied that they were two members of the same class of being. That was unacceptable because it implied that the Father, since he must have distinctive properties that distinguish him from the Son as a different member of the same class, is subject to defining or limiting properties and is not infinite or nonlimited in any respect.

Athanasius's use of *homoousios* in effect challenged the conventional Christian assumption, which Arius shared, that *all* relations of dependency on the Father must be the result of God's utterly free act of choosing to enter that relation. At least implicit in Athanasius's use of *homoousios* is the suggestion that God's will "to produce the dependent reality of creation is intelligible only if divine life is first conceived as itself an act of giving and responding, which is *free*, in the sense of being utterly unconstrained, yet *natural*, in the sense of not being the effect of a punctiliar act of conscious self-determination" (R. Williams 1987, 112). The giving and responding that constitute this divine life are, of course, partly the giving and responding that constitute the relations of begetting and loving between the Father and the Son. Abstractly speaking, the relation between Father and Son is as hierarchical for Athanasius as for Arius. The Father is self-subsistent, without a grounding *arche* (he is *anarchos*); the Son is eternally begotten of, and thus in some way is eternally dependent upon, the Father. It is just this eternal dependence of the Son on the Father that preserves the *monarchia* of God. The Trinity as a whole is the fundamental principle of reality because the Son (and, it was affirmed more explicitly later, the Spirit) are rooted in the Person of the Father who is, quite apart from the triune God's free "decision" to create reality other than God, the first principle and cause of the Trinity. However, just as the Persons of the Trinity are not members of different kinds of being (divine and creaturely), so too they are not three individuals of a single class whose respective individuality is defined by properties in addition to or restrictive of their common substance. It is precisely this structured dynamic that constitutes the divine life. It makes its creative act entirely natural, not in the sense that it is an unfree act ontologically necessitated by God's very nature, but in the sense that it is consonant with the character of the divine life, and thus in some way revelatory of the divine life, and not random or arbitrary.

In subsequent church councils called by imperial edicts, interpretations offered by Arius and others who, like him, had theological reservations about Nicaea's formulations were rejected. It may be too much to say that Athanasius's proposals prevailed, but they did set the general framework in which subsequent controversies were cast and through which properly Trinitarian understandings of God were discovered. In effect, Athanasius contributed a way of analyzing the relation between the Father and the Son in the story of the divine economy of salvation that was deemed to capture more adequately than did Arius's analysis how the dynamics driving that story are plotted. His way of analyzing the relation preserved the real distinction between Father and Son (as Arius's analysis did also) so that the story is moved along by genuine interactions between really different characters, while also allowing one to emphasize (as Arius's analysis did not) that it is a story about how God Godself, and not an inferior intermediary, comes among humankind to reconcile them to God.

The upshot of the controversies was a distinctive and conceptually very odd understanding of one way in which God relates to us: God comes among us as one of us. Jesus is *emmanuel*, the Hebrew for "God with us." The crux of this understanding of how God relates to us lay in how the "with" in "God with us" is understood. It is not simply that Jesus discloses or illustrates the general truth that God is on our side, in our corner, wishing us well, and working for our well-being through all that happens, although all that is also in some sense true. No, the claim was that in the one particular concrete human life of Jesus of Nazareth born of Mary, a life consisting of the distinctive sequence of events that constitute who Jesus is, God Godself—and not some intermediary being, inferior to the Creator in being but superior in being to all other creatures—shares our common lot, relating interpersonally with other human persons in a way that reconciles their distorted relationship with God. He simply is God giving Godself to fellow human persons.

Focus on this concretely particular way in which God relates to humankind did not supplant additional claims that God relates to humankind to create them and to draw them to eschatological consummation. To the contrary, as we saw, the claim that God also relates to us as our creator was a background belief that had to be shared by both sides to the controversy in order for them to make their respective points against each other. And, as we shall see, while the claim that God draws us to eschatological consummation can and must be distinguished from the claim that God also reconciles us, the relation between the two claims is so dialectical that each may serve as part of the background of theological explanations of the other. Focus on how God relates to us to reconcile us requires, rather than supplants, claims that God also creates and eschatologically consummates us.

The unenlightening conceptual tag for this strange way God relates to us as our reconciler is, of course, "incarnation." It points to a way in which God actively relates to us that is conceptually distinct from God relating to us as our creator or as our eschatological consummator.

Accordingly, our project here must explore the anthropological implications of incarnation as well as, but not as a substitute for nor as one instance among many of, the anthropological implications of God creating all-that-is-not-God and God drawing it to eschatological consummation.

Creedal Formulations

Adoption of a creed in AD 381 at the Council of Constantinople marks a decisive turning point in the history of Christian understanding of God. The theological conventions that Arius took for granted understood God cosmologically in terms of the contrast and relation between the ordered multiplicity of the cosmos (the creation) and its absolutely singular, self-subsistent *arche* or principle of being and unity (the creator "Father"). In its absoluteness, God can be related to the cosmos only through a distinct and dependent subsistent reality, Logos, who expresses or reveals in a rationally ordered multiplicity of ideas the singular and undifferentiated content of God's mind. The human mind can know and say some things about this revealed unity-in-multiplicity, but of God Godself "behind" the Logos nothing can be either known or said. Theology must finally be apophatic.

Post-Nicene theology tends to replace those cosmologically oriented conventions with christologically oriented ones. The distinction and relation between Son and Father in God's relating to us to reconcile us to God reveals and defines the divine life, and it is the divine life, not the cosmological monad, that is utterly simple and self-subsistent. (That, of course, sets up the question in what way "life," divine or otherwise, can be "utterly simple." But it only sets it up. It is some time in the history of theology before it is pressed strongly enough to become a major item on the Christian theological agenda.) The Father continues to be called "source" and "cause," but not in ways that suggest that there is an ontological "more" to the Father than the Son, something absolute in the sense of nonrelational, about which nothing can be said except that it "decides" to be self-determining as Father of a Son. In the conventions used by post-Nicene theology there is nothing of God's reality that is not expressed as relationship. Talk about the divine "nature" cannot be abstracted from talk about the Father's active relating to the Son in their conjoint relating, in the power of the Spirit, to humankind to reconcile it to God. Finally there is also an apophatic moment in such talk. That reconciling relationship, as well as the creative relationship, into which God enters with all creatures, in which the speaker is also caught up, cannot be cognitively distanced and exhaustively defined; so God's nature cannot be either. Nonetheless, it can be said that the ineffable mystery does not lie somehow behind God's relating, but precisely in and as God's active, self-involving, and self-expressive relating.

The implications of that shift for Christian understanding of God are still being explored. Some implications of the Nicene turn that are arguably inescapable might well be ones that Athanasius and his allies would have resisted as strongly as would their opponents at and after Nicaea. This leads, as Rowan Williams has observed, "to the odd conclusion that the Nicene Fathers achieved not only more than they knew, but a good deal more than they wanted" (1987, 22).

Adoption of the Nicene-Constantinopolitan Creed marked an anthropologically significant third moment in a movement toward properly Trinitarian understandings of God. The creed consists of a series of terse statements about the one God with whom Christians believe all human persons have to do. The statements fall naturally into three groups.

The text adopted at Nicaea was the basis for the first two groups of statements. The first group affirms belief in "one God, the Father, the ruler of all, maker of heaven and earth . . ." The second group affirms belief in "one Lord, Jesus Christ the Son of God, begotten as the only Son out of the Father . . . begotten, not made, *homoousios* ('of one substance') with the Father," who "for the sake of us human beings and our salvation, descended and became flesh, became human, suffered, and rose on the third day . . ."

The second is the most elaborated section of the creed, incorporating as it does important conceptual innovations: The distinction between Father and Son is now specified as a distinction in virtue of the Father's eternally begetting the Son, not in virtue of the Father's creating or making the Son; and without compromise of their real difference, Father and Son are also understood to be flatly equal in regard to their divinity, "of one substance" (*homoousios*). The Son is thus firmly located on the Creator's side of the ontological distinction between Creator and creation.

The third section of the Nicene-Constantinopolitan Creed affirms belief in the Holy Spirit. The text of the creed adopted at Nicaea had limited itself to "and [we believe] in the Holy Spirit." This was amplified in AD 381 at Constantinople to affirm the Spirit's relation to the Father by analogy with the way the second section of the creed characterizes the Son's relation to the Father. The council argued that it is appropriate to worship the Holy Spirit together with the Father and the Son. However, since it is only appropriate to worship God, the Holy Spirit must be said to be divine, on the Creator's side of Creator/creation distinction. Consequently in the third section of the creed the council affirmed, "We believe in the Holy Spirit, the Lord, the giver of life, who proceeds from the Father through the Son. With the Father and the Son he is worshiped and glorified."

The conceptual decisions the bishops made at Nicaea and at Constantinople were pregnant with changes in the way in which Christians understood God. These decisions stand without clear warrant in Scripture or well-established precedent in earlier tradition. For example, "begotten" is not used in the creedal sense in Scripture. Psalm 2:7 does say, "You are my son; today I have begotten you." But read historically, it is addressed to a new king of Israel who is being told that God has adopted him as a son. In its original context, "begotten" refers to status, not being. When, perhaps as an allusion to Psalm 2:7, "begotten" is used of Jesus in the New Testament (John 1:14; 18; 3:16; 18; 1 John 4:9), it is far from clear that it refers to Jesus' being rather than status. So too, while there is no clear biblical warrant for speaking of the Spirit "proceeding" from the Father and the Son, the term is adopted because it was different from "begotten," which was deemed a uniquely appropriate image for the Son's relation to the Father, and different from "created," which would put the Spirit worthy of worship on the wrong side of the Creator/creature distinction. Moreover, "proceeds" had no technical or theoretical connotations that could be misleading, and it did serve to stress the otherness of the Spirit to the Father. So too, *homoousios* is a term not found in Scripture, much less in relation to the Spirit. Indeed, in controversies leading up to and following the council, that was one of the strongest arguments against this innovation. Yet it is explicitly used in the creed to characterize the relation between Son and Father, and was generally understood to be implied in the remark that the Spirit "proceeds from the Father through the Son."

Clearly, in adopting the creed the bishops were not merely summarizing Scripture's stories of God's ways of relating to reality other than God. They needed only to stitch together Bible verses to do that. Rather, they were making decisions about how best to construe those stories insofar as they render the identity of God. Thus, by their creed the bishops were, among other things, giving broad hermeneutical guidance about how best to interpret Scripture. The bishops' decisions moved efforts to understand God Christianly in definite directions.

Nicaea is a Trinitarian creed, not a Trinitarian doctrine of God. Creeds and doctrines function quite differently. A doctrine—say, of the Trinity— is an effort to explain discursively an understanding of God as triune. To be sure, the creed has also been used didactically by Christian communities as the basis for instruction of religious inquirers or of persons seeking to join the community by baptism. The instruction takes the form of at least informal doctrine—that is, explaining and elaborating the creed, not just repeating it. The Nicene Creed has been used that way because of its more basic and proper use: as part of an act of public worship of God, it is a community's confession of faith in the triune God cast in terse verbal formulas. Its liturgical function has given the Nicene-Constantinopolitan Creed distinctive roles in regard to Christian doctrines of God. It should decisively shape any theocentric Christian doctrine of human being.

There is an indefinitely large number of possible Trinitarian doctrines of God. That is, there may be an indefinitely large number of possible ways in which to explicate, coherently interrelate, and elaborate on the affirmations made by the creed. Regarding such doctrines of God, the Nicene creed has traditionally functioned as the norm by which to assess relative adequacy of proposed Trinitarian understandings of God. In that regard, the creed functions meta-doctrinally, as a norm for assessing doctrinal proposals, not as such a proposal in its own right. What I mean throughout by "properly Trinitarian" understandings of God are understandings that arguably comport with this creed.

Of course, relative conformity to the creed does not by itself establish whether any particular doctrine of God is true rather than false, or even whether it is Christianly correct rather than incorrect. Additional types of arguments would need to be advanced to show whether a given doctrine of God were either true or Christianly appropriate. All that a given doctrine of God's conformity to the Nicene Creed establishes is that it is properly Trinitarian.

Regarding theological anthropology, the creed has filled three very different roles: existential, rhetorical, and methodological.

First, the creed's existential role: As noted above, the principal use of the creed is in the context of the liturgy. In their common worship, communities of Christian faith have used the creed to affirm their trust in God. Such use has both expressive and commissive force. That is, in the very act of affirming the creed as part of corporate worship of God, Christians have expressed who they understand themselves to be ("We are the people of *this* God, people whose lives are given us by God and whose personal identities are decisively shaped as an effort to respond appropriately to God understood in this way"). In the very act of affirming the creed as part of their worship of God, Christian persons have publicly committed themselves, with others, to a way of understanding the God with whom they believe all humankind has to do, an understanding of the ultimate context of their lives, an understanding of all else in relation to this God.

Utterance of the creed that has these types of force is existentially self-involving. That is, by using the creed in these ways ,Christians have shaped, as well as expressed, their personal identities. They have committed themselves not only to shape their understanding and talk of God by such use of the creed, but also to shape the ways in which they have understood and talked about themselves, along with all other realities insofar as God was related to those realities. As I shall have occasion to show in several different contexts later in this work, Christians' coming to understand God and the world in these ways requires their learning an array of concepts whose mastery is not merely an intellectual act; it involves deep existential change over time in their personal identities. A nearly random list of examples of Christianly important concepts whose mastery is existentially shaping would include concepts of God, creature, death, grace, flourishing, gratitude, glory, joy, faith, hope, love, sin, forgiveness, guilt, and repentance.

Clearly, the array of such concepts provides some of the subject matter for a Christian theological anthropology. Thus, the creed as used in worship functions as a privileged indirect source for theological anthropology just insofar as it directly helps shape the identities of the persons and communities that so use it.

Second, read against the background of arguments against Arius, the creed plays the role for anthropology of shaping the rhetoric appropriate to God's ways of relating to us. It tends to privilege images of dynamic relations to characterize more specifically God's ways of relating to us. The creed echoes the way Athanasius analyzed the plotting of the dynamics driving New Testament stories of the economy of salvation in a way that focuses on the personal interrelations between Father and Son. The identity of the Father is rendered, not by stories about God as source of all reality (God creating), nor by stories of God exercising sole governance over reality (*monarchia*), but by stories about God relating to Jesus. Conversely, the Son's identity is specified by reference to stories rendering Jesus in his relation to the One he called Father. Moreover, both sets of stories are needed to render the identity of God, and the understanding of God to which they point is a Trinitarian understanding explicated in metaphors drawn from a small set of interpersonal relations. That, in turn, tends to privilege the use of interpersonal relational terms in accounts of God's relating to us as our reconciler.

At the same time, despite the apparent force of the words "Father" and "Son," the creed's echo of Athanasius's way of analyzing the dynamics driving the story of salvation tends radically to qualify use of familial images for God's relating to human persons in general. Athanasius had urged a change in Christian use of the expressions "Father" and "Son." Before this controversy Christians spoke of God as "Father" in reference to stories of creation: as source of all being, God is Father of all. That includes us. Indeed, there is plenty of biblical warrant for understanding us as sons and daughters of whom God is the "Father." This approach makes it look as though, when the relation between God and Jesus is likened to relations between a father and a son, it is because it is an instance of a broader class of relations between God and all human persons that exists by reason of creation. However, Athanasius's reading of New Testament stories of salvation yields the insight that in this matter these stories' rhetoric effectively reverses background and foreground. Now "Father" is not an image for God's relation to creatures in general as background for characterizing God's relation to Jesus in particular. Rather, now "Father" is a name for One whose identity is constituted solely by eternally relating to another whose name is "Son." The relation is more like that of begetter to begotten than that of creator to creature. It is precisely this use of the metaphors "Father" and "Son" as names for two whose identities are constituted by their relationship of "begetter of/begotten by" that underwrites the unity of the two as one substance. Images of familial relations are thus especially privileged for use in stories rendering the identity of the One who is the triune God. The creed may begin naming the One who is "maker of heaven and earth" as "Father." However, read in the light of Athanasius's arguments, this may not be interpreted to mean that God is called "Father" in virtue of being Creator. Rather, the creed is telling us who the Creator is. The identity of the One who does make heaven and earth is normatively defined and disclosed by that One's relationship to Jesus Christ. The One with whom we have to do as Creator is the One Jesus called "Father."

But for that very reason, use of familial images in descriptions of God's relation to humankind as its creator must be qualified. The Son may be begotten, not created; but human persons are definitely created by, not begotten of, God. In no way are we of one substance with God. Properly speaking, there is not so much as a spark of divine substance in us. Here the importance to anthropology of the ontological distinction between God and creatures is especially clear: humans are firmly located on the creaturely side. If the Son himself teaches us to address God in the same way he did, as "our Father," the theological import of doing so must be understood carefully. Whatever may have been the historical Jesus' conscious or unconscious view of the matter, the reason for addressing God as "Father" cannot be that we *as creatures* have the same relation with the Father that the eternally begotten Son has. However, if we can in some way be drawn into the Son's own relation to the One he called "Father," then in that qualified sense we may be entitled to address God with Jesus as "our Father." The point would seem to be anticipated by the apostle Paul's characterization of persons drawn into Jesus' relation with God as God's "adopted" children (cf. Rom. 8:15, 23; Gal. 4:4, 5). Otherwise, given Athanasius's analysis of the dynamics driving canonical stories of salvation, unqualified use of the familial metaphors "father" and "son," and all expansions of the latter such as "sons and daughters" or "children," would be a seriously misleading imaging of God's relation to us as our creator and our relation to God as creatures.

Third, interpreted against the background of the controversies about Arius, the creed has two methodological implications for the structure of any Trinitarianly theocentric anthropology: (1) No exploration of the implications for theological anthropology of God's relating to human persons as their Savior may contradict or conceptually undercut the implications of God's relating to them as their Creator, and vice versa. (2) While Trinitarianly theocentric anthropological proposals will inescapably be indirectly christocentric epistemically, they need not derive their material content from Christology.

Regarding the first, recall that the Christian conviction that God relates to all-that-is-not-God, and so to us, as our creator functioned in the controversies leading up to Nicaea as a background belief shared by both sides of the controversies. The doctrine of creation was not bracketed, let alone rejected. To the contrary, it played a decisive role in the arguments both sides put forward. It functioned like a normative rule governing arguments. The rule could be formulated this way: no analysis of God's relation to Jesus and Jesus' relation to God in the economy of salvation may contradict or conceptually undercut the claim that there is an ontological distinction, though no ontological separation, between God who creates from nothing and all-that-is-not-God. Thus, an understanding of God's relation to all else as its Creator had a conceptual priority to understandings of God's relation to all else as its Savior.

I suggest that this rule governing how to go about trying to understand God more truly brings with it a corollary governing how to understand humankind theocentrically: no exploration of the anthropological implications of God's relating to human persons as their reconciler may contradict or conceptually undercut the implications of God's relating to them as their Creator. The anthropological implications of both relations need to be explored, but not as though one were simply an instance or subset of the other.

Second, despite the logical priority of doctrines of creation *ex nihilo*, properly Trinitarian understandings of God formed by this controversy are christocentric. That is, an understanding of Jesus Christ is decisively normative ("christocentric") for knowledge of God as triune. This follows if Athanasius's analysis of the dynamics driving the story of salvation is more adequate than Arius's analysis. Their controversy was christocentric; they disagreed about how best to describe God's relation to Jesus and Jesus' relation to God. They both acknowledged the ontological priority of God's creating to God's reconciling. After all, "reconciling" presupposes that there is something creaturely there to be reconciled, whereas creating *ex nihilo* presupposes that there is "nothing" there, and certainly nothing resulting from a prior reconciliation.

However, regarding God, Arius also made the doctrine of creation cognitively prior to the doctrine of reconciliation. For Arius, God's identity is rendered in the story of creation: the Creator is the One who, as it happens, also acts to save. Athanasius's move was importantly different. Without denying the logical priority of the doctrine of creation, and while concurring that the same God both creates and saves, Athanasius in effect insisted that canonical stories of the economy of salvation render the normative identity description of God. It is normative in that it warrants our understanding God in ways in which an analysis of canonical stories of God creating could never warrant and cannot preclude. As it turns out, understandings of God warranted by analysis of the economy of salvation are Trinitarian understandings. The upshot of Athanasius's move was that the question "Who is the One who relates to us to create us, to reconcile us, and to draw us to eschatological consummation?" is best answered by analyzing in particular the divine economy of reconciliation—that is, the story of the incarnation. For Athanasius it was best answered in a christocentric way, and the creed follows suit.

The last two points shape the procedure of my theological anthropology. If what we say about human persons is rooted in the ways in which God relates to us, and if God is understood in a Trinitarian way, then what we say will be christocentric, albeit only indirectly so. That most emphatically does not mean that everything we may say theologically about human persons must be derived from an analysis of the metaphysics of the incarnation. The argument of this chapter does not warrant an ontological christocentrism, as though the very being of human persons is constituted by and revealed in the being of the Son of God incarnate.

Indeed, so far as I can see, it is not necessary for most of the material content of Christian theological claims about human personhood to have any privileged source such as revelation, whether in Jesus Christ or elsewhere—though, of course, some of it may do so. Having a religiously privileged source for its content is not what makes an anthropology "theological."

Rather, what makes anthropological claims Christianly theological is that the selection of their contents, and the way that they are framed, are normed by claims about God relating to us, when God is understood in a Trinitarian way. And such Trinitarian understandings of God are cognitively christocentric. So when anthropological remarks are selected and framed in ways normed by claims about God relating to us, and when that God is understood in Trinitarian ways that are themselves epistemically christocentric, the anthropology will itself have been constructed in an epistemically christocentric way, but only indirectly.

From Historical Economy to Immanent Communion

It is hardly surprising that the creed adopted by the Council of Constantinople in AD 381 did not end controversies about how to understand Jesus' relation to God and God's relation to Jesus. Aside from the fact that Arius's allies were scarcely willing to give up their contention that the apparently victorious Athanasians dangerously mistold the Gospels' stories of the economy of salvation, the creed itself used novel concepts that were open to differing interpretations. In the early decades of the fifth century, continuing controversies yielded interpretations of the creed that mark an anthropologically significant fourth moment in the movement toward properly Trinitarian understandings of God.

In these controversies, focus shifted from analysis of the dynamics of God's economy of reconciliation in history to the quality of God's immanent eternal life. There have been two types of theological argument justifying this move, one arguing that the priority of the economic Trinity in the order of knowing entails claims about God's immanent life and the other arguing for the priority of the immanent Trinity in the order of grace.

The first type of argument is premised on the conviction that God's self-giving in the economy of reconciliation is also God's disclosing of Godself. This argument assumes that in freely self-determining to give Godself in the economy of reconciliation, God self-consistently remains God—that is, God remains true to God. It further assumes that God who is faithful does not mislead when God self-discloses. Hence, as disclosure of God, the economy of reconciliation is true to God. The argument concludes that if the economy of reconciliation is constituted by a triune dynamic, and if in that economy God is truly self-giving, then it must be true that the God who is self-giving in the economy is in some way triunely self-giving in God's own eternal life. It concludes further that, if God remains self-consistent in God's free self-determination to be self-giving in the economy of reconciliation, the character of God's life is not changed by God's relating to creatures to reconcile them. Hence God's life is in some way triune whether God freely relates to creatures to reconcile them or not. Thus, according to this argument, claims about the intrinsic trinity of God's life follow from claims about the triunity of God's economy of reconciliation.

The second type of argument is premised on the conviction that God's economy of reconciliation is free grace in which God is self-consistent. From God's side, that means (1) that God's self-determination in love to be self-giving in the economy of reconciliation is not necessitated by God's own being. God does not ontologically need to be self-giving in this way in order to be God. It also means (2) that in self-giving God is true to Godself, not changing in any way that involves self-contradiction or violation of God's identity. Now, the argument goes, we might declare the triunity of the divine economy to be flatly identical with the divine life. But in that case, the triune God's self-determination to enact the economy would be ontologically necessary; without it God would not be the God God is. But in that case, the economy would not be free grace. Rather, it would be ontologically determined. In the order of grace, there must be an immanently triune reality to God's life that is distinct from the triune dynamics of the economy of reconciliation and prior to it in the order of being. The free divine self-determination to enact the economy of reconciliation must be rooted in that immanent life. The claim about the triunity of God's immanent life cannot simply be another way of characterizing the economy.

Granted, if we are persuaded by the first step of the argument, we might still declare that, while the economy is constituted by triune dynamics, we should say nothing at all about the distinguishable and ontologically prior divine life in which it is rooted. We could grant the distinction between the economy, with its triune dynamics, and the eternal divine life while declining to affirm the triunity of the divine life. However, the argument proceeds, in that case we have failed to acknowledge and stress the implications of the conviction that God remains self-consistent both in God's self-determination to, and in God's enactment of, the economy of reconciliation. If God is self-consistent in enacting the economy of reconciliation, then the triune dynamics of the economy must in some way be consistent with the dynamics of God's eternal life. That consistency is what is named by talk of the triunity of God's eternal immanent life. In the order of grace, the triunity of God's eternal life is prior to the triunity of the economy of reconciliation.

These two intersecting arguments warrant distinguishing the triune dynamics of the economy, commonly called the "economic Trinity," from the triune dynamics immanent in God's life, commonly called in the West the "immanent Trinity." But they do not warrant separating the two. On the contrary, precisely because the economic Trinity is prior in the order of knowing, and the immanent Trinity is prior in the order of grace, they cannot be separated without suffering theological distortions in each.

For reasons we need not go into here, there has been a strong tendency in Western theology to separate them. Ever since Karl Rahner (1970) pointed out the theologically disastrous consequences of this separation, participants in the revived discussion of the doctrine of the Trinity have tended to rally to the slogan, "The economic Trinity *is* the immanent Trinity." I concur that the two must not be separated. However, the traditional types of argument outlined above have not been refuted and continue to warrant drawing a distinction between the two senses of "Trinity." It seems to me that if the "is" in the rallying cry's slogan means that there is no distinction between the two, then the priority of the immanent Trinity in the order of grace is denied and the graciousness of the economic Trinity is in question.

Assuming that these arguments warrant the shift of focus from the dynamics of the economy of reconciliation to the dynamics of the eternal divine life, I return now to explore the anthropological implications of that shift. The upshot of the shift of focus to the triunity of God's eternal life was an understanding of divine life expressed metaphorically as a perfect community in a communion among Father, Son, and Holy Spirit. As an effort to express this view of divine life more precisely, if more abstractly, a formula cast in technical terms became current: God is immanently one substance (Gr. *ousia*; Lat. *substantia*) in three "persons" (Gr. *hypostases*, pl.; sing., *hypostasis*; Lat. *personae*, pl.; sing., *persona*).

The formula "one *ousia* in three hypostases" is not in the Nicene-Constantinopolitan Creed. It is not even used much by the Cappadocians who formulated what became hallmarks of Orthodox explication of God's trinity. It developed as a summary of what is implied in the creed. It brings with it important implications for any theocentric account of human personhood according to which humankind's ultimate context is the triune God actively relating to human persons. The phrase "one *ousia*" is simply a reaffirmation of traditional Christian and Jewish (and certain pagan, and later Muslim) belief in the unity and singularity of God. "God is one substance" simply affirms that God is one unique reality of such a sort that it is a matter of logical and ontological necessity that there cannot be more than one God. The phrase "three hypostases" marks a conceptual innovation. Key to this development was the invention of a novel and uniquely Christian use of the Greek metaphysical term *hypostasis*. *Hypostasis* is conventionally translated in English as "person." However, because it has importantly different meaning than the modern term "person," I continue use of the Greek term to minimize confusion. We can bring out the implications of this term for anthropology if we take note of what was innovative about its use in Christian theology.

Development of the novel theological use of hypostasis was largely made possible by the Cappadocians, Basil of Caesarea, his brother Gregory of Nyssa, and Gregory Naziansus (see, e.g., Pelikan 1993, chaps. 5 and 15). The Cappadocians affirmed Nicaea's creed but worried that its own conceptual innovation, *homoousios*, could be interpreted in a way that undercut the real distinctions among "Father," "Son," and "Holy Spirit." If these three are all one in being, then perhaps they are not finally "other" than one another. Partly to block such interpretation, the Cappadocians formulated a technical distinction between *ousia* ("substance") and hypostasis ("person").

Any contemporary who had been paying close attention to the language used in the controversies and, indeed, in the creed itself, would have recognized that such a distinction was indeed novel. In fourth-century Greek, the two terms were ordinarily used vaguely in overlapping and interchangeable ways. *Hypostasis* literally means "standing or existing under." It has the same etymology as the Latin *substantia*, to stand [*stare*] under [*sub*]. In ordinary use, *hypostasis* normally had two meanings: "that which underlies or gives support to an object" and "the externally concrete character of a substance in relation to other objects" (see, e.g., LaCugna 1991, 66). Ironically, the Council of Nicaea had followed its promulgation of the creed by anathematizing anyone who taught that there were three *ousia* or three hypostases! Athanasius himself used the terms interchangeably as late as AD 369 (LaCugna 1993, 66). The Cappadocians' proposal was that *ousia* be used to designate what is common to the three and *hypostasis* be used to designate what is proper and distinct to each of the three. In their innovative technical use, a hypostasis was distinguished from *ousia* in two ways, which, it was easy to recognize, implied a third.

Relational categories were used to explain what a hypostasis is. Consider: "Father" and "Son" are relational terms, and the relations are both reciprocal and oppositional. The Nicenes tended to stress the reciprocity of the relations. This has the effect of underscoring the themes of derivation-in-equality, inter-Trinitarian causality, and the eternal dynamic giving and receiving that constitute the divine life. Medieval theologians, especially Thomas Aquinas, would later tend to stress the oppositional character of the relations: in the relations that constitute them, each of the hypostases is the one it is by virtue of ways in which it is not the other, but not by virtue of being a different "substance." Although such a stress has the drawback of suggesting that the differences between any one hypostasis and the other two is merely binary, it does serve to underscore the irreducible "otherness" of each hypostasis. In short, Father, Son, and Holy Spirit can each be considered a hypostasis in its own right if a divine hypostasis is understood to be constituted by its relationships to the other two hypostases. These relations, and these relations alone, are what are distinctive to each hypostasis, distinguishing it from the other two. It is not as though each of the divine hypostases has its reality in independence of the other two and subsequently enters into relations with them. Rather, each one has its reality *in* its relations with the others. That is what constitutes their unity or oneness in *ousia*.

On the other hand, each is really distinct from the other two. The irreducible distinctions among them are rooted in the fact that theirs are relations of opposition or contrast. Each can be constituted by its relation to the other two only if the other two are in fact irreducibly other than it. For the Cappadocians this was not just a claim about the irreducible personal identities of Father, Son, and Spirit, respectively. It was a metaphysical claim. They accepted that, as we saw in the previous two sections, the unsubstitutable identity, the "who," of each of the three is rendered its unique identity description by Gospel stories telling of their relations to one another in the economy of salvation. Beyond that, and based on that, the Cappadocians were promoting the metaphysical claim that what it is to be, respectively, Father, Son, and Spirit is constituted by their eternal reciprocal and oppositional relations to one another.

Before moving on to two more features of the Cappadocians' use of hypostasis, I need to justify a terminological decision I have made.

Although it is conventional to translate hypostasis in English as "person," it is very different from the modern concept "person." The difference turns on this: Modern concepts of the person take subjectivity, that is, self-conscious consciousness or self-aware awareness, to be constitutive of persons. Persons are subjects, centers of self-conscious consciousness. That is precisely what makes persons "subjects" and not "objects"—that is, things. The relations subjects have with other realities are relations "in consciousness." "Subjectivity" may be studied by the empirical psychological sciences, of course. However, it may also be used as an ontological category. It is commonly used that way when the reality or being of persons, in contrast to things, is understood to be constituted by consciousness. The Cappadocians' use of hypostasis, however, does not turn on the notion "subject as center of consciousness" (Barnes 2002; Turcescu 2002). The reciprocal oppositional relations that constitute each of the three divine hypostases are ontological relations that are not defined in terms of consciousness. They are defined as relations-in-being that are not necessarily constituted by being either "known" by each hypostasis constituted by them, or by the other two hypostases that relate to it. They are not necessarily relations "in consciousness." Reason and will together might count as the ancient equivalent of "subjectivity." They might or might not be ascribed to each of the divine hypostases; that remained a controversial topic. But if they were so ascribed, they were considered properties of something more fundamental in being, *viz.*, they were considered properties of their respective hypostases. There was conceptual room for speculation whether the relations might be conceived as willed relations or as cognitive relations. But the relations themselves were defined solely as relations-in-being, not "relations in consciousness." They were defined on the assumption of a "realist" rather than "idealist" ontology. Hence, simply in the interest of clarity I have deemed it better consistently to use "hypostasis" rather than "person."

The Cappadocians stipulated their technical use of hypostasis by noting a second thing. They pointed out that a divine hypostasis is constituted, not merely by its reciprocal oppositional relations to other hypostases, but by relations that are *generative*. The creed had adopted the metaphors "begetting" to characterize the Father's relation to the Son, "begotten" to characterize the Son's relation to the Father, and "proceeding from" to characterize the Spirit's relation to the Father. It was easy enough to add the metaphor "breathing" or "spirating" to characterize the Father's relation to the Spirit; although it is not in the creed, it has biblical precedent. These are metaphors drawn from various types of generative relations. The novel technical use of the term "hypostasis" was introduced to name the kind of metaphysical relations these are. A divine hypostasis is not just constituted by a relation; it is constituted by generative or productive relations of giving and receiving God's being, giving, and receiving precisely God Godself. This giving and receiving expresses the sheer fullness of divine being and is not caused by any inner lack in any hypostasis that leaves it needing to receive, nor any extrinsic constraint over any hypostasis that obliges it to give. Perhaps the best characterization is that this generativity occurs by God's free self-determination. Thus, the relations that constitute the hypostases are relations of divine self-bestowal freely given, and as such they are divine self-relations of free self-determination. God is freely self-giving, and in the giving of self is thus self-relating.

That the formula "one *ousia* in three hypostases" is a summary in technical and abstract categories of an understanding of the triune God as a community of communion came clear when a third feature of the Cappadocians' use of hypostasis came into view. It emerged as an implication of the claim that divine hypostases are constituted by asymmetrical reciprocal, oppositional generative relations. Because each hypostasis is what and who it is in its eternal relations to the other two, no one of them can be thought in isolation from the other two. In the eighth century, John Damascene suggested that the relation of each to the other two be characterized as *perichoresis*.

In Greek, *perichoreo* means "to encompass." Damascene was suggesting that the implication of the claim that hypostases are constituted by generative relations is that each encompasses the other two. When that idea was translated into Latin in the West it came out either as *circuminsessio,* which means to sit around (*circum-in-sedere*) one another, or as *circum-incessio,* which means to move around (*circum-incedere*) one another. The more dynamic character of the second translation is attractive because it underscores the dynamic characterization of the relations that constitute each of the three hypostases (begetter-of; begotten-of; proceeding-from; "breathed out"). Given this implication of hypostasis, the eternal life of triune God could be understood as a perfect community of three who, in their respective unsubstitutability for one another, eternally giving and receiving Godself, are in perfect communion eternally "dancing around" each other.

Thus the generative relations of giving and receiving, which simply are the hypostases' relations to one other, constitute a form of life that is communion in love. As LaCugna points out, given the decision to employ the concept coinherence, "While there is no blurring of the individuality of each person, there is also no separation. There is only the communion of love in which each person comes to be . . . entirely with reference to the other. . . . The model of perichoresis . . . locates unity . . . in diversity, in true communion of persons" (1993, 271). Indeed, it is not too much to say that this perichoretic community in a communion of freely self-giving love simply is the living God.

The shift in focus from God's economy of salvation in history to God's immanent eternal life marks a fourth logical moment in the process leading to historically fully elaborated Trinitarian understanding of God. It has an important implication for theocentric anthropology.

The character of God's eternal life privileges a distinct set of images for the type of existential "how" that constitutes human flourishing. The communion in self-giving love that constitutes God's life presupposes and requires that the beloved is an irreducibly other reality than the lover. Indeed, such communion nurtures the flourishing of the beloved precisely as other. The love that is God's life is not envious of the reality of that which is other. It does not seek to absorb the beloved. On the contrary, such love is a self-giving, a donation of God's own reality for the other. Furthermore, in this communion such love is reciprocal. The beloved loves the lover in a reciprocal self-giving that honors and fosters the otherness of the lover.

This is the character of the triune life that is the living God. It is commonplace to characterize this life as "mystery." Although Karl Barth grumped that "transcendence" is the most tedious concept in theology, "mystery" is surely a close runner-up, so loosely is it commonly used. It will be useful to pause to sort out several senses of "mystery" that are commonly employed in Christian secondary theology and indicate which of them are set aside in this project and which employed. First, we briefly review five theologically substantive explanations of "mystery," and second, we review three formal explanations.

A major reason the term "mystery" enters the Christian theological lexicon is that it appears in canonical New Testament texts. It is a quasi-technical term in the rhetoric of the apocalyptic tradition that is appropriated by some New Testament writers. As E. J. Tinsley summarizes it, "mystery" is used in these contexts in two distinctive ways: "First for the plan of God, the purpose of God in history, his eternal purpose and sovereignty; and second, for the thing or situation which is the medium by which the secret plan of God is disclosed," usually regarding the eschatological consummation of creation (1983, 386). Tinsley goes on to note that when New Testament texts refer to Christ as "the mystery of God," they mean that he is the unique medium through which God's plan in history is disclosed. Roughly contemporary with the use of "mystery" in the New Testament is its use in Hellenistic "mystery religions." There the mystery is a secret rite or ritual by which one is initiated into the immortal life of one of the gods. Perhaps the root of the difference between the two is that, whereas in New Testament texts Jesus Christ concretely enacts God's "plan" for the eschatological consummation of history in a public way, the rites and rituals of mystery religions are arcane. Canonical Christian texts and mystery religions both used the word "mystery" in relation to promises concerning immortality that were made within the cultural context in which Christians of the time lived in the first three centuries AD. It is not surprising that use of the term in mystery religions came to influence broader Christian use, so that among Christians also "mystery" came to be used in reference to rites and rituals leading to immortality, for example, baptism, Eucharist, the eucharistic elements, and incidents or scenes in the life or passion of Christ or the life of the Virgin Mary.

The presence of the term "mystery" in canonical texts also invites interpretations of the word in terms that may be alien to its historical home in apocalyptic rhetoric. The *mysterion* revealed in apocalyptic, God's plan for actualizing the promise of eschatological consummation, is secret before its disclosure and no longer secret thereafter. In Western theology, however, "mystery" has come to be associated with a thesis about human capacity to know God that is grounded in a thesis about the being of God. The cognitive thesis is that finite human beings are incapable of knowing the essence of the infinite God. The ontological thesis is that incomprehensibility is an essential property of God's being.

Given these theses, two things follow: If God Godself is to be known, and not merely God's plan for eschatological consummation, God's self-revelation is necessary; if it is truly God who is revealed, and incomprehensibility is one of God's essential properties, then it is necessary that God remains incomprehensible even in self-revelation. In a brief overview of the history of Western theology on this topic, Karl Rahner notes that while "Christian tradition has always attested this experience and doctrine of the incomprehensibility of God who comes to us as mystery" . . . yet "it cannot be said that the mystery was always emphasized enough" (1986, 1000). There was a tendency to explain the persistence of mystery after revelation as a function of humankind's pilgrim state in this life, which will be overcome eschatologically in the beatific vision. Thomas Aquinas gets it right: "Man's utmost knowledge of God is to know that we do not know him' (. . . *De potentia*, 7, 5 ad 14)" (Rahner 1986, 1001), strictly speaking not even in beatific vision (1000). Revelation may provide a basis on which to formulate claims about God that are objectively true in themselves, that is, in some way correspond with God's reality. But finally revelation does not provide a basis on which we can understand—"comprehend"—God; that is, no basis on which to understand how these claims apply to God truly.

"Mystery" is also used in Western theology in a broader way in the plural. For example, Rahner notes that Roman Catholic scholastic theology distinguishes two senses of "mysteries." In a wide sense, "mysteries" are not accessible to human beings unless they are made known by revelation "(*e.g.*, God's free decisions) but their essential meaning can be understood once they have been made known." In "the strict and absolute sense," however, "mysteries" are realities (or statements about them) that even when revealed cannot be fully understood in their essence or intrinsic possibility (1001). Granting that this is formally and logically clear, Rahner finds it problematic (1001). Theologically speaking, finite creaturely beings in themselves can never transcend the scope of types of being that the human mind is capable of knowing "to such an extent as to constitute a mystery in the strict sense. If such a mystery is in question, therefore, God as such must be involved, on himself and in his relation with man" (1002). Strictly speaking, mystery is singular. It is the being of God.

When plural uses of "mystery" are set aside and "mystery" is used only in the singular to refer to God's being, yet another meaning of the term comes into play. God may be self-revealed in and through finite creaturely things, persons, situations, events, visual and verbal images, and propositions, but these are not themselves "revealed mysteries." Strictly speaking, in revelation God does not communicate multiple pieces of information to human beings. In revelation God communicates *Godself* to human beings. This has been a major theme in twentieth-century theology, in both Roman Catholic theological projects like Karl Rahner's and in Protestant theologies ranging from Paul Tillich's to Karl Barth's. Rahner puts it this way: "This real self-communication (as an event which simultaneously makes itself known) necessarily shares in the character of incomprehensibility which belongs to God. For he communicates himself, not something finite and other than himself" (1002). Here "mystery" is what God communicates in God's self-revelation.

In Rahner's case, that leads to yet another theological sense of "mystery." Here it has its home in theological anthropology because it has to do with the ontology of human being when it is understood on the basis of a "transcendental deduction" of the conditions of the possibility of human consciousness as such. Rahner adopts the methodological thesis that an analysis of a phenomenology of human consciousness can exhibit the "transcendental" conditions of the possibility of the modes of consciousness that human beings in fact experience—that is, conditions that transcend every particular experience and structure all experiences. Centrally important among these is consciousness's "orientation towards mystery," its constantly "going beyond any comprehensible statement and raising a further question" (1002). Because this orientation to mystery is "the condition of the very possibility of cognition and freedom as such" it is "the ground of man's personal life as such" (1002). This structural feature of human consciousness is ontologically constitutive of human being as such: "Man's ground lies in the abyss of mystery, which accompanies him throughout life. The only question is whether he lives with mystery willingly, obediently and trustingly, or represses it and will not admit it, 'suppressing' it, as Paul says. Transcendence is transcendence into mystery" (1002). Since, on account of God's essential incomprehensibility, only God is mystery, to say that being-in-relation-to-mystery is ontologically constitutive of human being is to say that relatedness-to-God is constitutive of human being. God as mystery is at once immediately related to human being as the ground of the possibility of the consciousness that is the precondition of human cognition and freedom, and radically free from human being. "Mystery is the ground throughout, yet withdraws all the more; it is the foundation throughout but does not come under our control; it gives itself as all-encompassing and abiding mystery; we can speak in reaction to it but never really about it" (1002). In virtue of this ontologically constitutive relation that human being has to God as mystery, there is for Rahner a derivative, analogical way in which human being itself can be said to be "mystery" (see 1002).

In this project, unless otherwise stipulated, "mystery" will be used in the singular to refer to God's incomprehensibility to human cognitive capacities, to refer to revelation insofar as it is God's faithful communication of Godself precisely as incomprehensible, and in an analogical sense to characterize human beings as related-to by God, albeit on quite different grounds than those on which Rahner relies to make much the same anthropological point.

As used in theological contexts, "mystery" may also be explained in three formal ways. Writing in Oxford in the mid-1950s at the height of the philosophical influence of logical positivism and the philosophy of analysis, philosopher Michael Foster focused on the concept of mystery as a way to clarify the difference between the then current philosophical style and theology as types of rational inquiry. "Mystery" is generally used in a very broad way in reference to things we do not understand. In *Mystery and*

Philosophy (1957) he points out that the difference between philosophy and theology in regard to things we do not understand cannot lie in the fact that philosophy inquires about them by way of analysis, because theology does also (26). Rather, he suggests the difference can be brought out by noting formal differences among ways in which "mystery" is construed, respectively, in science, philosophy, and theology. Foster traces this from a two-part distinction by Gabriel Marcel (18) to the threefold distinction by Austin Farrer (19n1).

Science and the "philosophy of analysis" assume that nothing is really "mysterious." Therefore there "cannot be anything unclear that we can legitimately want to say" (17). Here "clear" and "clarity" are used in the Cartesian sense of "clear and distinct ideas." Unless a speaker is expressing ideas that are clear in this sense, the speaker does not communicate because the hearer cannot be said to understand what the speaker is expressing. In this sense of "clear," "we cannot be said to understand a truth that remains mysterious" (17). Science and the "philosophy of analysis" further assume that thinking "consists in answering questions" and that "if you want clear thinking, formulate your questions precisely" (22).

Accordingly, science construes something that we do not understand as a function of things we do not know about it. It construes it as a problem that can be solved, usually by asking well-framed questions about it that lead to the discovery of new information that solves the problem. Once solved, the problem ceases to be "mysterious."

"Philosophy of analysis" construes something we do not understand as a function of conceptual confusion. It construes it as a puzzle that can be dispelled by asking well-framed questions about it that lead to conceptual clarification. An example: On learning that the earth is a globe, a child finds it "mysterious" that people at the South Pole are not standing upside down because he conceives "right side up" and "upside down" relative to his own posture. Once he grasps the concept that "up" and "down" are relative to the center of the globe, the mystery goes away. Once solved, every puzzle ceases to be mysterious.

Theology also uses the word "mystery" to refer to things we do not understand. However, it leaves open the possibility that some things may in fact be genuinely and irreducibly mysterious. Accordingly, it addresses "mystery" on different assumptions about what makes it a rational inquiry and what makes for genuine understanding and communication about "mystery." Like classical Greek philosophy (see 31–37), Christian theology is interested in truth which "is the quality which Being [or, for Christians, God] has of revealing itself" (33). The critical difference between them is that, where for much classical Greek philosophy it is the nature of Being to be self-revealing and unhidden, for Christians God is hidden and God's self-revealing is a free and deliberate act (cf. 41). Further, precisely as self-revealed, God remains "mystery," that is, hidden. "God's hiddenness is derived from his holiness" (42), which is separateness from the world rather than separateness in the world from other things. This separateness is not the "uncanny," "weird," "occult," or "magical." Rather, Foster suggests, God's separateness is at once God's surpassing moral goodness, which is a property only of God (49, citing Hobbes!), and God's surpassing intellectual power, which is incomprehensible to us. Accordingly, as a form of thinking or rational inquiry, Christian theology is not a search for answers to our questions. "For Revelation is not an answer to our questions; God is prevenient in Revelation. Mystery involves Revelation and vice versa" (27). Such inquiry involves analysis and conceptual clarification if it is to communicate and is to be understood. However, "concept" must be understood appropriately. Here learning a concept involves existential shaping of one's identity. "Clarifying" a concept as much involves clarifying one's "forms of life" as it does clarifying one's "ideas." Here conceptual clarification is closer to the forming of *phronesis* than it is the forming of capacities for conceptual construction and theory making. As Foster puts it, such inquiry involves "something like a repentance in the sphere of the intellect" (46). It is repentance in response to God's self-disclosure, communicating Godself in God's holiness, which remains mystery to us precisely in its concrete self-revelation.

In this project, use of "mystery" will seek to conform to Foster's distinction between "mystery" on one side, and "problems" and "puzzles" on the other. In particular, the use of "mystery" herein seeks to hold together at least three clear features of the community-in-communion that is God's life and help make it incomprehensible to us (although presumably not to God!). First, as reciprocal self-giving out of fullness, not out of need, it is immeasurably rich life, inexhaustible in its resources. That, we may say, is the *glory* of God's life. Second, in its inexhaustible richness, it cannot be comprehended cognitively. We may apprehend it, but we cannot hope to comprehend it, to get our minds around it. It is impossible exhaustively to map it conceptually or to catch it all up in a net of theory. That, we may say, is the *incomprehensibility* of God's life. Third, if we think of God's life as God's self-relating, then we must say that in all of these reciprocal relations God is at once radically freely self-determining, so that God's self-giving in love is independent of and never exacted by the creaturely beloved other; and in self-giving God is true to Godself, never compromising divine love. That, we may say, is the *holiness* of God's life. The interdependence of its glory, incomprehensibility, and holiness, I suggest, constitutes God's life as a "mystery."

By just this life humans are engaged when the triune God relates to them. Therein lay its anthropological implications, for it defines human flourishing. By such engagement humans are called to analogous life which is their flourishing. Their flourishing lay in a community in communion analogous to that of the triune God, marked by mystery—that is, by analogous glory, incomprehensibility, and holiness, analogous to that of the triune God. Such life can only be analogous to the triune God's eternal life because humans are on the creaturely side of the creature/Creator ontological distinction.

The premises of this chapter have been that (a) if the theologically basic claims made about humankind by Christian theology are rooted in logically prior claims about God's ways of relating to humankind, then the way in which God is understood must have important implications for theological anthropology, and (b) Christianly appropriate understandings of God are Trinitarian. I have not tried to defend Trinitarian doctrine in this chapter. Rather, I have sought to bring out some anthropological implications of major moments in the historical movement from triadic references to God to properly Trinitarian understandings of God. The implications are both methodological and substantive.

Methodologically, it is important that the movement from triadic ways of referring to God to Trinitarian understanding of God was rooted in Christian communities' practice, fundamental to their common life, of interpreting biblical stories about God relating to humankind. The movement to properly Trinitarian understanding of God rested on the recognition that God relating to all that is not God to create it, relating to draw it to eschatological consummation, and relating to reconcile it are logically and ontologically distinct ways of relating. God relating to create has a certain logical priority to the other two. Moreover, narration of each way in which biblical stories tell of God relating requires a different rhetoric: God does not relate creatively by being one creature among many, but that is precisely the way in which God does relate to reconcile. Further, since it is reflection specifically on biblical stories of God relating to reconcile in Jesus Christ that leads to properly Trinitarian understandings of God, such understandings of God are cognitively christocentric. Accordingly, substantive anthropological claims governed by claims about the triune God's ways of relating to humankind will be cognitively christocentric, at least indirectly. It does not follow, however, that the substantive content of anthropological claims about what it is to be a human being must be derived from Christology.

Substantively, it is important for a theocentric theological anthropology that the movement to properly Trinitarian understandings of God was rooted in Christian communities' practices of worship in which at first triadic and later Trinitarian formulas were used. In the very broadest sense of "worship," those practices make up the communities' ways of relating to God in appropriate response to God's ways of relating to them. In that context, the implications of the movement toward Trinitarian understandings of God have largely to do with Christian theological answers to the anthropological questions, "Who are we?" and "How ought we to be?" In baptisms, in prayers of blessing at important moments in life, and in summary confessions of faith using the creed, communities of Christians self-involvingly identified who they were by relating themselves to the One whose story they trusted to be the story of God relating to reconcile them to God and by committing themselves to ways of being set into their worlds that would be appropriate responses to that One. Their Trinitarian understanding of that One warranted the qualified use of filial images to characterize who they themselves were: the adopted children of God to whom God relates in dynamic and generative ways analogous to parents' relations to their children. And it warranted a specific rhetoric to characterize the "existential how" which is their flourishing: participating in their own fashion in that community in communion which is the glorious, mysterious, and holy life of the triune God.

These are implications for theological anthropology of the movement toward a properly Trinitarian understanding of the One with whom we have to do as the ultimate context to which we unavoidably respond in some way. However, we have not yet explored the implications of a properly Trinitarian understanding of God for how each of the ways in which God relates to all that is not God, and hence the ways in which God relates to us, is to be understood. We need to explore the anthropological implications, not only of a Trinitarian understanding of the One with whom we have to do, but also of the One who has to do with us. I turn to that in chapter 3A.

All theology is anthropology
as a reflex of Christology.
PAUL LEHMANN

CHAPTER **2B**

The Kinds of Project This Isn't

Two points were made in chapter 1B about anthropological proposals in traditional premodern Christian secondary theology: (1) Those anthropological proposals do not constitute a particular theological *locus* but are scattered about in discussions of issues in other *loci*. (2) They are proposals made as part of secondary theological inquiry into the question "What is the logic of the beliefs that inform the practices constituting the common life of communities of Christian faith? What are the patterns of their formal relations to one another? How do they hang together? Are they coherent?" And so on.

In chapter 1B it was noted in passing that there are at least two other questions that have also guided inquiry in secondary theology: "What is the logic of coming to belief, or of coming to faith in God, with the result that one joins with companions in enacting the practices that constitute the common life of ecclesial communities?" and "What is the logic of the life of Christian believing, or the life of Christian faith?" Despite its awkwardness, I use both the expressions "belief" and "faith" in formulating these questions in order to acknowledge the variety of ways in which these terms are used in the practice of secondary theology and widespread disagreements about how the two differ from one another and how they are related to each other. I stressed that although both questions are entirely valid, indeed time-honored, in the practice of Christian secondary theology, this project in theological anthropology is not the kind of project that is generated by addressing either of them. I did claim, however, without further explanation, that it is a methodological mistake in secondary theology to conflate address to either or both the second and third questions with address to the first, as though answers to questions about the logic of coming to faith or of living the life of faith therewith also answer the question about the logic of Christian beliefs.

It is important to explain that claim and, thereby, to explain why this project does not address those two questions. It is important in large part because when anthropology becomes a theological *locus* in its own right in the modern period, it takes up many if not most questions about the logic of Christian anthropological beliefs within the context of a focus on the second question concerning the logic of coming to belief (far fewer addressed the third question, about the logic of the life of Christian believing). That approach places this project in a methodologically odd situation.

The questions, "What is the logic of coming to belief (or of coming to faith)?" and "What is the logic of the life of belief (or of the life of faith)?" certainly did not originate in modern theology. The former question has focused theological proposals defending the intelligibility and truth of Christian belief (or faith) since the days of the second-century Apologists, and the latter question has focused theological proposals concerning pastoral and spirituality issues throughout the history of Christianity. What is new in modern theology is the conjunction of address to these questions, on one side, and the emergence of anthropology as its own *locus*, on the other.

That conjunction is no accident. It is a commonplace that modernity places the practice of secondary theology, and indeed all the practices constituting the common life of communities of Christian faith, in a radically new social and cultural context. Its central challenge to those practices is to provide an apologetic for them—that is, to provide rationales why anyone ought to engage in such practices in the first place. One way in which to frame such a rationale is to develop faith-neutral accounts of what and who human beings are and how they ought to be set into their proximate contexts—that is, anthropological proposals that are persuasive to those who are not committed to enact the practices constituting the common life of ecclesial communities. Such anthropological proposals offer an attractive basis for an apologetic for making the transition from unbelief to belief or from unfaith to faith *if* they can persuasively show that there is something systemic about what and who human beings are, and how they ought to be set into their proximate contexts—something systemic that makes "coming to faith" or "living the faith" desirable or even necessary for flourishing as human beings. The systemic feature of human being that they disclose serves at once as the basis for a persuasive apologetic *argument* why one ought to move from unbelief to belief or unfaith to faith and as the basis of the internal unity of theological anthropology as a *locus* in its own right. Thus it is no accident that anthropology emerged as a *locus* in its own right in modern theology in conjunction with address to questions about the logic of coming to belief or coming to faith and the logic of living the life of belief or living the life of faith.

That conjunction places the present project in an odd situation. This project is at one with modern theological anthropologies in construing anthropology as a *locus* in its own right; but it rejects the assumption that grounds the unity of anthropological questions as a single *locus* in much theology in the modern period—namely, that there is something systemically inherent in human being, considered quite apart from any religious or theological commitments, that grounds the logic of coming to belief or coming to faith, unifies theological anthropological proposals into a single *locus*, and is a rational justification of the very project of making theological proposals about any topic.

This is the place to explain so ambivalent a relationship with most modern theological anthropology. The proposals made in chapters 2 and 3 about the God with Whom we have to do, and Who has to do with us, give some of the conceptual background for that explanation. This chapter is confined to what happens to theological anthropology when it is oriented to the question, "What is the logic of coming to belief or coming to faith?" So much twentieth-century theological anthropology has been oriented to that question that it provides an excellent test case of what systematically happens when an address to the question, "What is the logic of Christian anthropological beliefs?" is conflated with the question "What is the logic of coming to Christian belief or to Christian faith?" I would contend that pretty much the same things happen when analysis of the logic of Christian anthropological beliefs is oriented by the question, "What is the logic of the life of Christian belief or the life of Christian faith?" However, that analysis is not undertaken here.

Theological Anthropology and the Logic of Coming to Faith

The word "logic" in the question, "What is the logic of Christian beliefs?" is used in a different sense than it is in the question, "What is the logic of coming to belief or to faith in God?" In the former question, "logic" refers to the formal relations among beliefs: what particular Christian beliefs imply; what they might appear to imply but do not, and what blocks some apparent implications; how they relate to beliefs warranted by inquiries outside ecclesial practices, and so on. In the latter question, "logic" refers to a standard process, a kind of curriculum with its own internal logic, through which human beings are said to move in a transition from unbelief to belief or from unfaith to faith. The concept of such a standard process or life curriculum rests on an anthropological assumption: movement through the stages of such a process or curriculum is "standard" because both the stages and the drive to move through the stages are inherent in, and at least partly constitutive of, what and who human beings are; and actually moving through the stages is constitutive of how human beings ought to be set into their proximate worlds if they are to flourish.

There are important theological conceptual differences, of course, between belief and faith. However, what the question about the logic of moving from unbelief to belief or from unfaith to faith is getting at is broad enough to allow shorthand use of a single phrase to cover both. From here on I rely on the phrase "move from unfaith to faith" to cover both.

There is nothing distinctively modern about the project of making proposals regarding what it is that is inherent in human being and accounts for the fact that human flourishing depends on movement through a curriculum of standard "stages," what the "stages" are, and what the "drive" is that moves human beings through them. Framed conceptually in ways that are consistent with Boethius's sixth-century formula, "a human being is an individual substance of a rational nature," many of St. Augustine's anthropological proposals arguably provide at least the thematic basis for subsequent theological address to this question well into the seventeenth century. The basic structure of the argument goes something like this: As individual substances of a rational nature, human beings are inherently capable of both knowing and desiring the good, where "good" means at least that which is good for their well-being and flourishing and "knowing" is understood to be a type of union with what is known. Having a rational nature, they are free to pursue and actualize union with the good. As bodily individual, finite, radically contingent, mutable substances, their ultimate Good is that on which they depend for their being and value, known under various names, and by Christians known as "God." As rational substances capable of free choices and action, they are capable of disciplining their powers of intellect, will, and affection so that they are maximally focused on actualizing union with the good. They are capable of cultivating their powers' good habits—that is, the virtues that strengthen those powers, as the powers are exercised in their pursuit of the good. As free rational substances, they are also capable of (mistakenly) choosing lesser goods as their ultimate Good and investing their powers in pursuit of lesser goods as though they were their ultimate Good. When they do, their rational capacities to know their true ultimate Good are distracted, confused, and weakened.

Given all this, it can be said that inherent in human being is a drive to move through a certain curriculum of stages to the full actualization of human well-being and flourishing. The drive is human beings' inherent drive toward actualization of their relationship with their true ultimate Good. This is captured in the frequently quoted line in Augustine's prayer, "You have made us for yourself, and our hearts are restless until they rest in you." The restlessness manifests a desire. The contention is that desire for God as the true ultimate Good is inherent in human being. Augustine identifies such desire with what the New Testament calls "love for God." The stages of the curriculum are stages in the process of cultivating the virtues needed to focus human beings' powers on their true ultimate Good and, in addition, when they have confused lesser goods with their ultimate Good, stages in the process of correcting that confusion. For Christians, the sole context within which that process of correction is successful is God's unmerited love for human creatures—grace. It is as grace heals distracted and weakened human nature that human beings flourish as their innate drive toward union with God is finally actualized. The details of the stages of that process and how they are sequenced depend on the philosophical psychology that a theologian adopts.

Because rational nature embraces both cognitive and volitional powers, this general approach can be worked out in different ways. The crux of the differences is the question of whether coming to know some "good" even more deeply is the condition of coming to love it more profoundly, or whether coming to love it more is the condition of coming to know it better. Hence it is commonplace, if oversimplified and misleading, for survey intellectual histories to distinguish between more "intellectualist" and "voluntarist" versions. The first tend to identify the stages in the process as stages in an intellectual movement from truths about the structure and dynamics of reality that are most evident to truths that are deeper and more difficult to grasp, a process that moves one to ever deeper love for God by making God's reality ever clearer intellectually. The second versions tend to identify the stages in the process as steps in the transformation of the will from its captivity in love to lesser goods to love for the ultimate Good, so that it is more free to love God more profoundly and thereby in a position to know God—that is, to be united with God intellectually, more deeply. Either way, the stages constitute a standard curriculum through which human beings move from unbelief to belief, from unfaith to faith. The curriculum is standard because the logic of its stages and the drive to move through its stages are inherent in the very structure of human being. There is nothing distinctively modern about such a proposal.

What is distinctive about such proposals in modern secondary theology is that in framing anthropological proposals they turn away from the substantialist metaphysical concepts epitomized in anthropology by the formula, a human being is an "individual substance of a rational nature," and adopt the celebrated "turn to the subject." The turn, variously traced to René Descartes or to John Locke, has a complex history that need not be rehearsed here (see, e.g., C. Taylor 1989). The "turn" is expressed in various, and sometimes conflicting, ways in modern philosophy and the arts. Broadly speaking, where premodern theological anthropologies construe human being in substantialist categories as something given, a gift fully actualized, anthropologies that make the turn to the subject construe human being as a project, a process of self-constitution, a project of self-actualization that begins in mere possibility or potentiality and is only fully actual at its end.

The terms "self-constitution" and "self-actualization" suggest some kind of relation of the self to itself. It is often called simply the "self-relation." It is a very odd relation. From the perspective of classic substantialist metaphysics, a relation is a property of a substance, as size and weight are properties of physical substances and reason and will are properties of certain living substances. However, the self-relation by virtue of which subjects are self-constituted or self-actualized does not presuppose the reality of a subject whose property it is. Rather, the self-relation constitutes the subject. Pobably the closest to a historical theological precedent for such a notion of an entity constituted by a relation, but framed in classical substantialist terms, are traditional formulations of Trinitarian claims according to which each of the three hypostases of the one God is constituted by its relations to the other two hypostases.

However, two features that characterize the self-relation constituting a subject, according to the turn to the subject, distinguish it from the relations that constitute the three divine hypostases as they are understood in traditional doctrines of the Trinity. First, while consciousness, knowing, and willing may be attributed to each of the three hypostases of the triune God, it is a matter of theological controversy whether the relations that constitute each of them are fundamentally relations in consciousness. Indeed, insofar as those relations are relations of origin ("generated by," "breathed out"), they are traditionally understood as metaphysical relations that are prior in being to properties, such as consciousness, that may be attributed to the hypostases that they constitute. In contrast, the self-relation that constitutes a subject is in some way necessarily a relation in consciousness, although it is not necessarily self-conscious. Hence a "subject," unlike a "substance," is by definition, and therefore necessarily, a center of (perhaps un-selfconscious) consciousness. Second, the self-relation that constitutes a subject is a dialectical relation. Each of the three divine hypostases that is constituted by its reciprocal relations with the other two is distinct in reality—that is, it is irreducible in being to either of the other two. In contrast, each of the two terms of the relation that constitutes a "subject" (the so-called self relating to itself) is only conceptually distinguished from the other. In their relation, the two terms constitute one irreducible reality. The self-relation constitutes a single concrete subject, and the two terms are abstractions from it. Standard analogues for this kind of relation are such relations-in-consciousness as "self-awareness," "self-knowledge," "self-regulation," "self-determination," and "self-evaluation." In each case a conceptual distinction may be drawn between what is "aware," "knowing," "regulating," "determining," or "evaluating," and what is "known," "in awareness," "regulated," and so on. Each is what it is only by virtue of its relation to the other ("aware of"/"in awareness;" "determining/determined," etc.). But in concrete reality the two are one center of awareness, knowing, determining, and so on.

Important differences in the way the "subject" is understood in the "turn to the subject" depend (a) on differences in judgment about which kind of dialectical relation in consciousness is the most apt model for the self-relation that constitutes a subject, and (b) on differences in judgment about the concrete way in which the subject-constituting self-relation is a relation in consciousness. Below I suggest a typology of different judgments on these two matters in modern theological anthropology.

Before turning to it, however, recall why we are concerned with the proposals organized by the typology. Despite their differences, all the varieties of the theological-anthropological turn to the subject share two assumptions that are methodologically basic to most Christian theological anthropology in the modern period because they simultaneously ground the unity of anthropology as a single theological *locus* and exhibit anthropology's apologetic power—namely (1) that human being is constituted by some sort of process of self-actualization or self-constitution having a standard series of stages, moments, or steps through which one is moved by a desire or passion that is inherent in the process; and (2) that this process can be described in a faith-neutral way (hence its potential for the apologetic project) that can also be shown to be either identical in content with core Christian theological-anthropological claims or to entail them (hence its potential for the secondary theology project). Thus, the movement from outside to inside communities of Christian faith can be exhibited as the change in subjectivity that is precisely what one undergoes through the process of actualizing or constituting oneself as an authentic, flourishing subject. The stages from unfaith to faith are nothing else than the stages from potential subject to actualized subject, and vice versa.

Versions of the turn to the subject can be typologized according to their respective judgments about the kind of dialectical relation in consciousness that is the most apt model for the self-relation that constitutes a subject: self-affirmation, self-recognition, self-choosing, self-accepting. There may be more than one version of each type depending on the concrete character of the dialectic ascribed to the mode of self-relation that is privileged. There are relatively few pure instances of each type in theological anthropology, of course. In their anthropologies, theologians often address perceived inadequacies in one type by appropriating to it features of other types. But even when a given theological anthropology synthesizes more than one of these types, it tends to adopt one type as basic and subordinates the others to it.

Subjectivity Constituted by Self-Relating in an Act of Self-Affirmation

In theological anthropology in the modern period there are two prominent versions of this type. We may call one "moral self-affirmation" and the other "religious self-affirmation." They each involve both a claim about the concrete character of the act of self-relating in which a subject is constituted and a claim about the character of the dynamic that moves a subject through the act of self-relating.

1. The first version is indebted to the neo-Kantian philosophical tradition and is exemplified in the work of nineteenth-century theologian Albrecht Ritschl (see Ritschl 1966). According to this analysis, a subject is a moral agent constituted by a self-relation that has the concrete form of an abiding dialectical conflict between the subject as nature and the subject as spirit. In one aspect, a subject is bodied. It is located at some particular juncture in the causal nexus of inorganic and organic nature. Because the causal nexus is governed by the iron laws of cause and effect, nature is the realm of necessity and the movements of a subject as bodied are causally determined. In another aspect, a subject is spirit. The defining feature of spirit is a subject's freedom from nature's deterministic necessity by virtue of its self-aware exercise of its powers of self-critical rationality. As spirit, a subject is capable of two types of freedom from nature's causal nexus: cognitive and moral.

A subject can have a certain level of cognitive freedom of the causal nexus through its exercise of its powers of critical rationality by which it can transcend nature in discovery of the laws that rule in nature's causal nexus. Newton is the exemplar of that exercise of critical reason. Beyond that, by exercise of its powers of self-critical rationality, a subject can transcend nature by identifying and theorizing the systematic limits of human rationality. It can come to understand that all its knowledge of nature and its laws is limited to the access provided by sense experience, that it can know only what appears to consciousness by way of the senses and can never know things in themselves "behind" their empirical self-presentations, and that it plays a major role in constructing its several objects of knowledge and the world known as a whole or as a cosmos. Negatively, it can be shown by rigorous analysis that because subjects can only know phenomena that appear through sense experience, they never have scientific or theoretical knowledge of noumena, the reality of things in themselves "behind" their sensual appearances. Subjects cannot theorize their way to knowledge of the reality of God, or the reality of the cosmos as a whole, or the reality of the soul (i.e., subject) by exercise of their powers of self-critical reason. In such exercise of self-critical rationality, a subject is somewhat more free than it is in the exercise simply of critical rationality in that it transcends not only its given situation in nature, but also itself as simply given. Kant's *Critique of Pure Reason* exemplifies such an exercise of the power of self-critical rationality that defines "spirit."

However, this freedom is always dialectical and never absolute. The cognitive freedom that defines "spirit" is always dialectically related to nature, tethered to the particular juncture in nature's causal nexus where the subject's body is located and limited to what the body's sense organs can register from the perspective of that location.

A second form of freedom that defines "spirit" is moral freedom. Subjects know themselves to be accountable to moral duties. They are agents that are moral, not in contrast to immoral, but in contrast to amoral. They are moral agents in that they know themselves obliged to act in ways that deserve moral praise and that avoid moral blame by striving to do their moral duty. The moral imperatives that define their duty are inherent in the very nature of spirit because they are inherently rational. They are autonomous (*auto*: self; *nomos*: law; the law inside), not heteronomous (*heter*: other; *nomos*: law; the law outside). Since the rationale for their moral duty is inherently rational, subjects are capable of knowing their moral duties by the exercise of their powers of self-critical rationality. Thus, self-critical reason can show that subjects' sense of obligation to act according to duty is rationally justified. Such analysis also shows that rational justification of subjects' sense of moral obligation cannot be worked out consistently in a world in which, as obviously happens, good subjects suffer unjustly and the evil subjects prosper, unless one postulates the reality of subjects' life after death and the reality of a God who guarantees a postmortem righting of such injustice. Kant's *Critique of Practical Reason* exemplifies analysis of the exercise of this capacity of "spirit."

Rational analysis of acknowledged responsibility to act according to moral duty shows that the moral quality of an action depends only on its conformity to moral duty. Because the moral law is auto-nomous, inherent in spirit's self-critical rationality, action in accord with moral duty must be wholly indifferent to the attractions of pleasure or the fear of pain, whether grounded in bodily needs and impulses, in culturally inculcated tastes and values, or in the promises or threats of an external authority such as a parent or a god. Since it can be shown rationally that subjects *ought* to act only according to moral duty, and are capable of knowing what that duty is, by self-critical rational analysis and legitimation of their sense of obligation to act according to duty, it follows that they *can* act autonomously according to moral duty. "Ought" implies "can." That is, it implies that subjects not only have a relative, dialectical, cognitive freedom from nature's causal nexus, but that they also have an absolute moral freedom from nature's causal nexus. It implies that, as spirit, a subject is capable of acting in accord with moral duty and against the body's needs, impulses, and drives.

On this analysis, a subject's self-affirmation as moral agent is valued more highly than its self-affirmation as self-critically rational knower. A subject is fully actualized only when it struggles to relate to itself in ways that affirm that it ought to act in accord with moral duty, but such self-relating is not necessitated. This struggle is entered into freely. A subject might simply relate to itself in passive acceptance of its givenness as a cog in the mechanics of the causal nexus whose behavior is entirely determined by causal necessity. Then it would not at all be self-actualized as a subject. It might relate to itself entirely by way of exercising its powers of self-critical rationality, affirming itself as a knower of the world, actualizing itself as relatively and dialectically free of the causal nexus, standing, as it were, at its outermost limits as its rational observer and analyzer, but not absolutely beyond it as a moral agent. Even then it would not be fully self-actualized as a subject. On this analysis, a subject's self-affirmation as moral agent is valued more highly than its self-affirmation as self-critically rational knower.

Moral struggle is the concrete character of the act of self-relating that constitutes a subject. In exercising moral freedom, a subject as spirit is in conflict with itself as nature. Indeed, as a moral agent, a subject is constituted by a self-relation that has the concrete form of an abiding dialectical tension and conflict between the subject as nature and the subject as spirit.

The dynamic that accounts for a subject's actually relating to itself by affirming itself as, precisely, a moral agent (and not a mere theorizing knower), and doing so concretely through spirit's struggle against nature, is rooted in the subject's powers of self-critical reason. In its self-critique of its own nature-imposed limits, such reason inherently seeks freedom from those limits. Self-critical reason is itself the dynamic that inherently seeks freedom. Furthermore, through its critique of its own limits, it is capable of showing rationally that its freedom from nature can only be relatively realized by affirming itself as a theorizing knower but can be absolutely realized by affirming itself as a moral agent. That is, in affirming itself as one capable of exercising powers of self-critical rationality, a subject can live as one who is relatively freed from nature in the effort to know it by theorizing it. But in affirming itself as a moral agent, a subject can live as one absolutely freed from nature in the struggle to act according to moral duty and not according to the needs, impulses, and desires imposed on it by nature. The dynamic that accounts for a subject's actualizing itself as a subject by relating to itself by affirming itself as a moral agent is a function, not of the dialectic between the two aspects of every subject, nature and spirit, but in just one of its aspects, spirit—that is, self-critical rationality striving to be maximally free of nature.

Thus far, this analysis of the self-relation that constitutes a subject has not entailed any claims about relations either between God and human subjects or between human subjects and God. Analysis of moral self-relation has acknowledged that rational vindication of the validity of subjects' sense of being under obligation to act in accord with their moral duty requires the postulation of the reality of God. But it has denied that postulation constitutes a theoretical argument for the existence of God. In any case, it is only the postulation of the reality of God, not the postulation of any relation between God and particular subjects. Because a God-relation is conceptually absent from this analysis of subjectivity, it might appear that the analysis would not be easily appropriable into theological anthropology.

However, another factor in the way subjects are situated raises a new problem. The context in which subjects seek to affirm themselves as moral agents is deeply distorted by evil. This is taken seriously in Kant's profound analysis of radical evil in book 1 of *Religion within the Limits of Reason Alone* (1960). In consequence of this evil, precisely those who are self-actualized as subjects—that is, those whose self-relating takes the form of self-affirmation as moral agents through the struggle of spirit's conflictual dialectic with nature—will fail. They will become self-divided. The division will not be between nature and spirit, but between their good intention to act in accord with moral duty and the fact that their concrete enactments turn out not to accord with their moral duty. They become guilty of failing in fact to act in accord with their moral duty. That raises sharply the question, "What can sustain subjects in their process of self-actualization as subjects if the very project proves to be impossible?"

For broadly Ritschlian Protestant theology, this analysis of moral failure makes possible the appropriation by theological anthropology of this analysis of what it is to be a subject. The analysis of radical distortion of the context of human moral agency, and its consequences, can be adopted as a faith-neutral description of the same condition of the world that is described in Christian accounts of the fall, original sin, and their consequences. The analysis of subjects' self-division in the guilt inevitably incurred by morally serious agents, and not just by morally disengaged subjects, can be understood as a faith-neutral description of what Christians call the condition of sin and its guilt, echoing, perhaps, the apostle Paul: "For I do not do the good I want, but the evil I do not want is what I do" (Rom. 7:19).

The basic logic of Ritschlian theological proposals is this: Faith in the forgiving and reconciling love of God is alone the thing that can sustain subjects in their struggle to actualize themselves as moral-agent-subjects despite the guilt they will inevitably incur trying to act according to the imperatives of moral duty in a world distorted by radical evil, a guilt that signals their failure finally to actualize themselves as subjects despite their best intentions and high moral seriousness. "Faith" is not the name of a kind of knowledge of God; self-critical reason has shown that human rational powers are incapable of knowing God, in the proper scientific sense of "know." Nor is "faith" the name of a type of experience of God; self-critical reason has shown that human experience is limited to sense experience, and God is not an empirical object. Nor is "faith" the name of the act of postulating the reality of God, as a move in the rational vindication of subjects' sense of accountability to moral duty; that is an impersonal act. Rather, faith is a subject's personal relation to God. Faith is an act of personal trust that the historical life of Jesus discloses the nature of God's love as a love that forgives subjects' failure to act in accord with moral duty, affirms them as fully actual subjects despite their moral failure, reconciles them to one another as equally forgiven guilty agents whose mutual offenses have been put behind them, and motivates them to interact according to moral duty out of an ever deeper love for one another as together they build the reign of God on earth. When self-relating is conducted in the context of such faith in God's forgiving love, it is the faith in God's love that finally actualizes a subject as a moral agent, not the failed effort at self-relating through the struggle to act according to moral duty. For such theological appropriation of this type of analysis of subjectivity, that is what is meant by the Christian good news that subjects are justified by faith and not by works of the law.

The apologetic possibilities of this anthropological strategy are clear. The analysis of what it is to be a subject is faith-neutral and ought to be persuasive to modern minds. It is fully consistent with modern (i.e., Newtonian) scientific understanding of the causal nexus that constitutes the context of human subjects' lives and with modern (i.e., after the Kantian epistemological "Copernican"

revolution) understanding of the limits of human self-critical rational powers. The analysis cannot be accused of conceptually smuggling a relation to
God into an allegedly faith-neutral analysis. The God-relation consists solely
of faith, and it is a relation that is extrinsic to the self-relation that constitutes
a subject. Such a God-relation is not logically necessary to being a subject;
it is necessary only on the contingency that the context of subjects' morally
accountable action is distorted by radical evil and the guilt that subjects consequently incur necessarily. Furthermore, this relation of a subject to God does
not violate subjects' autonomy by subordinating them to an external, extrinsic
authority. Rather, this relation of trust is the condition of the possibility of subjects' self-actualization as moral agents and their realization of their freedom as
spirit under the conditions of radical evil.

Nevertheless, theological appropriation of this type of analysis of subjectivity is problematic both in regard to systematic theological issues and in regard
to the content of core theological concepts relevant to theological anthropology. It is systematically problematic in that it radically narrows the conceptual context in which anthropological topics are explicated theologically to the
conceptual pair: "sin" and "forgiveness and reconciliation" or "sin" and "grace."
God-relations are thereby fundamentally limited to God's relating to subjects
to forgive and reconcile and to subjects' relating to God in faith. It is difficult
to see how, in that conceptual context, one would explicate a claim that God
also relates to subjects in quite different ways—for example, to create them or
to draw them to eschatological consummation. This systematic problem generates interpretations of the material content of core Christian theological concepts that are problematic.

For example, the concepts of the world as creation and subjects as creatures
appear to be distorted. On this theological analysis of *anthropos*, nature names
the given that is the context of subjects' acts of self-affirmation. Formally, then,
nature fills the role filled by creation in traditional, premodern theological
anthropology. Materially, however, the two are not conceptually interchangeable. "Nature" is defined in terms of the deterministic causal nexus described
by Newtonian mechanics in which the concept of God relating to the nexus
can have no role. "Creation," by contrast, is defined in terms of God's relating
creatively to all that is not God, such that God's creative relating is an inherent
structural feature of what it is to be creation. When the context of subjectivity—
that is, the "world"—is understood as nature, it is understood at best to be resistant to subjectivity's freedom—that is, to subjects in the aspect "spirit"—and
at worst to be subjectivity's hostile enemy. Such a theological anthropology is
hard to distinguish from a Manichaean view of the world. In such a theological
framework it is difficult to see how to explicate the traditional Christian claim
that the larger context of which subjects are a part is good and that their proper
relation to God in respect of that context is gratitude.

Second, concepts of eschatological consummation and the Christian life
appear to be distorted. On this theological analysis of *anthropos*, "kingdom of
God" names the ideally just and peaceable society of mutual love that individual
subjects join with others to build, motivated by their reconciliation with one
another in consequence of God's forgiveness of them. Formally, then, "king-

dom of God" fills the role of "eschatological consummation" in traditional, premodern theological anthropology. Materially, however, the two are not conceptually interchangeable. "Kingdom of God" is defined anthropocentrically in terms of moral intersubjective relationships, such as justice, *agape*, and nonviolence, that accord with subjects' moral duty as subjects. "Eschatological consummation," by contrast, is traditionally understood theocentrically in terms of God relating to subjects to draw them to an intimacy of communion in community with God that they cannot otherwise experience. God's act of drawing subjects to this communion is traditionally called "grace." God's grace involves subjects' forgiveness, reconciliation, and deep moral change. However, these consequences of grace for subjects' sin and guilt in failing to act toward one another in accord with moral duty are ordered to something more basic—their relationship to God—which cannot be adequately explicated solely in moral categories. By contrast, when the significance of God's grace is understood in terms of an anthropocentrically understood kingdom of God, faith and the life of faith are understood moralistically. Faith is fundamentally understood as the subjective condition for living as a moral agent in relation to other moral agents in the midst of radical evil, rather than as a trusting response to being drawn into deeper relation with God. The life of faith is understood as fundamentally the moral life of subjects who are enabled by God's reconciling forgiveness to persevere in spirit's struggle to act in accord with moral duty and against nature's needs, impulses, and drives. Such a life's relation to God can be characterized as dutiful, obedient, and trusting, but it is difficult to see how it could be explicated as a life defined by liberty or joy.

Third, concepts of grace and, for that matter, of God, appear to be distorted. This theological analysis of *anthropos* assumes that the fundamental way in which God relates to human subjects is to forgive and reconcile them when they individually are guilty of failing to act in accord with moral duty and when they are estranged from one another by the tangle of reciprocal and mutual moral debts and trespasses generated by that failure. Lacking any larger context of additional ways in which God relates to subjects, this move systematically generates instrumentalized concepts of grace and God. When grace is basically understood as the forgivingness of God's love, it is understood as an instrument of remediation, a kind of analgesic for subjects' moral pain. Understood instrumentally, grace is understood in a Pelagianizing way. It serves as an instrument to assist individual subjects to exercise the powers they have anyway to act in accord with moral duty. In much premodern theology, by contrast, grace was understood as a substance that is infused into subjects' creaturely substance and empowers them to do what they cannot otherwise do. The conceptual scheme in which "substance" and "infuse" are at home may not have been theologically adequate. But the use of those terms to characterize grace and its relation to human beings at least makes it clear that God's grace is not fundamentally an instrument of remediation but a fresh creative act by God that has reality and value in its own right and is not simply a disposable instrument with mainly utilitarian value.

Similarly, and even more problematically, when God's relation to subjects in reconciling forgiveness has no larger context in God's relating to create and

God's relating to draw creatures to eschatological consummation, the question "Who or what is God?" can only be answered by the following: "God is whatever is the ultimate source of the reconciling love we experience in relation to Jesus, insofar as Jesus can be trusted to reveal the character of that love. We know enough about Jesus to characterize who he is; about the Origin of the love Jesus reveals we know nothing except that it functions as the origin of this love." In premodern theology, by contrast, the God who reconciles is identified as the God who creates *ex nihilo*, on whom all creatures are radically contingent for their being and value but who is not dependent on them for God's reality and value. The concepts of creation *ex nihilo* and radical ontological dependence are certainly not unproblematic, but they do make clear that God is to be understood as a reality in God's own right and not as a hypostatized function of other, lesser beings' problematic realities and needs.

Theological appropriation of analysis of subjectivity as constituted by a subject's act of self-affirmation through a conflictual dialectic between a subject as nature and as spirit is often dismissed as long discredited by the ease with which it was appropriated by Protestant theologians in Europe to justify the start of World War I and, later, by its failure to generate theological protest in Europe and North America to the rise of Naziism. Karl Barth dismissed it as a mere "episode" in the history of theology. However, it is arguably still the implicit theological anthropology of most American Christians, especially Protestants, theological "liberals," "moderates," and "evangelicals" alike, because it is the implicit theological anthropology of American civil religion. It remains culturally and theologically influential and is by no means merely a historical artifact.

2. A second version of this same type of analysis of subjectivity holds that a subject actualizes itself by relating to itself in an act of self-affirmation as a religious, rather than a moral, subject. The paradigmatic instance of theological appropriation of this version is the anthropology of Friedrich Schleiermacher's dogmatics (see Schleiermacher 1928). According to this analysis, a subject is essentially "religious." On this analysis, a subject is a center of consciousness constituted by a self-relation that has the concrete form of a continual process of self-actualization through a self-affirmation that takes the form of a dialectical tension, not between nature (which is not conscious) and spirit (which is consciousness's freedom from nature), but between two levels of immediate self-consciousness, one of which is consciousness of God. A lower level of consciousness, an immediate awareness (i.e., a self-awareness) of one's consciousness as determined by interactions with one's physical and social contexts, is called "sensible" self-consciousness. A higher level, an immediate awareness of one's consciousness as determined by a feeling of absolute dependence, is called "religious" self-consciousness. If "God" may be used to name the "whence" of this feeling of absolute dependence, then immediate consciousness of being absolutely dependent may equally well be called "immediate God-consciousness." In that case, a subject's immediate self-consciousness of being absolutely dependent simply is the subject's relation to God.

As different levels of immediate self-consciousness, neither of these is an objective consciousness—that is, a consciousness of an object that is "other" to the subject as a discrete "other." Consciousness of discrete objects is always conceptually mediated. What is in focus here is consciousness's immediate or nonmediated self-consciousness. In varying degrees, both levels are co-present in every moment of consciousness. Hence, a God-relation in consciousness is an inherent structural feature of subjectivity. That is why a subject's self-relation as self-affirmation is an affirmation of itself specifically as a religious, rather than moral, subject. This two-level structure of subjectivity as a center of consciousness is evident to us, Schleiermacher believes, if we will only engage in a little introspection.

Locating subjects' God relation within their immediate self-consciousness as its higher level is one of the major points at which the second version of this type of analysis of subjectivity differs from the first version outlined above. The two versions agree in rejecting a traditional construal of the God-relation as a cognitive act. It is not a relationship in reason. However, the second version of this type of analysis of subjectivity rejects the first version's location of the God-relation in connection with moral doing, as a necessary presupposition of a life of action in accord with moral duty. It urges that between them the broad categories "thought" and "action," "knowing" and "doing," prove conceptually inadequate to the complex richness of human subjectivity. They provide insufficient conceptual tools to analyze what it is to be a subject. A third category is required in addition, "immediate self-consciousness" that accompanies all moments of "knowing" and "doing," and is inseparable from them, but cannot be reduced to them. Immediate self-consciousness may be named "feeling" or, perhaps less misleadingly, "intuition," but in either case it serves to point out that in all their acts of knowing and doing subjects are always immediately present to themselves. Furthermore, this analysis urges, subjectivity's immediate self-consciousness inherently includes at its deepest level immediate self-consciousness of being absolutely dependent. If "God" is the name of the "whence" of that dependence, then God-consciousness, and thus the God-relation, is inherent in immediate self-consciousness rather than in either knowing or doing.

Like the first version of this type of analysis of subjectivity, this second version analyzes subjectivity as situated. However, where the first version construed subjects' context as a realm of necessity, a deterministic nexus of mechanical causal relations, the second construes it in an organic way, as a realm of developing forms of life, each instance of which must itself develop through a process of maturation that is specific to the kind of life it is. Accordingly, subjects also go through a specific maturation process, including a process of maturation of consciousness, that proceeds through a definite series of stages.

This developmental process is teleological. The drive to realize its *telos* is the dynamic that moves a subject through the standard curriculum of developmental stages by which it actualizes itself. The *telos* is a subject whose immediate self-consciousness is dominated by the feeling of absolute dependence—that is, by the "relation to God." When subjectivity is characterized by that state of immediate self-consciousness, a subject has affirmed itself as a religious subject and is then, and only then, a fully actualized subject. The subjectivity of a fully actualized subject is characterized by blessedness.

Unlike analysis of a subject's self-actualization as an act of self-affirmation as moral agents, analysis of self-actualization as an act of self-affirmation as a religious subject entails an intersubjective, rather than an individualistic, view of subjectivity. On this analysis, when a subject's God-consciousness unqualifiedly determines its sensible self-consciousness, so that its immediate self-presence (i.e., its immediate self-consciousness) is dominated by God-consciousness, there is a heightening of the immediate presence of other subjects to it ("species consciousness"). This heightening of species consciousness constitutes fully actualized subjects as inherently intersubjective or "social" subjects just to the extent that they are fully actualized as religious subjects. This is the *telos* of the stages of subjects' inherent developmental process as subjects.

Initially, however, an infant's consciousness does not differentiate between itself and, say, its mother. In time it develops into a more differentiated consciousness. As that process proceeds, the developing subject's immediate self-consciousness becomes increasingly dominated by the sensible consciousness that accompanies its growingly complex sense experience and physical activity. God-consciousness begins to develop at a later stage in the subject's process of maturation. It too needs to grow in power. However, as this higher level of immediate self-consciousness emerges, it is subordinated to the lower level of sensible consciousness that has had a head start in developing its power to determine the subject's immediate self-consciousness, accompanying all its doing and knowing. Because its dominance of immediate self-consciousness is the *telos* of the entire process, God-consciousness struggles to subordinate sensible consciousness to itself and thus to determine immediate self-consciousness so that it will be marked by blessedness. The dominance of God-consciousness does not come automatically, as though it were simply a function of subjects' maturational process. At some point, maturing subjects must take command of themselves to strengthen their God-consciousness to the point where it completely determines their sensible consciousness. That "taking command" constitutes their self-relation in an act of self-affirmation of themselves as religious subjects. It is a dialectical relationship between two levels within consciousness.

God-consciousness's dialectical relation to sensible self-consciousness clearly has the character of a conflictual struggle. However, because the process of a subject's self-actualization is teleological, inherently aiming at blessedness, it is only provisionally conflictual. Unlike the conflictual dialectic between nature and spirit in the first version of this type of analysis of the self-relating that constitutes a subject, here the initially conflictual character of the teleological character of the dialectic between two levels of immediate self-consciousness is destined to be overcome at the end of a subject's process of self-actualization.

The basic logic of broadly Schleiermachian theological proposals framed in terms of this analysis of subjectivity is roughly as follows: Since an immediate self-consciousness in which sensible self-consciousness is determined by God-consciousness simply is the blessedness at which the process of a subject's self-actualization is aimed, when the higher level determines the lower level with ease, so that the *telos* of the process of self-actualization is approached, immediate self-consciousness has the form of joy. In theological terms, fully self-actualized subjectivity—in which God-consciousness and sensible self-consciousness are co-present but God-consciousness determines sensible consciousness—is what is meant by experiencing the world (with which it is engaged in all knowing and doing) in relation to God—that is, "in God." The pleasure of such immediate self-consciousness is what is meant theologically by "blessedness." The fact that the co-present sensible self-consciousness is the condition of the possibility for such blessedness is what is meant theologically by saying that the world with which one is engaged in all knowing and doing is good and is God's gift (if no sensible self-consciousness for God-consciousness to determine with ease, then no blessedness). Moreover, since the contents of sensible self-consciousness are experienced as good when they are the occasion for, rather than obstacles to, the dominance of God-consciousness, they are experienced as contents ordered-to God-consciousness's determination of immediate self-consciousness. That is what is meant by the theological remark that they are ordered by divine providence.

On the other hand, when the higher level determines the lower level with difficulty, immediate self-consciousness has the form of pain. This pain is what is meant by consciousness of sin. The fact that in a subject's maturation process sensible self-consciousness emerges before God-consciousness and is pleasurable in its own right means that the possibility of its arresting the subsequent development of God-consciousness is inherent in the very nature of subjectivity. The further fact that every subject's maturational process is formed by its context in a social network of older subjects in whose subjectivities the emergence and empowerment of God-consciousness is already arrested means that it is inevitable that the growth in power of its own God-consciousness will also be arrested. That is what is expressed by the theological concept of fallenness. The consequence is that even when subjects do seek to take command of themselves to strengthen their God-consciousness so that it wholly determines their sensible self-consciousness, they find they are unable to do it and are embroiled in sin before they begin—that is, suffer a bondage of will in guilt, and are unable to bring it off. This situation is expressed by the theological concept of original sin.

Correlatively, any particular feature of nature or of society whose presence in sensible self-consciousness arrests the growing power of God-consciousness to determine immediate self-consciousness is what is meant by "evil." Nothing is evil except as experience of it arrests the development of the power of God-consciousness.

Specifically Christian religious consciousness is shaped by the immediate self-consciousness of the historical Jesus of Nazareth in which God-consciousness was powerful enough completely to determine his sensible consciousness with unqualified ease, so that his immediate self-consciousness was marked by blessedness. Since blessedness is the *telos* of the process of maturation through which subjects go, he instantiated the first fully actualized human subject, the end to which the entire project of human subjectivity moves. That is what is meant by the theological remark that Jesus is in his person the actualization of the *eschaton*, the end and goal of the project of human subjectivity's full self-actualization. The unqualified power of his God-consciousness is what is meant by the theological concept of Jesus as the incarnation of God. In interpersonal relationship with Jesus, other human subjects found that their own God-consciousness was empowered under his influence more and more to determine their sensible consciousness, reducing consciousness of sin and moving them toward full self-actualization as religious subjects—that is, toward blessedness. The empowering influence on others of Jesus' God-consciousness is what is meant by the theological concept of grace. The fact that the influence of Jesus' God-consciousness enables subjects to actualize themselves fully by affirming themselves as religious subjects means that they are preserved from any ultimate frustration of their movement toward blessedness. That is what is meant by the theological concept of "saving" grace. Since movement toward full self-actualization as a religious subject brings with it increased species consciousness—that is, increased intersubjectivity—one effect of the influence of the power of Jesus' God-consciousness on others is the rise of intersubjective communion among them. The theological name for that communion is "church." Finally, to an immediate self-consciousness wholly determined by its God-consciousness, all the contents of its sensible consciousness, including sensible consciousness of the person of Jesus, are experienced as ordered to its blessedness. That is what is meant by the theological concept of predestination to salvation by God's grace in Jesus.

The apologetic possibilities of this anthropological strategy are clear. The analysis of what it is to be a subject is faith-neutral and may be persuasive to modern minds. Even though cast in a pre-Darwinian form, it is compatible with a modern evolutionary and developmental view of both the organic and inorganic contexts of human subjects' lives. It is consistent with post-Kantian convictions about the limits of self-critical rationality. At the same time, it shows that while those epistemological limits rule out a traditional concept of God generated by metaphysical speculation about the ultimate first cause of all that is, there is an intellectually respectable alternative way of conceiving "God." Indeed, the analysis shows that everyone is in some degree conscious of God, even though many subjects do not attend carefully enough to the structure of their own consciousness to notice that they are already conscious of being absolutely dependent. Furthermore, unlike the traditional concept of an omnipotent and omniscient God who seems problematically to violate the integrity of subjects' immediate self-consciousness, this analysis of subjectivity yields an alternative concept of God as the condition of the possibility of subjects' having immediate self-consciousness. The apologetic force of the appropriation in theological anthropology of this analysis of human subjectivity is manifest.

Theological appropriation of this version of analysis of subjectivity as constituted by an act of self-affirmation has some advantages for theological anthropology. According to this analysis, God-relations are not limited to God's relating to subjects to forgive and reconcile them and, conversely, to subjects' relation to God in faith. God's relation in grace to sinful human subjects is conceptually located within a more basic, logically prior context (though not prior in the order of knowledge): subjects' feeling of absolute dependence that is structurally inherent in the immediate self-consciousness that constitutes them as subjects. This has four conceptual consequences for theological anthropology, each with its problematic aspects.

First, it has the consequence that immediate self-consciousness as a consciousness fully determined by God-consciousness is inherently social and not radically individualistic. This sociality is grounded in the way in which complete determination of sensible self-consciousness by God-consciousness heightens in particular the subjects' species consciousness—that is, the immediate presence to consciousness of other subjects.

However, this sociality is framed in a problematic way. It is sociality in the mode of conscious intersubjectivity, not in the mode of culturally expressed and socially organized power relations. A general feature of this entire analysis of the structure of subjectivity is that it systematically *interiorizes* subjectivity. The analysis stresses that subjects are situated in exterior contexts consisting of interacting powers of many sorts. It stresses that they have powers to interact with other realities in a shared public context. Nonetheless, according to this analysis, what makes a subject a subject and not an object is its utterly interior and private presence to itself unmediated by categories, concepts, or sense data, an immediate self-consciousness that constantly accompanies all its interactivity and underlies the sensible self-consciousness occasioned by such interactivity. When appropriated theologically, such analysis of subjectivity results in an anthropology that systematically brackets human subjects' inescapable involvement in exercise of various kinds of power and in various kinds of institutionalized arrangements of power. At the very least, such brackets problematically suggest that institutional arrangements of social, economic, cultural, and political power and their exercise are theologically neutral and irrelevant to a theological anthropology. At the worst it suggests that involvement in such arrangements of power objectifies subjects and renders their properly interior subjectivity inauthentic. This is anthropologically problematic because it appears to exclude from the realm of authentic subjectivity the reality that subjects are also, among other things, finite centers of power whose actual, concrete sociality is structured by complex arrangements of social, cultural, economic, political, and physical power. It is theologically problematic because it thereby appears systematically to exclude those features of subjects' reality from analysis of what it means to say that subjects are "creatures of God."

A second conceptual implication for theological anthropology follows from the first. An analysis that systematically interiorizes subjectivity may imply that subjectivity cannot be directly communicated and systematically eludes discursive articulation. Every effort to communicate subjective interiority directly distorts it by objectifying it. However this does not necessarily imply that subjects are hermetically sealed in their interiorities and cut off from communicative contact with other subjects and the wider world. Much theological anthropology in the modern period that adopts this analysis of subjectivity also adopts an expressivist view of subjects' action and speech as symbolic of the states of their subjective interiority. Their actions and speech are not expressive in the way in which a sentence in English and a sentence in Japanese are said to "express" one and the same thought. Rather, they are expressive in the way in which it sometimes is suggested that the works of creative artists are symbolically expressive of insights, attitudes, emotions, or moods that cannot be described "literally."

This has the important and problematic consequence for theological anthropology that when what is to be communicated in this manner concerns the God-relation, or other topics in relation to the God-relation (say, human beings), the communication cannot be interpreted appropriately as a statement whose truth or falsity can be assessed. The faith-neutral analysis of the structure and dynamics of subjectivity itself makes claims whose truth or falsity may be assessed. But theological remarks about God's relations to all that is not God and about the God-relatedness of realities other than God, especially human beings, must be construed as expressive "symbolic" utterances. All that can, and what must be, assessed about them is their adequacy as a symbolic expression of the speaker's otherwise inaccessible, wholly interior subjectivity. One result is that theological anthropology's engagement with anthropological wisdom grounded in other practices than those constituting the common life of communities of Christian faith is systematically ruled out a priori.

A third conceptual consequence of this analysis for theological anthropology: Because the God-relation is a structural feature of the immediate self-consciousness that constitutes a subject, the larger situation in which subjects move through the stages of the developmental process of their self-actualization as subjects can itself be conceptualized in terms of God-relatedness as "creation" rather than as "nature"—that is, as a context that is hospitable to the self-actualization of subjects characterized by a blessed immediate self-consciousness, rather than as context that is subject-hostile. Further, because that organic context is the condition of the possibility of having an immediate self-consciousness that includes a level of sensible self-consciousness that God-consciousness can then wholly determine, it can be called "good." The ghost of Manes is held at bay. The important consequence for theological anthropology is that human subjects' organic bodiedness is not inherently problematic but can rather be affirmed theologically.

However, this move is theologically problematic in at least two respects. As we noted above, the scope of subjects' own reality that is characterized as "creaturely and good" appears to be systematically limited to subjects' immediate self-consciousness of their intersubjectivity. It appears to exclude respects in which subjects are immediately self-conscious as centers of various kinds of objective finite power that they exercise in acting upon others. The ghost of Manes is kept at bay, but only, it appears, in the restricted territory of subjects' immediate mutual presence to one another in consciousness. Moreover, the content of sensible self-consciousness—the world—can be described theologically as "good creation" only in a systematically anthropocentric way. It can be affirmed to be "creature of God" and therefore "good" only in virtue of its playing a necessary supporting role in the developmental process through which human subjects become fully self-actualized. But, it appears, "good creature" cannot be affirmed theologically of the world in and for itself. As is often pointed out, especially in light of the ecological and environmental crises, this is a theologically dangerous anthropocentrism, opening the door to theological justification of instrumentalist and exploitative attitudes and practices in relation to nonhuman creatures.

There is a fourth conceptual implication for theological anthropology of this type of analysis of subjectivity. In theological appropriation of this analysis of subjectivity, there is as much warrant to characterize the larger situation in which subjects move through the process of self-actualization as "eschatological" as to characterize it as "creaturely." Because subjects' process of self-actualization is teleologically ordered toward a state of blessedness that at once terminates and stands beyond the temporally extended struggle by God-consciousness to determine sensible self-consciousness, it may be said theologically to be an eschatologically driven process whose eschaton is not an ideal intrahistorical society marked by justice, peace, love, and freedom (as it seems to be for the first version of theological appropriation of this type of analysis of subjectivity, outlined above), but in some way genuinely transhistorical. Thus, subjects' self-actualizing process of self-affirmation as religious subjects is itself concretely situated in a larger context that can be understood in one way as "creation" and in another way as "eschatological." Moreover, because the power of Jesus' God-consciousness, in which this eschaton is first historically actualized, can empower afresh the arrested development of the power of their God-consciousness in other subjects, Jesus' actualization of the eschaton can be called "grace." Indeed, it can be called "grace" in something closer to the full sense of an act of a new creation of other human subjects than "grace" merely in the sense of divine moral guidance and encouragement (as seems to be the case in theological appropriation of the first version of this type of analysis of subjectivity).

However, construing "creaturely" and "eschatological" as alternative theological characterizations of a single self-same larger context of a subject's process of self-actualization is theologically problematic for anthropology. To begin, it systematically absorbs human subjects' creatureliness into their eschatological consummation—that is, their full actualization. Human subjects, it seems, are not genuinely fully actual human creatures until their God-consciousness does in fact wholly determine their immediate self-consciousness, that is, only eschatologically. That appears to leave it indeterminate just how they are to be considered *in via*, between their births and their actualizations of their eschatological destiny. The same move appears to lead systematically to a theologically problematic characterization of other human subjects. As I noted above, because the grounds in this theological analysis for characterizing the contents of sensible self-consciousness as good creatures is their role in subjects' actualization of the dominance of God-consciousness in their immediate self-consciousness, it appears that they have the status of "good creatures" only instrumentally. Presumably, that includes other human subjects. Their bodies make them too part of the occasion of the sensible self-consciousness that some subject's God-consciousness struggles to determine wholly. An instrumentalist construal of the theological concept "creature" seems to lead to a problematically instrumentalist construal of other human subjects as "creatures." It appears that, although there is theological warrant for calling human subjects "good creatures," an instrumentalist construal of both "good" and "creature" excludes any affirmation of the integrity of their reality in and for themselves, quite apart from their instrumental roles in other subjects' process of self-actualization.

Subjectivity Constituted by Self-Relating in an Act of Self-Recognition

The modern period's turn to the subject produced a second type of analysis of what it is to be a subject. It construes subjectivity as a center of *self-aware* self-critical reason that actualizes itself through a dialectical process of self-recognition, rather than a dialectical process of self-affirmation (as in the first type of analysis, outlined earlier). "Self-affirmation" seems to presuppose that the subject already knows what she or he really is and needs only to affirm it. Considered informally, however, an act of self-recognition seems to presuppose that one does not initially know what one really is and needs to get some distance on oneself in order to recognize what and who one really is. Doubtless the most influential formalized developments of this type of analysis of subjectivity have come from the broadly Hegelian absolute idealist philosophical heritage (and its materialist inversion in broadly Marxist thought). These intellectual traditions count as instances of the turn to the subject only, perhaps, in an extended and ironic sense of the phrase. Nonetheless, they have forced important modifications in the turn which have influenced much theological anthropology in the modern period.

This second general type of analysis of what it is to be a subject begins with an assumption that the self-relation that constitutes a subject is a relation in reason. The defining feature of subjects is their capacity for rational knowledge of truth. Because truth is one, it must be some sort of coherent systematic whole. Accordingly, the defining feature of subjects is their capacity to seek the truth about reality as a whole, including truth about themselves and about Absolute Reality or God. This approach rejects both versions of the first type of analysis because it rejects their assumption that subjectivity is constituted either by a moral self-relation (first version) or by a relation in a-rational feeling (second version), on the grounds that they systematically exclude subjects and God alike from the scope of reason's grasp.

Although this approach may be a certain kind of rationalism, it shares with the two versions of the first type of analysis of subjectivity a rejection of the concept of reason that was assumed by early modern rationalist thought. Where early Enlightenment thinkers like Descartes and Leibnitz understood reason as the capacity for critical thought, and Kant reconceived it as the capacity for self-critical critical thought, Hegel reconceived it yet again as the capacity for self-aware self-critical thought. He accepted, as it were, the general analysis also stressed by Schleiermacher that the heart of subjectivity is a subject's immediate self-presence, but urged against Schleiermacher that what a subject was immediately self-present *to* is not an a-rational "consciousness" or "feeling," but rather reason. Rightly understood, self-critical reason is immediately but inchoately self-aware and seeks to know itself by relating to itself in an act of re-cognition. When it does so, a subject is self-actualized as finite spirit (Germ. *geist*)—that is, as a center of fully self-aware self-critical reason.

Like the two versions of the first type of analysis of subjectivity, this second type assumes that subjects are concretely situated in a larger context. Like them, it also accepts the general conclusion of Kant's *Critique of Pure Reason* that (*human*) reason's scope is limited. However, it holds that the limits that self-critical reason identifies for itself are not absolute and necessary but cultural and historical limits. They are relative and subject to change. This analysis holds that in reason's self-awareness it both grasps self-critically the limits of reason and in the same act transcends those limits to grasp the dialectic by which the whole of reality, inanimate and animate, is constituted as one unconditioned whole. It urges that the unlimited and unconditional character of self-critical reason's questioning shows that it is itself in some way infinite, cognitively at one with the dialectical character of reality as an unconditioned whole.

The upshot of this analysis is that as centers of self-aware self-critical reason, finite subjects are not cognitively cut off from the reality of the nonhuman context in which they are situated and are not antithetically alien to it. On the contrary, the logic of the dialectic of rational self-knowledge through which a finite subject actualizes itself as a center of self-aware self-critical reason is identical with the logic through which reality actualizes itself as a whole. This is an ironic turn to the subject because, rather than abandoning premodern theological anthropology's analysis of human being in terms of a cosmic context in which it is in some way at home, it introduces an alternative philosophical way of doing the same thing. Consequently this type of analysis has conceptual resources with which to give an account of subjects that dialectically integrates their subjective interiority into the objective exteriority of their physical, social, and cultural contexts.

On this analysis a finite subject is constituted by a dialectical process of self-constitution as finite spirit that emphasizes its situatedness by making its interactions with its situation constitutive of its reality as a subject. It is a finite subject in that it is limited by other realities with which it must interact. By the same token, insofar as the other realities with which it interacts are other subjects, it is inherently social. It is self-actualized as finite spirit through a dialectic between its own subjectivity and objectivity. The dialectic is this: As an autonomous center of self-aware self-critical reason, it is subjective spirit that manifests itself as a center of natural and moral energies. Exercise of such energies in the context of its physical, social, and cultural setting creates all manner of social, political, and moral structures and roles and material cultures. Collectively they constitute the context in which every finite subject interacts with other subjects and is constituted as "objective spirit." At the same time, every subject recognizes that its objective spirit or public self is an inadequate, even distorting, expression of its autonomy that oppressively limits its freedom. A subject as "subjective spirit" then seeks to correct this inadequacy in new concrete acts that constitute it as a somewhat different objective spirit which, in turn, as a subjective spirit somewhat changed by its memory of the history of its earlier inadequate efforts at self-manifestation, it recognizes its new and objective self to be an inadequate expression of its autonomy in new respects, and so on. In every repetition of this three-moment dialectic, the middle moment of self-alienation-in-self-objectification is necessary in order for a subject as a center self-aware self-critical reason to get the distance on itself that is required for a fresh moment of self-relation, and thereby a moment of fuller self-actualization, in deeper and more accurate self-re-cognition.

History is the story of objective spirit—that is, subjects as social and moral agents collectively giving subjective spirit concrete placement in constantly changing cultural and historical traditions that define a subject's identity. But history is also the story of subjective spirit's interactive, collective overcoming of successive modes of objective spirit and their forms of oppression in the direction of ever greater freedom. Finite subjects are constituted by this historically extended, progressive dialectic between subjective and objective spirit through which they come to full self-recognition. They are fully actualized, and history reaches its end, when objective spirit no longer oppresses them and their freedom is fully actualized.

On this analysis, if spirit, as self-aware self-critical reason, is capable of knowing its dialectical relation to own limitedness-by-reason-of-its-situatedness, it must be that it can transcend that situatedness. It must in some way be non-situated and unlimited—that is, infinite. It must not only be finite in some respect, but Absolute Spirit in another respect. As Absolute Spirit, it is constituted by the same dialectic by which finite spirit is constituted. Absolute Spirit is constituted by a nonsituated three-moment dialectic of self-recognition in which the entire world-historical process is the middle moment. The movement of the dialectic is this: Absolute Spirit (thesis: subjective Spirit), by manifesting or objectifying itself in world history as a whole (antithesis: objective Spirit), comes to an ultimate self-reconciliation in self-recognition (synthesis: actualized Absolute Spirit). The concrete character of the middle moment in this three-moment dialectic—world history—is critical. It is best articulated in Christian theological terms. World history is the moment in which Absolute Spirit—God—manifests itself as identical with finite spirit in a process moving from creation to the person of Jesus, culminating in his crucifixion—self-"objectified"—and, therewith, self-estranged, in incarnation. Correlatively, the historical person of Jesus also manifests that finite spirit is inherently one with Absolute Spirit. But this manifestation can happen concretely only in the form of conflict—the cross—because spirit's self-manifestation always involves inadequacy and the internal conflict of subjects' self-estrangement. The radicality of this divine self-estrangement is manifested in Jesus' death, which is to say, in the death of God. However, since this is a moment in a dialectic that constitutes Absolute Spirit, by definition God remains God through self-estrangement. Hence at bottom it is death that dies, and the bonds of finitude, including the bonds that limit finite spirit, are taken up into the infinite and are overcome. That is the significance of Jesus' resurrection and ascension.

This analysis of spirit as Absolute reintroduces a cosmic dimension into analysis of subjectivity after the turn to the subject. The full actualization of Absolute Spirit is at the same time the way in which the whole of objective reality, in all of its apparent heterogeneity of finite beings and apparent multiplicity of conflicting truths, is actualized as "reality-as-a-whole," unified in a single coherent truth, affirmed and transcended in the infinity of fully actualized Absolute Spirit's self-reconciliation.

There is a major anthropological implication of this analysis's cosmological side. Self-reconciled, not only is Absolute Spirit fully actualized, but finite spirit is also, because its essential freedom has finally been manifested in an undistorted and nonoppressive way in the resurrection and in Absolute Spirit's self-reconciliation. And in that actualization of finite spirit—of finite subjects—self-aware self-critical reason recognizes that finite spirit and Absolute Spirit are inherently one and are always unmediately present to one another. Indeed, it is recognized that Absolute Spirit's immediate presence to finite spirit is the condition of the possibility of the latter's freedom and its immediate presence to itself in self-aware self-critical reason. On this analysis, the God-relation poses no threat to the integrity of subjects' "subjectivity" or freedom.

According to this analysis of subjectivity, a general pattern of *self-manifestation-in-difference* characterizes the dialectic through which finite spirit and Absolute Spirit are both actualized. The pattern gives the analysis an attractive conceptual resource for a Christian apologetics showing that the logic of moving from unfaith to faith is inherent in the movement of every successful process of self-actualization of oneself as a subject. The issues the apologetic addresses are especially important to socially and politically engaged religious skeptics. The analysis seeks to show that the world-historical process, and subjects' process of self-actualization as subjects, are both rational processes leading to the ever-increasing freedom from oppression from self-alienation that socially and politically engaged subjects seek and, indeed, that the two processes have the same logic: just as finite subjects' self-recognition is actualized by a movement through self-manifestation-in-difference when they interact objectively with and in the objective world in which they are situated, so world history is a rational movement of the objective world toward greater freedom insofar as it is the moment of self-manifestation-in-difference of unsituated—Absolute—Spirit. Moreover, analysis of the logic of that movement, it is claimed, shows that what a concretely situated subject re-cognizes as it becomes fully self-actualized in self-recognition is that, precisely as a center of self-aware self-critical reason, it is inherently one with Absolute Spirit in its self-actualization through the world-historical process. The logic of the movement from unfaith to faith is a movement to self-recognition of oneself as a center of self-aware self-critical reason that is inherently one with God.

Analysis of subjects' self-actualization as a dialectical movement toward self-recognition through "self-manifestation-in-difference" has been enormously influential in theological anthropology in the modern period. Three features of this pattern are especially important theologically. Each, however, is also problematic for anthropology.

First, on this type of analysis a "God-relation" is a structural feature of the interiority of subjects who are nonetheless firmly located in the power relations and power structures of their physical, social, and cultural contexts. Indeed, it is a structural feature of subjects who engage so deeply in those objective contexts through their overtly public actions as to be integral parts of them, without compromise of their subjective God-relation. This is anthropologically important because it appears to overcome a theologically problematic systematic dichotomy between the public "objective" physical, social, and cultural world, on one side, and "subjective" interiority with its private "God-relation," on the other, that seems to be entailed by most other types of analysis of subjectivity after the turn to the subject. That systematic move has made some variants of this type of analysis of subjectivity theologically attractive to theologies that seek to emphasize the anthropological implications of intentional human obedience to divine commands and of the New Testament's witness to the in-breaking of God's eschatological rule, such as liberationist and political theologies.

However, this analysis of subjectivity may be theologically problematic just at the point where it appears to be theologically attractive because of the way it understands the relation between subjects, whether finite or Absolute, and their concrete actions. It understands subjects' concrete actions to be revelatory of the subjects who enact them. They are acts of self-manifestation. It explains how they reveal their enactors by saying that their actions express their subjectivities. That explanation appears to rely on a quasi-causal account of the relation between subjects and their self-manifestations in concrete actions.

It is a quasi-causal explanation in that, like the second version of the first type of analysis of subjectivity reviewed above (self-actualization as self-affirmation as religious subjects), they construe subjects' concrete acts as public symbolic expressions that are related to a subject's otherwise inaccessible and private interiority by being imaginatively caused or created to express it in a nondiscursive way.

In this context this is problematic in at least two ways. It is conceptually problematic because it seems to confuse the concept of human intentional action with the concept of human behavior. Much human behavior can be explained causally. When it is, the "cause" of the behavior and the "effect"— that is, the behavior itself—must be capable of being described independently of each other, or else the causal relation is vacuous. An intention, on the other hand, cannot be construed as a cause of which the action is the effect precisely because intention and action must each be described in terms of the other. Where the anthropological implications of intentional human action in response to divine commands or to the in-breaking of God's eschatological kingdom are focal for theological reflection, a quasi-causal account of the relation between subjects and their actions is problematic.

Construal of subjects' actions as expressive, and thereby revelatory, of their subjectivities is problematic in another, related way. In order to keep cause and effect really distinct in its quasi-causal account of the relation between subjects and their self-manifesting actions, such a construal seems to require a distinction in reality between human beings' subjective interiority, the cause, and their objective actions in the public world, the effects. That would seem to reintroduce a metaphysically dualist, "ghost in the machine" theory of human being that the turn to the subject was, in part, taken to avoid. In theological contexts that seek to develop holistic, psychosomatically unified accounts of human being, as much liberationist theology and feminist theology do, such a move would be theologically problematic.

Second, on this type of analysis a relative self-division in self-alienation is a necessary feature of finite subjects. Finite subjects' self-manifestations as objective spirit are inherently inadequate to manifest the full richness of a subjective spirit. This is anthropologically important because it serves to make subjects' elusiveness central to this type of analysis of subjectivity. The elusiveness is systematic. It is sometimes characterized as the "mystery" of subjectivity. However, while elusiveness is doubtless an aspect of the mystery of being a human subject, I shall argue that, theologically understood, the basis of that mystery lies elsewhere (see the coda at the end of this work). Nonetheless, this stress on subjects' elusiveness highlights a major feature of subjectivity. Doing so makes this type of analysis of subjectivity attractive to theological anthropology, especially because it cuts against both a popular culture and a scientific culture that assume that human behavior is a problem that can be exhaustively explained and solved in order to manipulate people to want to buy what they do not need, to vote against their interests, to produce more efficiently, to perform more effectively, to feel good despite their problems, or in order to fix their problems.

However, the explanation this type of analysis gives for subjects' systematic elusiveness is doubly problematic theologically. It explains subjects' systematic elusiveness in terms of the character of the dialectical self-relation by which a subject is self-actualized as a center of self-aware self-critical reason—namely, the three-moment dialectic of self-expression, self-manifestation-in-difference, and self-reconciliation. This type of analysis holds that that dialectic is the logically necessary logic of subjects' self-actualization. The middle moment of the three is necessarily an inadequate self-manifestation of the subject in order for the dialectic to proceed to its third moment. This analysis must reject the possibility that a subject and its self-manifestation might be identical, or even fitted to each other. The self-manifestation's inadequacy is necessarily grounded in its being some sort of distortion of the subject. On the other hand, this analysis also clearly wishes to reject the possibility that the real self stands apart from and behind all its manifestations. That would clearly reintroduce the dualistic "ghost (true subjectivity) in the machine (set of objectifying actions)."

Internal to the logic of this analysis there seem to be no controls over just what sort of inadequacy self-manifestations have in relation to the subjects they manifest. As the intellectual history of this analysis shows, it is open to a variety of very strong interpretations of that inadequacy. It is not just that individuals' uses of the languages of words, gestures, facial expressions, bodily movement, psychological structures, music, and the arts finally fail and mislead. Subjects' entire lived worlds, the complex of cultures and social institutions in which they live, are sometimes held necessarily both to distort the subjects who live in them and to express them in distorted ways. Action, speech, and lived world are alien to subjects or, more exactly, are the subjects in radically self-alienated form. What is theologically problematic about this are its evident affinities with aspects of gnostic outlooks (for a brief exploration of this problem, see Frei 1975, esp. chaps. 6 and 9; and, with a different agenda and in greater detail, O'Regan 1994).

This type of analysis of subjectivity's explanation of subjects' systematic elusiveness is theologically problematic for another reason. Subjects are held to be systematically elusive because they are necessarily self-divided between the subject and the subject's distorting self-manifestations. The distorting self-manifestations are the subject alienated from itself. The self-division is necessary because both are moments in the one dialectic that simply is the subject. Hence, on this analysis, to be a subject at all it is necessary to be, or go through a history of being, self-alienated. Understood within the larger context of Absolute Spirit's dialectical history of self-actualization, it is just this self-alienation that is overcome through the crucifixion and resurrection of Jesus. This type of analysis of subjectivity is problematic when appropriated by theological anthropology because of its consequences for the theological concept of sin. In terms provided by this type of analysis, sin is understood as subjects' self-alienation. However, in that framework, two conclusions follow. First, sin is basically explained in an anthropocentric way in terms of a misrelating of the subject with itself in self-manifestation, rather than theocentrically as a misrelating of human subjects to God. Second, because it is the necessary middle moment in the history of the dialectic through which subjects are constituted, sin is itself necessary. That raises the question whether human subjects can then be held accountable and blamed for sin and, indeed, whether sin is finally all that bad. If the answer is negative, has the concept of sin not been evacuated of its theological meaning?

Third, on this analysis of subjectivity, historicity is a necessary feature of subjectivity. For situated finite spirit, the dialectical process through which it is self-actualized has a history, and that process is what it is only as it is itself situated in "objective" public world history. For unsituated Absolute Spirit, objective public world history as a whole is the dialectical moment of self-alienation (crucifixion, the death of God) through which it moves to resolution in ultimate self-reconciliation (resurrection). World history is thus not the objectifying enemy of authentic authenticity. Rather, it is the story of both finite spirit's and Absolute Spirit's dialectical process of self-recognition through which they are ultimately fully self-actualized.

This stress on subjects' historicity provides a framework in which several anthropologically important theological concepts can be made intelligible to secular skeptics in ways that bear on the dominant concerns of persons actively engaged in cultural and political movements seeking liberation from oppression. For example: "divine revelation" can be understood, not as specific verbal communications from God, nor as particular extraordinary ("miraculous") events, but rather as history as a whole understood as the self-manifestation-in-difference of Absolute Spirit—that is, of God. This history, exhibiting a logic that drives to progressively increasing freedom, reveals that God is free, is the condition of the possibility of freedom, and therewith is the condition of the possibility of subjects flourishing. Similarly, the theological concept that human subjects bear the image of God can be understood in terms of their freedom, analogous to Absolute Spirit's freedom, to be self-actualizing and, in the process, to be the makers of their cultural and historical situations as in their concrete interactions they objectify themselves in ways that are self-manifesting-in-difference. Correlatively, theological ideas of sin and evil can be understood as any interaction or historical development that oppresses that freedom and limits its expression. A final example: The theological concept of the eschaton can be understood as the full actualization of freedom that is at once the goal toward which world history is driving, the full actualization of finite spirit as a center of self-aware self-critical reason, and the full actualization of Absolute Spirit. Indeed, in the context of this type of analysis of subjectivity, theological eschatology is a type of philosophical theology of history that demonstrates that historical change follows an internal logic that necessarily unfolds toward a particular end—the eschaton—which both drives historical change and makes it meaningful—namely, it actualizes self-aware reason's freedom.

However, the conceptual framework of this stress on subjects' historicity is theologically problematic. It seems to absorb the Christian theological concept of God relating to create all that is not God into the concept of God relating to draw all that is not God to an eschatological consummation, and correlatively to absorb the concepts of creation and creatureliness into the concept of eschaton. Whatever else it may mean, the theological concept of God relating to create all that is not God is a concept of God bringing into being actual realities other than God. And whatever else it means, the concept of those realities' creatureliness is a concept of their actuality, planted out by God, other than and over against God. In the framework under review, subjects' "historicity" is understood entirely in terms of the three-moment dialectical process through which subjects are self-actualized. Finite subjects, at least, are "actual" in the proper sense of the term only at the end of the dialectical process. "End" here means both the goal of the process and its full actualization. Insofar as the dialectical process is none other than world history, this end is the eschaton. If that is the point at which finite subjects are made actual, then, it would seem, it is the point at which they are created. "God relating to create" is identified with "God relating to draw to eschatological consummation."

That is problematic because it distorts both concepts. When they are not identified, the concept of God relating to create is the concept of God relating to give actual reality to finite creatures. It is assumed as the logically prior concept. Finite subjects' "creatureliness" is not their "eschatological consummation." "God drawing to eschatological consummation" is understood in contradistinction to it as God giving to finite subjects something above and beyond, but presupposing, what God gives in creating them. When the concept of God relating to create is absorbed into and identified with the concept of God relating to draw to eschatological consummation, there is no conceptual space for the distinction between the implications of each for finite subjects. "Eschaton" has lost its surplus of meaning over "creation." This generates the awkward conceptual problem for theological anthropology that it is impossible to know how to characterize human subjects theologically before their eschatological consummation. If their eschatological consummation is their creation as actual subjects, they are not yet actual subjects, nor actual creatures, throughout their lives in history (insofar as the eschaton has not yet come).

Other theological problems follow from this one. Theological concepts of sin and evil usually assume the logical priority of the concept of creation. "Sin" and "evil" are theologically explained as distortions or violations of what God creates. In Augustine's term, they are "de-gradations" of actual creatures. It is the logical priority of the concepts of God relating to create and of the creature-liness of all that God creates that is expressed in the symbolic characterization of sin and evil as a fall from created actuality. When creation is identified with eschaton, there are no actual human subjects to be distorted or violated until the end of their dialectical process of self-actualization. It appears that concepts of sin and evil have no role to play in theological accounts either of individual persons' lives leading up to their full self-actualization or of world history as a whole leading up to Absolute Spirit's self-actualization. Furthermore, it seems to leave us without conceptual resources for theological identification of, and comment on, the horrific evils that appear to play major roles in the world history that is declared to be, *tout ensemble*, God's self-manifestation-in-difference. Surely such systematic conceptual occlusion of evil is highly problematic theologically. It raises the question of whether this type of analysis of subjectivity as constituted by a dialectical process of self-recognition really can deliver on its promise of a conceptual framework for Christian theological anthropology that coherently holds together the set of anthropological claims that it seems to require given core Christian affirmations about the ways in which God relates to create humankind, to draw it to eschatological consummation, and, when it is estranged, to reconcile it to God.

Subjectivity Constituted by Self-Relating in an Act of Self-Choosing

The turn to the subject has produced in the modern period a third type of analysis of what it is to be a subject. It construes subjectivity as a center of consciousness that constitutes itself through a dialectical process that is more like an act of self-choosing than it is like an act of either self-affirmation (see the first type of analysis, above) or self-recognition (see the second type of analysis, above). Where "self-affirmation" seems to presuppose that one already knows what one really is and needs only to affirm it, and "self-recognition" seems to presuppose that one does not initially know what one really is and needs to get some distance on oneself in order to recognize it, "self-choosing" seems to presuppose that one is presented with several possible ways of being a subject and one needs to decide which one to choose. This stress on decision is, of course, a hallmark of existentialist analyses of subjectivity. The paradigmatic exemplifications of use of this type of analysis of subjectivity in relation to the question of the logic of coming to faith are writings attributed by Søren Kierkegaard to some of his pseudonymous authors. Whether the proposals of Kierkegaard's pseudonymous authors ought to be attributed to Kierkegaard himself is, of course, another question. Because it seems very doubtful that they should be attributed to him, I try to avoid suggesting that they are Kierkegaard's views.

In *Sickness unto Death*, Kierkegaard's pseudonymous author "Anti-Climacus" (Kierkegaard 1954) provides a paradigmatic formulation of this type of analysis (see 1954, 146). It analyzes subjectivity into a structure of internal acts of self-relating through which a subject is self-actualized as "spirit." This structure is used as a template by a great deal of twentieth-century, especially Protestant, theological anthropology. "Spirit" is not the name of one aspect of a subject, but is rather the whole self. A "self" is not a given but rather is a task or project to be actualized. It is a task because it is constituted by a set of relations some of which it does not enter into automatically or "necessarily," but only by freely deciding to enter them. The set of relations is structured in this way:

First relation: "Self" is a relation between body and soul (or consciousness?) that relates to itself. However, the relation between body and soul—the synthesis of the two—is not yet a self.

Second relation: "Self" is constituted by the fact that the interrelated soul-and-body pair relates to itself (second relation). Its relation to itself is constituted in an act of free decision about how to relate to itself. In this decision the "self" is set into and oriented toward its lived world in a particular concrete way that may be called its "existential how." In choosing a particular "existential how," it is choosing itself—the concrete version of itself it decides to be.

Later on in the text the author stresses that in relating to itself the relation is continuously conscious of itself as a relation, and conscious of the fragility of the relation, in a particular mode of consciousness: anxiety. It is anxiety about failing to be a self, failing to actualize itself. Such anxiety is a structural feature of subjectivity, and not a problem to be solved or a pathology to be cured. It is always an open possibility that the two terms or poles of the relation ("body" and "soul") will fall into some degree of disrelation. The most extreme degree, of course, is death. Short of that is the possibility of disrelation. That possibility constitutes its inherent fragility and finitude. The more extreme the disrelation is, the more intense the anxiety. The most intense degree of anxiety is utter hopelessness—that is, despair.

Third relation: The relation's relation to itself, and therewith its "existential how," can either be constituted properly, so that a self (i.e., "spirit") is fully actualized, or improperly constituted as a disrelationship. The structure as a whole defines what counts as the relation relating to itself "properly."

At this point "Anti-Climacus's" text appears to have a major ambiguity. It makes this purely formal claim about the first relation (the synthesis of body and soul): "Such a relation . . . must either have constituted itself or have been constituted by another" (146; the reference to "another" is repeated, 147).

The "another" is ambiguous. It might mean another human person, in which case the abstract formula itself entails an inherently social-relational view of subjectivity in which a God-relation has no structural place. Or it might mean God, in which case the abstract formula entails a God-relation as a structural feature of subjectivity.

"Anti-Climacus" argues against the possibility that the "body-soul synthesis" is a self-constituting relation on the basis of his analysis of consciousness of the self's fragility—that is, his phenomenology of despair. That phenomenology shows that there are two types of despair, despair of "not willing to be oneself" and "despairingly willing to be oneself" (147). If the body-soul synthesis were self-constituting, he argues, there would only be the first type of despair—that is, the despair of not being willing to constitute oneself, of "willing to get rid of oneself" (147). The condition of the possibility of the second type of despair is that the self-relation (body-soul synthesis) "cannot of itself attain and remain in equilibrium and rest by itself." This inability expresses the fact that structurally a subject as a body-soul synthesis (the first relation) can relate to itself (the second relation) so as to hold the first relation in equilibrium and rest only "by relating itself to that Power which constituted the whole relation" (first relation) in the first place (147). This "relating itself to that Power" is the third relation in the structure of relations constituting a self. In short, the condition of the possibility of phenomena of two basic types of despair is the structural "total dependency" of the self's relation to itself on "the Power which constituted it" (147). Because of that structural "total dependency," the relation's (body-soul synthesis) relation to itself must be mediated by its relation to the Power that constitutes it (third relation). Thus, the argument of "Anti-Climacus" against the possibility that the body-soul relation constitutes itself seems to require that the "another" that constitutes it is not some particular human other or others, for it could only be relatively dependent on any particular others, who, after all, come and go. Rather, the "another" must be a Power on which it has "total dependence." Arguably, a conventional name for that Power is "God."

In that case, "by relating itself to its own self and by willing to be itself the self is grounded transparently in the Power which posits it" (1954, 147). The decision in which the relation relates to itself in a way that is mediated by a relation to this Power is called "faith." Assuming that the Power is God, it is faith in God. That is one possible way in which a subject may choose to relate to itself, or, it may equally be said, it is one possible "self" that a subject chooses.

On this reading, which is generally adopted by theologians who appropriate this type of analysis of subjectivity, a God-relation is inherent in the structure and dynamics of subjectivity. It is the condition of the possibility of the phenomena both of subjects' despair and of their freedom to constitute themselves by an act of self-choice.

This Entire Set of Nested Relations Is the Structure of "Spirit"

Talk of a relation choosing to relate to itself in some particular way is obviously odd because "relation" is an abstraction. It is concrete subjects who decide to choose one way or another. However, the abstraction "relation" serves to remind that the terms of the relation, "body" and "soul," are shorthand for a concrete subject that is a living, organic, conscious, self-directing body, a psychosomatic whole in which body and soul are synthesized in very complex ways. When the relation chooses to relate to itself in a way that is mediated by its relation in faith to the Power that constituted it, it chooses itself as a relation that is already grounded in the God-relation. It is the choice of the proper self-relation because, in relating to itself that way, spirit is actualized. A subject constituted by the self-relation of self-choosing of this possible self is a subject whose "existential how" is religious.

The body-soul relation is free, however, to relate to itself in other ways. Their stress on this freedom is a point at which the pseudonymous writers' views clearly coincide with Kierkegaard's convictions. One of Kierkegaard's major polemical points against Hegel and the analysis of subjects' self-actualization through a dialectical process of self-recognition is that the dialectic makes a subject's movement through the process automatic and inevitable. In Kierkegaard's view it is important to insist, to the contrary, that subjects' movement to self-actualization as selves is their own free responsibility. Each must choose to decide the concrete character of its own selfhood. In each of the possible ways of relating to itself, other than through the mediation of faith, the relation is in disrelationship with itself and "spirit" fails to be actualized. In each case, a subject is conscious of the disrelation in despair. The pseudonymous editor Victor Eremita presents two of these possible ways to be a self (Kierkegaard 1959). In the first, the relation relates to itself immediately. Because it is not mediated by faith or by any substitute for faith, the relation it enters into with itself is uncritical. It has no basis on which to have critical distance on itself. Rather, it relates to itself by simply identifying with itself as it is given by the flow of its physical, psychological, and social-cultural experience, and relates to itself un-self-critically in terms of its society's conventions about what is an ideal and admirable self. Since this way of relating to itself is barely a decision at all, being no more than a decision passively to accept itself as given, this self-relating is a disrelation to itself. This is self in the aesthetic mode. Living it, a subject inevitably falls into the barely conscious despair of willing to get rid of itself as self-responsible, rather than willing to be responsible for the self it is. Nonetheless, this is one possible way of relating to oneself, one possible "existential how," that a subject can decide to choose.

In a second alternative to the religious "existential how," the relation relates to itself in a way that is mediated by the moral law and moral duty. The relation actively decides to relate deliberately and critically to itself as given through the filter of the demands of moral law and duty as criteria by which to assess and change the drives, impulses, felt needs, aspirations, values, and self-justifying rationalizations that the self as socially shaped immediately presents to itself. Constituting oneself by choosing to actualize concretely this possible way of being a self seems to be the same as constituting oneself by self-affirmation as moral agent (see above). The relation relates to itself actively in a project to actualize itself as spirit through becoming guiltlessly moral. It is a disrelation because it relates to itself solely in its own power to make decisions that regulate its interactions with its lived world according to moral law and demands. But this turns out to be a project that never can be completed. No subject in fact has the power to regulate its own life so perfectly that it remains guiltless, so that at no point in time would one have self-actualized as spirit. This is self in the moral mode. Living it, a subject inevitably falls into the acutely conscious despair at ever succeeding at willing to be itself.

This analysis of the structure of subjects as selves self-actualized through proper self-choosing provides conceptual resources for constructing a three-moment curriculum through which one must move existentially from unfaith to faith—into the religious mode of existence—in order to become a fully actu-alized spirit or person. It struck many mid-twentieth-century theologians as providing intellectual resources for a theological apologetic. The successive stages of the curriculum are, respectively, the aesthetic, the moral, and the religious modes of existence. Unlike the movement described by analysis of sub-jectivity as constituted by the dialectic of self-recognition, movement through the stages of this curriculum is not made inevitable by the logic of the dialecti-cal relation between the moments themselves. Rather, the relevant dialectic is internal to each of the first two moments: each self-deconstructs into despair. The despair does not necessarily propel one into the next moment. One may remain in either of the first two for one's entire biological life. The transition itself lies in a free decision to relate to oneself in a new way, choosing a different possible self, thereby constituting oneself in a new existential "how." Despair may not motivate such a transition, but it does provide the occasion for such a move. This type of analysis of subjectivity offers an intellectually powerful analysis of why the aesthetic and moral "existential hows" self-deconstruct. It does not depend on theological assumptions and may be persuasive to religious skeptics. The analysis of why living in both "existential hows" leaves one in despair rings true to secular experience. Moreover, it provides the conceptual resources of a philosophical psychology for diagnosis of widespread psychological suffering. It also provides conceptual resources of diagnostic analysis of the cultural artifacts, high and low, that express or reflect such suffering. It is no accident that much theological anthropology that adopted this type of analysis of subjectivity led into projects in theology and the arts. Further, the analysis of the movement from an aesthetic to a moral "existential how" shows, in a nontheological way, why the latter is, paradoxically, at once a fuller actualization of subjectivity and more intensely despairing than the former. It may make plausible the suggestion that a further move to the religious "existential how," by deciding to choose to relate to oneself in a way mediated by faith in God, will yield an existence even more fully actualized and rid of despair, though not of anxiety. The nub of the apologetic is the suggestion that the existential decision that will resolve the suffering of despair and actualize oneself in an act of proper self-relating is also the existential decision that constitutes the God-relation called "faith."

None of this, of course, amounts to a knockdown theoretical argument in defense of the rationality of faith in God. It is rather an existential argument urging the reasonableness of deciding to choose for oneself the possible way of being a subject represented by the religious "existential how."

In various combinations, permutations, and modifications, these three types of analyses of the structure and dynamics of subjectivity have been widely appropriated in theological anthropologies in the modern period. They are especially evident in the influential writings of otherwise very different, perhaps mutually exclusive, mid-twentieth-century theologians who self-consciously locate themselves after the turn to the subject, such as Reinhold Niebuhr's *The Nature and Destiny of Man* (1953); Emil Brunner's *Man in Revolt* (1947); the anthropologies in, respectively, the three volumes of Paul Tillich's *Systematic Theology* (1951, 1957, 1963) and in Karl Rahner's *Foundations of Christian Faith* (1978); and the theology in Rudolf Bultmann's essays on revelation, human historicity, Romans 7, faith in creation, the history of salvation, freedom, and living "between the times," collected in *Existence and Faith* (1960). Appropriation by such theological anthropologies of the types of analyses outlined above has had the advantage of providing a systematic structure by which to unify anthropology as a single theological *locus* and the structure of a broadly apologetic program for theology. It is not my contention that there is anything theologically problematic with either of those outcomes. Rather, my contention is that they do not serve each other. Insofar as they are helpful to the apologetic enterprise, these analyses of subjectivity provide conceptual templates for addressing the question, "What is the logic of coming to faith?" However, I wish to argue, precisely to the extent that they are helpful apologetically, such analyses of subjectivity distort addressing the question, "What is the 'logic' of Christian beliefs?" when they are appropriated to provide the unifying systematic structure for anthropology as a theological *locus* in its own right.

Against Conflating the Questions

The reason for this anthropological project's exclusive address to the question about the logic of Christian beliefs is the thesis that it is a profound conceptual and methodological mistake to conflate any theological project that attempts to answer the question of the logic of Christian beliefs with a theological project that attempts to answer the question of the logic of coming to faith.

This methodological thesis is not grounded in the fact that there are problematic features of efforts to identify the logic of coming to belief. There are also problematic features of efforts, like this anthropological project, to outline the logic of Christian beliefs. The fact that projects addressed to each of these three questions are problematic in different ways is not an a priori reason to set any of them aside. Each such project must be assessed ad hoc as to how persuasively it deals with the problems that are inherent in the effort to address the question it addresses.

Instead, my methodological thesis is grounded in the claim that it is a conceptual mistake in the practice of secondary theology. To conflate theological proposals addressed to the question of the logic of coming to belief with proposals addressed to the question of the logic of Christian beliefs, as though the former provided the answers to the latter, confuses two conceptually different kinds of inquiry. A functional account of how Christian concepts and beliefs may work—that is, the role they may play—in human beings' movement from unfaith to faith (or in living the life of faith, for that matter) is not the same as an account of what the beliefs mean, how they do or do not hang together, what they imply, how they may be freshly articulated most perspicuously, and so forth.

This conceptual mistake has serious systematic consequences in the practice of secondary theology. It leads systematically to at least four theologically undesirable emphases: utilitarian and functionalist trivialization of understandings of God and God's ways of relating to human beings, quasi-Manichean theological assessment of nonhuman creatures, anthropocentric and instrumentalist theological views of human beings' proper relations to nonhuman creatures, and an anthropocentric moralizing of accounts of Christian beliefs about human beings.

First, such conflation systematically leads to a theological anthropological denigration of human beings and a correlatively utilitarian and functionalist trivialization of God's relating to human beings.

Theological projects whose defining end is to answer the question about the logic of coming to faith focus, quite appropriately, on human sin and the problems it generates. They are inquiries focused and structured by the human condition construed as a problem. It is not construed as a problem in the sense of an intellectual wonder, much less a mystery. Rather, it is a problem in the sense of a weakness, a damaged integrity needing to be restored, a lost freedom needing to be liberated, or a disease needing to be healed. The typology, outlined above, of types of analysis of subjectivity appropriated by theological anthropologies after the turn to the subject repeatedly shows that the logic of becoming a fully self-actualized subject is the same as the logic of coming to faith if the human condition, the problem generating the struggle inherent in self-actualization, may be identified with the problem (sin) generating the struggle human beings are said, theologically speaking, to go through in the passage from unfaith to faith. The apologetic force of such theological anthropologies depends on that identification.

The theological methodological problem is not that these characterizations of human being are false or misleading. To the contrary, they are profoundly true and identify central practical and existential topics in Christian anthropology. Such theological characterizations do rightly denigrate human beings' weakness in certain respects.

However, such theological focus on human beings' weakness becomes problematic when it serves as the primary, and therefore the theologically determining, conceptual framework within which the anthropological implications of God's relating to humankind are worked out. The basic structure of theological anthropologies worked out in that context is a "God's grace/humans' sin" structure: The central Christian claim about God is that God relates to reconcile in the very odd mode of incarnation leading to crucifixion and resurrection (call it "saving grace"); therefore, the central Christian claim about human beings is that they must be in a condition of weakness, damaged integrity, lost freedom, or disease so profound (call it "original sin," "fallenness," "bondage of the will") as to require such an astonishing mode of divine relating for it to be overcome in the full actualization of human subjects. The apologetic force of this sort of anthropological project requires this structure. It has, however, the systematic consequence that Christian claims about other ways in which the triune God relates to all that is not God—for example, to create and to draw to eschatological consummation—are theologically marginalized.

That is not to say that these claims about other ways in which God relates to humankind, and their anthropological implications, are necessarily denied or ignored. It is to say that they are assigned the logical status of background beliefs. It must be acknowledged within this structure for theological anthropology that the central Christian claim that God relates to human beings to reconcile them when they are estranged assumes the validity of the logically prior claims that the God who relates to reconcile is also the God who relates to create human beings and relates to draw them to eschatological consummation. Nonetheless, according to this structure for theological anthropology, what Christian theology is chiefly about is the articulation of the central claim that God relates to reconcile and save fallen and sinful human beings. The systematic consequence for anthropology is that the anthropological implications of other ways in which the triune God relates to human beings are themselves assigned the logical status of background beliefs. They are marginalized.

Perhaps the most forceful expression of theological protest against these anthropological consequences of this way of conceptually structuring theological anthropology is Dietrich Bonhoeffer's often-quoted remark writing to Eberhard Bethge from Tegel Prison on June 30, 1944:

> Since Kant [God] has been relegated to a realm beyond the world of experience. Theology . . . has accommodated itself to the development by restricting God to the so-called ultimate questions as a *deus ex machina*; that means he becomes the answer to life's problems and the solution of its needs and conflicts. So if anyone has no such difficulties, or if he refuses to go into these things, to allow others to pity him, then either he cannot be open to God; or else he must be shown that he is, in fact, deeply involved in such problems, needs, and conflicts, without admitting or knowing it. If that can be done . . . then this man can now be claimed for God. . . . But if he cannot be brought to see and admit that his happiness is really an evil, his health sickness, and his vigor despair, the theologian is at his wits' end. It's a case of having to do either with a hardened sinner of a particularly ugly type, or with a man of "bourgeoise complacency," and the one is as far from salvation as the other.

By contrast, Bonhoeffer goes on to say a bit later,

> When Jesus blessed sinners, they were real sinners, but Jesus did not make everyone a sinner first. He called them away from their sin, not into their sin. . . . Never did [Jesus] question a man's health, vigor, or happiness, regarded in themselves, or regard them as evil fruits; else why should he heal the sick and restore strength to the weak? Jesus claims for himself and for the Kingdom of God the whole of human life in all of its manifestations. (1972, 341–42; see also 326–27)

A theological basis for such protest is the global judgment that Christian anthropological beliefs systematically hang on the claim that the primary implication of God's active relating to human beings is that human creatures are above all wondrously mysterious, good, and, in their finite way, strong. That is not simply negated or replaced by their profound distortions in sin; it is the abiding condition of the possibility of such distortion. The Christian claim that God relates to create all that is not God entails the claim that what God creates, including human creatures, are good in virtue of God relating to them creatively. It implies that human creatures in particular are a mysteriously complex mix of creaturely fragility and amazing resources of many kinds of strength. When the claim that the triune God relates creatively is taken as a theologically central claim, anthropology usually has a nature/grace structure (typical of catholic theology) or creation/redemption structure (typical of classic Lutheran and Reformed theology) that keeps primary focus on the goodness and strength of human creatures by virtue of God relating to them. The Christian claim that the triune God relates proleptically to draw all that is not God to eschatological consummation entails that the goodness of human creatures is confirmed by the eschatological glory for which they are destined and in which in some way they already participate. It implies that human creatures are a mysteriously complex mix of creaturely fragility and eschatological glory. When the claim that the triune God relates to draw all that is not God to eschatological consummation is taken as a theologically central claim, anthropology usually has a "creation/consummation" structure (characteristic of much late-twentieth-century theology of hope) that keeps primary focus on the goodness and glory of human being by virtue of God relating to them. I shall urge that each of these ways of systematically structuring theological anthropology is problematic in its own ways. However, they underscore an important systematic point about Christian theological anthropology: it is only as we begin to grasp the mystery of theocentric human being that we can also begin to grasp the profundity of human beings' distortion in the human condition.

Correlatively, when the human condition construed as a problem focuses and structures an account of the logic of coming to faith, God's relating to human beings is systematically construed in terms of its utility in fixing or healing that condition. God's relating is thus understood in terms of God's function of helping human beings cope with their condition. When that happens, God's relating to human beings is construed more as an analgesic or antidote to the human condition than as the ground of the mystery that is human being. When it is framed in that way, God's reality is understood in a fundamentally functionalist and even instrumentalist way.

But that is precisely what is ruled out by properly Trinitarian understandings of God. Functionalist and instrumentalist understandings of God are ruled out by Trinitarian understandings of God because they understand God's living reality to be constituted by the relations of free giving and receiving in communion among the triune "persons," relations whose reality is logically independent of God's "functioning" in any fashion relative to reality other than God. That is why I observed at the beginning of this chapter that the outline in chapter 2 of the anthropological implications of the stages through which properly Trinitarian doctrines of God developed provides the background against which an explanation is possible for the decision to address this project only to the question of the logic of Christian beliefs.

In sum, conflation of addressing the question of the logic of Christian beliefs about human being with address to the question of the logic of coming to faith systematically leads to accounts of Christian anthropological beliefs that are distorted by one-sidedly denigrating human beings and accounts of Christian beliefs about God that are distorted by threatening to trivialize God's relating to human beings in utilitarian and functionalist ways.

The same conflation has a second consequence that is theologically problematic for anthropology. It systematically tends toward a quasi-Manichean theological assessment of nonhuman creatures. "Nonhuman" means "nonsubjects"—that is, objects. We saw repeatedly in the typology of analyses of the structure and dynamics of subjectivity that theologies adopt after the turn to the subject (given above) that in one way or another "subjectivity" is defined, not merely in contradistinction to "objectivity," but as its opposite, the "nonobjectified." That move appears to be rooted in the intuition that, in opposition to the physical world understood in a modern, scientific way (certainly in a post-Newtonian way; perhaps also in a post-Einsteinian way), subjects are centers of free knowing or doing or feeling, that are constituted by the project of actualizing themselves by relating to themselves. Because subjects are bodied, self-actualization takes place within the physical world. Because the physical world as the realm of objectivity, is other than and incommensurate with subjectivity, subjects' self-actualization within the context of the physical world must take the form of a struggle against objectivity. The physical and cultural context of subjects' self-actualization is nature, the realm of causal necessity; a self-actualized subject is spirit, the realm of freedom and history. Ironically, although one of the aims of the turn to the subject was to provide an alternative to the dualistic conceptual framework of the earlier body/soul metaphysical analysis of human being, this move reintroduces a dualist nature/spirit conceptual framework. If nature and spirit designate to opposed realms of reality, conceptual dualism may count as an ontological dualism as well.

Conceptual and metaphysical dualisms easily become value (axiological) dualisms. If what one must struggle against in order to be oneself—to actualize oneself—is one's "enemy," then in some way nonhuman reality—"nature"—is "spirit's" enemy. Assuming that subjects' self-actualization has positive value, then the enemy that opposes that self-actualization has negative value. It is difficult to see how it is possible within the limits of such a conceptual framework to avoid the implication that nature is evil relative to subjects' self-actualization. In that case, when analyses of subjectivity are appropriated by Christian theology after the turn to the subject, if nature designates the world that is traditionally characterized as creation, it is difficult to see how it is possible to avoid the quasi-Manichean implication that nonhuman creaturely reality is evil.

The anthropological implication is clear. If nature is to be valued negatively, relative to subjectivity, because of its objectivity, that would seem to imply that human beings' bodies must be valued negatively. There is little question that such an implication is theologically unacceptable in Christian anthropology. Nor have Christian theologians committed to the turn to the subject been unaware of the need to provide grounds for blocking just that inference. For example, no one has worked more perceptively and subtly than Edward Farley in his extraordinarily rich interpretation of "a human condition" (*Good and Evil* [1990]) to show how sociological accounts of human sociality and scientific accounts of the biological aspects of personal being can be coherently integrated with an analysis of subjectivity. Yet the question must be asked whether it is really possible to head off a subjectivity/objectivity or spirit/nature divide by modifications and innovations within conceptual frameworks premised on the root intuition of the turn to the subject that subjectivity is definitive of the authentically human. Undoubtedly consciousness is a major feature of human being, of enormous importance to Christian theological anthropology. But is there strong theological warrant for adopting the claim that it is definitive of human being, such that anthropological proposals can only hope to be adequate if they are framed in terms of some analysis of the structure and dynamics of subjectivity? Perhaps theological interests require a more radical change in the conceptual conventions with which Christian anthropology has been working in the change to the subject.

Conflation of addressing the question, "What is the logic of Christian beliefs?" with addressing the question, "What is the logic of coming to faith?" has a third problematic consequence for anthropology. It leads systematically to a dangerous anthropocentrism relative to the rest of creation. If nothing else has done so, the environmental crisis has made it clear that anthropologies, theological or otherwise, are dangerous if they disengage human beings from the ecological web that is their physical environment in order to demonstrate human "superiority" over other forms of life. This danger is compounded when such anthropologies systematically make the interests of human beings the ground of the value of other forms of life in that web so that the latter have only instrumental value.

We saw above that inquiries into the logic of coming to faith are, by definition, systematically focused on human beings and their peculiar interests. The interests are to overcome living in falsehood or in inauthenticity or in despair or in meaninglessness. Such interests are entirely appropriate human interests. However, when answers proposed to the question about the logic of coming to faith are taken to constitute answers to the question about the logic of Christian beliefs about human being, they systematically frame accounts of the logic of Christian anthropological beliefs in ways oriented to human interests. Correlatively they systematically either marginalize or dismiss theological beliefs about nonhuman realities. Accounts of what and who human beings are and how they ought to be existentially set into their lived worlds that are systematically oriented to and framed in terms of major human interests are precisely the type of anthropocentric anthropologies that are dangerous to the entire living web of creatures, human and nonhuman.

Finally, such conflation leads systematically to an anthropocentric moralizing of theological anthropology. The theological ground for deeming theological moralizing of God's relation to human beings objectionable is the global theological judgment that Christian beliefs systematically hang on the claim that God's relating to all that is not God, including human beings, is grounded in God's free, wise, and generative love and not in human moral qualities, whether antecedent to or subsequent to God's relating to them. Insofar as the logic of coming to faith is a movement away from untruth, inauthenticity, despair, or meaninglessness, it is a movement away from sin and its consequences. Sin is peculiar to human beings, who alone among all the creatures are morally accountable. Theological projects whose end is defined by the question of the logic of coming to faith are projects focused on and systematically structured by the concept of sin and, correlatively, human beings as morally responsible agents. When addressing the question of the logic of Christian beliefs, especially anthropological beliefs, is conflated with addressing the question of the logic of coming to faith, anthropology becomes focused on and systematically structured by the practical problem of how to overcome human sin and make human beings morally acceptable.

The methodological problem is certainly not that the recognition of sin and its overcoming in salvation is an unimportant question. That is a central existential question in Christian anthropology. The methodological problem is that when this question becomes the focus and organizing theme of theological anthropology, the content of the anthropology is systematically anthropocentric in that it is exhaustively concerned with human failure, an exclusively intrahuman defect or distortion (sin) that is in need of correction. Correlatively, it construes human beings primarily as moral agents to whom God relates in terms of their moral worth and whom God must save when their moral worth is that of sinners. That is inconsistent with the global judgment that Christian beliefs systematically hang on the claim that God's relating to all that is not God, including human beings, is grounded in God's free, wise, and genera-tive love and not in human moral qualities. The irony is that, methodologically speaking, precisely because sin and salvation are centrally important to the logic of Christian beliefs, an account of the logic of overcoming sin in the move from unfaith to faith cannot be substituted for an account of the place of beliefs about sin and reconciliation in the logic of Christian beliefs without moralizing and moralistic distortions of the concepts under discussion.

This project in anthropology is confined to an exercise that addresses only the question, "What is the logic of Christian beliefs?" in an effort to avoid a denigration of human being and a correlative utilitarian and functionalist trivialization of understandings of God and God's ways of relating to human beings, a quasi-Manichean view of the physical world and human bodies, an anthropocentric view of the value of nonhuman beings and its implications regarding humans' proper relations to nonhuman beings, and an anthropocen-tric moralizing of accounts of Christian beliefs about human beings. It attempts to do that while nonetheless engaging the practical and existential themes that are inherent in Christian anthropology.

The One Who Has to Do with Us

The process leading to discovery of a properly Trinitarian understanding of God began with reflection on triadic liturgical formulas ("In the name of the Father, the Son, and the Holy Spirit") that were perceived to be related somehow to three sets of scriptural stories about the divine economy broadly understood. It shifted to reflection on the divine economy narrowly understood as the economy of reconciliation and its implications for understanding God formulated creedally. It shifted attention again from the economy of salvation to the immanent eternal life of the triune God imaged as a community in communion of free self-giving in love. The One with whom human persons must ultimately have to do is just this life constituted by the communion-in-community of the three perichoretic hypostases freely and in love giving and receiving Godself eternally. This is the One with whom we have to do.

Now the final anthropologically significant moment in the process of coming to a properly Trinitarian understanding of God turns on shifting focus back to the original topic: God's active relating to all-that-is-not-God, the One who has to do with us. The reflective process becomes a conceptual feedback loop. Unreflective use of "God" in the early moments of this movement toward Trinitarian understanding of God to designate the One who creates, eschatologically consummates, and reconciles is replaced by properly Trinitarian use of "God." Now it is the perichoretically triune God who is said to relate to all-that-is-not-God as its creator, eschatological consummator, and reconciler. However, this is not a matter of simply substituting one proper name for another, substituting verbal placeholders for "that with which we have ultimately to do." It involves a conceptual change that substantially complexifies the theological idea of "God relating."

This point is anthropologically important if human beings are to be understood in terms of their ultimate and proximate contexts, because the triune God's active relating to them simply is humankind's ultimate context, while the outcomes of that relating define their proximate contexts. The rest of this project consists in unpacking those implications.

Shifting Patterns

That the One who relates to humankind as their ultimate context is triune complexifies anthropological implications of that relating in subtle and substantial ways. The complexification arises from the interrelation between two features of the triune God's active relating to creatures.

On one hand, God is immanently a community-in-communion of three who are perichoretic in the dynamics of their interrelationships. There is a pattern or, in Greek, *taxis*, a certain asymmetry, to their *perichoresis*. The second hypostasis is eternally "begotten" of the first; the first is "begotten" of nothing. The third hypostasis is "breathed out" by the first and "proceeds" from the first and through the second. The first and the second hypostases are neither "breathed out" nor "proceed from" any other. Nevertheless they are co-equal and reciprocally encompass each other—as it were, "dancing around" one another. It is just *this* divine life that engages creatures when God actively relates to them. Because it is the perichoretically triune God who relates to creatures, all three hypostases are involved in each of the three ways God relates to creatures, but only in a certain pattern. Given *perichoresis*, it is not simply the Father who creates, but the triune God; it is not simply the Spirit who draws to eschatological consummation, but the triune God; it is not simply the Son who reconciles, but the triune God.

On the other hand, in each of the three sets of scriptural stories about, respectively, God's creating, eschatologically consummating, and reconciling, the pattern of relationships among the three hypostases changes. An account of those changes is not governed by the eternal pattern of asymmetrical relations among the hypostases that constituted the divine life. Rather, it is governed, or so I shall argue, by asymmetries among the three scripturally narrated ways in which the triune God relates to creatures.

The asymmetries are these:

1. Given the way the three sets of stories relate to one another as narrated, God's creating is ontologically prior to and logically independent of God's drawing creatures to eschatological consummation and God's reconciling them. God's consummating creatures and God's reconciling them both presuppose God's relating to create them, whereas God's relating to create them does not presuppose any other way of relating to them. If God has not first created (ontologically, not chronologically, "first"), there would be absolutely nothing either to consummate or to reconcile. Furthermore, nothing about the stories of God's creating entails that God

must necessarily also draw what is created to eschatological consummation or that God must reconcile them if they are alienated from God. Were it otherwise, neither God's relating to draw creatures to eschatological consummation nor God's relating to reconcile estranged creatures would be grace or gracelike. For grace is, by definition, not necessitated.

2. Given the way the three sets of stories are interrelated, God's relating to creatures to consummate them and God's relating to creatures to reconcile them are themselves complexly interrelated. Both are concretely enacted in the selfsame story about Jesus. Thus, *in concreto*, while distinguishable, they are inseparable.

Yet they are distinguishable precisely because stories of God relating to consummate creatures eschatologically are logically independent of stories of God relating to reconcile estranged creatures. Nothing about the stories of God drawing creatures to eschatological consummation entails that creatures must also be in need of reconciliation.

Nonetheless, as narrated, God's reconciling of creatures does seem to be partly dependent on God's drawing them to eschatological consummation. If God is drawing creatures to an eschatological consummation that is a creaturely participation in the divine life, marked by holiness, and if those creatures are in fact alienated from God and are thus unholy, then drawing them to consummation does entail reconciling them. In concrete actuality, the "ifs" do obtain.

In consequence of these asymmetries in the relations among the stories, in each type of story (about, respectively, creating, consummating, and reconciling) the relations among the three central characters (Father, Son, Holy Spirit) are plotted in a different pattern that gives each type of story a distinctly different character.

Formulated abstractly, these differences of pattern are the following: It is the Father who creates through the Son in the power of the Spirit; it is the Spirit, sent by the Father with the Son, who draws creatures to eschatological consummation; it is the Son, sent by the Father in the power of the Spirit, who reconciles creatures. These are not merely rhetorical appropriations of different relations to different hypostases for the sake of convenience in exposition.

I can bring out the anthropological implications of these shifts in patterns or *taxis* by exploring each in turn. Each is a preview of a separate part of this anthropological project as a whole. Taken together, they explain the structure of the rest of the project.

The Triune God Relating to Create

It is the triune God in its threefold dancing around that creates. Formulated abstractly, the plot of scriptural stories of God creating relates the three in a definite pattern: the Father creates through the Son in the power of the Spirit. Each phrase is significant.

To say that *the Father creates* is to stress that the triune God's creating, grounded in the divine love in which God's reality is eternally given and received among the three hypostases, is an inherently generative love. Since it simply is the triune God's being and life, such giving and receiving of Godself is not somehow a novelty that requires explanation when what is given is reality other than God. The love that God's self-relating enacts is not, for example, a response to some lovable reality that is already and independently "there" and whose attractiveness could explain God's loving it. In this giving and receiving, God is eternally self-consistent and unchanging. Furthermore, as triune, God has God's reality exclusively in this giving and receiving of Godself. No relation to reality other than God is constitutive of divine reality. The triune God is ontologically autonomous.

If the triune God is creatively related to reality other than God, it would be a relation in which God is true to Godself. Hence creating would itself be a generative relation of free and loving giving and receiving. It would be a relation generative of the reality of the other, rather than a response to its independent and anterior attractiveness—that is, it would be creative *ex nihilo*. It would be a loving giving of reality. For the creature it would be an ontological relation, a relation in being. Given both God's self-consistency and that God relates in love for the other in its otherness, it would be a relation respectful of the integrity of the otherness of the beloved creature; it would be a relating that does not violate the integrity of the other. Because God's reality consists of the relations among the three hypostases, this relation to reality other than God would not be constitutive of God's reality; God does not need any such relation in order to be God. Hence, if God is not only self-related but is also in fact related to creatures, that relation is ontologically radically free on God's side. If such a relation obtains, it obtains by virtue of the triune God's free self-determination, not by virtue of the relations that constitute God's being. At the same time, if the relation does obtain, then by God's free self-determination it is the case that in actuality God is not without God's other. Correlatively, as an enactment *ad extra* of the giving and receiving that constitute the triune God's own life, God's creative relating to reality other than God is a giving that is also at once God's invitation to realities other than God to respond to God in ways that are appropriate to the manner in which God has related to them and God's self-opening to receive their response.

To say that the Father creates *through the Son* is to stress that God's creating is rooted in an eternal dynamic relation in which Godself is given and received as God's intelligibly wise self-expression, God's "Word" in which is expressed God's glory, incomprehensibility, and holiness—the fullness of God's mystery. Because God's creating of reality other than God is rooted in the Son's relation to the Father, the character of the Son's relation to the Father has implications concerning what is created. It means that, as the Son is the self-expression of God, so also what is created through the Son, namely humankind's proximate contexts and humankind in them, are themselves in their own ways God's self-expressions of God's glory, incomprehensibility and holiness (see Rom. 1:19–21). That they are the triune God's self-expressions does not mean that humankind's proximate contexts are themselves necessarily fully intelligible. They may turn out to be intelligible to human beings only occasionally and in patches. However, as modes of God's self-expression, what the triune God creates does itself make intelligible, at least to human creatures, that God is mystery.

Further, the reciprocity in the giving and receiving between Father and Son that characterizes the triune life implies that the triune God's creative relating in giving reality to creatures entails that the creatures' appropriate response is a reciprocal giving to and receiving from God. Moreover, as God's wise self-expression—as created through the Son—humankind's creaturely proximate contexts mediate to human creatures, at least, a call to be wise for their own well-being in their response to the wisdom of God's own self-expression. In addition, because the triune God's creating them is rooted in the eternal dynamics constituting the relation between the Son and the Father, humankind's proximate contexts are created with a wisdom that makes them orderly enough and predictable enough for human creatures to learn to act wisely in them for their flourishing. Being wise for the well-being of the fellow creatures that constitute their proximate contexts, and for their own flourishing, is part of what constitutes human creatures' appropriate responsive relating to God in a loving giving and receiving that reciprocates God's loving giving and reflects the giving and receiving that characterizes the eternal relation between Father and Son.

To say that the Father creates through the Son *in the power of the Spirit* is to stress that God's creating is rooted in an eternal relation of divine self-giving and receiving, a love that is free. The third hypostasis is the breath of life eternally "breathed out" by the first hypostasis. The Nicene Creed characterizes the Spirit in its relation to all that is not God as "the Lord and giver of life." It is appropriate, then, to characterize "the power of the Spirit," in which the Father creates, as the divine triune love's vitalizing, enlivening, and empowering life-giving power. However, the "breath of life eternally 'breathed out' by the first hypostasis" is radically free, as unpredictable and uncontrollable as the wind. So the force of saying that the Father creates through the Son "in the power of the Spirit" is to stress that the Spirit's life-giving power in relation to that which is not God is radically free from ontological necessity and creaturely control.

Furthermore, the force of saying that the third hypostasis "eternally proceeds" from the first *through* the second hypostasis, which is the self-expression of God's wisdom, is that the third hypostasis is wise in its life-giving power and it empowers vitality ordered to wisdom. It is wise in its life-giving vitality in that its vitalizing and empowering of creatures is always accommodated to each creature's concrete particularity. And the vitality it empowers is ordered to making living creatures wise for their own well-being in their proximate and ultimate contexts.

These remarks on the theological formula "The Father creates through the Son in the Power of the Spirit" bring to light a central point about the logic governing exposition of the anthropological implications of the ontological relations "creator of" and "created by": it is a logic presided over by the preposition "to." God must be said to be related as creator *to* creatures, as One who is creature-ward, not as One who is among creatures nor as One who is between them. Use of "to" signals the way God is at once radically other than creatures and intimately near them in creating them. Otherness is the consequence of a nonreciprocal relation of dependence for being. Creatures depend on God's relating to them for their sheer reality. If the relation did not obtain, they would absolutely not be. On the other hand, God does not depend on the reality of creatures in order to be God. Did the relation not obtain, God would nonetheless be unqualifiedly God. "Nearness" follows from God's being the source of creatures' very reality. God is said to be closer to them—that is, ontologically more interior to them—than they can be to themselves. Traditionally this nearness has been characterized by metaphors drawn from transactions with matter (God "making" creatures), with living beings (God "nurturing" creatures), and with societies (God "superintending" and "governing" creatures), transactions that produce something good. However expressed, it is the intimate nearness of One utterly other than they in being.

Precisely because of the Creator's radical otherness from creatures in being, God's relation to creatures in creating them cannot be characterized in ways that assume that they share a common field of reality or a common frame of reference that we might hope to map conceptually and comprehend. As Creator, the triune God is simply not an item on the inventory list of the universe. That, however, is exactly what is assumed when God's relation to creatures is characterized in metaphors suggesting that, in creating, God is one among or between them. We must rely on the preposition "to" to express the radical otherness and radical nearness that are mutually implied in God's creative relating to all-that-is-not-God.

The remarks that compose part 1 of this project explore the anthropological implications of the formula, "The Father creates through the Son in the power of the Spirit." The preposition "to" presides over that exploration.

The Triune God Relating to Consummate Eschatologically

It is the perichoretic triune God that draws creation—and humankind as part of creation—into an eschatological consummation. Formulated abstractly, the plot of scriptural stories of God drawing creation to eschatological consummation relates the three in a different pattern: "The Spirit, sent by the Father with the Son, draws creation to eschatological consummation." The shift in pattern of relations among the three reflects not only the asymmetry of their eternal relations, but also the asymmetry of the relationships among the three ways (creating, consummating, reconciling) in which canonical stories tell of the triune God relating to what is not God.

The Nicene Creed names the Spirit as the "lord and giver of life." Where "the Father creates through the Son, etc." stresses the generativity of the relations constituting the divine life, to say "the Spirit draws creation to eschatological consummation" is to stress that the triune God's drawing creatures to eschatological consummation is grounded in the eternal giving and receiving of love, which comprises the divine life. That grounding means that if the triune God relates to creatures to draw them to eschatological consummation, it is a free enactment of love that draws creatures to participate in creaturely fashion in the triune God's own powerful life, symbolized biblically as the eschatological "kingdom of God" or, perhaps translated less misleadingly, the eschatological "rule of God." If God does so relate to creatures, it is an enactment of love. The triune God does not require such a relation with creatures in order to be God or have God's life. Nor can creatures exact such consummation from God. Thus, the point of stressing that God's relating to creatures to draw them to consummation is grounded in the eternal relations that constitute the triune God's very life is to stress that God can consistently relate to creatures in this way because of what God is, quite independently of whether the relation obtains. In enacting love to draw creatures to participate in God's own life, the triune God is at once self-consistent and freely self-determining. That is the force of saying "the Spirit," rather than the Father or the Son, "draws creation to an eschatological consummation."

To say that the Spirit "sent by the Father" draws creatures to eschatological consummation reminds that it is the Father who creates and that, while the relation "creator of" does not presuppose the relation "consummator of," "consummator of" does necessarily presuppose "creator of." The way this story is plotted, the Father sends the Spirit to draw to consummation that which God has (logically, not chronologically) "already" and independently created. The relation "consummator of" is asymmetrically related to the relation "creator of." God might self-consistently create that which God does not consummate, but God cannot consummate that which God has not even created. In the order of being (though not necessarily in temporal order), "creator of" is prior to "consummator of." Hence, any account of God's relation to creatures as "consummator of" and its anthropological implications is necessarily ruled in ways established by God's relation to creatures as "creator of" them and its anthropological implications.

To say that creatures are drawn to an eschatological consummation by the Spirit sent by the Father "with the Son" stresses three things. First, it

stresses that the Son's life defines the life into which the Spirit draws creatures. Eschatological life is nothing other than the life the Son has with the
Father in the power of the Spirit. That life is narrated in New Testament
stories of God relating to alienated creatures to reconcile them. Their plot
has a different pattern than the plot of stories of God's relating to creatures
to consummate them. As I shall show below, the relation between these
two sets of stories is asymmetrically dialectical. For present purposes that
means the following: in any account of the anthropological implications of
God's drawing humankind to eschatological consummation, characterization of that consummation must be ruled by accounts of the life the Son
has with the Father in the power of the Spirit whereby the Son reconciles
human creatures to God. As narrated, the concrete way in which God
relates to draw creatures to eschatological consummation simply is the
person of Jesus—that is, Jesus in his unsubstitutable personal identity as
that is rendered by stories, not simply of his resurrection and glory, but of
his ministry, suffering, and death. As narrated in the New Testament, that
concrete way in which God goes about drawing creation to eschatological
consummation is nothing less than the way of the cross.

Second, "with the Son" stresses that the triune God's drawing human
creatures into God's life is grounded in the self-expressiveness of the giving
and receiving that constitutes the divine life, and that self-expressiveness
is wise. Hence, the vitality into which human creatures are drawn by the
Spirit is not sheer, raw power. Rather, the ways in which we characterize it
must be governed by the way God's self-expressive Word itself characterizes divine life in its enactment of God's mystery.

Third, "with the Son" stresses that the triune God draws human creatures to eschatological consummation wisely. By the enlivening Spirit,
God's triune life engages human creatures in ways that are wise about what
makes for human flourishing, given what we are through God's creativity.
At the very least, this means that in drawing creatures to eschatological
consummation God does not violate their creaturely integrities.

These remarks about the formula "The Spirit sent by the Father with
the Son draws human creatures to eschatological consummation" bring
to light a central point about the logic governing exposition of the anthropological implications of the relations "consummator of" and "consummated by": it is a "logic" presided over by the expression "circumambient."
According to the relevant scriptural stories, the Spirit is circumambient,
interpenetrating communities of human persons to be between them. Use
of "circumambient" signals the distinctive ways in which God is at once
radically other than creatures and intimately near them in drawing them
to eschatological consummation.

Rather than the otherness and nearness of the ontological relations
"creator of" and "created by," this is the otherness and nearness of the historical and communal relations "consummator of" and "consummated

[margin note: eschatological as beyond history]

by." Here "otherness" is in consequence of the radical futurity of the eschatological life to which creatures are being drawn, its beyond-history or
eschatological character, such that we in our temporality are incapable of
generating it for one another through our shaping of historical developments. Relating to us in this way, the triune life is radically other than we
in being radically future to us.

"Nearness" is in consequence of the triune life already engaging us now.
The character of that nearness is expressed in traditional metaphors for the
engagement drawn from immediate sensory experience ("seeing," even
"tasting" God) or affective experience ("delighting," "glorying" in God;
"communing" with God). Such metaphors suggest that in consummating
us God relates to us on our own terms as creatures. Consequently this
relation cannot be expressed by the preposition "to," as used to express
God's creating them. The point of the latter is that in that relation God and
creatures do not share a common field. But here, the triune God relates to
creatures within the conditions of creaturely reality.

On the other hand, this relation cannot be expressed by the preposition
"among." To be among is to be near as one of several, each having its own
unsubstitutable identity. Where the several are human persons, identity is
strongly associated with having an identifiable face. However, the triune
God, as the Spirit sent by the Father with the Son, drawing creatures to
eschatological consummation, is not near them as just one more particular
reality among the many in the field of creatures. As rendered in biblical
narratives, the Spirit in its circumambience has no face and systematically
eludes personal identification. We must rely on the preposition "between"
to express the radical otherness and radical nearness that are mutually
implied in the triune God's drawing creatures to eschatological consummation.

The remarks that make up part 2 of this project explore the anthropological implications of the formula "The Spirit, sent by the Father through
the Son, draws creatures to eschatological consummation." The preposition "between" will preside over that exploration.

The Triune God Relating to Reconcile the Estranged

It is the triune God in its threefold *circumcessio* that reconciles estranged
creatures to itself. Formulated abstractly, the plot of scriptural stories of
God reconciling alienated humankind relates the three in yet another pattern: the Son, sent by the Father in the power of the Spirit, reconciles.
Here, too, the shift in pattern reflects not only the asymmetry of the eternal relations among the three, but also the asymmetrical relations among
the three ways in which God actively relates to what is not God.

[margin note: Again, beautiful, but does it align with Scripture?]

To say that "the Son reconciles" is to stress that the triune God's reconciling is grounded in the eternal divine self-bestowal in love which is
the divine life. The second hypostasis is constituted by the first's eternal

self-giving. That is the point of the Nicene Creed's phrase "The Son is eternally begotten of the Father." On that basis, if the triune God reconciles alienated human creatures, it is not by means of some instrument other than God that serves as a third-party mediator between God and creatures. Rather, it is by self-donation, God giving Godself, the Son, to human creatures. The giving and receiving that constitutes the divine life is recapitulated in relation to creatures. Thus, to say that it is the "Son who reconciles" is to stress that in reconciling the triune God is fully self-consistent, merely recapitulating among creatures the self-giving that is eternally its own life.

To say that the Son reconciles "sent by the Father" is to stress that the one who is self-donating is none other than the One who creates those who are being reconciled. The phrase reflects the fact that the relation "reconciler of" presupposes the relation "creator of": no creation, nothing to reconcile. Furthermore, the manner of reconciling is governed by conditions established by the relation "creator of." God's relating to creatures to reconcile them must not violate their creaturely integrity; rather, it must be enacted among them on their terms. "Sent by the Father" also stresses that while reconciling is a recapitulation among creatures of the eternal self-donation that constituted the divine life, it is neither a morally nor an ontologically necessitated recapitulation. Creatures have no moral leverage whereby they can exact such divine self-giving from God. In its fullness, the triune God's life of eternal giving and receiving has no need to give to what is not God in order to be itself. Hence, although God's relating to create is the ontologically prior presupposition of God's relating to reconcile, creating does not necessarily entail reconciling creatures if they become alienated.

To say that the Son reconciles sent by the Father "in the power of the Spirit" stresses two things. It stresses that the divine self-giving that reconciles is also powerful to enliven. God's reconciling not only overcomes the alienating effects of some deep deformity that overcame human creatures, it also empowers a deep and enlivening transformation of human creatures in community. Second, since the Spirit proceeds from the Father "through the Son," the phrase "in the power of the Spirit" stresses the qualification that God's enlivening reconciling is not merely powerful, but wisely powerful for creatures' flourishing. God reconciles in the power of God's wisdom.

These remarks on the theological formula "The Son, sent by the Father in the power of the Spirit, reconciles" bring to light a central point about the logic governing exposition of the anthropological implications of the relations "reconciler of" and "reconciled by": it is a "logic" presided over by the preposition *among*. The New Testament stories of God reconciling us are stories about Jesus of Nazareth, sent in the power of the Spirit by the One he called "Father," who, through his ministry among us of teaching and healing, proclaimed that the eschatological kingdom of God was breaking into history in and through his own person.

Accordingly, use of the preposition "among" to characterize God's reconciling relation to humankind signals the way in which, in reconciling, God is at once other than human creatures and utterly near them in yet a third sense of both words. Rather than either the otherness and nearness of the ontological relations "creator of" and "creature of," or the otherness and nearness of the historical and communal relations "consummator of" and "consummated by," this is the otherness and nearness of interpersonal relations that are at once physical and social.

Here the "otherness" is that of one human person as living body to another as living body, the otherness to each other of finitely free and responsible bodied agents sharing a common physical and social space and time, with all its possible creativity and fullness of life and its possible moral distortions and spiritual brokenness.

The nearness is the inseparable obverse side of the otherness; it is the closeness of intersubjective relations within shared social and physical time and space. This mode of God's nearness to us has traditionally been characterized by metaphors drawn from interpersonal transactions (God "forgiving," "reconciling," "ransoming") and from cultic transactions (God "expiating," "sacrificing"). Such metaphors suggest that, in reconciling us to God, God relates to us on our own terms as personal creatures. Hence this relation cannot be expressed by the preposition "to" as used to express God's relating to create us. These metaphors also suggest that, in reconciling, God comes near to us as an other with a very definite personal identity: Jesus of Nazareth. Hence this relation cannot be expressed by the preposition "between" as used to express God's relating to consummate us. Whereas in consummating us the triune God has no face, in reconciling us God has the face of Jesus. We must rely on the preposition "among" to express the radical otherness and intimate nearness that are mutually implied in the triune God's reconciling alienated creatures to God.

The remarks that constitute part 3 of this project explore the anthropological implications of the formula, "The Son, sent by the Father in the power of the Spirit, reconciles."* The preposition "among" will preside over that exploration.

"To," "between," and "among" point to irreducible differences among the three ways in which God relates to us. No single monolithic story can be told about God's relating to us. God's mystery eludes that, which means that there can be no single monolithic theological story to tell about what and who we are and how we ought to be. If the ways in which God relates

---

*Part 3 appears in vol. 2 of this work.

are irreducibly threefold, theocentric accounts of human persons will be irreducibly threefold. There is no single, simple Christian metanarrative. Nor can there be, parasitic on it, any Christian anthropological metatheory about human persons that can, at least in principle, systematically synthesize all relevant true claims about human being, Christian theological claims and otherwise. Human beings are in their own way too richly glorious, too inexhaustibly incomprehensible, too capable of profound distortions and bondage in living deaths, too capable of holiness, in short, too mysterious to be captured in that fashion.

*For Christians, scriptural interpretation
should shape and be shaped by the convictions,
practices, and concerns of Christian
communities as part of their ongoing struggle
to live and worship faithfully before God.*
STEPHEN FOWL

CHAPTER **3B**

The Concept of Christian Canonical Holy Scripture

In chapter 1B, I argued that one of the substantive standards of excellence internal to the practice of secondary theology is the accountability of the theological proposals made in secondary theology to canonical Holy Scripture. More precisely, it is accountability to biblical texts read *as* canonical Holy Scripture. The suggestion is that construing the texts, not simply as biblical texts, nor as scriptural texts, nor even as texts of Holy Scripture, but precisely as canonical Holy Scripture makes a difference to the ways in which they are read as authority to which the practice of secondary theology is accountable. The purpose of this chapter is to explain what I mean in this connection by "canonical Holy Scripture."

The reason that proposals made in the practice of secondary theology ought to be accountable to canonical Holy Scripture was said to be analytic in the nature of the practice of secondary theology. The practice of secondary theology critically examines the communities' received formulations of the beliefs inherent in the practices that compose their common life and shape their personal and communal identities, and to which they appeal in primary theology when they debate the adequacy or appropriateness of the ways in which their practices are currently being enacted. If the critique suggests that received formulations of these beliefs are inadequate, it is part of the practice of secondary theology to propose revised or entirely new formulations. Such proposals are made for the purpose of helping to shape the communities' practices so that they are more faithful to the communities' identity and their mission in the world. However, they are not proposals about the communities. They are proposals about how best to articulate who God is, how God relates to all that is not God, how to understand all other realities as God-related, and how best to respond to God in practices that compose the communities' common life.

Chapter 1B urged that, since the person of Jesus is decisive for the ways in which communities of Christian faith understand who the God is to whom they seek to respond appropriately, it follows that proposals made in the practice of secondary theology about who that God is must comport with the person of Jesus.

That is a substantive standard of excellence to which the practice of secondary theology is subject. Furthermore, chapter 1B urged, the practices that compose the common life of ecclesial communities seek to be appropriate responses to the ways in which God relates to all that is not God, including God's way of relating in the person of Jesus, as those ways of relating are explicitly or implicitly narrated, commented on, celebrated, longed for, alluded to, or assumed in various parts of canonical Holy Scripture. Since secondary theology is one of those practices, it follows that theological proposals about the ways in which God relates to all that is not God ought to comport with canonical Holy Scripture's accounts of the ways in which God relates. That is another substantive standard of excellence to which the practice of secondary theology is subject. This entire line of thought about secondary theology's standards of excellence addresses the question why its proposals ought to be accountable to canonical Holy Scripture. But it does not explain what the phrase "canonical Holy Scripture" means. The task of this chapter is to outline such an explanation.

After brief introductory remarks on "interpretation," the next four sections of this chapter will propose ways to use the terms "bible," "scripture," "Holy Scripture," and "canon" that may help minimize conceptual confusion and clarify aspects of a notoriously tangled debate about proper modes of disciplined study of biblical texts. They do no more than to stipulate meanings for these terms. The stipulations do not pretend to untangle debates about these terms, much less to solve the theological problems involved in those debates. In particular, they do not pretend to settle debates about what counts as responsible hermeneutical and exegetical practice. At most, these proposals could only hope to make it easier to state clearly what the relevant issues are and what the disagreements are among proposed resolutions of the issues.

The theses developed in this chapter are as follows: (a) study of texts is always governed by some type of interest or set of interests in the texts; (b) different types of interests construe the same texts as different types of things; and (c) the type of interest brought to study of texts, and the type of texts they are construed to be, bring with them distinctive ways of disciplining the study.

Disciplined study of the relevant texts, whether they are construed as "biblical," "scriptural," "Holy Scripture," or "canonical Holy Scripture," involves interpreting or explicating them, but what counts as significant interpretation or explication can vary depending on the interests governing the study. However, it does not follow that there are no constraints on interpretation. Interpretive relativism does not follow, such that any interpretation is as good as any another. Before exploring how different interests in the texts and different ways of construing the texts involve different ways of disciplining study of the texts, some remarks are in order about interpretation or explication of texts in general.

About Interpretation

It is commonplace to say that the task of interpretation of a text is to make clear the meaning of the text. The remark suggests that there is some "thing," perhaps some property, called the "meaning" of the text. It further suggests that that "thing" has describable features or contours that an adequate interpretation will make clear by describing them accurately. However, as Jeffrey Stout's important article (1982) pointed out a quarter century ago, that is to try to make one term ("interpretation") clear by using an even more obscure term ("meaning") to explain it. It raises the question, "What is the meaning of textual 'meaning'?" to which there are a very large number of competing theoretical answers. Hence, a theory of meaning may be a theory of any number of things. In that case, a "question of the form, 'What is the meaning of x?' retains all the ambiguity of its central term but none of the grammatical features that . . . would diminish its tendency to confuse" (Stout 1982, 3). The moral of this analysis is not that texts as such are wholly without meaning, except as it is ascribed to or imposed on them. Nor is the moral that the word "meaning" should be banished from discussion of excellence in the interpretation of texts. There are plenty of ad hoc contexts in which its use is appropriate and clear enough not to generate confusion. Rather, Stout suggests, the moral is that the task of interpretation ought not to be systematically defined in terms of explaining meaning.

If "interpretation" is not systematically defined in terms of explaining meaning, then we can simply set aside disputes over whether interpretation can and should be determined by a text's single and determinate meaning, or, alternatively, whether there is no such thing as meaning as a property of a text that could determine or control the act of interpretation. Such disputes can be set aside as misleadingly presupposing that there is an agreed-upon and standard meaning of "meaning."

Instead of defining the task of interpretation in terms of explaining a text's meaning, a counterproposal is, as Stephen Fowl puts it, to frame disputes about the interpretation of a text "in terms of varied and diverse interpretive aims, interests, and practices" which "will provide us with a much more manageable way of addressing interpretive disputes" (1998, 58). When that is done, it will be clearer that some interpretive disputes arise when interpreters who are pursuing the same types of interests in a given text disagree on how to apply the disciplined method appropriate to interpretation governed by their shared interests. It will also be clearer that other interpretive disputes are the result of bringing quite different types of interests to the texts, pursuing quite different interpretive aims, and consequently disciplining the study of the texts by the quite different methods required by different interests and aims.

When the task of textual interpretation is understood in this way, interpretation may, in Fowl's happy phrase, be characterized as always an "underdetermined interpretation" (56–61). On one hand, it is not determined by a text's single and determinate meaning. On the other hand, it is not undisciplined interpretation. It is not "anti-determinate interpretation" (40). On the contrary, the types of interests and aims the interpreter brings to study of the texts require that the study be disciplined in certain ways. That discipline, among other things, identifies and focuses the interpreter's attention upon features of the text that count as evidence for or against the type of interpretation that is governed by the interests and aims brought to the text. Even when those features make a particular interpretation overwhelmingly persuasive of its kind, they in no way establish that interpretation as the definitive account of *the* meaning of the text. They help to determine that interpretation in its kind, but they leave interpretation of the text underdetermined.

Now consider some ways in which the texts to which the practice of secondary theology is accountable may be construed, some of the interests and interpretive aims that may properly govern study of those texts construed in each of those ways, and some of the ways in which study governed by those interests are properly disciplined.

Bible

Let "bible" be used to designate either of two overlapping, historically contingent collections of ancient texts. One is a collection of texts originally in Hebrew that were written or edited into their present forms, at various times in diverse cultural contexts during three or four hundred years of the history of ancient Israel. Call it the "Hebrew bible." The second includes the texts of the first collection, in a somewhat different order, to which are added Greek texts written or edited into their present form, over a period of a few decades in the earliest history of the Christian movement. Call it the "Christian bible." Each "bible" can be adequately identified and described nontheologically—without reference to God. The scope of each collection is a bit indefinite and in any case is conventional and historically contingent. There are texts whose status in the collections is controversial because, while they appear in some ancient versions of the collections, they do not in others. The condition of the texts in each collection varies. There appear to be some passages that are so textually corrupted or garbled as to make it difficult if not impossible to be sure what they say. The texts in each collection represent a variety of literary genres and a multitude of kinds of subjects. They do not constitute any kind of systematic unity. Perhaps the only valid, if terribly broad, generalization about their content is that they seem largely to be about God and ways in which God relates to all or to some human beings, and about how human beings ought to conduct their lives, relate to God, and relate to one another.

Disciplined study of the texts composing the "Hebrew bible" and the "Christian bible" *as bibles* is generally governed by one, or both, of two interests. They may be studied with literary interests in their genres, the structure of their composition, the devices and force of their rhetoric, and how they make their arguments, if any. Or they may be studied with historical interest. This can go in any of three directions. The texts can be studied with an interest in the evidence they may provide to assist understanding of the ancient culture and historical period in which they originated. In that case, the texts may be of only instrumental historical interest in the service of historical inquiry into some other subject than the text itself. Or they may be studied with an interest to locate the texts in the cultural context in which they were written in order to discover ways in which knowledge of that culture can help explain significance of details in the texts. Or they may be studied with an interest in the history of the texts themselves, seeking evidence not only regarding the date and culture in which they were first written, but also evidence of influences on the original version of the text; evidence of sources, written or oral, on which they drew;

and evidence of subsequent editing, or sequences of editings, of a text. Responsible study of the text guided by these literary or historical interests must be disciplined by the critical disciplines that are standard in literary and historical scholarship.

These are not, of course, mutually exclusive modes of disciplined study of biblical texts. Features of texts identified by disciplined literary scholarship can play indispensably important roles in support of historical theses about the history of a text or its original cultural context; conversely, conclusions from disciplined historical analysis can play important roles in literary analysis of a text. Construed as "bible," these texts properly invite literary-critical and historical-critical study.

Scripture

Let "Scripture" be used to designate texts that play important roles in the life of religious communities. Such texts may play a variety of such roles: as objects of veneration; subjects of close study and teaching; sources of readings in individual and communal acts of devotion and worship; authority appealed to in making a case in a religious dispute, and so on. The texts composing, respectively, the Hebrew Bible and the Christian Bible are also "Scripture" in this sense. However, they do not exhaust the class of Scriptures. There are also, for example, Muslim, Buddhist, and Hindu Scriptures.

On this stipulation, the term "scripture" is understood in a religiously functionalist way in terms provided by the phenomenology of religion. The functions filled by Scriptures, and hence the Scriptures themselves, can be adequately identified and described nontheologically, without reference to God. Disciplined study of texts as Scripture is generally governed by an interest in religious phenomena. Such study may be disciplined by the "human sciences"—for example, ethnography, cultural anthropology, sociology, and so on. Such study requires as its background some theory of what religious phenomena are. Consequently, such study will also be disciplined by a philosophical phenomenology of religion that can provide a conceptual framework within which to explain what religious phenomena are, and, in particular, the role of Scriptures in shaping them. Study of Scripture is often comparative in character, bringing out the distinctive features of Scriptures and their role in one religious tradition by contrasting them to the role of other Scriptures in another religious tradition.

In the case of the texts making up the Hebrew and Christian Bibles, their responsible study as "bible" need not be mutually exclusive of their study as "Scripture," and vice versa. At very least, they may serve as checks on each other. For example, there is no reason in principle that some findings from study of these texts as Scripture cannot provide grounds for arguing that a particular thesis about the origin or role of a text (considered as "bible") in ancient cultic contexts is unlikely, given some well-established general characteristics of the ways in which Scriptures "work" in religious practices. Conversely, there is no reason in principle why some historical finding about the cultural context in which a biblical text was written, or a literary judgment about its rhetoric, cannot provide counterevidence that undercuts a thesis about how texts work as Scripture, suggesting that it is improbable.

Holy Scripture

Let "Holy Scripture" be used to designate texts that are lived with in the common life of certain ecclesial communities that *explicitly* trust that God works through the communities' employment of those texts to call them into being as communities seeking to respond appropriately to the ways in which God relates to them, to nurture and guide their common life, and, when their common life is not an appropriate response to God, to bring that to light and to correct it. At this point, the range of texts relevant to this stipulation concerning Holy Scripture narrows to the texts composing the Christian Bible. (Perhaps this stipulation also properly applies to the Hebrew Bible as lived with in the common life of Jewish communities, but that is for others to decide.) Just as clearly, Christians' "Holy Scripture" cannot be adequately identified or described precisely as Holy Scripture except by reference to God—that is, theologically. Construed as "Holy Scripture," they are by definition self-involvingly acknowledged as texts through whose use by the community God can be trusted to work to shape the individual and communal identities of members of the community.

Given the sense of "Scripture" stipulated above, these texts are properly designated as Scripture for such communities of Christian faith, since members of the communities do live with the texts in a multitude of self-involving ways that serve to shape their communal and personal identities. However, it is important to keep clear that the stipulated senses of "bible," "Scripture," "Holy Scripture," and "canonical Holy Scripture" that I propose here are not historical claims.

For example, it needs to be kept in mind that communities of Christian faith in the first century and a half AD would probably not have characterized the Greek texts with which they came to live in their common life—the Synoptic Gospels, the fourth gospel, and Pauline epistles—as "Scripture." In ancient Mediterranean civilizations, a necessary condition for texts filling the religious functions of "Scripture" was the texts' acknowledged antiquity. In early Judaism the Hebrew Bible functioned as Scripture in the sense stipulated above in part because its texts were deemed to be very ancient. It was natural for the earliest communities of Christian faith, newly separated from synagogues, whether by withdrawal or exclusion, to acknowledge the same texts (which they later read as "Old Testament") as what I characterize here as "Holy Scripture." However, although the newly written Greek texts with which they also closely lived *functioned* in their common life as Scripture, indeed as Holy Scripture, in the senses I am stipulating here, the communities themselves would probably not have called those texts "Scripture" because it was well known that they were not ancient.

The force, in this stipulation, of qualifying "Scripture" as "holy" is to emphasize that the ecclesial communities for whom the texts are "Holy Scripture" explicitly take their employment of these texts, in the practices that make up their common life, to be the medium through which the Holy God shapes their communal and personal lives. Further, the qualifier "holy" has the force of stressing that such ecclesial communities employ these texts in a multitude of ways in their common life in an existential trust that the Holy God has promised to work, in God's own free and unpredictable ways, in, through, and under the ways in which they live with these texts to form human lives so that they themselves, and the proximate social and cultural contexts in which they live and for whose well-being they are called to take responsibility, more nearly approximate holiness. The texts' holiness is not an intrinsic property of the texts. It is dependent on and derived from the holiness of God who, in free self-determination, commits Godself to work through them as they are employed in the communities' practices in response to God.

Traditional Christian doctrinal formulations of this point have been framed in terms of the ways in which the triune God relates to the biblical texts in the *taxis*, "the Spirit, sent by the Father with the Son," both inspires the testimony of prophets and apostles to the ways in which God relates to all that is not God, and illumines ecclesial communities as they live with those testimonies in various ways in their common life.

Ecclesial communities' acknowledgment that the texts of the Christian Bible are Holy Scripture, in the sense stipulated above, amounts to a self-involving performative act of acknowledgment that the texts have a certain authority in their common life. This is not an act of ascribing authority to the texts. It is an act of acknowledgment that the communities ought to live deeply with those texts in their common life because God is self-committed to work through the communities' ways of living with these texts to author life for them by forming new communal and personal identities. To characterize the texts as "Scripture" is to recognize their de facto functional authority. But to acknowledge them as "Holy Scripture" is to acknowledge the "ought." It is to acknowledge the texts' de jure, and not merely de facto, functional authority. I shall call this sense of Holy Scripture's authority as it is "lived with" in the practices composing the common life of ecclesial communities through which God is self-committed to author communal and personal identity, its primary authority.

It is important to distinguish this stipulation about authority from any historical claim about the process of canonization. What I define as Holy Scripture's "primary authority" largely coheres with one way in which "canon," "canonical," and "canonization" are conventionally used in historical controversies about the "process of canonization" in the early church. But the two are not identical. John Barton has argued (1997, 1–35) that historical debates about the process of canonization of the New Testament have been frustratingly inconclusive in part because they have not taken into account the different ways in which "canon" and "canonization" have been employed. The result is that disputants frequently talk past one another. He distinguishes two historically accurate stories that are told of the process of canonization. I take note of the first story here because it outlines the way in which I propose to use the expression "Holy Scripture," though not the way in which I propose to use the expression "canonical Holy Scripture." I shall reserve the second story for the next section of this chapter.

According to the first story, canonization was a spontaneous, largely unreflective process through which communities of Christian faith came to acknowledge certain early Christian writings as authoritative. It is a story of the reception of texts—first the texts of the Hebrew Bible, probably largely in Greek translation, and then new Christian texts, largely in the form of Gospels and letters. The process of reception was not a teleological process defined by a determinate product actualized only at the process's end. For example, it was not a process intentionally aiming to produce a Testament in Greek parallel to the older Hebrew Testament. The process of canonization, told in this way, did end in just such a set of texts subsequently called the "Testaments" of the "canon," but that was a matter of historical contingency. It was not the result of an inner logic driving the process of canonization to that outcome.

The evidence regarding which texts were so acknowledged largely consists of quotations in Christian writings in the patristic period from the Apostolic Fathers onward. The process of canonization, understood in this way, began very early. Barton relies on a sophisticated statistical study by Franz Stuhlhofer that analyzes data provided by the *Biblia Patristica* to measure how often these early Christian writings, including but not limited to texts that became the New Testament, were quoted throughout the patristic period "in relation to how often it ought to be quoted if all 'canonical' books were quoted *proportionately to their size*" (1997, 17; emphasis in original). This analysis shows that (in my words, not Barton's) if "canonical text" means a text acknowledged as authoritative for the common life of the ecclesial community, then "canonical" cannot be used as the name of a status a text either has or does not have. When "canonical" is understood in terms of the function texts may fill as "authoritative," it turns out that in the earliest ecclesial communities, it was not the case that texts either were or were not canonical. Rather, the statistical analysis yielded three clear classes of early Christian writing. There are texts that later came to be acknowledged as part of the New Testament—the Synoptic Gospels, the fourth gospel, and the major Pauline epistles. They are "cited substantially more frequently than one would expect, if all parts of the (later) New Testament had been equally important" (17). These texts were sometimes employed "alongside and in some relation to the Scriptures of Judaism" (24), even though they would not have been called "Scripture." There is a second distinct group of texts that later are acknowledged as part of the New Testament, but are cited by writers in the patristic period much less often than would be the case if all parts of the later New Testament had been equally important. Third, there is a group of texts that are either "scarcely cited at all or are cited only for purposes of rejection." "This group includes most of those that later decisions and decrees affirm to be non-canonical; even in the earliest period none of them is ever cited even so often as the books of the second class" (17). This three-group statistical analysis of early Christian texts "corresponds in principle to the theoretical position as set out by Origen and Eusebius, which thinks not of 'canonical' and 'non-canonical' books, but of books definitely accepted (*homologoumena*), books definitely rejected (*notha*), and a third category of disputed books (*antilegomena*). But the actual distribution of the books is not the same as theirs" (17).

On the basis of this, analysis Barton urges that entering the second century there was already a core of Christian writings that were widely acknowledged among communities of Christian faith as texts that *ought* to be lived with in their common life and therefore acknowledged as Holy Scriptures (as I am using the term) that are canonical in a functionalist sense of the term, even though the earliest church itself would not have called all of them "Scripture."

However, in the interests of conceptual clarity I opt in the next section to limit use of "canon" and "canonical" to a more restricted sense of the terms suggested by Barton's second story about the historical process of canonization. My stipulation there about "canon" and "canonical" does not rest on any historical judgment to the effect that the second story is more accurate. It rests rather on the conceptual freedom the second sense of "canon" and "canonical" gives to develop an understanding of the force of calling certain texts "canonical" consistent with this section's account of the force of calling the same texts simply "Holy Scripture."

Part of the importance of this section's remarks about the force of acknowledging biblical texts as "Holy Scripture" lies in implications of such acknowledgment for what counts as appropriately disciplined study of the texts. Acknowledgment of Holy Scripture's primary authority is a self-involving performative act. The very act of acknowledgment commits those who utter it to certain attitudes toward Christian biblical texts read as Holy Scripture. Collectively, they constitute an overall attitude of respect. I prefer to characterize this attitude as respect rather than reverence. Reverence is an attitude that tends to rule out criticism, much less rejection, of any aspect of that which is reverenced. But some features of some of these historically contingent and culturally conditioned texts, even when they are acknowledged to be Holy Scripture, turn out to be downright dangerous when they are uncritically used to shape communities' common lives and communal and personal identities. One is wise to have an attitude of respect, but not reverence, even for that which is dangerous!

This attitude of respect holds together several factors. The texts are respected as important and neither trivial nor ephemeral. Each text is approached with the attitude that it is intelligible and self-consistent. This does not rule out the possibility of interpretative problems and apparent internal inconsistencies in a text, which leads to another factor of the attitude of respect for Holy Scripture: each text is approached with the attitude that it contains depths such that it may have more than one layer of meaning. Finally, appropriate respect for Holy Scripture means assuming that each text may prove to be relevant in some way to the communal and personal lives of those who live deeply with the texts in the common life of ecclesial communities.

The last is a point easily distorted. The relevance that respect for Holy Scripture expects from the texts is not something imposed on the text by its readers. In order to stress this, it was a commonplace of neo-orthodox theological accounts of the authority of Holy Scripture to characterize the texts as words of personal address: "The Bible speaks to you." More recently there have been justified protests against interpretive strategies that are defended by agentic characterizations of Holy Scripture, as though a set of texts could, in some straightforward way, act intentionally on its readers. Granted that objection, it is nonetheless licit to read texts of Holy Scripture as though they were prefaced by the unwritten sentence, "You, reader(s), are among those about whom the following is written. This bears on you. Interpret accordingly."

Indeed, John Barton has pointed out that each of these attitudes toward texts of the Christian Bible read as Holy Scripture brings with it an interpretive or hermeneutical rule: read this text as profound; read it as self-consistent; read it as "full of mysteries"; read it as relevant to your own situation (1997, 134–45). To this list of hermeneutical rules, another needs to be added: in light of well-known human tendencies to be complacent, self-justifying, self-deceiving, and to legitimate their own interests by appeals to "authority," read this text of Holy Scripture critically and self-critically.

Engaged by readers with these attitudes, the texts constituting the Christian Bible are subject to disciplined study as Holy Scripture. Such study is governed most generally by existential interests in God's ways of relating to humankind, in who the God is that relates in those ways, in how to understand all other realities as God-related, and in responding appropriately to the ways in which God relates to all else. Human beings have these existential interests in the texts as people who identify with a community that reads the Christian Bible explicitly as Holy Scripture, and not simply as Christian "Scriptures."

The existential interests that govern study of the Christian Bible as Holy Scripture clearly focus primarily on God, and neither on the communities of Christian faith themselves nor on the individuals whose existential interests govern their study of the texts. As biblical texts, they tell, allude to, or assume stories about a great many subjects in addition to God: physical and nonphysical worlds, ordinary people and royalty, sinners and prophets, animals and angels and evil spirits. When studied as Holy Scripture, however, those same texts are properly studied insofar as their subject is God *pro nobis*, and in two ways at once: the texts are studied to see what they tell, allude to, or assume about what God is doing with, to, within, and through those other subjects, even in the case of texts in which God is not explicitly mentioned; and they are read as texts whose uses in ecclesial communities are themselves used by God to help define, nurture, and correct the users' personal and communal identities.

The existential interests governing study of the Christian Bible as Holy Scripture focus on God as the subject of the texts in a more particular way. As we saw in chapter 1B, those who have such existential interests in these texts are those for whom the person of Jesus is definitive for understanding who the God is to whom they seek to respond appropriately. Consequently, existential interests in God's ways of relating to humankind, and interests in responding appropriately to God's relating, are framed a priori in christological ways: who the God is who relates in all these ways is definitively defined by who Jesus is. That is, understanding God in terms of the person of Jesus is brought to disciplined study of these texts construed as Holy Scripture.

This does not mean that study of the Christian Bible as Holy Scripture is disciplined by christological doctrines, adopted a priori, and imposed upon the texts as a conceptual filter (read: "dogmatic procrustean bed") through which the texts are interpreted. Rather, because study of the Christian Bible precisely as Holy Scripture is governed by existential interests in God, the fact that God is understood in terms of the person of Jesus describes a particular field of inquiry in which endless questions grow about who God is, about the ways in which to characterize how God relates to all that is not God, about how to construe all other realities as God-related, and how best to respond to God's ways of relating. It defines a field of questions; it does not close off the questions before they can even be asked. Correlatively, the fact that God is understood in terms of the person of Jesus describes a particular conceptual space in which alternative and conflicting proposals may be formulated in conversation with the texts about how best, under present circumstances, to conceptualize beliefs about Jesus, about God, about how God relates to all that is not God, about what difference it makes that other realities are God-related, and about what count as appropriate responses to God's ways of relating. It defines a conceptual space in which proposals made in the practice of secondary theology can be formulated, criticized, and defended. It does not close off a priori any particular type of conceptual proposal concerning the type of questions that arise in the field it defines.

Here we approach the *telos* of this entire discussion of how different interests determine how biblical texts are construed and determine the ways in which study of the texts governed by those interests is properly disciplined. One of the standards of excellence inherent in the practice of secondary theology is that the practice be accountable to biblical texts studied as canonical (for the force of that qualifier, see the next section) Holy Scripture in ways governed by interests in the ways in which God relates to all that is not God, in who God is, in how other realities are to be understood in their God-relatedness, and in how humans best respond appropriately to God's ways of relating to them. Such study is disciplined, I am urging, in a distinctive way.

Such study of these texts, taken as Holy Scripture, is disciplined by a type of *phronesis*, practical know-how—that is, knowing how to enact practices in particular concrete circumstances. It involves practical reasoning. As practical know-how, it counts as a mode of critical and self-critical knowing. However, it is the "knowing" that is inherent in excellent enactment of a practice, rather than in the grasp of theory about the practice in abstraction from the concrete particulars of the enactment of a practice in a given context.

Excellence in practical reasoning requires the acquisition of a variety of competencies and dispositions. Just which competencies and dispositions are required depends on what practices in which one is engaged. We can distinguish between competencies and dispositions required for practical reasoning in general, and competencies and dispositions required for practical reasoning in the study of biblical texts read as Holy Scripture in particular.

Phronesis in general involves, at the very least, capacities for good judgment, imagination, and trained perception. Capacity for good judgment involves cultivation of certain dispositions. Once again, just which dispositions need to be developed depends on the particular practice in which *phronesis* is exercised. It seems clear that in general good judgment requires the cultivation of dispositions for measured deliberation; fair-mindedness in weighing the merits of alternative, even conflicting, ways in which to proceed in enactments of the practice; respect for the long-accumulated wisdom incorporated in received traditions about how to proceed in similar circumstances; prudence in assessing how far circumstances are and are not similar to the past; honesty about ways in which received wisdom have failed; humility in the face of the challenges confronting the practice in new circumstances; critical self-knowledge to counter tendencies to self-deception; decisiveness in judging; and so on.

In addition to those dispositions required for good judgment in general, good judgment in the particular practice of secondary theology guided by disciplined study of biblical texts as Holy Scripture requires acquisition of an additional range of dispositions that are part of an appropriate response to the ways in which God relates to all that is not God. Some examples: dispositions to respond appropriately in faith, hope, and love to the ways in which God relates to all else; the disposition to rejoice in God's ways of relating to all else, and the disposition to give thanks for them; the disposition to turn away from trust in something other than God as the ground of one's reality and value—that is, the disposition to repent; dispositions to commit oneself to a community of Christian faith, and to trust, respect, care for, be thankful for, and seek reconciliation with fellow members of that community; the disposition to share with the community in the ministry to which it is called in its proximate contexts to make them more just, free, and self-sustaining contexts for the well-being of human life; the disposition to trust that God will work through the ways in which the community lives with Holy Scripture in its common life to form and transform personal and communal identities; the disposition to hope in the possibility of such transformation for oneself and the community; and the disposition to engage in disciplined study of Holy Scripture collegially with others in the ecclesial community. *Phronesis* that can discipline study of biblical texts as Holy Scripture requires capacities for good judgment that presuppose dispositions such as these very traditional Christian virtues.

This partial catalog of the requisite dispositions adds nothing to the definition of the practice of disciplined study of Holy Scripture because it is entailed in the concept of the practice. Only someone with these dispositions would construe biblical texts as Holy Scripture in the first place. (For helpful discussion of the fundamental role of dispositions in study of Holy Scripture, see Fowl 1998, esp. chaps. 3 and 7. Cf. Rogers 1996, who shows how virtues and interpretation of Holy Scripture are interdependent in Thomas Aquinas.)

Phronesis also involves imagination. By "imagination" I mean what Garrett Green calls the "paradigmatic imagination" (1989, 49–54). The term names two interrelated capacities. It names the capacity to recognize the pattern in a complex whole that makes it the whole it is. Call it the whole's "constitutive" pattern. As Green points out, a pattern is an arrangement of elements in any medium (94). It can be imaged, although it may not be possible to picture it (consider patterns identified in subatomic physics that can be described mathematically but cannot be pictured). Where a picture would try to reproduce a constitutive pattern, an image exemplifies the pattern (93–94). Insofar as a pattern can function as "a *normative* exemplar of [the] constitutive structure" (66; emphasis added) of a complex whole, the pattern is a "paradigm" and the way in which it is imaged can function "paradigmatically." Second, "paradigmatic imagination" names the capacity to use an exemplary image of the constitutive pattern of a complex whole in various ways. For example, the paradigmatic imagination is "the ability of human beings to recognize in accessible exemplars the constitutive organizing patterns of other, less accessible and more complex objects of investigation . . . Imagination is the means by which we are able to represent anything not directly accessible, including *both* the world of the imaginary *and* recalcitrant aspects of the real world; it is the medium of fiction as well as fact" (66; emphasis in original). This is a heuristic use of an image of a constitutive pattern.

Phronesis that disciplines study of biblical texts as Holy Scripture relies especially on exercise of the paradigmatic imagination insofar as such study is governed by interests in the ways in which God is said to relate to all that is not God, in understanding who God is in terms of the person of Jesus, in understanding other realities as God-related, and in responding appropriately to the ways in which God relates to all else.

For example, biblical texts include accounts of different ways in which God relates to all else. These include stories of God relating to create and preserve it, to draw it to eschatological consummation, to reconcile and save it when it is estranged and in bondage to evil. These accounts can be construed as complex literary wholes. Disciplined study of them as Holy Scripture seeks to image the constitutive pattern of the more accessible of those accounts and use it heuristically to bring out the constitutive pattern of more complex, and therefore more obscure, accounts. Such study seeks to discern what differences there are, if any, in the constitutive patterns of narratives of God's different ways of relating to all else.

A second example: Holy Scripture includes several stories that can be construed as identity descriptions of Jesus, including three quite different Synoptic accounts of his life. Some of these accounts locate the story of his life in the context of longer stories of God's relations with ancient Israel. These stories constitute complex literary wholes. If the question who the God is that relates to all else is to be answered in terms of who Jesus is, then disciplined study of biblical texts as Holy Scripture must seek to determine whether there are exemplary instances of stories about Jesus construed in the context of longer stories about ancient Israel, whose constitutive pattern is paradigmatic of stories that give a description of Jesus' personal identity. And it must seek to image the paradigmatic pattern of the more accessible of these stories and use it heuristically to bring out the constitutive pattern of more complex, and therefore more obscure, accounts (see part 3 of this anthropological project*).

Phronesis that disciplines study of biblical texts as Holy Scripture also relies on the paradigmatic imagination insofar as such study is governed by an interest in responding appropriately in new and even novel circumstances to God's ways of relating to all else.

As a guide to appropriate response to God now, such study may seek to use heuristically its images of the constitutive patterns of Holy Scripture's stories of God relating to all else to illumine otherwise obscure patterns in the current events that are the community's new circumstances, patterns that may tentatively be construed as possibly the pattern of the way God is relating to the current situation. For example, it appears that in his second inaugural address in 1865 Abraham Lincoln imagined God relating to the events of the American Civil War in this fashion.

---

*Part 3 appears in vol. 2 of this work.

Or, as a guide to appropriate response to God now, disciplined study of Holy Scripture may use heuristically its images of the constitutive patterns of Holy Scripture's stories of other people's exemplary responses to God's ways of relating to them in their circumstances to illumine how to respond appropriately now to God's ways of relating in otherwise obscure current circumstances. For example, Wayne Meeks points out that in Philippians the apostle Paul aims to "shape a Christian *phronesis*, a practical moral reasoning that is 'confirmed to [Christ's] death' in hope of his resurrection" (1991, 333). In Philippians 2:1–11 Paul offers an image of the constitutive pattern of Jesus' story as the paradigmatic pattern that the Philippians should use to illumine how to respond appropriately to God in their different and otherwise obscure circumstances. In 3:2–16 Paul offers an image of the constitutive pattern of his own life and urges the Philippians to imitate him. Arguably, the paradigmatic pattern of Paul's story of his own life is the constitutive pattern of the story of Jesus' life. As Stephen Fowl points out, building on Meeks's exegesis, Paul's call to imitate himself is "really a call to imitate Paul's manner of practical reasoning, a practical reasoning based on what the Philippians see in Christ Jesus (2:6–11). This is not a wooden sort of identical repetition, but a 'non-identical repetition' based on analogy . . ." (1998, 196, quoting John Millbank's phrase; for Fowl's full discussion of this topic in Philippians, see 1998, 190–96).

Phronesis also involves trained capacities to perceive other human beings, oneself, and various features of the context of their communal and personal lives, in ways relevant to the practices that constitute their common life. Just what ways are relevant, of course, depend on the practice. However, in general, capacities for perception share the fact that they are capacities to perceive a complex object of perception as something: a line drawing as a duck or as a rabbit; an object lying in the road as a small dog or as a stuffed animal; a raucous social situation as a party or as a neighborhood fight, and so on. That requires an exercise of the capacity to imagine—that is, the ability to image the paradigmatic pattern that is the constitutive pattern of the complex whole that is the object of perception. Cultivation of such capacities for perception is inseparable from cultivation of imaginative capacities.

This distinguishes acts of perception from acts of interpretation. Interpretation is a deliberate and intentional activity. Perception is not. Either you perceive an ambiguous line drawing as a duck, or you perceive it as a rabbit. Your perception may switch back and forth between the two, a switch you may interpret by saying that the drawing is ambiguous. But you do not perceive it ambiguously as simultaneously a duck and a rabbit.

Perception is conceptually formed. The capacity to perceive "x" as "y" requires that one has mastered the concept of "y" and brought it to the act of perception. Excellent exercise of *phronesis* requires the cultivation of certain imaginative and conceptual capacities that are the precondition of abilities to perceive oneself, others, and the contexts we share in ways that are relevant to particular practices in which practical reasoning is to be exercised.

Phronesis that disciplines study of biblical texts as Holy Scripture relies on trained perceptual abilities, especially insofar as it is study governed by interest in responding appropriately to the ways in which God relates to the community engaged in the study. These are perceptual abilities trained by mastery of a distinctively Christian set of concepts. We have seen that perception involves perceiving "x" as "y." We have seen that the practices that make up the common life of ecclesial communities are conceptually formed, and that human beings' personal and communal identities are shaped by acquiring those concepts through their participation in those practices. Those concepts come to constitute the "y's" when they perceive "x" as "y." As their identities come to be formed, they come not just to know about these concepts but also to perceive themselves, others, and the contexts of their lives in ways shaped by those concepts. Thus they come to perceive the world as a whole, and the particulars in it, as creatures, as gift, as distorted, as redeemed, as promising, as God-related (see Kelsey 2005, 97–106). The distinction we noted above between the act of perception and the act of interpretation applies here. To perceive something, "x", as God's gift, as God-related, or, alternatively, as distorted, and so on, is not to interpret it. In an extended sense of the term, we are discussing ways of seeing the world, not an intentional and deliberative process whose result is an interpretation.

Inasmuch as the concepts that shape the practices that make up the life of ecclesial communities are different from those that shape the practices of the communities' host societies, they shape the perceptive abilities of the communities' members differently from the latter. The differences are a matter of degree, and do not necessarily affect the way every object of perception is perceived. They are, nonetheless, important differences.

The relation between study of Holy Scripture and this type of shaping of the students' perceptive capacities is circular. As Stephen Fowl puts it in this chapter's epigraph, "Scriptural interpretation should shape and be shaped by the convictions, practices and concerns" that form the communal and personal identities of members of ecclesial communities (1998, 62). On one hand, disciplined study of biblical texts as Holy Scripture is one of the practices through which their identities, and therewith their perceptual capabilities, are formed. On the other, the distinctive concepts that shape their perceptual capacities may make students of Holy Scripture more likely to perceive and focus on features of the texts that those whose perceptive capacities are shaped in other ways would not notice or consider relevant to their textual study.

In short, study of biblical texts as Holy Scripture that is disciplined by an appropriate *phronesis* requires cultivation of distinctive dispositions needed for the exercise of good judgment in explicating the texts; cultivation of imaginative capacities to recognize the constitutive patterns of texts construed as complex literary wholes, to formulate paradigmatic images of such patterns, and to use those images heuristically to illumine the constitutive patterns of more obscure complex wholes in the texts and in life; and cultivation of the imaginative and conceptual capacities required for perceiving features of the texts that are relevant to their role as Holy Scripture.

Study of biblical texts disciplined by *phronesis* is no less rigorously disciplined than is study of the same texts subject to literary, historical, or social-scientific disciplines. It is not even a type of discipline that is wholly different in kind from the others. Scholars who are skilled at studying biblical and scriptural texts in ways subject to literary, historical, and social-scientific disciplines are well formed by their training to study the texts in particular ways. Necessary conditions of such skill are mastery of a significant body of technical information and, perhaps, some theory or theories of interpretation. However, neither mastery of the body of theory nor, as Fowl points out, mastery of the technical information is sufficient to train skillful practice of study of these texts in ways subject to these disciplines. "The key virtue that [their] training seeks to form in professional biblical scholars is a type of practical reasoning or *phronesis*" (188), because technical information is not self-interpreting. "On its own it cannot identify and articulate interpretive problems" (188). Nor can theory of interpretation show, on its own, how it applies to particular texts. Hence, their professional training "seeks to form scholars who not only have technical competence, but who have the practical wisdom to know how to deploy specific elements of their technical knowledge in ways that contribute to the advancement, re-formulation, or reopening of particular interpretive disputes and discussions" (188). *Phronesis* is central to every discipline that is appropriate to each of the types of interest that may govern study of biblical texts. The fact that a distinctive type of *phronesis* disciplines study of those same texts as Holy Scripture does not make such study incommensurable with other types of their disciplined study.

There is no reason in principle that study of biblical texts as Holy Scripture cannot also be subject to literary, historical, and social-scientific discipline, as particular issues raised by particular texts call for it. Granted their interpretive indeterminacy, it is nonetheless evident that any responsible effort to explicate biblical texts as Holy Scripture must be a critical explication. It must ask relevant critical literary, historical, and social-scientific questions of the texts, and it must subject proposed answers to the standard disciplines of literary, historical, and social-scientific study of texts. The texts, after all, always represent some genre of literature and exhibit some synchronic pattern(s); have some history of transmission, interpretation, and, perhaps, editorial modification; and reflect in some way the societies and cultures in which they originated and in which they were subsequently employed in various ways. It is just those concrete texts, with their particular literary structures, histories, and socio-cultural contexts, not some set of literarily featureless and chaotic, ahistorical and culture-free texts, that are taken to be Holy Scripture. Study of Holy Scripture disciplined by appropriate *phronesis* must also be disciplined by the ways in which the study of the same texts is disciplined when they are studied as biblical texts and as Scripture if it is really to be disciplined study of the same texts as Holy Scripture.

Canonical Holy Scripture

Let "canonical Holy Scripture" be used to designate the collection of the very same texts (the Christian Bible) when they are explicitly acknowledged (Christian Holy Scripture) by certain communities of Christian faith to be a determinate set of texts whose employment by the community in many practices that constitute their common life is the medium in, through, and under which God works to call the community into being; nurture and sustain it; and, when necessary, correct and reform the ways they seek in their common life to respond appropriately to God's ways of relating to them.

"Canon" means a standard "ruler" (Gr. *kanon*, measuring rod). In this sense of the term, the canon of Holy Scripture, the standard measuring rod, can be identified by a list of the texts that make up the set.

For the practice of secondary theology, the force of acknowledgment of biblical texts, not only as Holy Scripture, but as *canonical* Holy Scripture (in the sense of "canon" outlined in this section) is to acknowledge that secondary theology ought to be accountable to this collection of texts as a set—that is, as an authoritative collection of texts, not merely a collection of authoritative texts (see Barton 1997, 9, citing Bruce Metzger). It is the collection as a set that is the standard measuring rod to which practice of secondary theology is in some way accountable *if* it is a practice of ecclesial communities that explicitly acknowledge this set of texts as canonical Holy Scripture. Not all communities that identify themselves as communities of Christian faith also identify who they are by this explicit acknowledgment of a canon of Holy Scripture. This stipulation of the meaning of "canon" applies only to those who do. Of course, canonical Holy Scripture is not the only thing to which such practice of secondary theology is accountable. Accountability to canonical Holy Scripture is only one of the standards of excellence inherent in the practice of secondary theology. What is to be explored here is the force of taking the texts that compose the collection of Christian Holy Scripture as a set, so far as the practice of secondary ecclesial theology is concerned.

The sense of "canon" I stipulate here coheres with the sense assumed in Barton's second story of the process of canonization. However, Barton warns against attempting to warrant contemporary proposals of canonical reading of Holy Scripture by appeal to any historical account of the process of canonization. Told in either of the two ways he identifies, one historical outcome is the same. Although "the Bible certainly was perceived as a single book by the end of the patristic period . . . ," it "was not read as a 'work' in the modern sense, as though it had a structure that yielded a continuous and ordered meaning. . . ." Instead, "It was perceived as something closer to a vast collection of (divine) aphorisms, rather as if the whole book were like the central sections of the book of Proverbs" (1997, 155). However, in contrast to patristic practice, I am urging that the practice of secondary theology is accountable to canonical Holy Scripture read as an authoritative set of texts that is a kind of whole, although not a literary or aesthetic "work." Consequently, I take seriously the recommendation with which Barton concludes a chapter on canon and meaning: "Canonical and synchronic readings need to be justified in their own right, as modern methods of exegesis, and not give hostages to fortune by claiming ancient precedent" (156). I seek to follow at least the negative part of that advice by confining myself to stipulating how I use terms like "canon" and "canonicity."

Barton's second story of the process of canonization involves ways of using the terms "canon," "canonical," and "canonization" that are paradigmatic of the use I wish to stipulate and can help clarify it. It is a story of ecclesial communities' efforts, not un-self-consciously and passively to receive, but explicitly and actively "to list and define which books should count as [Holy] Scripture" (27). As such, it is a process that does, over and over again in the work of different Christian writers, synods, and councils, aim at a product: acknowledgment of a list of texts that ought (de jure) to be used in practices making up the common life of communities of Christian faith.

This process is open to being told as a story in which canonization comes much later than it does in the first story. If the process of canonization can only be said to be completed when there is a list that is explicitly designated as the ecclesial community's acknowledged *kanon*, then the historical evidence makes it very difficult to date it before the fourth century. Athanasius's Festal Letter 39 of 367, Barton reports, is "the first unequivocal evidence for the use of the word [*kanon*] to mean a fixed list of biblical texts" (10) and the first "on which Scriptures are explicitly said to be 'of' or 'not of' the 'canon'" (12).

However, Barton argues, the second story need not be told in so restrictive a way. As he points out, "One should not think that an *interest* in identifying which books belonged in the Bible was new in the fourth century" (27; emphasis in original). The second story of the process of canonization can be told more broadly as the story of Christian writers making lists of texts that count as Christian Holy Scripture, a process already well established as early as Tertullian in the late second century. Tertullian "presupposes that the idea of the Church ruling certain books as 'not to be read' was no novelty" (27). The process of "canonization," understood in this way as a process of listing the texts that are an acknowledged set of Christian Holy Scripture, does not follow and bring to a conclusion an earlier process of passive reception of texts as Holy Scripture (first story). The second story is not the sequel of the first story. Rather, the two are historically concurrent.

Barton argues that such list making generally was "not part of an attempt to regulate which books Christians might or might not use, as though that were a matter of general doubt and difficulty" (28) in actual ecclesial practice. The context of some Christian writers' canonical lists was theoretical rather than ecclesial practice. Sometimes the theory was apologetic—for example, the effort to show skeptics that Christian thought is based on texts free of error and inconsistency. Sometimes, as in Jerome's theoretical argument against Augustine that only the Hebrew Old Testament, and not the longer Greek translation of the Old Testament (the Septuagint), could count as the Christian Holy Scripture because it was the Hebrew text that God inspired, the disputer continued in practice to cite texts he explicitly excluded from his list on the basis of his own theory. Some early Christian writers who do attend to ecclesial practice, such as Origen and Eusebius noting disputes in churches about the scriptural status of certain texts (e.g., Hebrews, Revelation, James, Jude, 2 Peter, 2 and 3 John), review the arguments pro and con, but do not select or reject the texts. "Thus," Barton notes, "exactly where rulings are needed, none is offered" (28). The context of other listings, especially those made by synodical decisions, is conflict with heresy. They concentrate on excluding texts favored by heretical groups. Here, too, the "approved" books "are not being selected from a potentially very much larger list, but simply recalled from immemorial tradition. . . , acknowledged to be (already) rightly held in reverence by the consensus of the faithful" (29). In all these cases of canonization as list making, Barton urges, "the aim is not to draw a line around these books, as though no others could *conceivably* be comparable" (29; emphasis in original). They do not imply that the list is necessarily closed. They do imply that certain explicitly excluded texts "do *not* measure up to those long received in the Church" (29; emphasis in original) and that at least the ones included on the list constitute the set of texts with which ecclesial communities ought to live in the practices that make up their common life.

That is the sense of "canon" (and therewith, of "canonical" and "canonization") I adopt here. This second story of the process of canonization is not offered as though it provided historical warrant for adopting this sense of "canon" rather than the sense of "canon" assumed in the first story. Instead, it is outlined because it exemplifies in a paradigmatic way the pattern of use of "canonical" that I adopt in this methodological proposal about secondary theology's accountability to canonical Holy Scripture.

The act of acknowledging the biblical texts to be canonical is as self-involving as the act of acknowledging them to be Holy Scripture. It amounts to the acknowledgment of the texts' authority, not only in their roles in ecclesial communities' practices, authoring determinate communal and personal identities, but more narrowly their authority as the set of texts, listed in the canon, to which the particular practice of secondary theology is accountable. The texts' authority in relation to secondary theology is derivative from the primary authority they exercise in the practices that constitute ecclesial communities' common life. Call it Holy Scripture's secondary authority as the authoritative collection of texts, and not merely a collection of authoritative texts, to which the practice of secondary theology is accountable.

In relation to the practice of secondary theology, modifying "Holy Scripture" with "canonical" in no way materially modifies the self-involving force (explored earlier) of acknowledging biblical texts as Holy Scripture. The complex attitude of respect toward the texts that such acknowledgment brings with it remains unchanged. So does the type of practical reasoning that such respect requires in order to discipline appropriately study of the texts precisely as "Holy Scripture" and the range of competencies and dispositions that such *phronesis* presupposes.

However, acknowledgment of the canonicity of the Holy Scripture to which the practice of secondary theology is accountable does amount to acknowledgment of certain formal features of the canonical set of Holy Scripture to which secondary theology is accountable.

For one, what is acknowledged as canonical is a set of canonically edited texts as received in Hebrew or Greek, or translated from Hebrew or Greek into some ordinary language. Historical-critical study of many of these texts shows that what is presently received comes at the end of a history of successive editings and redactions of earlier texts. It may show that the received text has many sources, some written, some perhaps oral, maybe some original to an editor or editors at one point or another in the history of the text. Such historical-critical insight into a received text's history of textual development can be helpful in identifying the theological interests that guided the successive editings that resulted in the received version of the text. What is acknowledged as authoritative for the practice of secondary theology, however, is only the collection of received texts, not their textual antecedents, if any. To characterize this collection of received texts as canonically edited is not to make an a priori and ahistorical suggestion that the texts were each and all edited with the intention of forming them into a canonical collection. Whether that is true of some of them needs to be argued case by case in appropriate historical fashion. To characterize this set of texts as "canonically edited" is only to underscore that what is acknowledged as canonical is a collection of texts in the edited versions in which they are received when they are acknowledged as "canonical."

A second formal feature of Holy Scripture read as a canonical set comes with the first. As we saw earlier, the set of texts received as "canonically edited" is, for historical reasons, formally organized into two parts, the Old Testament and the New Testament. John Barton points out that, in the context of the first story of the process of canonization, communities of Christian faith used as part of their functional canon new Christian writings (Gospels and epistles) they would not have called "Scripture," much less "Holy Scripture," because they clearly were not ancient. Their paradigm of Holy Scripture was the received set of ancient Hebrew texts that also were part of their functional canon. By the end of the second century, entering the third, as is clear in the writings of Clement of Alexandria and Origen, the new Christian writings came to be seen as "holy, ancient text[s], capable of containing hints of hidden meaning" (Barton 1997, 99). That is, they came to be acknowledged in the communities' practices as a New Testament of canonical (Greek) Holy Scripture in some kind of relation to the Old Testament of (Hebrew, in Greek translation) canonical Holy Scripture.

Acknowledging this bipartite set of texts as canonical entails acknowledgment of a third formal feature of the authoritative collection: it is some kind of "whole" that comprises two sets of diverse individual texts having very different properties.

One of the important contributions made to secondary theology by studies of these texts governed by, and subject to the disciplines appropriate to, literary, historical, and phenomenology of religion interests is the way they serve to discipline study governed by theological interests (in ways in which God relates to all that is not God, who the God is who relates in these ways, how to understand other realities as God-related, and what counts as appropriate ways of responding to God's relating). They discipline study governed by theological interests by making unavoidably clear the concrete particularity of each of the texts on the canonical list, how they differ from one another in their literary genres and rhetoric, their cultural assumptions, their theological assumptions and affirmations, their concrete historical occasions, and the particular situations to which they are addressed.

Sometimes this diversity is characterized as "polyphony." That musical metaphor can only be used with caution. It too easily tends to soften the sharpness of the differences among the texts, as if it suggests that each is a different voice in what is, taken all together, fundamentally a harmonious chorus. However, although the act of acknowledging Holy Scripture as a canon is an acknowledgment that it is in some sense of the term a "whole," it is not an acknowledgment that it can be unified by being harmonized. The range and depth of the diversity among the texts composing the canonical set is too great to be accommodated by the metaphor of harmony.

Sometimes the diversity of the canon is likened to the constituent parts of a literary work. That characterization brings with it a "hermeneutical imperative": "Read all these books as chapters in a single work" (Barton 1997, 152). "Work" is an aesthetic category. Its ascription to a writing, like its ascription to a piece of music or visual art, assumes that it is a more or less complex composition of parts that exhibits an overall, unifying pattern or structure that is in some way significant or meaning-laden and satisfies certain aesthetic standards. Think of a novel, a sonnet, a short story, or an epic poem. However, the occasion-specific character of most texts in canonical Holy Scripture, as well as the range and depth of the ways in which they differ from one another, cut against "work" as an apt characterization of the canon's wholeness. Reading the books of the Bible as chapters of a single work would systematically tend to smooth over and obscure those differences. To acknowledge Christian Holy Scripture as a canonical set is to construe it as some kind of whole, but (*pace* Barton 1997, 150–56) it does not entail that it is the wholeness of a work. Whatever sense of "whole" applies, the canon does not exhibit the wholeness of internally coherent unity—aesthetic, propositional, conceptual, or otherwise.

Nonetheless, to acknowledge Holy Scripture as a canon is also to acknowledge this collection of profoundly different texts as some kind of set, which suggests that the collection is in some sense a whole. Insofar as the set is read as the authoritative collection of texts to which secondary theology is accountable, it has the formal character of a certain kind of whole, a determinate space or field of narratives, concepts, and images in which the practice of secondary theology ought to find the paradigmatic patterns that govern its proposals about how best to formulate Christian beliefs about how God relates to all that is not God, about who the God is who relates in these ways, about how to construe other realities as God-related, and about the attitudes, dispositions, emotions, passions, and practices that count in current circumstances as appropriate responses to the way God relates. However, "a whole" and "wholeness" are formal characterizations at a very high level of abstraction. To stress that the canonical set of texts of Holy Scripture is, for all of its internal diversity, some kind of whole implies nothing about any particular way of characterizing what kind of whole it is.

It is important to underscore what acknowledgment of canonical Holy Scripture's wholeness does not imply. We have already noted that it does not imply that the canon of Holy Scripture is a closed set. In principle, it is logically possible that ecclesial communities might come to acknowledge additional texts as part of the set comprising canonical Holy Scripture, although it is entirely unclear through what procedures actualization of this possibility would have to pass.

Second, the wholeness of the canonical set does not imply that all the texts in the canonical set are equally important. Not all texts of canonical Holy Scripture are used equally frequently in the practices that make up the common life of communities of Christian faith. Among those practices, the practice of secondary theology is governed by interests in the ways in which God relates to all that is not God, in who the God is who relates, in how to construe all things as related to God, and in how best to respond appropriately to God's relating. In regard to this practice, Holy Scripture's canonicity does not entail that theological proposals ought to be accountable equally to each and every text of Holy Scripture. Rather, it entails that the set of texts constituting the canon comprises the field of narratives, concepts, attitudes, beliefs, images, and so on, that ought to guide the practice of secondary theology as its study of these texts is governed by its defining interests. Proposals addressing different theological *loci*, and different questions in regard to each *locus*, will find guidance in different texts. This leaves plenty of room for concrete enactments of the practice of secondary theology to hold themselves accountable to subsets of the canon of Holy Scripture for the purposes of that particular enactment of the practice in relation to the particular theological questions it is addressing in its particular historical and cultural context. Call such subsets the "effective canon" in regard to the particular theological questions being addressed. The formal wholeness of the textual field defined by acknowledgment of a canonical set of Holy Scripture does not rule out focus on more restricted ad hoc "effective canons" to which some particular enactment of the practice of secondary theology is held accountable.

Nor, third, does acknowledgment of the formal "wholeness" of canonical Holy Scripture entail any one type of construal of the texts of Holy Scripture. This is obvious and noncontroversial in relation to the use of these texts in most of the practices that constitute the common life of ecclesial communities. Some texts are construed as prayers and song; some as objects on which to meditate; some as sources of consolation, encouragement, self-examination, or wise counsel; some as moral injunctions to be obeyed; some are construed, in reflection on social and cultural issues, as paradigms of ideal social and cultural situations; some as the basis of acts of proclamation and exhortation; as material to be taught; as the subjects of suitably disciplined study, and so on.

However, the question of what counts as appropriate construal of texts of canonical Holy Scripture, given the canon's wholeness, is more problematic in relation to the practice of secondary theology. One of the standards of excellence inherent in the practice of secondary theology that is enacted by this project is that its proposals be shown to be accountable to canonical Holy Scripture. That forces the question, to which features or aspects of canonical Holy Scripture is it to be accountable? For example, since the purpose of secondary theology is to make proposals about how best to formulate the standards by which the adequacy of ecclesial communities' responses to God are to be assessed, does it follow that what it is primarily accountable to in canonical Holy Scripture is the propositional content of proposals made in those texts? Or, instead, is it accountable to canonical Holy Scripture construed as a set of "symbolic" expressions of a type of experience of God? Or, instead, account-able to the texts construed as projecting a possible way of being set into the world, an existential "how," that one might personally appropriate? (For more extensive elaboration of this notion of alternative construals of canonical Holy Scripture, see Kelsey 1999, chaps. 2–4, 8.)

Do different theological *loci*, or different kinds of questions within vari-ous *loci*, call for different kinds of construal of the very same texts of canoni-cal Holy Scripture? Is it appropriate to be inconsistent in this matter—that is, not to construe canonical Holy Scripture as having the same type of "force" in relation to each and all questions in every *locus*? In the practice of secondary theology, such decisions are unavoidable about how to construe the canonical Holy Scripture to which its theological proposals are accountable. However, although our exploration of the force of acknowledging biblical texts as canoni-cal Holy Scripture has shown that it entails construing the canonical set of texts as some kind of "whole," that "wholeness" is so abstractly formal that it cannot itself settle these questions. It cannot serve as a warrant for any particular theo-logical decision about how to construe the canonical Holy Scripture to which its theological proposals are accountable.

Nor, fourth, does acknowledgment of canonical Holy Scripture's formal "wholeness" entail any particular way in which Old Testament and New Tes-tament texts are to be related to each other. That is an interpretive or herme-neutical question that is settled on other grounds, not by acknowledgment of Christian Holy Scripture's canonicity.

One example of such "other grounds" is provided by the three-step history of theological "arguments from prophecy" in support of Christian claims about Jesus' status as the Messiah. As Barton points out, in the first historical step the earliest version of such arguments "presupposes the authority of the Old Testa-ment, and reasons as follows: if Jesus can be shown to be the one the prophets foretold, then his authority is thereby vindicated. . . . For a Jewish Christian . . . the crucial question . . . is whether belief in Jesus as the Messiah is compatible with this self-evidently authoritative collection of books" (1998, 70). Inciden-tally, claims about Jesus as Messiah were held accountable, not to the whole Old Testament, but to an "effective canon" of Old Testament texts, especially Isaiah and Psalms, which were taken to contain a concentration of christologi-cal prophecies. Here Old Testament texts are the hermeneutical lens through which the Jesus who is proclaimed as Messiah in communities of Christian faith is interpreted. When the Old Testament is related in this way to Chris-tian testimony to Jesus as the Messiah, the texts themselves tend to be read as straightforward testimony to Jesus. Already in Paul the Old Testament is read as though Christ were present in it. Barton cites early-second-century texts like the *Epistle of Barnabas* and Melito's *Paschal Homily* for which the Old Testa-ment is itself virtually a New Testament in which Christ is already speaking before the incarnation, saying nothing incompatible with what he would say later as the earthly Jesus (see 76, 77).

The second step begins no later than the early second century. The argument from prophecy "ceased to be a way of showing that Jesus was the continuation and only valid fulfillment of the religion, Judaism, which was already believed to be the one true revelation of God. Instead it became a way of showing that the Scriptures of Judaism ought to be accepted by Christians, too, since (however obscurely) they witnessed to the one in whom Christians *already* believed in any case" (72). It is likely, as Harnack argued, that this shift took place in Gentile communities of Christian faith in which it was not self-evident that the Old Testament is fundamental religious authority. For them, faith in Jesus as the Redeemer brought with it acknowledgment of the texts of the Old Testament as canonical Holy Scripture simply because they pointed to Christ. In writers like Tertullian and, probably, Justin, "the authority of the gospel accounts is taken for granted as the absolute starting-point for Christians" (73). Here Christian texts that tell, or comment on, the story of Jesus function as canonical Holy Scripture and serve as the hermeneutical lens through which the Old Testament is interpreted. One consequence of this shift is that, when a body of Christian texts is acknowledged as a distinct body of Holy Scripture, a "New Testament," that functions in the same way as the Old Testament had functioned, it is no longer possible to read the Old Testament as primarily a testimony to the gospel. Rather, it becomes "apparent that the teachings in the Gospel represent a fresh stage in divine revelation, and some kind of 'dispensationalism' will become the order of the day, with the Old Testament as that which Jesus took for granted but moved beyond, or as predictions or types which he fulfilled" (78).

According to Barton, the third stage in the history of the argument from prophecy comes when this "lurching" (73) from ascription of hermeneutical priority to the Old Testament, relative to canonical Christian texts testifying to Jesus as Messiah and Redeemer, to ascription of hermeneutical priority to the canonical Christian texts, relative to the Old Testament, eventually

> settled into a sort of equilibrium. The argument came to work as it were in both directions at once. It became an invitation to contemplate the divine *plan* in which old and new dispensations are in harmony. For this, it does not matter in which direction the argument runs—whether to show that the old scriptures validate Christ, or to vindicate the old scriptures by pointing out that Christ is their fulfillment and validation. . . . This results in a position where neither the New Testament is validated by the Old nor the Old by the New, but the providence and wisdom of God are proven by the congruence between the two. (74)

Acknowledgment of canonical Holy Scripture's purely *formal* "wholeness" provides space for such shifts in ways of reading the two Testaments in relation to each other, but it neither presupposes nor implies any one of them. They are hermeneutical shifts governed, as we have seen, by shifts in the theological interests and questions brought to study of the texts.

In sum, if it is stipulated that "canon" be used to name texts on the list of contents of an authoritative collection of texts (as opposed to a collection of authoritative texts) to which the proposals made in the practice of secondary theology are accountable, then acknowledgment of texts of Holy Scripture as "canonical" also amounts to acknowledgment of at least three formal features of the set: what is acknowledged as canonical is the received—canonically edited—version of the texts, not the oral or written sources of the received texts nor historically earlier strata in the history of the texts' successive redactions; that the set has an internal bipartite structure, "Old" and "New" Testaments; that the set is some kind of whole made up of texts that are so different from one another in many important respects as to be incapable of harmonization. The "wholeness" of the set of canonical texts, however, is entirely formal and does not imply that the set is necessarily closed; that all the texts in the set are equally important; that there is any one way in which to construe the force of canonical texts insofar as secondary theology's proposals are accountable to them; nor does it imply how Old and New Testament texts are to be related to one another in the process of holding secondary theology's proposals account-able to them.

The canonical set of texts thus defines a formal field of narratives, concepts, beliefs, images, attitudes, and expressions of emotions and passions, all of which concern ways in which God relates to all that is not God, who the God is who relates, how to construe other realities as God-related, and how best to respond appropriately to God's relating to which secondary theology's propos-als are accountable. But the formal features of this field do not have material implications about *which* narratives, concepts, beliefs, images, attitudes, and expressions of emotions and passions secondary theology is accountable to, or how they are to be related to one another.

The preceding sequence of sections explaining how I propose to use the terms "bible," "Scripture," "Holy Scripture," and "canonical Holy Scripture" warrants two conclusions about the kind of wholeness ascribed to Holy Scripture when proposals made in the practice of secondary theology are held accountable to canonical Holy Scripture. First, although to acknowledge Holy Scripture as canonical is to acknowledge that, formally speaking, it constitutes some kind of whole, it does not entail ascription to it of any particular kind of wholeness. Therefore, the kind of wholeness that Holy Scripture is assumed to have when secondary theology's proposals are held accountable to it must be grounded in something outside the biblical texts, whether they are studied as Bible, Scrip-ture, or Holy Scripture. Second, a major component, although not necessarily the only component, of that "something outside the biblical texts" is the set of interests that govern study of those texts. Those interests govern whether the texts are construed as Bible, Scripture, Holy Scripture, or canonical Holy Scrip-ture when they are studied. Consequently, the interests that govern study of the texts precisely as canonical Holy Scripture govern, though they do not wholly determine, how canonical Holy Scripture's "wholeness" is construed. I return to that question in chapter 12B.

PART 1

Created: Living on Borrowed Breath

Preface

The root question for this theological anthropology is, What does the specifically Christian conviction that God actively relates to us imply about what and who we are and how we are to be? The structure of the overall answer that I am proposing is grounded in the three-part specifically Christian background belief that the triune God actively relates to us in three interrelated but distinct ways: as One who creates, grounding our reality, and its value and well-being; as One who promises us an eschatological consummation and draws us to it; as One who reconciles us in our multiple estrangements. The task of part 1 is to elaborate on theological remarks grounded in the background belief that God relates to us creatively. It will cast this as a theology of birth, construing "to be created" as "having been born." Against the background of a description of our ultimate context in God's creativity (chap. 4A) and a description of our proximate contexts as the term of God's creativity into which we are born (chap. 5A), chapters 6 and 7 offer meditations on Job 10 as theological reflection on having been born as fellow creatures, body and soul, "individual and social," "private and public," placed in creaturely contexts to which they are organically integral. These chapters are each buttressed by chapters that, respectively, defend reliance on canonical Wisdom literature (4B), support a particular reading of Proverbs (5B), and propose a view about the relation between various forms of scientific inquiry and theological anthropology (6B). This provides the basis for a theological account of human creaturely flourishing in faith (chap. 8). This account of human creaturely flourishing has implications regarding who we are and how we are to be (chap. 9A). Correlated with this account of human flourishing is an account of distortions of creaturely flourishing in faith—that is, sin as inappropriate response to God relating creatively to all reality other than God (chaps. 10 and 11).

*The Ultimate Context
into Which We Are Born*

In modern systematic theology, "doctrines of creation" do remarkably little work (see Wingren, 1971; 1979). This is partly because much talk about "creation" and "creaturehood" in modern theology is terminally abstract. Even when one can understand it, it seems to make little difference in the broader project of Christian theology. A major challenge in this part of my theological anthropology is to clarify not only what it means to say that we are "creatures" of God, but what theological and practical difference it makes to say so.

Theologically speaking, human beings are God's creatures. The ultimate context into which they are born is God's relating to them as their creator. Human persons are born into complex networks of other beings that interact with one another and with specifically human beings in dynamic systems of energy and energy exchange that constitute their proximate contexts. The energy systems into which human persons are born can be conceptualized, analyzed, and causally explained in astonishing detail, at both micro and macro levels, physically, biologically, emotionally, socially, politically, economically, and culturally.

We learn all this from the physical, biological, and human sciences, which deliver more truths about human beings than we can hope to synthesize into a single comprehensive theoretical system. Beyond that, the human significance of these systems of energy is powerfully evoked for us in the work of artists in all cultures who deliver more insight about human being than any one of us can absorb in a lifetime.

Naturally, this raises a question: Other than making a pious gesture ("Just remember that this is all from God, and be grateful!"), what does a Christian theology of creation have to add concerning this context into which we are born and its implications for what it means to be human beings? Although a full-scale answer to this question would require a comprehensive and systematic doctrine of creation, in this chapter and the next I sketch a more modest response about the distinctive emphases that characterize a Christian theological account of creation, guided by witnesses to God's active creating that are found in canonical Wisdom literature. In chapter 5A, I suggest a theological account of the proximate context into which we are born, the realm of creaturely energy systems, and its anthropological implications; in the present chapter, I seek to clarify something more basic: the relation God has to us as our creator, the ultimate context into which we are born, and its anthropological implications.

In chapter 2A, I explored the rationale for understanding the Creator in Trinitarian terms. I add now that a Trinitarian account of God's creating needs to be guided and nuanced far more than they traditionally have been by canonical Wisdom literature's witness to creation. Because of Wisdom literature's widespread reputation for boring banality, this proposal will doubtless be met by many readers with something close to incredulity. Consequently, a rationale for privileging Wisdom's implicit theology of creation is developed in chapter 4B, some themes of which it will be useful to sketch right away.

Wisdom and Creation

We may take the Wisdom literature accepted as canonical by Protestants and Roman Catholics alike, namely, Proverbs, Job, Song of Songs, and Ecclesiastes, as one voice among many in canonical Holy Scripture, privileging its voice while attending to other voices in the canon that are both in harmony and in tension with it.

Walther Zimmerli's judgment seems now to be almost universally accepted: "Wisdom thinks resolutely within the framework of a theology of creation" (1976b, 316). Except for Proverbs 8:21–32 and Job, this creation theology is almost entirely implicit in biblical Wisdom literature. Wisdom's explicit interests center far more heavily on God's providential governance of the world. However, although an understanding of divine providence is logically and conceptually closely tied to an understanding of God's creating, the two are nonetheless distinct topics. In creating, God does not relate to any reality already extant. On the other hand, in managing creation (i.e., "providence," broadly understood), God is relating to reality that is already "there," fully actual and genuinely other than God. Canonical Wisdom's creation theology mostly functions as a set of beliefs that are background to the literature's explicit concerns about providence, a background against which it thinks about those concerns. However, for my anthropological purposes, canonical Wisdom's theology of creation is more important than its theology of providence.

What makes it important is the fact that, unlike most other biblical theologies of creation, canonical Wisdom's view of creation is conceptually separated from ideas of both reconciliation and eschaton. Canonical

Wisdom is remarkably silent regarding both redemptive covenant and the ultimate end or purpose of history. The creation theologies explicit and implicit in Genesis, Isaiah, and scattered New Testament passages arguably subordinate understandings of God's creating to understandings of God's actively relating to us to reconcile us (with the additional premise of a bondage from which we need to be saved), and subject the former to the narrative logic of the latter. The result in those cases is that the narrative logic of stories of God creating is bent under the pressure of the narrative logic of the stories of God relating to reconcile. Such bending is legitimate, for the stories in question are, after all, stories about God relating to reconcile, and stories of God relating to create are incorporated into them to bring out some important feature of reconciliation. Nonetheless, in such narrative contexts, stories of God relating to create are in some way skewed. Wisdom's theology of creation is conceptually independent of that pattern of thought and is not shaped by any understanding of God's active relating to reconcile creatures from the estranging effects of sin and evil. Consequently, in canonical Wisdom literature, stories of God relating to create are told for their own sake and are told in ways that do not bend their narrative logic.

There are theological contexts in which it is important to interpret God's creating in ways that are controlled by the narrative logic of stories of God's reconciling. However, if the hermeneutical significance attributed in chapter 3B to Trinitarian understandings of God is correct, stories of God's creating have their own narrative logic which should not be ruled by the narrative logic of stories of God's drawing creation to eschatological consummation or by stories of God's reconciling alienated creation. Wisdom's witness to creation firmly backs just that move.

The Creator's Relation to Creation

Canonical Wisdom literature's narrative of God relating to us as our creator constitutes one strand of the ultimate context into which we are born. The context that ultimately defines what and who we are and how we are to be is not the created cosmos. The creaturely realm is only the proximate context into which we are born. It, too, helps define what and who we are and how we are to be. But our ultimate context as creatures is the active creativity of God.

We share this ultimate context with all reality whatsoever other than God. This has an important implication for how we are to proceed in our effort to characterize God relating to us as our creator. We cannot start with God's relation to human subjects and then generalize it to all of creation. To do so would assume that what we say theologically about the rest of creation must be extrapolated from what we say about ourselves as creatures. It might suggest, indeed, that we extrapolate to the cosmos from what we say about ourselves as creatures because God somehow relates to the rest of creation through, or on the basis of, the way God relates to human creatures. Such a colossally anthropocentric assumption is theologically, not to say scripturally, unwarranted. Instead, precisely because we are part of reality other than God, the ways in which we speak of God relating creatively to reality in general must govern the ways in which we speak of God relating creatively to human persons in particular. This is what was right about the standard practice from the second through the sixteenth centuries of formulating anthropological remarks within the framework of a theological cosmology. In regard to human persons as creatures, we have to begin with some features of the big picture.

At the core of any theological account of the big picture is the following question: "How do we best describe the relation between Creator and creation?" If we allow mainstream canonical Wisdom's theology of creation to guide us, we will answer, "The relation between Creator and creature is best understood as God's being present to creation in hospitable generosity, free delight, and self-determining commitment."

The choice of the preposition "to" is important. The "creation-relation" is better understood as God being present *to* creation in commitment and free delight than as God being within creation as one entity *among* many, or as God being present *in between* or even "within" creatures.

Canonical Wisdom's background creation theology becomes explicit in few places. Two key passages are Proverbs 3:19, 20 and 8:22–31. They are narrative in form in only the most minimal sense of the word: They are in the past tense; they tell of something that happened; but they tell no extended story about it. Wisdom's creation theology involves no story explaining the process through which creation emerges; rather, it conveys some characteristics of God's active creating.

In Proverbs 3:20, creation happens abruptly. It erupts: the deeps broke open; the clouds drop dew. Indeed, active eruption will turn out to be characteristic of each of the three types of relation God has with creatures (creator-of, eschatological-consummator-of, redeemer-of).

In Proverbs 3:19, we learn that God does this "by wisdom." Then in 8:22–31 wisdom is personified as Woman Wisdom. She is the "first of his acts of long ago" (8:22). God's relation to her, the first of the creatures (through whom the rest are created? Cf. 3:19) is extraordinarily intimate. Wisdom personified is not God. For that reason, Woman Wisdom cannot simply be identified either with the second or with the third person of the trinity. Rather, Woman Wisdom stands in for creation, and God's relation to her is paradigmatic of the way God actively relates to creation as its creator.

In God's creating, Woman Wisdom "was beside him, like a master worker" (8:30a). The original is obscure enough that what is translated "master worker" might instead be translated "little child." In either case this is an intimate relationship: "and I was daily his delight, rejoicing before him always" (8:30b). On God's side we may call this intimate relation "love" but only so long as it is clear that in this instance that theologically smooth-worn word means neither *eros* as "needy love" nor *philia* as "love between equals" nor *agape* as "self-giving love." Rather, it is an intense, delighted, fair-minded attention to another in her particularity and otherness.

This type of love is a self-determined self-commitment by the lover to the beloved. As radically creative, such a love relation is best likened to a social institution embracing several parties and constituted by the dynamics and logic of giving and receiving gifts.

On one side is God's self-commitment to creatures. In creating, God is self-committed to the being and well-being of creatures precisely as ontologically other than God. That self-commitment is radically free. What is created does not obtain prior to or apart from God's relating to it in creative love. Hence it is in no position to earn or to exact this active relating from God. God's active relating has the status of a free giving, and what God creates has the status of a gift, precisely because it is the effect of an act of unexacted and unearned love. What God creates in affectionate and just attention, God values. What God values, God is self-committed to sustain and nurture. God keeps such commitments, not because having created them, God owes it to creatures to keep faith with them, but more basically because God is self-consistently faithful in loving, first to Godself and then to the beloved. That is, God is utterly trustworthy in God's self-determining self-commitments to creatures.

On the other side of this analogue to a social institution are creatures, including living creatures. They are receivers of the gift of themselves as concretely actual. This is a very peculiar type of giving and receiving. God's act of giving does not presuppose the prior actuality of the recipients of the gift. They do not chronologically or ontologically exist first so that God can then, second, give to them their concrete actuality. Rather, God's very act of giving creates them. Thus is God "to" the creation—that is, to the entire proximate context into which we are born and of which we are inextricable parts.

Finally, this relation is one that obtains solely at the Creator's free initiative. Canonical Wisdom's implicit theology of creation generally assumes that the Creator is radically free in relation to creatures, so free as to be elusive. The author of Ecclesiastes is particularly concerned to stress how difficult it is to discern where in the world God might be active, let alone discern just what God might be doing there. Similarly, Job's most powerful speeches acknowledge and lament that God's elusiveness makes it impossible for Job to have a showdown with God about the injustice he has suffered. God's creativity cannot be exacted from God. God remains creative at God's free initiative. Furthermore, lacking any genetic explanation of the origin of the world, canonical Wisdom literature has nothing like the suggestion in Genesis 1:1 that God's creativity was constrained to work with a chaos that was somehow already there. Wisdom's creation theology assumes that God's creating is radically free, neither exacted from the Creator nor constrained in the doing of it by any reality other than God. Nor do we find in canonical Wisdom literature any suggestion that, having entered into an ontologically intimate and self-committed relation with creation, the Creator has somehow lost freedom of initiative in creating. To the contrary, both Ecclesiastes and Job, pressing the boundaries of conventional Wisdom in different ways while remaining within them, stress the continuing freedom of the Creator in relation to the creation. Indeed, the very act of entering into such an ontologically intimate relation with reality other than God seems to be an exercise of the Creator's radical freedom of initiative. This is concretely how God goes about creating: a delighted, attentive freedom vis à vis creation, and a free delighting in creation.

In this delighted freedom and free delighting, God is hospitably generous, giving reality other than God time and space to be itself, genuinely other than God. Indeed, its otherness is the necessary condition of there being anything besides God for God to love freely and in delight.

When we hear the narrative accounts of God's creating in Genesis 1 and 2 against the background of canonical Wisdom's theology of creation, certain features may be foregrounded because they resonate with Wisdom. The relation between Creator and creation is marked by the same combination of freedom and intimacy. In Genesis 1:1–2:4a the Priestly editor (hereafter, P) has God talk the world into existence, and it erupts into being. On the one hand, God's creative word is utterly free and incomprehensible. In *Creation*, Claus Westermann (1974) points out that P, who insists throughout the Pentateuch that "all events have their origin in God's commanding word," underscores simultaneously the incomprehensibility and the total unconstrainedness of creation (42; cf. 115) by using the same locution ("talking reality into being") in regard to creation, without reference to preexisting matter or to any other addressee of the "word."

Furthermore, by preserving creation stories that rely on other characterizations of God's creative relating besides that it occurs "through God's word," P makes clear that the creation stories do not aim to give a single, definitive explanation of how creation happened. Rather, they simply affirm that God does create and that that divine creativity is the context in which fragile creatures, especially human creatures, live (5, 6, 11, 14).

Moreover, in the creation stories of Genesis, as in canonical Wisdom literature's creation theology, the Creator is pictured as immediately and intimately attentive to the well-being of creation. The Creator repeatedly declares the creation "good." Creation is "good" in the sense that it is good for the purposes to which the Creator is self-committed in creating. Creation is also "good" in the sense that it is beautiful. However, it is not beautiful as an object of disengaged contemplation. Rather, it is beautiful in the sense that it is experienced as reflecting the glory of the Creator when we engage it in its sublime splendor (61, 63). It is not "pretty," but it is in a certain way beautiful, perhaps more, in the sense of the "sublime."

In addition, in Genesis the Creator blesses animal creatures. Westermann stresses that "blessing" is a condition, a state of creatures, not an event. In blessing, God bestows life, growth, the power of fertility. In all this, the Creator is self-committed to animal creatures' well-being in their kinds across the generations (24, 46). Indeed, as Westermann reads the theological structure of Genesis in the context of its role in the Pentateuch as a whole, the specific role of Genesis 1:1–2:4 is the same as the whole of Genesis: to witness, not to how God creates and how creatures came to be, but to the fact that God relates to creatures in "blessing."

Beginning with Exodus, the rest of the Pentateuch mostly witnesses to God relating to humankind to deliver humankind from evil. In *Blessing*, Westermann (1978) stresses the difference and interrelatedness of these two ways in which God relates to creatures. Deliverance is episodic. It is told in stories of God acting to rescue, redeem, and liberate. It "is experienced in events that represent God's intervention. Blessing," on the other hand, "is a continuing activity of God that is either present or not present. It cannot be experienced in an event any more than can growth or motivation or decline of strength" (4). In the Pentateuch, the way in which God relates in delivering is understood to be so different from the way in which God relates in blessing that different types of verbs are characteristically used for each. God is said to "come" in epiphanies to deliver, but to be "present" in theophanies (i.e., present in theophanies *to* creatures) to bless (8–9). It is clear that it is the same God who relates in both ways. It is also clear that God relating to deliver presupposes God relating to bless. Only that which perdures, changes, and grows across time by God's relating to it in blessing is "there" to be liberated by God relating to it in deliverance. At the same time, neither of these two ways in which God relates may be construed as a mode of the other. In particular, Westermann insists, the Genesis account of God relating in creative blessing is misconstrued when it is taken, as von Rad does, to be simply the first moment in "salvation history" (10)—that is, in the history of God's events of deliverance. Thus, in the Pentateuch there is a "coexistence of God's two ways of dealing with his people" (6).

In these respects, while it lacks the note of delight, the creation story of Genesis resonates with Wisdom's picture that the Creator relates to creation at once in radical freedom and in self-committed ontological intimacy in a certain type of love, all of which is expressed in a rhetoric of "address."

Spirit, Son, and Wisdom

Our overall project in this section is to let Wisdom's creation theology guide our exploration of anthropological implications of God's relating to us as our creator. That immediately poses an apparent problem. Our project assumes a Trinitarian understanding of God according to which the triune God creates in the *taxis* "the Father creates through the Son in the power of the Holy Spirit." However, read in its canonical context, Wisdom's creation theology's references to the "Lord" may be understood to refer to YHWH even though YHWH is probably never named in canonical Wisdom texts. Just how do such references to YHWH relate to the Trinitarian formula?

It is God who creates. "YHWH" is the principal, though not the only, way in which Old Testament texts name God. Like a personal proper name, YHWH functions denotatively as a placeholder. By itself it connotes nothing about God. Trinitarian doctrines of God, on the other hand, offer identity descriptions of the same God based on christological grounds. Hence, the Christian theological claim is that God, called by the name "YHWH" in the Old Testament, and who is triune, creates. The description of God as "triune" conceptually entails certain characterizations of the way the Creator actively relates to creation. However, they are relatively abstract characterizations. When our discussion of the Creator's relating to creation is guided by Wisdom's creation theology, that abstractness can be filled in somewhat more concretely.

We can see more clearly how Wisdom's creation theology bears on a Trinitarian understanding of the Creator's relating to creation if we take the classical Trinitarian formula phrase by phrase.

The Father creates. This phrase gets its force entirely from its Trinitarian context and is not open to any direct nuancing by Wisdom's creation theology. Classically, the Trinitarian formula tells of the triune God's creating in a certain pattern: It is the "Father" who creates through the "Son" in the power of the "Spirit." It is not that the "Father" creates as YHWH, or instead of or on behalf of the triune God. Rather, it is the triune God who creates. However, God creates by actively relating in a certain way that is told most aptly in a particular quasi-narrative pattern: the Father creates through the Son in the power of the Holy Spirit.

What is conveyed by focusing the formula on the Father? In the context of a Trinitarian understanding of God, it stresses that the One who creates is intrinsically productive of divine reality constituted by an intimate communion of freely given reciprocal love among the three who are genuinely "other" to one another (Father to Son and Son to Father; each to Spirit and Spirit to each). Now, creatures are even more radically "other" than the Creator than the triune persons are "other" to one another. This is a difference in type of "otherness," not a difference in degree of "otherness": creatures are not divine, not God; the three persons are divine, are God. Accordingly, the triune God's creative relating to reality other than God is necessarily also characterized as a radically free productivity of reality to which the triune God is at once wholly other and yet to which God is also utterly intimate, more inward to the creature in regard to its sheer being than the creature can be to itself.

Indeed, the two points are dialectically related: A necessary condition of communion in radically free reciprocal love is that the depth of intimacy correlates directly, not indirectly, with the depth of the otherness. The more the genuine otherness, the deeper the possible intimacy; the deeper the intimacy, the more the otherness of the other is acknowledged, respected, and fostered.

Part of what is expressed by focusing the Trinitarian formula on "the Father" in regard to God's specifically *creative* relating to all else ("the Father creates through the Son in the power of the Holy Spirit") is a claim about God's relating creatively to all else, not a claim about either human knowledge of God's relating or human experience of God's relating. The claim is this: It is neither alien to God's reality nor extrinsic to God's reality that God relates creatively to reality other than God in such a way that their genuine "otherness" to one another and their intimacy to one another are dialectically interdependent. Some non-Trinitarian theisms characterize God's relation to reality other than God as its productive ground or source in such a way that God's otherness to all else and intimacy to all else are inversely related. Consequently either (or both) a relation of intimacy to reality produced by God's grounding or sourcing it, or a relation of otherness, is alien—that is, ontologically impossible, given God's own reality. Other non-Trinitarian theisms characterize God's creative or productive relation to reality other than God in such a way that, while it is not alien to God's reality, it is extrinsic to God's reality. On such views, while reality other than God may be created by or grounded in God, the specific character of the relation created by (or grounded by) God—namely, the dialectic of the dynamic between otherness and intimacy sketched above—is not itself grounded in the reality of God. However, when God is understood in a Trinitarian way, the character of God's creative relating is neither alien nor extrinsic to God's reality. The triune God's own reality as a life constituted by the dynamic of a self-giving that is productive of the genuinely-other-in-communion is itself the condition of the possibility of God's relating creatively to reality that is at once other than God (in a different mode of otherness) and in intimate communion. That is to claim that the character of the triune God's creative relating is universally grounded in the triune God's reality; it obviously is not a claim that only those who understand God in a Trinitarian way are related to creatively by God in this way.

"The triune Creator actively relates to creation," the Father through the Son in the power of the Spirit. "To" is perhaps the least misleading preposition to use to characterize God's active relating as Creator, but it is very abstract. There are many ways in which one reality can be "to" another. As the metaphor "Father" suggests, this is in some way a relation productive of reality, including ours.

There is a strong temptation to identify some analogue that will explain, or at least illuminate the dynamics, of this productivity by likening it, for example, to birthing or causing. However, the insuperable obstacle to likening God's creating the world to a mother's giving birth to a child is that like always gives birth to like: spaniels to spaniels and humans to humans. But the whole point of the idea of God actively creating is that what God creates is neither infinite nor divine but finite and secular. By contrast, the dynamism that constitutes the life of the triune God is best characterized as the Divine's production of the Divine. That is the only thing that even marginally commends biological birth as an analogue for God's life: "The Father eternally begets the Son."

To liken the relation between Creator and creatures to the relation between a cause and its effect is also problematic. Unlike birthing, causes are not necessarily productive of their like as effects. However, the concepts of cause and effect commonly employed in the modern world presuppose that causes and effects are events sharing a larger common context or field within which they are related to each other. Indeed, it is by reference to general regularities of that common field (the "laws of nature") that the relation between any given cause and its effects is explained. But the concept of God rules out the thought that Creator God and creatures share a larger common field embracing them both. Such a thought subordinates God to a reality greater than and more basic than God—namely, the context or field God as cause is supposed to share with creatures as effects. However, if one claims that there is a relation between two terms, it is one thing to describe the relation one is claiming obtains between them, characterizing it in the most accurate way one can; it is another thing to attempt to explain how the relation comes to be and, if it is a dynamic relation, how its dynamics work. In the case of the triune God's creative relation to all that is not God, it seems theologically wisest, in line with Wisdom creation theology's indifference to such topics, to rule out every effort to explain causally the dynamics of divine productivity of reality other than God and to attend instead to characterizing the ongoing relation that obtains between the Creator and creatures.

By focusing on metaphors associated with "Father," the Trinitarian creation formula, "The Father creates through the Son in the power of the Spirit," implies a first approximation of such a characterization: the triune God is freely present to reality other than God in such a way as at once unexactedly and unconstrainedly to constitute, sustain, and respect this reality's genuine otherness to God and, in a certain type of love, to be self-committed to an intimate communion with it for its ongoing being and well-being.

In the power of the Holy Spirit. What is conveyed by claiming that the triune God creates in the power specifically of the Spirit? Wisdom's creation theology does help give this somewhat more concrete content.

In classically Trinitarian doctrines of God, the Spirit is characterized as the Lord and giver of life. Hence, the phrase "in the power of the Holy Spirit" serves to specify further the relation between the triune God as Creator and God's creatures. The triune God is intimately present to living creatures in blessing as the source of their ongoing liveliness.

"Lord and giver of life" resonates with an important trope used in Wisdom's creation theology: Wisdom personified as a woman is characterized as life-giving, indeed as a "tree of life." She is the prime analogy for how God relates to creatures. As we have noted, Wisdom personified is not God. She is not to be identified with the Holy Spirit. Rather, she is a creature paradigmatic of the triune Creator's way of relating to all creatures. In Proverbs, Woman Wisdom makes human creatures wise in their creaturely contexts for their own well-being. She is an emblem of the aspect of creation the Creator uses for our well-being as human persons: creation's call to us, creation's placing us in a vocation to be wise in our actions for the well-being of our fellow creatures.

What matters is the manner in which Woman Wisdom makes human persons wise. Wisdom has power. But it is power understood in a particular way. In canonical Wisdom as well as in wisdom literature internationally in the ancient Near East, wisdom is conveyed by sentences cast in a limited number of stereotyped literary forms. However, what is theologically important is not the form of these sentences or their content but their force. They have pedagogical force; more exactly, they have evocative force. They most powerfully evoke wisdom in a student, not as written sayings, but as used orally (see the fuller discussion of this concept in chapter 5B). Canonical Wisdom literature preserves written sayings which, when used *viva voce*, teach wisdom, not by communicating information about wisdom, nor by communicating wise thoughts, but by evoking wisdom in students, making them wise themselves. This making is noncoercive and nonviolent. It does not involve violation of the creaturely integrity of the student. That is the sort of power Woman Wisdom exercises. As such, she is the emblem of how God relates to human persons in and through their creaturely context: giving life and well-being by calling, inviting, and evoking wisdom in us in ways that do not violate our integrity as human creatures.

If we let canonical Wisdom's trope of Woman Wisdom guide our account of the triune God's active relating to us as our creator, then we may characterize that relation more concretely. In creating, the triune God is present to us in the power of the Spirit, where "power" is understood as Wisdom's power. God is present to us not only in community that constitutes our being. God is also present to us in intimate community that constitutes our well-being in ways that respect the integrity of our otherness to God as human creatures.

Through the Son. What is conveyed by specifying that the triune God creates "through the Son"? Since the fourth century, doctrines of creation have interpreted "Son" by "Logos" and have interpreted "Logos" in Hellenistic philosophical fashion as a cosmological principle, the rational structure of God's mind. Hence, in classical Western doctrines of the Trinity, the expression "The Father creates through the Son" entailed, above all, that what the triune God creates is a cosmos given order in a Hellenistic cosmological sense of the term "order."

This is an order inherent in God's way of relating creatively to reality other than God because it is the order ascribed in a Hellenistic conceptual framework to God's own mind. It is exhibited in regularities in the interactions among creatures and the interactions among the several organs in each living creature. The orderliness of those regularities reflects the rational orderedness of God's active relating to creatures as their creator.

There are several features of this cosmological sense of "order" that have, as I argue in chapter 5A, problematic implications for the proximate contexts into which we are born. The "law of nature" reflecting the eternal rational structure of God's mind is an order that is static, unchanging, and unchangeable. Second, it is a teleological order. It is an order grounded in the end or telos for which each kind of creature was created. For example, the sun was created to the end that it give other creatures important conditions for life, such as light and warmth, and realizing that end simply is its actualization. As another example, human sexuality was created to the end that children be conceived and born, and sexual activity is truly actualized only when that end is realized. Or: The social institution of civil authority was created to the end that there be social order, security, and justice, and human communities are truly actualized only when that end is realized. Thus, the order of creation must be understood in terms of the defining end of each kind of creature. Third, these ends are themselves related to one another hierarchically. The realization of some ends is ordered to, and is thus in the service of, the realization of ends higher in the hierarchy. Since the order is static, the hierarchy of ends is also static. Most creatures, organic and inorganic, necessarily exhibit this order. Human and angelic creatures possessed of free will may act in violation of some features of this order and, violating the law of nature, fail to be fully actualized. If "Logos" signifies this sort of order, then what God creates "through the Son," who is the Logos, is a fundamentally static order.

Wisdom creation theology's tropes of Woman Wisdom evoking wisdom through the evocative force of wise "sayings" suggest an alternative interpretation of the Johannine Logos that brings with it a rather different understanding of "order" in the Creator's active relating to creation. The idea that "Logos" is better interpreted in terms of the Woman Wisdom of Proverbs than in terms of Hellenistic philosophical doctrines of a divine Logos is not new. As Jaroslav Pelikan points out,

> If we concentrate on the entire body of Christian literature rather than on the apologetic corpus [through the first three centuries AD], it becomes evident that the basis for the fullest statement of the Christian doctrine of the divine in Christ as Logos was provided not by its obvious documentation in John 1:1–14 but by Proverbs 8:22–31 (LXX)—which may, for that matter, have been more prominent in the background of the Johannine prologue than theologians have recognized. (1993, 186)

The proposal is not that Proverbs 8:22–31 should replace John 1:1–14 as the basis for an understanding of Jesus Christ as "Son of God," nor that the Johannine Logos be identified with the personified Wisdom of Proverbs. Instead, the proposal is that the Johannine passage itself is better interpreted in light of Proverbs rather than in light of Hellenistic philosophical categories.

We can show this by first attending to Wisdom's tropes for "saying" and "teaching." In its creation theology Proverbs uses Wisdom's conventions about teaching wisdom as a metaphor for God's creating: "The LORD by wisdom founded the earth" (3:19a). That does not mean, "The LORD founded the earth by relying on divine wisdom." Rather, canonical Wisdom is using conventions we have already noted about the pedagogical and evocative force of wise sayings as tropes for God's creating: the Lord evokes creation into being by speaking, using Wisdom's evocative discourse. As teacher is to student through speaking wisdom, so God is to creation through speaking wisdom—except for this major dis-analogy: Whereas the student is already there in front of the teacher, creation is actually constituted by God's act of speaking wisdom. (These claims about canonical Wisdom are warranted in more detail in chapter 5B.)

The metaphor in Proverbs for God's creative relating resonates with the account in Genesis 1:1–2:3 of God creating by speaking: "And God said, 'Let there be . . .'" Together, the accounts of God's creative relating in Proverbs and in Genesis might suggest that the most apt analogue for God's creative relating is the novelist creating a world as she at least subvocalizes sitting in front of her computer. However, this analogy obviously does not provide either a scientific or a metaphysical causal explanation of God's creativity of reality other than God. The Proverbs metaphor of God evoking the world into being as the teacher of wisdom evokes wisdom into being in the student does, however, suggest a claim about reality other than God: that God relates creatively "through Wisdom" means that reality other than God is sufficiently orderly to be a reliable context in which living creatures can adapt themselves to it, sustain themselves in it, and make their way toward enhanced well-being.

According to Roland E. Murphy, although Wisdom literature is "bent on discovering order, or orders, in the realm of experience and nature" (1990, 115), still the "orderly Greek *kosmos* (for which there is, in Hebrew, no exact word equivalent) was not the world in which Israel lived" (116), least of all the authors of canonical Wisdom literature. Murphy locates the difference in the fact that the authors of Wisdom literature did not ask the question, "What is the basis of the order into which we seek insight?" and, therefore, do not even imply the answer, "It is based on a universal and exceptionless structure undergirding reality," let alone the answer, "It is based on the universal and exceptionless structure of creaturely reality."

Instead, the writers of Wisdom literature sought to cultivate the capacity to discern order ad hoc in ordinary experience, both order in the relations between natural events and order in the relation between the moral quality of human actions and their consequences, and both in the context of their creation theology. Insofar as the Creator is free of the creatures and, in hospitable generosity, gives them space and time to be themselves, they "recognized a certain autonomy . . . in the actions and experiences of the world" (Murphy 1990, 115). Insofar as the Creator is intimately related to the creatures in delight and self-determined commitment to their well-being, Wisdom literature recognizes the Lord at work rewarding and punishing in accord with the moral quality of human actions. When such order is discerned it is localized, ad hoc, and patchy. It is formulated in rules of thumb or in "on balance" generalizations rather than in universal and exceptionless rules. The point of learning to discern such order is not to know the structure of reality but to become wise in one's actions for general well-being. The capacity to act in that way is more like *phronesis* than like *theoria*.

Now let canonical Wisdom creation-theology's metaphors for God's evocative speaking, rather than Hellenistic cosmological theories, guide our understanding of "Logos." The point is not that the fact that canonical Wisdom seeks a different sort of order in the world shows that Hellenistic philosophies were misguided in searching for cosmic order as they conceived it. Rather, this is an exegetical point: if what "logos" connotes in John 1 is governed by roots in and allusions to Proverbs 8, then the implications of characterizing God the Son as the eternal Logos need to be worked out in ways governed by canonical Wisdom's understanding of order. Canonical Wisdom literature assumes that the Wisdom through which God creates is the basis of such order as there is in creation. Therefore, construe "Logos" as Wisdom-discourse through which "the Father" talks the world into being—God actively speaking wisely to evoke a wise creation into being—and construe the "Logos" as God's call through that creation to human creatures to be wise in their actions for the well-being of creation. This is the way in which canonical Wisdom implicitly uses the rhetoric of address to characterize God's creativity, resonating with explicit use of parallel rhetoric in the creation stories of Genesis.

The Creator's Transcendence and Immanence

Actively creating us, the triune God is generously hospitable, present to us at once in freedom from us that gives us time and space to be ourselves, genuinely other than God, and in intimate delight in us, self-committed to our well-being in orderly proximate contexts.

This description challenges a conventional theological way of posing a question of the Creator's relation to creation: Is the Creator transcendent of creation, or is the Creator immanent in creation? There is a kind of logic governing conventional use of "transcendence" and "immanence" that tends to demand a choice: either the Creator is "transcendent," or the Creator is "immanent" in creation.

If one stresses God's immanence, one seems driven to think of reality as a single continuum embracing both creatures and Creator. In that framework, divinity may be thought of as one type of reality among many, a type shared perhaps with rational souls, the world soul, and sundry gods—as happens in classical Greek and Roman religion and related philosophical movements. As one mode of reality among many, God is in some ways as dependent on the others as they are on God. Or God may be thought as the fundamental principle of order and intelligibility, or the principle of change, or the principle of creativity, for the entire continuum of reality. But then God is as ontologically dependent on reality as a whole as it is on God. For then, in order to be actual, God ontologically requires some world of which to be the principle of order, change, or creativity. In both cases God's transcendence, and with it God's radical freedom in creativity, is compromised.

On the other hand, if one stresses God's transcendence, then one seems driven to think of reality as a vertical hierarchy of levels or types of being arranged in something like a pyramid, with God at the apex ("the Supreme Being") and all types of creaturely reality ranged across the degrees of being below God, from those most like God at the top to those least like God at the bottom of the pyramid. Here the Creator's transcendence is characterized by drawing contrasts with creaturely reality: In various ways all creatures are mutable, but God is immutable; in various ways creatures are limited, but God is limitless; creatures are produced or generated, but God is ingenerate; creatures are differentiated and complex, but God is simple; and so on. But then God cannot be said to be immediately and intimately related to every creature. At most, God is intimately related only to the level of creature most like God, and can be related to levels of reality further down the pyramidal hierarchy only indirectly through the mediation of the intervening levels of creatures. In that case, God's intimacy as One attentively delighting in creatures is compromised. Indeed, in this framework, the more one stresses the contrast between Creator and creature to underscore the Creator's transcendence, the smaller the scope of the Creator's direct involvement with creatures. When this conventional transcendence/immanence conceptual scheme is used, the Creator's transcendence of and immanence to creatures are inversely related, and stressing either inescapably involves compromising the other (see Tanner 1988; Placher 1996).

By contrast, the rhetoric employed in canonical Wisdom's creation theology challenges Christian reliance on this entire conceptual scheme. Kathryn Tanner (1988, esp. 37–48) has pointed out that it is possible to avoid the misleading constraints of conventional usage of transcendence and immanence by radicalizing both concepts. This can be done by following two rules. The two rules in fact generalize the pattern in which Proverbs 8 characterizes the Creator's ongoing active relating to creation:

1. Avoid talk of God the Creator as either identical with creation or simply contrasted to creation. Speak of God's transcendence in ways that go beyond identity and opposition with the non-Divine. Thus, we may use "freedom of initiative" (in creating) and "delight in creation" as metaphors from which we may abstract concepts, respectively, of transcendence and of immanence whose meanings do not rely on contrasting "opposition" with creation" to "identity with creation," or vice versa.

2. Avoid all suggestions of limitation in scope or manner of God's creativity. Speak of God's creativity as immediate and universally extensive. This does not rule out, of course, that God may also relate to creatures in mediated ways. It only rules out the claim that God must relate in mediated ways to certain levels or types of reality. Thus, "freedom of initiative" (in creating) and "delight in creation" may serve as metaphors from which we may draw, respectively, concepts of transcendence and of immanence whose meanings stress God's creativity as immediate and universally extensive and avoid all suggestions of limitation in scope or manner.

How shall we characterize the triune Creator's active relating to creation? As a free relating that in attentive delight constitutes creatures in being, each and all—as a delighting in each and all, a delighting in which God commits Godself to creation and its well-being in orderly proximate contexts. This is the ultimate context into which we are born: God's hospitable generosity, creatively relating, to us, free of creatures in creating and attentively delighting in them in their otherness to God, self-committed to that which is created.

Wisdom thinks resolutely within the framework
of a theology of creation.
WALTHER ZIMMERLI

CHAPTER **4B**

Why Wisdom?
A One-Sided Conversation
with Claus Westermann

Whereas Christian doctrines of creation have traditionally been warranted principally by appeal to Genesis 1:1–2:4, I shall rely in part 1 on canonical Wisdom literature to warrant theological accounts of humankind's contexts and nature as God's creation. Some backing needs to be given for this move.

Exegetical Arguments against Traditional Use of Genesis 1–3
Four exegetical arguments emerge from Claus Westermann's magisterial scholarship on Genesis (1984; 1995; also 1972; 1974; 1978) against traditional uses of Genesis 1–3 to warrant theological anthropological remarks.

1. The first exegetical point concerns the structure and role of Genesis in the overall structure of the Pentateuch. Westermann argues that the "central part of the Pentateuch tells the story of the rescue [it may equally well be termed 'deliverance'] at the Reed sea, Ex. 1–18. This event was the basis of the history of a people" (1984, 2). In Genesis, "The Yahwistic and Priestly syntheses of the Old Testament" relate this event with "an event at the beginning" by relying on preexisting traditions, so that "traditions which preceded Israel and from outside Israel penetrate what Israel has to say about God the creator, Yahweh, the God of Israel" (1984, 1–2; see 174, 121). Westermann's monumental commentary on Genesis aims to show, among other things, that the role of the book as a whole is that of an introduction to the Pentateuch.

Indeed, on this reading, Genesis provides two types of introduction to the Pentateuch's story of God's deliverance event at the Reed Sea. As concentric circles drawn around it, each introduction sets the deliverance story in a larger context, giving it a broader significance. "The relation of each circle to the central part is different. Hence their introductory functions are different" (1984, 2). Telling stories of the Patriarchs, chapters 12–50 "present the history of Israel before it became a people." The "story of the primeval events" in Genesis 1–11, however, places the central deliverance or rescue events in a second and "much wider horizon, extending them to world events in the broadest sense of the word" (1984, p. 2). Genesis 1–11 is a relatively late literary component in "Yah-wistic and Priestly syntheses of the Old Testament" (2), functions differently than the introduction provided by chapters 12–50, and is evidently separable from the rest of the book. "The different functions of these introductory sec-tions become very clear in the confessions of faith which draw together the tra-dition developed in the Pentateuch, Deut 26:5; Josh 24:2–4." There, "the stories of the patriarchs play their introductory role, while there is no mention at all of the primeval events" (2). To avoid confusion, I hereafter refer to the role of Genesis 12–50 as that of an "introduction," and the role of chapters 1–11 as that of a "preface" to the introduction.

Genesis 1–11, then, must be interpreted on its own terms as a relatively self-contained unity. That, in turn, has implications concerning the gist or *scopus* of chapters 1–3. If chapters 1–11 constitute a relatively self-contained unity, then—against all traditional exegetical practice—it is not self-evident that chapters 1–3 are decisive for interpreting the rest of the unit. It is true that chapters 1–3 make use of preexisting traditions about how the world came to be. However, it does not necessarily follow they are used in this context to say how the world, and with it humankind, came to be. It is also clear that these preexisting cosmogonies were theologically "bent" in the process of their use in the context of chapters 1–11. All the same, it is not self-evident that even bent they are used in this context to answer questions about cosmogony—that is, about the genesis of the cosmos. The question of their force or gist in this con-text must be answered by study of the unit of chapters 1–11 taken as a whole, not by a narrow focus on chapters 1–3 as though they were the hermeneutical key to the entire unit.

Whatever their particular force may be, what is already evident is that chap-ters 1–3, as part of the unit 1–11, function as part of a preface to a story about God's event of rescue at the Reed Sea and God's creation there of a people. They are in service to that story. Consequently, Westermann claims, "Biblical reflec-tion on Creation cannot be comprehended under a formula of belief in the same way as reflection on redemption. . . . The creation of the world is not an object of belief, but a presupposition for thought" (1974, 113–114).

His point is not, I take it, that biblical writers who presuppose God's creation of the world do not believe that God created the world. Rather, his point is something like this: Following von Rad's *Old Testament Theology* (1962, 1965), it may be said that at the heart of Old Testament theology lie such confessions of faith as Deuteronomy 26:5–9 and Joshua 24:2–4 that testify to God's deliver-ance at the Reed Sea. God's deliverance *is* an object of faith or belief, an object of existential trust by which a people's identity is formed. God's creating the world is a presupposition of that belief, but is not itself the object of such belief, —that is, faith or existential trust. In the Pentateuch it is not itself confessed in confessions of faith. Hence, if theology is reflection on belief as faith or existen-tial trust, biblical theological reflection on creation cannot properly be said to be reflection on religious belief but only on a presupposition of such belief.

2. Westermann makes a second exegetical point concerning types of writ-ing in Genesis 1–11: "Two different types of writing strike us immediately; we shall call them narrative and numerative. They are almost equal in extent. This is the only place in the Old Testament where genealogies [*i.e.* the numerative

writings] and narratives are put together in such a way. It is this that gives the primeval story its unique character" (1984, 3). Moreover, the numerative writings are formally the most important. They "form the framework of everything that is narrated in Genesis 1–11" (6).

Numerative writings. Westermann argues that the genealogies had their origins among nomad tribes and served as a sign of belonging (1984, 7). More exactly, he claims, their historical origins lie in narratives from which they were abstracted, becoming ever more formal until they survive only as lists of names (10). The genealogies provided, respectively, by Jahwist and Priestly editors of material in Genesis 1–11 have very different literary characteristics. (Hereafter "Jahwist" and "Priestly" are represented by "J" and "P.") The J genealogies are literarily varied and kept close to the narratives; the P genealogies are uniform, monotonous, systematized, and kept far from narratives (see 9–16). However, the P editor's literary spareness is especially effective in preserving the function such genealogies had in their original tribal contexts: to stress "the continuity of successive generations" (7).

The editors of Genesis 1–11 have used preexisting genealogical ways of expressing "the succession of generations as a succession of begettings" (1984, 16), but in the process they have bent what they borrowed in four theologically important ways. In each case, the bending comes under the pressure of a theological conviction about the uniqueness of Israel's God.

The first is this: There are no gods at all in either the numerative or the narrative writings in Genesis 1–11. There is only a unique Creator God who relates immediately to unique creatures (see 1984, 67). The P editor preserves the genealogical form of the cosmogonies being appropriated: Genesis 2:4 sums up the opening creation narrative with the words, "These are the generations of the heavens and the earth when they were created." However, no genealogy is given in which God figures as the first begetter of the heavens and the earth. Rather, the imagery of generation is brought under the control of the imagery of God's creative word as God relates immediately to each natural kind of creature, saying "Let there be . . . " The relation between Creator and creation is thus expressly not one of begetting.

A second way in which received numerative cosmogonies were bent is inseparable from the first. Internationally in the high cultures of the ancient Mediterranean world, cosmogony took the form of theogony, the begetting of the gods who in turn beget human kings. By contrast, while "the form of presentation is preserved" in Genesis 1–11, it draws a "clear line of distinction . . . between creation and the genealogy of the birth of the gods . . . The biblical genealogies describe the history of humankind only . . . ," and generic humans at that, neither gods nor kings (1984, 8). What is generated is utterly desacralized and in no respect divine. Genealogies can only begin after the creation of human creatures.

A third way in which the editors bent older genealogies when they used them concerns the relation between the genealogies in Genesis 1–11 and history. Whereas the Sumerian king-list genealogies, for example, are presented as part of history, the genealogies in the account of primeval history given in Genesis 5 are "on the other side of history" (1984, 9). They are entirely "abstracted from the historical character of the peoples mentioned" (9) and are not to be construed as the genealogies of historical individuals. That is the point, for Westermann, of calling Genesis 1–11 "primeval history." Primeval history is an account, not of the historical events of particular births, but of the necessary precondition of all historical events: The continuity of generations, "of growth, expansion, prosperity and fertility" (17). The force of the genealogies falls on the continuity of generation with generation, not on the historically particular persons who are born. That continuity is not itself an episodic event. It is rather a state of affairs that is, we might say, the proximate context and necessary precondition for any and all genuinely historical events. Of particular importance for the Pentateuch, it is the proximate context and precondition for political history.

The fourth way in which the editors bent the genealogical materials they borrowed is probably the most important for Westermann. The genealogies do not themselves refer to any special action by God. However, the P editor bent these genealogies by relating them "very clearly to the work of God in the blessing and its commission, 'Be fruitful and multiply;' 1.28." God's ongoing creative blessing is, we may say, human creatures' ultimate context. It is the ongoing continuation of God's creative power. Formed by the P editor's hand, what the genealogies describe is the effect of God's creative blessing. So too for the genealogies shaped by the J editor, "though no express blessing is found in his story. The creator made humans with the potentiality to increase their kind; this god-given dynamism is effective in the succession of new births which the genealogies report. It is the blessing that actualizes this potentiality, that makes possible the succession of births" (1984, 17). For textual support, Westermann draws attention to the wordplay involved in the names given to two children in Genesis 4:1 and 25, usually attributed to the J editor: "Now the man knew his wife Eve, and she conceived and bore Cain, saying, 'I have produced a man with the help of the LORD.'" (4:1). In Hebrew, "produced" resembles the word for "Cain." Second: "Adam knew his wife again, and she bore a son and named him Seth, for she said, 'God has appointed for me another child'" (4:25). In Hebrew "appointed" resembles the word for "Seth." Each verse suggests that begetting is the effect of God's creative blessing. In *Blessing*, Westermann takes pains to stress that in both types of numerative writing in Genesis 1–11, God's blessing is understood to be a constant relating to creation (1978, 4–8). As Westermann puts it in *Creation*, this constant relating imbues creation with a "forward-thrusting, ever pregnant power of becoming" (1974, 55).

These four ways in which the editors of the text of Genesis bent the genealogical tropes they borrowed from their host cultures address the question left open in the previous section: if the gist of chapters 1–3 is not to say *how* God creates the world, what is their force? The answer is: the force of the entire unit comprising chapters 1–11 is to characterize the broadest contexts within which the divine acts of deliverance recited in the rest of the Pentateuch are placed. The proximate context of God's acts of deliverance is the continuity of desacralized creaturely life, its "growth, expansion, prosperity and fertility" generation after generation. Its ultimate context is God's immediate relation to that proximate context in creative blessing. Since that is the force of the entire literary unit of Genesis 1–11, it is the force also of its subset, Genesis 1–3.

Narrative writings. According to Westermann, the genealogies of the numerative writings are used in Genesis 1–11 as the framework for narrative writings.

I take that to mean that the function and gist of the genealogies should serve as the hermeneutical lens through which the narratives are interpreted.

Westermann finds three groups of narratives in Genesis 1–11: creation, achievements, and crime and punishment. The groups are closely related to one another, even interwoven, and are closely related to the genealogies. These three types of narrative are found only in the primeval story of chapters 1–11 and not at all in the patriarchal stories of chapters 12–50. Furthermore, the narrative style of 1–11 is basically different from that of 12–50 (see 1984, 18–19). These are literary reasons for insisting that chapters 1–11 are a unit unto itself. They are also grounds for caution about taking the creation stories in Genesis 1–3 to express the point of the entire unit. If instead these narratives are read through the lens of the genealogies and *their* overall thrust, the force of all three classes of narrative taken together concerns the character of "primal time," that is, the character of the proximate and ultimate contexts of the divine acts of deliverance recited in the rest of the Pentateuch.

In their particular contents, these three classes of narratives replicate stories and motifs common to the mythologies of Israel's neighbors and predecessor cultures. The J and P editors of Genesis 1–11 were heirs to an already formed tradition that they adapted and refashioned. "They indicate clearly that their purpose is to pass on something that they have received and that it is not the result but prior to their confession of Yahweh as the savior of Israel" (1984, 64; note the allusion to 1 Cor. 15:3!). The primal histories narrated in the myths of Israel's neighbors were just collections of stories. The major change made by the J and P editors was to form them into one story, linking the primeval period with a history that begins with the call of Abraham (chap. 12) and leads, in turn, into the story in Exodus of God's act of deliverance at the Reed Sea.

In consequence of this editing, the three classes of narratives in Genesis 1–11 point forward as well as back. By being formed as the preface to the introduction (chaps. 12–50) to the Pentateuch, they are bent to refer forward and, in being bent, their force is changed. "What J or P wanted to say to the Israel of their day through this or that story need not necessarily agree with the intention of the story in an earlier Israelite or pre-Israelite form" (1984, 65). This holds for each of the three classes of narratives.

By their editing, the genealogies framing creation stories are ordered to the birth of Abraham, with the force of affirming that the same divine creative blessing which is at work "in the succession of generations leading up to Abraham is also at work in the line which takes its beginning from him." Furthermore, "The line of generations which leads from the birth of Abraham back to human beings who have not been born but have been created puts the birth of Abraham in a context analogous to the history of Israel as it moves from its beginning to its goal" (1984, 66).

By their editing, stories of crime and punishment in primeval history are ordered to the story of God's creation of Israel in the event of deliverance at the Reed Sea. In primeval history, "Sin, guilt and revolt are not the results of a long encounter with God as are the sins of Israel, which are condemned by the prophets. There is a conscious distinction. They belong to human existence as such and are common to all peoples in all places. The story of sin as part of the history of the people of God, as for example in Ex. 32–34, is set deliberately in the broader context of sin, guilt and punishment outside the history of Israel" (1984, 66–67). The same is true of human potential to sin. "The Old Testament," Westermann stresses, although it might be better to say more modestly, "Genesis," given Westermann's subject matter, "does not speak of a fallen creation or of a humankind fallen from grace; rather as it narrates the history of God's dealings with his people it draws attention to the many points in common between what is happening in Israel and what has been said about human sin and revolt at the beginning" (67).

As for stories of achievement, by their editing, such extra-Genesis stories are freed from mythology and oriented to Israel's future history so that what "humans achieved was neither divine nor was it extolled as such. Human endeavor and cultural progress were desacralized in Israel from the very beginning" (1984, 67). To be sure, God's creative blessing alone gives success to human efforts to achieve. However, as it was understood in Israel, "It is the person who is blessed; the person does the work; but human achievements in civilization do not acquire divine origin" (67).

However, even when edited as a preface that points forward to God's creation of Israel at the Reed Sea, these stories also continue to point backward. They point backward, not in the sense of "back in time," but in sense of "to the background." They remain the stories of primeval history, characterizing the proximate and ultimate backgrounds or contexts of historical events of deliverance, but are not themselves accounts of events in history. They continue to "trace back to its source the power which carries on [human] existence from generation to generation," that is, God's creative blessing (1984, 65). And they continue to characterize humankind's proximate context as marked by "sin, guilt, and punishment."

Westermann stresses strongly the important function played in relation to the Pentateuch by this backward thrust of its preface: the universal import of the divine deliverance at the Reed Sea that is the heart and "middle" of the Pentateuch. Genesis 1–11 "shows that God's punishment and forgiveness cannot be restricted to Israel alone, but must extend in some way beyond . . . to the broader horizon of sin and revolt as part of the human condition . . . " God's saving action, which begins in Genesis 12, "is concerned with humanity and the world and must be bound up in some way with the sin and revolt of humankind" (1984, 67).

Already we have strong exegetical reason not to privilege Genesis 1:26–31 and 2:4b–25 as the scriptural warrant and norm for theological anthropological remarks about human beings as creatures. It is just those texts that have figured most prominently in the history of Christian anthropology to warrant claims that human creatures are ensouled material bodies, created such that some particular human capacity or anthropological structure is the image of God, created in a state of original righteousness, and "fallen" from this prior state so that the image of God is damaged, obscured, or destroyed. These texts can be used in this role if they are assumed to be the lens through which Genesis 1–3, taken as a self-contained literary whole, is interpreted. However, that can be done only if Genesis 1–3 is interpreted outside its immediate context in chapters 1–11, and only if chapters 1–11 are, in turn, interpreted without consideration of their role in Genesis as a whole and without consideration of the role of Genesis in the Pentateuch as a whole. Read in that traditional way, Westermann insists, Genesis 1:26–31 and 2:4b–25 suggest that the central anthropological themes focus on one's own existential relation to God, the unnaturalness of death, that work is a curse, and so on, and warrant the individualistic existentialist anthropocentrism of a "creation and fall" anthropology (see 1974, 16). Clearly, Westermann's entire exegetical project on Genesis 1–11 undercuts any such use of Genesis 1–3. That fact alone, however, does not warrant my proposal that Genesis 1–11, including 1–3, ought not to be the Holy Scripture privileged in warranting theological remarks about human beings as creatures.

3. A third exegetical point by Westermann that bears on whether to privilege Genesis 1–3 in warranting anthropological remarks about human beings as creatures concerns translation of relevant Hebrew texts into modern languages. In what we have seen of his interpretation of Genesis 1–11 we have already encountered a distinction he draws between two ways in which the Pentateuch says God relates to humankind: creative blessing and deliverance. Translation of the Hebrew text into English has traditionally rendered "deliverance" as "salvation" (1978, 1) or "redemption" (1974, 115). Westermann argues that this translation is ambiguous and has introduced a systematic ambiguity into Christian theology.

"Salvation" and "redemption" conflate what the Pentateuch distinguishes: An event of divine deliverance (in Greek, *soteria*) and a state of divine creative blessing (in Latin, *salus*). Further, they tend to conflate a distinction between the event of deliverance and the state of having-been-delivered or rescued. "*Soteria* designates an act of deliverance and thus cannot designate a state of having been rescued. This latter meaning is represented in Latin translations by the word *salus*" (1978, 2) (the root of the English word "salvation") and in German by *Heil*. They express a condition, not an act or event. However Luther translated *soteria* as *Heil*, thus running together "event of divine deliverance" and "state of having been delivered." This ambiguity may lie behind long-standing disagreements between Roman Catholic and Protestant theologies about how justification (an event of deliverance?) and sanctification (a state of having been delivered?) are related to each other (see Anderson et al. 1985).

The layers of meaning in *salus* and *Heil* are even more complex. They designate a state or condition rather than an act or event all right, but originally they had nothing to do either with the event of deliverance or the condition of having been delivered. Rather, they expressed the state of being whole, healthy, intact, the state conferred by God's creative blessing rather than by God's event of deliverance. "The Hebrew equivalent for *salus* is not a word which means 'saving'; it is *shalom*, a word which expresses a state of well-being, especially well-being in community" (Westermann 1974, 115–16). These words continue to have that meaning, for example, when used in greetings. It may be that the state of having been delivered is also a state of being whole, healthy, and intact, but they clearly are not necessarily the same states. Theologically speaking, the state of being whole, healthy, and intact might be identified with any of three states: (a) the state human beings are in by God's creative blessing, (b) the state human beings are in "having been delivered" from the consequences of sin, which would be a restoration of their state of well-being by God's creative blessing *if* God's event of deliverance is primarily understood as an event of restoration of their pre-sin state; or (c) the state human beings are in by God's eschatological blessing.

To use such words as "Heil," "salvation," and "redemption" for both event and condition misrepresents the different force of different types of scriptural texts.

> From the beginning to the end of the biblical story, God's two [*sic*!] ways of dealing with mankind—deliverance and blessing—are found together. They cannot be reduced to a single concept because, for one reason, they are experienced differently. Deliverance is experienced in events that represent God's intervention. Blessing is a continuing activity of God that is either present or not present. It cannot be experienced in an event any more than can growth or motivation or a decline of strength. (Westermann 1978, 4)

This is the reason that, while he accepts von Rad's view that confession of faith in God's act of deliverance at the Reed Sea is the "middle" of the Pentateuch's salvation history, Westermann rejects von Rad's characterization of the Genesis creation story as the first event in salvation history. "Salvation history" is a history of events of deliverance centering on the exodus. "Creation" is not an event of the deliverance of anything from anything; it is not an event at all. It is the continuing condition or state of God relating in creative blessing, the condition that constitutes the ultimate and proximate contexts presupposed by any of God's events of deliverance.

4. Westermann makes a fourth exegetical point that bears on the question of the appropriateness of privileging Genesis 1–3 to warrant theological remarks about human beings as creatures when he attends to biblical endings, in addition to biblical beginnings, of salvation history.

He finds brief references to that ending in his exegesis of Genesis 1:1–2:4. Westermann claims that the P editor uses a novel and unique literary structure to integrate internationally shared stories of creation, conflating eight works of creation into six days of creation followed by God's day of rest. Thus the editor "has suggested the coming into existence of our world in successive stages . . . and, with the repose of the seventh day, has pointed to the continuation of this process as it moves towards a goal which transcends the works of Creation" (1974, 41). So too, the phrase "God saw that it was good" means it "corresponds to its goal," which turns out to be "rest on the seventh day" (61). Thus, the "course of human history" "runs to its goal just like the days of the week." And that goal is "the eternal rest which has been suggested in the rest of the seventh day" (65). Here we have a third distinct type of story: in addition to relating to all that is not God in creative blessing and relating to deliver humankind when that is needed, God relates to draw all that is not God to an eschatological blessing. The story of God's creative relating to humankind is told in Genesis in a way that is bent by a different story about deliverance, bent so as to point to an eschatological consummation of deliverance. It must be stressed that although Westermann's analysis argues for a hint of an eschatological allusion in the P editor's ordering of eight moments in the creation story into a sequence of six "days" whose "goal" is a seventh day of "rest," his exegetical analysis does not offer grounds for any particular interpretation of the metaphor of "rest" in the context of canonically edited Genesis. Just what it is "rest" *from*, and whether it necessarily entails cessation of all change and development in finite creatures that are drawn into such eschatological consummation, remains unspecified.

Westermann broadens his discussion of eschatological blessing in *Beginning and End in the Bible*, which deals with the entire Christian canon. The bulk of the Old Testament and of the New Testament may be stories of divine deliverance, but they are bracketed by the account of primeval history in Genesis 1–11, which prefaces them, and by Revelation, which tells of the end time. Where Genesis 1:1–2:4 had subtly pointed to the end time, Revelation does so openly. Westermann extends his characterizations of Genesis 1–11's account of primeval history to Revelation's account of the eschaton. Unlike what falls between, these texts are about a constant condition or state, not about events in history (see 1972, 3–4). If the primeval history of Genesis 1–11 renders God relating to all that is not God in creative blessing (rather than in events of deliverance), perhaps we may say that accounts of end time render God relating in eschatological blessing.

"Primal time and end time belong together and correspond to each other in that they belong beyond historical time. Primal time and end time are not the first and last sections of history; rather they constitute a framework for history in such a way that their essence is different from that of history" (1972, 27). Canonical narratives describing primal time and end time are written or edited in ways that order them to the history of God's acts of deliverance. Together, they express the necessary preconditions for any and all history of all people, including the history of divine acts of deliverance, but without being events in history.

This way of construing the relation has important consequences for interpretation of specifically Christian stories of divine deliverance. The latter, in turn, have several anthropological implications.

First, since the story of Adam in Genesis 1–3 is part of the primeval story of Genesis 1–11, it corresponds "not to Christ" as the decisive event of historical deliverance, as Paul has it in Romans 5, "but to the events of the end, and specifically to what is said about mankind as transformed at the events of the end, as for example, in Isaiah 65 and Revelation 21–22" (1972, 6). Consequently, it would require a misreading of the gist of the story of Adam and Eve in its context in Genesis 1–11 to use it to warrant an anthropological account of the sin and its consequences from which God delivers humankind in Christ.

Second, when the Adam-Revelation correspondence frames Christian stories about deliverance in Christ, the scope of the deliverance God brings in Christ broadens. As long as Adam is correlated with Christ, deliverance through Christ is limited to deliverance from sin and death, as in Romans 6. But when Adam is correlated with Revelation, then the features of the human proximate context from which Christ delivers humankind extends also to "the suffering which results from . . . being a creature" (1972, 7; see Rev. 21:4). Hence, theological anthropology of sin would be not only inappropriately, but inadequately, warranted were it to rely chiefly on Genesis 2:5–3:24.

Note that, if Christian theological anthropology is rooted in implications of ways in which God relates to all else, not only in creative blessing and in events of deliverance from the consequences of sin, but also in eschatological bless-ing, and if it were guided by Westermann's Adam-Revelation typology, rather than by Paul's Christ-Adam typology, it would be clear that the anthropological implications of God relating to deliver humankind from the consequences of sin would not only have to do with human beings' restoration to the state of God's creative blessing which was lost in consequence of their sin, but would have to do with human creatures' participation in a state of eschatological blessing that goes beyond the conditions of their creaturely blessing to remove the suffering to which their creaturely finitude makes them vulnerable. Following Wester-mann's lead here would result in stressing that although they are irreducibly different ways in which God relates to all else, God's relating to "deliver" and God's relating to bless eschatologically are interrelated and inseparable ways of relating that are together irreducible to God relating creatively.

Third, formulation of the eschatological significance of Christ must be guided by interpreting the story of deliverance in Christ through the herme-neutical lens of its brackets in Genesis 1:1–11 and Revelation. Fully "realized eschatologies" and their anthropological implications are ruled out. Wester-mann insists, "We cannot say that Christ is the end of history" in the sense that in him "the last day of judgment has broken in" (1972, 6). This is unequivocally indicated by NT passages expressing expectation of a future day when Christ will come and the day of judgment occur (1974, 6–7). True, although they give very different descriptions of it, in "both Testaments the goal of [deliverance] is existence in a new state, a state of well-being." However, Westermann goes on to say without nuance, "in neither Testament is this state an end" (1974, 34). He does acknowledge all the New Testament texts that "come very close" [!] to describing deliverance through Christ as an eschatological act. As Westermann continues the paragraph it becomes clear that what he wishes to deny is that the condition of the church community and of individual Christians in history have been eschatologically transformed so that they no longer experience sin, death, or suffering. Fully actualized eschatological blessing is not the end of deliverance in Christ here and now. It does not follow, of course, that what is not yet fully actual will therefore never be fully actualized.

On Westermann's reading, the anthropologically important positive thing that stories of primeval time and of end time do by bracketing the history of divine deliverance to which they are ordered is to locate that history in a universal context. Construed in the context of that bracketing, God's acts of deliverance at the Reed Sea and in Jesus Christ must be read to bear on all com-munities, not just that of Israel or the church (see 1972, 35).

Westermann's entire discussion of the correlation of texts about the end time with texts about the primal time suggests that, as prefaced by Genesis 1–11, the Pentateuch tells of three ways in which God "deals with mankind," not just two, "deliverance and blessing." Or, if not three ways, then the way of blessing is itself a complex intertwining of two distinguishable modes of God's relat-ing in blessing: creative blessing (primeval time) and eschatological blessing (end time). By stressing their similarities, he has clearly distinguished the latter two from scriptural accounts of God's deliverance. It was on that basis that he claimed that, according to the Bible, God deals with humankind in two ways: to bless and to deliver.

However, on the basis he himself used to distinguish these two, he ought on his own grounds to distinguish three ways in which God relates to all that is not God. He distinguished between the two on the basis of experience. Deliverance is experienced in events that represent God's intervention, but blessing is a continuing activity of God that can no more be experienced in an event than can growth or decline of strength. Granted that, on the same grounds a distinction may be made between God dealing with humankind to bless creatively and God dealing with humankind to bless eschatologically. If creative blessing can be experienced, although not in an event, it must be experienced as God actively relating here and now. But eschatological blessing by definition cannot be experienced that way. Since it is precisely what does not yet obtain, it can only be hoped for in response to some hints of a promise of it. Perhaps, as Westermann's exegesis of the seven days of creation suggests, it is a promise inherent in and sensed in the here-and-now continuity of generation after generation that constitutes the proximate and ultimate context of all history, including the history of deliverance.

These four exegetical points about Genesis 1:1–11 give reasons for a number of judgments about how not, and why not, to use all or part of Genesis 1–3 to warrant a theological account of human beings as creatures. By themselves, however, they do not yet make a case for completely excluding Genesis 1–3 from that role. Building on Westermann's exegesis of Genesis, the case for that judgment rests on a theological argument.

Theological Reasons for Not Privileging Genesis 1–3

In chapters 2 and 3A, I made a case for the claim that crucial moments in the discovery of a Trinitarian understanding of God have important anthropological implications. In chapters 1B and 3B, I made a case for construing the Bible as canonical Christian Holy Scripture and for construing the unity of that canon in a threefold way insofar as it is read as an account of God and God's three ways of relating to all that is not God. Its upshot for the present discussion is as follows:

A. Biblical texts are Christians' canonical Holy Scriptures for communities of Christian faith that acknowledge that it is by living with just this set of texts, in the power of the Holy Spirit, that Christian communities are called into being and are guided and corrected in their common life so that their communal and individual identities are constituted by their efforts to respond appropriately to that call from God. By definition, therefore, they are under obligation to assess the adequacy of their responses to that call by testing it against canonical Christian Holy Scripture. Insofar as their response includes ways of talking about God, the world, and themselves, that means that they are under obligation to acknowledge Holy Scripture as the authority norming that discourse.

B. For Christians, New Testament stories about Jesus of Nazareth decisively norm what they have to say about who God is. In that sense, Christian theology's access to knowledge of God's identity—that is, who God is—is Christocentric.

C. Analysis of New Testament stories about Jesus' relation to the One he called his Father, and that One's relation to Jesus, yield a Trinitarian understanding of God paradigmatically outlined in the Nicene-Constantinopolitan Creed.

D. Canonical scriptural texts include a wide variety of literary genres. However, stories have priority. Songs, law codes, prophetic visions, exhortations and denunciations, theologically laden moral or cultic advice, and admonition, and so on, all either presuppose some story as their literary and conceptual context or are commentary on some story.

E. Insofar as scriptural stories tell of God actively relating to what is not God, those stories may be ascribed to the triune God as their central character. This is not to claim that any of those texts state or imply a doctrine of the Trinity. But it is to follow well-established precedents of ascribing received stories about God to God as God is understood by those doing the ascribing.

F. There are three types of canonical scriptural stories about God relating to what is not God. They tell of God relating in creative blessing, in eschatological blessing, and to deliver and reconcile those who are alienated in some sort of bondage. They may each and all be ascribed to the triune God as the One who relates in each of these ways.

G. These three types of stories about God relating to what is not God may all be called narratives, but if so it must be acknowledged immediately that they are very different types of narrative. Some, mostly about God relating to deliver and to reconcile, are remarkably realistic. Some, mostly about God drawing to eschatological consummation, are more nearly fantastical narratives. Some, mostly about God creating, are hardly narrative at all, so few events happen.

H. If Holy Scripture is to guide and norm theological remarks about God's ways of relating to what is not God, the distinctive literary features of each of these types of narrative must guide and norm how each way the triune God relates is characterized.

I. The three ways in which the triune God relates cannot be collapsed into one another and are themselves interrelated in definite ways. Stories both about God relating to draw to eschatological consummation and about God relating to deliver and reconcile presuppose stories about God relating to create. Stories about God relating to deliver and to reconcile presuppose stories about why creatures need to be delivered and reconciled, but neither stories about God creating nor stories about God drawing to eschatological consummation do. Stories about God delivering and reconciling generally presuppose stories about God drawing to eschatological consummation, but the converse does not hold.

J. What gives Holy Scripture the wholeness it requires to serve as canon guiding and norming Christian remarks about God relating to what is not God, then, cannot be that it is literarily one long narrative with a beginning, middle, and end. Rather, what makes it the requisite whole is the complex of these three types of narratives about God relating to what is not God interwoven in just the pattern sketched above of asymmetrical dependence and independence of one another.

There is a major consequence of this way of construing the Bible as canonical Holy Scripture when it serves as authoritative guide and norm for theological remarks about human beings in light of God relating to them particularly in creative blessing: what should guide and norm such remarks are scriptural stories about God relating creatively to what is not God, not stories about God relating in either of the other two ways.

Westermann's exegesis does not just show why Genesis 1–3 ought not to be used as it traditionally has been to warrant theological remarks about God relating creatively in general and to humankind in particular. It also shows that the force of Genesis 1–11 as a whole is ordered to the Pentateuch's story of God's event of deliverance. That ordering bends the narrative logic of its creation story under the pressure of the narrative logic of the deliverance story. That is as it should be for a story serving as the preface to the deliverance story.

However, given the irreducibility of the three ways in which God relates to what is not God and the distinctive literary features of the scriptural stories that tell of each of these three ways in which God relates, a theological account of God relating creatively ought to be guided and warranted by the distinctive literary features of creation stories whose narrative logic is their own, and is not bent under the pressure of the narrative logic of another class of stories about God relating to what is not God. Westermann gives us reason to conclude that Genesis 1–3 does not provide such a creation story. Thus, the combination of my theological remarks about Christian Holy Scripture's canonicity and Westermann's Genesis scholarship warrant the conclusion that Genesis 1–3 ought not to be privileged as the canonical guide and norm for a theology of human creatureliness.

Reasons to Privilege Canonical Wisdom Literature

I propose privileging canonical Wisdom literature when scripturally warranting Christian theological remarks about God relating creatively to all that is not God because of two theologically important features of these texts:

1. In Walther Zimmerli's frequently quoted judgment, "Wisdom thinks resolutely within the framework of a theology of creation" (1976b, 316).

2. Canonical Wisdom literature makes no reference to the history of God's acts of deliverance or to God's self-disclosure in mighty acts in history, both of which are central themes in most of the rest of the Old Testament, and hardly any reference either to law or to cultic worship (see Zimmerli 1976b, 315). Unlike Genesis 1–3, its account of God relating creatively is not ordered to an account of God's mighty acts of deliverance and is not bent by the narrative logic of the accounts of God's acts of deliverance to which it is ordered.

By "canonical Wisdom literature," I mean those texts acknowledged as canonical by Roman Catholic and Protestant Christians: Proverbs, Ecclesiastes, Song of Solomon, and Job. As I read the texts, Proverbs conveys what we may call the conventions of mainstream Wisdom tradition as it thinks within the framework of a theology of creation. Song of Songs, Ecclesiastes, and Job may be read against the background of those conventions, but Ecclesiastes and Job press hard in different directions against those conventions. Expressly adopting Wisdom tradition's way of understanding all things in reference to God as their Creator, Job presses the conventions of the Wisdom tradition to see whether they can accommodate the notion of a person whose faith in God as Creator is an utterly disinterested faith. Explicitly adopting mainstream Wisdom's conventions, Ecclesiastes presses the tradition to see whether it can accommodate the view that everyday life lacks the sort of meaning that comes from a transcendentally overarching purpose or *telos*.

Of course, the texts in canonical Wisdom teach no dogmatic formulation about creation. The reality of God and "God is the creator of all that is not God" are expressly affirmed in only a few places in Proverbs and in Job. Generally, canonical Wisdom literature raises questions and makes affirmations that are urgent only if one does already live in trust in God the Creator. This trust in God is not yet itself a theology of creation. However, one cannot trust in God as Creator, nor can one frame either questions or affirmations about the upshot of such trust, without some concepts of God as Creator and some beliefs about God as Creator. Those concepts and (largely tacit) beliefs are at least the kernel of a theology of creation.

Furthermore, the texts that make up canonical Wisdom do not raise the same questions and do not necessarily make or assume exactly the same affirmations about creation. Brevard Childs nuances Zimmerli's judgment by noting that the variations within canonical Wisdom literature are all "a move to *expand* different aspects of wisdom through theological reflection within basically a creation theology" (1992, 189, emphasis added). The texts in canonical Wisdom may all think within the "framework of a theology of creation," but the framework turns out to be remarkably flexible, and different texts push its boundaries in various directions.

Abstracted from their canonical context as parts of Wisdom's voice in the canon, the trajectories of these ways of pressing the conventions of the mainstream scriptural Wisdom tradition obviously could go in a great many directions, some of them entirely subversive of mainstream Wisdom and of the canon's wholeness. My project is to try to hear them within the larger polyphony of canonical Scripture and to attend to what they imply about human beings as God's creatures. However, doing so must assume that these texts have indeed been canonically edited both as wholes themselves and as voices within the whole of the canon's polyphony.

Chapter 5B reviews the evidence for such editing of Proverbs. Similar reviews of other canonical Wisdom texts come in subsequent chapters. In none of these reviews do I say anything original. I have sought to learn from colleagues who focus their scholarly work on the study of the Old Testament. Presupposing the theological validity of the general case, I argued for a canonical construal of Christian Scripture (chap. 3B), I have sought to construct a coherent reading that brings out the normative bearing of scriptural Wisdom literature on a Christian doctrine of creation and, in that context, on Christian claims about human creatures.

*There is nothing better for mortals than to
eat and drink, and find enjoyment in their
toil. This also, I saw, is from the hand of God;
for apart from him who can eat or who can
have enjoyment?*
ECCLESIASTES 2:24–25

CHAPTER **5A**

Our Proximate Contexts as Created

Our Proximate Contexts as the Quotidian

What we are as human creatures has to be understood theologically in terms of God's creation as a whole, the proximate contexts into which we are born. But what does "the creation" mean? The theology of creation through which canonical Wisdom thinks suggests this answer: "the creation" denotes the lived world as the quotidian, the everyday finite realities of all sorts—animal, vegetable, and mineral—in the routine networks that are constituted by their ordinary interactions. Taken together, that network of realities defines the spaces and times of our everyday lives and provide us with fellow agents sharing those spaces and times. All taken together, they (we!) are a society of everyday being. For convenience, in this theology of creation I shall call it the "quotidian." What God creates is the quotidian. It is the proximate context into which we are born. Human persons are integral to it, as quotidian as everything else.

Wisdom creation theology's focus on the quotidian entails several differences from many doctrines of creation, classical and modern. They are best expressed in the negative. First, mainstream Wisdom's creation theology generally lacks any account of cosmic origins. It describes the relation of God the Creator to the quotidian as creature, but not the genesis of the quotidian. It does not suggest a developmental view in which God creates a set of fundamental physical principles and elementary particles and then the physical context of human life, followed by the biological context, followed at last by human life with its societies and cultures. Of course, it does not imply denial of any such view either. It simply does not touch on the question of how creation came to be. Nor does it suggest that the present context of our lives is a decline and fall from an actual paradisiacal state that God first created. Nor does what God created consist of an unchanging ontological structure, a set of metaphysical principles that constitute an order underlying the quotidian (see chap. 5B), giving it a modicum of normative order no matter how far it declines from this norm, and preserving it from declining altogether into nothingness. Once again, of course, Wisdom's creation theology is not necessarily inconsistent with a metaphysical thesis that such an order obtains; it simply does not raise the question or address the issue.

Nor is God's actual creation "noumenal" reality, a depth far more meaningful than the quotidian itself, of which the quotidian is mere phenomena or appearance. Nor does God merely create the conditions of the possibility of our having the sorts of conscious experience we do in fact have, the rest of reality being a social construct of our own collectively conscious, culture-shaped devising, which we invest with meanings and values of our own imagining.

Nor is God's creation a future state of the world, a state to which God will eventually bring the world through the ongoing movement of history. Wisdom's theology of creation lacks teleology. Creation-as-a-whole is not understood by reference to a transcendent end or *telos* beyond itself that it was created to actualize. For example, Ecclesiastes pushes the boundaries of mainstream Wisdom by exploring the following question: would trust that the quotidian is God's creation be unaffected by the suspicion that there is no ultimate goal or end whose achievement gives meaning to creaturely life? The writer's answer seems to be: trust that the quotidian is God's creation would be entirely unaffected (see chap. 4B). The concept "creature" in canonical Wisdom literature does not necessarily entail that "creatureliness" be understood in terms of ends that creatures are created to actualize.

No, the basic thrust of canonical Wisdom's creation theology is that what God creates is humankind's lived world in its concrete everydayness. Because, as we saw in chapter 4, canonical Wisdom thinks through a creation theology that assumes God's attentive delight in creation; canonical Wisdom itself assumes, in Iris Murdoch's wonderful phrase (1971, 34), a correspondingly attentive "compassionate and just gaze" upon the quotidian. The quotidian is not denigrated. Its dignity lies, not in the fact that it inherently refers beyond itself to transcendent reality, nor in its having an ontological depth more meaningful than itself, but simply in its being just what God creates in all its everydayness. This feature of Wisdom's creation theology serves to focus our effort to understand proximate contexts in their concrete quotidian everydayness.

At least since Hegel made the point in *The Phenomenology of Spirit* (1977), it has been conventional to characterize the concreteness of the everyday as its "locatedness" (*sittlichkeit*). Every quotidian is situated in the interactions of a multitude of energy systems: inorganic energy systems that can be analyzed molecularly, atomically, and subatomically; organic energy systems of varying complexity that appear to be emergent from inorganic energy systems; social systems that organize communal life with political and economic structures and arrangements of power; cultures whose repertoires of language, symbol, and practice systemically shape human affective, intellectual, and volitional energies. Further, each quotidian society with its culture constitutes a tradition handed over from generation to generation. These traditions are themselves internally fractured and conflictual. Nonetheless, traditions as processes of handing on themselves appears to be a type of energy nudging the social quotidian toward certain future states of affairs. Insofar as it is partly made up of human societies' cultural traditioning, the quotidian is socially constructed. Because it is always historical, and because histories are diverse, the quotidian manifests remarkable diversity. All of these are factors of every given quotidian's concreteness. However, they do not collectively situate the quotidian like an empty container into which the everyday is somehow placed by the Creator while these factors remain extrinsic to the quotidian. On the contrary, these factors are intrinsic to the quotidian. They are part and parcel of the everyday that God creates.

The decision to focus our theological account of the proximate context into which we are born on the quotidian does not absolutize any one concrete lived world. In particular, it does not entail an uncritical acceptance of the normativity of contemporary historically and culturally rootless, humanly meaningless, consumerist mass societies so easily critiqued as the offspring of unrestrained technological advances and uncontrolled, globalized free economy. To the extent that this is, in its broad-brush way, an accurate picture of our own quotidian, and it is for millions of persons, it is an "everyday" deeply deformed by evil. This may, roughly speaking, be our quotidian; it does not define "quotidian." Even a redeemed version would nonetheless be a quotidian.

These remarks remind us to relativize every instance of the quotidian. In all of the diversity of the quotidian *in concreto*, there is no one ideal or perfect instance of the everyday. To let Wisdom's creation theology guide our own reflections on human creatureliness is not to commit ourselves to being guided by every aspect and dimension of biblical Wisdom literature's picture of its quotidian. Canonical Wisdom literature's historical, social, and cultural location makes any such commitment extremely problematic. The quotidian taken for granted by canonical Wisdom literature exemplifies all of the features of concreteness noted above. Biblical Wisdom naively assumes that a particular type of society and its culture constitute the created and real world. It is a preindustrial agricultural society whose largely settled population lives in villages, towns, and small cities rather than scattered out on their land holdings. Its economy, grounded in farming and herding, sustains a vigorous merchant class. There are clear distinctions between rich and poor, but little evidence of extreme poverty or outrageous concentrations of wealth. This society is highly stable. Its culture is un-self-critically conventional, a culture of ancient traditions that are observed without question.

Arrangement of power in this culture surely classifies it as patriarchal. Men manage communities' public life; women manage the households, although in so doing women may also engage in trade and become relatively wealthy. Women are subordinate to men in legal and public matters, although in intimate relations there may be remarkable equality and mutuality. For example, mothers and fathers alike teach children wisdom.

Although the society assumed by biblical Wisdom literature is a deeply conservative society, social injustice and oppression are recognized as possibilities and protested when encountered. However, in canonical Wisdom literature there is not the remotest hint of the thought that the entire social-political arrangement could be radically different or should be changed to become systemically more just. Given the historical context, it would be absurdly anachronistic even to expect such ideas.

There is absolutely no good theological reason to idealize or absolutize this social world. To the contrary, there are plenty of good theological reasons for not doing so. My commitment to let canonical Wisdom's way of construing its world as God's creation guide my efforts to construe our own world as God's creation must not be confused with a commitment to nostalgic idealizing of the world Wisdom takes for granted as though it were theologically normative for all subsequent worlds. It is only fair to add that canonical Wisdom's creation theology shows no interest in absolutizing the quotidian it takes for granted.

The Quotidian, Practices, and the Human Vocation

As exemplified especially in Proverbs, canonical Wisdom's creation theology invites us to describe the quotidian in terms of human practices. By a "practice," I mean a form of socially established cooperative human activity that is both complex and internally coherent; is done to some end, though it does not necessarily have a product; and is subject to standards of excellence that partly define it (MacIntyre 1981, 175–283; see also Kelsey 1992, 118–24).

Wisdom's creation theology views what God creates in terms of several broad types of practices. It construes the quotidian in terms of practices in which human creatures interact with nonhuman creatures: practices involved in farming, working with domestic animals, making things (manufacturing). These practices also include studying other creatures in their own right ("Go to the ant, you lazybones, etc.," Prov. 6:6). Indeed, one major function of international Wisdom in the ancient Near East, especially Egyptian Wisdom, was to summarize encyclopedically information and insight about what we call the "world of nature" (e.g., regarding Proverbs, see McKane 1970, 51–210). That theme was preserved, especially in Job, when Israel's Wisdom literature was canonized.

Wisdom's creation theology also views the quotidian in terms of practices in which human creatures interact with other human creatures: practices of marriage, child rearing, managing households, preparing meals; practices of teaching and learning; practices of governing; practices of hiring and managing employees; practices of exchange in marketing and trade.

Finally, it views the realm God creates in terms of practices in which human creatures interact with social institutions: practices of securing justice and correcting injustice; of borrowing, lending, and managing money; and above all, practices of using language either truthfully or deceptively.

There is a normative edge to canonical Wisdom's construal of the quotidian—that is, God's creation—in terms of practices. Practices are subject to standards of excellence that partly define them. As I noted in chapter 4A, Woman Wisdom is the emblem in Proverbs of God's call coming to humankind through creation to be wise in each of the three types of human practices noted above, both for their own well-being and for that of the quotidian (see also chap. 5B). This means that the very context into which we are born has the force of a vocation regarding our practices: human creatures are born into a vocation, called to be wise in their practices. This vocation is the normative edge of their proximate contexts: the standard of excellence that partly defines human practices is wisdom. Human creatures may or may not respond to this call. Because human practices partly make up the quotidian, unwise or foolish practices deform not just individual lives but the quotidian—that is, creation itself. Wise practices yield the well-being of fully human, if dying, life; foolish practices yield a living death.

We can sharpen this profile of canonical Wisdom's concept of practical wisdom, and especially its normative edge, by contrasting it to concepts of wisdom in three other intellectual traditions.

In the tradition of classical Greek and Hellenistic thought, wisdom is understood in relation to a cultural assumption that there are three types of genuinely human life. They are contrasted to the life of a slave or peasant, which is not properly human because it is a life of sheer physical labor hardly distinguishable from the life of domestic animals.

One form of genuinely human life is the life spent in contemplation of that which does not change, the eternally true and good. Contemplation and practical action are viewed as in tension, if not mutually exclusive. Hence, the life of contemplation requires substantial material resources so as not to have to support oneself actively. The aim of contemplation—*theoria*—is reason's intuitive union with what is eternally true and good, in which the rational soul achieves the happiness of its full actualization. *Theoria* is reason's union with the eternal good; it is not, like modern "theory," a body of truths that might be applied in action. The fruit of *theoria* is *sophia*, wisdom. In the history of Christian thought, great confusion has been generated by using *sophia* to translate Hebrew words used in biblical Wisdom literature for "wisdom." Whereas *sophia* is defined by reference to what is timeless and unchanging and can be achieved only through contemplation that avoids the distraction of action, biblical Wisdom is practical and ad hoc.

At the opposite extreme is a second type of human life, *poesis*. It consists in the action of making things, whether it be furniture, houses, poems, or music. *Poesis* is a genuinely human life, unlike sheer brute labor, because it involves some kind of skill, *techne*, practical insight about how to make what one seeks to make. We might see *techne* as a certain kind of wisdom. However, as the fruit of long practice actively working with changeable materials, it is quite different from *sophia*, which is the fruit of inactive contemplation of the eternal. Moreover, *techne* is very different from biblical wisdom. Whereas in biblical wisdom one seeks the well-being of the quotidian, including one's self, *techne* is morally neutral. It is wisdom about how to make some particular type of thing, whether or not it makes for anyone's well-being.

A third type of human life, *praxis*, falls between *theoria* and *poesis*. *Praxis* is political action in which free males work together to govern a ~ethical~ city's—*polis's*—common life so that together they actualize the common good. This, too, is an elitist form of life, limited to free adult males with sufficient private resources to devote themselves to public affairs, seeking to sustain a common good that preserves their social status quo. Like *theoria* (union with the eternal good), what *praxis* aims to actualize is inherently moral (the public common good of the *polis*), unlike the morally neutral, privately enjoyed products of *poesis*. Far more than *poesis* and like *theoria*, *praxis* is sometimes deemed in this tradition to be a way in which a proper human life may be actualized. Indeed, the classical tradition is marked by a continual dispute between those who hold that human life is fully actualized in *theoria* and those who hold it actualized in *praxis*, and by debate whether the two are incompatible or can be combined in a single life.

Praxis requires a certain political know-how, a kind of practical insight called *phronesis*. Where *sophia*, as the fruit of *theoria*, is a wisdom about eternal and unchanging good and truth, *phronesis*, as the fruit of *praxis*, is a wisdom about the ever-changing political and social world. Thus, biblical wisdom practices are much closer to *phronesis* than they are to either *sophia* or *techne*. However, biblical wisdom is broader than *phronesis* because it is rooted in and bears on the well-doing and well-being of many more types of social practices than simply political action.

Wisdom is understood quite differently in ways shaped by modern philosophical idealist traditions, very broadly construed. Such traditions can be traced from Kant through Hegel to Marxism to Frankfort School and other post-Marxist critical social theorists, but also including certain philosophical phenomenological and existentialist thought that sees itself as the antithesis of Hegelian idealism. This is, of course, a set of intellectual traditions of ongoing disagreement and fierce reciprocal critique. Nonetheless, the disputants share some fundamental anthropological convictions: what differentiates human subjects from objects is that they are self-consciously responsible for their own self-actualization (however that is defined), and self-actualization is always oriented toward increasing human freedom. Such traditions assume a very different picture of what counts as fully actualized human life than does the ancient Greek and Hellenistic tradition.

The modern traditions adopted the ancient terms *praxis* and *theoria*. However, used against the background of very different anthropological beliefs, they mean something rather different. Here *praxis* means, not action ordered to a community's common life so as to actualize its common good as that has been traditionally conceived in the community, but rather action ordered to the realization of human emancipation or liberation from central structural features of the way the community has traditionally conceived the common good of its common life. Sometimes it is construed as action to free humankind from brute nature's constraints by creating civilization, a realm of freedom. Sometimes *praxis* is construed as action to liberate from oppressive social, political, and economic power arrangements within a given society. Sometimes it is construed as action to free human subjects from the constraints of civilization itself. In every case, however, *praxis* requires *theoria*, a body of theory explaining the laws governing changes in the realm of nature or explaining the dynamics of social, cultural, economic, and psychological change. In this tradition, *praxis* and *theoria* are dialectically interdependent: *theoria* is the moment of rational critical self-reflection within *praxis*. It presupposes that *praxis* is occurring, grows out of it to analyze *praxis*'s natural and social contexts, and then returns to critique and correct *praxis*.

Praxis in the modern sense is properly historical action. It is at once action embodied in some particular society and its culture, shaped by their histories; and it is action that does not just maintain and preserve the status quo "common good" of the society, but makes history, that is, effects changes over time in the direction of enhanced freedom in that society and its culture. Just this historicity of *praxis*, however, also makes it vulnerable to co-optation by the society in which it is enacted, in order to preserve and justify the society's oppressive power arrangements. Hence, *praxis*'s own *theoria* must provide a critical distance on the society and its power dynamics, a distance that is oriented by the core moral value of freedom. Thus, *theoria* is inherently moral-value oriented. It is not a value-neutral theory. It is a kind of wisdom.

At a very high level of abstraction, biblical "wisdom" has similarities to *theoria* as understood in these traditions. With them it presupposes socially and culturally embodied practices. With them it is at once rooted in and corrective of practices that aim at social well-being. However, there are at least two decisive differences. The wisdom celebrated by canonical Wisdom literature, as insight into very particular concrete situations in the everyday world, is far too ad hoc to lend itself to the sort of theorizing that constitutes *praxis's theoria*, including an anthropological theory about some core value orientation (say, freedom) ingredient in human creatureliness. The practices to which biblical wisdom is the dialectical companion are not defined by an orientation to the liberation of the human spirit. For canonical Wisdom literature, the vocation to wisdom does orient human practices, but it orients them elsewhere.

Wisdom is understood in a third way in the American pragmatist tradition. This tradition assumes that human action, rather than being oriented to the actualization of freedom, is more broadly oriented to the enrichment and complexification of experience. We might say that it understands human action and wisdom against background beliefs that make an aesthetic orientation (in a broad sense of the term) more basic to human practices than a moral orientation. On this view, theory is a kind of wisdom in service to action's success in enriching and complexifying experience. Such theory is relatively ad hoc. In idealist traditions, *theoria* often aims to be systematic and comprehensive, relating everything to everything else, to explain the dynamics of the actualization of free subjectivity-as-such, or the movement of history-as-a-whole, or the rules governing radical social and cultural changes as such and in general. The pragmatist tradition tends to be skeptical of such large-scale theorizing.

Overlaps clearly exist between biblical "wisdom" and the wisdom of "theory" in the pragmatist tradition. Both understand wisdom to be rooted in and corrective of human practices. Both are unsystematic and piecemeal. One difference is decisive, however. From the perspective of biblical wisdom, pragmatism's theory is too vulnerable to being co-opted by the social and cultural status quo. Lacking either an acknowledgment that we engage in practices within the embracing context of God's call to be wise, or a background belief that striving for some core moral value (such as freedom) is inherent in human nature, its view of the dialectical unity of practice and theory risks lacking a critical edge to give it distance on the particular society in which practice is embodied.

The distinguishing feature of the intrinsic standard of excellence, the normative edge, of human practices as understood in canonical Wisdom literature lies in the practices' intentionality as response. These practices are responses to God's call to human creatures, mediated by the quotidian, to be wise in their practices for the well-being of the quotidian, including themselves. The practices' responsiveness to God's call to wisdom defines them as just these practices, and that call is their normative edge. The relative excellence of enactments of these practices is measured by their appropriateness as, precisely, responses to God's call.

In applying this standard of excellence, mainstream biblical Wisdom's theology of creation lays remarkable stress on the right use of language. It stresses the normative connection between the character of practices of language use, on one side, and the quality of many complex practices that include speech practices on the other. Proverbs, for example, insistently draws attention to the connection between the character of our practices of language use—Are they truthful or deceitful?—and the character of the larger practices that include them: Do they lead to human well-being? Are they life-giving or death-dealing? The connection between the use of language and the life-giving quality of the practices that largely constitute the quotidian lies in the public status they share.

Recall that a practice is a form of socially established cooperative human activity. A society's culture provides a repertoire of practices that constitute its quotidian as a public space insofar as those practices are enacted by members of that society. Anyone born into that proximate context learns those practices and cooperates in them. The relations among the human persons who cooperate in practices are in large part determined by the ways in which various sorts of power (political, economic, social, and cultural) are distributed among the persons as they cooperate in common practices in the society. Given the way power is distributed in a particular society, some persons will exercise more power than others in cooperative practices. The varied distribution of power is one reason that practices are complex. Furthermore, the patterns in which various sorts of power are distributed and organized tend to become relatively stable and fixed over time; they become institutionalized. Insofar as practices are cooperative, socially established, culturally transmitted, and shaped by institutionalized patterns of power arrangement, they are inherently public. Such practices constitute the "public realm." To engage in such networks of practices is not only to acknowledge and, indeed, to manifest the institutional structures of a public realm. It is, in fact, to enact those institutions as the public realm here and now. Hence, to engage in a practice is inherently to be part of a public realm.

For their part, ordinary languages are also inherently public. Use of language is itself a socially established cooperative human activity that is complex, internally coherent, and subject to standards of excellence that partly define it. Of course, any ordinary language may be used in private. However, private uses of an ordinary language are parasitic on their status as public practices. Where a secret code or a private language is devised, its invention would seem to presuppose and to be parasitic upon some prior and surrounding public language. Furthermore, languages work properly when their use is tied up with practices, or forms of life, that are themselves public. To learn a language is, among other things, to acquire the conceptual capacities one needs to live as a member of the society that ordinarily uses that language, and to engage in the practices that constitute that society's public life. Conversely, a large part of learning most practices is learning uses of language that are inherent in the practices.

Accordingly, to engage in a practice properly requires using language truly in a threefold way. It involves using a language in ways that are true (i.e., fitting) to the nature and purposes of the relevant practice; true (i.e., faithful) to the persons with whom one is cooperating in the practice; and true (i.e., corresponding) to the realities of the larger public context of the practice. Canonical Wisdom literature's trope for use of language is "speaking." To use language in misleading and false ways is to "speak deceitfully," and doing so while engaging in a practice is to distort the practice. To distort the practice is to deform the quotidian public realm of which the practice is a constituent part. If the quotidian is what God creates, distoring the practice is to deform creation.

Such is the logic exemplified in the use of a trope in Proverbs that is the antithesis of Woman Wisdom: the adulterous woman. She is the paradigm of death-dealing folly. The adulteress uses the ordinary language of love to present herself as surpassingly desirable and to offer herself in love (7:14–18). She uses the language in a way that is true to the practices in question. However, she also uses this language to suggest that it is possible to enact loving and being loved in radical secrecy, not just in a private space and time temporarily protected from ordinary public space and time, but in a space and time absolutely disjoined from the quotidian public realm. Yet no such form of human life, and certainly no well-being of life therein, is possible. Using language in such a deceitful way is mortally dangerous. It is dangerous not simply because it risks incurring the murderous rage of the betrayed spouse (6:34, 35), but more profoundly because it threatens a basic condition of human life in a common public realm (2:18, 19). It is untrue to the realities of the larger public context of the practices. Therewith, it is finally faithless to the person being invited to cooperate in the practices.

Thus, the importance of the connection between practices of language use, on one side, and the life-giving quality of the practices that include language use, on the other side, lies in the public status they share in the quotidian world they largely constitute. Insisting on that connection makes important points in theological anthropology: as integral parts of God's creaturely quotidian, understood as networks of practices, human creatures are above all social, intentional bodied enactors of complex, cooperative practices that necessarily include practices of language use.

Excursus: Problematic Anthropocentrism?
This discussion invites an important objection that must be addressed immediately. The objection goes like this: Construing creation, and with it human creatures, as the quotidian, and then construing the quotidian, and with it human creatures, in terms of human practices, privileges a

particular model of the human person and a particular conceptual scheme with which to describe it. Focus on practices privileges an intentional-agent model of human personhood, and its attendant conceptual schemes. There are, of course, a variety of philosophical action theories. Nonetheless, an intentional-agent model of human personhood relies on a family of concepts presided over by concepts of practice, mental intention, and bodily action. Privileging such concepts, the objection goes, will inevitably lead to a radically anthropocentric view of creation, and therewith of human creatures. To do so puts into play a pattern of thinking that systematically elevates human creatures over the rest of the creation, for only human creatures are capable in the full sense of intentions and intentional actions and enacting practices, and so only they are really creatures. So far as their reality and value are concerned, all other creatures are reduced to the status of extensions or appendages of human creatures.

Before I rebut this objection, some concessions are in order. Later on I suggest that some versions of an intentional-agent description of human personhood, and the conceptual scheme it requires, do promise to provide a way to avoid the theologically objectionable tendency to dichotomize mental intention and bodily action, subjectivity and objectivity, interiority and exteriority, individual and society, private and public in descriptions of what human personhood is. It is also certainly the case that a theological construal of the quotidian guided by biblical Wisdom does not purport to give an objective picture of the creaturely realm—that is, a picture without perspective, point of view, or orienting interest. Nor does it purport to give a view of creatures from God's point of view. It is in this fashion human-centered in its way of knowing the quotidian. It is, we might say, epistemically anthropocentric. Indeed, we might wonder how it could be otherwise when it is human persons who are trying to understand the context into which they have been born as God's creation.

However, this perspective is not necessarily anthropocentric with regard to judgments of the reality and value of nonhuman creatures. It need not be or become ontologically anthropocentric. It does not assume or suggest that other creatures are real and have value only to the extent that they can serve as instruments that extend the scope and power of human persons' practices, rather than being real and valuable in their own right. Such a view *would* be ontologically anthropocentric. There is nothing in the invitation to view the quotidian in terms of human creatures' practices that implies the impossibility of our attending to fellow creatures with a compassionate and just gaze. Nor does it assume that other creatures' reality and value are constituted by their having been created to actualize purposes or ends entirely relative to human well-being. They are not created by God simply for us.

Indeed, canonical biblical Wisdom invites us to attend to the creatures that, along with us, make up the quotidian, as genuinely other than we in being and value. It invites us to do this, to be sure, from the perspective of those human practices whose guiding interest is the well-being of the quotidian, including human creatures. It is always conceptually possible for that interest to distort reflection from this perspective in an ideologically biased way, perhaps in the direction of an ontologically anthropocentric view of human creaturehood. However, the perspective provided by human practices does not necessarily entail this. Nor is there any systematic move that can be made in theology that will conceptually *guarantee* that such distortion will not happen. What we can do is be vigilantly self-critical in testing whether we have fallen prey to this danger.

The Quotidian as Finite and Human Perfection

What God relates to creatively, the proximate context into which we are born, is finite, and because it is finite it is experientially ambiguous.

"Finite" means "limited." Creaturely being is limited being. This is an ontological claim. The entire creaturely realm taken as a kind of whole, the particular proximate contexts into which we are born, and each particular physical creature that is a part of such contexts, including human creatures, are limited in being (I set aside reflection on the finitude of possible nonphysical creatures such as angels).

This is an ontological, not a numerical, claim. It may be that the number of individual creatures and of possible creaturely worlds is infinite. However, the ontological finitude of the creaturely realm, however infinite in number, is a function of its radical dependency for its existence on God's ongoing creativity. No particular constituent element, nor any universal dimension of creation, is inherently everlasting or exists necessarily. This point is summarized in the classical doctrinal formula that God creates *ex nihilo*, "from nothing." God does not create our proximate contexts out of a reality which, while genuinely other than God, is nonetheless co-eternal with God and as primordial as God (say, eternally preexisting matter). Nor is the world created by God out of God's own reality. "All that is not God" is not created out of anything. It is so radically dependent on God's continuing relating to it creatively that no aspect of it escapes that contingency. This claim is not an obscure effort to provide a hypothesis explaining how creation as a whole came to be. As Rowan Williams puts it, "The existence of the world is not a puzzling fact, as opposed to other, straightforward facts" for which the doctrine of creation might offer an explanation; "it is all the facts there are" (2000, 68). "Ontological finitude" describes a certain relation (radical-dependence-for-being) that the proximate context into which we are born (and we with it) has to God.

Every particular physical creature making up the quotidian is finite in at least two ways. First are the intrinsic limits to which creatures are subject. Every physical creature is a complex set of interrelated energy systems that is inherently subject over time to progressive disintegration. Energy becomes progressively less organized and eventually dissipates altogether, and the creature ceases to be. This claim, of course, is a highly generalized summary of the picture of physical entities that the life sciences give us. It is appropriated here to make a theological claim: The intrinsic limits of their organization of energy is the distinctive way in which physical creatures manifest their radical dependency on God's creativity. Their vulnerability to passing out of existence, to be succeeded by other creatures, simply is part of the way in which God sustains in existence a constantly changing realm of creatures. For theological anthropology, this implies that even when they are not killed by other creatures, human creatures "live on borrowed breath" (Crenshaw 1981, 198), and it is intrinsic to them that in the normal course of creaturely events they must sooner or later surrender what was borrowed.

Particular physical creatures' finitude is a function, second, of extrinsic limits to which they are subject. The innumerable networks of creatures of various kinds that make up the quotidian interact in infinitely complex fashion. They impinge on one another in rule-governed ways that inevitably involve the change and eventual destruction of each of them. The realm of physical creatures, which is the context into which we are born, is inherently accident-prone, as creatures inescapably damage one another. "Change and decay in all around I see"—that includes the "I" who sings the hymn.

One consequence of the finitude of creatures is that the quotidian is inherently ambiguous experientially. This ambiguity is rooted ontologically—that is, in the creatureliness of the quotidian. On the one hand, that which God creates makes possible the well-being of God's creatures in the ways appropriate to their kind. So the proximate contexts into which we are born simply are the condition of the possibility of our well-being as human creatures. Hence, what God relates to creatively, ourselves and our everyday worlds, may be experienced by us in delight and pleasure as, from our perspective, (relatively) good for us. On the other hand, the finitude of creation means that creatures are inevitably vulnerable to damage, deterioration, and destruction. The context into which we are born simply is the condition of the possibility of our undergoing hurt, loss, and death. Hence, that which God creates, ourselves and our everyday world, may be experienced, from our perspective, as threatening to us. On the pleasure-pain axis, that which God creates is profoundly ambiguous for us experientially. Hence, the sense in which their proximate contexts are "good" for creatures is relative to the basic nature of their creatureliness: they are "good" for a distinctive type of creature—namely, inherently finite creatures, not for creatures who are inherently incapable of being limited internally and externally, incapable of being vulnerable to damage and suffering, incapable of being subject to the ultimate disintegration of death. The well-being of which human creatures' proximate contexts are the condition is the well-being proper to thoroughly finite beings. Were they not finite in those ways, human beings would not be what they are—that is, the kind of creatures they are.

The theology of creation through which canonical Wisdom thinks is utterly realistic about finitude's experiential ambiguity. Its principal symbol for creaturely finitude is death. "The Lord gave, and the Lord has taken away" (Job 1:21b). The Creator who gives life also deals death. In canonical Christian Holy Scripture, this claim is not limited to Wisdom literature. Consider 1 Samuel, in the "Song of Hannah":

> The Lord kills and brings to life;
> he brings down to Sheol and raises up.
> (2:6)

This theological affirmation does not necessarily imply that the Creator is indifferent to creatures. Nor does it mean that the Creator is self-contradictorily also the un-Creator.

Rather, it entails at least these two claims: First, that the mode of reality that God creates in creating us and our proximate contexts is finite physical reality. That is the sort of reality in which the Creator attentively delights, and God's attentive delight in creatures necessarily respects the integrity of their reality, including their finitude and its vulnerability to disintegration. Second, it implies that creaturely change, including the destruction of creatures, is precisely the mode God's ongoing creativity takes. As I have noted, this creation theology posits no transcendent goal to God's ongoing creativity beyond the creating of reality genuinely other than God with which God, in creating it, enters into the community of being. This leaves us free, to be sure, to speculate about God's ongoing creativity as a goal-oriented evolutionary process through which God may be "moving" creation to a desired "end state" (see, e.g., Kaufman 1993, pt. 3). But canonical Wisdom's creation theology neither logically requires nor metaphorically suggests any such picture. Rather, it focuses on God's relation to just this everyday world, which is the proximate context into which we are born.

The theology of creation that is background to canonical Wisdom gives little conceptual room for ameliorating theologically the experienced ambiguity of the quotidian. For example, because it does not rest on an account of the origins of the everyday world, and in particular lacks any postulated paradisiacal earlier state of the world, this creation theology does not have conceptual space for a traditional theological distinction between what God created, which was unambiguously good for us, and what we experience now, which even in its physical particulars is a fallen and unqualifiedly degraded version of what God originally created. The ambiguity is inherent in precisely what God creates—that is, in finite creatures. Furthermore, Wisdom's creation theology does not allow us to distinguish between a transcendental reality, which God creates and which is unambiguously good for us and delightful, and its appearance, which in suffering we experience as bad for us. No, the ambiguity is inherent in the reality of creaturely finitude; it is ontologically inherent in finitude.

Guided by canonical Wisdom's background creation theology, I have made two theological remarks about the proximate contexts of which we are integral parts: the proximate contexts are thoroughly finite, and in consequence of their finitude they are experientially ambiguous. These remarks bear on the anthropological question, "What counts as a 'perfect' human being?" In much modern thought, the question about human perfection is cast as the question, "What is a 'real' or 'authentic' or 'fully realized' human being?" My theological remarks about human creatureliness imply an answer: the real and authentic human being is the ordinary, everyday human person. In the descriptive sense of "human being," it is trivially true that the everyday human person is a real human being, but in the normative sense of "human being," it is an importantly true remark. It is important because it warrants on theological grounds the abandonment of the notion of a perfect or the perfectly actualized human being. Clearly, this claim rests heavily on the distinction I invoked between two senses of our concept of human being.

The concept of "human person" has both descriptive and normative force. We use it descriptively to classify beings: this entity is a human person; that one is a very smart chimpanzee; that is a highly complex robot; and that is an angel (i.e., a type of nonhuman, nonphysical person). We also use "human person" normatively: at least in the modern world, depending in part on the historical and cultural period, some human persons are said to be less sincere, or less genuine, or less authentic, or less fully actualized persons than are others (e.g., see Trilling 1972).

Used descriptively, "human person" does not admit of degrees. One either does or does not belong in the classification "human person" (whatever the definition of that class may be). One either is a real human person, or one is not. Used normatively, however, "human person" does admit of degrees. One may be either more or less "really" a human person; or, as it is sometimes put, one may have either more or less fully "actualized" one's "real personhood."

The normative force of "human person" is dependent on the descriptive force of the term in one way and not in another. The normative force of "human person" presupposes its descriptive force because it requires a population class to evaluate. We can only evaluate, say, how authentic someone is in her human personhood if we have already satisfied ourselves that the entity in question is rightly classified as a human person. Normative judgments are made of entities according to their natural kind. However, descriptive use of "human person" may not adequately justify normative uses of the expression. The criteria that justify us classifying someone as indeed a human person may not yield adequate criteria by which to evaluate how far she has actualized her reality as a human person. Thus, the two ways in which we may use the expression "human person" may neither be separated nor collapsed into each other.

Return now to the question about the concepts of a "perfect" and a "fully actualized" human person. Strictly speaking, "perfect" means "complete," "lacking nothing." The idea that one might be a perfect human person who lacks nothing in regard to one's human personhood presupposes that there is (a) a single scale of possible degrees of completeness which is (b) comprehensive of all the relevant respects in which a human person might be complete. Such a scale would require a single-concept "human person" normative for all aspects of all human persons. Furthermore, the idea that one may in varying degrees "actualize one's true self" as a "person" presupposes (c) that there is a "true" self awaiting actualization, perhaps deep within, which serves as the norm by which to assess how fully self-actualization has occurred. *No true self*

However, given the descriptive concept of "human person" developed thus far in this theological account of what human persons are as God's creatures, no such normative concepts of human persons' perfection are possible, for two reasons. The features of the quotidian that constitute human creatures' intrinsic and extrinsic finitude make human persons too diverse to be subject to a single norm of human completeness that embraces every aspect of human personhood. The variety of ways in which individual human persons are concretely limited both intrinsically and extrinsically make them far too diverse in their finitude for there to be one scale of human perfect self-actualization comprehensive of all the aspects of human personhood that may be actualized. Second, the experiential ambiguity inherent in the quotidian makes it impossible to distinguish clearly between those lamentable features of persons' experience that are a consequence of their failure to actualize themselves adequately and those which are ontologically inherent in the concrete particularities of their finitude. Given the view of human creatureliness developed here, the real you simply is the quotidian you. *real you is simply the quotidian you*

The foregoing remarks involve a departure from most Western Christian theology about human persons as creatures of God. In Christian theology, everyday human persons born and living in the quotidian have consistently been deemed less than perfect, not fully actualized, incompletely real. The evidence for this judgment has been the experiential ambiguity of the quotidian in its finitude. Even when it has stressed that what God creates is precisely finite reality, Christian theology has traditionally deemed the quotidian "not what it's supposed to be" according to God's creative intent.

For example, in premodern theology the ambiguity of the quotidian was taken to be experiential evidence of a fall from an original perfection and an index of the range of the fall's effects. For Augustine and Western theology generally after him, the perfect human persons were located in the Garden of Eden before the fall. Even though all creation, including Adam and Eve, was understood to be finite, the perfection of the Paradise in which they were set at creation was understood to be experientially unambiguous. Adam and Eve were understood to be, respectively, perfect male and female historical human creatures in the strict sense of "perfect." They were taken to be perfect in their kind in every respect, not merely in regard to their morality or in regard to their relationship with God: they were understood to be adult human creatures lacking nothing—complete, in respect of physical development and beauty, bodily health, emotional health, social functioning, intelligence, and all the talents human persons can exhibit. They were understood to have been created fully actualized in this magnificent perfection.

It is essential to the logic of this traditional theology that Adam and Eve were not construed as ideal types. They were understood to be created by God as historically actual human persons perfectly realized in all respects. As such, they were together the single, comprehensive norm by which to assess the reality of all other human persons across history and cultures. Furthermore, their actuality was the prototype of the perfection that all of those raised in the last day in Christ will enjoy, albeit in spiritual rather than physical bodies. In this pattern of theological reflection, the eschaton was understood to include (though not limited to) the restoration of creation to its pre-fall perfection. Any account of the content of eschatological consummation was governed by the content of the theological description of originally perfect human creatures. The experiential ambiguity of the quotidian was taken to be experiential evidence of the fall from this perfection and an index of the range of the fall's effects.

By contrast, modern post-Enlightenment theology has tended to adopt some definition of "freedom" as the criterion of human perfection. It has read the Genesis account of Adam and Eve as a figurative rendering of an ideal type of human perfection—that is, perfect freedom. This focus on freedom narrows the range of respects in which human perfection may be assessed. Physique and health, for example, no longer enter in. Nonetheless, there is still a single, universally applicable standard of perfection: freedom.

In modern theology, freedom is understood, in varying combinations, as freedom in morally responsible action and freedom in self-expressive creativity. Both are defined contrastively—that is, over against something else that is already actual and must be overcome. It may be construed as freedom from the threats of nature "red in tooth and claw," with all of its instincts, drives, and exceptionless laws, and freedom for morally accountable and society-building behavior (Ritschl 1966). It may be freedom from the constraints of conventional culture and its unimaginative ways of thinking, and freedom for self-expression in any of a variety of possible media. It may be freedom from conventional routinized, mechanical, objectifying patterns of interpersonal relationship, and freedom for truly subjective relations to others in their concrete particularity and uniqueness (R. Bultmann 1960). Or it may be freedom from God as repressive, heteronomous "Lord," and freedom for being one's own lord transparent to "transcendence"—that is, being theonomous (P. Tillich 1951).

Various romanticist, existentialist, and psychological theories of the self, its constitutive dynamics, the forms of oppression to which it is vulnerable, and its modes of possible liberation, fund these pictures of perfect human freedom (see Passmore 1972, chaps. 9–12; C. Taylor 1989, esp. pts. 4 and 5). For theological purposes, such pictures of perfect human freedom find a typological instance in the story about Adam and Eve. Now, however, what is paradigmatic is the story of Adam and Eve's fall, not the story of their pre-fall paradisiacal state. In Eden they are in a state of innocence, which usually means "inexperience." Hence, by definition Paradise is experientially unambiguous. Once Adam and Eve actually seek to act or express themselves, or both, they simultaneously typify human perfection by seeking to actualize themselves—that is, actualize and exercise their freedom—and "fall" into an experientially ambiguous world. Being in Paradise is not being perfect; it is hardly "being" at all. On the scale of degrees of actualization of the real self, Paradise symbolizes the "hasn't even started to actualize self" pole. But neither is being in the quotidian the perfect actualization of human personhood. The quotidian, irreducibly ambiguous experientially, is the permanent enemy of freedom. One's reality is measured by the degree to which, rebelling against the quotidian, one transcends it. Perfection lies in the knife-edge between two alternatives. It characterizes human action that is both a rejection of the quotidian in an effort to transcend its bondage and a self-actualization out of the "dreaming innocence" (Tillich 1957) of Paradise.

[margin note: What about proleptically in Christ?]

The theological description I develop here of the proximate context into which we are born cuts against both of these absolutist pictures of human perfection. The real human person is, according to this picture, the quotidian human person. The real human person is God's good creature precisely in his or her quotidian everydayness and finitude, and not because they satisfy some one, universally applicable, ideal of a human person completely—that is, "perfectly," actualized in all respects. The status of "real" human person is not constituted by transcending the quotidian, any more than it is a degraded (i.e., "fallen") version of a historically once or future human perfection. One's creaturely human personhood may be normatively assessed in any of a variety of ways. But there is no single framework for doing that, no one universally applicable standard of human perfection. Theologically speaking, given this creation theology's picture of the finitude of the context into which we are born, there are many ways in which to be a "real enough" human creature, but there is no such thing as the perfect, fully actualized, truly real human creature.

The Quotidian and Evil

The quotidian is profoundly ambiguous in a second respect. It is morally ambiguous as well as ontologically ambiguous. In the everyday world pictured in canonical Wisdom literature, injustice and social disorder, dishonesty, betrayal of trust, lying, mistreatment of dependent persons, and cruelty are all realistically recognized. They are all already present in the context into which we are born. However, this ambiguity is depicted as one that ought not to obtain. Unlike the quotidian's ontological ambiguity, its moral ambiguity is not a necessary function of its finitude. In Wisdom's background creation theology, God does not create moral evil in creating the everyday. Evil is already present, but somehow as an a-rational, inexplicable intruder.

Because canonical Wisdom's creation theology is relational and not genetic, it does not even gesture toward explanation of the genesis of evil's intrusion into what God creates. In offering no account of the genesis of creation or of evil, it focuses entirely on the relation between God as Creator and the world as creation, and on the difference that relation makes for the creation. If Wisdom guides us in our effort to construe as creation the contexts into which we are born, it requires us to be absolutely realistic about the moral ambiguity of these contexts. And it suggests we leave the fact of evil's intrusion into creation unexplained, acknowledging it as mysterious.

In this framework, evil is defined by reference simultaneously to fellow creatures and to God. Here evil is defined as damage done to fellow creatures' well-being as finite creatures, damage that is contrary to God's self-commitment to finite creatures' well-being. Hence evil is in one way against creatures and in another against God. As I argue at somewhat greater length in chapter 10, this double way of defining evil requires that distinctions be drawn among senses of "evil." Some evils are damage done to the well-being of fellow creatures, human and nonhuman, by intentional actions of human creatures for which they are responsible and may be held accountable. Following traditional usage, I call such evil "moral evil." Such evil is the result of human actions that are inappropriate as a human response to the ways in which the triune God relates to humankind. I confine the word "sin" to name such actions. However, much damage is done to finite creatures simply by virtue of their finitude. I have urged that what God creates in creating finite physical creatures are members of societies of interacting finite centers of creaturely powers that are inherently accident-prone, vulnerable to damage from one another. In their vulnerable interactions, they inescapably do certain sorts of damage to one another. Although this seems to be true at subatomic, atomic, and molecular levels, both inorganic and organic, as well.as of the objects perceived in the every-day world, perhaps the most obvious emblem of the unavoidable damage-doing that correlates with finitude is the famous image of a food chain.

However, it is just such creatures that God declares "good." Whatever constitutes the well-being of creatures in their natural kinds, to which God is committed, that well-being does not seem to exclude such damage. Although from each creatures' own perspectives such damage is certainly against or bad for the creature, it does not so clearly seem to be against God. Otherwise physical finitude, at least in its organic forms, would have to be said to be somehow "against" God—that is, contrary to God's creative relating. If damage to creatures' well-being counts as evil only when it satisfies both the criterion of being against creatures and against God, then this type of damage that is inherent in finitude does not seem to satisfy the second criterion. I question whether much of what has traditionally _natural evil_ been classified as "natural" or "metaphysical" evil ought to be theologically named "evil" at all.

However, there are forms of damage to living creatures that, while apparently part of the damage to which their finitude leaves them vulnerable, are so horrendous that it is unimaginable that the triune God's affirmation of creation's goodness covers them. Damage of this sort to creatures seems surely to be against God as much as it is against the creatures. Perhaps every era has its peculiar emblem of such evil. At the turn into the twenty-first century, the most powerful emblem of such evils is the epidemic of AIDS.

In particular cases it can be extremely difficult to distinguish between such horrendous evils and the damage creatures suffer as an inherent part of their finitude. That does not invalidate the distinction between the two. It does urge theological modesty in declaring which forms of damage are, theologically speaking, to be counted as evil and which not. And it underscores the mysteriousness of evil.

In this project, however, the focus falls on moral evil. In that connection it is important to distinguish between evil as human act and evil as consequence of human action. In one sense, moral evil is a human action done against fellow creatures that avoidably and unnecessarily violates their finite creaturely integrity. In another sense, moral evil is the damage done by evil action to fellow creatures and to its actor, damage that abides after the action that caused it has ended. It is remarkable how frequently and consistently the general characterization of evil in Proverbs is violence—human action that violates other creatures.

If Genesis 3:1–4:16 is read through the hermeneutical lens of canonical Wisdom literature's creation theology, and especially through the lens provided by Proverbs, the emphasis in the Genesis account of the intrusion of moral evil into God's good creation falls on the story of Cain and Abel in 4:1–24 fully as much as on the story of Adam and Eve in 3:1–24. The two stories can then be read side by side as parallel concrete accounts of two of the many aspects of the moral ambiguity of the proximate contexts of finite, vulnerable, fallible human beings: The story of Adam and Eve explores ways in which dynamics of an interpersonal relationship between creatures with limited knowledge and unrestrained curiosity can leave them vulnerable to breaking faith with God, enacted in shame, evasion, and misrepresentation of the truth; and the story of Cain and Abel explores ways the dynamics of an egalitarian (fraternal) relation between brothers defined by kinds of work that are socially differentiated specializations (one a herdsman, the other a farmer), and subject to opposite and inexplicably unfair assessments of worth, leave them vulnerable to envy and rage enacted in violence. Such a reading of Genesis 1–11 counters conventional readings of the text that take 3:1–24 as the story of the origin of sin and evil in God's good creation and 4:1–16 as a story of one consequence and intensification of the earlier story. As Claus Westermann points out, in the literary structure of Genesis 1–11, these two stories are both part of "primeval history" that prefaces the Pentateuch's account of God's acts of redemption by describing the universal context of all human life in history (1984: 275–79, 288–300, 317–19), including its moral ambiguity.

It is also remarkable how frequently in the characterization of evil in Proverbs violence is connected to deceit, especially to deliberately deceitful misuse of language. This should not surprise us. We have explored above the rationale for this connection. What is added here is a dominant metaphor for evil: It is avoidable and unnecessary violence—that is, violation of the integrity of fellow creatures precisely in regard to their creatureliness, their everydayness.

Seen as such violation of fellow creatures in the quotidian, evil is a deformation of human creaturely practices and their human agents, at once parasitic on and corruptive of those practices and their agents. Evil deforms agents in their identities, in who they are, and in how they are to be, and not just in the moment of acting. Such deforming has ongoing corrupting force. By deforming the practice through which violence is inflicted, evil perpetuates itself across time in new enactments of deformed practices. Its rippling effect deforms the entire proximate context into which we are born.

As violation of creatures, evil is not a creature in its own right. It presupposes that there already exist human creatures and human practices capable of being deformed. Evil's presence in the quotidian presupposes, and so is parasitic upon, that context of creaturely being—that is, upon reality genuinely other than God in being, radically contingent on God for being, and the object of God's delight.

Mainstream canonical Wisdom literature generally expresses firm confidence that God continually acts in creation to establish justice by rewarding the righteous and punishing the wicked. Indeed, this conviction is a major motive for seeking wisdom: be wise so that you align yourself with the righteous. This confidence in God's providential righting of the moral balances cuts in two directions.

On the one hand, Proverbs, for example, complacently suggests that, if we conduct our lives wisely, which we are fully capable of doing, God's providence will unambiguously make for our well-being. Proverbs appears never to entertain the possibility that human beings who live wisely are sometimes afflicted, in apparent innocence, by horrendous suffering so intense it destroys their finite agency as creatures. It is Job that presses the conventions of mainstream Wisdom to explore how far its creation theology can acknowledge the reality of innocent suffering. But even here, Job himself preserves his agency throughout. Indeed, he does so nobly. Job notwithstanding, there do exist horrendous forms of suffering that do destroy their victim's agency. The very knowledge of such suffering by other persons can deeply and permanently corrode our lives with anguish. Given these realities, it is theologically necessary to block patterns of theological thought about evil that tend to replicate Wisdom's apparent complacency.

On the other hand, with varying degrees of emphasis, canonical Wisdom acknowledges that it can be very difficult to discern signs of God's providential righting of the balance of justice. This tends to undercut complacency about an inevitably experienced righting of the moral scales. Thus, Ecclesiastes acknowledges the reality of God's ongoing activity (e.g., 3:16–18), but stresses the ambiguities of the observable scene and expresses skepticism about the possibility of being wise to discern what God is doing in any particular case (e.g., 11:5). Proverbs acknowledges the ambiguities of the observable scene and the ambiguities of our wisdom (e.g., 16:25; 14:12), but optimistically stresses that in general and on balance the righteous prosper and the wicked are punished (e.g., 11:5). For Proverbs that pattern is not so much a "law," say, of history, but rather an "on balance" rule of thumb. Neither for Ecclesiastes nor for Proverbs does the conviction that God is at work in the everyday world to establish justice warrant the theological judgment that there are humanly discoverable moral laws built into the very structure of the quotidian, or "orders of creation," by which to guide our assessment of what makes for creatures' well-being and thus to identify what leads to their violation. Rather, Wisdom warrants at most exhortations to keep alert for occasional signs of God's arcane providential hand at work morally ordering the quotidian.

Thus the creaturely contexts into which we are born are morally ambiguous in two ways. First, they are morally ambiguous in that the complex interactions that make up the quotidian include human creatures' acts that are a tangle of morally good and morally evil actions. To the extent that the contexts into which we are born are constituted by networks of human practices, they cannot be described as unambiguously morally good contexts.

Second, one cannot claim that the skein of human interactions that make up the quotidian is unambiguously a moral arena in the sense that God's providence is clearly at work to reward the good, punish the evil, and set right the consequences of human violence. Signs of God's providential righting of the moral balance are not a steady-state feature of the quotidian. Rather, according to canonical Wisdom's creation theology, signs of God's providential preservation of a moral order break out in the quotidian like a small rash: patchy, intrusive, and unpredictable. God's providential action in creation is often eruptive, and what erupts are occasions in which evil is punished and righteousness rewarded with extraordinary clarity. These occasions are but patches on the broader spaces of the quotidian stained by violence.

Such occasions may be signs of God's hidden providence, but they cannot count as evidence of God's hidden providential moral rule. Were they taken as evidence, they might warrant the view that the quotidian is "really" unambiguous morally, that the ambiguity is only an appearance. For such events to count as evidence of God's providence, it would be necessary to be able to identify them without using a concept of providence. But, considered apart from the concept of providence, such occasions can be construed with equal probability as happenstances. They function as signs only when they are described using the conceptual framework of a doctrine of providence. What is important to see is that taken in the context of Wisdom's creation theology as signs (not "evidence") of God's moral rule, such events serve simply to underwrite the reality of the quotidian's moral ambiguity. Evil may be an intruder in God's creation and not part of it, but Wisdom's background theology of creation is entirely realistic about the real, if inexplicable, presence of that intruder.

The ambiguities evil generates in the contexts into which we are born are different in principle from the ambiguities its finitude generates. It is a matter of fundamental importance in theological anthropology to keep the two features of the quotidian conceptually distinct. Finitude is not an evil. It is not a problem to be solved, nor a predicament from which we need to be saved. And moral evil is not a logically or ontologically necessary consequence of finitude. Moral evil is not overcome by overcoming or escaping creaturely finitude.

Summary: The Quotidian as Gracious Gift

A theological account of our creatureliness as our having been born must begin with an account of the larger contexts into which we have been born. In chapter 4A, following the implicit creation theology through which canonical Wisdom thinks, I characterized the ultimate context into which we are born as God's active, creative relating to us in our interrelations with other creatures. This is an entirely gratuitous, active relating by God that is intimately free and freely intimate. It is a free relating because in it

God remains genuinely other, a relating neither exacted from God by us nor constrained by any feature of creation. It is an intimate relating in that in it God affectionately delights in the creation. God's free and creative love constitutes a relation with creation analogous to a social institution embracing several parties that is constituted by the dynamics and logic of an odd kind of giving and receiving.

In this chapter, also guided by Wisdom's creation theology, I have characterized the proximate contexts into which we are born as the quotidian in all of its accident-prone, experientially ambiguous finitude. The quotidian is a society of creatures instituted by God's self-commitment to their being and well-being in kind. Hence it is a society of fellow creatures that have parity with one another in being valued by God and parity in being radically contingent on God's ongoing creativity for their sheer existence. It is a society in which creatures interact in bewilderingly complex ways that inescapably involve their damaging one another. It is also a society in which moral evil is already actually present, albeit as an intruder. It is a society whose common history can be humanly meaningful, but only in quite patchy and ad hoc ways.

Precisely by having been born into such proximate contexts, we are integral to them and inextricable from them. Hence, what we are is just this: human creatures—that is, radically contingent, accident-prone members of the society of finite beings to which God is self-committed for its reality and its finite well-being in kind, a society that has already been distorted by moral evil before we are born into it. Moreover, as such we are born into a vocation from God, mediated through the quotidian, to be wise in our practices for the well-being of the quotidian.

Taken together, these remarks about the big picture warrant an even more basic theological claim about the contexts into which human creatures are born, and about the human creatures who are integral to that context. They are, severally and taken all together, in some way not only a gift, but a gracious gift.

Insofar as human creatures' ultimate context is God's utterly gratuitous continual relating to the quotidian, the sheer existence of the quotidian, and they with it, is in some sense a gift. A gift is a bestowal made freely and for the well-being of the recipient. God's creating is not simply a "permitting" or "letting be" (MacQuarrie 1966, chap. 10) of creatures to come into being. It is a positive bestowal of reality, done freely and in affectionate delight in the creature. However, as we saw in chapter 3A, it is "gift" only in an extended and odd way. It is the very act of God's gratuitous giving that constitutes—that is, creates—the receiver of the gift. In creating, God's gift to creatures is nothing other than the creatures themselves in the networks of their interrelationships. However, insofar as human creatures' proximate contexts are the quotidian itself—that is, God's creation—God's gift may more easily be understood as the quotidian gratuitously given to each human creature and each human creature gratuitously given to the quotidian.

Understood in this way, creaturehood is a gracious gift, but it would be misleading to call it "grace" without qualification. Christian theologians tend to use "grace" in conformity with one New Testament usage where it names God's action of giving Godself to human kind. God gives Godself as Emmanuel, one who may be encountered as One among us. And God gives Godself as Holy Spirit, the "advocate" or divine ombudsman of each human creature to all others, the systematically elusive "go-between" (J. Taylor 1972) committed to the whole family of God's people. However, in creating, God precisely does not give Godself. To the contrary, what God gives in creating is thoroughly other-than-God. Together, the Incarnate One and the Holy Spirit, with "first Person," are deserving of worship; the gift of creation is not.

Nonetheless, God's creating is truly gracious. The freedom of God's self-commitment in creating and the self-commitment of God's freedom in creating are formally identical with the free loving and loving freedom of God's giving of Godself. God's active relating to us as our eschatological consummator and God's active relating to us as our reconciler is grace properly speaking; God's relating to us as our creator is not. But it is certainly gracious.

We must move into theological anthropology if
we are to do justice to the wisdom literature.
ROLAND E. MURPHY

CHAPTER **5B**

Theological Reflections on Proverbs

The following offers theological reflections on Proverbs to back proposals in the previous chapter about our proximate context understood against the background of our ultimate context, God relating creatively to what is not God. In this chapter I pick up again a discussion of canonical Wisdom literature begun in the final section of chapter 4B. The justification for doing so was developed in the first two sections of that chapter.

These are theological reflections in two senses. They are reflections on Proverbs in its present canonical form and context. The justifications for privileging the received canonical form of the text are theological. I read Proverbs as part of the Christian canon. Theological reasons for reading Christian Holy Scripture this way have been outlined above in chapters 2B and 3B, where I argue that reading biblical texts in their canonical form and context does not involve ignoring or downplaying the results of historical-critical, form-critical, redaction-critical, or literary-critical studies of the texts. To the contrary, it provides one way in which to make constructive theological use of the results of such scholarship. Indeed, part of what it means to read biblical texts in their canonical form and context is to pay special attention to ways in which editors shaped them into the form they had when they were included in the canon. The critical scholarly work required to identify that editorial shaping underscores the importance of the fact that these texts have themselves undergone historical change, and it often suggests how best to construe the trajectory of that change and its theological significance.

Another part of what it means to read biblical texts in their canonical form and contexts is to pay special attention both to canonized texts in their individual integrity and to their differences from, tensions with, and interplay with other texts in the canon read in their individual integrity. The canon is a certain sort of whole, but that wholeness is not achieved by homogenization of the individual texts that make it up, nor is it a product of any internal and largely tacit systematic content. The canon is a chorus that is sometimes dissonant.

Hearing individual texts in their canonical setting requires paying attention to the distinctive pitch and timbre of different voices.

What follows are theological reflections in a second sense. They focus on the picture that Proverbs gives of how the Creator relates to creation and the sort of order that implies in the creation, two topics that are crucial to chapter 5A. I adopt this focus, of course, because I want to think about human beings as God's creatures in ways that are guided by canonical Wisdom literature's mostly implicit creation theology.

Canonical Editing of Proverbs

The claim that the received text of Proverbs has been canonically edited rests on two main contentions: First, that there is evidence that the contents of the book had their origin prior to the composition of the book and were in some sense gathered together in collections that constitute the present text; second, that these collections were themselves assembled through an editorial process that had canonical significance. I summarize the evidence for each contention below.

1. The sayings that are the content of Proverbs are part of a larger international phenomenon in the ancient world. There is "a significant area of common subject matter, literary form, and world view in Israelite wisdom and that of Egypt and Mesopotamia" (Crenshaw 1981, 212; see chap. 9; see also Childs 1979, 547–48; McKane 1970, 51–210; R. Murphy 1990, Appendix; see Crenshaw 1981, 212, for objections that "wisdom" is not the proper name for all of this literature). There are explicit references in the Old Testament itself to the wisdom of Easterners and the Egyptians (Gen. 41:8; Exod. 7:11; 1 Kgs. 4:30; Isa. 19:11–15) that place biblical Wisdom in a wider cultural context. There are impressive parallels between Mesopotamian texts and Job and between an Egyptian text and Ecclesiastes. Proverbs 22:17–24:22 closely parallels *The Instruction of Amen-em-opet* from Egypt's New Kingdom. Generally speaking, however, it is probably misleading to think of Israel at some point "borrowing" and adapting a hitherto alien "Wisdom." It may be better to say that Wisdom teaching was an integral part of the complex cultural mix out of which Israel itself historically emerged and, in one form or another, had always been part of its common culture. So far as cultural history is concerned, Wisdom may quite literally have already been there at Israel's creation.

The contents of Proverbs surely originated in a variety of social and cultural contexts. Even its original provenance in ancient Israelite society has proven very difficult to identify. Scholarly efforts to base it in one or two original social locations in Israel, such as the royal court or scribal schools, have been inconclusive. More persuasive is R. B. Y. Scott's commonsensical suggestion of "at least" six sources: (1) accumulated folk wisdom "based on the observation and evaluation of human experience and expressed chiefly in brief common sayings"; (2) education process in the home and later in schools; (3) specially gifted counselors to kings; (4) "the intellectual curiosity and moral concern of individuals engaged in a search for knowledge of the physical environment"; (5) the "institutionalizing of wisdom through a scribal profession"; and (6) "as a later development, the adaptation of oral and literary wisdom forms . . . for the purposes of conventional religious . . . instruction" (1970, 29).

In its present canonical form, Proverbs is a collection of collections of sayings. Some collections are expressly identified as such in the text by attribution to an "author." Proverbs 10:1–22:16 is called "The proverbs of of Solomon" in 10:1. Chapters 25–29 are identified in 25:1 as "other proverbs of Solomon that the officials of King Hezekiah of Judah copied." Proverbs 30:1–33 is identified as "The words of Agur son of Jakeh" in 30:1. Chapter 31:1–9 is identified in 31:1 as "The words of King Lemuel. An oracle that his mother taught him." On textual grounds, scholars have sought to identify further subcollections, though no one such proposal has won widespread agreement. Much of the material in these collections is commonly thought to be preexilic (i.e., before 587 BC). The present form of the text most probably dates from the postexilic period. It has long been recognized on literary grounds that chapters 10–22:16 are different from chapters 1–9, and it has often been argued that the material in 10–22:16 is older than 1–9. Chapters 10–22:16 are commonly referred to as "old wisdom." The difference between the two sets of chapters, however, might be only one of form rather than of age (see Childs 1979 547–48). Not much more than that can be said with confidence about dating this material.

A good deal more can be said about the function of Wisdom sayings in each of these collections in their original cultural settings. Their function there was clearly pedagogical. This literature was produced by practices of teaching and learning. In Mesopotamia and Egypt, Wisdom teaching was addressed to social and cultural elites. Mesopotamian Wisdom teaching seems to have mostly taken place in close relation to temples, training scribes for work in religious settings. In Egypt the teaching of Wisdom took place in close relation to the royal court rather than to religious centers. It aimed at preparing "actual or potential bureaucrats" (Crenshaw 1981, 214), scribes for the civil service or government officials (indeed, at least one text—the Instruction for Merikare—appears to be a pharaoh's instruction of his son in the twenty-second century BC).

The pedagogical force of the literature is reflected in its characteristic literary forms. The literature can take the form of relatively extended reflection, sometimes as a disputation or dialogue, on such themes as social disorder, justice, or undeserved suffering. These are found in both prose and poetry. Another characteristic literary form consists of lists of nouns that summarize current "encyclopedic knowledge concerning the different professions, flora, fauna, and so forth" (Crenshaw 1981, 224)—lists drawn up, perhaps, in an effort to impose order on rapidly growing funds of knowledge.

Most of this literature, however, takes a literary form that scholars usually call "sentences." Some sentences, especially in Egyptian texts, are direct instructions in the imperative mode: do this; don't do that. Mesopotamian texts tend to concentrate on instruction regarding spells, omens, magic, and sorcery. Other sentences are in the indicative mode. They are pithy and relatively impersonal observations about how things go in the world—"proverbs" in the ordinary English sense of the word. They have in common a condensed verbal concreteness.

This concreteness reflects how Wisdom's sentences function pedagogically. Wisdom is not verbally conveyed to another person abstractly, and the precision of its conveyance is not a product of rigorously defined concepts. Wisdom's sentences do not offer a grasp of a set of universally applicable rules, much less a body of theory. Rather, they elicit insight in a student by depicting concrete situations in the most condensed way possible, often by rendering the same situation in more than one way. As Gerhard von Rad stressed (von Rad 1972), they have the literary concreteness of good poetry. Sometimes this is accomplished through parallelism, poetic verse of two or three lines in which the second and third lines re-present the subject matter of the first line. Sometimes two lines agree, sometimes they appear to be antithetical, and sometimes the second or third lines advance the thought of the first without either agreeing or disagreeing with it. Precision in expression comes precisely by playing off against one another, contrasting rendering of the same situation. From the way in which he develops the term "poetic," I take it that this is von Rad's point in saying that "above and beyond their great differences in form and content" these writings are "all composed in a poetic form, they are poetry."

Ancient teaching was usually oral, and learning happened by rote repetition. Most Wisdom writings served, perhaps, as records of oral discourse, and perhaps as texts for oral performance. Thus, the literary forms used by Proverbs are inseparable from its function: To evoke ad hoc a certain kind of insight in regard to concrete situations.

2. There is literary evidence that this historically and culturally heterogeneous material at some point was deliberately collected and edited within a theologically significant frame as part of Israel's religiously authoritative Scriptures. The frame gives this collection of collections its canonical form as religiously authoritative Scripture. It also gives the collection a particular theological trajectory, which I am attempting to follow in my theological account of human creatureliness.

The frame consists of two editorial insertions, one at the beginning and the other at the end of the book, which bracket everything in between and provide the hermeneutical guide necessary for interpreting the book in its canonical form. First a superscription introduces Proverbs as a whole: "The proverbs of Solomon son of David, king of Israel" (1:1); then, in the next-to-last collection of proverbs ("The words of Agur son of Jakeh"), an opening expression of weariness with failure to learn wisdom and skepticism of its possibility (30:1b–4) is followed by an apparent rejoinder in which slight variants of 2 Samuel 22:31 and Deuteronomy 4:2 are conjoined:

> Every word of God proves true;
>> he is a shield to those who take refuge in him.
> Do not add to his words,
>> or else he will rebuke you, and you will be found a liar.
>> (30:5, 6)

Compare 2 Samuel 22:31, a part of King David's song of thanksgiving "on the day when the LORD delivered him from the hand of all his enemies, and from the hand of Saul" (22:1):

> This God—his way is perfect;
> the promise of the LORD proves true;
> he is a shield for all who take refuge in him.

And compare Deuteronomy 4:2, which is part of Moses' address to the people of Israel before they cross the Jordan into the promised land, at the point where, having rehearsed Israel's journey from Mount Horeb and its victories in Transjordan, he turns to teach the Israelites "statutes and ordinances":

> You must neither add anything to what I command you nor take away anything from it, but keep the commandments of the LORD your God with which I am charging you.

As Brevard Childs has pointed out (1979, 551–52), taken together these two passages acknowledge the religious authority of this collection of collections of sayings and serve to locate it as an independent voice within the canon that Israel acknowledged and Christian communities of faith adopted. It is very probable that attribution of this entire collection of collections to Solomon comes late in the history of the book's editing. So too, Proverbs 30:5–6, most scholars agree, comes from the final stages of the editing of the book. Both are editorial gestures that locate the book as a whole within a larger canonical literary context. Take them in reverse order.

Proverbs 30:5–6 puts the attentive reader on notice that this collection of collections and what it teaches have the same status as God's promises (e.g., to David) and God's law (e.g., as enunciated by Moses on the eve of the conquest of the promised land). It does not matter religiously or theologically that these materials originated at various dates and in diverse social and cultural contexts, some perhaps entirely outside of Israel. It does not matter that these materials make almost no reference to YHWH's saving acts in history, to YHHW's covenant with Israel, to Torah, or to cultic worship. It does not matter that these materials originated as human reflection on human experience and claim no revelatory origin. What matters is that these materials are acknowledged to have been appropriated by God as a medium for God's word to God's people. These collections of sayings are as religiously authoritative now as are the historical and prophetic scriptures—that is, they are part of the set of texts by which God calls, forms, re-forms, and nurtures the community of God's people.

At the same time, the superscription in 1:1 ascribes to Solomon both the collections of proverbs that are individually attributed to Solomon himself and collections that originally were and continue to be attributed to others. It ascribes the entire collection of proverbs to Solomon in a historical sequence. He is the "son of David, king of Israel." Solomon is thereby identified with his position within the total Hebrew tradition. It is in the light of that location that he is to be understood and this collection is to be interpreted. The superscription establishes an obvious connection with the "official" record of Solomon's place within Israel—that is, 1 Kings 3ff. (see Childs 1979, 552).

The fact that even when this entire collection of collections of proverbs is attributed to Solomon as its author, subcollections continue to be attributed to other authors, suggests that the attribution of "authorship" to Solomon is not so much an answer to questions about the origin of the text ("Who originally wrote this?") as it is an answer to questions about the grounds of its authority ("Why privilege this text of Wisdom in particular as distinctively normative for our common life of faith?"). Similarly, attribution of the Pentateuch to Moses grounds its authority in the covenanting history of YHWH with Israel and, in that context, particularly in the authority of Torah. So, too, attribution of Psalms to King David grounds their authority in the history of Israel's (ambiguously) divinely established monarchy and, in that context, perhaps particularly in cultic worship of YHWH at Zion. But Proverbs is attributed to one who, in 1 Kings, is explicitly linked to Eastern and Egyptian wisdom. Upon becoming king, Solomon prays to God for the gift of wisdom and is said to have been given it.

Thus, as Childs points out, the attribution of Proverbs to Solomon "does not seek to provide a secondary context on the basis of the Law and the Prophets from which to interpret the proverbs, but forms a connection only with the sapiential material within Kings . . . The title [superscription in 1:1] serves canonically to preserve the *uniqueness* of the sapiential witness against attempts to merge it with the more dominant biblical themes" (1979, 552, emphasis added) having to do with covenant, law, and monarchy. Thus, the canonical editing of Proverbs to ascribe it to Solomon reminds the reader that Proverbs is an independent voice in the canon.

It is no accident that, as scholars are fond of pointing out, canonical Wisdom literature, and Proverbs in particular, make no reference to the history of YHWH's saving acts, or to YHWH's self-revelation in mighty acts in history, which are central themes in most of the Old Testament, and hardly any reference either to Law or to cultic worship. The canonical editing of Proverbs functions to locate it within the canon of texts that the community acknowledges to be principal means by which YHWH calls, forms, re-forms, and nurtures the community. But the canonical editing of the text also serves to make it logically independent of other voices in the canon that render YHWH's acts to deliver and reconcile alienated people (and, we may add, logically independent of yet other voices that render YHWH's acts to bring God's people to eschatological consummation). By its canonical editing, Proverbs is located within the canon as a way of thinking about human existence in relation to God "within the framework of a theology of creation," but it does this in logical independence of the frameworks of theologies of deliverance and reconciliation or a theology of consummation.

The "Wholeness" of Proverbs

Granted that Proverbs has been edited in ways that direct us to read it as an independent voice in the polyphony of the larger context of canonical Scriptures, in what way is this collection of collections of proverbs an integral literary "work" that can be read as some sort of coherent whole that could have a theology of anything? Precisely in its canonical form the book's collections of sayings apparently lack any kind of overall organization, thematic or otherwise. Occasional individual sayings may be striking, but read straight through at a single sitting, the book is likely to strike a modern reader as a structureless anthology of apparently random collections of sayings, without literary form or aesthetic comeliness, and mostly banal: your basically boring book. Is there anything that makes a whole of it?

My proposal is that what makes Proverbs a whole in its canonical form is not its sapiential content (it's too disorganized) but its singular performative pedagogical force—namely, to evoke wisdom in us when it is properly used. Grounds for this suggestion lie in the implications of two ways in which its otherwise heterogeneous contexts have been edited into its present canonical form: (1) the role of chapters 1–9 in relation to the rest of the book, and, especially, (2) in counterpoint with 31:10–31.

The poems composing chapters 1–9, which include the major passages personifying Wisdom as a woman, may be taken as a unit consisting of materials probably coming from disparate sources subsequently edited into its present form (see, e.g., McKane 1970, 1–10, 362–69). However, as Zimmerli has observed, no matter how this unit of the text came to have its present form, it now fills a specific function by its placement at the beginning of this collection of collections. It serves as the "hermeneutical guide" (see Childs 1979, 189) to how to read the collection as a "whole."

Claudia Camp (1985) has developed the point by making notable suggestions about just how 1:8–9:18 works in literary counterpoint with 31:10–31 to make a whole out of this collection of collections of sentences. I examine in turn the function of each of these passages in Proverbs.

The unit of chapters 1–9 opens with a prologue that states the purpose of the collection and gives it theological location; thereafter the unit oscillates between exhorting us to listen carefully to instruction in wisdom and commending wisdom to us by celebrating its importance and value. The prologue declares that the book's purpose is pedagogical:

> For learning about wisdom and instruction,
>   for understanding words of insight,
>   for gaining instruction in wise dealing,
>   righteousness, justice, and equity; . . .
>
> (1:2)

Then the editor immediately adds lines that explicitly locate this purpose in a distinctive religious and theological context:

> The fear of the LORD is the beginning of knowledge;
>   fools despise wisdom and instruction.
>
> (1:7)

This editorial gesture is programmatic in the broad and loose sense that it explicitly announces what is mostly a background assumption of the entire book—namely, that responding to "the LORD" is the life-context of the search for wisdom. It is not a theologically programmatic statement in the sense that it announces a theme that will then be systematically developed in the rest of the book. Indeed, the relation between wisdom and the Lord, between "becoming wise" and "fearing the LORD", while not unmentioned in Proverbs, can hardly be described as a major explicit motif in the book. It is just that fact that has prompted scholarly arguments to the effect that the original context of wisdom teaching in Israel was "secular," and only relatively late in Israel's history was religious God-talk edited in by pious editors (see McKane 1970, 10–22). The theologically important point here, whatever the outcome may be of that scholarly debate, is that in its canonical form the text is edited to make two things explicit: (1) used properly, this book is to function pedagogically in regard to our becoming wise; (2) the necessary context of this pedagogy is appropriate response ("fear") to the Creator.

Exactly what sort of pedagogy? This unit as edited tends to focus, not on instruction in specific wise behaviors, but rather on commendation of the importance of seeking and attending to wisdom in the first place. The remainder of chapters 1:8–9:18 does move back and forth between recommendations of attention to wisdom (e.g., "My son [NRSV: child], do not forget my teaching" [3:1; cf. 1:10, 15; 3:21; 4:10, 20; 5:1, 7; 6:1, 3; 7:1, 24; 8:32]) and instruction concerning specific types of behavior. However, most sentences in this unit admonish us to pay attention to instruction in wisdom, immediately followed by the reason for doing so: Wisdom gives abundant life. Over and over again, using a rich variety of imagery, exhortation to seek wisdom passes over into celebration of the importance and life-giving value of wisdom.

Here lies the role of chapters 1–9 as, in Zimmerli's phrase, "the hermeneutical guide" to the book of Proverbs: This unit directs us to interpret this text by focusing on the ways in which it may be used with performative force to elicit wisdom in us so that we act in ways that are appropriate responses to God as Creator. Although some of the materials incorporated into this book do issue moral commands, as canonically edited they do not function primarily as instruction in ethics. Even though other materials do convey perceptive remarks about the human scene, as canonically edited they do not function primarily to draw our attention to interesting features of human experience that may have escaped our notice. As edited, traditional wisdom materials are not used to provide an abstract definition of wisdom; nor are they used to give rules to follow in order to become wise. At most, as edited, traditional wisdom materials serve to give concrete examples of someone in particular eliciting wisdom in someone else in particular in some particular context, and exhort us in our concrete particularities to go on in the same way in our own particular contexts. Thus, these materials, in all their relatively shapeless heterogeneity, are a whole in functioning together to elicit wisdom in our action as ones who live and act *coram Deo*, before God the Creator.

Camp extends this point by showing how the materials collected in Proverbs are literarily structured in the book's canonical form. It is clear on literary grounds that the poems of chapters 1–9, including those that personify Wisdom as woman, and the unit comprising 31:1–31 (the Ode to the Capable Wife) are distinct from the materials between them. Placed at the beginning and at the end of the book by the book's editor(s), they serve to frame it, like bookends giving it a definite beginning and end and thereby a minimal sort of literary wholeness.

Camp identifies nine images or, in one case, a "condensed tangle of images," shared by these two literary units that bracket the proverbs collected between them. These images repeat images already used in the intervening proverbs themselves (see Camp 1985, 191–207). In particular, she finds such strong resonances of themes and repetitions of images between the poems composing chapters 1–9 and 31:10–31, on one side, and chapter 23, which falls roughly halfway between them, on the other, that she ventures the hypothesis "that a conscious editorial effort was made to include within the body of the proverb collection a unit of instruction material [chap. 23] that corresponded to the thematic pattern being developed at the beginning and end of the book of Proverbs. The purpose of this move was to provide an extra 'stitch,' so to speak, in the seaming of the book" (201). Thus, the canonical editing of Proverbs shapes it into a certain kind of literary whole. The heterogeneity of the collected sentences and their nearly random and themeless order remain unaltered. What the editing provides is a literary, not a systematic or thematic, wholeness.

This editing of Proverbs is decisive for interpreting it theologically. The upshot of the book's canonical editing is that the book is not to be interpreted as a whole that is primarily about knowing and heeding particular wise ideas or knowing and following correct ethical commands. Rather it is about what wisdom is, and about our becoming wise ourselves in our particular contexts. In summary, the hermeneutical guidance provided by the editing that shapes the book into a literary whole is this: Proverbs is to be lived with (a) as a pedagogical book, (b) whose religious importance lies in its performative force to elicit wisdom in concrete situations (c) in the context of a lived commitment to the Lord (d) and as part, perhaps the core, of efforts to respond appropriately ("fear") to God as Creator.

The failure to keep all of this in mind accounts for the sinking feeling a reader in our culture may have, after reading several chapters of Proverbs at a stretch, that this literature is hopelessly banal. It is as though the sentences had all come out of the mouth of Polonius as he wanders around the Danish castle mouthing pretentious wise sayings to the king, to Hamlet, to his children Laertes and Ophelia. Why is it that if one momentarily forgets his name, one is inclined to identify Polonius as "the old fool"? It's not because the sense of his remarks is without insight ("To thine own self be true," etc.). It is because what he says so ponderously never relates to the concrete particularities of his world. His remarks always seem to float above the specific details of the immediate situation, or are connected to them only in ironic and unintended ways. Contrast the sentences of Proverbs. They are one-liners (or sometimes two- or three-liners). To be sure they have abstractable content, or sense, that can be stated propositionally, and they have a range of reference—that is, a variety of situations to which they may refer. But what is important about them is their performative force: They are to be used pedagogically ad hoc to elicit an attentive search for insight into what is going on in concrete moments of experience so that the student might act more wisely in those moments for her own well-being and that of her proximate contexts.

Tropes in Proverbs for the Creator's Relation to Creation

The account I gave in chapter 3A of how the triune God relates to reality other than God specifically as its creator developed two suggestions: that the description in Proverbs of God's relating to Woman Wisdom is a root metaphor for how God relates to creatures generally; second, that, because God relates to all other creatures through Woman Wisdom, she is also a metaphor for the fact that all human creatures in particular are created in being born into a vocation to be wise for the well-being of creation. Both suggestions rest heavily on interpretation of Proverbs' personifications of Wisdom as a woman. That interpretation deserves further explanation.

Two Women as Tropes for Wisdom

In Proverbs 1, after an exhortation to pay attention to instruction in wisdom comes a passage depicting Wisdom as a woman crying out in public places, aggressively calling us to embrace Wisdom (1:20–33). Repeatedly in chapters 1–9, brief passages characterizing Wisdom as a woman are interspersed among passages urging us to attend to instruction in Wisdom (3:13–18; 4:6–9; 7:4).

Wisdom is consistently presented as life-giving, the basis of human well-being. A major metaphor for Wisdom in Proverbs is the "life giving tree":

> She [Wisdom] is a tree of life to those who lay hold of her;
>   those who hold her fast are called happy.
>
> (3:18)

She gives life to us by authoring wisdom in us. That is how she is a "tree of life." In 8:35, 36 Woman Wisdom says of herself:

> "For whoever finds me [Wisdom] finds life
>   and obtains favor from the LORD;
> but those who miss me injure themselves;
>   all who hate me love death."

In 3:19–20, life-giving Wisdom is explicitly related to the creator. God created "by" wisdom;

> The LORD by wisdom founded the earth;
>   by understanding he established the heavens;
> by his knowledge the deeps broke open,
>   and the clouds drop down the dew.

This literary device is famously brought to a crescendo in chapter 8, where Wisdom is personified as a woman who "on the heights, beside the way, at the crossroads" (v. 2) takes her stand and calls us all to learn from her, celebrates the rewards of learning from her, and then reveals her astonishing identity:

> The LORD created me at the beginning of his work,
>   the first of his acts of long ago.
> Ages ago I was set up,
>   at the first, before the beginning of the earth.
> . . . .
> when he marked out the foundations of the earth,
>   then I was beside him, like a little child
>   [alt. reading: like a master worker];

and I was daily his delight,
 rejoicing before him always,
rejoicing in his inhabited world
 and delighting in the human race.
  (8:22–23, 29b–31)

Woman Wisdom is not God, for she is herself created (8:22). She is not creation as such; she was "created at the beginning of his work, the first of his acts
of long ago." She is a literary trope, a personification of Wisdom. Questions
about her ontological status (Is she an angel? Is she a divine being? Is she one of
the Persons of the Trinity? etc.) seem misplaced. What is appropriate is to stress
the relationships in which she stands and the roles she plays.

God has a definite relation to Woman Wisdom: God directly and immediately relates to her, and to all other creatures through her, being right beside her
(8:30) in creating and delighting in her. God's relation to her is the root metaphor for the way the Creator relates to all creatures. She, in turn, has a definite
relation to the rest of creation and a role within it. She lies at the foundation of
the creaturely realm, to which she gives abundant life and the guarantee that
creation is understandable (3:19). Her role is to call through creation to human
creatures to be wise themselves (e.g., 1:22–39). Furthermore, as the first of the
creatures and their foundation, she represents all creatures to God. Hence, her
relation back to God is a trope for how creation generally ought to relate to the
Creator, "rejoicing before him always" and in that context, also "rejoicing in his
inhabited world and delighting in the human race" (8:31).

Proverbs concludes (chap. 31) with another woman, the Capable Wife, who
also functions as a trope for Wisdom. She appears in an "Ode" which seems
to be an integral part of the final collection in Proverbs: "The words of King
Lemuel. An oracle that his mother taught him" (cf. 31). The Ode celebrates the
"Capable Wife" for her management of the complex affairs of a large household,
bringing food "from far away," providing meals, superintending servant-girls,
buying real estate, planting vineyards "with the fruit of her hands," weaving
and selling cloth, making clothes and selling them, being generous to the poor,
teaching wisdom, so that "her works praise her in the city gates." The Capable
Wife functions as a trope for the life-giving power of Wisdom in the quotidian,
in which what our own culture distinguishes as the private and public realms
thoroughly interpenetrate.

There is an impressive amount of literary similarity between Woman Wisdom and the Capable Wife (for the following, see Camp 1985, chap. 6). They
are characterized in many of the same ways, using a strikingly large number of
the same images. Both teach wisdom (1:8; 31:26 and 31:1–9); both are "more
precious than jewels" (3:15 and 8:11; 31:10); one will not lack for material gain
if one finds either (8:18; 31:10); nothing one desires can compare with Woman
Wisdom (3:15), and in the eyes of her husband, the Capable Wife surpasses
even the most worthy of other women (31:29). One should grasp Woman Wisdom and hold her fast (3:18), prize and embrace her (4:8), and love her (4:6);
so too one should put one's whole trust in a Capable Wife (31:11; cf. 5:18) and
be infatuated with her. Woman Wisdom calls all to the security and well-being
of her house (8:34; 9:1–6—which explicitly characterizes Woman Wisdom as

a capable manager of a household), and the Capable Wife is hospitable to the poor and needy. Woman Wisdom takes her stand and cries out in the gates (1:21; 8:3), and the works of the Capable Wife praise her in the gates. Regularly in chapters 1–9 the reality of Woman Wisdom must be carefully distinguished from deceitful appearances, and the Capable Wife must be distinguished from deceitful charm and vain beauty (31:30).

At the same time, there is a kind of antiphony between these two metaphors for wisdom. Present at the creation of the earth, Woman Wisdom has cosmic significance; the Capable Wife is utterly enmeshed in the quotidian. Woman Wisdom is active in the public realm, taking her stand in the streets and crying out in the city gates; however, true lovers of Woman Wisdom must find their way to her household. The Capable Wife, on the other hand, is active in the household, though her work regularly takes her into the public realm.

The differences between Woman Wisdom and the Capable Wife, functioning as literary tropes, exhibit an important distinction between two different senses of "wisdom" in Proverbs. The literary similarities and overlaps between the two bring out that these two senses are interrelated and inseparable. On the one hand, God's relation to Woman Wisdom serves as a metaphor for God's relation to creation in creating. On the other hand, the Capable Wife is a metaphor for that to which the Creator calls us in creating us, the vocation into which we are born.

Pedagogical Tropes for How God Relates in Creating

Thus far I have tried to establish three points:

1. The received text of Proverbs has been edited to ground its canonical status in the tradition of the authority of Solomonic Wisdom, which is independent of both the authority of the tradition of the covenant created with God's event of deliverance at the Reed Sea and its Torah, and of the authority of the tradition of the temple and its cultus.

2. The wholeness of Proverbs as canonically edited lies not so much in a literary structure that ties it together (for that is minimal) as in its single overall pedagogical force when used in the common life of the community that seeks to respond appropriately to the Lord's creating—namely, the force of evoking wisdom in those who attend to it "in the fear of the LORD."

3. Two dominant tropes in the text of Proverbs, Woman Wisdom and the Capable Wife, in their literary antiphony, function as root metaphors, respectively, for how God relates to that which is not God in creating it, and for that to which God calls creatures in creating them—that is, to be wise.

Together these points warrant the judgment that Proverbs is enough of a whole to fill the role of scriptural guide and norm for a theological account of God creating and human beings as creatures, is literarily governed by tropes that express a distinctive way of understanding God's creative relating to what is not God (i.e., "thinks within the framework of a theology of creation") and express what is appropriate human response to God creating, and does all this in a way that is independent of and not bent by the narrative logic of other types of scriptural stories that tell of God relating to deliver and reconcile or God relating to draw to eschatological consummation.

However, what has not yet been established is that the method in Proverbs of expressing *how* God relates creatively—while not bent by the influence of the narrative logic of scriptural stories of other ways in which God relates to what is not God—has an at least implicit narrative logic of its own that is distinct enough to norm and provide clear guidance for the formulation of a theological account of God's creating and its anthropological implications. The task of this section is to show that it does.

The major metaphor used in Proverbs for Woman Wisdom is "tree of life." This metaphor must be interpreted against the background of overall pedagogical force that makes Proverbs a whole. Woman Wisdom is a "tree of life" in that she authors or creates wisdom. As a tree nourishes life, so by authoring wisdom in her students Woman Wisdom nourishes life in them. If Woman Wisdom is a trope for how God relates to what is not God in creating it, then "tree of life" further specifies that relating: God's relating-to is an ongoing relating that nourishes life and is to be understood most adequately as an analogy with the way in which teaching and learning wisdom nourish specifically human life.

The "life" in question here is not limited to biological life. That is brought out by the contrast term in Proverbs to Woman Wisdom. Consistently the opposite of wisdom is folly, and where wisdom is said to lead to life, folly is said to lead to death. Folly is sometimes personified as the Adulterous Woman whose "way leads down to death" (2:18). It is not as though Woman Wisdom is being celebrated as the bringer of unending biological life, while the Adulterous Woman alone brings biological death. The issue between them is not immortality but overall human well-being. Thinking within the framework of a theology of creation, Proverbs celebrates our finitude and takes our inherent mortality for granted. What's at issue is fullness of life as long as it lasts and within the limits inherent in finitude. Folly, personified as the Adulterous Woman, yields a shallow, hollow, broken life, a life that is but a living death. Wisdom, personified as Woman Wisdom, yields a life that will eventually end in death but is lived richly and satisfyingly in the here and now of the everyday, a full though dying life.

I suggest later that it is theologically important to distinguish between the human well-being fostered by learning to be wise and human flourishing. Theologically speaking, both "well-being" and "flourishing" are anthropologically important human conditions. But they are different human "goods," the first grounded in the ways in which God relates to all else and the second in the ways in which human beings respond appropriately to God's ways of relating to them. Here we are reflecting on God's way of relating to all else creatively, so our focus is on what that way of relating entails in regard to human well-being when it is understood along the lines suggested by "mainstream" canonical Wisdom literature, of which Proverbs is paradigmatic.

The juxtaposition of the Adulterous Woman with Woman Wisdom brings out that becoming wise is itself in service of a dying life that enjoys well-being as long as it lives, just as being foolish is in service of a living death. Who authors wisdom in us does so in order to author life.

How does Wisdom do this? To answer this question, we need to analyze in more detail the ways in which Woman Wisdom and the Capable Wife in their complex interrelationships function as tropes for God relating to creatures and creatures' appropriate response to God.

It is conventional to distinguish in a metaphor between its vehicle and its tenor. For example, in the Psalmist's phrase "The LORD is my rock (and my salvation)," "rock" is the vehicle of this metaphor for the Lord, and its tenor is the array of associations with "rock" that are appropriate in the text's relevant literary, historical, and cultural context ("unchanging," "long-lasting," "steadfast," "trustworthy," "secure," etc.). In the personifications "Woman Wisdom" (in chapters 1–9) and the "Capable Wife" (in 31:10–31), taken as metaphors, "woman" is the vehicle of each metaphor, and its tenor is provided by the array of images of woman and of roles that are appropriately associated with women. These images illumine just how Wisdom is life-giving.

The tenor of these two metaphors cannot be just any images and roles for women that are familiar in the reader's own historical and cultural setting. They must be the range of images of women and roles for women in the historical, cultural, and social context in which Proverbs received its canonical editing and, at the very broadest, the range of images and roles for women found in the text's larger literary context in the canon. For our purposes, it is sufficient to take note of four images of women and roles for women prominently used in Proverbs itself, in chapters 1–9 and 31:10–31: woman as teacher and woman as lover and as beloved; and cross-cutting them, woman as effective verbal communicator and woman as manager of large and complex households.

(Claudia Camp argues persuasively that in the personification in Proverbs of wisdom as woman, a number of culturally familiar roles and images of women are drawn together. To identify them, Camp casts her net widely in ancient Israel's literature. Her principle of selection cannot but be determined at least in part by her self-admittedly speculative re-construction [1985, 16] of the social situation of early postexilic Israel and the unusually powerful, if largely informal, social and cultural roles it afforded women. However, even if, in a rush of scholarly caution, we bracket her historical reconstruction and with it part of her principle of selection of relevant images and roles for women, we still have at hand those images and roles for women that are explicitly mentioned or alluded to in Proverbs 1–9 and 31:10–31, and echoed elsewhere in the book. They are sufficient for our purposes. See Camp 1985, Prologue, chaps. 4–8.)

1. It is Woman Wisdom as teacher of wisdom who is life-giving. Here the tenor of the metaphor "Woman Wisdom" comes from familial roles. Woman Wisdom teaches as a mother—or father; both are cited interchangeably in Proverbs—teaching in the course of nurturing a child. It is a way of teaching that engages the entire person of the student, not only the mind, but also emotions, imagination, memory, will, and body.

The specific character of the teaching and learning interaction is important here. Wisdom is represented as coming to a student from the outside. It is significant that among the images and roles of women invoked in Proverbs 1–9 and 31:10–31, "birthing" or "mothering" never appear. Wisdom is not taught maieutically. Wisdom is not somehow mysteriously brought to birth in a student in the privacy of her personal interiority. Rather, Woman Wisdom teaches in public spaces.

This requires that Woman Wisdom be an effective verbal communicator using a natural language commonly used in a public space. Wisdom is elicited in students through conceptually formed exchange with a teacher that takes place in some social and cultural public space, uses some common language, and engages every aspect of the ones being made wise.

2. The tenor of Woman Wisdom as metaphor for wisdom in Proverbs is also provided by women as lovers and as beloved. This tenor makes Woman Wisdom a metaphor for the dynamics of teaching and learning wisdom. The dynamics of pedagogy in wisdom consist of a complex and subtle interplay between Wisdom's giving and others' receiving. As symbolized by Woman Wisdom, Wisdom (a) is always already there aggressively offering to give herself in love to everyone, but (b) wisdom is learned only by students' own passionately active seeking of Wisdom, so that (c) the offered gift is truly received only in the passionate interaction of giving and active receiving, an engagement, however, (d) that doesn't always happen, for wisdom is a mystery not always easy to find and always easy to confuse with deceptive solicitors of our love. Consider each of these points in turn.

(a) In chapters 1–9 Woman Wisdom is three times presented as one who actively calls everyone to wisdom. As we move through the three scenes there is a subtle and important series of changes in the way in which she is characterized. In the first scene she is described as calling in public places to warn of dire consequences to those who reject her:

> Wisdom cries out in the street;
>   in the square she raises her voice.
> .   .   .   .
> "How long will scoffers delight in their scoffing
>   and fools hate knowledge?
> Give heed to my reproof;
> I will pour out my thoughts to you;
>   I will make my words known to you.
> Because I have called and you refused. . . .
> .   .   .   .
> I also will also laugh at your calamity;
>   I will mock when panic strikes you."
>   (1:20, 22–24, 26)

Wisdom is already there before us, standing over against us in the public realm, calling us to wisdom and warning us of the consequences of loving folly instead. She calls in love, and her call here is love's own hectoring. There is something "out there" in creation extrinsic to us, not innate within us, that offers us wisdom, indeed, calls us to be wise in our agency.

In the second passage, the note of warning is missing and Wisdom is simply presented in public places calling everyone to learn wisdom from her, offering herself in love to those who will love her:

> On the heights, beside the way,
>   at the crossroads she takes her stand;
> beside the gates in front of the town,
>   at the entrance of the portals she cries out: . . .
> .   .   .   .

> "Take my instruction instead of silver,
>   and knowledge rather than choice gold;
> for wisdom is better than jewels,
>   and all you may desire cannot compare with her.
>   .   .   .   .
> I love those who love me,
>   and those who seek me diligently find me."
>   (8:2–5, 10–11; 17)

Here Wisdom is not only already there in the world, other than we, over against us, calling us to wisdom; not only is she present in the public realm, but she also presents herself as surpassingly desirable, and what she offers is nothing other than herself in love.

Here is the first moment in the dynamics of the pedagogy of wisdom. Wisdom is somehow already there in the created realm calling us to be wise in our agency. The offer is made in a love that is sheer spontaneous delight in humankind (see 8:30). In her call Wisdom offers us nothing less than herself. There is nothing esoteric about the offer or arcane about the call; the offer is made in a call that sounds in the public realm. Wisdom is to be learned by loving something genuinely over against and other than we.

(b) Woman Wisdom is characterized again in a third passage that brings out a second moment in the dynamics of pedagogy in wisdom. She is presented again, in public places, "the highest places in the town" (9:3), calling everyone to her to learn wisdom. However, this now-familiar scene is placed in a new context. Before she goes out to call, Woman Wisdom prepares a feast:

> Wisdom has built her house,
>   she has hewn her seven pillars.
> She has slaughtered her animals, she has mixed her wine,
>   she has also set her table.
> She has sent out her servant-girls.
>   (9:1–3a)

And then she calls everyone to come home with her to eat her banquet and drink her wine. She calls from the highest places in the town,

> "You that are simple, turn in here!"
>   To those without sense she says,
> "Come, eat of my bread
>   and drink of the wine I have mixed.
> Lay aside immaturity, and live,
>   and walk in the way of insight."
>   (9:4–6)

This presentation of Woman Wisdom resonates in two directions.

On one side, it resonates with the description of the Capable Wife in 31:10–31. Here the metaphor of Woman Wisdom as lover and beloved is cross-cut by the metaphor of her as capable manager. The Capable Wife manages the meal preparation and the deploying of her household help. In doing so she evokes the loving admiration of her husband. So, too, in 9:1–3 Woman Wisdom capably manages her household, perhaps with an extension of the connotations of "household." Does the remark in 9:1 that "she has hewn her seven pillars" allude to mythic accounts of the foundations of the earth? If so, the "household" she is managing, and the "banquet" she is preparing, have cosmic as well as domestic resonances. Here again, the literary interplay between the image of the Capable Wife in 31:10–31 and the image of Woman Wisdom in chapters 1–9 character-izes Wisdom as already there in the public world calling to us in love. Read in its interplay with 31:10–31, 9:1–3 suggests that the wisdom to which Woman Wisdom calls us makes for the sorts of order, perhaps both domestic and cos-mic, which human life requires for its well-being.

On the other hand, the description of Woman Wisdom in 9:1–3 also reso-nates with the description of the seductive "foolish woman" just a few verses later in the same chapter (13–18). Indeed, before encountering Woman Wisdom and the foolish woman in chapter 9, the reader has already encoun-tered four warnings in earlier chapters against the "strange woman" (2:16–19; 5:3–6; 6:23–35; 7:4–27). All four passages stress that she is seductive and that she leads to death; all but the second stress that she is an adulteress. The last of the four (7:4–27) in particular elaborates on her aggressive seductiveness in ways that echo descriptions in chapter 9 of both Woman Wisdom and the "foolish woman":

> She is loud and wayward;
>   her feet do not stay at home;
> now in the street, now in the squares,
>   and at every corner she lies in wait.
>   (7:11–12)

Against the background of these earlier warnings against the "strange woman," the trope of the "foolish woman" functions in chapter 9 as the liter-ary personification of foolishness in parallel with the way in which Woman Wisdom functions as the literary personification of wisdom. She too sits "on a seat at the high places of the town" calling to people to come home to "eat" with her:

> "You who are simple, turn in here!"
>   And to those without sense she says,
> "Stolen water is sweet,
>   and bread eaten in secret is pleasant."
>   (9:16, 17)

The "foolish woman" clearly is presented as erotically seductive. "Stolen water" and eating bread "in secret" have unmistakable sexual overtones.

Reading the account of Woman Wisdom in its literary interrelationships with the account of the "foolish woman" underscores that Woman Wisdom is being presented as just as much of a seductress as is the "foolish woman." There is the same dramatic movement in the descriptions of Woman Wisdom and of the "foolish woman": preparation of a meal at home, going out into the public realm to call others to come home to share the meal. The verbal par-allels between the two descriptions are so striking that it is difficult to suppose them to be merely accidental. The principal verbal difference between them is that the "foolish woman's" banquet offers only water, while Woman Wisdom offers wine!

The all-important practical difference between them is this. Responding to Woman Wisdom's call leads to well-being, but responding to the "foolish woman's" call leads to death:

> But they do not know that the dead are there [at her banquet],
>   that her guests are in the depths of Sheol.
>
> (9:18)

Part of the tenor of the metaphor "Woman Wisdom," then, is this: Wisdom's call is not just love's hectoring, as in 1:20–21. Nor is her call just love's offer of itself, as in 8:1ff. In the present passage (9:1–6), her call in love is intended to be seductive. Wisdom seeks to elicit an intensely erotic response, in the broad sense of desiring love, an *eros* born of lack and need.

What is the lack or need? The well-being of life depends on being wise in our agency. However, wisdom is not simply given with birth. We are not inherently wise. To the extent that we lack wisdom, we lack the condition for life's well-being. Acquiring wisdom is a need, and we will acquire it only by attending to it, by loving it, with an intense *eros*.

This is the second moment in the dynamics of pedagogy in wisdom. In love, Wisdom may offer herself, and do so in the public realm and not arcanely. All the same, the student must passionately seek to find her. Over and over again in Proverbs the reader is instructed, urged, enjoined constantly to seek out wisdom. On the one hand, Wisdom is characterized as already there, calling attention to herself, offering herself in love. On the other hand, we are constantly urged single-mindedly to search her out and find her.

(c) Learning wisdom thus involves a complex interaction between teacher and learner whose dynamics are like those of a relationship in which the lover is freely self-giving and elicits in the beloved a strong desiring love, and all in a way that makes for the beloved's well-being, but must nonetheless be actively sought and intensely desired.

Hence actually learning wisdom is explicitly likened to lovers' embrace:

> Happy are those who find wisdom,
>   and those who get understanding,
>
> . . . .
>
> She is a tree of life to those who lay hold of her;
>   those who hold her fast are called happy.
>
> (3:13, 18)

(d) However, pedagogy in Wisdom does not necessarily come to this happy consummation. Its dynamics are fragile and may easily malfunction. Overall, as a text with pedagogical force, Proverbs has a cheerfully confident tone. It is remarkably optimistic about the prospects of human agents actually learning to be wise in their agency. Nonetheless, around the edges even in Proverbs there are a few acknowledgments that the most earnest pursuit of wisdom may fail (cf. 14:12; 16:1, 2, 25). In particular, the collection of sentences introduced as "The words of Agur son of Jakeh" strikes a note of world-weariness at a frustrated effort to learn wisdom:

> Thus says the man: I am weary, O God,
>   I am weary, O God. How can I prevail?
> Surely I am too stupid to be human;
>   I do not have human understanding.
> I have not learned wisdom,
>   nor have I knowledge of the holy ones.
>   (30:1–3)

In Job and Ecclesiastes, on the other hand, canonical Wisdom literature presses against "mainstream" Wisdom's optimism as reflected in Proverbs.

Proverbs itself, in its canonical form, gives two principal reasons for this failure: Wisdom is both elusive and ambiguous. Wisdom's elusiveness is the obverse of the insistent exhortations in chapters 1–9 to seek wisdom and to pay close attention to instructions in wisdom. Wisdom is not just self-evidently available to a casual observer. She is elusive, and discerning Wisdom comes only by way of passionately attentive and focused pursuit. This is the ground of the possibility that Ecclesiastes presses so strongly, that Wisdom somehow hides herself precisely in offering herself.

Even when Wisdom presents herself, she is easily confused with her opposite. Although this ambiguity is only marginally noted in the collections of sentences gathered together in Proverbs, the root is underscored in the book's canonical framing in chapters 1–9. This collection introduced as "The proverbs of Solomon" includes the observation:

> There is a way that seems right to a person,
>   but its end is the way to death.
>   (14:12)

The observation is virtually repeated in a literarily distinct collection also attributed to Solomon (16:25). This second collection begins with a reminder of how ambiguous Wisdom may be to us:

> All one's ways may be pure in one's own eyes,
>   but the LORD weighs the spirit.
>   (16:2)

The root of Wisdom's ambiguity lies in something Proverbs underscores. It lies in the way in which Wisdom addresses our deep need for well-being in life, in the way Wisdom's seductiveness elicits in us an erotic love for her. In this regard, as chapters 1–9 repeatedly underscore, Woman Wisdom is all too easily confused with the seductive foolish woman and with the adulteress. We have noted that in chapters 1–9 there is a gradual shift from a picture of a seductive adulteress, apparently a stock literary figure in international Wisdom traditions, to a picture of the foolish woman as a personification of folly. We have also noted that the basic difference between the real and the counterfeit image of Wisdom is that the way of Woman Wisdom leads to life's well-being while the way of the foolish woman leads to death. Solicitations to Wisdom in concrete cases are, it seems, inherently ambiguous.

Just what is it about the counterfeit Woman Wisdom that is deadly? The answer lies in the view taken of adultery and the adulteress in 2:16–19; 5:3–14; 6:23–35; 7:5; and 7:6–27. The adulteress here is not a personification of folly, as 9:13–18 seems to be. Sometimes an adultery is just adultery—even in Proverbs.

It is significant that the figure used is that of an adulteress and not that of a harlot. Both are immoral, but in the relevant literatures the harlot is not deemed to be dangerous. To the contrary, she is socially tolerated (see Bird 1974, 66–67). A harlot conducts a business in which she enters into a system of exchange that necessarily observes some public—that is, generally shared—conventions and requires a certain amount of mutual trust. Like Rahab in Joshua 2:1–21, her line of work is publicly known and her house is easily identifiable. The adulteress, by contrast, is deemed to be dangerous, indeed deadly, and is not to be socially tolerated.

Why? The ways in which she is described in chapters 1–9 tie her deadliness to her misuse of language. Here, too, as with "woman as teacher," the force of the tenor "woman as lover" is crosscut by another tenor, "woman as communicator." The adulterous woman's dangerousness does not lie simply in her deception of her husband, violating the covenant trust between them, though that is noted (2:17). Nor does it lie finally in the fact that were her practice of violating covenants generalized it would absolutely destroy any larger social fabric. No, at bottom what is dangerous about her is her misuse of language. The single most common characterization of her is that she speaks with "smooth words" (2:16; cf. 5:3—"and her speech is smoother than oil;" 6:24—"smooth tongue"; 7:5; 7:21—"smooth words/talk"). The smooth words are mortally deceptive.

Wherein lies the deception, and why is it so dangerous? Perhaps we may explain it this way. Ordinary languages are inherently public. Where a secret code or a private language is devised, its invention presupposes and is parasitic upon some prior and surrounding public language. Furthermore, languages work properly when their use is tied up with practices of appropriate forms of life that are themselves public—that is, socially and culturally shaped. Indeed, to learn a language is, among other things, to acquire the conceptual capacities one needs in order to live as a member of the society that ordinarily uses that language and to participate significantly in its culture.

The adulteress in Proverbs uses the ordinary language of love to present herself as surpassingly desirable and to offer herself in love (7:14–18). And she uses it with skill and eloquence. However, she uses it to suggest that it is possible to enact loving and being loved in radical secrecy, not just in a private space and time temporarily protected from ordinary public space and time, but in an absolutely alternative world, in space and time absolutely disjoined from the public and the ordinary. She uses ordinary language to promise the possibility of life's well-being in a point of time and space entirely unrelated to the broad plane defined by the lines of our culturally and linguistically shaped social interactions.

That is utterly deceptive. No such form of life, and certainly no such well-being in human life, is possible. Here a language is used skillfully, but in total disengagement from all appropriate forms of life. In part, such misuse of language is dangerously deceptive because, simply as a use of language, it is so well hidden. However, it is dangerous at a deeper level than that. With her smooth speech the adulteress in Proverbs is using the familiar language of love in ways that threaten to destroy the very possibility both of genuine social interaction and of language itself, and therewith destroys the possibility of love. It uses an inherently public language tied up with inescapably social forms of life to promise and invite one into an alternative world of absolutely secret forms of life in which language is radically private—which is to say, it threatens to destroy the possibility of genuinely human forms of life. It is not dangerous simply because it risks incurring the anger of the betrayed husband (6:34, 35), but more profoundly because it threatens basic conditions of human life:

> for her way leads down to death,
>   and her paths to the shades;
> those who go to her never come back,
>   nor do they regain the paths of life.
>   (2:18, 19)

Conversely, a condition necessary for life's well-being is the truthful use of language: true to reality; true—that is, faithful, to conversation partners; true to the speaker's own intentions. Wise action requires true use of language.

Conclusion. Proverbs likens God's creative relating to what is not God to Woman Wisdom's way of making her students wise: God relates creatively as One addressing human beings in and through their public, everyday world with a call to be wise, placing them objectively in a vocation to be wise; addressing them with a call that engages all that they are by actively, though noncoercively, seeking to seduce in them a desiring love of wisdom born of need; offering, if embraced, to be the ground of their creaturely well-being—an offer, however, that can be received only by those who attentively and passionately seek to respond to God appropriately; and an offer that can fail to be received. This does not suggest any picture of how God creates that which is not God. It suggests, instead, a way of understanding the way in which God relates to all that is not God to sustain and nurture it in being.

Central to this way of characterizing the way in which God relates creatively are metaphors of truthful use of a common language. Truthful use of a common language, which includes keeping its use faithful to the forms of life of which the language is an integral part, is the theologically important necessary—though not sufficient—condition for the social, public practices that constitute human life. Calling creatures to be wise, God talks them into being in communities, communities of everyday social and public practices, including practices of use of common languages, communities whose well-being lies in responding appropriately (i.e., "in the fear of the LORD") to God's creative call, responding in passionate search for wisdom to which God in love woos them.

Accordingly, the ultimate context of our lives, God's creative relating to us, may be characterized as God constituting, sustaining, and nurturing reality other than God by freely continuing, in delight and love, to call it to be wise. This address is performative: it constitutes communities of language-use. And it is commissive on God's part: in the very act of calling to wisdom, God is freely self-committed in love to the well-being of that which is constituted by the call. So, too, the proximate contexts of our lives may be characterized as the public spaces and times constituted by everyday human practices, and the truthful uses of common languages that are integral to those practices. The relation between God and what God relates to creatively is thus analogous to a social institution, a society of beings, constituted by dynamics of giving and responding, in which God's address is a giving of reality and value, and the practices that make up the common social life of God's creatures are called to be formed wisely as responses appropriate to the way in which God has given.

Thus, as the book's central trope for how God relates creatively, "Woman Wisdom," in its literary relation to the trope "Capable Wife," provides a picture that is sufficiently determinate in its own right to guide and norm a theological account of God creating and of human beings as creatures. This trope is given its determinacy by the interplay among various tenors of its literary vehicle "woman." Thus, the picture in Proverbs of God relating creatively has its own internal logic that, unlike Genesis 1–3, is not shaped by being in service of any account of any other way in which God may relate to what is not God.

Wisdom: Well-Being and Order in Creation

The surface and explicit concern of canonical Wisdom points to another way in which Proverbs may guide and norm theological remarks about our proximate contexts understood as God's creature. It is obvious on the face of it that a major interest of Wisdom literature generally, and of Proverbs in particular, is God's providential rule in what goes on in the world, including human practices, both for the well-being of the wise and for the destruction of the foolish. It thinks about this too within the framework of a mostly implicit creation theology, at least in the sense that it thinks about providence in terms of a picture of how God relates creatively to the proximate contexts of human life. It is customary to characterize this interest in providence as an interest to preserve order in creation.

Arguably, the origins of the notion of "order" expressed by the materials collected in Proverbs lie in Egyptian Wisdom literature, but, once again, canonical editing of earlier Wisdom materials shapes the sense of the received term. Egyptian Wisdom tended to think within the framework of the concept *ma'at*. *Ma'at* is right order in nature and society, as established by the act of creation, and hence means, according to context, "what is right, what is correct law, order, justice and truth" (see R. Murphy 1990, chap. 8 and Appendix; cf. Morenz 1973, 111; Crenshaw 1981, chap. 9). *Ma'at* is at once an order inherent in reality to which human conduct should conform and an order that human agents are called on to establish. Although Egyptian religion knew many gods, the literature that focuses on the concept *ma'at* refers only to "god," who created the world in accord with *ma'at*. Thus Egyptian Wisdom too at least presupposes some sort of "theology of creation." This gives rise to the suggestion, which I argue is misleading, that the notion of order in Proverbs is best interpreted in its larger context if read as a concept analogous to *ma'at*.

It is precisely the background of commonalities between Proverbs and the international Wisdom literatures that highlights the distinctive twist that Proverbs gives the material it borrows and bends. Egyptian Wisdom focuses on the question, "Is there order in the world?" and answers, "Yes." *Ma'at* connotes a universally invariant lawlike order. It is objectively present in the pattern of events in the world and can be discovered by attending carefully to just those events. Students of Egyptian Wisdom are to learn to discern *ma'at* in their experience of the world and to live by it in their action in the world. The rationale for doing so is straightforwardly utilitarian: conforming to creation's order is the way to succeed as a bureaucrat. At this level of abstraction, *ma'at* no doubt overlaps quite a bit with that order which the sentences in Proverbs either invite us to discern or exhort us to obey.

However, if in their literary interplay, Proverbs chapters 1–9 and 31:10–31 provide the hermeneutical guide to the collection of collections of sentences bracketed between them, then this conceptual overlap with *ma'at* is subject to two important qualifications. These qualifications bring out the distinctive sorts of order that Wisdom provides as the condition of human well-being.

First, the editorial brackets subordinate the question, "Is there order in human experience?" to the question, "What is life-giving in human experience, what makes for the well-being of human life?" It is not necessary to choose between the general exegetical judgment that Proverbs is about discerning normative order and ineluctably restrictive structures in the world (so Crenshaw 1981, chaps. 1–3) and the judgment that it is basically about learning to live a fulfilling life marked by well-being (so Murphy 1990, chap. 8). The book is about both. The issue may rather be posed this way: which theme is in the service of the other? On that question, Murphy's judgment seems to me more persuasive. Granted, the sentences collected in Proverbs taken in abstraction from their common overall pedagogical force and from the brackets provided by canonical editing (chaps. 1–9 and 31:10–31), might arguably be said to focus generally on the same question as does Egyptian Wisdom: is there order in human experience? However, if their overall pedagogical force of calling to and eliciting wisdom ad hoc in particular contexts is honored and interpreted in ways guided by chapters 1–9 and 31:10–31, then the force of the sentences in Proverbs is understood differently. The central concern in Proverbs is human well-being. Acquiring capacities to discern how to order one's actions wisely for the well-being of one's proximate context is in the service of the concern for well-being. In Proverbs when the question about order is subordinated to the question about what makes for the well-being of human life—namely, being wise—the sense of order that is of interest is not a metaphysical order that ontologically grounds a type of natural law, but rather a more pragmatic, context realistic, goal-oriented-action sense of "order."

If the interplay between Wisdom personified in chapters 1–9 and the image of the Capable Wife in 31:10–31 is normative and definitive of Wisdom in Proverbs, then it is probably better to use the more concrete term "ordering" than the more abstract "order." What Wisdom establishes and maintains is the sort of active ordering that characterizes socially teleological personal agency, rather than a static and impersonal structure that is universally normative regarding human action in every concrete situation because it is built into the very structure of objective reality.

It is a teleological ordering. That is, it is the type of order that characterizes the relation between an act and its (more or less conscious) intention and helps make intelligible the relationship between a personal agent's intentional actions in the world and the state of affairs that obtain as a result of those movements. Consider, for example, some of what is involved in one of the actions attributed to the Capable Wife in 31:19, 24. The summary, "She intended to earn money by making a garment to be sold" makes sense of an otherwise baffling set of movements in which she weaves cloth, only to cut it up into pieces, only then to fasten some of them back together again with thread, and then after investing all that effort in it, to exchange it for money with a stranger in the market at the city gate. The very character of her actions actively orders the relationships in which she stands to a great many features of her setting—for example, thread, spindle, cloth and scissors, thread and needle, the physical marketplace, strangers in the marketplace, customary practices of exchange, and the current market value of linen garments. The remark, "She intended to earn money by making a garment to be sold," brings out that order, making the entire set of her movements intelligible.

It is also a social ordering. The Capable Wife shapes her actions according to more broadly accepted social practices so that her personal acts enhance other personal agents' enactments of their own intentions, rather than constricting or making impossible the exercise of their own agency. For example, shaping her actions according to more broadly accepted practices of fair exchange, she enacts her intention to acquire money (or something for which she barters the garment she has made) in such a way as to enhance another person's intention to acquire a garment, in contrast to enacting her intention in a way that frustrates satisfactory enactment of the other's intention to acquire a garment (say, by cheating her with shoddy goods), or, in the extreme case, renders the other incapable of intentional action (say, by violently binding and robbing her). So, too, in 31:15 the Wife manages her servant-girls. Assuming that she is capable in doing this, her intentional actions of assigning tasks to her servant-girls is done in such a way that it actively orders a set of relations among the servants and their respective immediate situations in which the servant-girls' own personal agency is, in a qualified way, to be sure, enhanced. The Capable Wife presumably does not treat her servant-girls as automatons, micromanaging their every movement. Rather, in her own managerial intentional action the Capable Wife orders a certain social space which is oriented to certain overarching purposes that she herself has set, in which her servant-girls' capacities for intentional action in relation to the Capable Wife's overarching purposes are not frustrated but enhanced.

Given the complex and artful literary relationships between 31:10–31 and chapters 1–9, personified Woman Wisdom, too, may be read as a quasi-personal ordering agency who, in delighting in human creatures, actively orders the cosmic household in a socially teleological way in order to enhance the personal agency of human creatures.

Woman Wisdom is a creature (8:22). She is not God, and there is no strong reason to interpret her as an attribute of God. On the other hand, as a creature, Woman Wisdom is not simply an allegorical trope for an orderliness, a canniness, a cunning inherent in creatures themselves. She is other than and prior to them in being. Wisdom is said to be that through which God created all other creatures. Such wisdom as they may exhibit is grounded in her. Her quasi-personal ordering activity is usually rendered in Proverbs as though done relatively ad hoc.

The literary interplay between Woman Wisdom in chapters 1–9 and the Capable Wife in 31:10–31 strongly resists being paraphrased into any metaphysical formulation. The most that this text leads us to say is this: (a) Just as the wisdom we may come to exhibit is grounded outside of us and elicited in us from without, so too the wisdom exhibited in creatures generally is grounded outside them and elicited in them. (b) Moreover, as is repeatedly pointed out in the sentences collected in Proverbs, the call to us to be wise is itself mediated to us through the wisdom exhibited by other creatures (e.g., "Go to the ant, you lazybones; consider its ways, and be wise," 6:6). It is through our fellow creatures that we receive the call to be wise in our own agency. (c) Moreover, it is not as though wisdom named some cosmic principle additional to God by which even God's creativity must be constrained. It is God who creates Wisdom, which, through fellow creatures, calls us to be wise and elicits wisdom in us. Interpreted in its canonical context, then, while the text does not necessarily imply that God's own creative wisdom is the ground and source of creaturely wisdom (it only says that Wisdom is the ground of creaturely wisdom, and that she is God's creature), it certainly does not serve to block any such line of thought. It simply leaves it an open question.

In sum, the force of Woman Wisdom as the definitive and normative metaphor for wisdom is just that the ground and source of wisdom in us is an ad hoc, quasi-personal, socially teleological ordering of the contexts and networks of our own personal agencies, an ordering that actively establishes and maintains the sorts of order that make for the well-being of human life. This is central to the concept of order in Proverbs when its interpretation is guided by its canonical editing. It may involve an adopting of the concept *ma'at*. But if it does, the adoption brings with it major adaptations. Whatever the amount of conceptual overlap between *ma'at* and order in Proverbs, the overlap is normatively subject to and so qualified by the logic of this socially teleological sort of order.

There is a second way in which the canonical editing of the book qualifies the concept of order that comes with Proverbs' despoiling the Egyptian's concept *ma'at*. In Egyptian Wisdom, *ma'at* names an order discoverable in the natural and social world taken in itself. The brackets that Proverbs 1–9 and 31:10–31 put around its collection of collections of wisdom sentences, however, serve explicitly and emphatically to relate natural and social order to God's active relating to creation as its creator. Egyptian Wisdom credited the presence of order in nature and society to the creative act of the god. God caused it. But Egyptian Wisdom literature could formulate its concept of order without necessary reference to the god, and it thought the order to be humanly discoverable without reference to god. Proverbs, on the other hand, interpreted in ways guided by its canonical editing, conceives order in nature and society only by way of reference to God. Here the God-relation is an essential part of the concept of order.

This point comes into view when we give up efforts to pin down Woman Wisdom's ontological status and attend rather to her literary role in Proverbs. In chapter 8, Woman Wisdom is presented as a witness to creation, a witness in whom God takes delight and who in turn rejoices and delights in God's creatures. Building on what was said above, we may add that what God delights in is Wisdom's ordering everything to God as its creator. Wisdom actively orders the world, then, not only by reference to what makes for the well-being of life, but also by reference to God. As the ground and source of wisdom in us, Wisdom actively orders the world, not on her own, so to speak, but by reference to God who in creating delights in Wisdom. The order she establishes and nurtures constitutes creatures' true relation to God. The order in question here is an orderedness-to-God. Any concept of order stateable without reference to God would be a different concept of order. This may well be an adaptation of *ma'at* and involve a good bit of conceptual overlap with it, but if it is, then the concept of order has been significantly modified in the process of adaptation.

In summary, Wisdom as the ground and source of wisdom in creatures is wisdom exercised by ad hoc ordering of nature and society that both constitutes creatures' God-relatedness and makes for creaturely well-being.

This, in turn, has two implications for understanding wisdom as an attribute that human creatures are called to exhibit and may come to exhibit. First, for Proverbs what makes an action wise is insight into how to act in the particularities of a given concrete situation so as to establish and maintain there that socially teleological order that makes for the well-being of human lives. We have seen that, abstracted from their canonical editing, the sentences collected in Proverbs either command particular behaviors in, or make sage but impersonal observations about, an astonishingly large number of concrete situations, and do so in a maddeningly unsystematic way. However, interpreted in ways guided by their editorial bracketing between chapters 1–9 and 31:10–31, they can be read with another, more unified pedagogical force. In all of their heterogeneity, these sentences have the force of calling human creatures so to attend to the concrete particularities of the actual situations in which they find themselves so that their actions in those situations establish and maintain the sorts of order in those situations that make for the well-being of human lives, both their own and that of others. Read this way, Proverbs is not simply a collection of many and diverse pieces of advice. Rather it has a single force: it seeks, through its pedagogical force, to make us wise in our agency in particular concrete contexts.

The second implication is this: acquiring capacities for the insightfulness that makes human agency wise is inseparable from learning to relate each concrete situation to God. The order to which Wisdom points in concrete situations is neither conceivable nor discernible apart from the situations' God-relatedness. Accordingly, learning to be wise involves acquiring two different but inseparable types of capacities. On the one hand, it involves learning how to refer each concrete situation in its particularity, including ourselves in it, to God. On the other hand, it involves learning to see each concrete situation, including ourselves within it, in the context of the larger network of its interactions with other situations and learning how to relate the entire network to God. To come to exhibit wisdom in our own agency is to learn how to act in ways shaped quite specifically by the God-relatedness of the situation in which we find ourselves in all of its concrete particularity. Part of the fear of the Lord that is the beginning of wisdom is to learn to see all things, and ourselves with them, in their God-relatedness as God's creatures.

In chapter 2A I noted that, since the "Son" is identified with the *Logos* of the Prologue to the Gospel of John, part of the force of the traditional Trinitarian formula "the Father creates through the Son" is to stress that God creates in an ordered, order-generating fashion. However, I noted, that leaves open the question, "In what sense of 'order'?" Classical Trinitarian theology tended to interpret "Logos" in Hellenistic philosophical categories according to which the answer is, "'order' in the sense of cosmological principles." I suggested that it would be less problematic to interpret "Logos" in terms of canonical Wisdom's sense of "order," especially the sense implied in Proverbs. The reasons in Proverbs for this suggestion are now evident.

If a Trinitarian doctrine of God relating creatively to reality other than God is guided by the creation theology of Proverbs, then the sort of creaturely order implied by "creation through the Son" is not an order that is constituted by timeless and unchanging cosmological principles "caused" to be there as the effect of the timeless and unchanging divine Logos. Rather, the ordering of creation that Proverbs points out in creation is an ordering defined and identified by reference to God. It is a quasi-personal, socially teleological ordering of events that, when detectable, is always ad hoc and situation-specific. This ordering of creaturely proximate contexts by God's creating them makes such reality intelligible, but only in terms of stories of what God is up to, what God's intentions are in concrete social circumstances. This quasi-personal, socially teleological sort of ordering of reality other than God precisely by God's creatively relating to it is the distinctive character of our ultimate context.

It is only by living completely in this world that one learns
to have faith. One must completely abandon any attempt to
make something of oneself, whether it be a saint, or a converted
sinner, or a churchman. . . . By this worldliness I mean living
unreservedly in life's duties, problems, successes and failures,
experiences and perplexities. In so doing we throw ourselves
completely into the arms of God. That, I think, is faith . . .
and that is how one becomes a man [sic.] and a Christian.
DIETRICH BONHOEFFER

CHAPTER **6**

To Be and to Have
a Living Body:
Meditation on Job 10

In chapter 4A, I proposed that, theo-
logically speaking, what we are as human creatures is determined by our
ultimate context: God creatively relating to us in a delighted freedom from
us and in freely delighted intimacy with us that places us in a context
analogous to a two-sided social institution. In chapter 5A, I proposed that
what we are as human creatures is partly determined by the fact that we
are inextricable and integral parts of the proximate contexts into which
we were born, the quotidian that is experientially and morally ambiguous,
yet nonetheless mediates a vocation that is ineluctably ours as creatures to
act wisely for the well-being of our proximate contexts. However, neither
chapter has proposed much about the content of what human creatures
are. I turn to that here. Taking our having been born to be our creation,
I propose to explicate human creatureliness through the lens of a theology of birth. The question we turn to in this chapter is, "What are the
anthropological implications of the fact of our having been born into such
ultimate and proximate contexts?"

I shall move from the particular to the general. I shall begin by reflecting theologically on Job's lament that he had ever been born (Job 10). Job's
story of having been born is told in two distinct ways, entwined tightly.
Together they also tell the story of the birth of every human person. The
distinction within narrative unity between the two ways of telling the story
renders the peculiarity of human creatureliness. Accordingly, this chapter moves through three steps: (1) an introduction locating Job's account
of his birth in its literary setting, (2) a reflection on the anthropological
implications of recounting Job's creation as the story of his having been
born a living body, and (3) a reflection on the implications of telling Job's
creation as the story of his being given a living body.

Introduction

Our theological reflections on the event of birth will be guided by Job 10:8–19, in which Job, boiling over with bitterness about his life, tells of his birth. This passage presents the climax of a series of exchanges with three friends in which Job challenges some of the conventions of mainstream Wisdom while continuing to seek that wisdom that is the link between disinterested "fear of the LORD" and human well-being (cf. Prov. 1:7; 4:7; 9:10, 9:13).

Job is presented as a man who has truly feared the Lord and has enjoyed well-being, only to lose his prosperity and be reduced to the most intensely constricting physical and spiritual suffering. Three friends, Eliphaz, Bildad, and Zophar, come to be with him. For seven days and seven nights they all sit together in utter silence, "for they saw that his suffering was very great" (2:13). Then Job breaks the silence with a long curse on the day of his birth, beginning thus:

> "Let the day perish in which I was born,
>   and the night that said,
>   'A man-child is conceived.'"
>
> (3:3)

In the context of conventional "mainstream" Wisdom, this is close to blasphemy. Two of Job's friends respond, each representing a different convention in mainstream Wisdom.

Eliphaz discerns in Job's losses and suffering the discipline of God, a punishment for sin that may wound but will also heal (5:17–18). But Job, Job's wife, the reader, and God all know that Job has not sinned. Job rejects Eliphaz's line with a strikingly modern psychological insight. He sees that his friend is reproving his words (6:25–26) because he is terrified by Job's calamity and fears Job's continued protests will just make everything worse (6:21). Perceiving that Eliphaz is more concerned with the way in which Job is dealing with his suffering than he is with Job in his suffering, Job challenges Eliphaz to look him in the face and deal directly with his concern.

Bildad proposes that the wise thing for Job to do is to repent of whatever the sin was that incurred this punishment and then "seek God and make supplication to the Almighty" for "surely then he will rouse himself for you and restore to you your rightful place" (8:5, 6). Conventional Wisdom holds that it is important but not sufficient, as Eliphaz had suggested, to recognize suffering as a discipline that will finally yield healing. More, Wisdom calls for repentance because suffering necessarily implies that sin has been committed. For conventional mainstream canonical Wisdom, the ultimate context into which we are born is governed by a law connecting innocence with prosperity and guilt with loss and suffering. Job's response exhibits a deepening of his grasp of Wisdom:

> "Indeed I know that this is so;
>   but how can a mortal be just before God?
> If one wished to contend with him,
>   one could not answer him once in a thousand."
>
> (9:2, 3)

The problem, deeper than the justice of the connection between folly and affliction, is the fact that the One who creates and is so involved in creation as to single out Job in particular for such affliction is at the same time too elusive and "other" than Job to be engaged in a discussion of the merits of Job's case:

> "For he is not a mortal, as I am, that I might answer him,
>   that we should come to trial together.
> There is no umpire between us,
>   who might lay his hand on us both."
>
> (9:32, 33)

The ultimate context with which Job has to come to grips somehow is not a law that in human affairs divine punishment always follows sin, but the fact that God relates creatively to him in a way that is at once directly and intimately engaged in Job's life and yet so radically free of it as to be beyond all contrasting with Job, beyond even the contrast "I and Thou in encounter."

Against this background, Job gives vent to his anguish at having been born.

> "I loathe my life;
> I will give free utterance to my complaint;
> I will speak in the bitterness of my soul.
> I will say to God, Do not condemn me;
>   let me know why you contend against me.
> Does it seem good to you to oppress,
>   to despise the work of your hands
> and favor the schemes of the wicked?"
>
> (10:1–3)

. . . . . .

> "Your hands fashioned and made me;
>   and now you turn and destroy me.
> Remember that you fashioned me like clay;
>   and will you turn me to dust again?
> Did you not pour me out like milk
>   and curdle me like cheese?
> You clothed me with skin and flesh,
>   and knit me together with bones and sinews.
> You have granted me life and steadfast love,
>   and your care has preserved my spirit."
>
> (10:8–12)

. . . . .

> "Why did you bring me forth from the womb?
> Would that I had died before any eye had seen me,
> and were as though I had not been,
> carried from the womb to the grave."
> (10:18, 19)

Job's negative attitude toward his having been born is perfectly clear. It lies at the heart of the contest about wisdom between Job and his friends. A theologically freighted and profound account of what it means to have been born is built into Job's complaints to God about having been born.

It is entirely apt theologically that Job's account of his having been created in his having been born is part of his protest against his having been born. The combination underscores the ontological ambiguity of finite creaturehood. Like all human creatures, in being created by God in and through his having been born, Job is a finite energy system that is part of proximate contexts consisting of networks of interacting finite energy systems that are ontologically ambiguous, both making for one another's well-being and damaging one another. It is just such damage that Job is protesting. These contexts are what God says "Yes!" to, as "just what God had in mind." God deems them "good" in the sense that God values them, but they are not necessarily desirable by human creatures. In Job's case, his protest against his having born, and hence against his having been created, may fairly be understood as an expression of anger at God for creating such contexts.

It is important theologically to note that such angry protest to God is not necessarily a faithless and inappropriate creaturely response to God's creative relating to human creatures. Job's protest is not only faithful to the real ambiguities of human creatures' proximate contexts, it is also faithful to God relating to them creatively. Job does not deny God, nor break relationship with God, nor disobey any command by God. On the contrary, Job persists in responding to God by actively seeking a face-to-face encounter with God in trust that God, in turn, will keep faith with Job. Under the circumstances, Job's anger with God is part of an appropriate response to God relating to him creatively. Under the circumstances, it is especially appropriate that Job's account of his creation is given as part of an expression of just such a response, for those circumstances are our circumstances also, and any account of our creatureliness that is guided by Job's account of his being created must be similarly faithful to and honest about the ontological ambiguity of God's good creation.

Job Created as a Living Body

There are two distinguishable ways in which Job tells this story of his having been born. They are wound together in such a fashion that no inconsistency exists between them. One account tells the story of Job's birth from a human mother, his coming to be as a living body, though not without

God's involvement. The other tells the story of Job's being given a living body by God. The difference is not that one tells a story about entirely natural processes effecting a particular natural outcome, and the other tells a story about God supernaturally doing something. Rather, the difference lies in the way God is involved in each. In this section, I focus on the first way in which Job tells this story.

The way Job tells it, his story is not simply an account of the moment of Job's birth, but the longer and more complex story of Job's having come to be born. It is the story of perfectly ordinary, entirely familiar natural processes. The story of the entire process of his having come to be born of his mother is also a story of God's creation of Job.

The rhetoric of this story is not unique to the author of Job. Probably it is simply the author's use of current understanding of what goes on in gestation. Such language is echoed, for example, in Psalm 139: "For it was you who formed my inward parts; you knit me together in my mother's womb" (v. 13). The metaphors reflect the science of the day:

> "Did you not pour me out like milk
> and curdle me like cheese?"
> (Job 10:10)

As H. W. Wolff suggests, perhaps the way in which poured-out milk curdles like cheese serves here as an analogy to help understand "the pouring out of the milky seminal fluid into the female organism and the development of a firm embryonic body that follows insemination" (1974, 97). On this telling of the story, then, what God creates in creating Job is one more instance of a familiar kind of living body—namely, a human one, that, having been born, exists apart from its mother but not independently of other living human bodies. As a living body, it is on a par with every other organic creature before God, at once utterly ordinary and a mysterious gift.

The way the story is told here, God is intimately involved throughout, from conception through gestation to birth. Unlike the biblical birth narratives of Samuel, Isaac, and John the Baptist, there is no suggestion in this story that Job's mother was barren so that his conception required God's special involvement. Rather, when Job complains, "Why did *you* bring me forth from the womb?" (10:18, emphasis added), the clear point is that God was directly involved in the entire process of his coming to birth. "Your hands fashioned and made me" (10:8); "Remember that you fashioned me like clay" (10:9).

Job's way of telling the story of his creation as the story of his having been born may guide the way we tell the stories of our creation by the triune God as stories of our having been born. What God creates in our having come to be born is actual human living bodies. That we now know immeasurably more than the author(s) of Job knew about the complex processes of gestation does not negate the story's theological point. Whatever the processes are, God is immediately, intimately, and inextricably involved in the processes that result in Job's having been born, processes in which Job has no say. The processes are already all there before Job is born; they are a given. God is directly and freely engaged creatively in all of them. Because God's involvement is unexacted and uncoerced, what is created in having been born is a gift, though it is but one instance among many of a perfectly familiar kind of living body produced through entirely ordinary and natural, law-governed processes.

The birthing in "having been born" must not be understood in a physiologically literal-minded way. It must be allowed to stand, not only for natural childbirth, but for any and all medical procedures by which a pregnant woman is helped to give birth to a live newborn.

The phrase "having been born" is important, not because of the precise character of any particular birthing procedure, but for its tense. It names a temporally extended process, not a punctiliar fact, a process begun in the past and now completed. It is a continuous process, itself continuous with processes that precede and follow it. There are no clear, sharp breaks that unambiguously mark its beginning or its completion. For reasons of convenience, we may decide to mark its beginning as the point at which a human sperm fertilizes a human egg. For the same kind of reasons, we may decide to mark its completion as the point when an actual living human body has been or could have been born—that is, delivered from its mother's body and able to live outside of her body and, indeed, quite apart from her under another's care. However, if we do, it must be acknowledged that "able to live independently of her [the mother]" is vague because there are no clear and fixed criteria by which to assess such an ability. Technological developments make it possible for ever more prematurely born infants to have been born and live independently of their mothers in artificial environments that replicate many features of their environment in their mothers' wombs, from which they cannot live independently. "Having been born," in the sense of "delivered from its mother's body and able to live independently of her," serves to identify the coming into being of an actual living human body, which is also God's creation of that actual living human body, as the completion of the process of gestation, but it does not, and in the nature of the case it cannot, specify a clear and distinct point in the process when it occurs.

We may restate the point of the first telling of Job's birth in language no less metaphorical but perhaps better suited to our own culture. Such restatement must rely on generalizations of at least two levels of inquiry in the life sciences.

Obviously, one is a generalization of research into the structures and processes involved in human reproduction and gestation. For our purposes here, the particulars of what such research shows do not matter. It may lack the bucolic charm of poured-out milk curdling into cheese, but a more modern rhetoric of molecular exchanges among biochemical energy systems can be used to tell basically the same story of our creation by God in our having come to be born.

The other set of generalizations on which a contemporary, if no less metaphorical, theological reformulation of Job's point in telling of his birth must rely is drawn from research into the nature of life itself—that is, research into the features of the structures and dynamics that are found universally in every form of life. If what is said to be created by God in our having been born are actual human living bodies, then the notion of "living body" needs to be clarified. It is important to note three broad generalizations about the structure and dynamics of every living body that arise from modern life sciences.

First, because the life of a living body cannot be understood except in terms of that body's dynamic relationship with its environment (salient aspects of its "proximate context"), biology (analysis of the life of a living body) is inseparable from ecology (analysis of the environment with which it interacts). Put in metaphysical categories, a living body's relation to its environment is internal to that living body's reality *qua* living, and conversely. As ecologist and evolutionary biologist Jeffrey Schloss points out (2002, 65), a consequence is that the concept of "living body" is ambiguous in current biology. It is ambiguous because "living body" (or "organism") may mean, roughly, an organism whose identity is defined by its skin, or it may mean an organism whose identity extends beyond its skin to include all the influences it has on its environment as it modifies its environment to enhance its own fitness. Its influences on its environment—that is, its dynamic relationship with its environment—partly constitutes its "living-ness." (See Richard Dawkins's [1986] notions of "skinless organism" or "extended phenotype.").

Second, living bodies are self-regulating sets of energy systems that seek to preserve internal homeostasis, a relatively persisting, self-organizing structure that does not dissipate the equilibrium of its various internal energy systems and resists entropy or thermodynamic decay. As such, the "life" of living bodies is goal-oriented or telenomic. Living bodies are systems that are "open at *two* ends, informational and energetic . . ." (Schloss 2002, 67; emphasis in original). On one hand, they act seeking sources of energy to sustain the homeostatic structure of their lives. On the other, they act seeking information about their environment, its resources and its threats. And each is the means to the actualization of the other. The interplay between living bodies' integral self-regulating homeostatic function and their integral self-directing teleonomic agency to fend off entropic disintegration may be viewed as the essence of life.

In that case, as Schloss points out (2002, 68), life admits of degrees. Living bodies not only are self-directing in telenomic ways. They must be able to identify their goals and to evaluate how well they were achieved. Different kinds of living bodies exhibit different ranges of powers "to engage and freely respond to the environment along increasing levels of spatial, temporal, and organizational scale through expanding powers of sensation, locomotion, and cognition" (2002, 68). These differing levels may be considered different degrees of life. Moreover, "the body is not only necessary *for* this awareness and freedom . . ."—that is, the body is not merely instrumental to life; it is the singular manifestation of it. "Disembodied" or immaterial life is just as dead—to itself and the world—as non-living matter" (69).

I urge that in the case of human living bodies the degree of life, and correlatively the concept of "living body," embraces social and cultural, as well as biological life inasmuch as capacities to develop ever more complex social and cultural forms of life serve to extend bodies' powers to engage and freely respond to their environments along increasing levels of spatial, temporal, and organizational scale.

Third are generalizations about death, predation, and the life of living bodies as outcomes of the evolution of life. Schloss claims that "there are no physiological or thermodynamic reasons why death must occur" to a living body. "The evolutionary interpretation of senescence is not that it represents either biological failure or necessity, but it is an adaptation *built in* to organisms, enhancing fitness by 'making room' for progeny. . . . The bottom line, however, is that death is not physiologically necessary but that it has proven evolutionarily valuable" (83). He points out that "the driving force of evolutionary change is excessive fecundity, and therefore random mutation is followed by differential transmission of those variants. It does not require—and often does not even entail—selective mortality. . . . So death is not necessary for evolution, and evolution would still occur if organisms were immortal in an unbounded environment" (83). "However, ecological settings are not unbounded. Therefore, although death is neither physiologically nor evolutionarily necessary, it is necessary if a habitat has finite resources and populations are reproductively increasing without emigration" (83).

As for predation, "We certainly cannot imagine earth's present major ecosystems functioning without a hierarchy of predation" (Schloss 2002, 83–84). Predators and parasitoids necessarily find their energy sources, after all, in what they kill for food. Three implications seem to follow from these features of the evolutionary biology of carbon-based life as we know it. A functioning ecology—that is, proximate context—without death would need to have either "an infinite [but, theologically speaking, creaturely] energy source, or organisms would not be reproducing" (84). Second, "energy flow through the ecosystem [or "energy exchange among sets of energy systems"] would have to reflect a balance of rates of energy utilization and productivity" (84). Third, "While death is not necessary for life, the *possibility* of death is necessary, that is, life entails the continual overcoming of entropic forces that, if unresisted, will degrade the function and organization of the living system. It is impossible even to imagine how we could have anything worthy of being called life apart from the reality of this tension" (84).

Thus, to say that God's creating us is God's immediate engagement in the processes comprising the extended event of our having been born as living human bodies means that God's free creativity is immediately engaged in the processes by which we each become a set of energy systems that are individually and collectively relatively self-regulating homeostatic structures exercising self-directed teleonomic agency that are integral living parts of complex exchanges of energy among energy systems that constitute their quotidian proximate contexts, whatever those systems are and however they may be best understood technically. The latter is the job of the sciences.

[margin note: God's immediate engagement of us as Creator]

Our meditation on Job 10 suggests nine core themes in a theology of human creatureliness that is normed by this canonical Wisdom text: What God creates in a human being's having been born is a living body that is (1) a gift; (2) actual (in contradistinction to "possible" or "potential"); (3) related to creatively by God in ways appropriate to its distinctive creaturely powers, but on a par with God's relating to every other kind of creature in regard to the freedom and intimacy of God's creative relating; (4) classified as "human" by its genetic structure; (5) constantly changing and developing; (6) inherently a center of a variety of powers; (7) finite in its powers; (8) inherently "mysterious" in the sense of being inexhaustibly complex both epistemically and ontologically; and (9) by virtue of God's creative relating, "good."

1. To tell the story of our having been born as the story of our creation by God, after the manner of Job's narrative, is to claim that our having been born as living human bodies is a gift by the triune God who is immediately and intimately involved in the process.

If the ultimate and proximate contexts of our having been born are God relating to us creatively in radically free intimacy, then God is inextricably involved in the processes that constitute, in the largest sense, our having been born. That can only be classified, I think, as an ontological remark about our ultimate and proximate contexts.

The same processes are also properly analyzed, described, and explained by the relevant sciences in a wholly naturalistic way—that is, in total abstraction from any consideration of or reference to God's involvement. However, the theological claim that these processes are located in the larger context of God actively relating to them blocks the tendency to construe the sciences' descriptions of these processes as having the status of ontological remarks about the concrete reality of those processes as parts of our proximate contexts. The theological claim is that, ontologically speaking, God relating to these processes is essential to their concrete reality. Consequently, descriptions of these processes that abstract from God's relating to them do not take the processes in their concrete actuality, but only describe certain aspects of them abstracted from their concrete reality.

This in no way invalidates the relevant sciences' explanations of the processes. It only challenges construal of them as sufficient ontological descriptions of "reality." Moreover, adding to the scientific explanations some theological remark such as, "Beyond all that the sciences know to say about these processes, it is the case that God is intimately involved in them," would add nothing to scientific explanations. Just what difference it does make to describe the processes of our coming to birth, understood in the broadest sense, in their ultimate context and not abstracted from it, is what this chapter seeks to explore in part.

The story of our births couched in the generalized naturalistic rhetoric of "interactions among energy systems" may be included without substantial modification in our longer story of God's creativity. This is the same God as Job's God, although we describe God in a Trinitarian fashion of which the book of Job's author knew nothing. To add that the triune God is immediately engaged with the entire given environment of networks of energy systems does not mean that God is yet one more energy system interacting with the myriad energy systems constituting the context into which we are born and the process through which we have come to be born. Such a notion of God would violate the rule identified in chapter 4A against conceiving God's immanence in such a way as to make God just one more item on the inventory list of the cosmos. Nor does the remark that God is immediately engaged with the entire environment of energy systems into which we are born mean that we have discovered an additional hitherto unidentified causal factor that might help account for something about the exchanges among these energy systems—something, perhaps, that nobody has thus far noticed needs to be explained. The point is rather that the entire set of energy systems is itself radically dependent on God's free creativity for its ongoing reality, so that its givenness has the character of a gift from God.

2. To tell the story of our creation after the manner of Job's narrative of his having been born is to claim that, in creating each of us, what the triune God creates are actual human bodies. "Having been born" is the event in the past in which a living human body emerged into actuality. What God creates in creating humankind is actual living human bodies, not merely the physical possibilities of there being living human bodies, nor merely the transcendental existential-ontological "conditions of the possibility" of human bodies' lives, nor the potentiality of living human bodies.

In order to clarify the point of distinguishing among "actual," "possible," and "potential," let us stipulate a distinction between possibilities and potentialities, and relate each to actuality, in the following way. The possibility of some state of affairs may be identified with already existing determinate conditions that are instrumental, whether by accident or deliberate action, to the actualizing of that subsequent state of affairs. These are physical possibilities of actual physical events. A possibility here is a *determinate* actual reality, or determinate set of realities, that is defined by reference to a determinate actuality for which it is the possibility. The presence in my kitchen of flour, yeast, salt, milk, a mixing bowl, an oven, and a baker are the possibilities of, later, a loaf of bread. The presence together on an open hilltop of a lightning storm and my tinder-dry wooden summer cabin, its tall chimney lacking a lightning rod, are the possibilities, later, of a house fire. However, whether physical possibilities are in fact instrumental to the coming about of the subsequent state of affairs does not depend entirely on them. The baker may not choose to bake; the lightning may not strike the cabin.

In this sense of possibility, if what is distinctively human about living human bodies is identified by human bodies' distinctive DNA, then the possibility of living human bodies may be identified in the broadest sense with the physical context, and its physical processes and physical laws, that make it possible for life to arise from abiotic matter, and distinctively human life to evolve, and any one of us in particular to be conceived and come to birth.

The possibility of living human bodies reaches further than that. Having been born entails that members of the class of human bodies have been located in proximate contexts that consist, as we saw in chapter 5A, of a multitude of organic relationships and culturally mediated psychological and social relationships. It is only in the context of such relationships that human living bodies are ever conceived and brought to birth. Only in such contexts are the lives and well-being of infant human bodies nurtured. Only such contexts make possible human bodies' learning to communicate, to interrelate, to take charge of their own lives, to acquire their own identities. However, to claim that God relates to us creatively in our having been born is to claim more than that God creates such physical and social possibilities of our having been born. It is to claim God's immediate and intimate creative relating to the process and event of each living human body having been born.

If what is distinctively human about living human bodies is deemed to be the distinctive character of human experience, then the possibility of living human bodies may be understood in a second sense. One or another type of human experience (consciousness as such, self-awareness, perception, willing, anxiety, courage, etc.) may be analyzed by a method of transcendental deduction to identify structures (usually called "existentials") that are transcendental in that they are found universally to shape actual, concrete, historically located, socioculturally conditioned human experience(s) (often called "ontic" experience) but are not themselves part of the content—that is, not the "objects"—of any particular actual experience. Not themselves the content of ontic experiences, the transcendentals are ontological rather than ontic in that they are the transcendental conditions of the possibility of human experience *being* what it actually is "ontically" on any given occasion—namely, specifically human experience. Here, too, possibilities are determinate realities defined by reference to the determinate actualities of which they are the possibilities. In this sense of possibility, if what is distinctively human about living human bodies is identified with the distinctive character of human experience, and if the presence of God to human consciousness can be shown to be one of human experience's transcendentals (say, the horizon of holy mystery that is the necessary background of every ontic experience), then God's creative relating to human consciousness is the transcendental condition of the possibility of what is distinctively human about living human bodies. However, to claim that God relates to us creatively in our having been born is to claim more than that God's creative relating is the condition of the possibility of living human bodies having the distinctive type(s) of experience they do have. It is to claim God's immediate and intimate creative relating to the process and event of each living human body having been born. God's immediate and intimate creative relating to the event of our having been born must be understood as relating as much to human living bodies as to living human experience or consciousness.

In contradistinction to "possibility," "potentiality," in the sense meant here, is a more or less complex dynamic system of some determinate kind that, given the right circumstances, will develop in definite, rule-governed ways into a dynamic system of a related but different kind. Given, among other things, the right circumstances of temperature differentials, wind pressure, and colliding fronts, complex weather systems of a certain sort will develop into the distinctive energy system called a tornado. Given the *emergence* right circumstances of nutrients in the soil, water, and sunlight, and the information contained in its genes, a buried acorn will develop into an oak sapling that will develop into an oak tree. Given the right circumstances, among other things, of nutrients and maternal resources, and the information contained in its genes, a fertilized human egg will develop into a zygote, which will develop into an embryo, which will develop into a fetus, which will be born a living human body.

Of course, these two heuristic examples of the difference and relation between a potentiality for *x* and the actuality of *x* are very, very different from one another. They can be laid alongside one another only when they have been very highly abstracted from concrete reality. However, together they serve to underscore a conceptual point: Every dynamic system that is a potentiality *for* some different, though related, dynamic system is also itself a concrete, determinate actuality of some kind. It is a potentiality only in relation to that into which it will usually develop in the near or far future. But in the present it is itself an actuality of some kind. This hour's storm system may be a potential tornado, but it is now actually a severe thunderstorm and not a tornado. An acorn may be a potential oak tree, but it is now an actual acorn and not an oak tree. A fertilized human egg, a human zygote, a human embryo, and a human fetus may each be a potential living human body, but what each is now is an actual fertilized human egg, human zygote, embryo, or fetus, and not, I would suggest, an actual living human body.

If what is distinctively human about living human bodies—the story of whose having been born just is the story of their creation by God—is the uniquely human DNA of what has been born, then the fact that human eggs and sperm, zygotes, embryos, and fetuses are potential living human bodies does not by itself settle the question whether they are themselves actual living human bodies. All that is clear is that they are now actual human eggs, sperm, zygotes, fetuses, and embryos and that, as such, except for human eggs and sperm, they are tissues of living cells having human DNA. If, however (following the way Job tells his story), the story of God's immediate and intimate involvement in our having been born is the story of our creation by God as actual living human bodies, the logic of that story of our creation cuts against classification of human eggs and sperm, zygotes, fetuses, and embryos as actual living human bodies. In this creation story, the actuality of a living human body does not consist in its being a tissue of living human cells having human DNA. Rather, its actuality as a living human body is a function of its having been born (past tense).

"Living human bodies" is a complex concept, partially unpacked in the points listed below. Together these points are designed to show how much more than possibility and potentiality, or even living human tissue, an actual living human body is. Actual living human bodies, I argue in chapter 7A, are personal bodies having unqualified dignity and value and deserving unqualified respect solely because they are God's creatures. That is a major part of what it means to claim that human beings are, not merely living human bodies, but living human bodily creatures. What "personal" means is the subject of chapter 7A. The point whose basis is being established here is that it is actual living human bodies that are personal bodies; possibilities of and potentialities for being living human bodies are not personal bodies.

[margin note: Can say same about all animals or plants]

Telling the story of our creation as the story of our having been born locates God's creative relating in the context of a set of creaturely developmental processes that are not marked by breaks, gaps, and discontinuities. There is no single point at which an actual state of affairs that is the potentiality for another, second state of affairs becomes the actuality of that second state of affairs. There is no single point that can be identified in the process from conception through gestation to birth at which potentialities for a new living human body become the actuality of a new living human body in its having been born.

Accordingly, the phrase "having been born" is in important respects ineradicably vague. It not only covers a variety of processes by which a living human body is delivered, from natural childbirth to Caesarean section. It also covers a large range of conditions of the newly born, from the fully developed newborn who certainly requires a complex support system to survive but no longer requires the support system provided by its mother's womb, to the radically premature newborn who requires what is, in effect, an artificial environment that substitutes for the environment of its mother's womb and is made possible by advances in the technology of neonatal care. "Created by God as an actual living human body through having been born" does not help to specify a moment of creation. It only specifies that "created by God" means "created as an actual living human body able to live apart from the body of its mother, although not apart from a complex physical and social network that is the newborn, newly created human being's necessary life support system."

3. Actual living human bodies, created by God in their having been born, are on a par with all other creatures so far as the immediacy and freedom of God's relating to them is concerned. Conversely, as their ultimate context, God's creative relating to nonhuman bodies is as immediate and free as is God's relating to human living bodies. God relates concretely to creatures in ways that are appropriate to their creaturely powers. Consequently, how God relates concretely to different kinds of creatures necessarily varies. But in regard to the intimacy and freedom of the relating, they are all on a par. Hence, the status of actual living human bodies within the ultimate and proximate contexts they share with all other kinds of creatures cannot be explicated by contrasting human living bodies to other kinds of creatures in regard to the freedom and intimacy of God's relation to them in their kind.

I am characterizing a relationship, not offering explanations of events. The rhetoric of networks of energy systems no more explains the processes that make and keep a human body living than does the story of Job's having been born a living body. This rhetoric is no more than a gesture in the direction of the several sciences and their findings. The important theological point is that God, described in a triune way, is immediately and intimately related to whatever may be the structure and dynamics of organic and inorganic creatures alike.

Recall the argument in chapter 4A that God's transcendence is not to be understood by contrast to creatures. Contrastive ways of characterizing God's relation to creatures bring with them the picture that God directly relates only to that which, though contrasted to God, is most like God. That view, in turn, tempts us to reason thus: Since God is not a physical

Compatible with multi-aspect monism

False declaration set up by the false logic of contrast. why/where unimportant

body, God must be directly related only to creatures that are nonmaterial, or spiritual, creatures. However, if God's relating to creatures is not understood in a contrastive way, then God ought not to be characterized as spiritual in contrast to physical bodily creature. *God as Creator is no closer to spirit than God is to physical matter.* All creatures, including purely spiritual creatures (if there be any) and human living bodies, stand on a par in regard to the fact that God directly relates to each of them in an intimacy that is directly, and not inversely, correlated with God's genuine "otherness" to creatures.

But again, isn't this just the common presence of Spirit?

God relates to different kinds of creatures on their own terms. Otherwise, in relating to them God would in some way be violating their integrities as just the kinds of creature they are. God's way of relating to creatures correlates with the array of powers and capacities a particular kind of creature has. Hence, God's way of relating to human creatures involves God's immediacy to ranges of powers and capacities that human living bodies have and some of which other creatures lack. Nonetheless, God is no more and no less immediately related to human living bodies than God is to any other kind of creature.

mediated by Spirit or not?

Contrastive ways of understanding God's relation to human creatures tempts us to form another problematic picture, which is blocked by noncontrastive characterizations of God's way of relating to creatures. If God is understood as spiritual reality in contrast to the human body's material reality, and yet God is understood to relate to human bodies, then it is tempting to form this picture: God's relation to human bodies must be mediated by some kind of creaturely reality in human beings in addition to their physical bodies—say, created "soul" or "spirit"—which both relates to their bodies and is more like God's reality than human bodies are, so that God can relate to this created "soul" or "spirit" and, through it, relate indirectly to human bodies. However, when God's way of relating to living human bodies is not understood contrastively, this entire line of thought is not required. On such a view there is no conceptual problem with the picture that in creating, God freely and intimately relates directly to human living bodies, just as God does to all nonhuman creatures.

Why not say this is what is referred to by Spirit.

Stress on the parity between the way God relates as Creator to human and to nonhuman creatures undercuts one type of argument for a metaphysical distinction in human beings between their bodies and their souls. The argument goes roughly like this: It is in virtue of God relating to them as their creator that human bodies live. But as spiritual reality, God cannot directly relate to material realities like bodies. Therefore, human beings must have a metaphysical principle of life that is itself spiritual and not material—namely, souls, to which God can relate as Creator and thereby, indirectly, be the source of life in those bodies.

If there are good metaphysical arguments on behalf of the ascription to human beings of nonextended, nonbodily souls in addition to their bodies, they must be another sort of argument. There may be such arguments (see, e.g., Cooper 1989; Davis 1993). Nonetheless, ascription of a nonmaterial soul or spirit to human living bodies is not required by the claim that God's continual relating to us as our creator is as immediate as it is universal.

[margin note: soul possible but not necessary]

4. If we rely on canonical Wisdom literature, in the form of the narrative in the book of Job of Job's creation, to norm our theological account of what it is to be a human creature, promoting stress on the actuality of what God creates in creating us, we need to clarify how we use the term "human" in this theological anthropology. In the phrase "actual living human bodies," "living bodies" names the actuality that God is said to create in our having been born; "human" only classifies it.

As used here, "human" is a descriptive term that may be used to classify, not just living bodies, but an array of living or formerly living things. It has wholly naturalistic criteria. Currently, the most decisive criterion of what counts as human is the genetic structure of *Homo sapiens*. "Human" may be used to classify certain genetic information found in nonliving matter (e.g., hair, bones, and teeth, or fossils of some of these, can sometimes be identified genetically as "human" hair, bones, or teeth). It may equally well be used to classify as human certain tissues of cells by their genetic structure (e.g., patches of skin, muscle, or brain tissue found, say, at the scene of an accident or crime can be identified as "human" skin, muscle, or brain tissue). It can equally well be used to classify particular living bodies as "human." Thus, the term "human" implies nothing about the ontological status of what it classifies. That is, it implies nothing about whether what it classifies is a complete living human body, a part of that body, or a nonliving part of such a body (i.e., whether it has the status of meat rather than that of flesh). Furthermore, used in this way, "human" has no normative or evaluative force. To classify correctly some piece of genetic information, some living tissue, or some actual living body as "human" implies nothing about how to value it or what obligations it lays on us.

The role of the word "human" in the formula "actual living human body" is to identify the subset of living bodies about which theological anthropological claims are made. It is the way to locate them, distinguishing them from other living (and nonliving) entities (e.g., chimpanzees, dolphins, robots, extraterrestrials, angels, demons, etc.). It is about the members of just this subset of the set of living bodies that theological claims are made about—for example, being "personal" creatures, ontologically dependent on God in specific ways, born into specific vocations, accountable to God in specific ways, promised eschatological blessing of a specific kind, alienated from God in specific ways, their identities distorted in specific kinds of bondage, reconciled in an odd way that makes specific differences to who they are and how they are to be, and imaging the image of God. The theological remarks make claims about living human bodies that go well beyond anything warranted by the naturalistic criteria used to classify the bodies as specifically human.

It will not do to rely on any theological remark about human beings, such as "bearer of the image of God," as the marker by which to identify to whom theological anthropological claims refer. That way lies a vicious circle. In order for such a theological identifier to be helpful, it would be necessary to identify which living beings are bearers of the image of God. A theological identifier of the referent of theological anthropological claims would create a closed circle of theological discourse that fails to hook up with our quotidian proximate contexts. Reliance on a nontheological identification of those about whom theological anthropological claims are made avoids that closed circle.

Of course, in addition to DNA, there are other naturalistic, atheological candidates for the role in theology of identifying marker of the population about which theological anthropological claims are made. Christian theology has long relied on the Aristotelian formula, "rational animal." Much nineteenth- and twentieth-century theology has relied on "conscious being," "self-consciousness being," "self-relating being," or "self-actualizing being." In the past few decades there have been proposals to rely on the formula "language user," "communicator," or "information processor."

There is plenty to dispute in each proposed marker of the class "human," but they all share one major drawback. Each relies on a property that undoubtedly characterizes most living human bodies, but only in varying degrees. Some of them, such as "rationality," "self-consciousness," and "language-using," appear to be missing in newborn human beings and only appear through a developmental process. Some disappear in the dementia of some of the aged, even though normal maturation may earlier have developed them to a high degree. Some are destroyed by accident or disease. Some never develop, through some malfunction of normal developmental processes. Were these characteristics employed strictly as the criteria of human beings' humanness, one would have to conclude that infants and profoundly damaged human beings were not human. But in that case, one would have to say that Christian theological anthropological claims do not apply to such living bodies, which is theologically unacceptable. To avoid that conclusion, it has regularly been necessary in theology to introduce mediating categories such as "potential 'human' living bodies" (e.g., infants) and "former" or "lapsed 'human' living bodies" (e.g., those who are profoundly damaged). These categories, mediating between the "genuinely human" and the "quasi-human," too easily appear to be euphemisms for "not really human." The advantage of a criterion based on *Homo sapiens* DNA is that it identifies in a more clear-cut way the subset of living bodies of which theological anthropological claims are made.

I have been arguing in this subsection that the way Job tells of his having been born as his creation by God suggests that the analogue in our cultural context for his way of identifying a living body as human is that body's DNA. This has a major negative consequence for certain speculative questions posed to theological (and other types of) anthropology, such as, "If artificial intelligence (AI) can be perfected to the point of being indistinguishable from human intelligence, would the machines (made of whatever material; the material would be irrelevant) count as 'human'?" "If so, should robots have civil rights?" "If intelligent beings are discovered on another planet in another galaxy, should they be counted as 'human'?" If the answers are "Yes," then the next round of questions must be theological: "Do Christian theological anthropological claims then also apply to such 'beings' as artificial intelligences, robots, and extraterrestrials?"

On the basis of the discussion to this point, the answer to the second round of questions is clearly "No." If (a) what theological anthropological claims refer to are what God creates in our having been born, then (b) what God creates in our having been born is actual living human bodies, and the identifier of the class of human living bodies, is (c) human DNA. AI is an abstract operating program for a computer, not a concrete body of any kind; robots are not organic—that is, "living bodies"; extraterrestrials presumably do not have human DNA.

There may be a great many theological remarks to be made about AI, robots, and extraterrestrials. Given Christian beliefs about the triune God's relating to all that is not God in both creative and eschatological blessing, there are remarks to be made about their creatureliness and their eschatological consummation. Whether there is anything to be said about their estrangement from God, and therewith about the triune God's relating to them to reconcile them to God, would depend on knowing quite a great deal about the ways in which they are capable of responding to God. It is not self-evident that human beings are capable of knowing much about that. In any case, the specific content of theological remarks under these *loci* will not be identical with the content of anthropological remarks under the same *loci*. Whatever their content, they will be remarks about AI or robots or extraterrestrials and not about human living bodies. In principle there is no reason that there could not be such AI theology, robot theology, or extraterrestrial theology. However, while such theologies might have analogues to theologies rooted in the triune God's relating to humankind, they would not be such theological anthropology simply extended in scope to cover God's relating to these other kinds of beings. Instead, such theology would need in each case to be based on how God in fact relates to each of these (AI, robots, extraterrestrials) in its kind, not on how God relates to humankind. It cannot simply be assumed that we know the character of that divine relating on the basis of what we know of God's relating to humankind.

The issues addressed in this subsection are the theological issues that have been at the core of anthropological debates about monogenism generated initially by pre-Darwinian versions of the theory of the evolution of the species. Traditional Christian anthropology uncritically interpreted Genesis 2 and 3 as a historically accurate report of the origin ("genesis") of humankind from one ("mono") human couple who had come into being as fully actualized perfect specimens of humankind. The monogenism of humankind was official church teaching both by confessional Protestant (see Hodge 1872, 1857) and Roman Catholic communions (see Rahner 1961, 229–96). The evolutionary theory of the origin of the species raised for monogenism the formal issue whether Genesis is true in these regards. It also raised material systematic issues. Charles Hodge saw these issues acutely. Although he was committed to a very conservative scholastic Calvinism in the tradition of Francis Turretin, he held a pre-Darwinian optimism about the harmony of science and revelation. The apparent challenge to scriptural inerrancy did not bother him very much. He was mistakenly confident that the conflict was only apparent and could be resolved regarding the question of the "special creation" of the first human couple.

The systematic issues, however, were more serious in Hodge's view. They turned on the possible denial that all subsequent humankind had had its origin from one human couple. The systematic issue is important because it turns on the importance of the claim that humankind is one family in the full, ordinary biological sense of the term. For Hodge, the consequences ("original sin") of the first couple's disobedience for all future human beings depends on their belonging to the same family. Much in Christian theology, Hodge saw, depends on a strong theological claim about the solidarity of humankind, and the clearest, least artificial, by no means utopian, model of solidarity is familial.

Hodge overlaid the extended-family solidarity of humankind with the conventions of a so-called federal covenant, according to which certain members of a family can properly represent each and all other members in such a way that the decisions and actions the representatives undertake count as decisions made or acts done by each and all. For Hodge, the consequences of the first human disobedience apply to all their descendant family because of such a covenant God had made with the first couple and their family, not because the consequences are passed on genetically. Correlatively, by virtue of a divine covenant with the human family as a family, and not just as an aggregate of individuals, the saving effects of the work of Christ can only bear on other human beings if they are, by virtue of the incarnation, all one family. This is the way Hodge interprets the parallel the apostle Paul draws in Romans 5:12–21 between the way "one man's [Adam's] trespass led to condemnation for all" and the way "one man's [Christ's] act of righteousness leads to justification and life for all" (5:18). But, in Hodge's view, if humankind had emerged out of the evolutionary process at different times and in more than one place, it does not constitute one family, and both the doctrine of original sin and the doctrine of redemption are systematically undercut.

The anthropology developed here has no commitment either to Hodge's view of Scripture's inerrancy or to his federal theories of divine covenants. However, it does require a strong claim about the solidarity of the human family. The theological importance of the claim lies in the way it grounds the solidarity of humankind in human beings' bodies and, more exactly, in those bodies' shared DNA. It cuts off at their roots all challenges to the full inclusion of any individuals in the class "human beings" on the grounds of their apparent biological gender, their race, their sexual orientation, or their physical or mental abnormalities. A given living body either has human DNA and counts as a human living body or it does not. Neither differences in development of sexual organs nor differences in characteristics by which individuals are assigned to socially constructed racial types are relevant to the question of whether a given living body belongs to the class "human living bodies." It is striking that modern genetics appears to establish that "modern" *Homo sapiens* (sometimes named *Homo sapiens sapiens*) has in fact evolved from a single African mother, perhaps as recently as seventy thousand years ago. Perhaps this finding may serve as at least a symbol of the validity of the intuition about the theological importance of the solidarity of humankind that lay behind Hodge's monogenism.

5. As we have seen, the way Job tells the story of his having been born as the story of his creation makes it clear that he understands that his birth comes as the outcome of a process of development from his conception to his being delivered from his mother's womb. Understanding Job's creation by God in terms of his having been born as the outcome of a process of development signals a larger point about what it is that God creates in relating creatively to Job. The actual living human body that God creates not only has been born as the outcome of a process of development, but is inherently a reality that is continuously changing and developing in various ways toward various outcomes for the rest of its life as a living human body.

Premodern Christian theological anthropology assumed that what God created in creating human beings were adult human beings, perfect (i.e., completely actual in every possible respect) in their kind, from whom all humankind are descended. (Irenaeus is the major, but only partial, exception. Although he proposed that Adam and Eve, as historical figures, were not only "inexperienced" but "immature," he too assumed they were biological "adults.") Traditional Christian theological anthropology was well aware, of course, that subsequent generations of human beings are born as relatively helpless babies and must go through complex and relatively long processes of physical, emotional, and intellectual maturation, which require a great deal of nurture and support by adult human beings, before they become adult human beings themselves. However, only adulthood was assumed to be the condition of fully actualized human creaturely being. The only significant processes of change adults go through are moral and spiritual, and those processes could be considered developmental only in the sense that they may take the form of recovery of the moral and spiritual capacities for love for God with which adult humans were originally created and subsequently lost.

In different ways, Søren Kierkegaard (1980) and Friedrich Schleiermacher (1928, 269–315) in the early nineteenth century explored the theological anthropological implications, especially regarding doctrines of sin, of a developmental picture of the evolution of humankind that does not assume the creation of a perfectly actual adult human pair as the progenitors of humankind. Schleiermacher also relies on a developmental view of individual human consciousness to help explain the fact and nature of sin. However, his analysis of the dynamics of sin and redemption seems to assume that it is only mature adult consciousness that is capable of redemption—that is, capable of undergoing the process of overcoming sin (under the influence of Jesus' God-consciousness) whose outcome is a fully actual human being. Kierkegaard's phenomenology of consciousness seems to assume that it is only adult consciousness that is capable of relating to itself in the way that constitutes it as concretely actual "spirit"—that is, an actual human being. Both approaches appear to assume that fully actual individual human being presupposes completion of an individual's maturational process. Neither appears to have conceptual space for the generalized claim that developmental, maturational processes are constitutive of actual living human bodies. That general claim, however, is basic to the understandings of all aspects of living human bodies yielded by the various sciences, understandings that contemporary members of communities of Christian faith take for granted in the educational, medical, therapeutic, child-raising, dietary, and artistic practices that partly constitute the proximate contexts they share with their neighbors.

To emphasize that developmental processes are constitutive of actual living human bodies raises, however, an important theological question for this anthropological proposal. The question is how to understand the relation between the newly born actual living human body, on one hand, and the various stages or moments in the process that precedes and leads up to its birth, on the other. If, following Job, a human creature's creation is its having been born as a living human body, it would seem that it has not been created until it has been born. Consequently, moments in the process leading to that birth would seem not themselves to be part of that creature's history. On the other hand, it is clear that in some way the one who has been born is the same as the one undergoing the processes leading to its birth. It would be odd to deny that the pre-birth moments are indeed part of the newly born creature's history. That is, perhaps, the core background theological puzzle in debates about the morality of abortion:

(margin handwritten notes:) ✱ Humans as developmental by nature, not static

what is the ontological status of the unborn? Even though modern scientific understanding of the complexities of the process are qualitatively different from the ancient Near Eastern understanding reflected in Job, the form of the theological question is unchanged. Presumably it is a question the author(s) of Job could have understood as well as we do.

Neither canonical Wisdom literature nor any other voice in canonical Christian Scripture provides much guidance in addressing this puzzle. There are a few passages of scriptural witness to God's knowledge of the speaker before his birth—for example, "Before I formed you in the womb I knew you" (Jer. 1:5); "The LORD called me before I was born, while I was in my mother's womb he named me" (Isa. 49:1b). However, such passages do not make claims about the ontological status of the unborn, and they do not warrant ontological conclusions about this puzzle. At most, such passages are testimonies to God's intentions for the particular speakers' lives. Granted traditional beliefs about God's omniscience and foreknowledge, such passages claim at most only that God's intentions for these particular lives are antecedent in the order of being, but not in the temporal order, to their creation as actual living human bodies.

However, we have found that the way Job tells of his creation does suggest three theological claims about the moments of the process that precedes Job's having been born that have some bearing on our puzzle. First, God directly relates creatively to each moment. What is actual at that moment, insofar as it is actual, is God's creature. As God's actual creature of one determinate sort, it is also potentially a number of other actual creatures of other determinate sorts. Second, each moment consists of a tissue of living human cells, but a tissue of living human cells does not by itself necessarily count as an actual living human body. As we noted above, a fertilized human egg dividing and subdividing into a tissue of living cells with human DNA classifies as an actual zygote but not necessarily, as such, as an actual living human body. A given tissue of living human cells may have the ontological status of being a potential embryo and a potential fetus and a potential human living body, but what it is is an actual zygote. Developed further, the tissue of cells is an actual human embryo that is also a potential human fetus and a potential human living body. Developed further, the tissue of cells is an actual human fetus and a potential human living body. At each moment in the process "what it is," is, theologically speaking, an actual creature. Like all else that is other than God, an actual tissue of human living cells is a creature of God. Third, by God's creative providence the tissue of cells may develop into an actual living human body, say, Job. However, none of the moments in the process is itself Job's actual living body. Each is actually something else and potentially Job's actual living body. Each of the salient moments in the process preceding Job's having been born is indeed a moment in the history of Job's actual living body having been born, even though none of the moments itself *is* his actual living human body. That is actualized, and not without God's involvement, only by Job's having been born. Hence, while each of the moments in the process that precedes a human living body's having been born is indeed part of that human living body's history, it does not follow that any of them, or the entire process as a whole, are *what* God creates in the living human body's having been born. According to this theology of birth, what God creates through its having been born is simply that newly born actual living human body. Apart from its having been born, it has not yet been created, although other creatures with human DNA may have been created—tissues of living human cells, an actual zygote, an actual embryo, an actual fetus—that were the potentialities of an actual living human body having been born.

"Having been born" is the marker by which actual living human creatures are distinguishable from potential living human creatures. This theological remark is different from a traditional theological remark that the viability of a living human body within its mother's womb is the marker that the fetus has received from God its newly created immortal rational soul, therewith received the image of God, and has become an actual—even if as yet unborn—human living body. The theological premise in this view is that until God joins an immortal rational soul to a fetus, it cannot count as a new human creature. The difference between the two theologies of human creaturehood is ontological. Although the anthropological proposals being made here rely on a distinction between potentialities for an actual living human body, on one side, and the actuality of that living human body, on the other, they have not invoked the concept "immortal rational soul" to explain the actualization of the potential. Nor have they invoked the theological concept of the image of God. As a marker of the distinction between potential human living bodies and actual living human bodies, "having been born" is more straightforwardly naturalistic than "implantation of an immortal rational soul."

6. Like all living creatures, actual living human bodies are each centers of actual power that are genuinely other than God's power while nonetheless dependent on God for their reality and value. Living human bodies are inherently relatively powerful agents. Framing an account of the creation of human beings and, correlatively, an account of their creatureliness in terms of their having been born as living bodies privileges one set of characteristics of human beings as especially important theologically: the sheer energy of their vitality, their inherent power.

That human creatures are centers of power would seem so obvious as to be trivial were it not the case that modern Christianity seems to be as uncomfortable with the inescapable fact of human power as earlier generations of Christians were with human sexuality. Recurrent theological claims that faithfulness to God requires the abandonment or denial of power and the embrace of powerlessness, when left unqualified as they often are, amount to a call for the denial of our creatureliness. To be God's human creature simply is to be a center of finite power. Far from being an act of faithfulness, denial of this fact would be a fundamental act of faithlessness to the Creator.

More accurately, in being created by having been born, living human bodies are centers of a large variety of powers. This variety is brought out by the rhetoric of exchange among energy systems of various types. A living human body is itself a relatively self-regulating set of energy systems that, having been born, is set into an environment of other energy systems that inevitably have significant effects on that human living body through exchanges of energy. Conversely, as a relatively self-regulating set of energy systems, a human body is born into an environment of other energy systems on which it inevitably may and does have significant effects through exchanges of energy. To speak of ways in which a living human body *may* impinge on its proximate context refers to the body's capacities; to speak of events in which it *does* impinge on its context refers to its agency.

Some of the energy exchanges that constitute some of the systems constituting a human living body—for example, some of its biochemistry— are basically the same in all living organisms. Some are basically the same in all mammals. However, by virtue of the ways in which energy is organized to constitute them, human living bodies generally have a distinctive array of capacities for specific types of self-regulated behavior that involve more complex, more long-range, and more flexibly modulated planning than that of which any other kind of living body is capable.

Many capacities of human living bodies are inherently socially and culturally shaped. That we have been born presupposes at the very least a society of parents and, usually, other adult human creatures in a multigenerational extended family, possibly with other children, which, with its local culture, provides part of the necessary conditions for both the conception and the survival of the newly born. The living human body that is born is capacitated for and requires some degree of life in such a society. Moreover, the fact of one's having been born itself creates a significantly new society simply by the fact that a new living body has been added to the complex of culturally mediated relationships that constituted an earlier society. The introduction of a new child inevitably changes the micro-society of the family in which it is nurtured and reared.

Living human bodies' capacities for self-regulated behavior need to be continually nurtured and empowered by social interaction with other human beings. That social exchange itself necessarily involves some sort of material culture, however rudimentary. Centrally important to any such culture is its repertoire of images, symbols, myths, rituals, and significant gestures. Each of these is conceptually determinate. The concepts are publicly shareable insofar as they are expressible in an ordinary language. Thus, the culture's repertoire of images, symbols, myths, rituals, and

significant gestures is inseparable from its language. This linguistic repertoire is the principal medium through which living human bodies' capacities for self-regulated exercise of their powers are given definite shape
and organized patterns. Hence, the interplay between a culture's language
and living human bodies' specific capacity for language is an essential
feature of human creatures. Living human bodies' capacity for language
amplifies and complexifies all of their other powers (see, e.g., Pinker
1995).

Thus, the concept "living human body" needs to be capacious enough
to include not only networks of organic energy systems organized, for
example, into respiratory, digestive, circulatory, and neurological systems,
but also networks of energy organized in social and cultural systems.

Clearly, "energy" means rather different things when used in these various ways. But they are not absolutely different meanings. There are overlaps and family resemblances among these uses that allow us to make a
very broad but nonetheless significant generalization: the same rich and
complex array of types of energy systems and their networks of exchange
characterize all human living bodies. But "energy systems" is just another
way of referring to "systems of powers." Human living bodies are centers
of real power exercised in exchanges with other centers of power, thereby
constituting their shared proximate contexts.

Christian theological anthropology has traditionally privileged certain
ranges of these powers as humankind's "higher powers." Premodern theology tended to assume that they are the intellectual powers. Modern theology has tended to assume that they are powers of consciousness. In either
case, they are deemed "higher" for two broad reasons. They are judged to
be the powers that set human living bodies apart from all other kinds of
living bodies because no other kind of living body possesses them. Also,
they are judged to be powers that either are not rooted in the body or are
powers that make it possible to transcend the body. Intellectual powers
are held to be rooted in a nonmaterial soul, while the lower powers were
rooted in the body. Powers of consciousness are held to be human subjects'
ecstatic capacities, their capacities to stand outside the lawbound determi-
nateness of their objective physical bodies in the radical freedom of their
subjectivity. In both regards, these powers raise human beings above other
creatures.

It is no longer clear that either "intelligence" or "consciousness" name
some one human power. Following Howard Gardner's (1993) pioneering
work, psychologists have sorted out several distinguishable types of intelligence. "Consciousness" is perhaps best understood as a placeholder for a
set of distinguishable human powers. Moreover, it is increasingly clear that
any account of the metaphysical status of either type of power must take
into account their physical grounding in human beings' living bodies (see,
e.g., Damasio 2003). In that regard, they are on a metaphysical par with all

other human powers. Living human bodies undoubtedly have ranges of powers that either are not shared at all by other kinds of living bodies or are not shared in the same degree. But it is only as actual living bodies that they have the powers they do have.

There are important metaphysical questions about living bodies and their powers. It may be that these questions cannot be answered coherently and adequately without, say, invoking the distinction between body and soul. They are interesting questions for philosophical-theological speculation prompted by dogmatic theological claims about human beings as, precisely, creatures. They are not explored here. The only point being made here is that any theologically adequate metaphysical proposal must cohere with the theological claim that what God creates in our having been born are centers of a variety of powers that are rooted in living human bodies.

7. Human living bodies are finite centers of power. Stress on finitude is inherent in a Christian theological concept of a living human body. The basis for this claim has been laid in earlier accounts of our ultimate and proximate contexts.

By virtue of having been born, living human bodies are made integral and inextricable parts of proximate contexts, societies of fellow creatures analogous to a social institution. They are all radically dependent on God's free creativity for their continuing actuality.

These contexts are ontologically ambiguous in two ways, both of which limit human living bodies' powers. They are inherently accident-prone. Living human bodies are ontologically ambiguous, first, because each is located in and constituted by an environing network of relations with other creaturely centers of power that have effects on each body, constraining it in many ways, often violating it, sometimes destroying it. Second, living human bodies' proximate contexts are ontologically ambiguous in that each living body inescapably survives by consuming other creatures, living and nonliving. Some degree and type of predation, in a very broad sense of the term, is built into the dynamics necessary to sustain their lives. Living human bodies are finite in the sense that each is located in an environing network of other lives, some of which sustain themselves at their expense and in which they can only sustain themselves if there is a supply of other living bodies on which to feed.

Human bodies are also finite in that the energy of each is inherently limited in definite, if not always knowable, ways. "Each creature eventually ceases to be" may be reformulated as "Each finite energy system eventually disintegrates" (assuming an appropriately broad concept of "energy"), or "Each finite center of power eventually ceases to be powerful" (assuming an appropriately broad concept of "power"). Hence, as living bodies, human creatures are inherently fallible and defectible. They inherently may and do defect from levels of energy exchange and from levels of exercise of powers that they once enjoyed.

Consequently, it is important that the concept "living human body" stress human creatures' neediness and desire. Finitude entails not only interaction, but also interdependence or mutual need among fellow creatures. Human creatures are inherently needy in a multitude of ways that correlate with the multitude of energy systems that constitute a human living body. They may, of course, become deluded about what they truly need, but if so, it is a distortion of neediness. Neediness itself is constitutive of creatureliness, not a failure of it.

So too, in self-regulation of their powers, human creatures inherently desire what they need. Like neediness, desire is not a deformity of human creatureliness. To the contrary, it is the principal motive of human living bodies' exercise of their powers in interdependent interactions with fellow creatures.

This stress on human neediness and desire is in line with canonical Wisdom. Indeed, as H. W. Wolff takes pains to point out in his study of Old Testament anthropologies (1974, 10–25), need and desire are features of human creatureliness prominently stressed in all the voices in the Old Testament chorus. The point would seem too obvious to be worth noting, were it not for long traditions of distortedly one-sided Christian rhetoric suggesting that desire in particular is a sign of a deformity that fully actualized human creatures would overcome. But, to overcome desirousness would amount to overcoming creatureliness itself. To attempt that would be faithless to the Creator.

8. Created by God in their having been born, living human bodies are intrinsically mysterious. They are mysterious in regard both to knowledge and to being.

Their complexity makes living human bodies mysterious objects of knowledge. Let us call this their "epistemic mysteriousness." Even though they are far from fully understood, living human bodies are knowable and known in astonishingly subtle and complex detail. In classical theology, that knowability has been grounded in the Trinitarian formula that we are created by the "Father *through* the Son" who is the fundamental principle of all intelligibility. Indeed, the formula grounds this knowability in the very life of God: we are created by the font of all reality through its own Wisdom, by virtue of which everything created is capable of being known.

We are capable of being known, but not necessarily capable of being known exhaustively. The mystery of human living bodies is not that which is thus far unknown about them. Their mysteriousness as objects of knowledge lies, rather, in what is known, or more exactly, in the ongoing process of coming to know them. Knowledge and ignorance of living human bodies appear not to be inversely related. Expressions such as "pushing back the frontiers of knowledge" misleadingly suggest that growth in "knowledge" is an incremental gain on the finite territory of "ignorance." What seems to happen instead is that with every "advance" in knowledge, new and unimagined ranges of ignorance open up. What grows incrementally is a sense of the astonishing complexity of living human bodies in the broad sense of the term outlined here. Living human bodies are inexhaustible objects of knowledge. This inexhaustibility is their espistemic mysteriousness.

Living human bodies are mysterious in a second, more basic sense. Let us call it their ontological mysteriousness. The sheer fact that the networks of energy systems constituting a living human body and its proximate context are "there" itself gives cause for wonder and intense amazement. What solicits such wonder is ontological mystery—that is, the contingent fact that these energy systems in their complex interactions exist. To say that their actuality is radically contingent on God's creativity does not explain creatures in a way that dissolves this mysteriousness. It merely locates that mysteriousness in the context of God relating to all that is not God.

9. The rhetoric I have elected to use in explicating our creation as our having been born as living bodies suggests a sense in which, by our creation, we are deemed to be good as creatures. What is true of the myriad energy systems by which we came to be born is also true of us as living bodies who have been born: as Creator, God actively relates directly to us in our having been born as the sort of living bodies we are, with the distinctive array of powers that characterize our species. Since this free creativity is self-involving on God's part, in creating us God is self-committed to respect and nurture us as living bodies rather than resisting or threatening to violate us as living bodies as long as we live.

Furthermore, as respected and nurtured by God, we are valued by God. That is, God deems us "good" precisely as the sort of living bodies we are, not despite, but precisely as finite centers of power, prone to causing and suffering damage, thoroughly ambiguous both morally and ontologically. Created by God's free and immediate involvement in our having been born, our goodness as living human bodies is not a function of any of the properties characterizing our living bodies. We are not deemed "good" by God as an assessment of our energy, beauty, creativity, or wisdom. Nor is the goodness we are deemed to have a function of any exercise of any of our powers in bodily actions. We are not deemed "good" by God insofar as we consciously and intentionally exercise our powers in ways that make for the well-being of our fellow creatures and our shared proximate contexts. Nor is it a function of any role we may fill in the larger ecology of the society of creatures. It is not because in filling the roles we inescapably fill in the ecology of our proximate contexts that we are deemed "good" for fellow creatures—that is, contributory to their well-being as opposed to being inherently and unavoidably destructive of their well-being, or at least good in that sense for some of them some of the time. Thus, the sense in which actual living human beings are deemed "good" is different from the sense in which their proximate contexts are experienced as morally ambiguous, at once "good" and "evil," precisely because they do at once nurture and frustrate the well-being of the creatures whose networks of interdependence help constitute those very environments. Rather, the goodness of actual living human bodies is grounded in exactly the same way, and is of the same sort, as the goodness of all other creatures: it is grounded in God's self-commitment to valuing creatures in delight with them for what they are, valuing them in the free and delighted intimacy and the intimate and attentive freedom of God's creative ongoing active relating to them.

Job Created as One Given a Living Body

Thus far we have been reflecting on the first of two ways in which Job tells the story of his having been born. It has been the story of Job's being a living body born, we may say, through normal channels, but not without God's direct involvement.

Job tells the same story a second way, as God's directly giving a living body to Job.

> "You clothed me with skin and flesh,
>   and knit me together with bones and sinews.
> You have granted me life and steadfast love,
>   and your care has preserved my spirit."
>   (10:11, 12)

A subtle shift in verbs and pronouns deserves attention. In the first way of telling the story, God was directly involved in Job's having come to be born *as* a living body so that Job *is* a living body; in this second way of telling the story, God gives a living body directly *to* Job so that Job *has* a living body. In both tellings of the story, God is immediately and directly involved as one freely self-committed to what God creates. However, the change from Job's being a living body to his having a living body suggests some distinction between Job and his living body—a distinction, but not a separation or dichotomy.

Why doesn't the story of Job's creation by God in Job's having been born *as* a living body suffice? I suggest the following answer: the story of Job's being given a living body is necessary for the account of his creation to be adequate to its larger literary context.

The larger literary context of the second story is Job's protest: his horrendous and undeserved suffering signifies that, at least in Job's own case, God has broken God's commitment to creatures. The premise of this complaint is that in creating human beings, God has established something like a two-sided social institution. We saw in chapter 5A that the ultimate context into which we are born—God's ongoing creativity—is best likened to just such a social institution embracing several parties and constituted by the dynamics and logic of giving and receiving gifts. The appropriate response to God's gift of creation is faithfulness to God. Human creatures are accountable to God for that response.

Accordingly, Job acknowledges that it is appropriate for God to ask him to account for his behavior. He recognizes that he has an obligation both to his friends and, more basically, to God to answer the question, "Is my behavior innocent, or have I sinned?" Indeed, Job yearns for an encounter with God in which God can demand such an account, and Job can, as it were, answer, "My behavior is innocent of sin, innocent of faithlessness to You!" In so doing, Job implicitly acknowledges that he is capable of responding with a true account. He is not only response-able (e.g., in lament and bitter outrage), but also account-able for his response (e.g., God can ask Job to account for his outrage in the face of God's display of the complexity and range of God's creativity). What Job protests, however, is that while he has faultlessly kept faith with Creator God, his suffering shows that God has been faithless to God's commitment to creature Job.

It is the human capacity for response and account giving that requires that the story of Job's creation as his having been born distinguish between (but not separate) Job and his living body.

Job is, by God's gift, able to respond to God. Furthermore, he is responsible to God in a distinctive way: he is not only capable of responding to God, but also of being held accountable for his response. Job's response to God and giving an account to God of his ways of responding to God are exercises of powers he has simply by being the actual living human body that he is. However, responding to God appropriately and giving an account to God of those responses are self-reflexive exercises of those powers. Responding appropriately involves exercise of powers to self-regulate the exercise of other powers as one interacts with other creatures. Giving accounts of one's responses involves exercise of powers to monitor, assess, and explain one's responses. In that respect, they are analogous to many other exercises of human powers—for example, responding appropriately to other creatures, including other human beings, and giving accounts of those responses at least to other human beings (and to oneself).

It is commonplace to note that the terms "self-regulation" and "self-monitoring" name a relation between two terms, "I," as in "I regulate x" or "I monitor x," and "myself," where "x = myself." It is tempting to suppose that it is a relation of the same sort as the relation between "I" and "car" in "I steer the car," except for the oddity that "I" and "myself" are one and the same, whereas "I" and "car" are not. The oddity is sometimes signaled by characterizing the relation as a distinct type of relation—namely, a "self-relation." It is not necessarily problematic to construe "self-regulating" and "self-monitoring" as the names of relations. "Relation" is a very abstract notion. "Self-regulating" and "self-monitoring" arguably express a grammatical relation between the subject of an intentional action, "I (regulate/

monitor)," and the intentional object of that action, "myself." "Myself,"
"herself," "themselves," and the like are, after all, grammatically speaking,
reflexives.

Accordingly, the claim, "Job's creation is Job's being *given* a living body
by God, so that not only is it the case that Job *is* his actual living body, but
it is also the case that Job *has* his actual living body," can be understood
as the claim that Job's creation in his having been born is complex enough
to require description in two different stories: (1) a story about God's creative relating to Job—namely, "In having been born, I was created a living
human body by God"; and (2) a story about the consequence for Job of
his creation in his having been born—namely, "In having been born as a
living human body (i.e., as a living body with the complex range of powers
of human bodies), I was given a living body and made response-able to
God and account-able to God for the character of my (bodied) responses
to God." Both are faithful stories of Job's creation by God. Neither is an
adequate account of Job's creation as a living human body taken apart
from the other.

What is problematic is the equation of this grammatical relation with
a relation between two different actual entities. That way lies a metaphysically dualist analysis of human being. A distinction between "mortal
body" and "immortal rational soul" has been the most common version of
this analysis in Christian theological anthropology. Metaphysically dualist
anthropological theories may or may not be problematic as metaphysical
theories. What is problematic is any suggestion that they are entailed by
the grammatical relation expressed in reflexive expressions such as "I regulate myself," "I monitor myself," and so on. The claim that Job's account of
his having been born as his creation by God requires both a story (a) of his
being an actual living body, and (b) his being given an actual living body
for whose responses to God he is accountable, does not by itself entail a
metaphysically dualist theological anthropology.

The second recounting of Job's creation as his having been born also
tells our stories of creation. Our being created by God must be told as
stories of God giving a living body to each of us. Hence, the second story
of Job's birth can guide our reflections on our own births as God's creating
us in a distinctive way.

This second recounting of Job's birth story brings with it implications
regarding three topics of major importance to theological anthropology:
(1) the restricted sense in which human creatures are each unsubstitutable
for one another, (2) the nature of the dignity of human creatures, and (3)
the unqualified respect each human creature deserves.

1. In light of the second description of Job's birth as his creation, we may
say that in certain definite but quite limited respects, human creatures are,
precisely by virtue of God's relating to them as their creator, unsubstitutable one for another. The first telling of Job's (and our) creation by God in

our having been born as living bodies underscores our inherent relationality and irreducible sociality as members both of the society of all creatures and of societies of human living bodies. By contrast, the second telling of God giving a living body to Job underscores that precisely as relational and social beings we are each not only finite centers of power, but in certain respects novel and unsubstitutable centers of finite power.

We must keep clear the limits of this theological claim about human beings' unsubstitutablity, for it is easily exaggerated. We are not absolutely unsubstitutable. For example, we are not unsubstitutable by virtue of the roles we play in social energy systems. In fact, there are many respects in which we are entirely substitutable for one another, each of us representing an instance of one or another social process in which we are eminently interchangeable with many others. It is obvious that another person can be substituted for any given occupant of such roles as national president, college dean, town dog-catcher, church pastor, store manager, salesperson, customer or consumer, or village ne'er-do-well. Even within relatively small and intimate social groups such as the family, when described and analyzed as systems—that is, analyzed in terms of recurring and characteristic patterns of interaction and of social and psychological roles—each human being can be shown to hold a place and role that may be filled by others as well. A Christian theological account of our creatureliness has nothing to gain by decrying such analysis and description of the roles human bodies fill, and certainly nothing to gain by denying its truth. It is simply part of our creatureliness.

Nor does the theological claim about the unsubstitutability of human persons one for another rest on the view that each human being is characterized by a unique and radically free interiority. The latter claim rests on some version of a picture of human being in which a strong and systematic distinction is drawn between our radical determinedness (i.e., by "the laws of nature"; call it our "exteriority" or "objectivity") and our radical undeterminedness (i.e., "freedom"; call it our "interiority" or "subjectivity"). On this view, while our exteriority is determined by its physical and social-cultural contexts, our interiority is independent of any context and, hence, "truly" free. On this view, such interiority continually expresses itself in ways for which no other human creature's interiority could be substituted. Hence human beings are unsubstitutable. There may be strong reasons in support of such a picture; my point here is that those reasons do not lie with logical necessity in a Christian theological account of our creatureliness that comports with the implications of Job's accounts of his having been born.

The most that a theological account of our creatureliness yields in regard to the claim about our unsubstitutability is this: by our birth as our creation, God has placed us in a context constituted by the dynamics of giving and receiving the gift of creation. This is the ultimate context in which human beings must be understood by virtue of their creation. In that context, we each are called to respond faithfully in the presence of, and in company with, our neighbors, to the faithfulness of God's creativity. None can respond to God in place of another. No one is accountable for another's response to God. It is in being responsible and accountable, to the extent that we are capable, that we are each unsubstitutable by any other human living body. Absent this context, it would be difficult to find strong reasons for stressing our unsubstitutability by one another.

"Response" to God must be understood broadly here. It designates the response of a concrete human creature and it involves the full array of whatever powers and capacities the creature has. Certainly, it includes types of intentional action that are normally classified as moral. Hence, faithful response to God includes keeping promises to God, acknowledging the truth to God, and the like. But it also includes types of response often classified as aesthetic ("delighting in the glory of the Lord") and affective ("joy," "fear"), for whose intentional formation, clarification, and deepening one can be held accountable. In creating, the triune God directly relates to each human creature as a living body; accordingly, faithful response to God engages the full capacities and powers of an entire human creature as a living body, not merely some peculiarly spiritual dimension of the creature.

There is a great variety in the range of human creatures' capacities for intentional responses to neighbors and to God, as well as the richness of those capacities. They normally vary according to stages of maturation. That is why it is appropriate to hold adults accountable for their responses in ways that are not applicable to children, and why we expect a broader range of responses from older children than from younger ones. It may be that among adults there is a normal or average range of the capacities of intellect, emotion, imagination, and insight called into play in their responses to God. However, we must note the many adults whose relevant capacities were significantly limited at birth, as well as others whose capacities have been damaged in the course of their lives by accident, disease, or self-destructive behavior. The theologically important point remains: human living bodies are unique and unsubstitutable one for another in the accountability each has for whatever response each is capable of making to God relating creatively.

A theologically appropriate individualism is evident here. It is not the atomic individualism of existential aloneness, as though one were somehow created a human person first in isolation, and only subsequently joined with others in society. As outlined in chapter 5A, the proximate contexts into which we are born make us social beings all the way down, and all the way up to our responding to God as well. Hence, I am not accountable to God for the way I respond to God's creative relating all by myself. Rather always, and from the origins of my being, I am accountable for the way I respond as a member of a society of fellow human creatures, all of whom

[margin note: Faithful response → includes aesthetic and affective dimensions]

are also accountable for their responses to God relating to them creatively, and by whose network of relationships with me my capacities to respond and to give an account of my response are empowered and shaped. But I, only, give my account; I give it in onliness, though not alone.

2. Human beings' inherent accountability for their response to God provides the theological basis on which the peculiar dignity of human creatures is to be understood. Dignity inheres in human creatures' concrete actuality by virtue of the fact that the triune God has directly related to them as their creator. In the practice of secondary Christian theology, human dignity must be understood, I suggest, theocentrically. That is, it *must* be understood in terms of the way God relates to us creatively. Human dignity is thus *ex-centric,* grounded and centered outside human creatures.

Such a theocentric concept of human dignity differs in important respects from what is arguably the dominant modern concept of human dignity in the West, even though the practical applications of the two converge and overlap. The prevailing modern concept of human dignity understands it as a human being's absolute value as an end in herself. It is an absolute value in that it is not relative to nor a function of anyone else's inclinations, immediate projects, or overarching life goals. This value or end makes a human being an end in herself in that it is an objective self-existent end rather than a subjective end that is an object of others' inclinations or free choices. As an end in itself having absolute value, a human being's value is permanent, such that no circumstance can diminish it. It is incommensurable with the value of any project that could be accomplished by treating a human being as merely an instrument, or with the value of any desire that could be satisfied by using a human being as a means to that satisfaction. And it is unsubstitutable such that its value cannot be quantified and nothing can compensate for its loss.

The classic expression of the practical upshot of this concept of human dignity is Immanuel Kant's second formulation of the categorical imperative: "Act in such a way that you always treat humanity, whether in your own person or in the person of any other, never simply as a means, but always at the same time as an end" (1959, 96). Although the absolute value of a human being cannot be produced or reduced by any human being's actions, the categorical imperative implies that in their relations with one another, human beings must honor that value, seeking to maintain and promote it. This involves restraint, refusal of any action that abases another human being to the status of a mere means to the actor's own subjective ends. Kant himself restricts the word "respect" to such restraints. Honoring another's absolute value also involves actions that positively further a human being's value, making the other's ends the actor's own. Kant calls this "love." As Gene Outka (1986) points out, the concept of human dignity that is currently culturally dominant generally uses "respect" more broadly to cover what Kant calls "love" as well as what he calls "respect."

The second formulation of the categorical imperative is worded to cover both relations to others and relations to oneself: "Act in such a way that you always treat humanity, *whether in your own person or in the person of any other*, never simply as a means, but always at the same time as an end" (Kant 1959, 96). "Whether in your own person or in the person of any other," your duty is to treat "humanity" as an end and not merely a means by promoting its happiness and its moral perfection. However, respect for human beings' dignity must be nuanced to take into account fixed structural differences between one's relations to another and one's relating to oneself. One can only develop one's own moral perfection. Consequently, the categorical imperative can only imply that one has a duty to develop one's own moral perfection. It cannot imply that one has a moral duty to develop another's moral perfection, since only that "other" has the capacity to develop its own moral perfection. Conversely, it cannot be a moral duty to promote something one already desires in any case. Hence no one can have a moral duty to promote his or her own happiness, which he or she necessarily desires. However, the categorical imperative does imply that one has a moral duty to promote other human beings' happiness.

There is clear overlap between, on one side, the imperative to respect human beings as ends in themselves that is entailed by this concept of human dignity, and, on the other side, the ways in which that imperative is nuanced in practice to take into account fixed structural differences between one's relations to another and one's relating to oneself and the imperative to love one's neighbors as oneself that is entailed by the theocentric concept of human dignity implied by acknowledgment that God relates to human beings creatively (see part 3, chap. 22).

However, there are at least three major differences between the two concepts of human dignity.

These differences arise when it is asked what the justification is for ascribing such dignity to human beings. First, where the theocentric concept of human dignity proposed here justifies the ascription of absolute value to human beings on the grounds that God relates to them creatively and calls them to a certain vocation, the culturally dominant concept of human dignity justifies ascribing dignity to human beings on the grounds that "humanity" differs from animals by virtue of two capacities: to be self-determining, and to adopt rules that are acknowledged to be binding on all rational beings including oneself. Critique of the latter holds that it rules out ascription of dignity to human beings who are incapable of self-determination or do not exhibit the rational capacities that would classify them as rational beings. The objection is that it justifies ascription of dignity on too narrow a basis that would exclude infants and the rationally impaired, removing such human beings from the class of those deserving the respect that treats them "never simply as a means, but always at the same time as an end." When the justification for ascribing respect-demanding dignity lies in God's relating to human beings creatively, however, the ground for ascription of dignity expands to cover all actual living human personal bodies.

A second difference has to do with the location of that which is said to have dignity that demands respect. Kant's formulation distinguishes between humanity and its location in persons, "whether in your own person or in the person of any other." Apparently "humanity" is a property universal to and abstracted from all concrete, actual human "persons." In the *Groundwork of the Metaphysics of Morals*, Kant identifies this property with the autonomy of the rational will that is bound up with the moral law, makes one "free of all laws of nature," and constitutes "the ground of the dignity of human nature" (1959, 103). The critical point here is that for Kant this property marks a radical qualitative discontinuity between human beings and all animals. Outka (1986), for example, brings this out by locating Kant's concept of this property in a larger context in Kant's thought. In the *Critique of Practical Reason* (1956, 166), Kant famously remarked, "Two things fill the mind with ever new and increasing admiration and awe . . . the starry heavens above me and the moral law within me," and then goes on to say that the moral law within "reveals a life independent of all animality and even of the whole world of sense . . . a [purposive] destination which is not restricted to the conditions and limits of this life but reaches into the infinite." Outka adds, "Here is the point perhaps at which Kant comes closest to a doctrine of the *imago Dei*" (1986). If it is a doctrine of the *imago Dei*, it is a doctrine that identifies the *imago* with a nonphysical property of human beings that is, or comes close to being, a participation in divine being as opposed to seeing physical human creatures as the *imago*. All the same, it is just that property, and not a human person's particular, singular, concrete "personhood," that constitutes human persons' humanity. That property is the same in all particular, singular concrete "persons." The location of the dignity that deserves respect is that nonbodily divinelike property. It is that property, humanity, that deserves respect, not particular, singular concrete persons as such. Persons are to be respected only insofar as they share that property. A theological worry about this way of "locating" the dignity that deserves unqualified respect for living human personal bodies is that it looks like one more conceptual door opening into a metaphysically dualist anthropology that allows no conceptual space for positive theological assessment of human physical bodiliness as God's creation. When the justification for ascribing respect-demanding dignity lies in God's relating creatively to living human persons in community, however, the dignity that deserves respect is located in those actual living human personal bodies in their concrete particularities.

A third difference exemplifies a long-standing critique of the way in which the culturally dominant concept of the dignity of human beings is conventionally justified. Kant appears to have tried to defend on purely secular grounds a concept of the dignity of human beings that is historically rooted in Jewish and Christian religious traditions, where it is warranted by the claim that the dignity is a function of the way God relates to human beings. Secular as well as theological critics doubt that it is possible, absent reference to God and God's ways of relating to human beings, to develop a persuasive justification for adopting the concept. This culturally dominant concept of the dignity of human beings has its historical home in Western cultures, which may help make it seem intuitively self-evident. But it is not part of other cultures and its presuppositions are by no means intuitively self-evident universally. Obviously, this critique of the culturally dominant concept of human dignity is avoided by the alternative concept proposed here that is theocentrically formulated from the outset.

Because theocentrically understood human dignity is inherent in our creation in our having been born, it is not a function of the distinctive array of powers and capacities we have by which to respond appropriately to God relating to us creatively. Much less does our dignity consist in our exercise of those capacities and powers in acts of response to God. As we have noted, human creatures vary considerably in their range of capacities and powers. As we shall see, in sin they in fact fail to exercise those powers and capacities appropriately in response to God. However, neither restricted capacities nor failure to exercise them in appropriate response to God diminishes the dignity of human creatures. Our dignity is not a function of our capacities or achievements in moral heroism or in cultural creativity, in liberation from social oppression or in the human spirit's freedom from the constraints of brute nature. Our dignity is inherent in the sheer gift-character of creation.

Human creatures' dignity is not the same as creaturely goodness. As we saw in the previous section, human living bodies are deemed good in their kind because they are freely valued by God in exactly the same way as are all other creatures in their kinds. It is precisely *as* good living human bodies that we have a distinctive dignity. However, our creaturely goodness, understood as God's valuing us in delighting in us, is not identical with our dignity. We have dignity solely by virtue of the fact that in our having been born, God sets us in a relation with our creator in which the Creator is self-committed to us in certain ways and we are thereby made response-able to God and account-able for the character of our responses. Thus, human dignity, like creaturely goodness, is eccentric.

3. From this understanding of human dignity we can speak theologically of respect for human creatures' dignity. There are certain logical features of a morality of respect for human creatures: (a) Respect for the human dignity must be universal. (b) It must be practical. That is, respect must be construed in such a way that makes a difference in persons' actions with respect to one another. (c) Respect for human creatures' dignity must

override any other interest one might have in regard to them. (d) Respect for a human creature's dignity must be objective. That is, we do not confer dignity, much less the value "good," upon any human creatures by respecting them. Rather, respect is an acknowledgment of human dignity that obtains prior to and independently of its being respected (see Downie and Telfer 1970).

The crucial theological point is this: by creating us in our having been born living human bodies, God sets us into a social institution in which we are, with neighbors, accountable to God for our reception of the gift of our creation and in which we are under obligation to acknowledge the claim our neighbors' dignity makes for respectful response to them. Appropriate response to God and respect for neighbor are distinguishable but inseparable in Christian reflection because they are both grounded in the logic of giving and receiving which is inherent in the story of the peculiar way the triune God goes about actively creating us.

Were we to confer dignity on fellow human creatures by respecting them, we could equally well withdraw what we had conferred. We could decide that certain types of human creatures lacked dignity. Under certain circumstances it might be arguable that certain groups of human creatures that, we decide, lack dignity, do in fact pose some sort of threat to the rest of us. In that case, there would be license for genocide. Doubtless in an enlightened, humane, and scientific culture like our own, it would be a rational, scientifically justified and humanely enacted genocide, but genocide it would be nonetheless.

These remarks about the ground of human dignity raise a question for the most morally honorable and impressively humane of our secular neighbors (see Downie and Telfer 1970, chap. 5): absent God—or more exactly, God directly relating creatively to us—on what basis can we claim an inherent dignity to human beings which, because it is inherent, must be acknowledged by us in all other human living bodies in overriding and practical ways, rather than being ascribed to them by us?

The natural next step in theological reflection is to ask: In what does respecting the dignity of human creatures consist? The answer to this question would be a major part of a full-fledged theological ethics or moral theology. It is enough here to note that acknowledging the dignity of human creatures, where dignity is understood in the way outlined above, involves two broad types of intentional action, one positive and one negative. Positively, respecting the dignity of human creatures involves taking actions to nurture the well-being of such capacities and powers as they may have for their own accountable response, with their neighbors, to God who gives them living bodies and to the neighbors with whom they share proximate contexts through which come God's call to act wisely for their well-being. Negatively, it involves avoidance of violence. That is, it involves avoiding actions that in some way violate the capacities for accountable response,

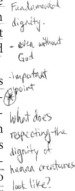

and violate the dignity and unsubstitutability, of any human creature. Therewith, it also involves actions to protect human creatures from such violation.

The two stories of Job's birth as his creation are entwined tightly together in Job 10. I have relied on each of them to guide a different set of theological reflections on what human beings are as creatures of God. In the next chapter, I rely on the way in which the two versions of Job's birth story are entwined to guide further reflections on what a human creature is.

CHAPTER **7**

Personal Bodies:
Meditation on Job 10

Job 10 entwines two tellings of Job's creation in his having been born. This entwining renders the peculiarities of human creatureliness with a richness that neither telling of the story could do alone. In the previous chapter, I focused on the implications of the differences between the two for a theological understanding of what human creatures are precisely as living human bodies. Having unbraided the two and reflected on the anthropological implications of each separately, I turn now to the anthropological implications of the fact that in Job 10, the two tellings are in fact wound together. Against that background, we then listen to the voices of creation stories in Genesis 1–3. This yields, I suggest, a picture of human creatures as not simply a type of living body— namely, human living bodies—but as personal living bodies that (1) are ontologically integral but subject to disintegration, (2) are personal in virtue of the status before God and within creation that is given to them by the peculiar way in which the Creator relates to them, (3) are created as fully actual personal bodies who may or may not also be perfect persons, (4) are set by their creation in the society of creatures as first among equals, and (5) as all of the above, are terminal individuals.

Much of the theological work usually done in anthropology by the notion of "image of God" is done here by the theological notion of the "personal" proposed in this chapter. The concept *imago Dei* is reserved for its proper theological home in the Coda, where the triple helix of inter-relations among the anthropological implications of the three canonically narrated ways in which God relates to humankind are explored. Reasons for that reservation are offered there.

Integral and Fragile

In the book of Job, ways of recounting the story of our having been born as the story of our creation are necessary in their literary interplay if a theological understanding of human beings' creaturely integrity is to be rendered adequately.

What a human creature is precisely as creature, in all of its complexity (sketched in chap. 6A), has an integral ontological unity that is inherently fragile. It both may and does dis-integrate. However, what counts as "violation" of a living human body, understood precisely as "creature," must be considered carefully in light of a theological understanding of its distinctively creaturely ontological integrity. The creaturely integrity of human creatures is not their physical biological integrity, which may be violated by some kind of physical assault. A human living body retains its ontological integrity precisely as human creature even though it has been so severely assaulted, for example, as to have lost limbs or even physical mobility. Nor is its creaturely integrity identical with its psychological integrity. A human living body retains its ontological integrity precisely as human creature even though its emotional integration has been so disrupted for psychodynamic or chemical reasons as to become profoundly psychotic and nonfunctioning. Nor is its creaturely ontological integrity identical with moral integrity. A human living body retains its integrity as human creature even when it has deeply compromised itself morally. In all of these circumstances, a human living body is nonetheless there as the specific kind of living bodied creature it is—namely, human. By God's gracious creative hospitality, she or he is still, in company with other creatures, God's genuinely "other" partner in a community of discourse, called by God to be wise, and capable of responding in some manner to God, even if only, like many living creatures, by its sheer mute living presence before God. This is because creaturely ontological integrity of human creatures lies not in their physical, psychological, or moral centeredness but in their ex-centeredness. It is rooted in the peculiar ways in which God actively relates to them as their creator, the ground of their reality and value.

Accordingly, far from their creaturely integrity being violated by God actively relating to them creatively, God's relating is the very condition of their having any creaturely integrity at all. God's creative relating is essential to what it is to be a creaturely living human body. Nevertheless, the creaturely integrity of living human bodies is fragile just because it is a function of God relating to it creatively. Absent such relating, they ontologically dis-integrate as human, living, bodily creatures. Absent God's creative relating, human living bodies absolutely are not.

The analysis of human creatureliness in previous chapters also stressed as a correlative point that what living human creatures are as finite creatures includes this: they are profoundly dependent on other creatures to be who and how they are in concrete actuality. Hence, it is part of what they are—that is, it is among their essential properties—that they both actively relate to and are actively related to by other creatures in ways that help construct their respective concrete identities. The consequences of other creatures' active relating to me are so interior to me as to be essential to making me the concretely particular human living body that I am, with the quotidian personal identity I actually have ("who" I am) and the concrete way in which I am in fact set into my proximate contexts ("how" I am). This in no way counts as a violation of my creaturely integrity. To the contrary, this type of dependence on other creatures is an essential condition of my creaturely integrity having the concretely actual personal identity it does in fact have. As a consequence, however, the concrete actuality of each human creature's creaturely integrity—who and how he or she is in concrete actuality—is fragile through and through. The integrity of human living bodies' personal identities is inherently capable of dis-integrating.

The fragility of such integrity clearly is a function of its essential finitude, since it is an essential part of what a given human living body is to actively relate to and be related to by other creatures in ways that help construct their concrete identities. Consequently it is always possible that those interrelations will damage those living human bodies' identities in various respects and to various degrees.

As living bodies, human creatures are especially vulnerable to such damage because they inherently must develop from immature to mature states, and must mature in regard to a large range of powers and in regard to a large range of capacities to regulate the exercise of those powers. The powers themselves may develop in varying degrees in different individuals and, once developed, may weaken, or they may fail to develop entirely. Human capacities for self-regulation can weaken and fail, in part as a result of something human beings suffer and in part as a result of something they do. They can, for example, fail to develop adequately or they may develop distortedly because of physical accidents. Or they may fail to develop because the societal and cultural contexts in which such capacities must be nurtured and formed fail adequately to nurture and form them.

These capacities for self-regulation may also weaken and fail because of what individuals do or fail to do. For example, consistent failure to keep faith with one's neighbors and to keep promises one has made to them may erode and finally threaten to destroy the systems of social energy that constitute the immediate society's common life. Furthermore, a failure intentionally to cultivate and deepen my capacities for faithfulness in my relations with my neighbors may, over time, so weaken my capacity to take charge of my own behavior that eventually I consistently fail to keep faith with those neighbors. As one loses capacities to be intentionally in charge of one's own behavior, one puts one's relatively integral unity at risk. It undergoes some degree of disintegration.

Thus, as the examples given above of biological, psychological, and moral loss of integrity suggest, human creaturely disintegration may proceed along several different dimensions of the complex life of human living bodies. In each dimension, creaturely disintegration is a matter of degree.

Its ultimate degree is its death. And if dead, then a human living body is no longer "there" as a genuinely other partner to God in a community of discourse. Precisely its creaturely integrity has then been absolutely negated.

Here a crucially important theological point must be repeated: while the doctrine of creation proposed here stresses God's continual creativity and refuses any fundamental difference between "God relating to us creatively" and "God persistently relating to us sustainingly," its logic entails no theological claim that having created human living bodies, God is thereby committed to preserving them in being indefinitely. In creating them, God is self-committed to whatever their well-being might consist of under the particular conditions of finitude that make up their actual proximate contexts—but only as long as they live. What God creates in creating human creatures has its proper creaturely integrity, but it is nothing other than just this essentially fragile creaturely integrity. Such creaturely finitude makes their deaths essential possibilities. Relating to us creatively, God creates dying life.

To convey such distinctively creaturely integrity, both of Job's two ways of telling the story of our birth as our creation must be held together. Each telling of the story taken alone has problematic anthropological implications that are blocked when it is held together with the other telling of the same story. Alone, each would yield anthropological judgments that either deny the complexity of human creatures or deny their integral creaturely unity.

For example, telling our creation through the story of our having been born as living human bodies stresses our sheer givenness. This might imply not only that a human creature is a living body with a certain DNA, but that the relation between human creature and biologically human living body is that of mathematical identity. A further implication might reasonably be drawn that theological anthropology is compatible with an ontologically reductive physicalism or materialism. That is, it might arguably imply that such a theological anthropology is compatible with the view that the set of law-governed physical processes into which the natural sciences analyze a living human body gives an exhaustive account of its reality. Call this the metaphysically physicalist view of the creature.

not reductionist

However, further analysis of the concept of "living human body" suggests that it is so complex that an exhaustive reduction of it to a set of natural processes is implausible. A theologically significant part of this complexity is brought out by the second way of telling the story of our creation: we are created by being given a living human body by God, to whom we are then accountable for at least some of that body's behavior in response to God and to fellow creatures. Hence, human creaturehood is *physical, but related to God's* not simply a given but a project—namely, the project of so regulating our bodied behavior that it is an appropriate response to our neighbors and to the ways in which God has already related to us. This theme is a central point of existentialist theological anthropologies and is well warranted by the second way of telling the story. Because the two ways of telling the story are woven together in Job's account of his having been born, the second story's focus on living bodies' responsibility and accountability for the way in which they regulate their own action serves to block the possibly reductionist implications of the first.

On the other hand, as noted in chapter 6A, to tell of Job's birth as his being given a living human body by God implies a distinction between Job (or you) and his (or your) living body, which could be construed as a hierarchical metaphysical dichotomy. That is, it may be taken to imply not only that "you" and the "living body" are two distinct and ontologically independent entities, but also that the "you" to whom a living body is given is more basic to your creatureliness than is the living body itself. The "you" (whatever "you" are) to whom a living human body is given would seem to be prior to and ontologically more basic than the living body, because only if you are somehow already really there could anything be given to you. On such a supposition, unless God creates "you" first and most basically—that is, ontologically "first"—nothing exists to whom God may then give a living body. That which receives the gift of a living human body would be the real you. Moreover, it would seem that the living body is not integral to your reality as a creature. Granted its priority in the order of being, the "you" would be nonetheless real were no living body in fact ever given to it. In short, we could infer from the second way of narrating our creation, taken in isolation from the first, that the real human creature is this mysterious you and not the living body, which is only secondarily real and is, by its birth, given to you. Call this an ontologically dualist view of human creatures.

When this second way of telling of our creation is entwined with the first way of telling it, then the latter serves to block these possible implications of the former. Describing human creatures as living bodies, as well as being given living bodies, conveys that being a living body is integral to human creatureliness. It is not secondary to—and, as it were, metaphysically optional in relation to—a nonbodily entity identified with the real you. It affirms that the real you is none other than this living human body that has been born of particular parents at a particular time and place in a particular society with its particular culture.

Furthermore, the interweaving of the stories conveys that complexity as part of a larger and more fundamental story about the particular, concrete, and complex way in which God creatively relates to humankind. It conveys the particular way in which God relates to us in creating us—namely, that God's way of relating to us creatively is at once to be involved in the processes of our being born instances of a specific type of living body and, through those processes, to give us living bodies for whose responses to God God calls us to give account. The complexity-in-unity of the story

Job tells of his creation as his having been born renders the complexity of the way in which God relates to us creatively to constitute each of us as a unity-in-complexity.

Moreover, an adequate account of the integrity of what God creates in creating human beings, the integrity of just that unity-in-complexity, requires the telling of these two intertwined stories to bring out the "eccentricity" of that integrity. Told in this fashion, the double-stranded story of our creation as our birth focuses on the fact that this is an integrity whose basis lies not in the creature in its own right, but in God's continuously active relating to creatures as their creator.

Such integrity is fragile. As we have seen, there is a wide variety of ways in which we can fail to be in charge of our living bodies and their actions, and innumerable degrees of failure in each. This vulnerability to disintegration through both what individual human beings suffer and what they do is an inherent fragility. Such vulnerability is an aspect of finitude rooted in human living bodies' constitution as living bodies complex enough to be given over, in some measure, into their own charge.

God's continuous creating of us, for all of God's self-commitment therein to our being and well-being, does not necessarily entail that God will protect us from the consequence of accidents, or from failures by others that may sometimes incapacitate some of us to be properly in charge of ourselves, nor from the ways in which we ourselves culpably fail to take charge of ourselves. In relating to us as our creator, the triune God is directly and intimately related to each of us as One who gives us space and time to be ourselves. What we are by God's creative relating simply is: Human creatures as fallibly integral living bodies, capable of being in charge of certain ranges of their behavior for which they are accountable, and susceptible to various types of disintegration of their integral unity.

Personal Bodies

Such living human bodies in their fragile creaturely integrity are, in a properly theological sense of the term, personal living bodies. It is on the properly theological sense of "personal" and, by extension, "person," that I want to reflect in this section in ways guided by Job 10 and by Genesis 2:4b–3:24 read in the light of Job 10. Throughout this discussion, "personal," and by extension "person," are used only in reference to human creatures. I bracket use of the same terms in reference to God (as in, "God is personal," or "God is a person") and in reference to nonhuman creatures (as in, "Angels are persons," or "Sufficiently complex robots are persons").

It is very important, I believe, for Christian theological anthropology—at least Christian theological anthropology written in English—to be self-critically reflective about its use of such terms as "person," "personal," "personhood," "personality," and the like. "Person" and "personal" do have technical and properly theological meanings as used in the context of

Trinitarian doctrines of God. However, I contend (see chap. 7) that it does not necessarily follow that that sense of the terms also constitutes their properly theological sense as used in theological anthropology.

"Person" and "personal" are also used in a variety of distinguishable but overlapping ways in ordinary secular discourse in modern Western cultures. Those uses are deeply connected to some anthropological assumptions embedded in those Western cultures that are profoundly problematic from a Christian theological point of view. A properly theological sense of "personal," and related concepts, would be one that uses such terms in ways that make it clear what is appropriated and what is modified or challenged in the host culture's reigning anthropological assumptions.

There are two ways in which conventional uses of "personal" (and related terms) in ordinary discourse and properly theological uses in Christian anthropologies do typically overlap. The first is that "personal" serves as the name of one of two main classes of predicates that are commonly ascribed to human beings. The name of the other class is "bodily" or "material" predicates. The latter are typically deemed to be "impersonal" predicates. Whereas members of the latter class of predicates are usually thought of as a human being's physical properties (e.g., "He is tall, thin, slightly stooped, and usually moves briskly"), the former are usually thought of as a human being's mental properties, including intellectual (e.g., "He is smart"), emotional (e.g., "often mildly depressed"), moral (e.g., "uncompromisingly honest"), and imaginative properties (e.g., "and typically he's literal-minded"). In a classic essay analyzing the relations between the ways in which these two classes of predicates are ascribed to human beings, P. F. Strawson (1959) dubbed these two, respectively, "M-predicates" (presumably for "material predicates") and "P-predicates" (presumably for "personal predicates").

However, Strawson went on to argue a thesis about the concept "person" that is misleading from a theological perspective. He argued that in our ordinary use of (English) language, the concept of "person" (in contradistinction to the concept of "personal," which he reserves to name one of these two classes of predicates) is a logically "primitive" concept. That is, it is a concept that cannot be explained by being analyzed into any other, logically more basic concepts. Thus, according to Strawson's analysis, in the conceptual scheme we use to describe, analyze, and discuss human beings, neither M-predicates nor P-predicates name that of which they are predicated. The concept we have of the "of which" cannot be explained by being analyzed into any subset of either class of predicates. Neither class of predicates is somehow "more basic" than the other in relation to human beings. Rather, "person" is used to designate that which is logically more basic than both classes of predicates, that of which both M-predicates and P-predicates are predicated. The content of the concept of person simply is that of which both M-predicates and P-predicates may and must be predicated.

It does seem to be true that both ordinary discourse about human beings and theological anthropological discourse involve an informal logic according to which some such primitive concept must be employed. If one does not call that which is designated by Strawson's primitive concept "substance," in one of Aristotle's senses of the term (namely, that of which other things are predicated, but which is not itself predicated of anything else; *Metaphysics* 4.8), one will have to introduce another term whose use fills the same function as "substance." Were "person" actually used consistently and exclusively in that way, it would make for greater clarity in ordinary discourse about human beings, and it would make it easier for theological anthropology to explain itself by using quite straightforwardly the conventional tropes of ordinary discourse. However, it simply is not clear that "person" is typically used in ordinary discourse as the primitive concept for that of which M- and P-predicates are predicated. Other terms, notably "individual," "subject," "ego," "self," "spirit (i.e., *Geist*)," "thou" (in express contradistinction to both "I" and "It"), and "agent," are regularly used in just that way. Such terms bring with them various connotations that function as background (and theologically problematical) beliefs about what that of which M- and P-predicates are predicated really is. That is, they function as quasi-technical metaphysical concepts that, I suggest, stand in considerable tension with some core claims of Christian theological anthropology. This is one of the reasons that Christian theological anthropology ought to be cautious about simply appropriating the family of concepts centered on the concept(s) of person that are current and powerful in Western cultures (see chap. 9B).

Conventional uses of "person," "personal," and related terms and properly theological uses of the same terms overlap in a second way. In both contexts, "person" and related terms are used with both classificatory and evaluative forces.

As we have noted before, on one side "person" is used as a way to classify certain of the beings we encounter. Some beings, we say, are persons and others are not. Several different types of standards are conventionally used in ordinary discourse in Western cultures to draw this classificatory distinction. Especially important in modern Western cultures are psychological standards. A being counts as a person if its behavior is marked both by its expressivity of complex and more or less organized emotions in response to fellow creatures, especially in response to other creatures (i.e., human living bodies) that are similarly expressive emotionally, and by a certain subtlety of sensibility with respect to other creatures' emotional expressivity. "Person" signifies a being that either now has, or is capable of developing, such sensibility and emotional life. Inanimate objects and nonhuman living beings are usually classified as not-persons because they lack and will never develop such capacities. By contrast, normal human infants are classified as persons because they will develop such capacities.

A second type of standard that beings have to satisfy in most modern Western cultures in order to classify as persons is, in a certain sense, moral. At issue here is not the question of whether a given being is moral or immoral, as though only moral beings count as persons. Rather, the issue is whether it is appropriate to hold the being in question morally accountable for its actions or, if not now, to expect that in time, as it "matures," it will become appropriate to hold it morally accountable for its actions. Thus, for example, while nonhuman animals that are kept as house pets may be strikingly expressive emotionally and exhibit remarkable sensitivity to their owners' emotions, so much so that by psychological standards they might be seriously nominated as candidates for the class "persons," according to this second, moral standard they are regularly classified as not-persons because they are not now and will never become morally accountable for their actions. On the other hand, given the moral standard, normal human infants and sometimes, far more controversially, human fetuses are classified as persons because, while they cannot be held morally accountable for their actions now, they can be expected to develop into beings who can be held accountable in that way.

A third, more ancient type of standard that beings have to satisfy sometimes in certain circumstances in modern Western cultures in order to count as persons is intellectual. A being is a person if it is rational. Of course, the definition of "rational" continues to be subject to debate. The intensity of the debate is at least in part a sign of the continuing importance of this type of standard for classification as a person.

Note that while the distinction between "person" and "not-person," when drawn according to some or all of these three types of standards, often coincides with the distinction between "human being" and "nonhuman being," it is also the case that "person" is often used in ordinary discourse in ways in which the two distinctions do not coincide. Using these types of standards, the distinction "person"/"not-person" is often drawn between two beings, both of whom are acknowledged to be, nonetheless, human beings. For example, a human child born massively brain damaged or a human adult who is in an irreversible coma or has suffered massive brain damage and lives in a vegetative state will be said to be not really a person. Given these standards by which to classify beings as persons, under certain circumstances it can be said that a given human being cannot be classified as a person.

On the other side, "person" is also commonly used with evaluative force. That is, to declare a being as belonging to the class "persons" is thereby to declare that that being intrinsically has a distinctive value that lays a moral claim on all other persons. Ripping the formula out of its conceptual context in systematic Kantian moral theory, modern cultures use "person" to designate beings that "are always to be treated as ends and not as means only," as intrinsically having a certain dignity that ought always to be respected. To classify beings as "persons" is therewith to commit oneself to avoid certain ways of relating to them (e.g., relations that exploit them, disrespect their dignity as persons, treat them merely as means to my own ends) and to adopt certain ways of relating to them (e.g., ways that always respect their dignity as persons, consistently treat them as ends, i.e., goods in their own right and independent of their utility for me, and foster their well-being).

In both ordinary discourse about human beings in Western cultures and in properly theological Christian anthropology, "person" is used with classificatory and evaluative force. The combination of classificatory and evaluative force is no accident in either sort of discourse. However, just what the connection is between the two logical forces with which "person" is used is not self-evident. Theocentric reasons can be given of why "person" must be used with both kinds of force. However, it is far from clear why "person" must be used with both kinds of force in ordinary secular discourse.

If one brackets God's relation to humankind, it is not difficult to show that using "person" with evaluative force has valuable instrumental consequences in reinforcing the sort of relationships among persons that sustain the stability, order, and relative peace of their common life. Treating one another as though every other was an end in herself or himself and deserving of unqualified respect is socially functional. Left at that, however, the "as though" is indistinguishable from "because we just decided to do it this way." If evaluating other human beings as "persons" is a matter of useful social convention, such evaluation can as easily be withdrawn when it seems socially functional to withdraw it. Under those circumstances, whole classes of persons can lose their status as persons at any moment, or never be granted it when first encountered. The experience of South American Native peoples when first "discovered" by the Spanish, and the experience of Jews, Gypsies, and homosexuals in Nazi Germany testify that actualization of such possibilities is neither rare nor distant in time.

An alternative to explaining, by an appeal to social conventions, why evaluative use of "person" should be conjoined with classificatory use would be to show that some (or all) of the standards by which a being is classified as a person (descriptive force of "person") necessarily entail that that being must also be evaluated as an end in itself never to be treated as a means only, whose dignity unconditionally deserves respect (evaluative force of "person"). Such an argument would show that the combination of classificatory and evaluative forces in the proper uses of "person" is a rational necessity. However, it is far from clear that such an argument can be made in respect of any of the types of standards according to which beings count as persons (for a helpful review of a variety of such arguments, culminating in a broadly Kantian proposal with a clear, if downplayed, theocentric structure, see Downie and Telfer 1970).

Failure of such arguments leaves the field to the conventionalist explanation of the conjunction of classificatory and evaluative uses of "person" in ordinary secular discourse. That leaves the door open to horrendous possibilities. The apparent groundlessness of the conjunction of classificatory and evaluative uses of "person" in ordinary discourse is yet another reason that theological anthropology would be wise to be very cautious about simply appropriating the uses of "person," as well as related and substitute terms, that are current in theology's larger host cultures.

Here I propose a theological concept of "person" in Christian anthropology that overlaps with the two ways in which "person" is also used in ordinary discourse about human beings in Western cultures, but avoids the dangers in the latter. Let use of "person" in Christian anthropology be guided both by a reading of Job 10 and by a reading of Genesis 2:4b–3:24 in light of Job 10. Guided by a meditation on Job 10, the previous chapter developed the theme that "body," in the phrase "living human body," signifies something more complex than a particular natural kind of biological organism, amazingly complex as that undoubtedly is. It developed the thought that "living human body" is constituted by a set of energy systems—psychological, intellectual, social, and cultural—all of which are given to us at birth and some of which are subject to our regulation, for which we are accountable. Furthermore, entailed in that proposal was the notion that in some way all of those energy systems are rooted in certain capacities of human beings as living human bodies, biological energy systems, a natural kind of organism. We can build on that here if we listen to the creation story in Genesis 2:4b–3:24 against the *cantus firmus* of Job 10's double-stranded story of Job's having been born as his creation. The two sets of texts together, I suggest, bring to focus a distinctively theocentric concept of "person." The thought here is that human creatures are constituted as personal beings by God relating to them, rather than by certain types of creaturely capacities—emotional, moral, or intellectual— which qualify them to count as entities called "persons." However, God relates to human creatures to personalize them in a different way than God relates to them to create them. In creating, we saw in chapters 5A and 6, God relates immediately and directly; in constituting those same creatures as "personal" living bodies, God relates to human creatures indirectly through the medium of the quotidian and, especially, through its ordinary languages.

The contrasting narratives in Job and Genesis of God's creation of human beings assume that a human creature is, in Paul Ricoeur's phrases, the unity of a "personal body" with its own "capital of heredity" (1966). We have used the body's human DNA to stand for its "capital of heredity," but the "heredity" also includes a complex mix of cultural, social, and linguistic factors; here we are exploring the meaning of the phrase "personal body." Personal bodies are called "personal" because of a distinctive way in which God relates to them, not because of the ways in which they relate to God. The analogy suggested by Job and Genesis for the distinctive way in which God relates to creaturely human bodies to personalize them is "address." It is an active relating by God to human creatures that is mediated by some culture and, usually, its ordinary language that constitute a kind of social space and time in which human creatures may respond appropriately to God.

In this way of using the terms, "personal" is logically prior to "person": it is only because human creaturely living bodies are "personal" that they may, for that reason, also be called "persons." God's address to creatures presupposes actual human creatures in all of their complexity, but it does not privilege any particular set of human creaturely capacities, emotional, moral, or intellectual. Those creatures to which God relates in this distinctive way are, *for that reason and no other*, "personal bodies." As a kind of shorthand expression, "personal bodies" may then be called "persons," but being "a person" is not a function of any particular human power or set of them.

Nor is "person" used here as a primitive concept, a surrogate for "substance" used to designate that of which various properties are predicated. Rather, the primitive concept, that of which Strawson's M-predicates (e.g., "organic body with human DNA") and P-predicates (e.g., psychological, social, intellectual, and cultural energy systems) *and* the predicate "personal" are all predicated, is "actual creaturely human living body." To characterize that body as "personal" or, in shorthand, to classify it as "a person," is to acknowledge that it has a certain status before God, not a certain array of powers.

These ways of using "personal" and "person" are guided by reflection on Job 10 and Genesis 2:4b–3:24. One of the most prominent features of the Job and Genesis stories of the creation of human beings is the way in which they tie together their understanding of human creature and language use by God. The way they both narrate it, in relating creatively God is self-committed to a type of public space, constituted by the dynamics of God's giving and human creature's receiving the gift of creation. Both Job and Genesis 2:4b–3:24 assume such a space, in which God addresses the human creature and in which human creatures may or may not address God. Such space is analogous to a public space constituted by a covenant-like social structure and the use in it of an ordinary language. In creating, God commits Godself to relating to human creatures by addressing them through the conventions of their proximate contexts and, in particular, through their ordinary languages. Thus, according to both Job 10 and Genesis 2:4b–3:24—and in slogans prominent in Protestant theology in the first third of the twentieth century—"God addresses humankind," and "Humankind may address God."

From this theocentric perspective, what defines human creatures as "personal" is not a set of properties they have logically and ontologically prior to being addressed by God, say, cognitive or affective capacities that constitute their "addressability"—that is, capacities that make possible their being addressed by God. Rather, it is precisely the actuality of God's relating to them in address that creates them, not just as actual living bodies (in that regard, God's creative relating is direct and immediate), but more particularly as personal bodies having just such capacities for relating to one another through the use of a language (in that regard, God's personalizing relating is indirect and mediated). They are "persons" inasmuch as the living bodies that God creates are personal bodies (as opposed to impersonal bodies) by virtue of the distinctive way in which God creatively relates to them indirectly: through their creaturely proximate contexts, and in particular through use of an ordinary language. God, as it were, talks living human bodies into being personal.

Note in passing that this feature of the Job and Genesis accounts of God relating to humankind further complexify the picture of that relating developed in chapters 5A and 6. There it was shown that, guided by the creation theology of Proverbs read in light of Job 10's account of Job's creation in his having been born, God's creative relating to humankind must be said to be concurrently an immediate and a mediated relating. As we noted in chapter 4A, God's creative relating to humankind and to all other kinds of creatures is unmediated by any other reality; that is the point of saying God's creating is *ex nihilo*. That relating constitutes them as human creaturely living bodies. It is their ultimate context as creatures. God's creative relating is at the same time a call to human creatures to be wise for the well-being of their proximate contexts, a call that is mediated through human creatures' fellow creatures and their shared proximate contexts. To this we may now add that God's mediated, indirect creative relating to human creatures in the call to be wise for their proximate contexts is therewith also God's constituting the human creatures addressed by that call as not only creaturely living bodies but as personal bodies.

"God addressing" characterizes human creatures' ultimate context. In that case, much will depend on the sort of the addressing that is involved. Job and Genesis render this "addressing" in markedly different ways. The next few paragraphs seek to establish the point that hearing the J account of how God addresses human creatures in Genesis 2:4b–3:24 will require us to nuance what we are led to say when we listen to Job's account of the same thing.

In Job, God is long silent. For its part, the human creature is free to speak much, indeed, to be downright voluble in putting questions to God. On Job's side this questioning is an intentional bodily action. This is not a dialogue solely in the mind; it cannot be described adequately as a series of purely mental acts.

God does not quickly respond. Indeed, Job's complaint early on is that because God cannot be encountered as "I to Thou," Job lacks an umpire, a "mediator," to get them together. God's silence does not imply, for Job, that God has become disengaged from the space of public use of language to which God was self-committed by the very act of creating. Had Job thought that to be true, there would have been no point in continuing to address God. When God does finally speak in Job 38, it is no equitable exchange of views. Job has questioned God; now God questions Job:

> "Who is this that darkens counsel by words without knowledge?
> Gird up your loins like a man,
> I will question you, and you shall declare to me."
>
> (38:1–2)

God's speech is confrontive. But it is neither judgment nor threat of punishment. Rather, it is a rhetorical questioning that is a piece of verbal performance art displaying God's glory as Creator:

> "Where were you when I laid the foundation of the earth?
> Tell me, if you have understanding.
> Who determined its measurements—surely you know!
> Or who stretched the line upon it?
> On what were its bases sunk,
> or who laid its cornerstone
> when the morning stars sang together
> and all the heavenly beings shouted for joy?"
>
> (38:4–7)

It is as though the text should read in summary: "Job demanded an explanation from God, and God obliged. 'Sit down and keep quiet,' God explained." Even so, the text privileges the use of human language as the medium of personhood.

Following the book of Job's characterization of God's way of relating to Job, we may say of ourselves also that we are constituted as personal living bodies by God's relating to us in speech that performatively displays God's glory as Creator. Later, when God draws Job's attention to the variety of animals, God's address to Job is mediated through fellow creatures when they are attended to in their relation to God, that is, when they are attended to precisely as creatures whose creatureliness displays the glory of God. Thus, human creatures' proximate contexts mediate to them their ultimate context insofar as the latter is God actively addressing them.

The person-constituting relation between human creatures and God is rendered rather differently in Genesis 2:4b–3:24. It is modeled on speech-acts of commanding rather than questioning. Having created the man, the Lord God plants a garden and puts him in it. The Lord permits the man to eat "freely" of the fruit of every tree in the garden, but commands him not to eat of the tree of the knowledge of good and evil, "for in the day that you eat of it you shall die" (2:17b). The command comes from the One who is the source of life, and it is meant to protect the man from death. The entire narrative assumes that God and the man share in a community of discourse. As Westermann points out, there can only be command where there is speech (see 1974, 89–91). The command is clear enough in one way, but because it lacks any rationale it is incomprehensible in another. The man can accept it only in trust that the One who issues it means him well and, in particular, means to protect him from death. Thus, Westermann observes, "There cannot be command and the consequences of command without a personal relationship to the one who issues the command" (1974, 91). Indeed, the command creates the social space required by just such a relationship. The command entrusts the man with the freedom to say either "yes" or "no" to the command and the capacity to be accountable for his answer. Thus, the command creates the "possibility of something happening between God and man" (Westermann 1974, 90)—namely, the "happening" of a relationship that personalizes a human living body. In its own way, Genesis 2:4b–3:24 renders human creatures' ultimate context as "God addressing them."

The personal character of human bodies is also closely tied to language use in Genesis 2:4b–3:24's account of the human creature's proximate context. Throughout the narrative, reciprocal address between human creatures and Creator is as intimate, simple, and apparently nothing out of the ordinary as is speech among the human creatures. We read that "out of the ground the LORD God formed every animal of the field and every bird of the air, and brought them to the man to see what he would call them; and whatever the man called every living creature, that was its name" (2:19). As Westermann points out, "They receive names only inasmuch as they are animals who have been given a function in man's world, and so it is only man himself who can give them a name. . . . It is speech that makes the world human" (1974, 85). None of the animals is a fit helper for the man. Only at this point in the story does the Lord create the woman. The man's first response to her in "jubilant welcome" (Westermann, quoting Herder, 1984, 231) is speech: "This at last is bones of my bones and flesh of my flesh" (2:23). Later, when the man and the woman have disobeyed and eaten fruit of the forbidden tree, God questions the man and the woman and announces the consequence of their actions.

Use of the metaphor of God "addressing" human creatures in Genesis 2:4b–3:24 differs from Job's use of the same metaphor in an important respect. Job's use of the metaphor does not necessarily imply that the creatures who are addressed by God are capable of responding to God in the give-and-take of a conversation. In that regard, it is similar to the use of the same metaphor in Genesis 1:1–25 where God is represented as relating creatively to the heavens and the earth and all that is therein by "addressing" them, calling into being, through the formula, "Let such and such be done," an array of creatures that are not characterized as capable of responding reciprocally to God in conversation. By contrast, in Genesis 2:4b–3:24, God is represented as "addressing" only a subset of creatures, "the" man, "the" woman, and "the" mysterious talking serpent, who are capable of engaging in reciprocal conversation with God.

Although the character of the exchange in Genesis 2:4b–3:24 is quite different from that in Job 10, in Genesis, too, God and human creatures share a public space created at God's initiative in giving the gift of concrete actuality, a public space constituted in part by use of some ordinary language. Job 10 and Genesis 2:4b–3:24 alike suggest that human creatures are "personal" in virtue of the fact that in speaking to them God grants them a status in a social space that is constituted by God's giving the gift of concrete actuality and by the human creatures' response in some mode (not necessarily in speech) to the gift of concrete actuality—including the response of ignoring or denying its character as gift. Theologically speaking, the "personal" is therefore necessarily a public reality. Indeed, it is a social construct—that is, the construction of a society by God through the social practices of language use.

Because we are made personal by God's relating to us through the use of ordinary language, being a personal creature is not itself a task or a project that one may or may not actualize. It is a status out of which one may or may not intentionally live. Nor is being personal a function of how one relates to other human creatures; our loving interactions do not personalizes us. Likewise, being personal is not, in this theological sense of the term, a function of how we relate to nonhuman creatures. Our triumphant transcendence over impersonal nature does not make us personal subjects. Personhood is not even a function of how we relate to God. Nor is our personhood a function of those properties of human nature that make any of the above possible—for example, the transcendental structures of our consciousness. Theologically speaking, our personhood is entirely a function of how God relates to us in creating us—namely, a relating mediated by using some ordinary language in a public space constituted by use of that language, and using the social conventions presupposed by uses of the language. The "possibility" *in us* of our being addressed by God, our "addressability"—and hence, our status as persons—follows excellently from the actuality of God speaking to us, and hardly at all from anything else.

In short, it is not as though what God creates in relating creatively to humankind is living human bodies that subsequently may or may not develop into being personal, and if they do may become personal in varying degrees. Were that the way in which "personal," "person," and related terms ought to be used in Christian theological anthropology, it would leave the evaluative force of those terms disconnected from God's creativity. That would open conceptual space in which it could be thought that those of God's creaturely human living bodies that do not mature to satisfy the standards they must meet to count as "persons," or having done so do not continue to meet those standards, are therefore not deserving of unqualified respect. Rather, "personal" is a status in which God locates all creaturely human living bodies simply by the peculiar mediated as well as immediate way in which God relates to them creatively. The full answer to the question of what God concretely creates is, "*personal* living human bodies."

Of course, human persons may or may not intentionally act out of that status, may or may not put that status into practice. They may act in ways that simply ignore or deny the fact that they ineluctably do have this status. They may or may not act as "persons" in the sense of the term "person" proposed here. If they do respond appropriately to God's address to them, they respond out of their status as personal creatures; they respond to God as persons, and in that sense they have a personal relation with God as Creator.

Actual and Perfect Personal Bodies

Another set of differences within similarities between Job 10 and Genesis 1 and 2 concerns the relation between being actually personal and being perfectly personal—that is, being personal in a way that satisfies some absolute standard of how personal bodies ought to be.

One of liberal, humane secular culture's deepest suspicions of classical Christianity is that at the end of the day Christianity holds that most human beings are not really human or fully persons. The root of this persistent suspicion is the Christian view that human beings are profoundly sinful and in consequence are physically, morally, and emotionally imperfect compared to ideal, normative humanity for which Adam in his freshly created original righteousness is the mythical symbol. According to this suspicious reading of Christian anthropology, since Christians hold that Adam and Christ alone were both fully actual and fully perfect human persons, Christian anthropology must hold that in their sinful imperfections the rest of humankind are not, strictly speaking, fully actual either as "human" or as "persons." Correlative is secular culture's suspicion that Christians who claim that their own imperfections are being overcome by God's grace cannot, if they are consistent, unambiguously respect as persons those others in whom sin is not being overcome.

Classical theological anthropology was guided by a reading of Genesis 1 and 2 as a narrative that culminates in the story of the fall in Genesis 3. As we have previously noted, the texts were interpreted as having the following narrative logic: The historically actual first man and woman were created in a world without sin and evil. These adult human creatures were not only fully actual, they were also perfect in every respect. Because sin and evil were unknown in the social space into which they were set by God's creative act, that social space, too, was normatively ideal.

The man and woman's initial perfection plays two functions in the subsequent narrative of their disobedience of God. First, their disobedience introduced change into the narrative for the first time; because of their disobedience, something new must happen. Since their initial state was absolute human perfection, this new development could only have the form of a decline from perfection. That is the only direction in which absolute perfection can change. Absolute perfection, after all, by definition cannot change for the better.

Second, the first pair's initial absolute perfection—what the tradition called their "original righteousness"—serves as the norm by which they and all those affected by the consequences of their disobedience must now be measured. Their subsequent imperfection is assessed by reference to this norm.

It has been conventional through much of the history of Christian theology in the West to understand this norm to be not only very high but absolute. "Perfect" means complete. Adam and Eve's created perfection was understood, not just as the perfection Adam and Eve in fact actually had—a perfection appropriate to and so relative to their physical, psychological, and intellectual particularities—but as the standard of the complete perfection all actual human creatures should have as created by God, regardless of their idiosyncratic particularities, and lack only because of their sin.

It is just such readings of Genesis 1–3 that give rise to secular culture's suspicions about the upshot of Christian belief concerning the status of imperfect human persons. If Genesis 1:1–2:4a and 2:4b–25 norm what Christians hold about the relation between being an *actual* personal body and being a *perfect*—that is, complete—personal body, then it would seem to follow that actual human personal bodies are created by God in a state of fully actualized and absolute perfection. Indeed, this has been taken to be the meaning of God's judgment that what had been created was "very good." In this framework, "good" and "perfect" are interchangeable notions. It does seem fair to conclude that, within the context of such a doctrine of creation, being an actual human person necessarily implies being a perfect human person. But from that it seems to follow that human persons, like us, who are not in fact perfect are therefore not, properly speaking, fully actually human either.

It should be noted that this problem does not automatically disappear if, acknowledging that scientific accounts of the origin of humankind make the historicity of Genesis 1–3 incredible, theologians read those texts as myths symbolic of the human condition rather than as history. It is still necessary to think through carefully the theological use of the concept of human perfection and its relation to a theological understanding of actual human creatures.

It is especially important to do this in any theology that wishes also to speak of sinful human persons becoming perfected by God's grace—not just improved, but increasingly being made perfect. In such contexts, "perfection" implies that some absolute standard is being approached, even if only asymptotically. What one standard of perfection could be absolute for all aspects of all personal bodies?

Identification of human perfection with human actuality is a theological muddle, and a conceptually unnecessary one. It can be clarified if we let Job 10's double-stranded telling of Job's birth as his creation guide our theological reflection and govern our identification of the theologically salient features of Genesis 2 and 3.

Job 10 Heard in Contrast to Genesis 1 and 2

As we have seen, both Job 10 and Genesis 1 and 2 depict the creation of human creatures as the creation of actual personal living human bodies, and not merely as the creation of possible personal bodies, or as the creation of the conditions of the possibility of human creatures actualizing themselves to be personal bodies, or as the creation of potential personal living human bodies.

However, Job 10 and Genesis 1 and 2 differ in two important respects. In the first place, Job 10 tells of Job's having been born as his creation, the beginning of a single actual infant personal human body. The larger literary context of chapter 10 in the book of Job clearly assumes that the one whose birth is his creation will grow and change until he becomes an adult male. Newborn Job's maturation from biological, psychological, and intellectual infancy into adulthood is inherent in his actuality as a personal body. As a personal body, he must have a personal history. The history of his maturation involves, although it is not limited to, mastering, and being formed by, myriad concepts, conceptually determinate beliefs, and conceptually formed emotions, passions, feelings, attitudes, and policies for action. It includes learning to speak an ordinary language by which to express and communicate all of the above, acquiring powers to be an interlocutor with other human creatures and with God.

The immaturity of newborn, newly created Job does not imply that he is at that point an imperfect personal body according to some absolute norm of human perfection. The narrative logic of Job 10 in its larger literary context suggests, rather, that "perfect" is best used of human creatures in relative rather than absolute ways: this infant Job may be perfect as infant, although for that reason imperfect as adult. He may be physically perfect—completely "normal"—but neither perfect nor imperfect morally since he is not yet capable of responsible intentional action or of giving an account of his actions; and he may be perfect in relating to God in that he responds to God in ways appropriate to an infant. Neither his actuality as a personal body nor his perfection are brought into question by his infancy.

As a personal body, Job will mature, mastering and being formed by concepts, beliefs, emotions, and so on, appropriate to the social institution into which he is set by his birth, his proximate context of complex networks of giving and receiving in relation to fellow creatures and in relation to God, an institution constituted by God's gift of concrete actuality. However, this social institution, including ordinary language, is prior to Job's undertaking the tasks of maturation. It is prior not only in time, but also in the order of reality. It is the precondition in reality for Job's being created a personal body. Job's birth is his creation precisely because, in his birth, infant Job is set by God's creative relating into the proximate context of that already-actual social institution. Thus, by his creation in his having been born, infant Job's status as personal body is already actual. Although his actuality as a personal body requires that he have a history—which includes that he develop and mature in some respects, actualizing a variety of capacities and powers—nevertheless his status as a personal body is not itself actualized by him in and through that process of actualizing his capacities and powers. Nor can it be taken away or diminished by any failure to actualize his capacities and exercise his powers appropriately. On the contrary, his status as a personal body is the precondition of his setting out on his personal history of actualizing his capacities.

By contrast, in the two Genesis creation stories, Adam and Eve cannot actualize their capacities because they start off existing as already fully actualized adult human persons. Above all, they are created with already fully actualized powers to be interlocutors with God. No maturation of any sort can be part of their actuality. As perfect personal bodies, they can have no history. History would imply change, and given their perfection, change could only be change to imperfection. According to the narrative logics of these two creation stories, infancy or any other stage on the way to maturation, as well as any decline through disease or accident from fully actualized adulthood, is imperfection. What God creates in the condition of absolute perfection is fully actualized adults and nothing less.

A second major difference between Job 10 and Genesis 1 and 2 has to do with the character of the proximate context God gives us in creating us. In the Genesis creation stories, the first man and woman are created in a world without sin and evil. Their proximate context—Eden—is "perfect." As we have seen, this is necessary to the narrative logic of the traditional construal of the larger story in Genesis 1–3 of which the creation stories are but the opening: the story of humankind's defection from absolute perfection, God's deliverance from which is narrated in the remainder of the Pentateuch. The perfection of the initial situation lies in the interconnections among the perfection of the first pair as persons, their surroundings, and their relation to God. That initial absolute perfection sets up the possibility of the central story about God's initiative, first with Noah and again with Abraham, to restore the initial community between humankind and God that has been lost. However, the same narrative logic implies a theologically problematic equation of human perfection with human actuality.

According to Job 10, on the other hand, the concrete version of the social space into which Job is set at his creation is, as a simple matter of fact, distorted and deformed by sin. This fact about their social world is well known among the human creatures, who are persons by virtue of God addressing them through that world. In Job's world, for example, it comes as no surprise that in so weighty a matter as his controversy with God, his human interlocutors will all be male. Women, specifically Job's wife, daughters, and daughters-in-law, are entirely marginal. This is already a world in which social power is unequally distributed between men and women. Job himself participates in and is deeply shaped by that version of the social space God institutes in creating us, even though throughout the book Job consistently maintains that he personally is sinless.

The way this narrative renders our proximate context, it cannot be assumed that actual human creatures are, simply on the basis of their having been created, absolutely perfect human persons—that is, normative for what actual human persons should be like. Moreover, "perfection" is understood here only in terms of human creatures' ways of relating to God. Job and his human interlocutors acknowledge the possibility that actual human creatures may vary as to whether they respond properly to God.

On the other hand, Job steadfastly insists that he has responded properly and has done nothing to deserve his suffering. In this rendering of our proximate context, it is conceivable that some individual persons might be perfect in their relating to God. Yet both those like Job who are perfect in some respect, and those who are not, are fully actual personal bodies. Thus, the narrative logic of the double-stranded story of Job's birth, read as the story of his creation, is able to keep it clear that human perfection is conceptually entirely distinct from human actuality. The imperfections of personal living bodies in no way bring into question their actuality either as human or as personal bodies.

In short, the way in which Job 10 tells of Job's birth as his creation implies three anthropologically important distinctions:

First, by casting the story of Job's creation as a story of his having been born, the text keeps the actuality of personal bodies sharply distinguished from any question about those personal bodies' having actualized any particular capacities. To the contrary, it is inherent in being an actual personal body that one have a personal history of change and maturation through which a multitude of capacities are actualized.

Second, both by casting Job's creation as the story of his having been born and by narratively rendering his proximate context as already morally ambiguous, the text assumes a relative rather than absolute concept of human perfection. "Perfect" must be said relative to a particular person's history and relative to distinguishable aspects of that personal body's life—for example, physical, emotional, intellectual, and God-relating aspects.

Third, by rendering Job's proximate context as morally ambiguous, the narrative logic of Job 10 keeps personal bodies' perfection sharply distinguished from their actuality. There is no hint of a conceptual problem about affirming that someone is both a fully actual and fully personal living human body and, at the same time, profoundly imperfect. The first depend on how God relates to the creature; the second depends on how the creature relates to God.

Genesis 1 and 2 Heard against the Background of Job 10

Combined with a point made earlier about the goodness of creatures, these distinctions help to clarify the muddle that is too frequent in Christian discourse about the relation between human imperfection and human goodness.

Chapter 5A argued that what God creates is a good gift solely by virtue of the way in which God relates to it. Unexacted and uncoerced, God creates. So creating is "gracious," and what is created has the character of a gift that is valuable because God values it. But created personal bodies are perfect only by virtue of how they receive this gift in their response to God, that is, by virtue of how they themselves actively relate to God. What human creatures are by God's creative act is good; how they are in response to God may or may not be "perfect"—that is, may or may not be an appropriate response to the specific way in which God is relating to them. However, the degree of perfection of their response to God has no bearing on whether human creatures are actual personal bodies deserving of unconditional respect.

Heard in a way framed by Job, Genesis 1:1–2:4a and 2:4b–25 need not suggest either that the first pair's perfection is identical with their goodness as creatures or that it is identical with their full actuality as adult human personal bodies. Granted, the first pair as created is characterized in these stories as both fully actual and perfect. Their creaturely goodness necessarily follows from their creaturely actuality. However, does their perfection also follow from their actuality? The muddle we have been dealing with assumes that the answer is "yes." But there is nothing about the movement of the stories to require us to answer one way or the other.

When Genesis is heard in the context of Job, one may answer, "No." Adam and Eve are concretely actual and good by virtue of God's relating to them as Creator. They are also—apparently *very* briefly!—perfect in their response to God. Indeed, it is precisely when that relation changes that they cease being normative for the rest of us. However, the fact that, upon creation, they do respond to God properly does not derive by necessity from the way God relates to them as their creator.

At least since St. Augustine, the central Western theological tradition has held that in addition to relating to the first pair as Creator, God related to them in a logically independent way: God graced them with resources

key:
Created good and gifted personal dignity
But can still progress to 'perfection'

to relate back to God in appropriate response for the gift of creaturehood (the "grace of perseverance"). This is the root of the classical distinction between nature and grace: regarding even the first couple, before sin came on the scene, a distinction exists between the gift God gave at creation ("nature") and the extra gift God super-added to nature ("grace"). In my construal of these matters in this project, the distinction has been drawn as a distinction between God's active relating to humankind as their creator and God actively relating to them as their eschatological consummator. The upshot of the distinction in this case is the same, however: that human persons are good follows from the fact that they are concretely actual, whether as infant or as adult, healthy or diseased, faithful to God or faithless, because of the way God relates to them as their creator. What I propose is that whether they are perfect does not follow from their actuality, but only from the way in which they, in turn, relate to God, perhaps assisted by God's (superadded) grace. In contrast to the traditional reading of the Genesis creation stories, the grounds they provide on this reading for affirming the goodness of personal bodies are entirely independent of the grounds they provide for affirming or denying personal bodies' perfection. In their disobedience, the perfection that characterized the first pair is lost, although they remain fully actual living human personal bodies.

Following the narrative logic of Job 10, and of Genesis 2 and 3 read in the context of Job 10, we may generalize the anthropological point: human creatures' actuality depends on God directly relating to them creatively; their status as persons depends on God speaking to them, as though using a common language, in a way that places them in a social space constituted by language use, a space in which they may respond to God through their own use of language. Neither claim is qualified by whether those creatures are in fact perfect personal bodies. Indeed, there is no absolute standard for human physical, mental, or emotional perfection. The only theologically relevant sense of perfection is defined in terms of the appropriateness of personal bodies' response to God's relating to them.

Personal Bodies and Other Creatures

Another way in which classical theological anthropology is profoundly problematic is the picture it gives, guided by Genesis 1:1–2:4a and 2:4b–25, of the proper relation between human and nonhuman creatures. I urge that here, too, Job 10's two entwined ways of telling of Job's having been born as his creation offers needed correction of the problematic trajectories of the narrative logics of the two Genesis narratives of the creation of humankind.

Job 10 leads to a picture of human creatures as particulars—that is, particular instances of familiar energy systems of various sorts. It has led me to stress in this chapter that what God creates is concretely actual—if biologically, psychologically, and socially immature—living human personal bodies. Read in the larger context of mainstream canonical Wisdom, this emphasis reinforces the relational and holistic picture of human creatures developed in chapter 5A. According to that picture, every human creature must in the first instance be understood in terms of its relationships to its proximate context, its ecological, social, and cultural environment. These relationships, set in the larger context of God's ongoing creative relating to human persons, are constitutive of what those personal bodies concretely and particularly are as creatures. At the same time, this is a picture according to which every human creature must be understood in its own right as a complex and relatively fragile, partly self-regulating network of inter-related and interpenetrating types of systems of energy—biological, psychological, social, and cultural.

In Genesis the P (1:1–2:4a) and J (2:4b–25) accounts of the creation of humankind resonate with Job 10 by locating human creatures in relation to the rest of creation, but each in a strikingly different way. The two ways in which the story of Job's having been born is told clearly set him in the larger context of biological and social life. However, unlike the two creation stories in Genesis, Job's story relates the human creature to other creatures in a noncontrastive way. Indeed, the first telling of Job's having been born as a living human body stresses the way in which Job as creature is on a par with other living creatures. By contrast, according to Genesis, as Benno Jacob put it, "In chapter 1 man is the pinnacle of a pyramid, in chapter 2 the center of a circle" (quoted in von Rad 1961, 75). In both cases, what God creates in creating human creatures is defined by way of a contrast with nonhuman creatures.

Thus, the way in which Genesis 1:1–2:4a moves from God's creation of cosmic order (light) against chaos (darkness, water), through the creation of various classes of creatures (plants, marine animals, birds, land animals) clearly presents the climax of the whole movement as the creation on the sixth day of humankind:

> Then God said, "Let us make humankind in our image, according to our likeness; and let them have dominion over the fish of the sea, and over the birds of the air, and over the cattle, and over all the wild animals of the earth, and over every creeping thing that creeps upon the earth." (1:26)

The picture given by Genesis 1 stresses the glory of human creatures, not their parity with other creatures as creature. Human creatures' glory here is their dominion over all other creatures (1:28).

This dominion is a complex relationship. On the one hand, it signals that human creatures are inextricably related to other creatures; this is conveyed by God's blessing on human creatures. Although upon creating them God blesses both water creatures and air creatures with fertility, God does not so bless land creatures until human persons are also created, and then the blessing appears to be directed at the human creatures. As Westermann observes, this blessing "embraces the very existence of man and the life of the beasts. The blessing is 'natural' to man, and man is just not 'natural' without that [the blessing of fertility] which links him with the rest of creatures" (1974, 50).

On the other hand, human creatures are understood by contrast to the rest of the creatures, to whom they are superior. The blessing given to human creatures goes beyond fertility; it includes "dominion" over all other creatures. The glory of human creatures is thus their kingly status in relation to other creatures. The verb used in "fill the earth and subdue it" is also used of the rule of the king (e.g., in 1 Kgs. 5:4; Ps. 110:2; the same thought is conveyed in Ps. 8; see Westermann 1974, 52). The deeper background of this equation of human creatures' glory with their kingly status in relation to other creatures may be the age-old struggle between human creatures and deadly animals. However, the "dominion" in question is ordered, not to the exploitation or extermination of other animals, but to their well-being. In their kingly role, human creatures are to be mediators, the protectors and preservers for other living creatures, to actualize the blessing "Be fruitful and multiply."

Thus, read together as separate voices in the chorus of canonical Holy Scripture, Genesis 1 and the Job-based account of human creatureliness mutually nuance each other. Genesis 1 stresses that human creatures' creaturely glory resides in a certain primacy in relation to the rest of creation, a note missing in Job; but read in the light of Job 10's story of Job's having been born as his creation, this stress on humankind's glory is qualified by the reminder that while in some sense humankind may be first among other creatures, it is only the first among equals.

In contrast to this picture of humankind's relations with other creatures, Genesis 2:4b–24 (the J version) clearly locates humankind at the center of the circle of humankind's lived world. This is a thoroughly anthropocentric picture of the proper relation between human and nonhuman creatures. Humankind defines the circle. It is served by the rest of creation, which in turn is understood in the context of humankind's lived world. Plants are created to delight and nourish human persons. Animals are created in order to be partners for the first man, but none are adequate to being "helpers"—that is, equals. So God creates a woman from Adam's rib to be a genuine partner who is of his kind. According to this picture, genuine partnership for human creatures requires that both partners be equal as instances of human living bodies ("bone of my bones and flesh of my flesh" [2:23]; other animals fell short on this score), and yet each partner must be genuinely other than and complementary to the other partner (see Russell 1979, esp. chap. 2). Thus, this creation story stresses that it is inherent in human creatures to need other bodily creatures to relate to them, not only for their bodily nourishment, but also for delight and for partnership; and, if it is inherent to need, then it is inherent to desire other creatures not only for nourishment, but also for delight and partnership. God's creativity blesses human creatures with just what they most need. Where the P account of creation (Genesis 1:1–2:4a) stresses the glory of the human creature, the J account (2:4b–24) stresses the blessedness of the human creature.

Like the account of Job's birth as his creation, the two Genesis accounts of the creation of *adam* (in Gen. 1, "humankind"; in Gen. 2, "a man") stress the inherent relationality of human creatureliness. But where Genesis 1 focuses on the character of *adam*'s relation to other creatures, Genesis 2 focuses on other creatures' relations to *adam* as sources of nourishment, delight, and partnership for needy and desiring humankind. The first sees the relation as a vocation on the side of humankind in regard to other creatures; the second sees the relation as a creaturely blessing on humankind given in other creatures by God.

Taken by themselves, the Genesis creation stories might fairly be thought to imply a particular view of the nature of nonhuman creatures: they have no reality in their own right; they are inherently instruments for humankind; their reality is ordered to the nourishment, delight, and, in some degree, partnership of human creatures. When nonhuman creatures are understood in this fashion in terms of their relationship with human creatures, there is nothing to check a purely exploitative relation by human creatures with nonhuman creatures except, perhaps, enlightened self-interest. These are precisely the themes in classical theological anthropology, guided by such a reading of these texts, that are extremely problematic pictures of human creatures' proper relationships with nonhuman creatures.

However, this sort of metaphysically anthropocentric picture of the relation between human and nonhuman creatures is blocked when the Genesis creation stories are understood in the light of the story of Job's having been born as his creation. As previously noted, Job 10 leads us to stress that in their relationality human creatures are, as creatures, on a par with nonhuman creatures. It is true that in the broader canonical Wisdom literature represented by Proverbs, the literary context within which Job is to be interpreted, human creatures also have a vocation that other creatures do not have—namely, to be wise in their action, as far as finitude allows, for the well-being of other creatures. However, human creatures who fail in this vocation are nonetheless still genuinely human creatures in their own right. So, too, it is true that human creatures need and desire nonhuman creatures to relate to them as blessings. But to be the occasion of blessing for a human creature does not constitute any nonhuman creature's reality as creature. Nonhuman creatures that are source neither of nourishment, nor of delight, nor, in some degree, of partnership are nonetheless actual and good creatures in their own right. (Consider the mosquito.) Being blessed by God through nonhuman creatures is of the well-being of human creatures; but it is not of the essence of nonhuman creatures to be such blessings.

Terminal Individuals

Thus far I have explored ways in which Genesis 1:1–2:4a and 2:4b–25 nuance Job 10's account of Job's birth as his creation as a particular personal body when they are read in ways governed by Job. These texts back a stress in theological anthropology on the particularity of Job—and, by extension, of each of us—as personal bodies, as instances of quite familiar kinds of complex, integral, and finally mysterious centers of finite powers. Now we need to add that Job 10 also shows that each such human creature is not only a particular instance of various sets of creaturely energy systems having many instances, but is also, by its creation, something utterly new and unsubstitutable, a "terminal individual" (Hartt 1957) accountably responsible for its use of its "capital of heredity."

Job's twofold way of telling of his birth led us to stress that human creatures are set by their creation into a social institution constituted by the dynamics of God's giving the gift of creation and human creatures receiving that gift, where the gift's reception constitutes, consciously and intentionally or not, acts of response to God. Human creatures are accountable for the way they make use of their "capital of heredity" in their response to God. "Capital of heredity" refers to the entire array of senses of life in which a human body may be said to be a living body.

As we have seen, "life" must be ascribed to human living bodies in several senses. Human living bodies' life is psychological and social life and not just biological life; psychological and social life, furthermore, is always inescapably mediated by some culture and its language. Accordingly, the life of human living bodies is by definition one lived in and shaped by the public space constituted by interlocutors sharing the same culture and its language, and cannot be separated from such public space. This "life" is, in Ricoeur's image, "capital" for whose investing—or squandering—in patterns of human action and practices each personal body is accountable. In particular, each is accountable for investing this capital in actions and practices that are appropriate as a response to the way in which God has already related creatively to her or him. Job 10 has led us to stress that each personal body is created utterly new and unsubstitutable in this accountability.

Thus, Job 10 leads us to stress that what God creates in creating each human living body is a terminally individual personal body. It is a personal body that is terminal to two lines of questioning. It is terminal in responding to fellow creatures and to God. Who responds to them? None can substitute for me; only I can respond to them for myself. Second, it is terminal in the giving of an explanatory account of intentional actions. How come just this intentional action by me? Finally the answer is, "I did it."

This does not contradict the claim that human creatures are thoroughly relational. The fact that we are relational all the way down does not entail that each of us is relational all the way up to the point of giving an account of her investment of her own particular "capital of heredity." Here the onliness we noted before comes into play: I do not give an account of my response to God and to my neighbors alone, for I am a thoroughly relational creature; however, I am the terminal responder, only I, though not I in lonely isolation. To be unsubstitutable in this way is to be—beyond a particular instance of some larger class of entities—a terminally individual personal body.

In summary: What does God create in human creatures? Guided by Job 10 and, heard against its background, Genesis 1:1–2:4a and 2:4b–25, we are led to say that what we are, are

— Actual human living personal bodies that are centers of various types of powers, who, precisely as living bodies, are on a par with all other creatures, being but particular instances of sets of creaturely energy systems of which there are many other instances of the same type.
— Personal bodies who are particular instances of energy systems by virtue of which, like all creatures, they are themselves thoroughly finite, fragile, and vulnerable to disintegration.
— Personal bodies who, precisely *in* their finitude, fragility, and vulnerability, are deemed by God to be good.
— Personal bodies who have as their glory a vocation to care for non-human creation's well-being, and have as their blessing other creatures on whom they are dependent to meet their needs and desires for nourishment, delight, and partnership.
— Personal bodies set by their creation into a social space instituted by God's creative act, and constituted by the dynamics of God's giving the gift of concrete actuality and human creatures' reception of that gift.
— A space in which human creatures are placed by their creation as utterly new and unsubstitutable, with a dignity that calls for unqualified respect.
— A space in which human personal bodies' responses to God are enacted through the exercise of their powers.
— A space organized by the ways in which those creaturely powers are arranged.
— Personal bodies that are terminally accountable for the ways in which they each respond to God's gift.
— Personal bodies that are, finally, inexhaustibly mysterious.

CHAPTER **8**

Faith: Flourishing on Borrowed Breath

A fundamental Christian claim is that the triune God actively relates to humankind creatively. I have suggested that when this claim is articulated in ways largely guided by biblical Wisdom traditions, it brings with it the anthropological remark that human beings are actual human personal bodies living on borrowed breath. That their breath of life is borrowed does not imply that the life of their living human bodies is not their own. A living human personal body's life is its own in the sense that it simply is that human creature. However, a human creature does not own her bodied personal life as though it were a piece of property. Rather, the life of her living human body is borrowed in that her accountability to God for the way that life is lived as a response to God's creative relating to her puts her more in the position of a steward of a loan than that of an owner of a piece of property.

Theological anthropologies in Western traditions frequently move directly from the implications of some such doctrine of creation to the anthropological implications of doctrines of the fall and sin. Mainly under the influence of Augustine, the fall is conventionally understood as a universal decline from created absolute human perfection, evil as the consequences thereof, and sin as culpable human failure to live in accord with that perfection. However, I have argued against theological endorsement of any one picture of an absolute and ideal human perfection. Lacking such a picture, the fall, evil, and sin can hardly be construed as a decline from it and a culpable failure to accord with it. Instead, I suggest, sin and evil are best understood, not in contrast to an absolute ideal of human perfection, but in contrast to the glory of God expressed in God's creative relating to us as personal bodies.

Given that the triune God relates creatively to personal bodies, constituting them as living bodies and giving them living bodies for which they are called to be accountable, human beings' creaturely flourishing must be understood in two interrelated senses. This twofold flourishing defines human creaturely glory. In a modification of the remark by Irenaeus that provides this chapter's epigraph, we may say that the glory of God is a flourishing personal body. The point may be made more concretely: insofar as human creatures are accountable to God for the way in which their borrowed living bodies are oriented in their proximate contexts, the concrete content of their flourishing simply is a set of practices in their quotidian proximate contexts that make for the proximate contexts' well-being for their own sakes, and not for the sake of some further quotidian-transcending outcome. Such practices are personal bodies' ways of responding faithfully to the peculiar way in which the triune God goes about relating to them creatively. Such practices are the concrete content of faith in God, understood both as *trust* in God as ground of their being and value and as *loyalty* to God's own creative project. Accordingly, the aim of this chapter is to trace the systematic connections among theological concepts of human flourishing, the glory of God, human wisdom, and faith in God. I shall begin with two sections that examine the concept of God's glory. That leads into two further sections exploring ways in which the concept of God's glory is related to a twofold theological concept of human flourishing. On that basis, one side of that twofold concept of human flourishing can then be explained more concretely by an analysis of what counts as "appropriate" human response to God's call to be wise in action in the quotidian for its well-being. Finally, I develop the suggestion that the proper theological name for such appropriate response to God's call to be wise is "faith," which consists of nothing other than "wise human action in the quotidian for its well-being for its own sake." Hence, it is precisely in faith that personal bodies flourish as the glory of God.

The theological understanding of human flourishing developed here implies some answers to the perennial anthropological questions, "Who are we?" and "How are we to be?" which are explored in the next chapter. Only against that background can we turn in the following chapters to the topics of sin and evil.

Expressing the Glory of God

God's glory is the full richness of God's reality. Karl Barth captures this point in his suggestion that "divine glory" be understood as the totality of all the perfections of God's reality in God's self, rather than as one among many divine perfections (1957, 643–44). God is glorious in and of God's self, yet "God's glory" is a relational concept. In its biblical uses relative to God, "glory" connotes at once God's self-expressive self-giving—relating outward, as it were, to genuine others—and God's attractive beauty—relating to others by drawing them toward God.

"Glory" is the usual English translation of a variety of biblical Hebrew and Greek words. It translates Hebrew terms connoting adornment (*hadar*, e.g., in Ps. 90:6) and beauty (*hod*, e.g., in Ps. 8:1, and *tiphereth*, e.g., in Isa. 46:13). Most frequently, however, it translates *kabod*, which connotes honor, weight, heaviness, or, we might say, gravitas. The third-century BC Greek translation of Hebrew Scripture, the Septuagint, used by many early Christians, translated *kabod* in Greek as *doxa*, which connotes splendor. The Septuagint's use of *doxa* probably influenced the New Testament writers' frequent use of the term. "Glory" is the usual translation of *doxa* as used in the Greek New Testament.

On the face of it, a phrase like "God's glory" is simply about God. However, so far as biblical uses of such phrases are concerned, this is oversimple. Donald Evans provides a careful analysis of biblical uses of such phrases as "the glory of the Lord," "the glory of God," and "glorifying God" in *The Logic of Self-Involvement* (1963; see esp. 174–96). On his analysis, "God's glory" in its biblical uses has "a three-fold reference: An *inner divine quality* is expressed through certain *impressive observables*, evoking a correlative *human feeling-Response* [*sic*] *and acknowledgment*" (174; emphases in original).

What is important for my purposes is that the three referential uses of such phrases in biblical contexts are inseparable, which warrants the remark that personal bodies are the glory of God. The inseparability of the three referential uses of "God's glory" (and similar phrases) is rooted in the expressive force of biblical uses of "glory" in relation to God. And it is the expressive force of biblical uses of such expressions as "the glory of God" and "God's glory" that makes glory a relational concept.

This concept can be brought out by reflection on what Evans calls the "self-involving" force of biblical uses of such terms. I shall take in reverse order the three references Evans identifies. As used in biblical contexts, utterances like "God is glorious" have the force of expressing the speaker's feelings in response to something that expresses God's glory. In biblical contexts, these feelings are typically some mix of gratitude, jubilation, fear as awe, and fear as terror. Perhaps we may call them collectively "doxological" feelings. This is one way in which biblical uses of "glory" in relation to God are expressive.

Furthermore, as used in biblical contexts, such utterances have the force of committing the speaker to an array of attitudes (e.g., that fellow creatures are gifts), passions (e.g., for the well-being of fellow creatures), and dispositions (e.g., in all circumstances to refer all things to God) that are appropriate responses to that which expresses God's glory. Thus, the utterance "God is glorious" is self-involving. That is, the very act of making the utterance not only expresses a certain set of feelings but also involves the speaker in commitments to a range of attitudes, passions, and dispositions that are coherent with the doxological feelings. Hence, we may dub such attitudes, passions, and dispositions "doxological" as well.

It is already plain that it is impossible to explain the biblical use of "God is glorious" in reference to the speaker's feelings without also referring to the "impressive observable" to which the feelings are a response—that is, the second of the three referential uses of the phrase that Evans disentangled in biblical contexts. Evans (1963) dubs "glory," and the like, "Aptness-words" (174). Here "glory" is used, not in reference to the speaker's doxological responses, but in reference to something observable that is impressive in such a fashion that it is apt to evoke just these responses. Hence the utterance has not only self-involving but also performative force: in saying "God is glorious," one is performing an act of acknowledgment. One is acknowledging that something observable is such as to evoke the feelings one is expressing and the attitudes and dispositions to which one is committing oneself. Thus, use of "glory" in reference to a certain range of human feelings and commitments is inseparable from its use in reference to certain impressive observables to which one is responding appropriately in saying, "God is glorious."

Here the relevant impressive observable is a proximate context viewed as expressive of God's own glory (and, it may be added, the impressive observable relevant to God drawing humankind to eschatological consummation is the risen and transfigured Christ, and the impressive observables relevant to God's reconciling alienated humankind are God's events of deliverance in Israel's history and, normatively, the crucifixion and resurrection of Jesus of Nazareth). Indeed, that is why the proximate context is impressive in the requisite way: it expresses God's glory. To express that I am so *im*pressed by my proximate context as to respond doxologically (saying—among other things—"God is glorious") is at the same time to acknowledge that my proximate context itself is *ex*pressive of God's glory. It is not just human persons who express God's glory; the quotidian does also.

Now, our proximate contexts certainly are observable in their finitude and their moral and ontological ambiguity, but they do not seem to be self-evidently expressive of divine glory. Evans stresses biblical recognition of the world's ambiguity in these regards (194). In biblical contexts, "God is glorious" does not rest on a context-less, value-neutral description of the world. Rather, the assumed background of biblical uses of such phrases is a picture of the proximate context as a two-sided social institution of discursive giving and receiving constituted by the triune God's self-involving and performative creative address, which invites creatures' own self-involving and performative responses. It is a context defined by the reciprocal commitments of God and creatures. Adopting, however implicitly, this picture of the proximate context involves a judgment about the proper conceptual context within which to understand the world most concretely: the world is best understood in terms of the conceptual framework specified by this two-sided social institution. So understood, our proximate contexts in all their ambiguity are nonetheless lived in as contexts expressive of God's own glory. Thus, the utterance "God is glorious" also has the force of a judgment (or, in J. L. Austin's technical terminology, the "verdictive" force [1962, 88]): our finite quotidian context, in all its ambiguity, is most appropriately lived in as expressive of God's glory.

Already we have been using "God is glorious" in reference to God's own intrinsic glory, the first of the three referential uses of the phrase that Evans distinguished. Use of "God is glorious" as an acknowledgment is impossible without its concurrent use to make a truth claim: "God is (intrinsically) glorious." Here the expressive force of the word "glory" as used in biblical contexts shifts. "God is glorious" not only expresses the speaker's response to something, it also acknowledges that God is self-expressive, naming God's self-expressiveness "God's glory." God's own glory is God's arresting splendor. It is the splendor of that which is ultimately important and commands utmost attention. God's splendor is arresting in virtue of God's gravitas (*kabod*). God is ultimately important in attractive fashion. As that which is ultimately important, God is splendidly beautiful. God's splendor is the dazzling brilliance of God's beauty (Heb.: *hadar, hod*; Gk.: *doxa*), such that, in a line from Walter Chalmers Smith's hymn, God is "in light inaccessible hid from our eyes." Without reference to God's own glory, it is not possible to articulate acknowledgment of that to which God creatively relates—that is, our creaturely proximate contexts and us with them is so impressively expressive of God's glory that it is apt to evoke doxological feelings and commitments in response.

Thus, in biblical contexts "the glory of God" is a relational concept: God's glory is God self-expressively relating to another in a distinctive and peculiar fashion that evokes reciprocal relating in response. It is the self-expressive character of God's glory that makes inseparable the threefold reference of biblical uses of "glory of God."

Our Ultimate Context as the Glory of God

The peculiar way in which the triune God relates to us creatively, our ultimate context, expresses the glory of God and so is itself, in a derivative sense, the glory of God. Put in technical Trinitarian language, humankind's ultimate context is "the Father relating creatively to all that is not God through the Son in the power of the Spirit." Part of the point of that technical formulation is to underscore the peculiar way God relates creatively to all that is not God: God relates creatively directly to all that is not God wisely—that is, through the divine wisdom (the Son). This relating is marked by both radical freedom and hospitable generosity. God creatively relates to all that is not God by an utterly free self-determination. In this relating God's Wisdom generously shares reality with that which is not God and hospitably gives creatures their own time and space to be and become themselves. God's creative relating thus expresses two of the perfections of God's reality: freedom and hospitable generosity.

This brings out the relational character of God's glory. If God's glory is the full richness of God's reality, inclusive of God's perfections of freedom and hospitable generosity, then God's glory at once attracts as something beautiful, drawing the other into relation, and, in free hospitable self-giving, goes out to relate directly to the other. To be sure, God's glory is not contingent on God creatively relating to reality other than God. God does not need to create in order to be gloriously God. The going out in self-giving and drawing toward as attractive value that constitute the gloriousness of God's reality simply *are* the relations among the three persons that constitute life of the immanently triune God. Accordingly, God's glory is relational whether or not God creatively relates to reality other than God.

Because the triune God is intrinsically glorious, God's creative relating to reality other than God is derivatively glorious in that it expresses God's own glory. It is expressively derivative, not causally derivative. God's intrinsic glory is not the cause of which the glory of God's creative relating is the effect. Causes and effects have to be identified in conceptual independence of each other, but expressive action (e.g., "joyous action") cannot be specified independently of the inner condition it expresses. Thus, our ultimate context is (derivatively) the glory of God.

Flourishing as Dying Life

I am suggesting that the glory of God defines human creaturely flourishing. However, what counts as "flourishing" is relative to what flourishes. It is actual living human personal bodies' flourishing that we seek to understand, not God's. In the case of a human creature, what flourishes must be understood theologically not only in terms of its ultimate context but also in terms of its proximate contexts.

Recall some themes developed in earlier chapters: Understood in terms of its proximate context, a human person is a type of being that at once (a) is a living body set into a society of beings, living and nonliving, interacting as systems of physical and sometimes cultural-linguistic energies, and (b) has this living body on loan. It lives on borrowed breath and is alone accountable for the fundamental orientation, dispositions, policies, emotions, passions, and beliefs that shape its living body's interactions with fellow creatures. The integral unity of such a one, at once being a living body and one who receives a living body on loan, is constituted by its ultimate context—that is, by the triune God creatively relating to it in both direct and indirect address. By God's direct address, God is more intimately related to personal bodies than they are to themselves, constituting them in reality as genuinely other than God. God's creative indirect address, mediated by quotidian proximate contexts, is a call to be wise for their own well-being and that of their proximate contexts. It is God's address to them in this dual call that constitutes living bodies as personal bodies. The task here is to identify the consequences of our proximate contexts for the idea of human flourishing.

"To flourish" means both "to blossom" and "to thrive." There are connotations of each sense that are useful here; there are other connotations that must be excluded. So my use of "to flourish" and related terms must be somewhat stipulative. "To blossom" is to manifest the type of beauty of which a given life is capable by virtue of God relating to it creatively. "To blossom," in a metaphorical sense, is also to be on the way to providing both fruit, on which contemporary others' flourishing may depend for nurture and support, and seed, on which a subsequent generation's life may depend. The range of metaphorical uses of "seed" and "blossom," of course, extends much more broadly than simply to procreation. In all these senses, "flourishing" may be used metaphorically to characterize a certain type of human life. But "to blossom" and "to bloom," used metaphorically, may also connote maximal good health. I shall argue that health, whether physical, emotional, intellectual, social, or cultural, is at best a problematic metaphor for what is meant theologically by human flourishing. I seek to qualify radically that connotation in theological use of the term.

As for "to thrive," its root is Old Norse, "*thrifask*, to have oneself in hand." Used metaphorically of a certain type of human life, that too is theologically appropriate. However, used metaphorically, "to thrive" may also connote both "to grow luxuriantly" and "to prosper." I seek to exclude both of these senses, the first because it unqualifiedly reintroduces health as a metaphor, and the second because it introduces wealth and achievement as metaphors definitive of human flourishing.

Understanding human beings in terms of their proximate contexts foregrounds two themes fundamental to a theological idea of human flourishing. It stresses, first, the fact that what may flourish is radically finite. It is life lived on borrowed breath. Personal bodies are inherently relational beings, limited by their dependence on others and by others' dependencies on them. Because it is the flourishing of finite creatures who are integral parts of the thoroughly finite quotidian, human flourishing is something quite different from utopian life in a paradisiacal setting free of social and physical stresses and conflicts. Human persons' flourishing in their kind is inseparable from the flourishing of all creatures in their kinds. Hence human creatures' glory, whatever it is, lies neither historically behind the quotidian (in Eden) nor ahead of it (in the "kingdom of God"). Nor does it lie above the quotidian in transcendence of the everyday. It lies rather in human creatures being dedicatedly active for the well-being of their everyday proximate contexts as citizens of the society of creatures that comprise the quotidian.

Moreover, as living bodies, their life within the quotidian is always a life toward death. Life lived on borrowed breath is a dying life. It must resolutely be kept clear that the creaturely human flourishing of which we speak is the flourishing of dying life.

At the same time, understanding human creatures in terms of their proximate contexts also stresses that, precisely as dying lives, they express God's glory just because they are part of that to which God relates creatively. As we have seen, "God's glory" is a relational concept and, in biblical contexts, both God's creative relating and that to which God creatively relates are expressive of that glory. In John Calvin's phrase, our proximate context, the created world is intrinsically "the dazzling theater" of God's glory (1960, 61). Personal bodies are not just the audience; they are part of the performance of God's glory.

Personal Bodies as the Glory of God

If (1) the triune God's own glory is relational in its expressivity; (2) and if the peculiar way in which God creatively relates to reality other than God (i.e., our ultimate context) is expressive of God's glory and thus is itself (derivatively) the glory of God; (3) and if that to which God relates creatively (i.e., our proximate contexts, including ourselves) express that same divine self-expressive relating and thus are themselves (derivatively) the glory of God; then, (4) inasmuch as flourishing personal bodies are parts of their proximate contexts, they too are (derivatively) the glory of God. Indeed, because human persons both are living human bodies and have living human bodies on loan, they are the glory of God in two related senses.

Flourishing as Living Bodies

In one sense, flourishing personal bodies are the glory of God simply as living human bodies. As part of all that exists by virtue of God's utterly intimate creative relating, personal bodies are in their own fashion the glory of God. Indeed, their "fashion" is a remarkably rich expression of God's glory. The more complex the powers of a creature, the more richly it expresses God's glory. The difference between more and less rich expression of God's glory is not a difference of degree on some scale or continuum of "expressivity of God's glory." It is rather a series of differences in the complexity of their modes of expression. Different creatures are God's glory in different modalities; they simply express God's glory in different ways.

Hence the theological concept of the flourishing of human creatures in particular is a highly relative concept. Christian understanding of human persons as God's creatures does not entail any abstractly ideal and absolute standard of human flourishing against which the degree of flourishing of each and every human life could in principle be measured. Not even the life of Jesus provides such a standard. Instead, what counts as the flourishing of any given human life must be understood concretely in terms of the particular finite array of powers and capacities that that given living body has and the particularities of the finite networks of relationships in which it has been set in its proximate contexts across time. Given that flourishing personal bodies are living bodies with a remarkably rich and complex array of types of powers, they are the glory of God in their own distinctive modes simply as living bodies creatively related to by God. If nothing else, the complex physiology of living human bodies, as construed within their proximate and ultimate contexts, is in itself an "impressive observable" expressive of God's glory.

That remark immediately invites the question whether only healthy lives are the glory of God. That question, of course, is only the camel's nose of a larger problem of evil. Are the infant suffering from failure-to-thrive syndrome and the elder suffering from Alzheimer's disease not the glory of God even though they are God's creatures? Aspects of the topics of sin and evil are taken up in later chapters. Here it is sufficient to point out that the question assumes that health is the index of flourishing, Christianly understood—an assumption I wish to challenge.

In a theocentric anthropology, human flourishing ought to be understood in relation to God. I suggest that expressing God's glory—that is, being derivatively the glory of God—is the index of human flourishing. Flourishing human bodies are not the glory of God because they are healthily flourishing; theologically speaking, they are deemed flourishing to the extent that even in extreme unhealth they are nonetheless in some mode (derivatively) the glory of God.

"Health" is problematic as an index of a human flourishing (theologically understood) because "health" and "unhealth" are usually understood functionally; indeed, "dysfunctional" has come to be used almost interchangeably with "unhealthy." The criteria of the "healthy" functioning of energy systems are self-referential. To the extent that an energy system functions to maintain itself in its immediate environment and to grow, it is healthy; to the extent that it does not, it is unhealthy. A self-referential index to human flourishing is problematic in an anthropology that seeks to understand human persons, not finally in relation to themselves and their proximate contexts, but excentrically, in relation to God as the center of their reality and value "outside" themselves.

Of course, a healthy human living body is preferable to an unhealthy one. For that matter, for any personal body, thriving in the sense of prospering is preferable to being impoverished. These are common themes in canonical Wisdom literatures. Proverbs has "Solomon" (or is it Woman Wisdom, as at 1:20ff.?) enjoin the hearer,

> My child, do not forget my teaching [of wisdom],
>   but let your heart keep my commandments;
> for length of days and years of life [presumably healthy life]
>   and abundant welfare they will give you.
>
> (3:1, 2)

The theme that being wise will make life bloom and thrive reverberates in both mainstream wisdom—for example, Proverbs—and in its internal critics—for example, Ecclesiastes. Wisdom literature cuts against any theological tendency to play down the importance of healthy and prosperous life. Furthermore, in that literature this theme has very broad application because "life" is construed broadly to embrace several dimensions: biological, emotional, intellectual, social, and cultural, each of which may at any particular time be relatively healthy or unhealthy.

It is clearer today than ever before that the health of each of these dimensions is interdependent with that of the other dimensions in complex ways that are not now well understood. It is also clear that a certain minimum degree of biological health is the necessary condition of any degree of health whatever in the other dimensions of human life. The infant that for genetic reasons will never mature biologically, the infant born radically retarded, the mature human living body afflicted with advanced stages of neurological diseases such as Alzheimer's, and any human living body that has slipped into coma, although they all continue to live, simply do not have the powers needed for the emotional, intellectual, social, or cultural dimensions of human life. Some greater degree of healthy human life is preferable because it is a necessary condition for the exercise of the complex array of powers, wherein human persons may distinctively express God's glory simply by being living bodies.

Nonetheless, I suggest, personal bodies in extreme states of unhealth continue in their own ways to express God's glory. It is not in virtue of their unhealth or health that God creatively relates to personal bodies in those conditions; and it is not in virtue of either their unhealth or health that they are the glory of God simply as living human bodies. Rather, they express God's glory in virtue of the minimal degree of functioning life they still do have as the condition, as it were, of their profound dysfunctions. So long as they do physically live in virtue of God self-expressively relating to them, those suffering extreme unhealth also are in their own ways the glory of God. The index of their flourishing as God's glory is not any sort of health, but simply the fact that God's creative relating to them is inherently self-expressive of God's own glory. In all the ambiguity of their dying lives, as God's creatures they express God's glory. They constitute the limit cases of living human bodies as the glory of God.

Flourishing as Having Borrowed Living Bodies

Personal bodies may be the glory of God, not only in virtue of being living bodies, but also in virtue of having living bodies on loan. Sharing reality with their proximate contexts by divine wisdom's direct creative address, they are also called by divine wisdom's indirect address, mediated through their quotidian contexts, to be wise for their own well-being and that of their proximate contexts. That their living bodies are on loan means that they are accountable to the Lender for the ways in which they deploy them in their proximate contexts. In this regard they are the glory of God as they flourish in the quasi-technical sense of "thrive"—that is, have themselves wisely in hand. To the extent that they take charge of themselves wisely for their own well-being and that of their proximate contexts, actively responding to God's call to be wise, to that extent they are the glory of God in this second sense of the term.

This has a further general consequence for a theological concept of human flourishing. Not only is what counts as any particular personal body's flourishing relative to her particular range of powers, it is also at any given time in her life a matter of degree. The degree to which any particular personal body may take itself in hand ("thrive") so that it is able to manifest the beauty of the emotional, intellectual, and social grace of which it is capable and is able to nurture both companions and descendants ("blossoms") may vary considerably.

Flourishing in Wise Action for the Quotidian's Sake

Personal bodies flourish in being (derivatively) the glory of God. An understanding of human creatureliness guided by the creation theology through which canonical Wisdom literatures think allows this thesis to be formulated more precisely in two respects. Personal bodies are the glory of God as they flourish in appropriate response to their vocation to (a) wise action for (b) the well-being of the quotidian (c) for its own sake.

Flourishing in Action

The account given of our proximate contexts in chapter 5A was guided by mainstream biblical Wisdom literature's stress on the human practices that make up our everyday lived worlds. When these practices are enacted as responses to God's call, they aim to be wise for the well-being of our proximate contexts. Hence, the wisdom to which we are called is a practical wisdom. I adopted the following definition of human practice: a practice is any form of socially established cooperative human action that is complex and internally coherent, is subject to standards of excellence that partly define it, and is done to some end but does not necessarily have a product. The human actions that make up practices are specified by their intentions. If it is in wise practices that human beings flourish in the sense of "thrive," it follows that they flourish as they act intentionally. They flourish in their human acting. More exactly, they flourish in action in the here-and-now quotidian world.

A Christian theological anthropology that takes human creatureliness as seriously as it takes the promise of human eschatological consummation and the good news of the reconciliation of estranged human sinners has, it seems to me, overridingly strong reasons to hold to a picture of human persons as fundamentally bodied agents, not patients, bodily enactors of intentions, and only as such also passive registers of passing modifications of consciousness and of interior acts of existential self-relating resolve.

For the Well-Being of the Quotidian

The overall goal of the action in which personal bodies flourish is entirely formal: the well-being of the quotidian for its own sake. Such action seeks to protect the integrity of creatures from violation. Posed positively or negatively, this is a formal goal in that it implies nothing about what counts as the well-being of the quotidian. This "formality" is already implicit in the fact that the wisdom to which our creaturely vocation calls us is not only a practical wisdom but a concrete, ad hoc wisdom. Such wisdom is a kind of insight into particular situations in the quotidian and what will make for their well-being.

Such insight requires two types of capacities. Isaiah Berlin famously distinguished two types of thinkers: the foxes who cover a great deal of intellectual territory and have a synoptic sense of the conceptual topography of a broad area of inquiry, and the hedgehogs who patiently stay in one circumscribed intellectual area and stubbornly root away at its conceptual difficulties until they know one topic thoroughly. Although he does it in a very different context, Charles Wood's use of Berlin's simile (1985, 67–68) suggests a way to characterize the capacities needed for ad hoc practical wisdom. The call to be wise is a call, we may say, to exercise capacities for both discernment and vision.

On one side, ad hoc practical wisdom about how to act wisely for the well-being of fellow creatures requires capacities to discern what makes for the well-being of particular fellow creatures in their particular situations. According to canonical Wisdom literature, we are born into a vocation to be wise for the well-being of our fellow creatures, but biblical Wisdom offers no body of theory about what makes for their well-being. Instead, this vocation is an invitation: look and listen carefully and figure it out for yourselves; it doesn't matter where you learn what makes for creatures' well-being or how it is discovered. When our practices are not guided by such discernment, they run the serious risk of violating the integrity of our fellow creatures and, because we are so deeply interdependent, of ourselves as well. Personal bodies flourish in wise action that is discerning about what makes for the well-being of particular fellow creatures in their particular situations.

On the other side, ad hoc practical wisdom concerning the everyday world requires capacities for a certain synoptic vision of the creaturely quotidian precisely in its God-relatedness. Basic to canonical Wisdom literature's background creation theology is the conviction, equally clear, though with different nuances, in Proverbs, Ecclesiastes, and Job, that God is continuously active in the quotidian to sustain it. It would be misleading to call this an implicit theory about a created natural causal order in the world. As chapter 5B tried to show, it is more accurate to call it an implicit claim that overall and in general there are reliable patterns in the interactions of creatures within the society of being. As we have seen, there is a strong strand of skepticism in Wisdom literature that human creatures, in all their ambiguities, are capable of grasping what God is doing in the quotidian with enough clarity and confidence to guide their own actions.

None of this rules out, of course, that some theory of natural law might be theologically warranted on some basis other than an account of what we are by virtue of God's creatively relating to us. Nor, alternatively, does it rule out the possibility that a deontological account of duties universally ascribable to human creatures and formulated as necessary a priori imperatives might be warranted theologically on some basis other than an account of our creatureliness considered in itself and for its own sake. It only means that an account of our creatureliness normed by canonical Wisdom literature, and by other scriptural voices read in its light, does not warrant either type of theory.

What canonical Wisdom literature does claim that we are called to do is learn to construe fellow creatures and ourselves precisely as creatures, as dependent on God's continuous creative relating to us. That divine relating is central to every creature's integrity and to the integrity of the everyday world as a whole. When our practices are not formed by such a vision of our fellow creatures, the circumstances within which we act, and ourselves as agents, we risk doing violence to fellow creatures' integrity. Personal bodies flourish in wise action that has learned to envision its proximate contexts within the ultimate context of the triune God's actively relating to them creatively.

For Its Own Sake

Just as the creation theology through which scriptural Wisdom literature thinks is not shaped either by the story of God's events of deliverance nor by a picture of a form of human life lived in covenant under Torah; neither is it shaped by the story of God promising to draw creation into an eschatological consummation "beyond" the quotidian. The integrity of creatures comprised by the quotidian, considered either singly or in the complex networks of their interactions and interdependencies, is not defined by reference to some goal lying beyond the quotidian itself. In this creation theology, God's relating to us as Creator gives us no theologically superior goal for our projects beyond the well-being of the quotidian. This has at least two implications for wise human action in practices seeking the well-being of the everyday world.

1. There is an important implication for theological anthropology's assumption about personal bodies as historical agents that calls into question major themes in both traditional and modern theological anthropology.

Mainstream biblical Wisdom regularly assumes that the Creator's hand moves providentially in human affairs, working God's own purposes in history. This might suggest that the historical context of any one personal body's life ought to be understood theologically in a totalizing way. That is, it might suggest we understand history as a single totality, as one long project with a single determining internal logic and unified into a whole by the actualization of a final and definitive goal for which God created the entire world-historical process in the first place. In that case, personal bodies would find well-being only in action that is consonant with God's action, seeking to actualize the goal that is history's end. However, biblical wisdom's background creation theology undercuts all such totalizing views of history and their anthropological implications.

Christian theologies, ancient and modern, in which the doctrine of creation plays a major role have been dominated by various totalizing views of history based on the claim that God not only creates, but creates precisely in order to realize a goal through and beyond history. In this context the idea that God has a "plan" for history has often been taken to suggest that God has a script that the drama of history will follow, or perhaps a diagram of the relations of proximate historical ends to proximate historical means through which God will achieve God's goal for the creative project as a whole. In some versions the incarnation simply is that goal (notably in Irenaeus, Schleiermacher, Barth, Rahner). In others the incarnation is the means God has chosen to deal with the threat, introduced by sin, that history will fail to actualize its God-given goal for it (notably in Augustine, Thomas Aquinas, Calvin).

Since the Enlightenment, atheological but equally totalizing views of history have dominated Western cultures. Of course, they differ from one another profoundly. Classical economic and political liberalism holds that human history moves inexorably toward the maximization of human happiness, driven by a combination of rational self-interest and the hidden hand of the economic mechanisms of the free market. Various Hegelianisms view world history as a single movement through which Spirit, understood as rationally self-conscious freedom, both finite (i.e., human) and absolute (i.e., divine), comes inexorably to self-actualization through something like a maturation process driven by an intrinsic dialectical logic. Classical Marxism sees all history moving inevitably toward maximization of human freedom through a process driven by a dialectic inherent in successive forms of economic organization. In one way or another, they all underwrite the view that, at least over the long haul, history is marked by incremental progress toward its goal. Of course, such a view is usually subjected to all manner of qualifications: the line of development is not straight; there have been and will be many setbacks in the movement toward history's goal; indeed, the fact of progress is not easily discernible in any one generation. Nonetheless, overall cultural, medical, technological, educational, economic, social, even governmental incremental progress (not just change) across the centuries is claimed to be real.

At least since Reinhold Niebuhr's critiques (1953, vol. 2, chaps, 1, 6, and 7), a standard theological objection to them all has been that unlike Christian views of history, they ignore both the fact of human sin that derails history's roll toward actualization of its goal, and the fact that sin cannot be eliminated from history by historical action. Penetrating as that critique is, it fails to move on to a necessary correlative critique of the Christian theological tradition itself. That tradition, after all, is a part of the intellectual antecedents of modern totalizing views of history. The modern views are in many ways secularized versions of the Christian theological tradition's own totalizing views of history based on doctrines of creation that interpret divine providence in overall goal-actualizing ways.

An understanding of human creatureliness guided by biblical Wisdom literature, however, will be deeply skeptical of all totalizing pictures of history. To be sure, mainstream biblical Wisdom as reflected in Proverbs appears to be optimistic about the possibility of a certain kind of change for the better in history. A great many of the wise sentences it anthologizes stress that practices of deceit, betrayal, oppression, injustice, violence, and bad government lead, not to well-being, but to death. The call to be wise that comes through the book construed, not as a disparate collection of such sentences, but as a canonically edited whole, is a call to repent and avoid such practices. It is a call for a certain kind of historical change. However, it does not come close to implying that all wise historical changes, just because they are wise, cumulatively move toward actualizing some overall goal for the whole of history.

Ecclesiastes pushes against the conventions of mainstream biblical Wisdom to stress this point. The Teacher never denies divine providence and at least indirectly affirms it: "for apart from [God] who can eat or who can have enjoyment? For to the one who pleases him God gives wisdom and knowledge and joy; but to the sinner he gives the work of gathering and heaping, only to give to one who pleases God" (2:25–26). There is no clear textual basis for supposing that the Teacher is either insincere or satirical in his indirect affirmations of providence. The Teacher's famous skepticism has rather to do with our capacity to discern just what God is doing or what God's goal may be: "Just as you do not know how the breath comes to the bones in the mother's womb, so you do not know the work of God, who makes everything" (11:5; see 8:16–17). He never suggests that it is sin that darkens our insight. He seems rather to associate the limits of our knowledge with limits imposed by creatureliness.

He goes further. Even if God's providential hand is hiddenly at work in history, history is not to be thought of as moving by incremental steps in a line, either straight or crooked, toward actualizing an overall goal. The Teacher is famous for his opening announcement:

> What has been is what will be,
> and what has been done is what will be done;
> there is nothing new under the sun.
>
> (1:9)

Instead of incremental development in history, what God's hand brings is a series of different periods or "times" in history: "For everything there is a season, and a time for every matter under heaven" (3:1; see 3:2–8; 8:6). These are periods for different undertakings and interactions, each having its own goal. The call to be wise in our agency is partly a call to discern what it is currently time *for*, what types of interactions and practices are appropriate given the nature of the time.

This is not a cyclical view of history. Granted, on this view nothing absolutely unprecedented ever happens. The same types of events keep happening. But there is no suggestion that there is some one sequence of times that regularly recycles. Even less is it a progressive view of history. There is no suggestion that the "times" follow in some sequence that incrementally moves human history toward actualization of some divinely chosen goal for the entire creaturely project.

We are called to wise action for the well-being of the quotidian for its own sake and not for the actualization of some goal beyond it. In creating, God does not set any such goal. Understood in ways guided by canonical Wisdom literature's background creation theology, the historical context within which we are called to act is not itself some one divine project made into a totality by God's continuous actualization of a world-historical goal. Personal bodies have a vocation in celebration of the quotidian for its own sake and not for the sake of any further goal. They flourish in wise action for the well-being of the quotidian. That well-being is to be understood in terms of the particularities of their fellow creatures, not in terms of some goal transcending them.

2. When human creatures are understood in ways guided by canonical Wisdom literature's background creation theology, they are understood to flourish in wise action that seeks the well-being, for its own sake, of the quotidian, which includes themselves. Not only has that theme an implication for anthropological assumptions about personal bodies as historical agents, it also has an important implication for the way in which they view their own lives. It resists the picture that a properly human life is one lifelong project of self-actualization.

In the abstract, the picture of a properly human life as the project of self-actualization is a plausible and theologically inviting thought. It is in its own way a totalizing picture of human life. Cast in the terms we have been using, it is the picture that in being called to be wise in action for our own well-being as well as the quotidian's, we are called to the lifelong project of actualizing ourselves as wise persons. The well-being of the quotidian for its own sake, for which we are called to be wise in action, includes our own well-being for its own sake. According to such a picture, what makes a human life a single and meaningful whole is that it has been totally committed to some sort of project, perhaps that of becoming a wise person.

Some basic assumptions of such a view are that life is meaningful when it is worth living, and that what makes life worth living is that it is lived as a whole that is integrated as a whole by some central value. Total commitment to a project provides such a value. It is a total commitment when it engages the total array of powers a person has. Such total commitment to a project binds up one's time and energy into an integrated whole constituted by the time-extended actualization of the valued project. Such a view of properly human life is not necessarily an individualistic view. Engaging in any of the types of project that are acknowledged to make a meaningful whole of one's life requires a social context because it requires interactive engagement in a variety of socially established practices.

Two versions of such a view are frequently encountered in contemporary culture. In one version, what makes a personal body's life authentically human is its total commitment to some relatively long-term project whose outcome or product is valued: a successful career in some socially valued role or occupation; artistic creation; being a morally good person according to a recognized definition of moral goodness; and so on. In the other version, what makes a personal body's life authentically human is that one actualizes one's true "self." Such a life has no product beyond itself. It is made an integral, and hence meaningful, whole by being itself one lifelong project of self-actualization. This may have a secular version, often in humanistic psychology, which supposes that each of us has within us a potential true self that needs to be actualized and can be actualized by our own efforts if we practice the right therapy or spiritual disciplines. Or it may have a theocentric version which holds that each of us is actualized only as we, by God's grace, relate to God by saying "yes" to God. Indeed, this version is the basic thesis of some intellectually powerful theological anthropologies on the current scene (Rahner 1961; 1978, pts. 1 and 3; Boros 1965). In either version, the story of such a life can be told in a single well-formed narrative that renders that life as a single and coherent totality.

However, canonical Wisdom literature's call to us to be wise in our agency in the quotidian does not warrant any such picture of the lives of personal bodies. Indeed the voice of Ecclesiastes speaks against it. Here it is especially important to hear Ecclesiastes within the chorus of canonical Wisdom and not as an undialectical negation of biblical Wisdom. Mainstream canonical Wisdom, as represented by Proverbs, optimistically affirms that God is at work in the quotidian to maintain its well-being. In particular, it affirms that God is at work to preserve the moral well-being of the everyday, seeing to it that the wise righteous are justly rewarded and the foolish wicked justly punished. Its call to us to act wisely for the well-being, especially the moral well-being, of the everyday world is a call to live in ways that are appropriate responses to the way in which God is already at work in that same world. Its call is always ad hoc, a call to us in particular situations to act wise for the well-being of those particular situations. It is never a call to be wise as such and in the abstract, as though actualizing ourselves as generically wise personal bodies constituted our well-being. Granted, though it neither implies or affirms the idea, Proverbs is arguably consistent with the view that an authentic and meaningful human life is one lived as a lifelong project of actualizing itself as a wise life. Nonetheless, Proverbs does not itself warrant such a view.

Ecclesiastes never explicitly repudiates mainstream biblical Wisdom's affirmation of God's governance of human affairs. However, the Teacher consistently presses against the conventions of mainstream Wisdom to test how far they will stretch. Especially in his famous negativity ("Vanity of vanity, all is vanity"), the Teacher presses against those conventions to see whether they can accommodate the view that human lives committed to wise practices in the quotidian may be meaningful in ways that are not contingent on their having some one overarching goal—whether, we may add, it is the goal of self-actualization or some other. He repeatedly moves through a three-stage pattern of reflection. He begins with reports of observations of long-term human life-projects (e.g., commitment to occupations, 3:10ff; acquiring riches, 6:1ff; even engagement in cultic worship, 5:1ff). Each of these is described not just as one project among many, but rather as a life project whose goal outlasts and so lies beyond the everyday: a legacy for posterity; honor; friendship with God. He then judges that each is finally "vanity and chasing after wind." He regularly concludes with a recommendation that we focus our lives on the particularities of the everyday world, engaging in short-term projects whose goals are nothing more than our well-being in the practices that make up the well-being of the everyday world.

The first instance of this pattern in the book ties it to the Teacher's own life. After announcing that the world's constant change is not marked by the emergence of any genuine novelty and that "there is nothing new under the sun" (1:9b), and following a self-introduction as "king over Israel in Jerusalem" (1:12), the Teacher reports that seeking to live wisely he undertook a long-term building project: "I made myself gardens and parks" (2:4, 5), bought many slaves, acquired much wealth, enjoyed many pleasures. By his society's standards, actualizing this project is a great life achievement. More, in actualizing this achievement he thought he actualized himself. Engaging in this project constituted his personal identity: "*I* became great and surpassed all who were before me in Jerusalem" (2:9; emphasis added). But then, taking note that he would die as surely as will fools who do not bind the time and energies of their lives into any project whatever, he judges that what he had done was vanity and chasing after wind (2:11–23).

The Teacher then proposes an alternative picture of how to be wise for one's own well-being: "There is nothing better for mortals than to eat and drink, and find enjoyment in their toil. This also, I saw, is from the hand of God; for apart from him who can eat or who can have enjoyment?" (2:24–25). The juxtaposition of this recommendation with the immediately preceding judgment that it is vanity and chasing after wind to seek self-actualization in long-term projects, especially some one lifelong project, gives it the force of saying this: rather than binding the time and powers of one's life to a single lifelong project that transcends and unites quotidian moments in order to make one's life a meaningful whole, it is better to focus on short-term projects that constitute the everyday world.

This recommendation is a straightforward celebration of personal bodies as part of the quotidian taken in its dependence on God creatively relating to it ("for apart from him who can eat or who can have enjoyment?"). Its background is the stress on creaturely finitude that lies at the core of biblical Wisdom's background creation theology. The Teacher repeatedly notes that what reduces life-totalizing projects to "vanity and chasing after wind" is the universal inevitability of death. If life were made meaningful only by the actualization of some life-unifying project, even that of self-actualization, then death will inevitably undercut that meaning. In the context of this creation theology, death has its proper role in the quotidian. It is not inherently evil. The Teacher's is not a tragic vision of life holding that human goods are inescapably doomed by powers of futility and evil. The Teacher's view is simply realistic. In celebrating personal bodies as part of the quotidian, he also celebrates death's role in the everyday.

Wisdom's call, mediated through the quotidian, to be wise in action for the well-being of the everyday is always ad hoc. It is a call to be wise for the well-being of the given quotidian in its particularities here and now for its own sake, not for the sake of some ideal state whose transcendentally future actualization alone will be this everyday world's proper well-being. Since the everyday includes the personal bodies who respond to this call, it is also a call for them to act wisely for their own well-being as quotidian creatures *in* the given everyday world for their own sakes and not for the sake of some ideal "self" in whose actualization alone will they be authentic and meaningful human lives.

The ground of meaning in human life is eccentric to that life. What makes their lives meaningful wholes is not that they have been unified by the lifelong project of actualizing their true "selves," but simply the fact that the triune God has been creatively relating to all of the shorter- or longer-term projects in whose practices they concretely interact with fellow creatures as they "eat and drink, and find enjoyment in their toil," than which "there is nothing better for mortals" (2:24). Unlike the meaning of lives unified as wholes by life-totalizing projects, the meaning of lives engaged in ad hoc quotidian projects cannot be undercut by the inevitability of death. The meaning of such lives is grounded on God's creative relating to the quotidian, not on a goal actualized through the projects themselves, a goal that death dissolves. It is in the actions and interactions of such practices that personal bodies, who are accountable for the way they are set into their proximate contexts, flourish as the glory of God.

Flourishing in Faith

To flourish as personal bodies who are responsible to God's address and accountable for that response is to be the glory of God, and flourishing lies in responding appropriately to the triune God who has already related creatively to us. The name for such appropriate response to God as Creator is "faith." To be faithful to God is, to paraphrase H. Richard Niebuhr's formulation (1960, 16–23), to live in our proximate contexts trusting God as the ground of our being and value and being loyal to God's own project—namely, our creaturely proximate contexts. "Trusting God as ground of our being and value" is an appropriate response to God's creative direct address to us; "being loyal to God's project" is an appropriate response to God's creative indirect address.

What count as trust and loyalty is defined by that to which they are responses, in this case the triune God. Accordingly, a Trinitarian understanding of God will qualify our characterization of responsive faith. Put formulaically, faith is trust in and loyalty to "the Father through the Son in the power of the Spirit," mirroring in response the way in which the Father creatively relates to us "through the Son in the power of the Spirit."

"Flourishing in Faith . . . through the Son"

To say that faith is trust in and loyalty to the Father "through the Son" is to stress that faith is faith in God precisely in the peculiar way in which God relates to us creatively—namely, a self-committing way defined by the interplay in divine Wisdom between freedom and hospitable generosity. In short, as trust in and loyalty to the triune God, faith is a response to our ultimate context as God relating to us creatively. What makes faith the *appropriate* response is that it reciprocates and reflects God's faithfulness to us in our proximate contexts. To express in this fashion the way in which God relates to us is to be, derivatively, the glory of God.

Construed this way, faith is perhaps better understood as a personal body's responsive attitude than as a virtue. Virtues are settled and long-lasting dispositions to act or respond in a variety of circumstances in specific ways. Classically, moral virtues are dispositions to act in morally good ways, such as courageously and justly. By only the slightest extension the idea can cover dispositions to think in good ways, such as truly and rigorously—that is, intellectual virtues. The idea can arguably be extended further to cover dispositions to have certain emotions, such as pity and gratitude (Harak 1993). They are emotional virtues. Each virtue is a shaping of one kind of human power so that it may be exercised in a definite way. However, virtues shaping one kind of power do not necessarily shape another. Courage, for example, is a moral, but not an intellectual or an emotional virtue. Faithfulness to the triune God, however, is not the determinate shaping of some one kind of human power. Like a virtue, faithfulness is a long-lasting shaping of a personal body. However, faithfulness to God cuts across all of a personal body's powers. It is an attitude orienting them all in a definite fashion. Hence, as a condition of a whole complex personal body, faith is itself complex.

Faithfulness to God is a complex responsive attitude because what it responds to is complex—namely, the expression of God's glory in the peculiar interplay between hospitable generosity and freedom that constitute our ultimate context. Faithfulness is basically commitment to an array of practices that enact trust in and loyalty to God's free hospitable generosity. Some of them are practices that express certain emotions, passions, and feelings. Since such enactments would be insincere if their enactments did not in fact have the relevant emotions, passions, and feelings, faithfulness must also include certain affections. Further, since faithfulness to God, both as an array of practices and as a set of affections, is conceptually formed and specified, it necessarily involves mastery of certain concepts and commitment to certain beliefs.

What unifies this complex responsive attitude is the fact that in its complexity this disposition is a single response to the singular glory of the triune God that is expressed in the way God relates creatively to personal bodies. As one, albeit complex, appropriate response to the glory of God by creatures capable of being held accountable for their attitudes, faithfulness to God glorifies God—that is, is itself expressive of the glory of God.

Faith construed as an attitude does have much in common with virtues. Virtues are conceptually defined and specified. Indeed, acquiring a virtue is in large part a matter of deeply learning the relevant concepts. A major part of learning the concept of justice is learning to recognize in very different circumstances what would count as just behavior. An even deeper learning of the concept involves learning how to be just oneself— learning the disposition to act in appropriately just ways in various, perhaps unanticipated and even unprecedented, circumstances. Thus, the very process of learning such concepts can be existentially self-involving, a process by which the learner is personally shaped in certain definite ways as an agent, thinker, or feeler, becoming, say, just, clear thinking, or grateful. Like a virtue, the attitude of faithfulness is conceptually formed. As a responsive trust in and loyalty to the triune God, faithfulness supposes, however implicitly, certain beliefs about God and God's trustworthiness,

God's perfections, how God relates creatively, what the project is to which God is loyal, and the relations among the foregoing beliefs. Faithfulness to the creative triune God includes not just the knowledge that the church teaches such beliefs or that some persons believe such things. More, it includes the disposition oneself to affirm such beliefs as true. It also supposes on the part of faithful persons some grasp of the concepts employed in such beliefs. Furthermore, insofar as faithfulness involves mastering a set of concepts and affirming a set of beliefs, it also involves a process that is existentially self-involving. Because faithfulness to God is the ongoing effort to respond appropriately to the way in which God has already related creatively to us, the process is a continuous effort to keep the practices of one's life shaped by concepts and well-warranted beliefs about that divine relating. In this way, faith as trust in and loyalty to the triune God deeply defines who one is.

In short, personal bodies flourish when they glorify God. Simply as living bodies, they flourish insofar as their sheer existence as living bodies interdependent with their proximate contexts reflects God's glory; insofar as they are borrowed living bodies for whose responses they are accountable, personal bodies glorify God by responding appropriately to the way in which the triune God relates to them creatively—namely, respond in faith. In the first case they flourish in the sense of "blossom," and in the second in the sense of "to have oneself in hand."

"Flourishing in Faith in . . . the Power of the Spirit"

To say that faith is trust in and loyalty to the Father "in the power of the Spirit" is to stress that faith is a blessing given, not a state acquired or achieved through self-discipline. Thus far, following a trajectory in canonical Wisdom's creation theology, I have been suggesting that wise action in and for the quotidian for the quotidian's own sake is the concrete content of human creatures' faithful response to the triune God's creative relating to them. However, according to biblical Wisdom's background creation theology, wisdom is finally a free blessing from God. If wise action in and for the quotidian is the appropriately faithful response to God's creativity, the faith too is a blessing freely given as God is with us circumambiently "in the power of the Spirit."

It is easy to think otherwise, reading Proverbs. It can make wisdom sound like a commodity one might acquire:

> "The beginning of wisdom is this: Get wisdom,
>   and whatever else you get, get insight."
>   (4:7)

The opening of the poem containing this exhortation to acquisitiveness explains how one gets wisdom and insight:

> Listen, children, to a father's instruction,
>   and be attentive, that you may gain insight.
>   (4:1)

This makes it sound as though one could learn to be wise simply by attending carefully to Wisdom tradition's sentences that elicit insight.

However, as we have seen (chap. 5B), the basic units of Wisdom literature are short sayings or sentences addressed to particular aspects of concrete situations in life. They are often juxtaposed to contrasting and apparently contrary sayings about other aspects of the same situations. The friction between sayings seems designed to elicit insight into the particularities of actual creatures in actual settings. "Listening" to such instruction is hard work, an active, struggling listening.

Making it even harder work is the fact that wisdom is ambiguous. This is a clear note in Proverbs. It is not as though wisdom is plain to see, once one gets the hang of it. It is far too easy to confuse folly with wisdom:

> There is a way that seems right to a person,
>   but its end is the way to death.
>   (14:12; see 16:25)

Identifying what is wise is not easy; nonetheless, we are called to listen to the sages' teachings as the way to the insight that yields wisdom.

It is tempting to push this theme in biblical Wisdom one step further. It would be easy to suppose that such texts imply that the very struggle to gain insight into wisdom from the sages' "sentences" itself cultivates and sharpens our ordinary capacities to see and hear what is present in our proximate contexts. The struggle would thus be understood as a kind of discipline of imagination, emotions, and intellect by which we make ourselves insightful. Biblical Wisdom literature clearly assumes that such disciplines have a social context. They take place in practices in which human creatures interact. The payoff of the hard work of subjecting oneself to the sages' discipline would be the acquisition of wisdom.

However, Proverbs and canonical Wisdom literature generally insist that wisdom is finally a gift from God:

> For the LORD gives wisdom;
>   from his mouth come knowledge and understanding.
>   (2:6)

Listening properly, and the disciplines it involves, are a necessary but insufficient condition for becoming wise. It is finally necessary for God to give the wisdom. The structure and dynamics of divine giving and human receiving that constitute the social institution established by God's creative relating also characterizes the vocation to wisdom into which we are born in our being created. Wisdom is free, a gift given in the freedom of God's hospitable generosity; but it is not cheap, for its reception is nothing other than the continual social disciplines of the struggle to be insightful.

If wise action for the well-being, for its own sake, of the everyday world, including ourselves as part of the quotidian, is the concrete content of human creatures' faithfulness to God, then faith too must be said to be a gift from God. It is a gift given in and through the practices that make up the common life of our quotidian proximate contexts. In the conventions of Trinitarian understandings of God, of which canonical Wisdom knows nothing, this may be expressed by saying that personal bodies have such faith "in the power of the Spirit, sent with the Son from the Father."

CHAPTER **9A**

Doxological Gratitude: Who We Are and How We Are to Be as Faithful Creatures

Thus far, our exploration of anthropological implications of the basic Christian claim that the triune God relates creatively to all that is not God has yielded remarks in response to the "What?" question. The full complexity of what we are as creatures, I suggested, is best conveyed by telling two different but inseparable stories about our being created in our being born: one a story about our being created as living human bodies, and the other about our being created in being loaned a living human body for whose orientation toward, and practices in, its proximate contexts it is accountable. I promoted the phrase "personal bodies" as a placeholder for the entire set of remarks about what we are in virtue of God's double way of relating to us creatively, at once directly and indirectly. It follows from those remarks, I urged, that personal bodies are the glory of God *both* insofar as they simply are living human bodies *and* insofar as they orient themselves in their proximate contexts in ways that are appropriate responses to the peculiar way in which God has already related to them creatively. In regard to the former, I proposed, lies their flourishing in the sense of "blossoming," whether in health or unhealth, simply as the living bodies they are. In regard to the latter—that is, in orientations and practices that are shaped as appropriate responses to the way in which God relates to them, I proposed, lies their creaturely flourishing in the sense of "thriving," having themselves in hand. And the fitting name for the fundamental attitude comprising such orientations and practices, I suggested, is faith.

These remarks in response to the "What?" question suggest further remarks in response to the other two perennial anthropological questions: "Who are we?" and "How ought we to be?" I turn to them now.

Senses of Personal Identity

I have characterized the questions "Who am I?" "Who is she?" and "Who are we?" (asked by members of a community about that community) as questions about personal or, in the last case, communal identity. What is being requested is a description of a personal body, possibly oneself, or a description of a community of personal bodies, that is maximally adequate to her, his, my, or their concrete uniqueness across time in various circumstances precisely as a personal body or a community of personal bodies. An important clue to the sense of "identity" intended here is the fact that answers to "Who?" questions that are deemed maximally adequate to precisely personal (or communal) identity are normally given in selected types of stories about the personal bodies or communities of personal bodies in question. The types of stories told to describe a personal identity are selected because they do two things (see Frei 1975, chaps. 4 and 9).

On one side, they are selected because they tell what a personal body is like without contrasting or comparing her to other personal bodies. Instead, the stories are selected because they tell of intentional actions the person has done in certain circumstances, or has undergone in certain circumstances. The stories describe a particular pattern of intentional actions done and undergone by the subject of the "Who?" question. Let us call these patterns of intentional action done or undergone in certain circumstances "patterns of intentional interaction." The stories are selected because what they narrate her doing in particular circumstances as she interacts with other personal bodies "was just like her." The stories, we say, capture "who she most basically was." "That was Jane through and through. In doing that," we say, "she was most truly and fully herself." "You want to know who St. Francis was?" we ask. "Here are stories of what he did and underwent in which he was most characteristically himself." "You want to know what the community of ancient Israel was? Here is a story of something it did and underwent in which it was characteristically itself."

Such stories do not describe what a given personal body is like by comparing or contrasting him to other personal bodies. These stories are not selected because the patterns of intentional interaction they exhibit represent or illustrate some condition that, by comparison with others, can be shown to be a condition of humankind as such, or can be shown by contrast to others' stories to be a condition of a specifiable subclass of human person. Rather, such stories describe the subject of a "Who?" question entirely by reference to the subject's own intentional interactions within its given circumstances. The patterns of intentional action they exhibit do not illustrate or represent anything more general; they constitute the personal identity of the subject of a "Who?" question at the time in which the narrated intentional interactions occurred. They may constitute the subject's personal identity at that point in time even when the interactions change the personal body profoundly.

On the other side, stories are selected that express the subject of a "Who?" question, not at a particularly characteristic moment of interaction, but as she or it persists through change across time. They are stories of self-manifestation-in-difference. The differences—that is, the subject's changes—are certainly real; yet the subject remains the self-same subject through the changes. These stories, too, are neither comparative nor contrastive. They are told solely in reference to the subject of the "Who?" question about its own interactions with its circumstances.

Furthermore, they are not told as though the interactions they narrate merely represent or illustrate the "real identity" or "true self" of a personal body that somehow lies "behind," "beneath," or as the "outcome" of the sequence of behaviors themselves. These stories are not told in a way that draws an implicit comparison or contrast between the person's behaviors, on one side, and some underlying identity on the other. To the contrary, these stories are selected as the appropriate ways in which to describe the subject of a "Who?" question precisely because in their very way of telling stories of the subject's interactions they hold together as a single whole a series of diverse behaviors that serve, in their differences, to manifest a persisting unity. Simply by the way in which such stories are told, they render the self-manifestation-in-difference of personal bodies. Such stories render their subjects' personal identities, not behind or at the end of a sequence of actions, but precisely in those actions.

Left at that, however, this explanation of the concept of personal identity remains an ambiguous phrase. What is being asked for in "Who?" questions requires more clarification not only for the discussion of the "Who?" question in this part of the project, but for parallel discussion in parts 2 and 3 as well. To that end it will be useful to distinguish this concept of personal identity from four other senses of the phrase that might be confused with what is asked for in "Who?" questions.

First, "Who is she?" might be confused with a request to identify one person out of a group. That is, it might be a form of the question, "Of all the people at this party, which one is she?" However, where "Who?" questions may be asked equally well of myself as of others, it would make no sense for me to ask the identification question about myself ("Of all the people at this party, which one am I?"). An adequate answer to the "Who?" question intended here might provide a uniquely identifying description by which to pick her out of a larger set, but help in picking an item out of a set is not what is being asked for by the question intended here.

Second, the sense of identity intended by a "Who?" question is not mathematical or strict logical identity. "Who is George Washington?" is not a poorly framed form of the question, "Is George Washington identical with the first president of the United States?" Nor is "Who am I?" an obscure form of the question, "Am I identical with the eldest child of Mildred and Hugh Kelsey?" The answers to the latter two questions are undoubtedly, "Yes." However, what constitutes "identity" in the phrase "personal identity" is more complex, marked by genuine change across time while remaining self-same. Such identities are identities in the loose sense of "identities-in-difference," not identities in the strict sense of simple logical or mathematical identity.

Third, the sense of personal identity intended by "Who?" questions might be confused with the psychological phenomenon sometimes referred to as a "self-image." The psychological notion of a self-image is thought to be a useful psychological diagnostic tool. Persons' self-images may be either unconscious or conscious, or both in different respects. In either case, they may be realistic or distorted. Distorted self-images are sometimes said to contribute powerfully to persons' dysfunctional and self-destructive attitudes and behaviors. Behaviors and attitudes expressive of distorted self-images are perceived to be misleading about who that person really is. They tend to prompt the question, "Who is he *really*?" and, in cases of extraordinarily perceptive self-reflection, "Who am *I* really?" Such questions presuppose a distinction between the misleading picture of personal identity in a distorted self-image, on one side, and a "real personal identity" on the other. As we have seen, the sense of personal identity assumed by "Who?" questions refers only to the latter.

Fourth, the sense of personal identity asked about in "Who?" questions is not necessarily the sense of identity assumed by philosophical discussions of the question, "What constitutes the perduring identity of a temporal and physical entity across time and through change?" That question is a standard and important topic for projects in systematic metaphysics. Widely debated answers, for example, propose that what constitutes the perduring identity of a human being through temporal and spatial changes is that throughout it has one and the same soul, or that it has one and the same physical body and set of memories, or that throughout it is one and the same substance of which locations in different places and moments of time are merely changing accidental properties. The answers that philosophers propose are metaphysical principles of identity. In the case of the illustrations, the proposed metaphysical principles of identity are, respectively, soul, physical body and memory, and substance. Each of them is given its precise meaning by the systematic metaphysical theory of which it is a part.

Metaphysical principles of identity may or may not also be answers to the "Who?" question in view here. It depends on whether the answer proposed by a systematic metaphysics construes the identity of any given personal body as an illustration or representation of something that somehow lies behind or beneath or as the outcome of the person's (or community's) history of interactions. If the proposed answer does that, it is addressing a question about identity that uses the term "identity" in a different way than it is in the "Who?" question in view here. For the personal identity in question here is an identity-in-difference, an identity that is not one of several possible illustrations or representations of more basic universal principles that somehow underlie or transcend change and difference. Answers deemed adequate to "Who?" questions doubtless bear implications for the metaphysical question. Conversely, the philosophical inadequacy of certain answers proposed to the metaphysical question may well suggest ways in which certain answers proposed to the "Who?" question are also inadequate. Nonetheless, the sense of identity addressed by the metaphysical question is not the same sense of identity as that addressed by "Who?" questions.

The "Who?" questions discussed in this and subsequent parts of this anthropology request a description of the identity of a personal body, possibly oneself, in a sense of the term "identity" that is not necessarily exclusive of any of the other senses of "identity." The personal bodies or communities of personal bodies of whom "Who?" questions are asked no doubt can be picked out of larger sets, are strictly identical with what is described in uniquely identifying descriptions of them, do have self-images that may be distorted, and their perdurance through time and change may be constituted by a metaphysical principle of identity. Nonetheless, the sense of identity assumed by "Who?" questions is importantly different from each of these alternatives.

Who We Are as God's Creatures

According to mainstream canonical Wisdom's theology of creation, God relates to us creatively in a twofold performative and self-involving address. On one side, by God's direct address we are each created part of a society of interacting beings. Irreducibly other than one another, creatures constitute a society of networks of interactions of giving and receiving in which they are ineluctably interdependent in a wide variety of ways. All together they are radically dependent for both reality and value on God's continuous creative relating to them. So their relating with God constitutes something like a society with a certain institutional structure, in which God gives and creatures receive reality and value and in which creatures give and God receives their response to God's giving. On the other side, by indirect address through the medium of the quotidian, God calls human creatures to be wise in their practices. Thus, more by its canonical editing than by the materials thereby formed into a literary whole (or so I argued in chap. 4B), Proverbs makes the anthropological claim that the very context into which human creatures are born places them in a vocation. A personal body's appropriate response to this call to be wise, I urged in chapter 7, is faith as trust in and loyalty to the triune God as the ground of her reality and value. Engaging all of a human creature's powers, faith is one way in which a personal body, responding appropriately to the peculiar way in which God has related creatively to her, is the glory of God precisely by glorifying God.

Granted the limitations of the root analogue of "divine address," understanding our creatureliness in ways guided by canonical Wisdom literature's creation theology does nonetheless bring with it two interrelated answers to the question, "Who are we as God's creatures?"

In that God creatively addresses us directly, the answer is: we are finite creatures empowered by God to be and to act, to give and to receive in our own places and times, creatures whose personal identities are defined by our responsive trust in God. Faith as trust is the attitude that "who I am" is this: one radically given to by God. The giving is radical, at the root (Lat. *radix*) of my being. It is the giving, not of this or that power or experience, but of finite reality other than God, sheer thereness.

Second, in that God creatively addresses us indirectly through our everyday proximate contexts, the answer to the "Who are we?" question is: we are finite creatures called by God to be wise for the well-being of the quotidian, including ourselves; hence our personal identities are appropriately reflected in our responsive loyalty to God's own loyalty to the quotidian and its well-being. Faith as loyalty is the attitude that who one is, is defined by nothing other than the triune God's free and hospitably generous gift of reality within a society of interdependent finite beings genuinely other than God, constituted in being as a society by God's call to respond wisely to God's giving of reality, a society to whom God gives the space and time to live out their socially interrelated responses to God, a society to whose well-being God is self-committed.

The second of these answers means that I am not radically given to in a primal isolation, but only as a member of the interrelated society of creatures. Hence, my personal identity is inherently an identity *in and through* relations of giving and receiving with fellow creatures. Thus, I have my personal identity only in giving to others, so that they are to a certain degree inherently dependent on me, and in being given to by others, so that I am inherently dependent on them. As one radically given to, I am at once a finite giver and receiver, at once depended on and dependent upon others. If trust in the triune God defines my personal identity, it orients me in a distinctive way to my proximate contexts, making it clear that personal identity defined by faith as loyalty to God is inherently world-affirming and not world-denying, defining us as creaturely citizens of the quotidian and not as creatures who are citizens of some other, transcendent, and far better world who are merely passing through this one.

This is the appropriate attitude to our proximate contexts to the extent that it is an attitude of trust in and loyalty to the way in which God's own self-commitment to the same contexts expresses God's glory. Probably the most apt characterization of faithful persons' attitude to their proximate contexts is reverent and awed doxological gratitude for hospitable generosity of God's gift of those contexts. Reverent and awed doxological gratitude is the context of the fear of the Lord that is the beginning of wisdom.

It expresses the glory of God by glorifying God. According to John Calvin, glorifying God by doxological gratitude is what it means to image God as we were created to do (1960, 1.15.3; see Gerrish 1982, 154). The entire life of those oriented to their proximate contexts in doxological gratitude is a complex act of referring all things to God. As the epigraph to this chapter says, such lives "would not make sense if God did not exist."

In this way, too, personal bodies who so take themselves in hand as to flourish—that is, so as to be personally defined by faith as trust in and loyalty to the triune God's creative project—are, derivatively, themselves the glory of God. However, while responding to God in doxological gratitude is one aspect of the way in which personal bodies are the glory of God, it does not constitute their personal identities. Theologically speaking, human persons' identities are given them by God and are not achievements constructed by their own effort, not even their efforts to respond appropriately to God. Such identities are most aptly described in certain stories of interactions that personal bodies undergo rather than ones they enact—namely, stories of God relating to them creatively in both direct and indirect address.

Thus, personal bodies' identities are given to them by God in two interconnected ways. Question: "Who are we as God's creatures?" Answers: "We are those radically given to by God," and "We are those called by God to be wise for the well-being of our proximate contexts, including ourselves." The interconnections between these two answers are important.

On one side, the second answer to the question, "Who are we as creatures?" serves to specify the first. It specifies that because God's address to us is inseparably both indirect through our proximate context and direct, we are called and empowered by God not merely to be, but to act; not only to receive, but to give; not solely and "spiritually" for and to God, but more broadly for the well-being of our very material proximate contexts that are God's own projects.

On the other side, the first answer to the question radically qualifies the second in at least two ways. First, the only "I" who can be safely called to be wise for the well-being of the quotidian is one who is radically given to directly by God and who is, therefore, radically dependent on the Divine Giver. Those whose personal identity is framed by appropriate intentional response to God relating to them in that way are under perpetual injunction not to confuse their response to the call to be wise for the well-being of the quotidian with a seizure of autonomous sovereignty over their proximate contexts to exploit them to their own advantage, and they are under a perpetual demand to surrender false pretensions to such sovereignty when they do confuse the two.

Second, the first answer to the question, "Who are we as creatures?" makes it clear that while I have my personal identity only in and through relations with other creatures of giving and receiving, my personal identity is not given to me by them in their assessment of me and it does not depend on their judgments of me. My personal identity is free of them, grounded elsewhere. I am radically given to directly only by the triune God. Faith as trust responsive to God's giving is the attitude that my right to be and act, and the justification of the time and space I take up being and acting, is not contingent on my meeting the needs or acquiring the approval of any of those finite others to whom I give and from whom I receive in the society of creatures. Faith is the attitude of trust in God's radical giving of reality as alone definitive of my personal identity: a finite creature called and empowered to be, to act, and to give in my own place and time. Your personal identity is defined by God alone and not by any creature. It is eccentrically grounded and defined.

Faith, Doxological Gratitude, and Existential Hows

A personal body's appropriate response to the triune God's call to be wise, I urged in chapter 7, is faith as trust in and loyalty to the triune God as the ground of his reality and value. Engaging all of a human creature's powers, faith is one way in which a personal body, responding appropriately to the peculiar way in which God has related creatively to him, is the glory of God precisely by glorifying God.

Faithfulness to God's creative relating to us involves an attitude to our proximate contexts that is best described, I suggested, as the "fear of the LORD": reverent and awed doxological gratitude. Reverent and awed doxological gratitude to God for our proximate contexts is appropriate both to the hospitable generosity of God's free creating and to God's own self-committed loyalty to the society of creatures constituted by God's creative address.

Part of the point of stressing that faith is trust in and loyalty to the Father in the power of the Spirit is to underscore the theological importance of certain cautions in the use of the notion of existential hows. At least since Kierkegaard's use of it as a quasi-technical term, "how" has come to have distinctive meaning in existentialist and existential-phenomenological theory, both religious and secular. There, broadly speaking, it is often used to refer to the way in which a personal body in her concrete particularity actively disposes of herself in, orients herself toward, and situates herself within the concrete particular proximate context in which she finds herself. She does not have actual concrete existence except in some such setting. However, her existence in that setting is not simply a given. It is a task. Indeed, in these intellectual traditions it is only her act of taking charge of how she situates herself subjectively in her setting that constitutes her concrete existence.

In much existentialist thought, the idea of existential hows supposes (a) that the power definitive of human persons as persons is the power to be so freely self-relating that they can determine for themselves the way they are situated in their contexts by their own free existential decision; (b) that this self-relating is an act of personal consciousness or "subjectivity"; (c) that the hallmark of subjectivity is an ontologically ungrounded, and in that sense absolutely free, self-determination of consciousness; and (d) that each person's how is constituted individualistically in a radically free and solitary act of decision. Indeed, the criteria by which each existential how must be assessed are (1) whether it clarifies and intensifies, or obscures and diminishes consciousness; and (2) whether it preserves and enhances, or subverts, ontologically ungrounded free self-determination.

My use of "how" in a theocentric account of human flourishing is designed to acknowledge that, as those who are accountable for the responses of their borrowed living bodies, human creatures are indeed accountable for so taking themselves in hand that their way of being set into any proximate context is an appropriate response to the way in which the triune God has already related to them creatively.

However, stressing that this is a response "in the power of the Spirit" underscores three Christian convictions that substantially modify three conventional existentialist suppositions.

First, to say that faith is a response to God "in the power of the Spirit" reminds us that *what* is constituted in reality by God's wise utterance addressed, both directly and indirectly, to a personal body "in the power of the Spirit" is a receiver of a borrowed living personal body for whose responses she is accountable to God. Among that living body's powers are some that, because of their interconnectedness with one another, may be conceived together as her powers of consciousness or subjectivity. But that which responds appropriately to the triune creating God is not simply a center of consciousness or a subject (not even a subject constituted by intersubjectivity), but an objective personal body with a far more complex set of powers than just those constituting "consciousness," complex as they are. Theocentrically speaking, "human person" cannot be easily resolved simply into "center of consciousness." Hence, the "hows" we speak of are not just modalities of subjectivity. They are concrete ways of being self-situated in proximate contexts that involve all of a personal body's entire array of powers.

Second, my use of "how" in theocentric contexts substantially modifies apparent tendencies in parts of the existentialist tradition to construe the subjective act that constitutes any given existential how as a conceptually unformed decision, a purely volitional mental act independent of and prior to any conceptual cognitive mental act. In contrast to that, to say that faith is a response to God "in the power of the Spirit" reminds that personal bodies' acts are always conceptually formed by the communities of which those personal bodies are members and by their traditions. The "Spirit sent from the Father with the Son" is the triune

God circumambient in communities of faith, working among other media through the communities' traditions of speech and action to form personal bodies' identities. The forming is conceptual. Persons whose identities are defined by faith in God are accountable in their onliness, one by one but not alone or in isolation, for the ways in which they situate themselves in their proximate contexts. However, the ways in which they are self-situating are not of their own private devising, utterly unique to each person. Rather, they are conceptually formed by the faith community's shared practices of speech and action, where "practice" means a socially established cooperative activity that is complex and internally coherent.

Recall some ways in which this notion of practice is loaded with theoretical commitments: (1) "Activity" means, not human bodily behavior generally, but intentional behavior in which act and intention are dialectically related; (2) intentional actions are practices when they are socially established, cooperative interactions that (3) are coherent, (4) have goals but not necessarily products, (5) intrinsically have standards of excellence, and (6) can be all of the above (socially established, coherent, goal-oriented, and with standards of excellence by which they are assessed) only insofar as they are conceptually formed. Accordingly, although what communities of Christian faith deem to be appropriate practices of speech and action in response to the triune God's way of relating to them may change as their proximate contexts change over time, they cannot be changed by individual private fiat. They can only be changed as the community's practices through processes involving the community's use in its public life of a common language to express the array of concepts that give form to that shared public life. That array of concepts is used to define, differentiate, and warrant a range of ways in which personal bodies may be self-situated in their proximate contexts as expressions of appropriate response to God relating to them creatively.

Each person may have his own idiosyncratic variation on the range of ways of being situated in any given shared proximate context that are made available by the communal traditions he shares. But he could have a privately unique how only if he had a genuinely private language of Christian faith which he could use to formulate truly unique concepts, ones only he could grasp, to give definition to his peculiar way of situating himself in his proximate context. But a purely private language of Christian faith is a self-contradiction. Consequently, while each personal body is accountable for the concrete way of being situated in any given proximate context—a how he appropriates from an array of possibilities made available by the community with which he has identified himself—faith's hows themselves are not given definition by each person's individual and utterly private decision. Rather, they are given definition by the practices of speech and action that constitute the common life of their community of faith lived in the power of the Spirit.

Third, my theocentric use of "how" substantially modifies the apparent tendencies of parts of the existentialist tradition to construe the subjective act that constitutes any given existential how as radically autonomous. To say that faith is a response to God in the power of the Spirit reminds us that God's continuous direct and indirect creative relating is the condition not only of personal bodies' reality, but also of their activity.

It would be insufficient to construe God's creative relating to human persons as the ungroundedly free divine positing of ungroundedly free creaturely self-positers, as though God's direct creative relating to creatures, including finitely free human creatures, were not a continuous relating that constantly impinges on the intentional interactions that constitute their ongoing practices. When it is evident, the view that God does not constantly relate to personal bodies in their practices would seem to be an existentialist version of classic deist construals of God's creativity in which, once God grants creatures objective reality other than God, God ceases actively to relate to them in their acting.

Nor is the triune God's continuous creativity inversely related on a sliding scale to finite personal bodies' intentional interactions, as though the more God acts, the less space and time creatures have to act, and vice versa. On the contrary, the two need to be thought of as ontologically correlative. The notion that human personal bodies' existential freedom is only conceivable as ontologically ungrounded freedom is flatly rejected. Appropriate human response to God is necessarily free human personal action in the power of the Spirit. Dependency on the triune God in the *taxis* "the Spirit sent with the Son by the Father" is an ontologically necessary condition of the free self-determination of genuinely finite human persons of faith. In that framework, enacted faithfulness to God is itself a gift of God.

With these three modifications of familiar existentialist uses of the word "how," we may say that the attitude of faith is lived out concretely in certain existential hows that are expressive of doxological gratitude. Indeed doxological gratitude may be lived out in an indefinitely large number of concrete hows, for they vary not only with the set of human powers they engage but also with the particularities of their concrete proximate contexts, which constantly change.

Hovering over this entire discussion of doxological gratitude is the dark cloud of possible ridicule. Commending doxological gratitude too easily sounds like an endorsement of continual and really annoying utterances of pious remarks, regardless of circumstances: "God be praised" uttered as the sheriff serves foreclosure papers on your home, "Thank you, Jesus" as the furnace breaks down on the coldest night of winter. Far worse than prompting annoying displays of piety, it may sound like a theological imperative that persons undergoing the horrific bodily pain and emotional suffering of advanced cases of HIV/AIDS, bone cancer, and the like must nonetheless be doxologically thankful for their condition if they are to be faithful to God relating to them creatively. Pastorally, such an admonition would be profoundly faithless to the patient and, in suggesting that God "sent" such a condition, blasphemous. However, commendation of reverent and awed doxological gratitude does not necessarily imply or endorse such remarks. Two considerations bear on this.

Recall, first, that doxology is the appropriate response to God's glory in Godself, or more exactly, the appropriate response to the hospitable generosity of the triune God's glory *in se*. Further, on that basis, doxology is appropriate response to the (derivative) glory—that is, the hospitable generosity—of God's creative relating to all that is not God. It is not praise for anything God has done, does, or will do for us in the events of our lives, not praise for God's providential governance of creation. Rather, it is praise for creation's ultimate context.

Recall, second, that gratitude, precisely as doxological gratitude, is appropriate response to God for the glory of God expressed in our proximate contexts. It is thanks for those proximate contexts, including fellow human creatures whose practices in large part constitute them, as expressive of God's glory and thus as themselves derivatively the glory of God. But, to be concrete about it, that means it is doxological gratitude for our proximate contexts in their quotidian finitude. It is just that everyday finitude that is derivatively the glory of God. But that means that appropriate response to God includes doxological gratitude for our proximate contexts in their experiential ambiguity, since their finitude is at once the possibility of our proximate contexts being good for us and the possibility of their damaging us, both in ordinary, bad enough ways and in horrendous ways. Doxological gratitude, then, is gratitude for the sheer thatness of our proximate contexts, including ourselves, for what they concretely are; it is distinctly not necessarily gratitude for everything human creatures do and undergo in those proximate contexts. Pious self-expression and Christian admonition or pastoral care that fails to observe these distinctions are distorted expressions of doxological gratitude and are faithless pastoral care.

Recall, also, that personal bodies express doxological gratitude in their practices only insofar as they receive living human bodies from God and are accountable for the ways in which they respond to God. Insofar as they simply are living human bodies, it is the living bodies themselves that express the glory of God. Consequently, doxological gratitude may be expressed in a multitude of ways made possible by personal bodies' array of powers: powers of intentional bodily action, of forming determinate emotions and passions, of learning and knowing, of cultural creativity (including the creation and maintenance of social institutions), of imaginative self-expression in many media, of creating and fostering interpersonal relations, and the power of using language. Furthermore, to express doxological gratitude, these powers may be exercised in differ-ent ways in different circumstances at different times. The multiplicity of concrete ways in which personal bodies may express doxological gratitude is thus a function of both the rich multiplicity of powers that personal bodies have and the variety of bodily, social, and cultural circumstances in which they may exercise those powers over time. Moreover, among the differing circumstances in which doxological gratitude may be expressed are circumstances of limited or diminished human powers. When certain of a personal body's powers do not develop as they normally do, or when they are lost, she may express doxological gratitude by other powers, per-haps without speaking at all. If her powers are profoundly diminished in her undergoing horrific evil, her ability to respond to God in doxological gratitude is diminished and she is not accountable before God and her neighbors for doing so. Under such circumstances, it is no distortion of her trust in and loyalty to the triune God when she ceases to express doxo-logical gratitude by engaging in cooperative practices.

Granted these qualifications, then, we may say this: each concrete way in which a personal body does orient herself to and situate herself within her proximate context may be called her "existential how" at that moment. When it is shaped by faith's loyal response "to the Father through the Son in the power of the Spirit," any such "how" may be a concrete expression of doxological gratitude.

Flourishing in Faith: How We Are to Be on Borrowed Breath

No inventory of hows expressive of faith is possible. However, what faith is loyal to is at once that to which the triune God is self-committed by the Father's creative address "through the Son in the power of the Spirit," and the peculiar way in which the triune God relates creatively both directly (the interplay among wisdom, freedom, and hospitable generosity) and indirectly (the call to be wise mediated by our proximate contexts). The intersection between these two generates a rough three-part typology of existential hows expressive of doxological gratitude. Each of the three types of existential hows is enacted in a type of practice of Christian com-munities of faith.

1. *Practicing wonder.* One type of faithful persons' existential hows is the practice of wondering at that which God has given them as fellow giv-ers and receivers in their shared proximate contexts. Wonder at fellow creatures is gratitude's doxology in which God's creaturely gifts are each and all referred to God. It is a way of being loyal to the fellow creatures to whom God is loyal simply by being attentive to them, attending to them in their concrete particularities. To attend wonderingly to fellow creatures in their concreteness is to attend to them not only in their radical depen-dence on God across time but also in their interdependence with fellow creatures across time.

The "across time" qualifications are essential. To attend in wonder to fellow creatures in their concreteness is to wonder at the pastness of their present, to wonder at them in the network of relationships out of which they have become what they are, to attend to them as temporally changing creatures.

Learning to practice wonder involves discipline. It is hard-won partly because wondering is a complex practice.

(a) It involves learning a certain respect for fellow creatures in their own right, for their gift-character, for their sheer given otherness to oneself and to each other. Learning to respect them for their own sake means learning to set aside one's own interests, which focus our attention to fellow creatures on their possible utility for us. The discipline of learning to respect them just as what they are in their everyday otherness is thus partly an ascetical discipline cultivating a disposition to transcend one's interests in the other's possible utility. As a way of being loyal to the project to which God is self-committed, it is also partly a moral discipline cultivating a disposition to let the fellow creature be in its own right.

(b) Learning to wonder at fellow creatures also involves learning to attend to them in certain sensory ways. Wonder's sensory attending is not a blank stare or untutored hearing. It attends to a fellow creature in its concrete particularity *as* God's creature—*in* God's relating to it. Here sensory perception and conceptual mastery interpenetrate in a certain aesthetic experience. Learning to attend to an "other" in its concrete particularity as God's creature involves cognitive discipline to master—for example, the concept of creature. It also involves aesthetic discipline to cultivate capacities to see, hear, smell, and touch fellow creatures as they are actually given and not in ways preformed by conventional stereotypes.

Here it is critical to distinguish between, on one side, the quotidian in the sense of the everyday lived world that is, by God's creativity, our proximate context, and on the other side the quotidian in the sense of hackneyed experience. The latter is aesthetic attention to a creature as an instance of a stereotype that abstracts it from its concrete particularity as, precisely, God's creature. In an essay on "The Loss of the Creature," novelist Walker Percy captures the difference between these two types of aesthetic experience. He contrasts the experience that García López de Cárdenas had when he first discovered the Grand Canyon and wondered at the sight, and a modern sightseer's experience of the canyon. It is almost impossible for the latter to gaze directly at the canyon, Percy says,

> because the Grand Canyon, the thing as it is, has been appropriated by the symbolic complex which has already been formed in the sightseer's mind . . . The thing is no longer the thing as it confronted the Spaniard; it is rather that which has already been formulated—by picture postcard, geography book, tourist folders, and the words *Grand Canyon*. As a result of this preformulation, the source of the sightseer's pleasure undergoes a shift. Where the

wonder and delight of the Spaniard arose from his penetration of the thing itself, from a progressive discovery of depths, patterns, colors, shadows, etc., now the sightseer measures his satisfaction *by the degree to which the canyon conforms to the preformed complex. . . .* The highest point, the term of the neighbor's satisfaction, is not the sovereign discovery of the thing before him; it is rather the measuring up of the thing to the criterion of the preformed symbolic complex (1975, 47, emphasis in original)

which abstracts it from its concrete particularity.

Stereotyped perceptions are preformulated in that they see and hear the other as one among many possible instances of some one already-formulated type, rather than in its unique concrete particularity. Such perceptions are literally prejudiced in the pejorative sense of the term. They are prejudged to be just more instances of the same type of perception expressed by a stereotype. Just as the pejorative sense in which such hackneyed perceptions are "quotidian" must not be confused with "quotidian" in the positive sense of the everyday lived world that is our creaturely proximate context, so, too, the pejorative sense in which such perceptions are prejudiced must not be confused with the positive sense in which, as Gadamer (1990, 277–307) argued, "prejudice" is a condition of understanding in the "human sciences."

Learning to wonder at fellow creatures involves both a conceptual discipline and an aesthetic discipline that together capacitate one to pay sensory attention to fellow creatures in their concrete actuality without assimilating them to preformulated types. For persons also shaped by a consumerist culture dominated by the powerful stereotyping images in which creatures are packaged for merchandising purposes, learning to wonder will also involve ascetical disciplines that liberate them from the grip of such images on their sensory perceptions.

(c) Learning the practice of wonder at fellow creatures also involves learning to be curious about them in a certain way. It is a committed rather than idle curiosity. As one type of existential how seeking to be loyal to God's loyalty to creation, wonder at fellow creatures involves a curiosity about them that is committed to their well-being. It is a passion to understand them ever more truly, a passion for inquiry. However, it must be a disciplined passion. If it is going to yield deepened understanding of fellow creatures, such curiosity involves the intellectual discipline that cultivates capacities for critical and self-critical inquiry publicly conducted and honestly reported.

It is also a curiosity committed to understanding fellow creatures in their particularities. Learning to be curious in this specific way involves a discipline that cultivates a disposition to respect fellow creatures' concrete actuality. Given the nature of disciplined inquiry, this is an odd combination of intellectual and moral discipline. On one hand, the complexity of fellow creatures requires that inquiry must methodologically simplify its subject matter. It must focus on one aspect of its subject abstracted from the others, or the inquiry becomes unmanageable. Such abstractive simplification is as unproblematic in the physical and life sciences as it is in any humanistic inquiry. Nonetheless, abstracting in this fashion means inquiring into the creature taken out of many of its relations with other creatures and entirely out of its relation to God the very relationships that constitute its concrete actuality.

Moral respect for the integrity of the complex actuality of the creature under study therefore requires what we might call the metaphysical disposition to refuse all intellectual moves to equate one or some of the results of various abstractive inquiries with a metaphysical account of the subject's concrete actuality as such. This is, perhaps, doxological wonder's version of A. N. Whitehead's refusal of "the fallacy of misplaced concreteness."

As one type of faithful persons' existential hows, the practice of wondering is a complex of respect for fellow creatures, sensory attending to them, and curiosity about them. Learning the practice of wonder involves moral, conceptual, aesthetic, and intellectual disciplines that form and nurture diverse dispositions to engage fellow creatures in certain ways. None of these disciplines is itself an existential how. Rather, these disciplines shape and nurture human powers to be the competencies persons need in order to situate themselves ad hoc in their proximate contexts in ways that are faithful responses to the way in which the triune God has already related creatively to them.

2. *Practicing delight.* A second type of faithful persons' existential hows is enacted by the practice of delighting in fellow creatures. It is doxology's gratitude for fellow creatures, a practice loyal to God's own wise delight in God's creatures (Prov. 8:31). It is an engagement with fellow creatures as they are given and self-giving here and now. However, delight is not necessarily a spontaneous engagement. As a way in which to respond appropriately to the triune God's creative relating to us, delighting in fellow creatures is a practice that must be learned.

(a) Delight's usual spontaneous and unstudied feel is misleading. What we delight in, and how we relate to it, is conditioned by a multitude of things we have already learned to do, feel, and think. Like the faithful persons' practice of wonder, delight is a complex practice learned through a variety of disciplines.

It involves learning to rejoice in the sheer givenness of fellow creatures. Faithful joy is an affective response not to be confused with euphoria, global elation, or generally "being happy." Nor is it a spontaneous response to others simply in virtue of their otherness. Taken in abstraction from their proximate and ultimate contexts, others are often anything but occasions for spontaneous rejoicing. Joy has a more definite object and occasion. It is an affective response to particular fellow creatures' reality in and for themselves specifically as God's creatures. So it is an affection given definition in part by the discipline of mastering the concept of finite creature. It is also an affective response of praise of God. To look on a fellow creature with joy is a doxological act, so it is an affection given definition in part by the discipline of mastering such concepts as God and creating *ex nihilo*.

However, looking on something or someone, whether with joy or otherwise, can be a disengaged, even distancing act. "I'm so happy for you" does not necessarily entail that I am engaged with you. Delight, on the other hand, is inherently engaged with what it delights in. It is delight that keeps joy in solidarity with what it rejoices over.

(b) Learning to practice delight in fellow creatures also involves learning patience to give fellow creatures their own space and time in which to be themselves. In this way, delight is an appropriate response to God's hospitable generosity in giving us our own space and time in our proximate contexts. Fellow creatures are delighted in, not because of their utility for us nor because they are transparent, or somehow point beyond themselves, to God, but because of the concrete reality that God gives them in the present. Hence, learning to give objects of our delight space and time to be themselves involves a moral discipline that fosters dispositions to engage the objects of delight in ways that preserve and nurture them in their own spaces and times. What this concretely means in practice depends, of course, on the kind of creature in question. Most generally, it means dispositions actively to engage creaturely objects of delight in ways that preserve and nurture both them and their necessary ecological contexts.

Learning this also involves ascetical discipline. My delight is self-destroying if it expropriates the object of delight, making it an extension of my self-defined and self-managed space and time, or if it absorbs the object of delight into myself, making it an extension of my personal body. When that happens, there is no genuine other in which to delight. Learning to practice delight in fellow creatures thus involves ascetical disciplines that check our tendencies to expropriate or absorb the fellow creatures in whom we delight.

(c) Learning to practice delight also involves learning to love properly the objects of our delight. To delight in a fellow creature is to be attracted to it. As delight in a fellow creature, the attraction is a species of desiring love. Of the three senses of love that are conventionally identified by the Greek names *eros*, *agape*, and *philia*, delight's love of fellow creatures is perhaps closest to *eros*.

Agape is defined by God's way of loving estranged creatures that become, in their estrangement, unlovely. It is a committed love that creates, rather than responding to, the beloved's value and persists even when the beloved, in indifference and hostility, is utterly unattractive. Indeed, it persists at the risk of profound cost. Human *agape* in response to God's *agape* can only be a finite imitation of God's love. Delight's love is different in principle because it is responsive to the other's attractive, God-given value.

Classically, *philia* is a reciprocal love between those who have equal status in a hierarchical structure and who are engaged in a common project—say, creating a good society. The equality in question may be abstract, a social or legal status abstracted from the concrete particularities of each party's abilities, resources, and personal history. *Philia* can also be understood as the reciprocal love that can develop among people who have very different social or legal status but are equally dependent on one another in some shared task or ordeal, a small military unit in battle, say, or the crew of a small craft surviving a terrible storm, or a highly competitive athletic team. Or the equality that grounds the reciprocity of *philia* may be understood as the equality that characterizes a certain kind of friendship. Delight's love is different in principle because it is love for fellow creatures in the concrete actualities each is by virtue of God relating to it creatively. The delight whose practice is one type of existential *how* that is expressive of appropriate response to God's creative relating is different from any of these senses of *philia* because it is a love by human creatures *as* creatures for other creatures *as* creatures in their concrete particularity in their own right, and not in regard to status or shared goal-oriented struggle or friendship they share with the one who delights. Creaturely lover and beloved are concretely equal simply by virtue of God's creative relating to each.

Eros has been understood in different ways in modern Christian religious thought. Most broadly, it is desiring love born of need. Otto Piper seemed to identify it with sexual desire or, as he called it, "sexual sympathy" (1941, 34). However, although *eros* includes the sexual desiring with which it is most commonly identified, it is usually understood more broadly in theological contexts as rooted in all of the ways in which human persons are needy because of their relative dependence on fellow creatures and radical dependence on God. Seen in this way, *eros* is a passion attracted to its beloved by the latter's perceived capacity to satisfy some need of the lover.

However, the movement driven by that passion between the desirer and the object of desire is ambiguous. It is on this point that interpretations of *eros* begin to differ substantially. In his enormously influential theological study, *Eros and Agape* (1953), Anders Nygren, following a classical interpretation of *eros* represented especially by Plato's *Symposium*, defines it as the "love of desire" (133). It is the lover's passionate movement drawing the object of love toward, and indeed into, the lover. The love object is attractive because it promises to satisfy the lover's need if only it can be internalized or absorbed by the lover. For Nygren, *eros*'s motive is egocentric. "*Self*-love is the very essence of Eros" (179, 137). Far from being sexual desire, the paradigm of *eros* for Nygren is the intellect's passion to comprehend and order the entire universe, to bring it into itself and subject it to the intellect's control. Even though this intellectual passion ultimately reaches out of this life as "man's way to the Divine" (133), its full movement is one of seeking to draw the divine toward—indeed, into—oneself. Seen this way, *eros* always is at risk of undercutting the otherness of the beloved, whether creaturely or divine.

On another understanding, represented in different ways by Freud (1959) and by Denis de Rougemont's analysis of the roots of modern romantic love in Medieval traditions of courtly love (1956), *eros* is the lover's passionate movement away from herself. De Rougemont defines it as "boundless desire," . . . "a desire that never relapses, that nothing can satisfy, that even rejects and flees the temptation to obtain fulfillment in the world . . . It is *infinite transcendence*" (62). *Eros* differs from sexual desire in that while sexual desire seizes the opportunity to satisfy itself, *eros* understood as Freud and de Rougemont do is precisely a passion for reaching out, not for satisfaction. It would contradict itself if it allowed itself to be fulfilled in this life. At its most extreme, it is a desire for death and self-extinction in the infinitely "perfect" that is "beyond." For *eros* understood in this fashion, the love object is attractive because it promises return to a primordial or transcendental unity from which the lover has been alienated. That original unity may be a preconsciousness oneness with the mother, lost by birth into individuality and regained, at least symbolically, only in death's oblivion. Or it may be a transcendently good substance of which the lover is an alienated fragment whose reunification may be mediated by a love object that points beyond itself to the transcendent Whole. In either case, the lover's passion is driven by an underlying need to be made whole again by reunion with that from what she is alienated. On this understanding, *eros*'s motivation may be as egocentric as it is on Nygren's understanding. But one understands it as a movement pulling to and the other as a movement reaching out to lose oneself. Where *eros* threatens to undercut the otherness of the beloved on the first understanding, it is at risk on the second understanding of undercutting the otherness of the lover.

Part of learning the practice of delight in fellow creatures is to learn to love in a way that is like *eros*, rather than *philia* or *agape*, in being a desiring love attracted by the perceived value of its love object. However, delight's love is a desire for fellow creatures that is born of the lover's doxological gratitude for himself as God's creative gift, quite as much as it is born of doxological gratitude for the beloved as God's creative gift. His gratitude cannot faithfully praise the way God creatively relates to him if it moves him to undercut his own otherness as a personal body by driving him toward self-transcendence into another mode of reality. Neither can the desiring love born of such gratitude. It loves fellow creatures as creatively related to by God, not as actively relating to God in such a way as to be translucent or even transparent media through which the lover may so unite with God as to surrender the burden of concrete otherness. Thus is delight's love unlike *eros* understood one way.

So, too, delight's love is a desire for fellow creatures as partners in the networks of giving and receiving that compose the society of beings constituted by the triune God's creative address. Gratitude for fellow creatures' actuality cannot faithfully praise the way God creatively relates to them if it moves a faithful person to undercut fellow creatures' otherness by absorbing them into the one expressing doxological gratitude. Neither can the desiring love born of such gratitude. It is indeed attracted to fellow creatures because they offer to give what satisfies the creaturely lover's creaturely needs, but it is attracted to them, not as raw materials to be appropriated, exploited, and absorbed by their lover and laying no claims on their lovers. It is attracted to fellow creatures as God's creatures. It construes what it loves as, by God's creativity, renewable resources, offering gifts for the lover's reception, and needing gifts the lover may offer them in return. Thus is love's delight unlike *eros* understood in a second way.

Learning to love fellow creatures in delight at them involves forming the lover's passion conceptually by the intellectual discipline of mastering certain concepts under which the lover construes both herself and the beloved, notably the concept of the creation as a society of beings comprising their interactive giving and receiving from one another, and the concept of creation as a society of beings constituted by God's continuous creative address to them. It involves moral discipline of a lover's passion that capacitates the lover to desire fellow creatures in ways that focus on their interdependency, and not on either party alone or abstracted from the network of their giving and receiving, so as to negate neither the lover's nor the beloved's creaturely otherness.

3. *Practicing perseverance.* A third type of faithful persons' existential hows is enacted by the practice of perseverance with fellow creatures in interactions of giving and receiving within the society constituted by God's creative address. This perseverance is not that which Hebrews 11 celebrates, and of which it takes Abraham to be the paradigmatic instance. That perseverance is a faithful person's steadfastness on a journey to the divinely promised eschatological "city that has foundations, whose architect and builder is God" (Heb. 11:10). Rather, what is in view here is a faithful human creature's perseverance in her vocation to be wise for the well-being of the quotidian which we have understood, following Ecclesiastes, to have no *telos* other than to flourish as itself in all its variety of kinds of creatures. It is a perseverance in loyalty to fellow creatures that mirrors God's loyalty to them even when—indeed, especially when—we and our fellow creatures suffer evil, whether self-inflicted or not. John Calvin (1960, 3.2.17) makes this point strikingly by selecting as the paradigm of faith's perseverance, not Abraham, but King David, who suffers

the grievous evil he brings on himself and his kingdom by murder, adultery, and deceit; expresses in Psalms (which Calvin assumes he wrote, see 3.3.11) a keen sense of his abandonment by God; and nonetheless repeatedly repents and returns to the Lord, persevering in his loyalty to his vocation from God.

Perseverance is doxological gratitude's loyalty to God's call to be wise for the well-being of the quotidian; and therein it is loyalty to and trust in the triune God's loyalty to God's creative project despite God's apparent indifference to, or even apparent abandonment of, the project. On one side it is faith's loyalty in spite of and in face of evil and God's apparent absence. On the other side, perseverance is faith's hopefulness that God's commitment is itself trustworthy and will in time manifest itself.

If to wonder at fellow creatures is to attend to the pastness of their present, and if to delight in them is to attend to their present givenness, then to persevere with them is to be loyal to the future of their present. To persevere with them is to trust that while God's freedom in relating creatively may make it impossible for us to see just how God is being hospitably generous at present, it also invites us to be alert to ways in which God's hospitable generosity will surprise us as a future emerges out of the present quotidian no matter how deformed by evil.

Like learning practices of wonder and delight, learning practices of perseverance with fellow creatures requires discipline. Learning it is hard-won because perseverance, too, is a complex practice. To persevere with the present quotidian is not just to survive in it; it is to act for its well-being in the very midst of its deformities by evil. So, learning to persevere involves the moral disciplines that nurture dispositions to act prudently and justly in the quotidian.

Because it is oriented to the well-being of the present quotidian, learning to persevere with it also involves disciplines of our perceptual, imaginative, and cognitive capacities to nurture competencies for both discernment and vision concerning the quotidian. As noted in chapter 8, discernment requires that perceptual, imaginative, and cognitive capacities be disciplined to be capable of paying close attention to particular creatures, to do so intentionally, and to so in ways that as far as possible set aside self-interest and the biases it introduces, in order to learn what truly makes for their well-being as creatures. And vision engages a range of human capacities to form and hold together a synoptic picture of creatures in their concreteness. That means to discipline our perceptive and cognitive capacities so that they habitually understand fellow creatures, each creature in itself and all together, as creatively related to by God, a picture that refers them all to God.

Learning to persevere also involves discipline of our cognitive capacities in ways that nurture capacities to say with precise, accurate, and full truth just what the condition of the quotidian presently is. Perseverance with fellow creatures in the midst of evil's deformations rests on realism. Willed ignorance, avoidance, or denial of the present quotidian's evil condition subverts perseverance.

Efforts to discipline so diverse a range of human capacities arrayed here are obviously interdependent. Prudent and just acts need to be discerning acts guided by a vision of the quotidian's needs and possibilities as a whole, and both are defeated if they are not guided by truthful accounts of the present condition of the quotidian for whose well-being they are concerned.

Bodily lives whose concrete ways of being set into their proximate contexts are particular enactments of faith communities' practices of wonder, delight, and perseverance are, as Cardinal Suhard said, lives that testify to God's peculiar way of relating to them creatively and "would not make sense if God did not exist."

Identity, Practices, Competencies, and Hows

This part's account of what it is to be a human creature and in what our flourishing consists has yielded accounts of who we are and how we are to be as God's creatures. They are, so to speak, our *what*'s own *who* and *how* to be. We are those who are both radically given to by God's direct creative address and placed in a vocation to be wise for the flourishing of our quotidian proximate contexts by God's indirect creative address. We respond to our vocation appropriately when our response is faithful to God, trusting in and loyal to God's own loyalty to God's creative project. Concretely speaking, we enact our response to our identity-defining vocation in the concrete ways in which we situate ourselves in our proximate contexts— that is, in our existential hows.

As a faithful personal body's particular way of situating herself within a given quotidian, her how is her particular orientation at a given time and place at once to her proximate and her ultimate contexts. Each such how is concretely shaped in part by the particularities of the given quotidian, but it is also shaped by practices of a community of Christian faith in which she is engaged and by the competencies she has acquired in learning to engage in those practices. Indeed, the concrete way in which she situates herself within the quotidian is an enactment of some of those practices and an exercise of competencies nurtured by the disciplines required to learn them. For those whose personal identities are given definition by faith—that is, by responsive trust in and loyalty to the triune God who relates to them creatively—these are practices of wonder at, delight in, and perseverance with the fellow creatures that make up the creaturely quotidian. Thus, these practices are not themselves concrete hows, but rather types of existential hows that concretely enact the practices in particular and ever-changing contexts.

Learning these practices involves the disciplining of a rich array of personal bodies' capacities. Note how theological address to the questions, "Who are we?" and "How are we to be?" has circled back to the question, "What are we?" My account of who we are as creatures and how we are to be presupposes that what we are simply as creaturely human personal bodies essentially and necessarily includes a certain array of capacities.

However, capacities are not yet competencies. The competencies that must be acquired to learn how to engage in the practices that constitute the life of faith, such as wonder, delight, and perseverance, are not innate. They themselves must be formed by various disciplines. Given that we are creatures radically given to, and hence dependent on, the triune God, they are not learned autonomously in solitary self-discipline.

That they are learned requires the power of the Spirit and, in that respect, they are gifts of the Spirit. That is why the more or less formal disciplines through which they are learned are traditionally called "spiritual" disciplines. More exactly, they are disciplines that properly constitute a creation spirituality since they bear on learning practices definitive of how we, as related to creatively by God, ought to be existentially set within our proximate contexts. The traditional theological name for the entire process of formation, of which this is the aspect related to God's creativity, is "sanctification."

The point to be made here is that the triune God's actively relating to us to sanctify us does not happen apart from God's relating to us creatively. The capacities disciplined in the power of the Spirit to become competencies for the practices in which we communally live out faithful response to God are capacities rooted in our personal bodies. They are not capacities unique to persons of Christian faith that are somehow supernaturally implanted by the power of the Spirit in addition to the capacities given us by God creatively relating to us. They are all part of *what* we are by God's creativity. Hence an exhaustive account of what we are as human creatures would need to inventory all these capacities, itself an exhausting task. And an unnecessary one. It is sufficient to note that this account of how we are to be as creatures underscores the theological reason for remarking on the plasticity of what we are as human creatures. The lives of personal bodies can be formed in the most amazing variety of ways by various types of discipline of their rich and complex array of interrelated capacities.

Such disciplines shape and nurture human capacities into definite competencies, both dispositions and powers to interact in determinate ways in quotidian proximate contexts. I use "act" broadly here to cover acts of intellect, perception, and the affections as well as intentional bodily acts. These competencies have traditionally been called good *habitus* or virtues. In this discussion, several such powers and dispositions have figured prominently: respect, prudence, and justice as virtues of intentional bodily action; truth, vision, discernment, and mastery of Christian concepts of creature, creation, and Creator as intellectual virtues; delight's joy and love as affective virtues. These *habitus* are not themselves "hows" either. Rather, they are the competencies that personal bodies exercise when they situate themselves in their proximate contexts in practices faithful to the triune God's creatively relating to them.

Such competencies, at least those concerning intentional action, are the subject matter of the tradition of virtue ethics. Arguably, intellectual and affective virtues ought also to be part of the subject matter of ethics. However, I do not consider the account given here of how we are to be as creatures to be part of a theological ethics. Theological ethics would need to theorize each of these virtues far more than has been done here. A full-blown theological ethics would require far more reflection to clarify just what counts as a just or prudent or respectful act, what counts as mastering a concept or speaking the truth, what counts as loving another with delight's love. It would likely need to build intellectually on other types of inquiry in addition to a theocentric anthropology. What this section of this theocentric anthropology does provide is a theological conceptual context that a theological ethics might find to be at once an intellectually nurturing home and an intellectually provocative point of departure.

Basic Unsubstitutable
Personal Identity

The concept of personal identity was introduced in chapter 9A and reappears often in each of the parts of this theological anthropology, sometimes explicitly qualified as "quotidian" personal identity, sometimes as "basic" personal identity, sometimes as "unsubstitutable" personal identity, sometimes as both of the latter two. The way in which the expression "personal identity" is used in this theological anthropology was contrasted negatively in chapter 9A with some other well-established uses of the expression "identity of persons," in order to minimize confusion. However, noting what the phrase does not mean in this theological context goes only a little distance to clarify what it does mean. This chapter seeks to explain more fully the phrase and some reasons for using it.

"Personal Identities" vs. "Identities of Persons"

It is no part of this project to defend a claim about what the English word "person" really means in theological contexts or otherwise. Indeed, chapter 7 urged that, for the purposes of Christian theological anthropology, it is wise to avoid altogether the use of the substantives "person" and "self," and more abstract related terms such as "the person," "the self," "personhood," and "selfhood," to name the subject matter of theological anthropology—as in the remark, "Christian theological anthropology elaborates 'the Christian concept of the human person,' or 'the Christian understanding of human personhood,'" Used in that way, "person" and related terms are used to name members of a distinctive class of actual concrete entities. Instead, chapter 7 proposed, it will be less misleading to use the adjectival form "personal" to characterize the task of theological anthropology as the elaboration of a Christian understanding of what makes human creatures "personal creatures." Used in that way, the term "human creature" is used to name members of a distinctive class of concrete entities, and "personal" is used to characterize those entities in a certain way. Part of the task of this chapter is to develop more fully some reasons for adopting these proposals. What is to be noted here is that, given adoption of these proposals, the phrase "personal identities" does not mean "the identities of entities called 'persons.'" Rather, "personal" qualifies "identities" in a certain way, without specifying which entities it is whose identities are thus qualified.

One of the reasons for urging that the proposals made in theological anthropology not be framed as proposals about an entity called "person" is that, in both theological and nontheological contexts, the word "person" has a variety of intelligible meanings. The meanings vary with how the word is used in different discursive contexts and subject to different interests. Each of them is a valid meaning of the term in its context. It is not possible to show that some one of them is what the word "person" *really* means.

In Christian theological contexts, for example, different ways of using the word "person" have developed that are governed by theological interests specific to different theological *loci*:

— In the context of the traditional Christian doctrine of the Trinity, as developed by the fourth-century Cappadocians, God is one substance in three "persons" who are distinguished from each other solely by certain "incommunicable" or unshareable properties—namely, the unique way in which each is related to the other two. It is not clear that this concept of person can be generalized to cover human beings. Strictly speaking, it is a concept of person appropriate only in the context of the doctrine of God because only God is capable of having the eternal generative relations ("begetting," "begotten," "proceeding") that differentiate the three divine "persons." These are relations in being. Furthermore, the eternity of these relations is conceptually inseparable from their nonmateriality. God has no body. Human beings, on the other hand, live in time and have material bodies. Moreover, since the three relations that constitute the divine "persons" in their differentiation from one another are profoundly different from one another, and each is unique to the "person" it differentiates, the word "person" may be ambiguous in this context. The concept of person may be different in each case. If this sense of "person" is to be generalized to cover human creatures as well, it would seem to be possible only by an analogical (or controlled equivocation) use of the term that blurs its equivocal character and is so extended that its illuminating power would be very dim.

— Arguably, Richard of St. Victor retrieves key insights in this Cappadocian analysis in his twelfth-century definition of "person" (in the context of Trinitarian discourse) as "an incommunicable existence of divine nature." For him the "incommunicable existence" of each divine person consists of (1) the fact that it has its existence in itself and not in anything else, and (2) its originating relation—that is, where it has its being from, as understood specifically in terms of Richard's analysis of God's eternally self-giving love. Because neither of these can be shared or communicated with any other, they constitute a distinct divine person. Arguably, this marks a significant distinction between the Cappadocians' concept of person and Richard's. Both may result in controlled equivocations ("analogies") in their uses of "person." For the Cappadocians, the differences in relations of origin that distinguish the divine persons from one another are differences in ways in which the richness of divine being inherently spills over or gives itself as another who is nonetheless divine. Because divine "being" is (in the modern sense of the term) an "impersonal" category and inherently unknowable to finite minds, human beings have no analogues in their own experience or knowledge of themselves that can be used to control the equivocations in this Trinitarian use of the term "person." For Richard, on the other hand, divine being is understood in terms of divine "love" which (in the modern sense of the term) is a "personal" category that has analogues in human experience and self-knowledge. Perhaps on that basis, Richard is able persuasively to sort out similarities and differences among types of divine love that can serve to control equivocal use of "person" in reference to the divine Trinity. If Richard's concept of "divine person" can be generalized to cover human beings, it can only be done by abstracting the defining characteristics of a human person from God's nontemporality and nonphysicality so that they reduce to a human being's personal identity (it has its existence in itself and not in anything else) and its constitution through the "other's" love of them.

— A different theological concept of "person" was explicitly developed in the fifth century by Boethius in the context of traditional christological (rather than Trinitarian) doctrine interested in clarifying the way the Incarnate Son of God is one "person": A person is "an individual substance of a rational nature." In such a concept, a person is not constituted through its relationships to any "other," but only by its individual subsistence as a concrete instance of a particular kind of being—a "rational" kind. While it may clarify questions in Christology by addressing christological conceptual interests, this concept of person would not be adequate in the context of the doctrine of the triunity of the one God. God's (one) nature is itself "individual substance of a rational nature." To define the three divine persons in the same way would yield doctrinal incoherence and polytheism. On the other hand, because it disregards relations as constitutive of persons, this concept does not raise any conceptual issues about the differences between divine and human individuals and may easily be generalized from the Incarnate One to cover creaturely persons such as bodied human beings and nonbodied angels. Perhaps for that reason, it was dominant in much medieval theology and philosophy. Insofar as "rational" (in "rational substance") is understood to be not only the capacity to know truth, but also the capacity for free action, this is a sense of the word "person" that is conceptually open to the claim that human persons are above all centers of agency capable of exercising their distinctive array of powers freely and intentionally in public space. Insofar as the "substance" (as in "rational substance") that is specifically human is understood as "formed matter," this is a sense of the word "person" that is conceptually open to the claim that bodiliness is in some way essential to being a human person. That claim, of course, has been the subject of much metaphysical debate in Christian history. What is significant about this concept of person is that it makes that debate possible.

In the quite different context of legal discourse, "person" is used in yet another way, governed by core legal interests:

— In U.S. law, for example, "person" is used to refer to any member of the class of parties that have standing in the law and have relevant legal rights in relation to a given case, a class that equally includes individual human beings and legally chartered retail corporations like Wal-Mart, financial corporations like Citibank, or manufacturing corporations like Boeing. Conceived in this way, persons are not constituted by their relations, nor are they constituted through the "other." Moreover, while in certain cases human beings may lose their legal status as persons if they can be shown not to be of sound mind, it is not evident that rationality is definitive of corporations' legal standing as persons. It is striking that, insofar as legal standing is the ground of a variety of types of social, economic, and political power, this is a sense of the term that defines "person" in terms of possession of power in the public realm.

Undoubtedly the most influential meaning of the word "person" in the discursive contexts of modern Western cultures has been governed by the Enlightenment's interests in human liberation from arbitrary, unjust, and oppressive authority—that is, from heteronomous, political, social, moral, and religious authorities. Furthermore, as Christoph Schwoebel points out, as it arose in the eighteenth century, the "modern" use of "person" "appeared most prominently under the guise of the theme of the perfectibility of humanity" (1991, 169). Anthropology arose as an independent theological locus in the eighteenth century and was from the beginning framed in terms provided by a distinctively "modern" concept of person:

— This is the concept of person that comes with the Enlightenment's celebrated "turn to the subject": A person is a morally perfectible, autonomous center of self-aware consciousness, in contradistinction to non-self-aware, nonconscious "things" that are subject to physical determinism. A person is a "subject" in contrast to an "object." Insofar as "consciousness" may be—indeed, must be—analyzed in relational terms, this concept of person is open to elaboration in the thesis that persons are constituted through the "other." It is less clear how a concept of person as center of consciousness can be used to develop an account of human persons that systematically includes scientific knowledge about persons as bodied, how and why their living bodies function, and how consciousness is related to their bodies. It is also less clear how a concept of person as center of consciousness can be used to develop an account of human persons, not only as subjects of experiences of personal and nonpersonal others and imaginers of possible actions in the privacy of their subjective interiorities, but as active agents in a public world.

These uses of "person" overlap in many ways and arguably exhibit numerous family resemblances. No doubt there are additional uses of the term. However, it would be wrongheaded to postulate some one core, basic, or essential meaning underlying or shared by all of these senses of "person." There is no basis on which to argue that one or another of these meanings of "person" is the real or true meaning of the term, of which the rest are at best partial distortions or one-sided uses.

It is commonplace, for example, to explain the meaning of the word "person" by observing that the word has its historical roots in the classical Greek *prosopon*, "face," and the Latin *persona*, "mask," which were used to refer to the mask through which an actor speaks or to the role an actor plays. However, it cannot be argued that the real or fundamental meaning of the word "person" is the social role a human being plays, or the more or less stylized self-presentation through which a human being expresses herself or himself to others, on the historical grounds that the origins of the English word "person" are the Greek *prosopon* and Latin *persona*. While it is sometimes illuminating, the etymology of a word does not determine its meaning.

Nor can such a thesis be argued on cultural-anthropological or sociological grounds. There is a highly influential narrative of the development of the modern "category of the person" that grows out of "the work of the French school of sociology," influenced especially by Émile Durkheim, and summarized in a celebrated 1938 essay by Marcel Mauss, "A Category of the Human Mind: The Notion of Person; The Notion of Self" (1985, 1–25). The narrative outlines "the succession of forms that this concept [of "self," *moi*] has taken in the life of men in different societies, according to their systems of law, religion, customs, social structures and mentality" (3).

1. On the basis of the reports of anthropological field studies of the Pueblo of Zuni, American North-West Indians, and Australian traditional cultures, Mauss generalizes that "a whole immense group of societies" (Mauss 1985, 12) construe their common life as a sacred drama and that an individual's name identifies which of the limited number of roles (*personages*) in that drama is his or hers, identifies his or her status in the society, and identifies his or her kinship relations with ancestors who filled the same role, all of which is expressed by the mask the individual wears in social rituals.

2. The next stage is the rise of awareness of "the individual, of his consciousness—may I say, of the 'self' (*moi*)" (Mauss 1985, 13). Mauss thinks there is evidence that this concept first emerged in India, and then in China, but in both cases the "self" was considered to be composite and dissoluble. Rome's is the most important culture to "have made of the human person a complete entity, independent of all others save God" (14). The context of this development is the evolution of Roman law. "'[P]erson' (*personne*) is more than an organizational fact, more than a name or a right to assume a role and a ritual mask. It is a basic fact of law. In law, according to the legal experts, there are only *personne*, *res*, and *actiones* . . ." (14). The fundamental "independence" of human persons from one another (i.e., their individuation) is rooted in the fact that their rights and responsibilities before the law are independent of anything anyone else is or does.

3. This development is reinforced and enriched by the Latin and Greek moralists (200 BC–AD 400) who add to the juridical meaning of *persona* a moral one, "a sense of being conscious, independent, autonomous, free and responsible" (Mauss 1985, 18).

4. Christianity introduces the next step by making a sacred "metaphysical entity of the 'moral person'" (Mauss 1985, 19). Mauss holds that Christianity's stress on the indissoluble "one," first in regard to the divine persons, but then also regarding the church, led to its stress on the irreducible metaphysical

oneness of the human person: "The person is a rational substance, indivisible and individual" (20). Moreover, for Mauss, this Christian concept grounds the unity of the human person in its sacred, although created, soul.

5. The final step to the "category of the 'self'" (*moi*) involves a shift from the person as a metaphysical and sacred being to the person as a "psychological" being (Mauss 1985, 21). It is a shift from conceiving of the person in metaphysical terms related to "substance" to conceiving it in terms related to "consciousness." In such figures of the early Enlightenment as Descartes, Spinoza, and Leibnitz, the person was still conceived in metaphysical categories, although the definitive function of the metaphysical soul was discursive, clear, and deductive thought. Mauss holds that it was the sectarian religious movements of the seventeenth and eighteenth centuries rather than the early Enlightenment philosophers who provided "the basis on which is established the notion: the 'person' (*personne*) equals the 'self' (*moi*) equals consciousness, *and is its primordial category*" (21; emphasis added). Although it embraces current understanding of "the psychological" as the dynamics of the affections, broadly construed, Mauss intends "psychological" to cover more. Kant, the Pietist, "made of the individual consciousness, the sacred character of the human person, the condition for Practical Reason." He posed, "but did not resolve," the question "whether the 'self' (*moi*), *das Ich*, is a category" (22). "It was Fichte," Mauss contends, "who made of it [individual consciousness] as well the *category of the 'self'* (*moi*), the *condition* of consciousness and of science, of Pure Reason" and of all action (22; emphasis added). As the phrases I have underscored emphasize, Mauss seems to be arguing that the distinctively modern "psychological" understanding of the person that arises at the last moment of his narrative not only construes "person" in terms of consciousness, rather than metaphysically in terms of a concept of "substantial soul," but construes consciousness as a "category," presumably in contradistinction to a mere "concept." As he puts it at the end of a one-sentence summary of his narrative, the last moment of the narrative is a move from "person" as "sacred being" to "person" as "a fundamental form of thought and action" (22), perhaps a "transcendental" category that provides the framework that defines the range of application and meaning of all possible statements about the nature of human beings.

Mauss is clear and emphatic that his intent in telling this narrative is to impress on his readers that the concept of "person" has changed profoundly several times across human history. The modern notion of the person may function as a (transcendental?) category for those who are formed by modern cultures, but it is not universal or innate in human consciousness. There are many other possible ways of understanding the person. The modern category of the person is historically very recent. It has developed out of earlier concepts, but Mauss is not, apparently, arguing for any type of logical necessity to that development.

The irony of Mauss's narrative, however, is that it is told in a way that is open to being read as an argument for the superiority and, in some not very clear way, the inevitability of the modern category of the person. This possibility is a function, I think, of the narrative being cast as a retrospective story of a teleological process. It is made a single, continuous process by its *telos*, which is already known at the beginning of the story. That *telos* is the modern psychological category of the person. The story is told retrospectively from the perspective of the realization of its *telos*. That unavoidably gives the impression either that the moments in the process that came before the *telos*'s realization inevitably lead to that realization because they are all organic to the process of the *telos*'s unfolding, or that the narrative is misleading and unpersuasive because the moments have been preselected from a much larger array of data, cherry-picked because they seem most clearly to anticipate or prefigure the distinctively modern understanding. The first impression is reinforced by Mauss's opening observation that "the notion [person; self (*moi*)] has assumed" different "forms" at "various times and in various places" (1985, 2), and by his concluding observation that this type of "social anthropology, sociology and history . . . all teach us to perceive how human thought 'moves on'" (22). Is there some one notion that undergoes a process of metamorphosis over time, perhaps unfolding according to its inner logic? People think, and change what they think. But what does the moving when thought moves on—perhaps reason itself, according to its inner logic? Either way, the essay's narrative reads as though haunted by Hegel's ghost. Mauss's explicit intent for the essay rules out its narrative as the ground for declaring the modern psychological meaning of "person" to be the word's real meaning; the reading the essay too easily invites, however, offers nothing but a bad argument for the same thesis.

One reason for adopting chapter 7's proposal that theological anthropology not be framed as a discussion of the properly Christian concept of person is the variety of valid senses of the word "person" already at work in theological and nontheological contexts, and the impossibility of showing that one of them is the basic or correct meaning of the term. Granted that proposal, the phrase "personal identities" does not mean that the topic for discussion is the nature of the identities of entities called "persons." Rather, as chapter 7 urged, "personal" in the phrase "personal identities" should be understood to qualify in a theocentric way the identities of entities not specified by the phrase itself (but specified in chapter 6 as "actual living human creaturely bodies").

But, it might be asked, why should not a project in Christian anthropology stipulate a technical theological concept of "person"? It need not be claimed to be the real meaning of the word that is fundamental to all other valid uses of the term. It need only be claimed to be the correct way of using "person" in the practice of Christian secondary theology addressing the locus of anthropology.

Excursus: The Power and Inadequacy of the Modern Concept of Person

The major problem with framing a Christian anthropology as a theological concept of person lies in the inherent power and current cultural dominance of the modern concept of person. A theological anthropology will have theological reasons for affirming some of the features of the modern concept that make it powerful. However, in other respects the modern concept of person is finally insufficient to articulate its own Enlightenment interests, and is in any case inadequate to central Christian theological interests. Consequently, a theological anthropology that is framed in terms provided by the modern concept in order to acknowledge and affirm theologically some part of what makes it a powerful concept would also need to modify the concept radically, and in some respects to distance itself from it. The difficulty is that the cultural dominance of the modern concept of person is so strong that it is next to impossible in the context of modern culture to employ its central terms, especially the term "person," in a way that does not also implicate the very features of the modern concept of person that need to be revised or rejected for theological reasons. Readers of, or listeners to, theological anthropological discourse that is framed in terms provided by the modern concept of person will inevitably associate it with, and infer from it, the key assumptions about what it is to be a person that are conventionally ready at hand in modern culture, including theologically problematic assumptions, no matter how skillful the theologian's conceptual strategies may be to set limits to the modern concept so that one goes only so far with it and no further. Analyses by Michael Welker, Hans Frei, and Christoph Schwoebel show ways in which the modern concept of person is powerful and ways in which it is at the same time insufficient to explicate the most important Enlightenment interests it was created to serve and is inadequate to explicate core Christian theological anthropological interests.

In "Is the Autonomous Person of European Modernity a Sustainable Model of Human Personhood?" Michael Welker (2000) characterizes the modern concept of person in ways very like Mauss's characterization of the "psychological" concept of person, although he emphasizes more than Mauss did the theme of autonomy. The parallel with Mauss is neither surprising nor controversial. There is broad consensus about the character of the concept of person that is dominant in modern Western cultures. Welker begins his analysis of the modern concept of person by invoking the origin of the word "person" in the Greek *prosopon* and Latin *persona* that "refer to the mask through which an actor speaks. The expression can also signify the actor who wears the mask, and the role played by the actor" (96). Welker invokes this word study, not to mount an etymological argument in support of a thesis about a singular meaning of the word "person," but as a heuristic device to focus the problem that the modern concept of person has been developed to solve. Welker suggests that "mask" is an illuminating trope for the modern concept of person. "Mask" holds together "the concrete individual (the actor), the typification on the basis of the role, and the condition of being adjusted and attuned to a public spectrum of expectations (the role and its performance)" (96). What is of "utmost importance to modern mentalities" is (1) "the polarity between, on one hand, human singularity and uniqueness and, on the other hand, abstract human equality, as well as" (2) "the mediation between these two poles" (96, 97). Accordingly, the concept of person has to be able to hold coherently together (presumably, that is what "mediating" does) *the individual as a 'unique one' and the individual as 'an example or representative of the species'* " (96), all of which individuals are in some way equal in the abstract and therefore interchangeable, substitutable for one another and hence, apparently, not "unique." "Mask" is a good trope for that mediation; as conceived in the modern concept of person, "The person represents such mediation" (97). Perhaps we may say that, conceived in this way, a person simply *is* the mediation of these poles.

This mediation is complex. Welker shows well how the trope of the mask brings out the complexity. The mediation "has to operate, so to speak, both in front of the mask and behind the mask" (2000, 97). "In front of the mask," an individual person's human uniqueness and her abstract equality with all other individual persons have to be mediated objectively for her outside surroundings and public world. Call this the objective and public dimension of a person. It is a complex task. By it, "the individual mediates to the outside world uniqueness and equality, non-disposability and security of expectations" (97). "Behind the mask," an individual's human uniqueness and equality have to be mediated subjectively and for the inside. Call this the interior and private dimension of a person. By it the individual "mediates and differentiates himself and his perceptions and stylization of himself" (97). The mediating that is necessary "behind the mask" is, if anything, even more complex than the mediating that is necessary "in front of the mask." The mediating of human uniqueness and equality that constitutes the interior dimension of a person is itself inherently self-conscious and therewith self-reflexive. It involves both the differentiation of "I" and "self," as the subject and object of one's self-consciousness of the interior mediating going on "behind the mask," and the mediation of "I" and "self." This differentiating and mediating of "I" and "self" "we attribute to subjectivity" (97). "The person, visualized by the mask, is the interface both determined by and turned towards the outside world, and determined by and turned towards the inside" (97). Welker stresses that conceived this way, a person in both her public dimension mediating "in front of the mask" and her private dimension mediating "behind the mask," "adjusts and attunes herself both consciously and unconsciously in accordance with a broad spectra of expectations . . . " (97). Sometimes these expectations are presented pre-formed by the outside world and simply adopted; sometimes they are presented by the outside world, modified, even transformed, and adopted; sometimes they are presented and resisted; sometimes they are created and adopted by the person herself. Like the "mask," as conceived by modernity the person is at once "the concrete individual (the actor), the typification on the basis of the role, and the condition of being adjusted and attuned to a public spectrum of expectations (the role and its performance)" (96).

Welker warns that the sheer complexity of these mediations means that the modern concept of person is vulnerable to a number of commonsense confusions, mixing up "person, individual, subjectivity, the 'I,' etc." This confusion

> provokes a welter of different one-sided and reductionist conceptions of personhood . . . Very different elements of personhood or constellations of these elements can be grasped as *the* person, or even made the criterion for "the person," such as an unsteady and bizarre individuality following his inclinations (the "post-modern individual"), a subjectivity which gives security of expectations but is socially quite unadapted (the Bogart type), an abstract "I" seeking to become his own self (the identity-search figure), a self turning with the change of public moral pressure (the typical petty-bourgeois individual), or a personality who controls the social environment with a strong sense for resonance (the success-type in market societies), to name only a few. (2000, 98, 99)

Despite such vulnerability to reductionisms, the modern concept of person has "tremendous integrative power" (Welker 2000, 101) with respect to the Enlightenment interests it was designed to serve. Central to those Enlightenment interests are the values of individual human uniqueness, the abstract equality of all human individuals, the autonomy of human individuals, and human perfectibility. In contrast to premodern concepts of person, modernity conceives the person as *not* something simply given, *not* determined by inherited traditional family status and social roles, by traditional class and social structures, or by traditional expectations of one's own social and familial roles and modes of self-presentation. As conceived by modern cultures, a person is autonomous in the sense of being free from all such unquestionable and unchangeable cultural and social determinism. Rather, a person is conceived by modern cultures as constituted by (1) the concrete way in which she mediates or holds together "I" and "self"; (2) the concrete way she interiorly holds together "behind the mask" her individual uniqueness and her abstract equality with every other person as her private dimension, shaped in large part by the set of expectations she adopts to form that concrete mediating that constitutes her private dimension; (3) by the concrete way in which, in the outside world "in front of the mask," she holds together her individual uniqueness and abstract equality with every other person as her public dimension, formed in large part by the set of expectations she adopts to shape that concrete mediating that constitutes her public dimension; and (4), above all, by the concrete way in which she holds together the two acts of mediating that constitute her private and public dimensions.

As conceived by modern cultures, a person is autonomous not only in the sense of being free from predefinition by unquestionable and unchangeable cultural and social determinisms, but also by being free for choices among a large array of different ways in which to hold these polarities together. The corollary of such autonomy is that the

> person of modernity must *continually regain the unity and constancy of the person* by, on the one hand, striving for *coherence in rule-governed self-direction* and, on the other hand, *dominating one's corporeal, sensual nature.* The "agonal self" [the classical Greek concept of person, Welker 2000, 102] is thus interiorized and verifies autonomy in an enduring battle with itself and in a continuous process of triumphing over self. . . . Autonomy has a dynamically exemplary effect on other human beings, inasmuch as it summons them to become increasingly steady and increasingly perfected selves. In theory at any rate, this reciprocal process is supposed to lead to a steady increase in the moral and rational coherence of the entire community. (103)

The cultural power of this modern concept of person has been its capacity to coherently integrate in this manner Enlightenment interests in human individual uniqueness, human equality, human autonomy, and human perfectibility.

That conceptual power makes the modern concept of person attractive to Christian theological anthropology because there is a way in which, like the Enlightenment, it too is interested in stressing human individual uniqueness, human equality, and human freedom—although whether the human freedom it values is isomorphic with Enlightenment autonomy is not so clear—and human perfectibility, at least eschatological "perfection" construed as "sanctification."

Welker points out that this modern concept of the person amounts to the *"subjectification of the person"* (2000, 99; emphasis in original). That is, what is most valued about a person, "what modern consciousness holds to be holy about the person seems to lie behind the mask: self-reference and familiarity with one's own self; the ability to refuse demands from the outside world, to say 'no' and to be self-determining; free subjectivity in her differentiated adjustment and attunement of the 'I' and the self; the free cultivation of individual capabilities in the process of education based on one's own power and authority" (99). Accordingly, were it uncritically appropriated by Christian theological anthropology to provide its conceptual framework, it would amount to the "subjectification" of theological anthropology as well.

In *The Identity of Jesus Christ* (1975, chap. 9, esp. 94–101), Hans Frei offers a brief sketch of a second trope that can serve heuristically to bring into slightly different focus the same set of polarities, and the same mediating of the polarities, that the trope of the mask brings into focus as the structure of the modern concept of person. The trope is "self-expression," if "self-expression" may be understood abstractly as a dynamic of "self-manifestation-in-difference." If Welker's trope of the mask helps explicate the modern concept of person by focusing on the way it addresses interests central to the Enlightenment, Frei's trope of "self-expression" helps explicate it by focusing on the way it addresses interests central to Romanticism (see Lukes 1973, 3–23; C. Taylor 1989, 355–92). Frei's trope suggests that the most apt way to conceive subjectivity—that is, the self-reflexive mediating of "I" and "self," subject and object of self-consciousness—is as "expressivity"; and the most apt way to conceive subjectivity's mediating of individual uniqueness and abstract equality in terms of some set of acknowledged expectations (i.e., the mediating that goes on "behind the mask," which constitutes the interior and private dimension of a person) is "self-expressivity." The "self" is the unique "I's" expression of itself to itself as both unique and equal to all other individuals; and it is framed in terms of a set of acknowledged and generalizable expectations. The trope also suggests that "self-manifestation-in-difference" is the most apt way to conceive the mediating that goes on "in front of the mask," the mediating of individual uniqueness and abstract equality in terms of a set of acknowledged and generalizable expectations in the outside world, which constitutes the objective and public dimension of a person. As a mediating in the outside world of the polarity also mediated interiorly, it is a manifestation in public of a self-expressiveness that is otherwise inaccessible, private to the individual's subjectivity. As an objective public manifestation, it is a manifestation-in-difference—that is, in an objective medium rather than in the immediacy of subjective self-reflective self-presence.

This trope has, perhaps, been dominant in modern Western culture under the influence of Romanticism and the latter stages of the Enlightenment. It is powerful because it suggests a way to conceive the relation between the person-constituting mediating that goes on behind the mask and the person-constituting mediating that goes on in front of the mask (i.e., using terms suggested by the trope of the mask). "Mask" is an illuminating image for an interface, a line at which are simply juxtaposed two different kinds of mediating poles that together constitute a person, according to modernity's concept of person. Beyond that, "self-expressivity" suggests a way to conceive how those two types of mediation are related to each other: They may be conceived as two moments in a single, if complex, dialectic that just is a person. A person is not to be identified with the expressive I. Nor is it to be identified with the self-reflexive dialectic of I and self that constitutes subjectivity. Nor is it to be identified with subjectivity's self-expressive interior mediation, or holding together, of its individual uniqueness and its abstract equality, which constitutes the interior and private dimension of a person. Nor is a person to be identified with its public holding together of its individual uniqueness and its abstract equality, framed in a set of acknowledged expectations, which constitutes the objective and public dimension of a person. Rather, a person is to be identified with the entire dialectic of private self-expressivity self-manifested publicly—that is, "in difference." Furthermore, the dialectic is not to be confused with a process having an internal logic that defines the dialectic as the movement it is in a logically or ontologically necessary way. On the contrary, what the dialectic concretely is in any given case depends on contingent choices about the concrete way in which the I expresses itself to itself and the concrete way in which that internal self-expression manifests-itself-in-difference outwardly.

The trope of self-expression helps focus the reason that the modern concept of person involves the subjectification of the person. If what constitutes a person is the entire dialectical movement of self-manifestation-in-difference, then the person is not to be understood as constituted by a logically and necessarily unfolding process. Rather, it is constituted by a dialectic that is driven by the inherent expressivity of the I. Because in this dialectic self-manifestation—in-difference is by definition an inherent moment in the dialectic constituting a person—it is inherent in the dialectic (and in the person) to be involved in "the different." However, that which is manifested-in-difference is *not* itself integral to the publicly accessible "different." Rather, it is the utterly interior I, inaccessible but inherently expressive, whose self-reflexive self-expressivity constitutes subjectivity, as understood through the trope of the mask. When analysis of the modern concept of person focuses on the expressivity of the I, it clarifies why an analysis that focuses on the interface between behind the mask and in front of the mask shows the concept to be a subjectification of the person because it shows that the concept assumes a certain priority of the behind-the mask-subjective-dimension of the person.

Analysis of the modern concept of person focused by the trope of expressivity brings out another part of the power of the concept. It shows that in addition to powerfully integrating anthropological interests that the Enlightenment most values, the modern concept of person also provides two conceptual spaces in which deep differences among versions of the modern concept of person can emerge without ceasing to be the modern concept.

One such space is opened by the self-reflexivity that constitutes subjectivity itself, the interior act of I expressing itself as self: just how transparent is the I in its self-expression? The modern concept of person leaves space for a range of opinion about this question. At one pole, perhaps best represented by Descartes's formula, "I think, therefore I am," is the assumption that subjectivity is or can be wholly transparent to itself. The "different" in which subjectivity's self-expression is self-manifest may be "objective," but it can consist of transparently clear and distinct ideas. Perhaps the other pole is best represented by Freud, for whom central features of subjectivity are opaque, either obscured or entirely repressed by subjectivity's self-reflexive self-expressivity. The "different" in which subjectivity's self-expression is self-manifested is an objectification of subjectivity's self-expression (in dreams, jokes, slips of the tongue, myths and symbols, conveyed in speech, writing, and the arts) that distorts and obscures what is being manifested, while leaving clues to what it is that is being distorted. It is not so much that the intractability of the media of the self-manifestation makes it unavoidably a distorted and obfuscating manifestation. Rather, self-manifestation-in-difference is anything but transparent because the self-reflexive act of self-expression that constitutes the subjectivity that is manifesting itself is *itself* anything but self-transparent. These two poles, and the differing views that fall between them, are all variations on the modern concept of person as the dialectic of "self-expressiveness-self-manifested-in-difference." They can disagree among themselves because that concept leaves open the question of the degree to which subjectivity's self-expression is transparent.

A second conceptual space for differing versions of the modern concept of person is opened by the phrase "in difference." What are the relevant media of self-manifestation, and just what sort of difference is the "difference" between that which is "self-manifested," on one side, and the medium in which it is manifested, on the other?·Not much help is given toward answering that question by the very abstract remark that it is the difference between subjectivity and objectivity, such that self-manifestation always involves the objectification of the subject. That may be true, but the question is how to understand the difference between "subject" and "object." The "different" is the objective medium in which the subject manifests itself. The open question is just how adequate or how resistant is the objective medium of self-manifestation? Here too the modern concept of person leaves space for a range of opinion. At one pole, perhaps best represented by Romanticism, is the view that self-manifestation-in-difference primarily occurs in a medium consisting of the human body: its facial expressions, gestures, and "body language"; its vocalizing in talk and song; and its shaping of matter in regard to line, color, space, and volume in the various arts. Such media are different from that which is being manifested in being corporeal and publicly accessible, rather than being noncorporeal (spiritual) and privately inward. Such media are not wholly transparent to that which is being manifested in that they do not allow for exhaustive self-manifestation. However, as far as they go, they are capable of serving as the media of genuine self-manifestation. A different type of view holds that the media of self-manifestation include, not only the body as the register of the self-expressivity that constitutes subjectivity, but also the givens of an already structured society and its cultural traditions, including its language and symbol system, and its ways of organizing and distributing social, cultural, economic, and political power and status. Different aspects of different cultures (but not necessarily all) are different from that which is being manifested, not only in being publicly objective rather than privately subjective, but also in that they prove to be more or less resistant to serving as media for self-manifestation-in difference. Indeed, some aspects of at least some cultures prove to be repressive and oppressive of subjectivity's inherent self-expressivity. In this version of the modern concept of person, some but not all of the media of self-manifestation are different from that which is manifested simply in the sense of being objectively and publicly available rather than subjective and privately inward, while others are different in the sense of yielding only objectifications of what is being manifested that profoundly distort them. In the latter cases, the entire dialectic of self-manifestation-in-difference constitutes a concrete person who is constituted as self-alienated and self-contradictory. At the far pole of this range of opinions is the view that all possible media of self-manifestation-in-difference are hostile to subjectivity's self-expressiveness. On this view, objectivity as such is repressive and oppressive of subjectivity. It fundamentally distorts subjectivity's self-expressiveness into that which is nonsubjective. Hence all self-manifestation-in-difference, through the body as well as through all social and cultural givens, is in fact self-manifestation-in-self-contradiction. On this version, since the person-constituting dialectic of self-manifestation-in-difference intrinsically entails the person's involvement in the different, the modern concept of person is inherently a concept of the person as necessarily self-alienated in the full dialectic of its self-manifestation-in-difference. This version of the modern concept of person appears to have strong structural parallels with late antiquity's gnostic and Manichean concepts of of person: The difference between that which is manifested ("subjectivity" in the modern case; "soul" in antiquity) and the medium in which it is manifested-in-difference ("objectivity" in the modern case; "matter" in antiquity) is not merely "differentness." It is the difference between that which is valued and that which is inherently hostile to what is valued. That order of difference easily slips into the difference between good and evil.

Thus, the trope "self-expressive" helps bring out the power of the modern concept of person not only to integrate anthropological themes especially valued by Enlightenment culture, but also to provide a framework in which two types of significantly differing versions of the modern concept of person can be explicated, contested, and defended. This power makes the modern concept of person attractive to Christian anthropology because it provides a context in which to formulate accounts of traditional claims about human fallenness and sin that are coherent with the culturally dominant concept of person. The distorting effects of sin and the fall on human persons can be elucidated as persons' self-alienation in their public self-manifestations. The one exception to this theological attractiveness is the gnostic-like last version of the second type of version, which, if adopted by Christian anthropology, would entail also adoption of a Manichean picture of physical and social reality as inherently evil and no part of God's good creation.

Christoph Schwoebel suggests a third trope that can serve heuristically to bring into focus the same set of polarities, and the same mediating of the polarities, that are focused in different ways by the trope of the mask and the trope of self-expression. His essay, "Human Being as Relational Being: Twelve Theses for a Christian Anthropology" (1991), suggests how the rather more abstract trope of "relational being" (141) can serve heuristically to bring into focus certain features of the structure of the modern concept of person. "Relational being" is an appropriate trope for the set of acts of "holding together"—mediating—the pairs of polarities that constitute the modern concept of person as understood in light of the trope "the mask." Each mediation is a way in which two poles are related: I and self related; individual uniqueness and equality related interiorly in terms of acknowledged expectations ("behind the mask"), constituting the subjective and private dimension of a person; individual uniqueness and equality related publicly in terms of acknowledged expectations ("in front of the mask"), constituting the public and objective dimension of a person; and the subjective and objective dimensions of the person related to each other.

The trope of relational being helps focus the dynamic and autonomous character of the modern concept's subjectification of the person. As conceived by the modern concept of person understood in light of the trope of relational being, each of the mediations that constitute a person is a dynamic act of self-relating (in a nontechnical sense of "self"). Indeed, when understood in light of the trope of relational being, the entire dialectic of self-manifestation-in-difference (which the trope of self-expression shows constitutes a concrete person) is seen to be a complex act of dynamic self-relating. And insofar as that dialectic is driven by the person's subjectivity, it is understood as a fundamentally intrasubjective self-relating. Moreover, as an act of self-relating, the concrete act of mediation could have been made in another way. The person's autonomy is rooted in this ability to relate the mediated poles to each other in different ways, thereby concretely constituting itself as one of several alternative possible persons.

Analysis of the modern concept of person focused by the trope of relational being brings out yet another aspect of the power of the concept. It shows that, in addition to powerfully integrating anthropological interests that the Enlightenment most values and providing conceptual space in which deep differences can emerge among versions of the modern concept of person, not only about the character of the difference between the self's subjectivity and the objectivity of its self-manifestation, but also about just how transparent is the I in its self-expression, it also provides conceptual space for deep differences about the character of its acts of self-relating. The act of self-relating that constitutes the person, as conceived by modern consciousness, may be understood as a subject's act of self-choosing (among alternative ways in which concretely to be itself; cf. Søren Kierkegaard); or an act of self-affirmation (saying "yes" to itself; cf. Karl Rahner); or an act of self-acknowledgment (relating to itself as one already affirmed by God; cf. Rudolf Bultmann); or relating to itself as an act of sheer willful self-assertion (cf. Friedrich Nietzsche); and so on. Differences on this score generate different versions of the modern concept of person. Part of the power of the modern concept of person is its capacity to generate such variations without ceasing to be basically the same concept.

This conceptual power makes the modern concept of person attractive to Christian anthropology because it promises to provide conceptual space in which to introduce a reference to God, a space that is otherwise missing in the modern concept of person. Theological anthropology can appropriate the modern concept of person as a culturally familiar way to think about what it is to be a human being that at the same time offers a culturally intelligible way to explain a theologically central claim about human persons' "God-relation." Concrete acts of mediating the poles that constitute a person—that is, concrete acts of self-manifestation-in-difference—can be construed as acts of choosing oneself as a subject (i.e., choosing oneself as a relation between I and self) that is itself already related to by God in being constituted as a relationship in the first place (cf. Kierkegaard 1954). Or as acts of affirming oneself as a subject (constituted by the relation in self-consciousness between I and self), the horizon of whose self-consciousness is the mystery of holy being, for whom religion's name is "God" (i.e., affirming oneself as a self-reflexive or self-present center of consciousness, one of whose transcendental conditions of possibility is a concurrent unthematized relationship in consciousness to God, an affirmation that is inherently also a "yes" to God; cf. Rahner 1978). Or as acts of acknowledging oneself, in a response to an event of the proclamation of the gospel that is called "faith," as one whose life has been made worth living by having already been related to by God's grace in the concrete event of proclamation (cf. Ogden 1960); and so forth.

Not only does the trope of relational being serve heuristically to bring out aspects of the theologically attractive power of the modern concept of person, it also serves to place the concept in a larger context. Understood in light of the "relational being" trope, the modern concept of person conceives the person as constituted by intrasubjective relations, relations within self-reflexive consciousness between the two poles that must be mediated in several polarities that structure a human person. However, intrasubjective relations are only one kind of relation in which persons stand. As Christoph Schwoebel (1991) points out, the relative abstractness of relational being allows intrasubjective relations to be located in a larger array of types of relations—for example, human persons' relations with "other parts of the animal world and its common microbiological structures" (141); "their social relations to other human beings"; or their creation of "symbolic systems of communication that regulate the relation of human beings to the natural world and their forms of social organization" (142).

Locating the intrasubjectively relational modern concept of person in this larger context helps bring out an important point about all of these modes of relationality: they can be used in anthropology generally, and in theological anthropology in particular, in either nonreductionist or reductionist ways. As Schwoebel points out, "A nonreductionist [anthropological] analysis has to retain a multi-dimensional view of human relatedness, but can nevertheless claim that one specific relation in which human beings exist forms the perspective from which to interpret the others." By contrast, a "reductionist [anthropological] analysis is basically one-dimensional. . . . [It] claims that the dominant relational dimension that forms the basis for . . . [the] approach is the only dimension of human being in the sense that all other dimensions have to be explained as specific developments from the fundamental dimension" (1991, 142). This distinction applies as much to the modern concept of person as to any other. Not only is it vulnerable, as Michael Welker points out, to reductionist versions of itself, its richest and most powerful formulations are also liable to reductionist uses.

Michael Welker and Christoph Schwoebel identify major ways in which all versions of the modern concept of person are unacceptable from a theological perspective. For one, Welker argues, the modern concept's "subjectification" of the person worked well "as long as it took place in environments whose communicative structures were dense and closely connected, and as long as it was directed against powerful, stable and stratified public institutions and hierarchical forms of organization and order . . . The one-sided concentration on the processes behind the mask made sense as long as the conditions existing in front of the mask and with respect to it were densely ordered and relatively clearly definable" (2000, 99, 100). However "withdrawal 'behind the mask'" has become problematic as "strong hierarchical public institutions are substituted by market-type configurations and media-stimulated pluralistic developments" and "human beings have to act in thinly structured or relatively diffuse public environments" (100). Welker finds that these "displacements" were first grasped by North American cultural critics like C. Lash and R. Sennett, expressed in phrases like "the minimal self," "the culture of narcissism," "the decay and end of public life," and "the tyranny of intimacy" (100). When the distinctively modern concept of person is no longer powerful to integrate the core Enlightenment anthropological values it was designed to mediate, it becomes much less attractive as a means by which theological anthropology can elucidate a Christian anthropology that is intelligible and persuasive to people of modern consciousness.

Even if in present social and cultural circumstances the modern concept of person were capable of integrating the Enlightenment anthropological values it was designed to mediate, Welker points out, its subjectification of the concept of person would still leave it unable "to grasp the authenticity of the unique corporeal and sensual person" (2000, 104; emphasis omitted). Moreover, it "underestimates the [historical, social, and cultural] contextuality of morality and the mutability of rationality" (105; emphasis omitted), and "it cannot assign any clearly definable place to the way in which human beings are shaped by modernity's social and cultural processes of differentiation" (105). We may generalize these observations as follows: in subjectifying the person, the modern concept of person has proven incapable of illuminating the relation between the "outer" and the "inner" dimensions of the person and has left itself conceptually unable to integrate the entire "public dimension" of the person (cf., 98).

Schwoebel identifies several additional ways in which all versions of the modern concept of person are not only unattractive but intrinsically unacceptable from a theological perspective. Their unacceptability follows from an analysis of Christian theological anthropology's core claim. From a Christian perspective, anthropology not only claims "that the relationship of humanity to transcendence is the dominant perspective from which all other relationships should be understood. It claims, more specifically, that the relationship of God to humanity is the key to the understanding of all relationships in which human beings exist, *including humanity's relationship to God*" (1991, 143;

emphasis added). As the emphasized phrase suggests, God's relationship to human beings is not to be conflated with "humanity's relationship to God." The name of humanity's relationship to God is "faith," understood, not primarily as a mode of inward subjectivity, but as "a form of life," bodily life in public spaces (145) whose "basic orientation . . . is in accordance with God's relationship to humanity" (146). God's relationship to humanity is, concretely speaking, the "revelation of the Father through the Son, in the Spirit" (144). Faith is "passive" inasmuch as it is an intentional response to God's ontologically prior relationship to human beings in the person of Jesus, a response that is wholly focused on what it is responding to and therefore is wholly formed by that to which it is a response. However, faith is "active" inasmuch as it is a form of life that is in active conformity with Christ's human response to God (cf. 151, 152). It is a life that constitutes "eschatological existence" because in its conformity with Christ it participates "in the relationship of humanity to God which is the purpose of God's will for his creation" (147). As a response, faith—that is, human beings' relationship to God—is secondary to and dependent upon God's relation to human beings in the person of "the Son sent by the Father with the Spirit." Hence, Christian theological anthropology not only claims that "the relationship of God to humanity is the key to the understanding of all relationships in which human beings exist, including humanity's relationship to God," but more than that, "it asserts that the relationship of God to humanity can only be adequately understood as the basis for human relational being, if it is understood as the relationship of the *triune* God, Father, Son and Spirit to humanity" (143; emphasis added).

Schwoebel's analysis of Christian theological anthropology's core claims brings at least three "corollaries" about the theological unacceptability of the modern concept of person (Welker's analysis of the modern concept of person in light of the trope "the mask" leads to a similar theological analysis of the theological concept of faith and a critique of how the modern concept of person is unacceptable because it distorts it [2000, 105–12]).

For one, if God's relation to human beings in "the Son sent by the Father with the Spirit" is "the dominant perspective from which all other relationships should be understood," then it follows that in principle "adequate and complete knowledge of what it means to be human can neither be read off the empirical findings of the different anthropological disciplines, nor developed from the reflexive character of human self-consciousness" (Schwoebel 1991, 145). On one side, this clearly rules out "any attempt at grounding the definition of human personhoood on a comparison with non-personal nature . . ." (154). Any such attempt would be incomplete as a definition of personhood, and false if it claimed to be complete. On the other side, since it is clear that the modern concept of person is grounded in analysis of "the reflexive character of human self-consciousness," the modern concept is also ruled out in principle as an acceptable concept for use in theological anthropology. Theological anthropologies based in either of these approaches would be examples of reductionist anthropological projects.

Second, any "attempt to derive the character of personhood from reflection on interpersonal human relationships or on intra-personal self-reflection is . . . ambiguous, because from the perspective of faith all social and reflexive relations of the human person reflect the dislocation and disorientation of sin" (1991, 154). Since it is clear that the modern concept of person is grounded in analysis of "the reflexive character of human self-consciousness," it proves for this reason also to be unacceptable for use in theological anthropology.

The third corollary of Schwoebel's analysis of Christian theological anthropology's core claims leads to a more formal "meta-level" reason that it is unacceptable to use the modern concept of person in Christian anthropology. The corollary is this: "the understanding of personhood based on conformity with Christ in faith remains incomplete unless it is developed in its full Trinitarian sense" (1991, 154). This is the case for Schwoebel because human beings' relationality is properly understood only on the basis of their relationship to God (i.e., faith) as a response, secondary to and dependent for its shape and content upon, the logically and ontologically prior relationality among Father, Son, and Spirit that constitutes the triune God's own life. The argument goes something like this: (a) The ground of human beings' relationality (in the order of being), and the key to proper understanding of all relationships in which human beings exist (in the order of knowing), is God's relationship to human beings. (b) God's relationship to human beings is a triune relationship, "the Son sent by the Father with the Spirit" ("economic trinity," a term Schwoebel does not use). (c) The condition of the possibility of the triune relationality of God's relationship to human beings ("economic trinity") is the inherent relationality of the three divine "persons" that constitutes the triune God's life ("immanent trinity," a term Schwoebel does not use). (d) Therefore, the inherent relationality of the triune God is the condition of the possibility, not only of proper understanding, but also of the reality of the relationality that constitutes human being. However, (e) it does not follow that "the concept of the person characterizes the relational being of humanity in analogy to the relational being of God in the persons of the Father, Son and Spirit" (155)—a least not without important qualifications.

Human and divine concepts of person cannot be "analogical" in the sense of *analogia entis*, Schwoebel argues, on the (perhaps dubious) grounds that doing so "would lead to the well known difficulties of positing the concept of being as a *terrium comparationis* between humanity and God which would contradict the fundamental truth that all being is the result of God's creative and sustaining agency" (155). Barth's proposal that analogy be understood as *analogia fidei* might be more adequate, but only if "faith" is understood, not merely "epistemologically as the mode in which we perceive the analogy between God's relational being and human relational being, but ontologically as the way in which human relational being is constituted and restored through the relationship of the Trinitarian God to humanity" (156). (f) Such an ontological interpretation of *analogia fidei* entails the conclusion toward which Schwoebel has been arguing.

It is a conclusion, not about the material content of the concept of person, but about its conceptual status. If the "analogy" between human person as relational being and divine person as relational being is understood in this way, it "is strictly interpreted as *analogia transcendentalis*, both in its ontological and its epistemological sense." That is, "'person' has the conceptual status of a category and not [that] of a classification concept. *It determines the meaning and range of application of all possible statements about a human person and provides the framework in which statements about what human persons are can be made.* This implies that personhood is an ontologically primitive category: it cannot be derived from any other concept and cannot be adequately defined through any other category" (156; emphasis added).

I take it that the force of the phrase *analogia transcendentalis* is something like this: Just as in discussion of the relational being of divine persons, "person" has the status of a "transcendental" (filling the functions Schwoebel outlined in the emphasized sentence above), and so too in discussion of the relational being of human persons, "person" has the status of a "transcendental" and functions in the same way. In each case it is an ontologically primitive concept; in neither case can it be derived from any other concept or be adequately defined through any other concept. Stressing that the two "transcendentals" are at most related as analogies, the phrase *analogia transcendentalis* brings out that the concept of divine person and the concept of human person are not the same concept. Indeed, it brings out the categorical distinction between divine and human relational being. The analogy works only one way: since "The Trinitarian God is the condition for the being of human persons as well as the condition for knowledge of the truth about the being of the human person" (Schwoebel, 156), but not vice versa, the concept of divine person functioning as a transcendental in theological reflection on divine relational being is the formal condition for the concept of human person functioning as a transcendental in theological reflection on human relational being. Nonetheless, precisely because it is an ontologically primitive concept, the transcendental concept of human person cannot be derived from or defined through the concept of divine person. The nature of the relations that constitute human person, properly understood in terms of God's relationship to human beings, cannot simply be read off any account of the relations that constitute the triune divine persons.

This last point about the concept of person in theological anthropology concerns its formal status, not its material content. However, insofar as the modern concept of person is derived from or defined through concepts of intersubjective relations, intrasubjective relations, self-consciousness, self-reflexiveness, self-expression, and self-manifestation, its status is that of a classificatory concept, not a category (in Schwoebel's sense). Therefore, it is unacceptable for use in theological anthropology, which requires a concept of person that is an ontologically primitive concept which cannot be derived from or defined through other concepts.

Although they do not explicitly argue for the thesis that it should not be adopted, Michael Welker and Christoph Schwoebel give strong reasons not to adopt the modern concept of person in Christian theological anthropology. The tropes of the mask, self-expression, and relational being help bring to focus a number of features of the modern concept of person that have made it a powerful concept in modern Western cultures and, for that reason, very attractive to modern theological anthropology as a way in which to explicate Christian anthropological convictions in a fashion that is both intelligible and persuasive within the context of modern culture. However, not adopting the modern concept of person·is not so easy to do by Christians who gave grown up in, now live in, and whose consciousness is thereby deeply formed by modern cultures and their reigning concept of the person. As Peter Berger and his associates write, "Modern consciousness is rather hard to get rid of" (1973, 215). Culturally speaking, "Demodernization in advanced industrial societies has limits that may be shifting but are nonetheless quite firm. . . . These limits are grounded in the necessity of maintaining the fundamental technological and bureaucratic machinery of the society. This means that demodernization, and the social constellations created by it" (including "modern consciousness") "will be parasitical upon the structures of modernity" (222).

Nor can the modern concept of person be eliminated from theological anthropology simply by providing an alternative theological concept of person. So dominant is the modern concept in modern culture, and such is its power that, it seems to me, it is virtually impossible to use the English word "person," however much it is qualified, without leading the listener or reader to absorb what is said or written into this already-well-known concept of person. The very use of the word "person" to name the subject of the discussion would invite confusion of the received modern concept of person with what is proposed as a theological alternative, regardless of how explicit, clearly different, and intellectually powerful the theological formulation of the alternative concept might be. The systematic irony of every polemical strategy that might be employed to distance a proposed theological concept of person from the unacceptable modern concept of person is that the more one compares and contrasts the preferable concept to the unacceptable one, the more the preferable concept is defined in terms of the inadequate concept. Even if it is only defined by negation of the unacceptable concept, the preferable concept ends up sounding like a new, improved version of the unacceptable one. To turn an unacceptable concept on its head simply leaves one with an unacceptable upside-down concept.

Because there are strong theological reasons not to adopt the modern concept of person, I suggest—going beyond anything either Welker or Schwoebel suggests—simply setting aside completely the word "person" as the name for the subject of theological anthropology. In chapter 7, I concurred that theological anthropology requires a logically primitive concept of human being that is not derived from or defined through any other concept. I think Schwoebel is correct that such a concept functions as a "category" (in his sense of the term) in theological anthropology. That is, among other things, this primitive concept determines the meaning and range of application of all possible theological statements about a human person and provides the framework in which statements about what human persons are can be made. For example, as I urged in chapter 7, theological anthropology's primitive concept determines that claims about human being employ a theocentric conceptual scheme that is simultaneously classificatory and evaluative. One could use the English word "person" to express this concept, calling it the "Christian theological concept of person." After all, one is free to stipulate technical meanings of words as one chooses. However, for the reasons reviewed above, I urge that that would be misleading and that it would be wise to retire the word "person" from this role in theological anthropology, at least temporarily. In place of "person," I have urged in this part of this work that anthropology's primitive categorical concept be expressed by the phrase "human creature," and that "personal" be used to underscore the conjointly classificatory and evaluative character of properly formulated theological claims about human creatures.

"Basic Personal Identity"

Perhaps the sense of the phrase "personal identity" intended in this theological anthropology project is best brought out by clarifying the kind of question to which a narrative description of someone's personal identity would be the appropriate answer. To ask who someone else is or who one is oneself is to ask about her, his, or my "personal identity" in the sense of the phrase intended here. As noted in the first section of this chapter, in the sense intended here, "identity" is not qualified by "personal" because it is the identity of an entity called a "person." Rather, in the sense of the phrase intended here, "identity" is ascribed to beings of the category "human creatures" understood theocentrically—that is, in terms of God's relation to them and their relation to God; and, as the second section of this chapter urges, the qualifier "personal" in the phrase "living human personal bodies" stresses that the phrase "human creature" has the logical status of a category that rules that all theological remarks about human beings, including their identity descriptions, must cohere at once with both a theological description of what it is to be a "living human personal body" (i.e., "creature") and the evaluative judgment that human living personal bodies have unconditional and immeasurable worth and dignity just because God relates to them.

The sense of the term "identity" that is at work here is rooted, I think, in a very particular intuition about the integral dynamic singularity of each human creature's life across time in community and its proximate contexts. "Singularity" expresses an aspect of the intuition that "individuality" and "uniqueness" might appear to express equally well, but do not. "Individual" and "individuality" are abstract. Each living human personal body in community is a concrete individual whose individuality consists in being one of many possible, and otherwise interchangeable, concrete instances of the class *Homo sapiens*. But the fact that an individual's individuality is specified as one instance of *Homo sapiens* shows that the term "individual" is used in a way that abstracts from everything else that is true about her or him. As "individual," she or he is indistinguishable from anyone else except numerically. Being an individual instance of x is an abstraction from the concrete particularity of a living human personal body in community. So, too, each living human personal body in community is unique in many respects, though not in all. Specification of a respect in which a given living human personal body is unique requires abstraction of that respect from the rich complexity that constitutes her or his concrete reality. For many purposes it is helpful or even necessary to take human beings as individuals or to specify respects in which they are unique. However, the intuition at work here is this: when the intent is to describe who a given human creature is in a way that holds together a description of who she or he is as a concrete human creature and the evaluative judgment that she or he is of unconditional and immeasurable value and dignity, as is required when such description is determined by the category "human creature," it must be a description that conveys that her or his unconditional and immeasurable value and dignity lies in the full complexity and richness of her or his life across time in proximate contexts as a concrete living human personal body related to by the triune God in three distinguishable ways. It does not lie in his or her abstract individuality as an instance of *Homo sapiens*, underlying, as it were, all the other respects in which they might be alike or different from others. Nor does it lie in one of those respects that is unique to that individual, or a set of such respects, abstracted from the full complexity of the concrete human creature. To be sure, "individual," "unique," and "singular" are terms used in ways that often overlap. In her or his singularity, a living human personal body is an individual instance of *Homo sapiens*, and of a lot of other classes as well. And in her or his singularity, each of them is also unique in many ways. The way I use "singular" is largely stipulative. "Singularity" is used to pick out the inseparable conjunction of value, dignity, and messy complexity of detail that, following the intuition underlying this notion of "personal identity," constitute a concrete living human personal body's identity across time in its proximate contexts, including community with other human creatures, as related to by God. Given the singularity of the personal identity of a concrete living human personal body, an adequate description of that identity needs to render at once what she is like in her singularity and that she is of unconditional value and dignity in, and not somehow behind or underlying or despite, the complex and not necessarily very orderly details of her life across time.

The terms "life across time," "in community," and "in their proximate contexts" express another aspect of the intuition about human creatures that lies behind the concept of "identity" that is in view here. The intuition is that a human creature's identity resides in his singular way of conducting his life—that is, in his singular ensemble of ways of acting, interacting, and interpreting or acknowledging what befalls him across time with other human creatures in community in their shared proximate contexts. On this intuition, a human creature's identity is not constituted by a static inventory of physical features, powers, virtues, vices, traits of temperament, sensibility, beliefs, commitments, genetic lineage, cultural heritage, intersubjective relationships, and so on, including in the inventory also the item "a singular life." Rather a human creature's personal identity is the integrally dynamic singularity of his intentional actions and interactions with other human creatures in their shared proximate contexts and his way of interpreting the significance of what befalls him and of relating to it. He may relate to what happens to him by interpreting it as coherent with his identity in his actions and interactions to date, or interpreting it as a threat to his identity to be resisted and denied, or interpreting it as a gift that enriches his identity to be acknowledged and affirmed. His identity lies in the sequence of these dynamic intentional interactions and events of interpretation that cumulatively are integral to one singular life. "Integral" does not necessarily mean that this sequence of actions, interactions, and appropriations is "orderly," "coherent," or even—in the psychological sense—"well-integrated."

It only means that everything in the sequence is part and parcel of that human creature's identity. They are not simply a random collection of actions, interactions, and events, but rather constitute his life because they are *his* actions, interactions, and events; and he has his identity, as the one whose they are, in them and not beneath (as their sub-sistence that stands under them) or behind (as their antecedent metaphysical cause) or ahead of them (as the ex-istence that merges out of them and stands in front of them). The singularity of that identity lies in the peculiar ways in which that human creature engages in those actions, interactions, and appropriations.

The singularity of a human creature's identity might be thought of as her peculiar style or styles of engaging in those actions, interactions, and appropriations, so long as "style" is not thought of as artifice. The singularity of a human creature's identity is not a style that necessarily makes him stand out from the crowd. It is not to be conflated with nonconformity. Much less is it to be confused with the magnetic, attractive, glowing, creative, powerful personality, celebrated in what Warren Susman calls "the culture of personality" (1984, 271–85). Both a global policy of nonconformity and assiduous cultivation of personality can best be seen, perhaps, as defensive strategies against the threat of absorption into an anonymous and oppressively conformist mass culture. The intuition behind the concept of "identity" under discussion here is that every human creature has a singular identity. It is not a defensive strategy. It does admit of degrees of vividness so far as an observer is concerned. The singularity of human personal identities can range from a blandness that is scarcely noticeable to the intensity of self-dramatization that generates celebrity status. Regardless of its degree of vividness, however, singularity is inherent in being a living human personal body.

The peculiar styles or ways in which a human creature engages in intentional actions, interactions, and interpretative relating to the events that happen to her are not something she unchangingly stands behind and picks up or puts down. Rather, the intuition is, she is who she is in those ways or styles of acting, interacting, and appropriating. Over time, the peculiar ways in which a human creature engages in the actions, interactions, and appropriations that constitute her life may well change. Those changes are themselves integral to who she is. In their peculiar concreteness, those changes are themselves part of her singularity. Such changes are an important part of what is dynamic about human creatures' identities. To give an adequate identity description of a human creature, in the sense of "identity" in view here, is to describe the dynamic singularity of the ways—and the singularity of the changes of those ways—in which, across time and in community with other human creatures in their proximate contexts, she engages in the sequence of actions, intra-actions, and various interpretive relations to what happens to her that are integral to her life.

As was noted in chapter 9A, the intuition about integral dynamic singularity of each human creature's life across time in community and its proximate contexts that lies behind the sense of "identity" in view here means that the identity question addressed by this project in theological anthropology is different from some other quite familiar identity questions. The identity question in view here is not a question about how to identify a particular human being in the midst of a group ("Which one is he?"). That question is answered by a few descriptive remarks that are sufficient to help to contrast him with others and pick him out of the crowd. Given the particular makeup of the crowd, those remarks help us to identify his singularity in the moment. But they do not describe him in his singularity in every context in which he lives, with which he interacts, and in which he changes over time. Nor is the identity question a question about what constitutes his numerical and logical self-identity through change across time. That is a metaphysical question. Whatever its answer, it must by definition be something itself unchanging. A description of such a principle of identity cannot be a description of a personal identity understood as a dynamic singular life across time in its proximate contexts.

Much less is the identity question, in the sense of "identity" intended here, the same as the question we sometimes ask of someone, including oneself, whose behavior on some occasions is radically different from her behavior on other occasions: "Who is she, *really*?" That question invokes a distinction between who someone appears to be outwardly and publicly and who she "really" is inwardly and privately. By assuming the identity of her "real who" with her nonapparent inward and private identity, the question simply presupposes the validity of the subjectivizing modern concept of person. It implicitly identifies the identity description that would answer the question, not with a description of the apparent identity, but with a description of the real identity. That, however, runs counter to the intuition that lies behind the "who question," the identity question that is in view here, for the intuition in question assumes that a living human personal body's publicly available—that is, "apparent"—identity is as fully a genuine part of its identity as its "inner"—allegedly "real"—identity, no more, no less. Doubtless there are cases of living human personal bodies about whose identities we have the intuition that they are extremely ambiguous and puzzling, suggesting deception in self-presentation. Such a case does raise the question, "Who is he, really?" But that is not the intuition that lies behind the type of identity question in view here, and it takes a quite different kind of identity description to answer it.

It needs to be stressed again that noting these differences does not amount to the suggestion that only the sense of "identity" that is rooted in the intuition of the integral dynamic singularity of each human creature's life across time in community and its proximate contexts is the correct or valid sense of "identity." Each of these senses of "identity" is used for important intellectual work in various contexts. The task here has merely been to clarify the sense of the word that is important in this theological anthropological context.

The sense of the word "identity" as used in this context is also not identical with the sense it has in such familiar, largely journalistic, uses in contemporary culture as "racial identity," "ethnic identity," "sexual identity," "gender identity," and, in relation to all of the above, "identity politics." The two are not identical, but they do partially overlap. In subsequent chapters, this partial overlap is signaled by a distinction between "quotidian personal identities" and "basic personal identities." To clarify the distinction, and its relation to the sense of "identity" in relation to "identity politics," I shall explain each term in order.

In chapter 6, I urged that God relates creatively to each living human personal body in its having been born into some physical, social, and cultural quotidian proximate context that is itself also God's creature. Through a prolonged maturational process, human creatures are profoundly formed by the quotidian proximate contexts into which they are born and in which they live. The social and cultural aspects of those quotidian worlds hand on already formed—traditional—ways of acting and interacting with other human creatures in community, the humanly constructed cultural and social dimensions of their proximate contexts, as well as with the nonhuman dimensions of their proximate contexts, and also traditional ways of interpreting and relating to everything that happens to them. This includes ways of appropriating racial, ethnic, gender, and sexual differences. All these ways of acting and interacting involve the array of expectations that, we saw above, the person as conceived by modernity must mediate in both its inward and private dimension and its outward and public dimension.

Quotidian worlds vary tremendously regarding the freedom they allow human creatures to revise or resist the ways in which the quotidian shapes how they act and interact, interpret, and relate to what befalls them. In some quotidians, traditional forms of acting and interacting, interpreting, and relating to have the force of fate, given and inexorable. In others, varying degrees of latitude are allowed to human creatures to accept, revise, or reject them. Appropriation of the quotidian's formation in all of these respects decisively shapes human creatures' singular identities. In other quotidians, in which the modern concept of person is dominant, human creatures are relatively free to express themselves subjectively and to manifest-themselves-in-difference objectively in ways of their own devising. In so doing they are as free to reject or radically revise expectations laid on them by their quotidian worlds regarding race, ethnicity, gender, and sexuality as they are to accept them. We may call whatever identity a human creature develops in its interactions with its quotidian proximate context its "quotidian identity."

A human being's quotidian identity is always a negotiated combination of a social construct or constructs provided by the quotidian proximate context and an original self-construct by the human being. The self-construct not only involves some degree of acceptance or rejection of the received forms of action and interaction, and forms of interpretation of what befalls the human being, and forms of how to relate to what befalls, that are laid on human creatures as expectations by their proximate contexts. It also involves some assessment of the relative importance of each of those received expectations in the total ensemble of the human being's personal identity. Moreover, the self-construct aspect of quotidian identities involves some degree of originality, however slight or subtle, in the peculiar ways in which a given human being concretely enacts the expectations its proximate context lays on it, the concrete ways it goes about playing the roles assigned it, and the concrete ways it occupies the status to which it is assigned.

Especially in the case of quotidians in which the modern concept of person is dominant, human creatures' quotidian identity will include particular, consciously formed, explicit racial, ethnic, sexual, and gender "identities."

However, because the singularity of concrete quotidian identities inherently includes many more aspects than those identified by racial, ethnic, sexual, and gender markers, their partly socially constructed and partly self-constructed quotidian identities will include such aspects but will not be simply identical with them. To the extent that "quotidian identity" means the manner in which individuals identify themselves in the context of modern culture and the structure of consciousness that it brings with it, their identity can be described as having four aspects, according to Peter and Brigitte Berger and Hansfried Kellner's study of "modernization and consciousness" in *The Homeless Mind* (1973). Partly socially constructed and partly self-constructed modern quotidian identities are "peculiarly open" in the sense that they are "peculiarly 'unfinished'" as they enter adult life. "The modern individual is peculiarly 'conversion-prone'; he knows this and often glories in it. Biography is thus apprehended both as a migration through different social worlds and as the successive realization of a number of possible identities" (77). It is "peculiarly differentiated" in the sense that, because modern individuals live in a plurality of social worlds and "the structures of each particular world are experienced as relatively unstable and unreliable," "the individual seeks to find his 'foothold' in reality in himself rather than outside himself" (77, 78). "One consequence of this is that the individual's subjective reality (what is commonly regarded as his 'psychology') becomes increasingly differentiated, complex—and 'interesting' to himself. . . . Something that is constantly changing is supposed to be the *ens realissimum*" (78). Modern quotidian identities, third, are "peculiarly reflective" precisely because their proximate contexts confront them "with an ever-changing kaleidoscope of social experiences and meanings" (78). This reflectiveness "pertains not only to the outside world but also to the subjectivity of the individual and especially to his identity" (79). Finally, modern quotidian identities are "peculiarly individuated" in the sense that the "bearer of identity as the *ens realissimum*, quite logically attains a very important place in the hierarchy of values. Individual freedom, individual autonomy and individual rights come to be taken for granted as moral imperatives of fundamental importance, and foremost among these individual rights is the right to plan and fashion one's life as freely as possible" (79).

From a theological point of view, however, quotidian identities, including modern ones, are themselves included in a larger context for which the term of art here will be human creatures' "basic identity." In each of the three parts of this project, theological anthropological claims are generated on the basis of a theological account of human beings' proximate contexts as understood within the larger context of their ultimate contexts constituted by the triune God relating to all that is not God, respectively, to create, to draw to eschatological consummation, and to reconcile when it is estranged from God. One of the anthropological implications of that distinction between proximate contexts and their enveloping ultimate contexts is the distinction between human creatures' integral dynamically singular quotidian identities and their basic identity. Their basic identity is who they are by virtue of the triune God relating to them. Put anthropomorphically, their basic identity is who they are, not simply as their partly socially constructed and partly self-constructed identities are accessible to and describable by others, nor as their identities are interiorly accessible to and describable only by themselves, but who they are by virtue of God relating to them to create, to draw to eschatological consummation, and to reconcile when they are estranged from God. Their basic identity is who they can know themselves to be as they respond appropriately in faith, hope, and love to the triune God's threefold way of relating to them.

A different aspect of living human personal bodies' basic identity is derived in each of the three parts of this work from a different way in which the triune God relates to all that is not God.

1. The triune God relating creatively defines human living bodies' basic identity in a double way. Inasmuch as God directly relates to them creatively, the answer to the question about who they are is, "We are those who are radically contingent on God's call to be and to act, to receive and to give well-being and flourishing, in generous hospitality in our own time and place as far as our finitude allows, to fellow creatures." Inasmuch as God indirectly relates to them creatively through their quotidian proximate contexts, the answer to the question about who they are is, "We are those who are called to be wise in our actions for the well-being of our quotidian contexts."

2. The triune God relating to draw all that is not God to eschatological consummation defines living human personal bodies' basic identity in a second double way. On one hand, the answer to the question about who they are is, "We are those who are elect by God, not for special status or a special role in contradistinction to others who are not so elect, but for a distinctive relationship with God in community with all other human creatures, which is our eschatological consummation; we are those who have this destiny." On the other hand, the answer to the question about who they are is, "We are those to whom the catastrophe of final judgment is now happening."

3. The triune God relating to draw estranged living human personal bodies to reconciliation defines their basic identity in a third way. The answer to the question about who they are is, "As those who are structurally reconciled with God 'in Christ,' we are those who have their personal identities 'in' Christ's identity, as the plot or narrative logic of God's relating to reconcile us by way of Incarnation becomes the plot or narrative logic of the dynamic of our own singular identities." These are not three basic identities, much less three alternative basic identities, but three aspects of one basic identity given to living human personal bodies by God.

Living human personal bodies' basic identity is God's gift. Their basic identity is not a potentiality whose realization is most desirable and into which human creatures may, or necessarily will, develop in time. Nor is it a logical possibility that human creatures may or may not appropriate in self-involving subjective acts that are existentially formative. Christian anthropological claims about human creatures' personal identity have the force of a claim that human creatures already actually have this identity by virtue of the triune God relating to them. Basic identity has the ontological status of actuality, not ideality.

Accordingly, living human personal bodies' appropriate response to this gift is not to actualize it existentially or internalize it psychologically in acts of self-reflective subjectivity. Perhaps human creatures can actualize or internalize logical possibilities, making them their own in self-involving acts that are existentially shaping. However, one cannot actualize what is already part of one's own actuality. And one may not even try to actualize what is another human personal body's actuality. The first is self-contradictory; the second is an effort to absorb the other into one's own actuality that violates the other's integrity as a fellow living human personal body. What a human creature may do by way of appropriate response to God's gifts of actualities is to acknowledge them, rather than realize them or actualize them. In this case, "acknowledgment" consists of a human creature living out the three aspects of their God-given basic identity and doing so concretely as the integrally dynamic singular quotidian identity it in fact now is. That concrete quotidian identity is "who" acknowledges its own basic identity by living in congruence with it. The human creature's quotidian identity is not replaced by its basic identity. Rather its quotidian identity is taken up into its basic identity and, across time, is shaped by it.

In one of the few cases where concession of the obvious is at the same time an important theological claim, it is stressed in each of the three parts of this project that living human personal bodies are fully capable of living as though the three aspects of their basic identity do not obtain, are not in fact their basic identity, indeed have nothing to do with their personal identities. Human beings can live quotidian identities that totally ignore the gift of their basic identity. They can live quotidian identities that do not wholly ignore their basic identity, but rather fail to cohere with it so that they amount to distortions of it. They can live, as it were, at cross-grain to themselves. In that sense, they can live with divided identities. Each would be an identity consisting at once of a quotidian identity defined by some negotiation between roles, status, and expectations projected onto them by their proximate contexts and the degree of their own willingness to actualize those roles, status, and expectations, their relative weighting of the importance of each of those roles, status, and expectations, and their creativity as to the ways in which they concretely enact those roles, status, and expectations, on one side, and a basic identity on the other side defined by God relating to it but wholly unacknowledged by it. In each of the three parts of this project, a fundamentally different way in which a living human personal body can live as a divided identity at cross-grain with itself is explored as bondage in a living death. It is "sin in the singular"—that is, in the singularity of one's personal identity. Such a divided identity is akin to bondage because it cannot be self-overcome. It cannot be done because it is a self-contradictory project: Who would it be that would take steps to overcome the self-division except a self-divided, self-contradictory identity, or some community of them? Who would enact any self-healing or interhuman other-healing practice as self-contradictory agents in self-contradictory—sinful-in-the-singular—ways?

Excursus: Describing Personal Identities

It is the dynamic character integral to the singularity of human living personal bodies' identities that warrants the point made repeatedly in this project that narrative is the most appropriate form for descriptions of personal identities. Obviously, an identity description cannot report every action and interaction by a given human being, every interpretation of what befalls that human being, or every way in which she relates to what befalls her, the sequence of which comprise her life in community in various proximate contexts across time, or all the ways in which her particular style of doing these things changes across time. However, a narrative can concurrently achieve two descriptive goals: (1) It can give relatively brief stories that exemplify ways of acting and interacting and ways of interpreting and relating to what befall her, that are "just like her," "her when she is most fully herself," that are selected because they achieve the goal of conveying "what she is like"; and (2) it can give a more extended story of her life as a whole that can achieve the goal of rendering who she is as a singular agent in her peculiar way(s) of acting in her proximate contexts, including communities of fellow human beings, and being acted upon by her proximate contexts.

By the first strategy, narrative can convey what Hans Frei calls the "ascriptive subject" to which we conventionally ascribe both physical and mental or psychological properties when we attempt to describe their identities in nonnarrative ways. However, the properties we ascribe are abstractions that (with the exception of Duns Scotus's celebrated theory of "haecceity," a property of a person that only he or she has, e.g., Moses' "mosesinity" or Cleopatra's "cleopatrinity") may equally well be ascribed to other ascriptive subjects. But what we want is a description of the singular way she is or enacts these properties across time, and does so as a kind of ensemble. The singularity of the person's identity slips through the network of ascribed properties, no matter how complex and dense the network. It is the ascriptive subject that the modern concept of person conceives as an inherently self-expressive subject to which we ascribe the publicly available properties that are its self-manifestation-in-difference. However, unlike ascription of a network of abstract properties, brief anecdotal stories can convey who the ascriptive subject is in her or his singularity without ascribing abstract properties to her or implicitly comparing her with others who share the same properties.

By the second strategy, narrative can achieve the goal of rendering the singularity of her identity across time and change as the singularity of the identity of a living human personal body as intentional agent. Premodern metaphysical descriptions of human beings as agents of intentional acts offered a description that avoided the type of disjunction between the interior and private and the outside and public aspects of personhood that we have seen is problematic in the modern concept of person. Premodern analysis does this by construing the relation between intentions, to which the agents who form them have privileged access, and actions, which take place in public and are observable to others, as a dialectical relation rather than as an event-cause-and-effect relation. In explanation of events, causes and effects must themselves be events defined independently of each other, or the explanation will be viciously circular. But intentional actions can only be described dialectically in terms of intentions-to-act and enacted intentions. The agent of intentional acts is understood as an integral whole.

However, premodern metaphysical description and analysis of agents' acts typically distinguishes between the agent's being and its operations. Its intentional acts are among its operations. They are accidental to its being, which is logically and ontologically prior to its operations. In the case of intentional agents, "being" is described as "rational substance," perhaps as a "rational soul." Although it is materially different from the dualist disjunction in the modern concept of person between subjects' "subjective inside" and "objective outside," this metaphysical "being/operations" distinction is another problematic anthropological dualism. On the other hand, a narrative of an agent's actions in and interactions with its proximate contexts, and its interpretations of and ways of relating to what befalls it in those contexts, can render that agent's singular identity across time and through change in a way that holds both the agent and its circumstances, and its actions and its identity, together in dialectical tension without having to make either pole prior to the other pole or either pair prior to the other pair. Furthermore, the plot or narrative logic that structures the movement of the narrative, and makes it the narrative of a given agent in her singular identity rather than a mere chronicle, can render the peculiar ways of acting, interacting, interpreting, and relating that constitute the singularity of the identity whose narrative it is.

"Unsubstitutable"

The identities of living human personal bodies are repeatedly characterized in this project as "unsubstitutable." The term calls for some clarification.

Individual human beings are usually considered to be substitutable for one another in regard to many of the roles they fill. The understudy in a play or an opera substitutes for the principal actor on occasions when the latter cannot perform the theatrical role. There are substitute teachers to fill the social role of teacher when the regular teacher is unable to do so. Within limits, human beings can be substituted for one another in filling roles. The limits have to do with how precisely the role is defined. Conceivably, it might be the case that there is a surgical procedure so complex that only one living surgeon has the skill to perform it. In that case, that surgeon would be unsubstitutable in regard to filling the role of performing that procedure. Her unsubstitutability would be a function of the historical accident that at a particular moment in time she is the only one capable of filling the role. She would be contingently unsubstitutable.

The case is different when opera buffs insist that "nobody can substitute" for their favorite diva, or when professional baseball fans declare that "nobody can substitute" on the mound for their favorite pitcher. This, too, is a claim of contingent unsubstitutability. It is made about certain human beings in relation to roles they play. However, I suggest, it is not finally a claim about their substitutability in filling those roles. Rather, it is about their substitutability as occasions for others' pleasure and admiration. Roles are defined independently of the description of any individual human being's personal identity. Hence, it is proper to say that a role can be filled by any of several individual human beings who can be substituted for one another in filling the role. This is said at a high level of abstraction. An individual human being is an abstraction from some concrete living human personal body. An individual human being is a numerable instance of the class "living human beings"—living *Homo sapiens*. If the opera is performed, some singer fills each role and another could have substituted. If the professional baseball game is played, some player fills each role and another could have substituted. However, concretely speaking, a human being, simply *as* "human being," does not fill any role. In concrete actuality, it is some living human personal body in her or his quotidian and basic identities who fills a role. And, filling the role as who she or he is, filling it in her or his personal identity, she or he fills the role in ways that are peculiarly and singularly her or his own, ways integral to her or his quotidian identities. The distinctive way each goes about filling the role is a function of the historical accident that only she or he has the specific mix of physical capacities, natural talent, sensibility, relevant intelligence, history of training and coaching, and experience that are integral to her or his quotidian identity and that she or he exercises in filling the role with a particular power, subtlety, and grace. What the opera buffs or the baseball fans are declaring to be unsubstitutable is not the presence of a particular individual human being in a given role in a performance of a given opera or in the playing of a particular ball game, but the delight and admiration a favored singer or athlete occasions in performing their roles in their own singular ways. Because the delight and admiration that are contingent on features of the quotidian identity of the favored singer or athlete, which could have been different, the singer's or athlete's unsubstitutability is a contingent unsubstitutability. Nonetheless, it is not their unsubstitutability in regard to a role, but an unsubstitutability in regard to their personal identities.

The sense in which "unsubstitutable" is used in this project in the phrase "unsubstitutable personal identity," however, is neither the contingent unsubstitutability that might be ascribed to the human being who is the sole human being capable of filling a given role, nor the contingent unsubstitutability of particular living human personal bodies who, on account of their personal identities, occasion pleasure and admiration because they fill certain roles in peculiar ways that no other can. Instead, "unsubstitutable" is used here in sense of "absolute unsubstitutability."

Incidentally, since chapters 18, 19A, and 19B refer to Jesus' unsubstitutable personal identity, it is appropriate to note in passing that what is said here about that phrase applies to its use in reference to Jesus in his humanity as much as it does to its use in reference to any other living human personal body. Many of the titles traditionally ascribed to Jesus are the names of roles: Lord, judge, revealer, king, priest, prophet, messiah, savior, and so on. It is conventional to note that these roles are ascribed to Jesus in analogical ways. I have just urged that roles are properly defined without reference to the description of the personal identity of anyone who might fill them. Consequently, any given human being could be declared "unsubstitutable" in a given role only contingently. However, Christians have traditionally described Jesus as unsubstitutable as the one who fills the roles named by his "titles."

The theological issues this apparent conflict raises are complex and require a larger theological context than is provided here. However, four brief points can be made. First, if Jesus' personal identity (however it may be described) is unsubstitutable absolutely and not contingently, and if the analysis above of the sense in which human beings are substitutable for one another is correct, then it is not an unsubstitutability relative to his filling any roles whatever. If this claim is correct, second, his personal identity is not defined by the roles named by his titles. If it were, the meaning of the titles would be defined by the roles they name, roles already well known to us independently of who Jesus is—that is,well known independently of his personal identity. Rather, it is his personal identity that defines what those titles mean. That is to say: Granted that the titles are used of Jesus analogically, it is the description of the identity of Jesus that provides the rules that govern appropriate analogical use of the titles in regard to Jesus. Third, in relation to Jesus, at least some of the titles probably cannot be conceived as roles that he fills, not even analogically. The test question, I think, is whether a dynamic relation that is strictly singular can be conceived as a role. An example: Theologically speaking, the triune God's actively relating to create all that is not God (i.e., relating "cosmically") is strictly speaking a singular relating. If all that is not God is created, it is created. The creative relation is singular. In principle it is not a role that needs to be or can be repeated. If that can be granted, then what about the triune God actively relating to save all reality other than God from the consequences of its estrangement from God, and doing so concretely once and for all in and through what Jesus does and undergoes? It too is a cosmic relating. Is it not also, strictly speaking, a singular active relating by God? In that case, being savior is not a role. In being "Savior of the world," Jesus is not filling a role (for which someone else, at least in principle, could be substituted for him). In his personal identity, he would have to be said to be absolutely unsubstitutable as Savior. This opens into a final point. What has been said thus far is restricted to Jesus' personal identity in his humanity. It is quite another question what it might mean to speak of personal identity in regard to the three nonbodied eternal persons of the triune God, or in regard to the nonbodily triune God as such (is the triune God either a person or personal, and if so, in what sense?), or in regard to the divinity of Jesus.

In general, living human personal bodies' personal identities are absolutely unsubstitutable in at least three respects. First, no other quotidian personal identity can be substituted for the quotidian personal identity that simply is who a given living human personal body is. That human personal body's quotidian personal identity can change radically. However, a narrative description that renders that identity must include an account of the change and the short- or long-term differences it makes. The singularity of human creatures' integrally dynamic identities means that in principle their quotidian personal identities are inalienable. No other identity can be substituted for them. Given the sense in which "identity" is used here, this is a conceptual point. Strictly speaking, "identity theft," in this sense of identity, is an incoherent expression.

It is important to note this sense of the "absolute unsubstitutability" of personal identities because it sets a firm limit to the sense in which one living human personal body can imitate or, in a certain sense, participate in the personal identity of another living human personal body. This is an important point, because just such participation in Jesus' identity is claimed in chapters 19A and 20A to be a major aspect of human beings' basic identity. Imitation of another's personal identity can never amount to a replication or cloning of it. In the sense of the term adopted here, a human being's quotidian "personal identity" lies in the sequence of acts, interactions, and interpretations of, and responses to, what befalls it that constitutes the life of a living human personal body in community in its proximate contexts. The life of another human being cannot consist of the same sequence; therefore the personal identity of another human being cannot lie in that same sequence. That is as true of Jesus' quotidian personal identity as it is for any other human being's quotidian personal identity. While the sequences of actions, interactions, and so on, that constitute other human beings' lives may be similar to the sequence that constitutes Jesus' life, they cannot be identically the same as his. Accordingly, while they may be similar in some respects, the quotidian personal identities they have in those sequences cannot be identical with the personal identity Jesus has in the sequence that constitutes his life. They cannot simply appropriate Jesus' inalienable quotidian personal identity as their own. They can only imitate it at some distance.

Then in what sense can other living human personal bodies participate in Jesus' personal identity? Clearly they cannot participate in it in the sense that their quotidian personal identities replicate his so that the two identities become indistinguishably one and the same, or in the sense that the sequences of acts, interactions, and so on, that constitute their respective lives somehow become segments of the sequence that constitutes Jesus' life and in which he has his personal identity. However, the quotidian personal identities of other living human personal bodies can come to participate in Jesus' personal identity formally, in the following way. The dynamic movement of the sequence of acts, interactions, and so on, that constitutes the human life in which a living human personal body has its personal identity has a certain pattern. Narrative descriptions of that identity convey the pattern by the plot or narrative logic that structures and drives the movement of the narrative, however loose or simple or apparently uninteresting it may be. The inalienable quotidian personal identities of living human personal bodies may be said to participate in Jesus' inalienable personal identity "formally" to the extent that the pattern of the movement of the sequence of acts, interactions, and so on, that constitute the lives in which they have those identities begin to be shaped by the narrative logic of the life in which Jesus has his personal identity. When that happens, the personal identities that participate in Jesus' identity are identities that coincide with rather than living at cross-grain to, at least one aspect of their basic identity—namely, the aspect constituted by the triune God relating to them to reconcile them by way of incarnation to God when they are estranged from God.

Living human personal bodies' personal identities are absolutely unsubstitutable in a second respect. They are absolutely unsubstitutable in regard to their responsibility for the acts, interactions, interpretations of what befall them, and responses to what befalls them, that constitute the different lives in which they have their respective quotidian personal identities. The individual acts and so forth may be contingent on accidental features of their proximate contexts. But the human being who did them did so in his or her quotidian personal identity and in none other. That identity may change radically over time. However, the changes are themselves moments in the sequence of acts and so forth that constitute a human being's life and in which she has her identity. The changes do not terminate one personal identity and begin another *de novo*. The personal identity in which a human being did the acts and so on that make up its life remains unsubstitutably the identity that is responsible for those acts and so on. No other personal identity can substitute in regard to that responsibility. That is a metaphysical claim that the relation between quotidian personal identities and the acts and so forth that constitute the lives of living human personal bodies makes the unsubstitutability of their personal identities absolute and not contingent on any accidental features of their proximate contexts. It is in their inalienable quotidian personal identities that human living personal bodies are terminal and absolutely unsubstitutable for any other in the order of responsibility.

Third, living human personal bodies' quotidian personal identities are absolutely unsubstitutable in respect to certain ways in which they have value and are loved. Loving is at very least a valuing of the beloved. Living human personal bodies are loved in their concrete quotidian personal identities, not in the abstract as "individual instances of *Homo sapiens*." Consequently, precisely as beloved, one personal identity may succeed another, one may even displace another, but no one personal identity can, strictly speaking, substitute for another as beloved. As beloved, a personal identity is unsubstitutable. Substitution in intentional relationships can happen in a relationship defined by a role or by exploitation, but not a love relationship focused on the other in his or her inalienable quotidian personal identity.

Erotic love and love as friendship are contingent on a host of accidental features of shared proximate contexts, of who meets whom, of peculiarities of sensibilities, of what and who one finds loveable, and so on. Correspondingly, the unsubstitutability of the personal identity of the one who becomes the beloved is contingent; once the beloved has become the beloved, however, her or his personal identity is unsubstitutable by any other human creature in respect of being the beloved. But the beloved might not have become the beloved. It is a contingent matter. However, living human personal bodies are also intrinsically valuable and are to be loved in their personal identities for that reason. As parts 1, 2, and 3 of this project argue, they are to be loved simply for what and who they are by the triune God's creative relating, by the triune God's relating to draw them to eschatological consummation, and by the triune God's relating to reconcile them. They are inherently to be loved because their *basic* personal identities make them absolutely unsubstitutable in their dignity and value, precisely in their quotidian identities, by virtue of God's relating to them in creative, eschatologically consummating, and reconciling love. Living human personal bodies' quotidian personal identities are unsubstitutable as beloved in this way in regard to their *basic* personal identities, and because what is valued in their being beloved is inherent in what and who they are, rather than being contingent on accidents of their proximate contexts, it is an absolute unsubstitutability.

Unsubstitutible Personal Identities and Individualism

Clearly, this project's attention to living human personal bodies' unsubstitutable personal identities focuses on human beings as individuals. The question of what constitutes a personal identity is in part the question of what distinguishes one particular concrete human individual from another. The question of how best to describe the unsubstitutability of a human being's personal identity is in part the question of how best to describe her personal identity in a way that brings out what it is about her human being's personal identity that keeps her from ultimately being interchangeable with any other human being. "Individual" is a very abstract notion; an individual human being's unsubstitutable personal identity is the concreteness of her individuality. A thesis to which this anthropology returns in each of its parts is that a relatively adequate description of an individual human being, even granting that it can never be exhaustive, would be a description that conveys or renders his or her unsubstitutable personal identity.

However, contemporary theological anthropologies include a good deal of polemic against strands of individualism alleged to be implied by much traditional theological anthropology and to be explicitly affirmed in characteristically modern or Enlightenment theological anthropology. These attacks on the typically modern individualistic concept of human being rooted in the Enlightenment help explain the attractiveness to current theological anthropology of various lines of postmodern thought. And objections to individualism seem to underlie widespread theological interest in relational views of human being in current anthropology, whether postmodern or not. Therefore, the question arises of whether this project's attention to living human personal bodies' unsubstitutable personal identities entails yet one more individualistic anthropological proposal in theology.

The question as posed cannot be answered in a straightforward way because closer analysis shows that "individualism" is used in so many different ways that, unless further specified, it is extremely ambiguous. In *Individualism* Steven Lukes (1973) isolates eleven "of the basic ideas of individualism by indicating broad conceptual outlines, partly by definition (positive and negative) and partly by historical allusion, but with no suggestion that the elements isolated are either mutually exclusive or jointly exhaustive" (44). The elements he identifies seem to me to fall into three classes. One class consists of five different types of individualistic explanation of certain human phenomena. A second class of one consists of a second-order methodological commitment to individualism in explanations of certain human phenomena. A third class of five consists of characterizations of the individual that cut across the five types of explanation because they are, usually tacitly, presupposed as descriptors of the individual who figures in the explanation. Lukes's sorting of the ambiguities in common uses of "individualism" is critical as well as analytic. It is helpful to the effort to clarify whether, and in what way, this project yields an individualistic anthropology.

"Individualism" means different things in different kinds of inquiry seeking to explain certain human phenomena. Lukes identifies five such senses:

1. "Political individualism" proposes an explanation of the conditions under which government works best. It consists of a set of ideas central to classical liberalism, relying on a picture of society whose members are "'independent centers of consciousness' [quoting Robert Paul Wolff], . . . independent and

rational beings, who are the sole generators of their own wants and preferences, and the best judges of their own interests—which can be identified by consulting them or observing what they desire and aim at" (Lukes 1973, 79). Political individualism includes a view of government "as based on the (individually-given) consent of its citizens . . . ," a view of political representation "as representation, not of estates or social functions or social classes, but of individual interests . . . ," and a view of the purpose of government "as being confined to enabling individuals' wants to be satisfied, individual's interests to be pursued and individuals' rights to be protected, with a clear bias towards *laissez-faire* . . ." (79, 80). Otherwise conflicting views of the relation between individuals and society, such as conservativism, socialism, and pluralism, join in disputing political liberalism as "both naïve and mistaken" in viewing "the individuals forming society as 'independent centers of consciousness', as the sole generators of their own wants and preferences. Their consciousness is rather seen as (partially or wholly) socially determined and their wants and preferences as socially and culturally patterned" (86).

2. "Economic individualism" proposes an explanation of the conditions under which a nation's economy is most vital. "It is a belief in economic liberty" (Lukes 1973, 88). It holds that "a spontaneous economic system, based on private property, the market, and freedom of production, contract and exchange, and on the unfettered self-interest of individuals, tends to be more or less self-adjusting; and that it conduces to the maximum satisfaction of individuals and to (individual and social) progress" (89). Economic individualism "amounts to the justification of certain culturally specific patterns of behaviour (such as the systematic pursuit of profit maximization . . .) and the institutions and procedures within which such behaviour is developed" (88). Referencing Gunner Myrdal, Lukes notes that despite its claims to "value freedom," it can be plausibly argued that economic individualism "is inherently normative, tending to present the core institutions of capitalism—private property, the market, free competition, etc.—as meeting the requirements of efficiency and equity" (91).

3. "Epistemological individualism" proposes an explanation of the nature of knowledge and the conditions under which human beings have it. It "asserts that the source of knowledge lies within the individual" (Lukes 1973, 107). Descartes provides a rationalist version in his theory that knowledge of the external world and the past is grounded in the knower's certainty of her own existence, on the assumption of God's veracity. However, Lukes urges, "The paradigm epistemological individualist is perhaps the empiricist, who holds that (individual) experience is the source of knowledge, and that all knowledge arises within the circle of the individual mind and the sensations it receives" (107). Generally, epistemological individualism is contrasted to theories "which hold that knowledge is, at least in part, the product of what Wittgenstein called 'forms of life' and is to be tested as genuine by reference to a public world" (109). From that perspective, it is open to two related objections, "first, an appeal to a public world, and, second, to a shared 'inter-subjective' language, as preconditions or presuppositions of knowledge" (109).

4. "Religious individualism" proposes an explanation of how human beings are truly and properly related to God. Defining it "as the view that the individual

does not need intermediaries, that he has the primary responsibility for his own spiritual destiny, that he has the right and duty to come to his own relationship with his God in his own way and by his own efforts," Lukes characterizes it as "both a religious doctrine and, by implication, a theory of the nature of religion" (1973, 94). It "points to two further and important ideas: spiritual equality and religious self-scrutiny." In its more extreme forms it "bases religious certainty on the individual's act of faith" (96), evidently making it a form of religious epistemological individualism. In this vein, since Pascal, Lukes takes Søren Kierkegaard to be "the most profound and influential exponent of religious individualism" (97). Lukes observes that religious individualism "evidently embraces a wide range, from the most communal forms of Protestantism to cults of private mysticism" (95). Lukes cites, apparently approvingly, Ernst Troeltsch's judgment that religious individualism's core stress on the individual's unmediated relationship with God is rooted in the religious movement of the Reformation, and not in the secular movement of the Renaissance (cf., 94), and Werner Stark's amplification that it arose in opposition to the Catholic view of God's relationship to the whole of humankind (rather than to the individual) and of the "collectivity of the Church as the mediator of redemption" (95). Lukes associates the practice of "religious self-scrutiny" especially with "Calvinism" (95). He cites Troeltsch's opinion that such self-scrutiny "tended to make the individual increasingly egocentric" (95).

5. "Ethical individualism" proposes an explanation of morality. It defines morality as "essentially individual" (Lukes 1973, 99). Lukes distinguishes between "ethical egoism" and "ethical individualism." Ethical egoism, which was popular in Great Britain from Hobbes to the early Utilitarians, "postulates the *object* of morality as exclusively individual" (100), viewing the "sole moral object of the individual's action" as "his own benefit" (99). This view has often, although not always, been underpinned by a psychological egoism, "according to which men always act in their own interests" (99). In contrast to that, ethical individualism holds that "the *source* of morality, of moral values and principles, the creator of the very criteria of moral evaluations, is the individual: he becomes the supreme arbiter of moral (and, by implication, other) values, the final moral authority in the most fundamental sense" (101). Lukes takes Nietzsche and Kierkegaard as the paradigmatic examples of ethical individualism (see 101), although he names C. L. Stevenson's "emotivism" and R. M. Hare's "prescriptivism" as other versions of it (see 104). Lukes suggests that ethical individualism "can be seen as the philosophical consequence of taking the idea of autonomy seriously and carrying it to its logical conclusion" (101). He also urges that it is "intimately linked with the view that facts and values are logically distinct, that no empirical description of the world compels us to adopt any particular set of moral evaluations or principles, or even limits the range of our possible value preferences" (101). Indeed,

> Ethical individualism is a position which can only be maintained by someone whose language embodies this distinction between fact and value, that is, a language whose moral vocabulary enables him to make statements which are distinctively either factual or evaluative . . . as opposed to the moral vocabularies of earlier periods of our history or of other, less 'indi-

vidualistic' cultures, where central moral terms such as 'chivalry,' 'honor,' 'piety,' and so on are an intrinsic part of an established structure of roles and obligations and are in their contexts of use ineradicably both descriptive *and* evaluative. (102)

These five senses of individualism constitute one class of "elements" that Lukes has isolated in his analysis of the various ways in which the term is used. The theological account of human being developed in the present work does not entail any one of them, nor any combination of them. Indeed, it would be very difficult to show the coherence of any of them with this anthropology. Political individualism and economic individualism assume that human beings are "independent centers of consciousness" who are the sole generators of their wants, preferences, and values. But this project in theological anthropology goes out of its way to stress that it is essential to what human creatures are that they are social agents in shared public proximate contexts that are partly structured by cultural traditions and shared language that shape human beings' wants, preferences, values, and ways of construing themselves, one another, and their worlds. So, too, epistemological individualism is challenged by this anthropology's insistence that Christian claims, in this case about human being, are grounded in and shaped by the practices of communities of Christian faith—that is, by "forms of life," and by shared uses of a common language. Even when discounting the theologically dubious proposals about the origins of religious individualism in the Reformation's critique of medieval Roman Catholic practices and its special affinities with Calvinism, it is nonetheless the case that its core claim about human beings' unmediated relationship with God flatly contradicts this anthropology's systematic reliance on the claim that many of God's relations to human beings and all human relations to God are mediated. There is, perhaps, more prima facie similarity between ethical individualism's stress on individuals' responsibility for the moral values they cherish, the moral principles they follow, and the moral ends for which they strive and this anthropology's insistence that each human being is "terminal" in the order of responsibility—that is, the order of ability to respond to questioning about the moral quality of their lives—and in the order of accountability—that is, the order of ability to give an account of the moral quality of their actions, in short, for their own decisions of "how" they orient themselves to God and to their fellow human beings. However, insofar as ethical individualism requires a systematic bifurcation between descriptions and evaluations, it is incommensurable with the conceptual scheme of a theological anthropology like this one whose conceptual structure is presided over by the concept "personal" (as in "living human *personal* bodies"), whose use is ineradicably both descriptive and evaluative. Not only are these five senses of individualism not entailed by this anthropology, they are basically inconsistent with it.

A second class of elements that Lukes (1973) has isolated in his analysis of the various ways in which individualism is used consists of a single idea. "Methodological individualism" does not propose an explanation of any human phenomenon. Rather, it is "a doctrine about explanation which asserts that all attempts to explain social (or individual) phenomena [i.e., attempts to explain human phenomena] are to be rejected (or, according to current, more sophisticated versions, rejected as 'rock-bottom' explanations) unless they are couched wholly in terms of facts about individuals" (110). The doctrine "advances a range of different claims in accordance with how much 'society' is built into the supposedly explanatory 'individuals'" (118). This can range across the following spectrum: (a) genetic makeup, brain-states, and the like; (b) aggression, gratification, stimulus-response, and the like; (c) cooperation, power, esteem, and the like; (d) enactment of practices like cashing checks, saluting, voting, and the like (see 118). "Methodological individualism," Lukes concludes, is "an exclusivist, prescriptive doctrine about what explanations look like. In the first three forms," which restrict relevant explanatory "facts" to either types (a), (b), or (c) above, "it excludes explanations which appeal to social forces, structural features of society, institutional factors, and so on, while in the fourth form," which includes explanatory "facts" of type (d) above, "it only appears to exclude such an appeal" (122) because it "builds crucial social factors or features of society into allegedly explanatory individuals. . . ," with the result that "the social phenomena have not really been eliminated; they have been swept under the carpet" (121–22).

The theological account of human being developed in the present work certainly does not lead to an anthropological individualism in the sense that it relies on methodological individualism. Not only does it not entail methodological individualism, its methodology is contradictory to methodological individualism. In particular, this anthropological project stresses theological reasons for attending to social structures and forces when offering explanations of how faithful, hopeful, and loving personal identities are formed, flourish, become distorted, bound, set free, and eschatologically consummated—namely, that social structures and forces should be considered as integral a part of God's good creation of human beings in community in their proximate contexts as their physical bodies and their various physical, sensory, affective, imaginative, and cognitive powers are considered part of God's good creation.

A third class of elements that Lukes (1973) isolates in his analysis of the various ways in which individualism is used consists of five characterizations of the individual that cut across individualistic political, economic, epistemological, religious, and ethical explanations, as well as methodological individualism, because they are, usually tacitly, presupposed as descriptors of the individual who figures in the explanation. They are as follows:

1. *Dignity*, the "principle of the supreme and intrinsic value, or dignity, of the human being" (Lukes 1973, 45; emphasis omitted). Lukes judges that this idea "has the logical status of a moral (or religious) axiom which is basic, ultimate and overriding, offering a general justifying principle in moral argument. He holds that its "most impressive and systematic expression" is found in the writings of Immanuel Kant, for whom human beings exist as ends in themselves, and not merely as means for arbitrary use by others, and that human beings must therefore in all their actions, whether directed at themselves or to other rational beings, always be viewed at the same time as an end.

2. *Autonomy*, or self-direction, "according to which an individual's thoughts and action are his own, and not determined by agencies or causes outside his control. In particular, an individual is autonomous (at the social level) to the

degree to which he subjects the pressures and norms with which he is con-
fronted to conscious and critical evaluation, and forms intentions and reaches
practical decisions as the result of independent and rational reflection" (Lukes
1973, 52). Lukes notes that Thomas Aquinas seems to have been the first to
express this idea clearly, that it is found in the Reformers' writings about con-
science, and is a major theme in the Renaissance, as well as being a central
theme in the Enlightenment (see 52, 53). It is "neutral with respect to the issue
whether or not morality is relative and, in particular, to whether moral values
are subject to individual choice" (57). Hence, while it does not entail ethical
individualism, such as Lukes attributes to Kierkegaard along with Nietzsche, it
is entirely compatible with it.

3. *Privacy*, the idea of "a private existence within a public world, an arena
within which the individual is or should be left alone by others and able to do
and think whatever he chooses . . ." (Lukes 1973, 60). The private realm as a
space for socially unregulated and unmonitored thought and action is a positive value in modern liberalism rooted in the Enlightenment. It is the basis of
the value placed on the institution of private property, construed as a physical
possession with which one is free to do what one wishes, as virtually an extension of one's physical body. Isaiah Berlin also links privacy to the idea with
"negative liberty," based on a sense of the sacredness of personal relationships,
that has been part of liberalism's justification for insisting on civil liberties and
individual rights. Construed slightly differently as a space for an inner religious
life in which "*secret* [esoteric?] knowledge of and communion with God" is
achieved, privacy is also a value in the tradition of Christian mysticism. By
contrast, much of the ancient world considered it a negative value—in Hannah Arendt's phrase, a "privative trait" of a life like that of a slave that "was not
permitted to enter the public realm" (60).

4. *Self-development*, "an ideal for the lives of individuals"—an ideal whose
content varies with different ideas of the *self* on a continuum from pure egoism to strong communitarianism. Where the idea of privacy is rooted in the
Enlightenment, the idea of self-development is rooted in Romanticism. For the
early Romantics it was an antisocial ideal, calling for the individual to be set
apart from and hostile to society. In Germany it developed "into a theory of
organic community" (Lukes 1973, 69) in which individuality "is predicated of
the *Volk*, or the State" (69), which is to develop its unique communal spirit.
Especially through John Stuart Mill, the idea of self-development also entered
the liberal tradition. In that context it was more extra-social than anti-social,
calling for the individuals to pursue their own paths, free of social pressure. The
idea also entered Marxist theory through Karl Marx's anthropology, according
to which self-development is essentially communal (see 70, 71). In that context
it is highly social, calling for individual "self-development *through* community
with others" (71; emphasis added). In each version, self-development "has the
status of an ultimate value, an end-in-itself . . ." (72).

Where dignity, autonomy, privacy, and self-development name values or
ideals that describe the individuals who are key to various types of individualistic explanations of human phenomena, a final descriptor of those individuals
whom Lukes isolates as a basic idea of individualism has a different logical

status. It "specifies, not a value or an ideal, but rather a *way* of conceiving the individual (which is not, however, morally neutral)" (Lukes 1973, 73; emphasis in original).

5. Lukes refers to the *abstract individual*, "with *given* interests, wants, purposes, needs, etc." (73; emphasis added).

> The crucial point about this conception is that the relevant features of individuals determining the ends which social arrangements are held (actually or ideally) to fulfill, whether these features are called instincts, faculties, needs, desires, rights, etc., are assumed as given, *independently of social context*. This givenness of fixed and invariant human psychological features leads to an *abstract* conception of the individual who is seen as merely the bearer of those features, which determine his behaviour, and specify his interests, needs and rights (73; emphasis added)

In this view, "Society and the state are pictured as sets of actual or possible social arrangements which respond more or less adequately to those individuals' requirements. Social and political rules and institutions are, on this view, regarded collectively as an artifice, a modifiable instrument, a means of fulfilling independently given individual objectives; the means and the end are distinct" (73). Alternative conceptions of the individual that are essentially social were advanced by counterrevolutionary and conservative Romantics; by Auguste Compte and the so-called Positivists; by sociologists and social psychologists, notably Émile Durkheim and the pragmatist George Herbert Mead; by Hegel and English idealists; and by Karl Marx. Lukes cites Marx's critique of abstract individualism as especially penetrating: "*Man* is not an abstract being, squatting outside the world. Man is *the human world*, the state, society." "Man is in the lost literal sense of the word *zoon politikon*, not only a social animal, but an animal which can develop into an individual only in society. Production by isolated individuals outside society . . . is as great an absurdity as the idea of the development of language without individuals living together and talking to one another" (75, 76, quoting, respectively, *Marx's Contribution to the Critique of Hegel's Philosophy of Right: Introduction*, written in 1844, and *Introduction to the Critique of Political Economy*, written in 1857).

The abstract individual is the individual to whom dignity and autonomy are ascribed and whose privacy and self-development are ultimately valued. It is the individual who is declared by methodological individualism to be the key factor in explaining human phenomena, and it serves as the key explanatory factor in political, economic, epistemological, religious, and ethical individualism. However, it is not a concept of human being that is entailed by the anthropological proposals advanced by this project. As a concept of individual human beings abstracted from their social, cultural, and historical proximate contexts such that their instincts, faculties, needs, desires, rights, and so forth, are assumed to be given independently of their proximate contexts, it is flatly contradictory of this anthropology's insistence on human creatures' essential locatedness in the quotidian worlds of their proximate contexts.

Steven Lukes's conceptual analysis of the ambiguities of ordinary uses of "individualism" is helpful, not only in distinguishing this anthropological project from common senses of "individualism," but also in clarifying some tangled issues in intratheological disputes about individualism.

What is the Christian theological objection to an individualistic concept of human being? What would be a theologically more acceptable alternative concept? It is not uncommon to read in theological anthropology that a theologically adequate anthropological concept would be a "relational" concept of human being (or of the "human person," or the "self," used virtually interchangeably) rather than an "individualistic" concept. Broadly speaking, the theological argument for this claim seems to be that a relational concept of human being would provide conceptual space and conceptual resources in which to explain in "personalistic" categories core theological claims about the dynamic intersubjective relational sociality that is the necessary condition of creaturely human life and its flourishing; the dynamically relational character of the image of God that marks human beings as human; the dynamically interpersonal relational character of bondage in sin, oppression, and evil that estranges human beings from God and one another, distorting the image of God; the dynamically interpersonal relational character of reconciliation to God and one another and the process of transformation of sin's distortions of human being (i.e., "justification and sanctification by grace through faith"); and the dynamically intersubjective relational character of eschatological consummation of that process of transformation in human beings' eschatological consummation in a creaturely participation in the life of the triune God that is itself inherently relational and dynamic in its own interpersonal way. In contrast to this, it is claimed, an "individualistic" concept of human being only provides conceptual space and conceptual resources in which to explain these theological anthropological claims in static and impersonal categories in terms of universal, and often hierarchical, structures of human beings' status and roles vis à vis one another and God (often construed on the model of a contract or covenant), structures of rules governing human beings' appropriate actions in those status and roles, and legalistic and moralistic schedules of rewards or punishments for following or violating the rules. An intuition underlying this preference for relational rather than individualistic concepts of human being is that relational concepts allow for coherent characterization of theologically significant relationships with God and fellow human beings as relationships somehow internal and intrinsic to human being and conducive to its flourishing, while individualistic concepts only allow characterization of them as external and extrinsic relationships that threaten the integrity of human being in its fundamental individuality.

However, as Steven Lukes's analysis of senses of individualism shows, a contrast between individualistic and relational concepts of human being as though they were mutually exclusive does not hold up historically or conceptually, at least not if social relations really count as relations. Many if not most of the senses of individualism that he sorted out among the ambiguities of ordinary uses of the word are individualisms that can, and historically have, embraced social concepts of the individual as well as egoistic concepts of the individual. Among concepts of the human individual are coherent social concepts of the individual. In general, individual and social concepts of human being can no more be played off against each other in theological anthropology than they can in any other type of inquiry concerning human being.

Furthermore, sociality is only one kind of relationality. If individual concepts of human being cannot be played off against social concepts of human being, neither can they necessarily be played off against relational concepts of human being in general. If there are some kinds of relations that human beings might have to realities other than themselves that are mutually exclusive of an individualistic concept of human being, that would need to be demonstrated case by case. It cannot be deduced a priori from an alleged contradiction in principle between relational and individualistic concepts of human being. I suggest that an individualistic concept of human being is not as such problematic in theological anthropology, if for no other reason than because it is conceptually impossible to talk about human beings without acknowledging that they are not only social beings standing in and shaped by many kinds of relations, but also are concrete individuals who are not wholly reducible to mental constructs abstracted from concrete social entities.

There is, however, a genuine issue in theological anthropology about the kind of concept of "individual" that is theologically acceptable. It can be couched as a choice between the concept of an abstract individual and the concept of a concrete individual. As we have seen from Lukes's analysis, a concept of the "abstract individual" is a concept of an individual whose instincts, faculties, needs, desires, rights, interests, purposes, and so on, are simply given as properties of a center of consciousness that is independent of its social, cultural, and historical contexts. It is the modern concept of the person that, as we noted above, Michael Welker argues is theologically inadequate. It may be formulated in a variety of ways, from a concept of an egoistic individual to a concept of a social individual that is understood relationally at least in regard to social relations and the intersubjective and intrasubjective relations that are required for social relations. However, it seeks to conceptualize individual human being and its instincts, faculties, needs, desires, and so on, in abstraction from the concrete particularities of its social, cultural, and historical contexts. The contrasting concept of a "concrete individual" is of an individual whose instincts, faculties, needs, desires, rights, interests, purposes, and so on, are, in varying degrees, modified, shaped, or even constituted by the structures and dynamics of its social, cultural, and historical contexts. It seeks to conceptualize individual human being in its concrete social, cultural, and historical locatedness rather than by abstracting it from its locatedness. The difference between the two is a difference in view, not about whether human individuals are both individual and in some way relational, but about in what way they are *at once* individual and relational. The concept of abstract individuality can coherently include the view that social relations are necessarily a property of individual human beings, but holds that they are a property of a center of consciousness whose instincts, faculties, needs, desires, rights, interests, purposes, and on some views, its *inherent sociality*, and so on, are given independently of, and logically prior to, its social, cultural, and historical contexts. In contrast to that, according to the concept of concrete individuality, an individual human being's instincts, faculties, needs, desires, rights, interests, purposes, and so on, are a product of some type of reciprocal dialectical relation between an individual and its context. A concept of concrete individuals leaves a great deal of conceptual room for differing views of just how the dialectic between an individual and its contexts works.

I suggest that polemics in Christian theological anthropology against anthropological individualism are aimed at abstract individualism in theology, which is deemed to be theologically problematic. The polemics are framed much too broadly when couched as polemics against individualism in general. Given that abstract individualism lies at the heart of the modernist intellectual tradition from the early Enlightenment onward, represented especially powerfully in modern culture by classical liberalism, it is pretty certain that it is the real target of theological polemics that appropriate the insights of postmodern thought, whose polemical target includes precisely that concept. However, abstract individualism has been the target of theological polemics in a number of Christian theological movements well before the rise of postmodernism. These include theological anthropologies influenced by such disparate intellectual movements as sundry Hegelianisms, various Marxisms, certain existential phenomenologies such as that of Alfred Schutz, the "sociology of knowledge" (especially Émile Durkheim, or Karl Manheim, or, more recently, Peter Berger), Whiteheadian or Hartshornian process metaphysics, and American pragmatism.

Insofar as the target is abstract individualism, the anthropological proposals promoted here have explicitly joined the theological polemic against individualism. The proposals advanced here do not tacitly imply such abstract individualism. However, as this project's repeated focus on questions about human beings' unsubstitutable personal identities shows, it stresses the importance of concepts of concrete individualism in the practice of secondary Christian theology for specifically theological reasons.

Two things I ask of you;
    do not deny them to me before I die:
Remove far from me falsehood and lying;
    give me neither poverty nor riches;
    feed me with the food that I need
or I shall be full, and deny you,
    and say, "Who is the LORD?"
or I shall be poor, and steal,
    and profane the name of my God.
PROVERBS 30:7–9

CHAPTER **10**

Sins as Distortions of Faithful Existential "Hows"

Creaturely human personal bodily life is finite, dying life lived on borrowed breath. Lived wisely in faith, it flourishes as the glory of God. However, lived foolishly in distorted faith, dying life becomes a living death. It obscures God's glory. The distortion of faith that is enacted in foolish living is sin; the living death that it causes is one type of evil. It is important for theological reasons, I believe, to distinguish clearly between sin and evil. The failure to do so generates unnecessary confusions in theological anthropology. I suggest that the difference can be brought out this way: where "sin" must be defined theocentrically as a distortion of proper human response to God, "evil" may be defined in a creature-centric way as violation of creatures' integrities. I begin this chapter, therefore, with remarks about the concept of evil that are guided by canonical biblical Wisdom literature's background creation theology.

Evil: Fools, Falsehood, Violence, and Living Death
A persistent theme in biblical Wisdom is that while wise practices in the everyday lead to life, foolish practices of a certain sort lead to death. In the Proverbs lexicon there is a distinction between two categories of fools and foolishness. One is that of the inexperienced and simple, such as those to whom the opening verses of Proverbs are addressed. Theirs is a foolishness that can be outgrown as, seeking to respond appropriately to the way in which God creatively relates to them, they become wise—or at any rate, wiser. The other is the foolishness of scoffers and scorners who refuse to respond appropriately to their vocation to be wise. The latter foolishness leads to death. In this chapter, only the second type of fool is in view.

What is striking in the explanation of foolish practices in Proverbs is its consistent association of violent practices with false speech.

The mouth of the righteous is a fountain of life,
but the mouth of the wicked conceals violence.
(10:11; cf. 10:6)

Violent practices are active relations with fellow creatures that violate them. That includes violations that lead to biological death (e.g., Prov. 11:30). But in Proverbs, violence has a broader range than that. It covers practices that violate fellow creatures by belittling them (11:12), by slandering them (10:18), even by enticing them into "a way that is not good" (16:29). It also includes practices that violate the network of interactions which makes up quotidian social life by introducing strife in the home (17:1, 14, 19; 20:3) and strife in the community by being quarrelsome (26:21) or by meddling in others' quarrels (26:17), by false witness (19:5) and gossip (11:13; 20:19), by "[winking] the eyes" at evil (16:30; cf. 10:10), by whispering (26:20, 22), or (of special importance to those who are short on sleep) by inappropriately loud pious talk:

Whoever blesses a neighbor with a loud voice,
rising early in the morning.
will be counted as cursing.
(27:14)

Practices that violate fellow creatures and the shared everyday world lead to a death that is not necessarily the end of biological life, but is usually a common life that is a living death.

One thing shared by this entire range of types of violating interactions is that they are all human actions to which use of language is integral. Mainstream canonical Wisdom has a strikingly high view of the power of speech for good or ill:

When words are many, transgression is not lacking,
but the prudent are restrained in speech.
(10:19)

With their mouths the godless would destroy their neighbors,
but by knowledge the righteous are delivered.
(11:9)

To watch over mouth and tongue
is to keep out of trouble.
(21:23)

And it links untruthful speaking with violating practices:

The words of the wicked are a deadly ambush,
but the speech of the upright delivers them.
(12:6)

> Death and life are in the power of the tongue,
> and those who love it will eat its fruits.
>
> (18:21)

This link between false speaking and violating practices brings out an important anthropological point. Personal bodies' violating practices are inseparable from untruthful uses of language. Like all human practices, practices that violate other living creatures, and the networks of giving and receiving that make up their common life, are socially established and cooperative. As socially established, such practices have a certain determinacy because they are conceptually formed. Anyone who engages in them has to have learned the relevant concepts as part of learning a common language. Since the practices are cooperative, anyone who engages in them has to share that language and use it with others who cooperate in the practice. For a practice to continue and for it to be effective, language use among those engaged in it, even when it is a violating practice, has to be relatively truthful and reliable. Hence there is at least a minimal degree of truth-telling among conspirators in a deception. However, for a practice to violate others' lives it must also in some way engage those who are violated. The violated must somehow be co-opted into the practices, at cost to their well-being. That can only be accomplished by untruthful use of some common language, by lying and deceitful speech.

Such lying speech may be untruthful in any or all of three ways. It will certainly be untrue to the ones being violated. It will be untrue to whatever trusting relationship they have with those who violate them. It may also, second, be untrue to facts, so that it misrepresents, denies, or obscures circumstances and features of the practices that make them violating. And it will be speech untrue to those doing the violating, misrepresenting, denying, or obscuring their motives, dispositions, interests, and intentions.

Such lying speech need not be employed deliberately, with conscious intent to deceive. To say that some person has lied to others and deceived them naturally suggests that the lying and deceit was intentional. However, a society's conventional ways of employing an ordinary language can serve to mislead both hearers and speakers by obfuscating and distorting reality. When those ways of speaking are uncritically employed, speech may be said to be systemically lying and deceitful even though no speaker intends to lie or deceive anyone. Wisdom's reference to lying and deceitful speech can as accurately characterize systemic as intentional lying and deceit. Correlatively, those who are violated through practices of lying and deceitful speech need not be consciously co-opted into such practices. They need only engage in the practices uncritically, and engaging in them will be costly to their well-being. That is different from their consciously and deliberately allowing themselves, perhaps out of desperation, to be co-opted by violating practices that depend on systematically lying and deceitful speech, because those practices appear to offer the only way in which to survive in their particular proximate contexts.

Understood in the context of its background creation theology, canonical Wisdom's link between untruthful speech and violating practices may guide theological reflections on the nature of evil.

Evil may be understood as violation of creatures. Understood in this way, evil is any violation of what creatures are by God's creative relating to them. It is violation of what the violated ones are, either as instances of some natural kind or as individuals in their particularity. In the case of human creatures, accountable for their response to the triune God, evil may also be violation that distorts the personal identities (who they are precisely as creatures) of the ones violated. And evil may distort the ways in which the ones who are violated are existentially set in their proximate contexts (how they ought to be precisely as creatures). Furthermore, in the case of human creatures, those who violate others by enactments of certain practices violate themselves as well.

This is not the place to develop a full-blown theological taxonomy and explanation of evil, but six unsystematic remarks are in order.

1. "Evil" is here defined theologically relative to creatures as they are creatively related to by God. If God relates to what is not God in other ways as well—say, by drawing it to eschatological consummation or by reconciling its estrangements—then there may be additional senses of "evil." These additional senses of "evil" would be defined by reference to creatures as actively related to by God in those additional ways. That is a contingent matter, dependent on God's free self-determination. There can be no a priori logic by which to generate a theological Christian taxonomy of evil that would comprehend all of these senses of evil systematically. In the context of a discussion of human beings as creatures, evil is defined by reference to what creatures are by God's creative relating.

2. Adopting canonical Wisdom's dominant image for evil as violence against fellow creatures, and trading on the relation between violence and violation, we may develop that image further: in the context of the triune God's creative relating to all that is not God, evil is always a distortion of a creature in one or more respects. Hence, "evil" is not the name of a reality in its own right, other than fellow creatures and other than God. The creature is the reality in its own right. Evil may be violation of a particular creature (as happens by disease or accidental injury or violation of a network of social relationships in which certain creatures are located, as when a mother and her young are scattered, or when a human community disintegrates). Evil is a distortion of creatures, but not the transformation of creatures into some other type of reality than they are apart from the distorting violation. Thus, evil's reality is parasitic on creatures' reality. It follows that evil cannot be a reality in its own right. Given this account of evil, the notion of something purely evil as such would be a category

mistake. Rather, on this understanding, evil is a condition of creatures whose reality and value are grounded in God's creative relating.

3. A third unsystematic remark about a theological concept of evil is that violated creatures, victims of evil, remain centers of energy. As something a creature undergoes, "violation" implies the creature's passivity. It may involve weakening of the creature as a finite center of energy. However, as a condition that a creature has undergone, "violation" does not imply the absence, nor does it necessarily imply the weakening, of a creature's energy. What it does imply is some distortion of the creature's energy. Hence, evil as violation may just as well be an active and powerful condition of a creature as it may be a passive condition.

This remark fits poorly with two major Western theological traditions about evil. Much theology since the early nineteenth century has echoed Schleiermacher's contention (1928, 315–24; see 338–40) that evil is simply the way people experience and interpret certain events when their consciousness of God has severely dimmed. Were their God-consciousness not so dim, they would experience and understand God's presence even in evil events. This comes too close to making evil into an illusion, an unreality created by the state of our consciousness and projected onto fellow creatures. In Schleiermacher's case it does not finally come to that because, on his account of it, the experience of evil is a very real experience of suffering that has powerful and real consequences for one's well-being. Nonetheless, the reality and power of evil situations is bestowed on them by the state of our consciousness, rather than being inherent in evil situations independently of our mode of consciousness of the evil. By contrast, I want to stress that we neither ascribe nor bestow reality and power to evil conditions or situations as evil; rather, we acknowledge their reality and power as we suffer from their energetic reality.

Alternatively, in the Augustinian tradition, evil is understood as the privation of being. On this view, to be is, by God's creative fiat, good; evil is a loss or privation of some degree of being, and hence a loss or privation of goodness. Evil is related to a creaturely reality as disease is related to a living body. The diseased body is still a real and living body, but in some respect(s) it is corrupted, diminished. So, too, when evil afflicts God's creature, the creature is still a real creature and (since what God creates is always good) is therefore still good. Nevertheless, if the created cosmos may be thought of as a hierarchy of creatures having different degrees of being, a creature afflicted by evil has slipped a grade in being and value. It is ontologically de-graded. It is diminished both in being and goodness. This has the theological merit of stressing that evil conditions and situations are real, independent of our consciousness or understanding of them. It also avoids suggesting that evil is a powerful being in its own right. Thus, it is the polar opposite of the claim that evil is merely the construction that dim God-consciousness puts on one's circumstances. Evil is the corruption of a created being, not a being in its own right. However, this view has the drawback of tending to suggest that evil is a weakening of creatures and their powers, not a distortion of their powers, which, far from weakening them, may focus and intensify their powers in dangerous ways.

4. At the same time, it must be added that as a violation of creatures as centers of energies, evil is often a systematic distortion of creatures as energy systems. This gives evil a certain over-againstness relative to personal bodies' individual and collective intentional actions to correct, heal, or even eliminate particular violations of fellow creatures. Some distortions brought by violations of creatures tend to have the power to resist ameliorative or transformative efforts. In the case of personal bodies this means that the evil each undergoes may so distort his energies that, even though he himself longs for and seeks their correction, the distortions may have, as it were, a life of their own, resistant of efforts to change them. In the case of communities of human bodies, this means that distortions of the practices that make up their common life may become so systemic to their common life that they persist over time as particular personal bodies enter and leave the community and powerfully resist efforts by members of the community to modify or transform them.

5. Understood as the violation of finite beings insofar as they are creatively related to by God, evil may be said to damage their well-being but not to damage their flourishing as God's glory. In chapter 7, I stressed that creatures' flourishing is defined by God's glory and is independent of their well-being. Well-being is an abstract and relative notion that must be concretely defined in each case by reference to what a given creature is. What human creatures are as living bodies by God's creativity is and remains the glory of God, no matter how much their well-being is damaged by evil violation. Consequently, violation of their creaturely integrities in no way undercuts human creatures' dignity and their inherent claim on their neighbors for unconditional respect. On the other hand, the fact that who they are and how they are to be is also the glory of God becomes very ambiguous and obscure when they are violated by evil.

6. Finally, personal bodies' actions that violate fellow creatures are inseparable from untruthful use of language. Human action that violates fellow creatures is always done in a social and cultural context, is parasitic on that culture's language and its conventions of significant gesture and action, but uses them untruthfully. Hence, like all human action, action that violates creatures and their interrelationships is done and experienced in ways that are conceptually formed and (usually) linguistically shaped. However, it is also the case that action that violates other creatures—that is, causes evil— is done and experienced in ways formed by untruthful uses of language. This is not to say that all action that violates fellow creatures is action that intends to violate them. The lying and deceptive language used in common by violator and violated alike may be deceptive precisely in the ways

it obscures from both violator and violated the violating consequences of the action it helps form. Nor is this to say that untruthful speech always forms the motives of intentional violation of other creatures. The motives of intentional acts that unintentionally violate other creatures may well be formed by truthful uses of language. Nonetheless, the violating practices that are enacted in intentional actions that unintentionally violate fellow creatures are inseparable from untruthful uses of language.

Sin: Folly, Distorted Faith, and Living Death

In contradistinction to evil, I suggest that human creatures' "sin" is best defined as "living foolishly in distorted faith." Sin is folly—that is, an inappropriate response to the triune God relating to us creatively. The opposite of living in "the fear of the LORD" that leads to life, to sin is to live in distorted faith in God. To sin is not simply to live in the total absence of any trust in or loyalty to God and God's own cause, although that may be its limiting case, but to live in a trust and a loyalty that are distorted versions of an appropriate response to God's active creating.

This proposal is guided by biblical Wisdom's view of sin as folly. In mainstream biblical Wisdom tradition, as represented by Proverbs, "folly" designates human practices in which untruthful use of language and violations of fellow creatures are combined. In this literature, "fools" designates human creatures who scorn their vocation to be wise in their practices for the well-being of the quotidian. Their practices are designated "foolish" because they do violate the well-being of the quotidian, including their own well-being. They are self-destroying practices, leading to living death.

"Folly" enacts an orientation to the quotidian that is the opposite of "the fear of the LORD." Proverbs regularly connects the fear of the Lord with wisdom, knowledge, and life. The prologue to the book concludes with this theme, although it is not to be interpreted as a programmatic statement for the book as a whole:

> The fear of the LORD is the beginning of knowledge;
>   fools despise wisdom and instruction.
>
>   (1:7)

The fear of the Lord can be flatly identified with instruction in wisdom:

> The fear of the LORD is instruction in wisdom,
>   and humility goes before honor.
>
>   (15:33)

The fear of the Lord is explicitly associated with life:

> The fear of the LORD prolongs life,
> but the years of the wicked will be short.
> (10:27)

Indeed, a later sentence identifies the two:

> The fear of the LORD is life indeed;
> filled with it one rests secure
> and suffers no harm.
> (19:23)

In the context of biblical Wisdom's background creation theology, "fear of the LORD" is personal bodies' appropriate response to the peculiar way in which God relates creatively. In this context, "fear" does not have the sense of "terror." Rather it has the sense of a doxological gratitude that is reverent before and awed by the hospitable and radically free generosity of God's creativity.

Negatively speaking, fear of the Lord is the opposite of folly—that is, the conjunction of untruthful speech and violating practices:

> I, wisdom, live with prudence,
> and I attain knowledge and discretion.
> The fear of the LORD is hatred of evil . . .
> and perverted speech I hate.
> (8:12, 13)

Conversely, the opposite of fear of the Lord, according to Woman Wisdom, wisdom personified, is scorn of the call to be wise:

> Because they hated knowledge
> and did not choose the fear of the LORD,
> would have none of my counsel,
> and despised all my reproof,
> therefore they shall eat the fruit of their way
> and be sated with their own devices.
> (1:29–31)

Understood in the context of its background creation theology, canonical Wisdom's picture of folly may guide theological reflections on the nature of sin, in contradistinction to evil, that are developed along a trajectory set by Wisdom but which go beyond anything Wisdom literature itself affirms.

Properly speaking, then, sin is not the name of a subset of evil. Evil is defined by direct reference to creatures as they are related to creatively by God. Evil is violation of what and who creatures are and how they are to be. Sin, by contrast, is defined by direct reference to God. It is defined theocentrically; it is always "against God." It is not fundamentally constituted by a mis-relating to ourselves and to our neighbors but by a mis-relating to God.

As inappropriate response to God, sin causes distortions of personal bodies even though sin is not itself a violation of personal bodies, but rather a violation of human bodies' appropriate way of relating to God in response to God's relating creatively to them. In particular, sin causes distorting violations of the one who sins. As we shall see below, it leads to distortions of their existential set in the everyday world (their existential hows) and distortions of sinful personal bodies' identities (their "who"). Moreover, as distortion of appropriate human response to God's creative relating, sin leads to a mis-orienting or mis-focusing of finite energies, but it does not necessarily weaken them. It may rather lead to their amplification. Sin may have effects that violate both the sinner and her fellow creatures, but such violation is not necessarily a diminution of their energies and powers. Thus, if faith, as the fear of the Lord, leads to life, then sin, its grotesque distortion, leads to distorted life, to living death. Sin's consequences, thus, just are evils in the sense of "violations of creatures."

Sin and the evil that it causes are negative mysteries. Defining sin relative to God as an inappropriate response to God, and acknowledging that it leads to evil distortions of oneself and of fellow creatures, helps not one bit to explain either the presence of sin in the quotidian or the presence of evil. This is consonant with a remarkable fact about the creation theology through which biblical Wisdom thinks. Just as it offers no account of how God creates, it offers no account of how evil entered creation, even though, especially in Job, it has a realistic view of the presence of evil in the everyday. Such evil cannot be fully explained by saying that human sin causes it and introduced it into the quotidian, for then the question is why sin is present in the quotidian. And sin cannot be fully explained by pointing out that evil already present in the everyday has the effect of distorting personal bodies as energy systems so that when they enact shared practices they do so in distorted—sinful—ways. Such an explanation leaves open two questions. Explanation of sin by reference to the effects on human creatures of preexisting evil simply pushes the question back a step: why was such evil already present? Second, if one simply accepts the (inexplicable!) fact of the existence of evil prior to sin and postulates that sin arises as a (misguided!) effort to correct the evil by our efforts alone, thus weakening and distorting trust in God (i.e., falling into sin), the question would remain why human creatures would undertake so misguided a venture.

The wisdom of silence in the face of the question, "How come sin?" is captured by Kierkegaard's slogan in *The Concept of Anxiety*, "Sin posits itself" (1980). Every theological explanation of how sin entered creation either turns out to be circular, presupposing the very thing it sets out to explain, or explains it away by reclassifying it as another type of evil. For example, explaining sin by sin, Schleiermacher attributes each individual's sin to the fact that each one is born into a social matrix already characterized by sinfully dim God-consciousness. To break out of circular explanation, he accounts for the sinfulness of the communities into which we are born by a developmental drag inherent in human creaturely maturation. As humankind develops, sensuous self-consciousness develops more rapidly and powerfully than God-consciousness so that the latter cannot intensify to the point of governing the former (1928, 271–75). The dimming of God-consciousness and its power to shape communal life simply is the sinful context into which subsequent generations are born (282–306). Thus, the emergence of sin is a function of structures and dynamics inherent in creaturely finitude. Such an explanatory move, however, fails to explain the emergence of sin as evil that is not related to God's creativity. It simply reclassifies such sin as an instance of the class of evil that is a function of God's creativity (330–38). By contrast, Augustine attempts to use the Genesis 3 story of Adam, Eve, and the serpent as the basis of a genetic explanation of how sin and evil entered creation. He traces its origin back to the serpent's already sinful deceptive powers as a tempter. He then attempts to explain why the serpent is evil, although created good by God, by reference to a quasi-biblical myth of the pre-Adamic fall in which the highest angel succumbs to the temptation to rebel against God, becoming Satan the tempter. At each turn, the key explanation relies on vulnerability to being tempted, which may imply sinfulness, as well as an effective tempter, which already implies sinfulness in the tempter (see R. Brown, 1976).

The point of Kierkegaard's slogan, I take it, is that such circularity is no accident. The logic of a doctrine of the good God's creating a good world *ex nihilo* makes it a conceptual point that "sin posits itself." If sin unrelated to God's creativity is present in the everyday world, that is a fact to be acknowledged. But it is an ab-surd fact that cannot be factored into contributing causes, a surd all the way down. Nothing about either God, the world as God's creature, or the relations between them explains it or implies an explanation.

Sin is a type of negative mystery. It is not mystery in the sense of something in principle explicable but about which we presently have insufficient information for an explanation. Nor is it mystery in the sense of something too richly complex for our finite minds to be able to grasp its rationale. Rather it is mystery in the sense of something undeniably real but a-rational, without cause or reason. Hence, to pose the question, "How do you explain the presence of sin and evil in the created realm?" is to fall prey to a conceptual mistake. To attempt to answer it is to fall into the same confusion.

Appropriate response to God's creativity is faith, that is, trust in God as ground of our reality and value and loyalty to God's own creative project.

Therefore, sin defined theocentrically as personal bodies' *in*appropriate response to God's creativity is a distortion of just such faith. Leading to living death, sin inflicts on the sinner a distortion of its life. It is a radically absurd negative mystery that is energetically powerful, distorting at once sinner, fellow creatures, and the networks of relations in which they interact. Sin causes a subset of a type of violation of human creatures, but that is not what makes it sin. Where evil is defined by reference to the creatures violated by it, sin is defined by reference to God: sin is distortion of appropriate response to the peculiar way in which the triune God relates creatively to all that is not God.

Of particular importance for theological anthropology, sin as distortion of a personal body's faithful response to God is at once distortion of that living body's personal identity and distortion of how that personal body is set into its quotidian proximate contexts.

Distorted Faithful Existential Hows

Sin against the triune God relating to us creatively is, in one way, distortion of faith's loyalty to God's creative project. As distortion of faith's loyalty to God's creative project, sin is a distortion of personal bodies' orientation to their proximate contexts that are largely made up of networks of interactions among fellow creatures, whereas sin as distortion of trust in God is a distortion of personal bodies' orientation to their ultimate context. Sin in the latter sense, as distortion of faith's trust in God's creative relating to us, is taken up in the next chapter as an aspect of sin in the singular, a distorted quotidian personal identity that binds one in a living death. Sin in the former sense, sin as distortion of faith's loyalty to God's creative project, is what we take up here as sins in the plural, distortions of faith's existential hows.

Loyalty to God's project entails doxological gratitude, a distinctive orientation to our proximate contexts. That orientation may be expressed in an indefinitely large number of ways of being set into our proximate contexts. Or, in the sense of the term used in the previous chapter, we can express doxological gratitude in an indefinitely large number of existential hows. Correspondingly, sin as *dis*loyalty to the triune God's creative project can also consist of an indefinitely large number of existential hows.

There is no reason that such hows may not express a certain sort of gratitude for and celebration of the familiar everyday world. However, attitudes and passions of gratitude and celebration are made specific by the determinate character of their objects, of what it is they are thought to be grateful *for* and in celebration *of*. Faith's doxological gratitude is distorted when the quotidian as actively related to by the triune God in God's peculiarly free and hospitably generous way is not the occasion for gratitude and celebration, and the triune God creatively relating to the quotidian is not the One to whom the gratitude and celebratory praise are addressed.

Such distorted doxological gratitude is a personal body's orientation to her proximate contexts. It may be expressed in an indefinitely large number of existential hows. It is such hows that are sinful, expressive in various ways of personal bodies' distorted loyalty to the triune God's creative project and enacted in sinful practices. Certain practices are properly called sinful just because they enact those hows in the everyday world.

In chapter 8, I suggested the multitude of existential hows expressive of faith's loyal doxological gratitude for our proximate contexts—although no inventory can be made of them because they are indefinitely many—may be roughly typologized by their enactments as practices of wonder at, delight in, and perseverance with the quotidian. Correlatively, the multitude of ways in which our orientation to our proximate contexts may express distortion of doxological gratitude can be typologized as practices that are sinful distortions of delight, wonder, and perseverance. Distorted practices of delight, wonder, and perseverance cause evil in that they violate the integrities of finite creatures, but they are sinful in that the existential hows they enact are lived lies. Such hows are ways of being oriented to our proximate contexts that are false in several respects: They are untrue to the triune God's creative relating to our quotidian proximate contexts, they are untrue to quotidian fellow creatures in their concrete particularities as creatively related to by God, and they are untrue to the complex integrity of the personal bodies who engage in such practices.

1. *Distorted practices of delight, for example, are sentimental.* Delight is doxology's gratitude for our proximate contexts within their ultimate contexts, delight in finite fellow creatures as they are given to us by God here and now. It is distorted when it becomes delight in fellow creatures in abstraction from their finitude, in abstraction, not so much from God's relating to them, but from the concrete particularity in which they are constituted by God's creative relating to them. Such abstractive delight in fellow creatures necessarily involves speech that is untrue to the actual quotidian precisely as God relates to it.

In distorted delight, the interplay is dissolved among personal bodies' capacities for rejoicing in fellow creatures, for being patient with them, and for a certain love of them. Delight's joy is informed by the concept "finite creature." As an affective response, it is made determinate by the way in which its present objects are conceived—namely, as finite creatures. Such delight is distorted when its objects are conceived in abstraction from their finitude, as though finitude were a shadow that would rule out positive affective response to them. Delight is sentimental when its objects are falsely idealized as though they were free of intrinsic and extrinsic limits, conflictual contexts, and vulnerability to damage and destruction. Sentimental positive affective response to fellow creatures may take any of a number of forms, ranging from complacency to euphoria about a falsely pretty everyday world. American popular culture, especially in its celebration of family values and of wilderness values, is one vast solicitation of just such sentimental distortions of delight. In their sentimentality, such responses are inappropriate to the finitude of their objects. For that very reason, they are disloyal to God's freedom to create finite creatures truly worthy of joyful response precisely in their finitude. Practices that express such sentimental affective responses are sinful distortions of a faithful response to God.

Delight's patience with finite fellow creatures is distorted when it is separated from joy in those creatures. Creatures' finitude calls for the patience to engage objects of delight in ways that preserve and nurture both them and their ecological contexts so that they have time and space to be themselves. Unconditioned by joy in fellow creatures precisely in their finite particularity, one who patiently engages them will either try to conform them to idealized pictures of the everyday or, oblivious of their otherness, will try to expropriate them as extensions of his own space, time, and personal projects. Even when they are patient, both ways of engaging fellow creatures are sentimental in their denial of the ineluctably finite otherness of fellow creatures. Such distorted patience is an inappropriate response to God's hospitable generosity in giving us our own time and space to be ourselves in our own proximate contexts. Practices that express it are sinful distortions of faithful response to God.

Separated from joy in and patience with fellow creatures, delight's needy love of its objects of delight is also sentimentally distorted. If not conditioned by delight's joy in fellow creatures precisely as finite and by patience with and for them in their finite otherness, love desires them as though they were not genuinely other. It tends to absorb the objects of its desiring love into itself, destroying the love relationship by evaporating the beloved other. Or it desires them as not finally finite, as media so transparent to unlimited, unconditioned transcendence that by loving them one can elevate oneself into union with the infinite Whole, thereby escaping one's own burden of finite otherness. In either form, such distorted love for fellow creatures is an inappropriate response to the hospitable generosity and freedom of God's creativity. Practices that express it are sinful distortions of loyal response to God and God's project.

2. *Distorted practices of wonder are exploitative.* Wonder is gratitude's doxology for its proximate contexts' having come to be as they are. Whereas to delight in the quotidian is to attend to its present givenness, to wonder at it is to attend to the pastness of its present, to attend to the present in the context of its connections with the past out of which it has emerged. Wonder is distorted when it attends to fellow creatures as though they were concretely actual in all their particularity in abstraction from God creatively relating to them precisely in and through their past, in and through their having come to be. Such abstractive wondering at fellow creatures necessarily involves speech about the quotidian that is untrue to God's creatively relating to it.

In such wondering the interplay of personal bodies' capacities for certain kinds of perception, respect, and curiosity is dissolved. Fellow creatures are always perceived as something. In general, perception is formed or "filtered" by some set of concepts. Thus, being perceived as creatures is a condition of creatures' being properly respected as creatures. In distorted wonder, perception is separated from faithful respect for fellow creatures' concrete particularity. Lacking faithful respect for its objects, such perception invites exploitation of what is perceived. When perception is separated from faithful respect for fellow creatures, they are perceived as instances of stereotypes. Stereotypes are rigid and simple sets of highly general concepts. They distort wonder's proper perception of the quotidian because they are inadequate to the complex particularities of fellow creatures as related to by God. The rigidity of sets of stereotyping concepts makes perception imperceptive of the glorious diversity of fellow citizens in the quotidian society of being. This is especially dangerous morally when the fellow creatures are personal bodies and the stereotyping perceptions are racist, sexist, and classist. But it is also morally dangerous when the fellow creatures are of any natural kind whatever and the stereotypes are instrumentalist and utilitarian. Such perception construes a fellow creature this way: Here is an instance of something that may contribute to our project; that over there is an instance of what restrains or is hostile to our project; this can be turned to a profit; that is valueless. Stereotypical perception of creatures is an inappropriate response to the wondrous freedom of God's creativity. Practices that enact such response to God are sinful distortions of a faithful response to God.

Correlatively, wonder's respect for fellow creatures requires perception of them in their particularity as related to creatively by God. Perceived stereotypically, the quotidian may be valued for the potentialities it offers to enhance perceived human well-being. It may also be respected for its threatening power, and even for its astonishing complex beauty. However, astonishment at its complex beauty will be trumped by its valued potentialities for human well-being; respect for its power will simply cause any actualization of its valued potentialities to be undertaken very carefully. Wonder at fellow creatures separated from respect for them is inherently exploitative of the quotidian. It is inhospitable to fellow creatures whose status in the divinely created society of being is not dependent on their contribution to the well-being of human creatures. It is inappropriate response to the hospitality of the triune God's creativity. Practices that express it are sinfully distortions of loyal response to God and God's project.

By the same token, wonder's curiosity about fellow creatures is distorted apart from proper perception of and respect for them. The types of inquiries generated by faithful wonder's curiosity may, for the sake of intellectual convenience, abstract their immediate subject matter from the creative relation into which God enters with them and from their relations to fellow creatures as creatures. Such abstracting is routine and appropriate in the several sciences. However, wonder's curiosity may not simply identify the results of such inquiries with a metaphysical account of fellow creatures' concrete actuality as related to creatively by God. Unchecked by wonder's respect for and perception of the everyday in its relation to God's creativity, such inquiry is inevitably in service of exploitation of the quotidian. Failing to inquire into fellow creatures in their concrete actuality precisely as creatures, it is inappropriate response to the generosity of God's creativity. Practices that express it are sinful distortions of loyal response to God and God's project.

Exploitative practices of wonder are both evil and sinful, but for different reasons. Exploitative practices of wonder count as evil practices because they violate the quotidian, but they count as sin against the triune God because they actively engage the quotidian in abstraction from what it concretely is as God actively and creatively relates to it. Inappropriate responses to the hospitably generous and free way in which the triune God relates creatively to all that is not God, they are distortions of practices of wonder that are loyal to God and to God's project. They express distortions of doxological gratitude's existential hows, its ways of being oriented to its proximate contexts.

3. *Distorted practices of perseverance are self-abnegating.* As doxological gratitude's loyalty to God's call to be wise for the flourishing of the quotidian for its own sake, practices of perseverance are ways of indwelling the quotidian that are loyal to God's own loyalty to God's creative project. Such loyalty perseveres in the face of God's apparent absence from the project, engaging in practices for the well-being of the everyday world and the creatures it constitutes in the midst of experienced evil. Where practices of delight attend to the quotidian's present, and practices of wonder attend to it as developing out of its own past, practices of perseverance attend to the future that grows out of the everyday world's present. Perseverance is distorted when it engages the presently given quotidian as though it had no future, as though God's creative relating to it were not extended across time. In that case, there can be no content to the vocation to be wise for the quotidian's flourishing. If the everyday present has no future, we cannot be called to be wise for its well-being in the future, and there is no vocation to which to be loyal. Such an orientation to our proximate contexts is inappropriate response to the triune God's hospitable and free generosity in relating to us creatively.

In distorted practices of perseverance, the interconnections between vision and discernment of the quotidian are severed. When vision's synoptic picture of the quotidian loses touch with acute perception of creatures in the ambiguities of their concrete particularities, it denies either or both the reality of evil present in the quotidian and the quotidian's continuous dependence on God's creative relating to it. Such vision denies the moral and ontological ambiguity of the everyday. Conversely, when quotidian creatures are discerned in their ambiguous particularities but not against a background synoptic vision of the everyday world as nonetheless ongoingly related to creatively by God across time, then fellow creatures are discerned as inhospitable, perhaps threateningly so, and meaningless. When connections are thus severed between faithful discernment and vision, stories are told of our proximate contexts that are untrue either or both to their moral and ontological ambiguities and to their relation to their ultimate context. Such untruthful speech distorts the practices of perseverance that it informs.

When perseverance is thus distorted, the practices in which personal bodies indwell the everyday world become self-abnegating. Discerning only the quotidian's threats of violation and not its creatureliness, they may envision the everyday world as unambiguously evil and become cynical defensive practices to stave off annihilation and to survive as long as possible. Envisioning proximate contexts as unambiguously inhospitable, personal bodies' practices may discern each being in its particular otherness as inherently meaningless. Such practices turn into survival practices that are utterly indifferent to the well-being of the quotidian for its own sake. Against the background of such a vision of the everyday world, the very idea "for its own sake" is meaningless. In such practices living human bodies may act aggressively for their own survival in the quotidian. But they do so willing not to be creaturely personal bodies. That is, they negate themselves precisely as creaturely personal bodies. Or in such practices, living human bodies may passively resign themselves to the perceived meaningless of others in their particularities and to the envisioned indifference of the everyday world. Such practices are called "not willing to be a self" by Søren Kierkegaard (1954, 146, 180–94), "sensuality" by Reinhold Niebuhr (1953, 228–40), and "sloth" by Karl Barth (1958, 403–82). In such practices, human living bodies negate themselves precisely as ones to whom living bodies have been given on loan, for whose disposition in their proximate contexts they are accountable. Such practices express an orientation to the quotidian that is an inappropriate response to the hospitable generosity of God's creativity. Such practices are sinful distortions of loyal response to God and God's project.

Collectively, distortions of practices of wondering at, delighting in, and persevering with our quotidian proximate contexts are enacted in existential hows that are inappropriate responses to the peculiar way "the Father through the Son in the power of the Spirit" relates to us creatively, disloyal to God and God's creative project. Such ways of being oriented to our proximate contexts are grotesque distortions of doxological gratitude's appropriate response to God's creative relating. They are sinful hows enacted in sinful practices.

Sins are sins against God. What has been explored here are types of sinful hows that are against God in the sense of distortions of faith's loyalty to God and God's creative project in response to the hospitably generous way in which God relates creatively. Such hows are innumerable. However, since the loyalty to God that is truly appropriate response to God's peculiar way of relating creatively is made specific by a distinctive interplay within it of delight in, wonder at, and perseverance with fellow creatures, distortions of such loyalty can be typologized along axes defined by various ways in which delight, wonder, and perseverance may be separated from one another in the existential hows by which personal bodies are set into and oriented toward their proximate contexts.

However, typologizing sinful hows in this way might suggest that only those consciously responding to God's creativity but doing so in distorted ways can and do adopt sinful hows. That raises questions whether personal bodies (a) whose distortions of loyalty to God are not conscious or (b) who do not seek to respond to God at all can be said to be set into their proximate contexts in sinfully distorted hows.

In response to the first question, I observe only that at no point in the discussion of existential hows in this chapter and the last has conscious intent been part of the definition of an existential how. There is no reason in principle why someone's how could not count as a distortion of faith's loyalty to the distinctive way in which God relates creatively even though it was unconsciously adopted and unconscious of being such a distortion. Enactments of the practices in which such hows are expressed entail conscious intentions for the most part, but the hows expressed in those practices do not. Thus, what makes such distorted existential hows sinful need not be conscious.

The second question raises a more serious problem. "Response" is usually used to characterize certain intentional actions—for example, when someone is said to seek to respond appropriately to God. Distortions of such intentional response to God might be said to be sinful distortions of personal bodies' spiritual or religious life. They may be distortions of a sincere and pious intention to respond to God, but they are sinful distortions nonetheless. It is important to begin analysis of the Christian concept of sin with distortions of the spiritual life, and not with distortions, say, of economic or political or professional life, in order to block the received convention that sin is the contradictory of sincere spirituality or earnest faith. It is important to begin here, furthermore, because no other distorted existential hows are more dangerous to fellow creatures and to the proximate contexts shared with them than distortions of faith's loyalty to God and God's creative project.

However, "response" may be used as a descriptive term without reference to intentionality. It may be used to describe a living creature's behavior in the third person from the point of view of an observer ("Her behavior is thus-and-so") rather than from the point of view of her first-person account of the behavior ("I was intending to do thus-and-so"). With regard to the fit between a creature's behavior and its context, it is conventional to observe in this third-person fashion that the behavior either does or does not respond in certain ways (adaptively, efficiently, fittingly, etc.) to the concrete conditions of its context. Such characterizations of a creature's response to its context may equally well embrace both creatures' intentional and conscious actions in that context and nonintentional and even nonconscious behavior. It is in this latter sense of "response," inclusive of more types of human behavior, that the term has been used here.

Accordingly, the existential hows of persons who consciously do not intend to respond to God at all and of persons who are not conscious of the very possibility of responding to God, whether appropriately or inappropriately, may nonetheless be assessed as to whether their hows are in fact appropriate as loyal responses to God's way of relating creatively. Personal bodies whose "set" and orientation in their proximate contexts are subjectively indifferent to God relating to them creatively or are intentionally an effort not to respond to God's alleged creatively relating certainly are not spiritual or religious existential hows. They are the limiting cases of sinfully distorted versions of loyalty to God and God's creative project.

Sins in the Plural

What count as sins in the plural, I suggest, are a multiplicity of concrete existential hows expressive of disloyalty to God rather than a multiplicity of specifically sinful individual human actions.

Traditionally, theological accounts of sin have distinguished between sin (in the singular) as a state or condition of fallen human creatures (i.e., original sin) and sins (in the plural) as a variety of intentional acts (i.e., actual sin). Sinful acts (in the plural) are traditionally defined either by reference to the harm they do to others (sins against the neighbor's created "nature") or by reference to violations of God's positive law (sin against God, doing either what God's law forbids or failing to do what it commands). Neither definition of sin in the plural is quite adequate. The first fails to keep clear sin's theocentricity, conflating sin with what I have called "evil." The second is more clearly theocentric, but construes sin as violation of a code of rules rather than a violation of a relation marked by free and hospitably generous giving on one side and doxologically grateful receiving on the other.

If sin is understood relationally as personal bodies' inappropriate response to the triune God's having already related to them creatively, then the sense in which sin is plural is best understood as individual enactments of practices that express a multiplicity of existential hows that are sinful distortions of loyalty to the triune God relating creatively in hospitable generosity and to God's own creative project. Since, as I argued above, existential hows may be either unconscious or intentionally distorted versions of faith's loyalty to God and God's creative project, it follows that sins as enactments of such hows may be involuntary (see R. Adams, 1985) as well as intentional.

Sinfully distorted existential hows certainly have consequences for human action. As personal bodies' orientations to their proximate contexts, hows give definition to the practices in which human persons engage in those contexts. However, what is sinful about enactments of such practices is not that such human actions work against the well-being of the quotidian and are thus disloyal to it. Such practices do that and hence do count as evil. But what makes them sinful is that in any given case such practices are expressive of just how some personal body is set in his or her quotidian proximate context as someone disloyal to the triune God's creative project. Such practices are thus expressive of existential hows that are the fundamentally inappropriate response by human creatures to God's creative relating to them.

One consequence of this way of understanding sin in the plural is that it makes it impossible to systematize sin by identifying some root cause or motive for the multiplicity of sins. The Augustinian tradition, for example, tends to identify self-love as the root underlying cause or motive of all sins. Self-love is inordinate love of self. It is a distorted version of human creatures' appropriate response to God—namely, love for God. In self-love, human creatures love themselves with the love appropriate to God, love themselves as the final good of their lives, as though they were God. Relying on an analysis of the dynamics of love for God, it is then possible to argue that such misplaced and distorted love for God is the cause or motive of the entire array of sinful acts. All sinful acts can be shown to be systematically interrelated because of their common root in inordinate self-love. The popular, simplified version of this tradition, relying on folk psychology, sees all sins as systematically motivated or caused by selfishness. The corollary is that if people would just quit being selfish, they would quit committing sins.

Another example locates the systematic root of all sins in pride, understood as willful assertion of one's self and one's interests as trumping in value anyone else's interests. Reinhold Niebuhr revived this tradition in an intellectually powerful analysis of the dynamics by which pride causes or motivates an enormous array of sinful actions (1953, 186–203). Although he formally distinguishes two registers of sins, those of pride and those of sensuality, perhaps better named "sloth," it is arguable (see Saiving 1962; Plaskow 1980, 62–73) that his explanation of the second reduces it to a subset of the first so that finally pride is made the cause of all sins whatever.

A systematic theology of sin might be possible were there just one root to sin, some single basic cause or motive of the entire multitude of sins. We may leave aside the uncertainty whether self-love and pride are thought to be motives or causes of sins and the related and vexed questions whether motives are reasons for personal action or their causes, and, indeed, whether reasons are a type of cause or something else all together. No matter how such conceptual questions are resolved, another conceptual point undercuts their theological relevance. It is the point that we have already made: sin posits itself. The concept of sin as against God is the concept of an a-rational surd in the everyday world, something in principle inexplicable. To agree to offer a theory of the single cause or motive of sin that systematizes its multiplicity would betray a failure to grasp the concept of sin against God.

Precisely because human existence is not a system, human sins do not form a system. Just as there can be no systematic, comprehensive taxonomy of the variety of existential hows that might be expressive of faith in God creating—that is, loyalty to God and God's project—so there can be no systematic taxonomy of their distortions as sins. "Disloyalty to God's creative project" does not name either the cause or the motive of any human practice and the actions it embraces. "Disloyalty to God" simply characterizes certain practices. A Christian theocentric doctrine of sin ought to offer an explication of a Christian concept of sin and a description of certain violated aspects of quotidian reality; it does not have the job of offering genetic explanations of those sinful and evil aspects of the everyday.

CHAPTER **11**

Living Death: Sin as Distortion of Trust in God

Exploration of answers to the perennial question, "What are we?" that are suggested by canonical Wisdom literature's stories of God relating creatively to all that is not God brought with it a pair of remarks in answer to a second perennial question, "Who are we?" As ones directly addressed creatively by God, who we are is this: Those radically given to by God, given sheer "thereness." Hence, our personal identities are appropriately reflected in our responsive trust in God as the ground of our reality and value. As ones addressed creatively by God indirectly through our everyday proximate contexts, who we are is this: Finite creatures called to be wise for the well-being of the quotidian, including ourselves. Accordingly, our existential hows are genuinely faithful when they appropriately reflect our responsive loyalty to God's own loyalty to the quotidian and its well-being.

Sin in the Singular: Distorted Faithful Personal Identities

Considered in the context of God relating to us creatively, or so I argued in the last chapter, sins (in the plural) are against God. They are enactments of human practices that are defined by existential hows that express distorted versions of loyalty to the triune God and to God's creative project. Sin in the singular, I propose in this chapter, is also sin against God and is best understood as a living human body's personal identity distorted in an inappropriate trusting response to God relating to her creatively.

"Personal identity" is used here in the sense outlined in chapter 8. There I suggested that we use the concept of personal identity when we want (a) to speak, not of human beings' abstract or numerical identity in general, but to speak of them as beings each of which has its own particular and idiosyncratic memories of interrelations with others, with their shared proximate contexts, and with themselves, and exhibit a willingness to be answerable for actions in which their own intentions have played a major part; (b) to say of such personal identities that they are in some, though not all, respects unsubstitutable by any other personal identity; and (c) to say that this remembering and accountable someone is himself or herself one and the same at some important point in time as well as over a length of time. It is about just this personal identity that we ask the question, "Who is she? Who is he?" Such questions about personal identities are distinct, not only from questions about logical or mathematical identity, but also from epistemological questions about how to identify the same person in different places and times or within a group, and from psychological questions about someone's self-image, although it overlaps with each of these questions.

In this part of this work, we focus on human creatures as related to by God creatively here and now, and on their response to the way in which God relates to them creatively here and now. Hence our focus in part 1 is on human creatures' present orientation in and to their proximate contexts, not on their "future-ward orientation" or "past-ward orientation" in and toward those contexts. If, as I have been arguing, faith in God here and now entails a distinctive personal identity, then sin's distortions of faith in God entail distortions of that identity. Such a distorted identity is defined by what a personal body acknowledges to be the ground of its reality and value here and now. That distorted identity is not discontinuous with the identity he has simply by virtue of the triune God's direct and indirect creative address to him. Rather, it is a distorted version, a parody, of that identity. It is the identity of a life lived at cross-grain to who it is called to be, at cross-grain to the personal identity it objectively has by God's direct and indirect address. Such a distorted identity is, I shall argue, a bondage to a living death.

Distortions of faith involve distortions of the relation between faith's trust in the triune God and faith's loyalty to God and God's creative project. Hence, distortions of faith lead to three types of distorted personal identities: personal identities defined by conflating trust in God with loyalty to God's project; personal identities defined by trust in God without loyalty to God's project; and personal identities defined by personal bodies' trust in and loyalty to themselves and their projects alone. Each involves false speech about the triune God's odd way of relating creatively to all that is not God, about proximate contexts, and about personal bodies, both that of fellow human creatures and that of the speaker with distorted personal identity. All three of these distorted personal identities are marked by existential bondage in a specific type of un-freedom.

Bound in a Distorted Identity: Trusting in the Quotidian

Because they are radically given to by the triune God in regard to their very reality and value, living human personal bodies are fundamentally dependent on God for their reality and value. Such dependence is not a violation of what they are as human creatures. It is the condition of the possibility of their being what they are. Furthermore, fundamental dependence on the triune God defines who they are so profoundly that, while they may elect to live as though their identities were defined in some other way, if they do elect to live in that way their personal identities remain distortions and parodies of who they are by virtue of God's creative relating. When their quotidian personal identities are defined by acknowledgment of some aspect of their quotidian proximate contexts as the basis of their reality and value, their personal identities are distorted in a bondage of limitless dependence on that by which they consider their identities to be defined, whatever it may be. The distinction between fundamental dependence and limitless dependence marks the difference between personal bodies' basic personal identities and their distorted quotidian personal identities.

For example, human creatures' quotidian personal identities are distorted when they are not only loyal to God and God's creative project but also trust that project or some aspect of it, rather than God, to ground their reality and value. Such distorted identity comes with a distorted response to God that conflates trust in God's direct creative relating to us as the ground of our reality and value, with loyalty to God's creative project and its well-being.

Such personal identities may really be defined by loyalty to God's creative project. Thus there is a religious or spiritual version of this general type of distorted personal identity. Personal bodies may have such identities self-consciously, prepared to acknowledge explicitly God's call mediated to them through the everyday world to be wise in their practices in the quotidian for its well-being. They are ready to affirm that who they are is defined by just that vocation. Or they may have such identities entirely implicitly. Such are a-religious or secular versions of this general type of personal identity. Without making any theocentric affirmation, the pattern of the practices in which such personal bodies engage in the quotidian may in fact nonetheless be an appropriate response to God's free and hospitably generous gift of reality in a society of interdependent finite beings. Theologically speaking, the personal identities of the latter may as truly fit the definition of loyalty to God's creative project as the former, even though they do not explicitly affirm God's creative relating and may not know to affirm it.

Like personal identities defined by appropriate response to God's creative relating, such distorted identities are concretely shaped by their historicity, by their particular locations across time in particular societies and cultures. Such identities are inherently identities in and through relations of exchange, of giving and receiving, of interdependence with fellow creatures. All of these exchanges may well make for their proximate contexts' well-being. These are relations shaped by the cultural particularities of the languages of speech, significant gesture, image, social role, and so forth, which are the medium of their interactions. This is as true of this general type of distorted identity as it is true of identities defined by appropriate response to God.

The distortion of such personal bodies' identities comes when personal bodies trust in precisely those particular concrete practices of exchange, of giving and receiving to ground their reality and value as personal bodies. In that case, their personal identities are defined by the particular ways in which their fellow human creatures define them in interactions of giving and receiving, for the practices themselves are socially constructed and employ a conventional, socially shared common language of speech, image, symbol, and gesture.

Personal bodies' identities may be passively distorted in this way. In their interactions with us, fellow creatures may perceive us in terms of stereotypes. A pre-formed identity is bestowed on us as the price of our participation in practices composing our everyday lived world. This, of course, is what happens routinely in networks of interactions conducted on terms defined by stereotypes about race, gender, age, social class, intelligence, physique, education, type of occupation, and the like. Because stereotypes are faithless to the concrete particularities of the human creature being stereotyped, they distort perception in ways that manifest sinful disloyalty to God and God's project.

A personal body who, in loyalty to the quotidian and its well-being, trusts in just those networks of exchange to ground his reality and value will for that reason require such acceptance. As the price of acceptance, and thus as the price of securing his reality and value as a personal body, he may passively accept his fellow creatures' stereotypes of him as definitive of who he is. His quotidian personal identity is one who is a more or less clear instance of such-and-such a stereotype. Since the stereotypes defining the bestowed identity are sinfully distorting, the passively accepted personal identity will also be distorted. His reality and value are acknowledged by himself as well as by others as nothing else than what they are perceived to be by fellow creatures. Such personal identities are passively defined as minimally agentic, scarcely at all the agents of their own lives.

Or personal bodies' identities may be actively distorted by trust that the networks of exchange constituting the quotidian themselves ground human persons' reality and value. Inherent in the social and cooperative practices that constitute personal bodies' networks of interactions are standards of excellence. Depending on the character of the practice, the standards may pertain either or both to the enacting of the practice or to its outcome or product. These standards of excellence are as historically conditioned and culturally relative as are the practices themselves. In loyalty to the quotidian and its well-being, a personal body may also trust the excellence of her enactment of practices that make up the everyday world to ground her reality and value. Her reality and value as an agent wise in her actions in her quotidian proximate contexts are a function of the excellence of her enactment of practices that make up the common life of those everyday worlds. She does not passively accept an identity bestowed on her; she actively earns an identity by satisfying standards inherent in the social practices in which she interacts with fellow human creatures. Her personal identity is highly agentic. It is defined, not truly, but as enacted, as one who meets or exceeds the standards (alternatively: norms, rules, laws) by which we measure the excellence of enactments of practices that constitute our everyday world.

Not that excellence is necessarily sought in all the practices that make up the quotidian. Part of the agency exercised by personal bodies with such identities is control of which range of practices in particular will define their identities—whether the practices of a successful career in an organization or profession, a successful entrepreneur, a successful parent, a responsible citizen, a celebrated good neighbor, and not excluding the practices of a truly spiritual person. Fellow human creatures acknowledge rather than bestow such personal identities as earned and due.

At this point, our initial distinction between passively and actively distorted personal identities begins to dissolve. On one side, personal bodies who actively distort their personal identities nonetheless passively accept as the criteria of their reality and value the standards of excellence inherent in some of their proximate contexts' practices. On the other, personal bodies who have passively distorted identities may nonetheless actively seek to satisfy the stereotypes on whose terms their identities are bestowed on them.

Whether initially defined passively or actively, such personal identities are sinfully distorted in that they are deficiently eccentric. In appropriate response to the triune God's creative relating, whose generous giving is always ontologically prior to and not contingent on human creatures' responding, *un*distorted personal identity is defined by trust in God alone as the ground of personal bodies' reality and value, albeit a trusting that takes place only in and through interrelations of giving and receiving with fellow creatures. The Center trusted to give reality and value is ontologically prior to and independent of creatures' response because it is eccentric, outside personal bodies and their networks of interdependent giving and receiving. As genuinely eccentric to us, the triune God gives reality and value without receiving either, and gives both before receiving any response from us to the giving. By contrast, in the type of distorted personal identities examined here, personal bodies not only have their identities in and through their culturally located interdependent exchanges with fellow creatures, but they also trust just those exchanges to ground their reality and value. Since their centers of reality and value lie within the quotidian, they are genuinely outside any particular given personal body within that quotidian. But such centers of reality and value are not eccentric to the entire network of interrelations which make up the quotidian, of which the personal bodies are themselves parts. Hence, personal identities defined by trust in them are deficiently eccentric. They are finally untrue to the peculiar way in which the triune God relates to them creatively.

Personal bodies whose identities are distorted in this general way are in bondage to limitless dependence. Rowan Williams distinguishes helpfully between limitless dependence and fundamental dependence (2000, 70), and I shall expand somewhat his sense of limitless dependence. In fundamental dependence, one's personal identity is defined by dependence on—that is, trust in—that which truly is the ground of our reality and value and is in no way dependent on us for its reality and value, the triune God relating to us creatively. Fundamental dependence is a nonreciprocal eccentric relation. Limitless dependence, on the other hand, is a function of the interactive character of the networks of practices of exchange that make up the everyday lived world. In these networks of giving and receiving, personal bodies are deeply dependent on one another. Each of the others is a fellow creature who had to be given to before it is capable of giving anything. In limitless dependence, one's personal identity is defined, as Williams says, by endlessly "accumulating dependent relationships to things, persons, institutions" (70) in order to secure one's reality and value. By the same token, to expand Williams's point in the other direction, one's identity is therewith also defined by one's being endlessly depended upon by others in their efforts to secure their reality and value. Precisely because personal bodies are social beings, the project of grounding their reality and value in the social projects constituting their common proximate contexts is necessarily a social conspiracy of reciprocally limitless interdependence.

The project of grounding one's reality and value in the network of endless reciprocal dependency will fail. It will fail because limitless dependence ties personal bodies in bonds to the fellow creatures on whom they depend and who depend on them to define their identities, bonds that can only work if they dissolve the ways in which we are each an other. When we trust in interdependence with fellow creatures to ground our reality and value, our genuine otherness from one another is in jeopardy. On one side, we are constantly in danger of "becoming the raw material of other identities" (Williams 2000, 71) that depend on our accepting them as instances of their favorite stereotypes or on our conspiring in their practices, and our acknowledging their achievements as measured by standards of excellence inherent in those practices. We thus are bound to them, co-opted into fellow creatures' projects by which they define their identities.

Conversely, we are bound to fellow creatures in whose stereotyped perceptions of us, or in whose acknowledgment of our achievement of excellence in the shared practices, we trust to ground our reality and value. Since we passively or actively conspire with them in the same practices, we absorb them into our project of securing our reality and value, dissolving their otherness to us and defining them as extensions of ourselves, but only at the price of being conscripted into their projects, eroding our own otherness to them. Thus, limitless dependence binds personal bodies to fellow creatures in ways that are untrue to the concrete creaturely otherness of both themselves and their fellow creatures, making them a threat to the integrities of their proximate contexts.

There is a structural contradiction in personal identities distorted in this general way. It makes them dangerous to their proximate contexts. That personal bodies whose identities are distorted in this general way genuinely are loyal to God's creative project is shown by their loyalty to the call to be wise in their practices in the quotidian for its well-being. However, what is at issue here is the aspect of appropriate response to God's creative relating that consists, not in loyalty to God's creative project and its well-being for its own sake, but in appropriate trust in God to ground one's reality and value. The distortion of appropriate response to God that generates the issue here is the substitution of appropriate loyalty to God for trust in God, as though the former (loyalty to God and God's project) were simply another name for the latter (trust in God as ground of reality and value). When the former is substituted for the latter, response to God in trust is distorted into personal bodies' trusting to other finite creatures to ground their reality and value. When they do so they become caught in an endlessly regressive search for creatures who are suitably dependable. What is needed is a center of reality and value capable of giving reality and power without itself having first to receive either reality or value. No fellow creatures, nor the networks of all fellow creatures taken as a whole, is ontologically prior in all giving, not itself in need of having been given to before being capable of giving. Hence, personal identity defined by trust in exchanges with fellow creatures to give a personal body its reality and value can only be lived, in Williams's phrase, as the "constantly fearful and cautious negotiation of . . . identity" (2000, 72) in "a compulsive search for 'piecemeal' securities, the shoring up of identity by exploiting *specific* facets of every environment which threatens to swallow" us (Williams 2000, 18; emphasis in original).

A personal body's distorted identity is self-contradictory. Such identity defines a personal body as one committed to the well-being of the quotidian for its own sake; at the same time it defines the same personal body by its exploitative search for dependable grounds of its own reality and value. That exploitative search turns quotidian fellow creatures, nonhuman and human alike, into successively disposable instrumental means to the end of securing its own reality and value. That contradicts the project of acting wisely for the well-being of the quotidian for its own sake. Ironically, although it focuses exclusively on loyalty to God's creative project, the structural self-contradiction of such distorted personal identity makes it dangerous to God's creative project. It is untrue, not only to the peculiar way in which the triune God relates creatively, but also to the quotidian of which it is a part and, in its structural self-contradiction, to itself.

When a personal identity's definition by loyalty to the quotidian is not regulated by also being defined by trust in a genuinely eccentric ground of reality and value, the lie at its core makes it destructive and self-destructive.

Bound in a Distorted Identity: Trust in God without Loyalty to the Quotidian

Human bodies' quotidian personal identities are also distorted in bondage to abstractions of themselves when they truly are defined by trust in God to ground their reality and value, but are not also defined by loyalty to God's creative project. This is the converse of the first type of distorted identity.

Such personal identities really are defined by trust that is a fundamental dependence on that which is free of and eccentric to the quotidian and directly grounds the quotidian's reality and value. But they are not defined by trust in and through interactive practices in the quotidian enacted in loyalty to its well-being for its own sake. Such identities are defined in terms of "being," as in: "Who are they? They are those whose reality is a gift directly given to them by the Creator"; they are not defined in terms of "interacting," as in: "Who are they? They are those who faithfully interact as they are called to interact (i.e., for the well-being of the quotidian, including themselves)." Indeed, such identities are defined on the assumption that trust in a radically free and eccentric center of reality and value is mutually exclusive of identity-defining interactions within the quotidian.

Such personal identities are distorted, not only because they are inadequately defined by trust in a radically eccentric center of reality and value entirely apart from loyalty to God's creative project, but also because they are defined by trust in something other than the triune God. As I took pains to show in chapter 3A, when God is understood in a Trinitarian way, God cannot be conceived as somehow in competition with the quotidian for our trust and loyalty. The assumption that the two are mutually exclusive betrays a different understanding of the ground of the quotidian's reality and value than the understanding formulated in properly Trinitarian doctrines of God.

The trust that defines distorted quotidian personal identities of this alternative general type of distortion may indeed be "religious" trust. It may be trust in a reality understood to be transcendent of the world, but not One understood to relate to the world in the peculiar way disclosive of God's triunity. Or it may be "spiritual" trust in transcendence-as-such experienced as mysterious. Or it may be a purely secular trust in timeless and universal transcendental values whose actualization constitutes personal bodies' proper reality and value.

To trust any of these as ground of one's reality and value is to trust that which can only be construed by a distancing negation of the quotidian: a reality transcendent of the everyday; transcendence-of-the-world-as-such; or transcendental values that do not just instance or manifest themselves in the world, but have to be actualized through struggle against the world. Trust in such as these defines personal identities in quite a different way than does trust in the triune God's relating to us in free and graciously hospitable creativity.

Personal bodies whose identities are defined solely by trust in a ground of reality and value, and not also by loyalty to the quotidian and its well-being, are distorted in bondage to themselves. Certainly, human persons with such identities do in fact interact with fellow creatures in common practices in their proximate contexts. However, those interactions do not define who they are. They inescapably have relationships of interaction with fellow creatures, but in their cases those relationships do not go deep enough to shape and help define their identities in any fundamental or decisive way. Their identities are defined independently of and prior to any exchange involving giving to and receiving from other creatures. Hence, caring for the well-being of others and being cared for by them are entirely incidental to their identities. They are not physically or socially solitary, of course. They live with other human creatures. Nonetheless, who they are is defined by each one's radically solitary relation of trust in God as the ground of her or his reality and value. Defined solely by reference to themselves and their individual responses to God, "who they are" is by definition "ones bound to themselves, fundamentally to the exclusion of others."

Because their quotidian personal identities are fully defined independently of and prior to any exchange of giving to and receiving from other creatures, the identities of such personal bodies are also defined abstractly. They are defined in abstraction from the historically and culturally conditioned networks of time-extended practices that make up the proximate contexts in which such personal bodies are concretely located. Such identities are timeless and unchanging. They may be construed as actual, the true selves that personal bodies have by virtue of a genuinely transcendent ground of reality. Or they may be construed as timeless ideal possibilities, ideals of their true selves that await actualization by personal bodies. By the way they are defined, such personal identities are distorted in bondage to their assumptions about their unchanging and unchangeable true selves, actual or ideal.

In their untruthfulness to themselves, to their fellow creatures, and to the ground of their reality and value, personal bodies with this general type of distorted quotidian identity violate their proximate contexts. They may engage in practices that make for the well-being of their proximate contexts, but they do so in ways that make such practices of no importance to who they are. They do it incidentally, in perhaps somewhat detached ways, perhaps condescendingly, perhaps sentimentally, perhaps ironically, perhaps cynically. Defined by a trust in a ground of reality and value that is not mediated by loyalty to the well-being of their proximate context and its network of relationships with fellow creatures, the identity they have cannot change, grow, or have a history in and through such practices. It cannot be vulnerable to any exchange of giving and receiving with fellow creatures.

When a personal identity's definition by trust in a radically prior ground of reality and value is not made historically concrete by also being defined by loyalty to the quotidian, there is ice at its core.

Bound in a Distorted Identity: Trusting in and Loyal to Oneself Alone

There remains, of course, at least the logical possibility that a personal body's identity might be defined neither by trust in a radically eccentric ground of reality and value nor by loyalty to the quotidian and its well-being, but simply by trust exclusively in oneself and loyalty exclusively to one's life, as one lifelong project. Such personal identity is distorted in bondage to the deep darkness of delusion about itself.

Such personal identity is radically self-defined in a Promethean gesture, wresting reality and value out of the perceived nothing of its proximate contexts. It is the general type of distorted self-identity that was taken to be paradigmatic of human fallenness in mid-twentieth-century neo-orthodox rediscovery of the profundity of traditional Augustinian and Reformation doctrines of sin. Its paradigmatic status is best caught, perhaps, in the English title of Emil Brunner's acclaimed study of sin, *Man in Revolt* (1947, esp. 114–204. The German title was *Der Mensch im Widerspruch*, which means something somewhat less dramatic, such as "Humankind in Contradiction"). This type of personal identity has been explicitly celebrated by otherwise very different types of thinkers in the modern West, both Romanticist (think N. Kazantzakis) and existentialist (think F. Nietzsche and J. P. Sartre). Heroic, and often self-dramatizing, instances of this type of personal identity have not been unknown in modern Western societies. Doubtless there have been many more un-self-dramatizing but nonetheless willfully self-assertive persons who have in fact implicitly defined themselves in this way, overcoming unimaginable obstacles in a struggle to secure their own reality and value. The personal identities of such persons are no more defined by trust in and loyalty to practices of exchange with fellow creatures in their shared proximate contexts than they are by trust in and loyalty to the triune God. Such personal identities are defined by amazing acts of sheer will. It is understandable that personal bodies having such identities are thought to be capable either of extraordinary acts making for the well-being of quotidian fellow creatures, or of acts that violate the quotidian in extraordinary and extraordinarily destructive ways.

However, we may doubt that there are in fact very many personal bodies with such identities. For one thing, it seems very rare that a living human personal body has the capacities so powerfully to assert itself that it at least appears to define itself without the interdependence that comes with all social and cooperative practices. It takes the personal resources of Milton's Satan to be up to that. Moreover, it is not necessary to ascribe this Promethean type of distorted self-identity widely to humankind at large in order to explain such horrendous evils as totalitarian oppression, the Holocaust, and ethnic cleansing. All that is required for such evil, we have learned, is an everyday community of personal bodies whose identities are distorted, to adapt Hannah Arendt's phrase about evil, in the most banal of ways.

Personal bodies whose identities are distorted in this general way are in bondage to the deepest of self-delusions. Such personal identities are certainly not bound to fellow creatures. Nor is their bondage to whatever they construe to be their "real selves," to which they recognize they may be faithless and must struggle to be true. Such personal bodies do not need to acknowledge any timeless and ideal "real self" other than the de facto powers of their given personal body. Rather, they are in bondage to the delusion that they can secure their own reality and value entirely by their own powers. Their personal identities are defined by just that delusion. At the heart of such personal identities is a deep darkness.

Bound Identities and Obscured Creaturely Glory
Sin in the singular is distortion of a personal body's identity as a whole. To say that the dynamics of a distorted personal identity places one in some kind of bondage, therefore, is to say that to be in sin (in the singular) is to be a personal body in bondage.

This is, of course, one major theme in traditional doctrines of original sin. In traditional interpretations, original sin designates two conceptually distinct but closely interrelated subject matters: (1) a certain condition or predicament in which human persons universally find themselves, globally called fallenness, and (2) a genetic account of how humankind came to be in this condition or predicament, usually tracing it to Adam and Eve's original—historically first—sin (see Gen. 3) by which the entire human family somehow "falls" from the condition in which God had created them.

If we set (2) aside, we see that traditional theological analyses of (1) tend to stress five features of original sin as the human predicament.

First, it is universal. All human creatures are born into it. Second, it is, in Calvin's phrase, "adventitious." It is not a change in what human creatures are. To use a classical distinction between essential and accidental properties of a substance, the condition of original sin does not involve any change in the essence or nature of human creatures; it is an accidental property. Third, in it death has a certain power it would not otherwise have. There is disagreement whether human creatures would not die at all were it not for this predicament of original sin, or whether it is only that death, which would happen in any case, now has a certain power over human creatures that it would not otherwise have. Fourth, all persons born into the condition of original sin are born into guilt. There has been disagreement whether to understand this as a share in Adam and Eve's guilt for the original act of sin, or whether to understand it as guilt that subsequent human persons properly incur for themselves. Fifth, in the condition of original sin, human creatures are in bondage. This has often been characterized as a "bondage of the will," especially by the sixteenth-century Reformers.

My discussion of sin in the singular has been confined to description of a predicament that personal bodies find themselves in when their identities are distorted. The genetic explanation side of traditional doctrines of original sin is set aside on the conceptual grounds that "sin posits itself," and consequently attempts to offer a genetic account of original sin as predicament fall into conceptual confusion.

Thus far, this discussion of sin in the singular explicitly overlaps traditional accounts of original sin regarding its adventitiousness and its bondage. In order to keep it as clear as possible that sin in the singular is not somehow essential to human creatures, I have analyzed it, not in connection with discussion of what human persons are as creatures, but in discussion of human creatures' personal identities: who they are as creatures. What a human person is as creature cannot change without the creature ceasing to be human, but her personal identity can change radically without alteration of her nature as human. In order to keep it as clear as possible that it is entire personal bodies that are in thrall to sin in the singular, I have explored sin as distortion, not of some one power such as will, but of human creatures' personal identities, which engage all of their powers. And I have tried to show how such distortion places them in one or another kind of bondage. It is a profound insight of traditional doctrines of original sin that human creatures can be and are in a bondage that is not essential to their being human creatures.

Such bondage rules out one specific type of freedom for personal bodies having distorted personal identities. While having a personal identity is an aspect of what it is to be a personal body, no one particular personal identity is an aspect of what it is to be a personal body. Explication of what it is to be a personal body leaves open the question of just who that personal body is. So far as the nature of human creatures is concerned, it is in principle possible that any particular quotidian personal identity may change across time in various respects. To the extent that a quotidian personal identity is partly defined by its culturally shaped interactions with fellow creatures in their shared historically conditioned proximate contexts, such change is highly likely.

However, distortion makes one type of change in personal identities impossible. Distorted personal identities are incapable of undistorting themselves. This is a conceptual point, not a quasi-empirical generalization about human creatures' powers. As creatures given living bodies on loan, personal bodies are accountable to the triune God for the disposition of their personal bodies in their proximate contexts. Their personal identities may be defined in undistorted ways by appropriate response to the odd way in which the triune God relates to them creatively, namely by faith's trust in God as ground of their reality and value and loyalty to God and God's creative project. In that case, it is the peculiar way in which the triune God relates to them that defines personal bodies' personal identities. Or personal identities may be defined in distorted ways by inappropriate responses. In either case, it is precisely as the concrete personal identity that one is, as who one concretely is, that each one responds to God and is accountable for its response. Its response constitutes its orientation to its proximate context and is expressed concretely in how it is existentially in the everyday world.

Now, if a personal body's quotidian identity is distorted, it is as just that distorted quotidian personal identity that he seeks to make whatever changes he may make in the fundamental way he is disposed in his proximate contexts. A distorted "who" orients herself in the everyday world distortedly, albeit with great freedom regarding the concrete hows in which she expresses her distorted orientation. Hence, it is a conceptual point that personal bodies whose identities are distorted cannot redefine any particular distorted quotidian personal identity in an undistorted way. Who is it that seeks to redefine the distorted identity? None other than a distorted quotidian personal identity exercising its powers. Distorted, personal identities alone or conjointly may change the concrete hows in which their own identities are expressed, but what is expressed continues to express the same general type of distortion. Or perhaps, through their interactions, they may even change the general type of distortion of their identities. In either case, however, the deep sense in which they are in bondage is that neither they themselves nor any of their fellow human creatures with distorted personal identities can redefine their distorted identities by exercising their powers to enact faithful—undistorted—responses to the triune God relating to them creatively.

Affirmation of bondage in distorted personal identities does not entail a global denial of freedom of choice to personal bodies whose identities are distorted. It remains an open question whether, within limits set by their finitude, they are free to choose among alternative possible practices and actions, objects and relations. What is denied is that they are free to change the fact that in making any and all such free choices, who makes the choice is a distorted personal identity. That is to say, they are not free to enact such choices as enactments of trust in and loyalty to the triune God relating to them creatively.

This discussion of sin as distorted personal identity also touches implicitly on the three remaining major themes in traditional teaching about original sin: its universality, its guiltiness, and the power of death in it.

A basis for the theological claim that bondage in sin in the singular is universal was laid out in the account given above of human personal living bodies' proximate contexts as the triune God's creation. Guided by biblical Wisdom's background creation theology, chapter 5 developed an account of our proximate contexts that stressed their ontological ambiguity. Following canonical Wisdom, it sought to be utterly realistic about the reality of evil and sin in the creaturely quotidian, so that they are also morally ambiguous. It follows that every personal body is born into an everyday world that is already constituted by exchanges of giving and receiving among personal bodies whose existential hows and personal identities are sinful. Chapter 6 proposed that our creation be understood as our having been born, so that it is clear that while we are created as something concretely actual and not just ideally possible, it is also the case that what God creates in creating us is something inherently developmental in nature. Since personal bodies' identities are at least in some degree partly defined by interactions with fellow creatures as they mature and develop, it follows that every personal body born into the quotidian is going to have its identity shaped by such interactions. If the others with whom they interact already have distorted personal identities, their interactions will be distorted and younger personal bodies' identities will in turn be distorted. We are not created with distorted identities, but we are all born into them. Hence, the universality of bondage in distorted personal identities.

The guilt that accompanies sin in the singular is a theme at once more vague and more complex than its universality. Just what we are guilty of is vague. If one declines to interpret the story of Adam and Eve's disobedience and expulsion from the garden of Eden (Gen. 3) as the genetic explanation of the reality of sin in the singular, at very least on the grounds that it is poor exegesis, then there is no biblical basis for the claim that subsequent generations are born somehow already sharing in Adam and Eve's guilt for their action. To the extent that we are co-conspirators in the social practices in and through which our personal identities are distorted, and once we have matured to the point of being accountable for our response to God, we may be said to be guilty of distortion of our own identities. But that is not the same as guilt for the fact of the universally shared predicament of sin in the singular.

These observations assume that "guilt" is being used in an objective moral sense. It names the burden of having violated a personal relation with God, disobeying God's direct command, becoming vulnerable to punishing consequences. "Guilt" is not used here in the subjective sense of an awareness of having culpably violated a relationship with God—that is, "feeling guilty." Rather, "guilt" names a status before theological standards regarding relationships with God, a status one has objectively whether one is aware of it or has acknowledged it or not—namely, the status of one who has in fact violated a relationship with God and is in fact subject to the consequences of that violation.

However, I suggest, the objective status one enters by violating relationship with God by responding inappropriately to God's creative relating might better be designated by impurity before God than by guilt before God. Subjective awareness of this status might better be described as feeling shame rather than feeling (subjective) guilt. If so, the dynamics of impurity before God need to be outlined.

Probably the central biblical metaphor for that dynamic is the stain that violates something by soiling or dirtying it. A rhetoric of impurity and stain, used to describe conditions like sin and estrangement that we consider to be moral or spiritual conditions, strikes readers in modern Western cultures as "archaic" in large part because its imagery relies so blatantly on dirt, which seems to us neither morally nor spiritually charged. At the same time, modern Western people continue to use this rhetoric when they describe experiences of having been violated, or experiences of discovering that they had, all unaware, been complicit in violating another, by saying that they felt "soiled" by what they had undergone or had done. The inconsistency is not surprising, considering the ambiguity of the symbolism. As Paul Ricoeur points out in the *Symbolism of Evil* (1967), although the rhetoric of stain never is abstract enough to escape association with "the half-light of quasi-physical infection" by impure matter and "the magic of contact and contagion" that is alien to "modern culture," it is nonetheless the case that even in its most ancient literary expressions, "defilement was never literally a stain; impurity was never literally filthiness, dirtiness" (35), but was always a "*symbolic* stain" (28; emphasis in original).

In connection with human personal bodies' relationship with God, the rhetoric of stain expresses a dynamic of human movement away from God. I suggest that that movement characterizes the condition of human personal bodies in bondage to the distorted personal identities analyzed here—that is, in bondage to sin in the singular. As a stain on a beautiful garment obscures its splendor, moving the splendor out of view for the eye of a beholder, so being born into the predicament of sin in the singular moves a creature in the direction of being out of view for God's eye even though God declares the creature good. Having a distorted identity to which one is in bondage is "sin in the sight of the Lord" and needs to be "washed away." A related sensory simile expands the range of the dynamic of impurity before God expressed by "stain": As the terrible odor of a seriously ill loved one can move one away from them even as one seeks to tend to them, so being born into the predicament of personal bodies in bondage to distorted identities may be likened to a "stench in the nostrils of the

Lord" that moves one away from God and needs to be washed away. Being born into such an identity is offensive and, as it were, makes God wretch even as God relates creatively to the violator in hospitable generosity.

The range of the dynamic of impurity before God expressed by "stain" can be expanded by another simile drawn from traditional cultures' practice of driving violators of the society's mores "outside the camp." This simile moves the force of the rhetoric of impurity closer to that of the rhetoric of guilt: just as violations of the rules that norm the practices constituting the common life of a society move the violator outside that society as one who thereafter lives literally as an outlaw, neither constrained nor protected by society's laws, so violation of the relationship with God that, by God's creative address, constitutes a society of beings with which God identifies Godself initiates a movement of the violator toward the outside of that society, and therewith away from community with God.

In short, the burden of original sin, traditionally expressed in the theological symbol of original sin's guilt, is the dynamic of impurity before God that is internal to the objective status of those born into proximate situations in which their personal identity comes to be defined by inappropriate response to God's creature relating. It is a dynamic of progressive or, more exactly, regressive movement away from God, the ground of one's reality and value. One is not culpable ("morally guilty") for having this status or for being subject to this dynamic. Because the dynamic moves toward an ultimate dissolution of human personal bodies' reality and value, they need to get out of this status and to be free of this dynamic.

A basis for the theological claim that bondage in sin in the singular is a life in which death rules was laid out in the account given earlier of the finitude of human personal living bodies. Guided by biblical Wisdom's background creation theology, chapter 6 developed an understanding of human creaturely finitude according to which mortality and dying are inherent features of what it is to be a personal body. Hence it cannot be said that somehow adventitious distortion of personal identities causes personal bodies to die. It does, however, give the inevitable reality of death a terrible power over personal bodies with distorted identities.

For those whose agency of their own lives is systemically undermined in personal identities distorted by acquiescence in others' stereotypes of them, and who nevertheless trust their acceptance of those stereotypes to ground the reality and value of their lives, death ceases to be a universal feature of living and becomes the dominant good, the liberator to be longed for. To live with no possibility of being the agent of one's own life is to live not just a dying life, but the living death of the radically oppressed. To live such a life, as one whose personal identity is distorted by trust that others' stereotypes of oneself can define one's identity in a way that grounds its reality and value, is to live a living death without resources capable of transforming it. For living human personal bodies with this type of distorted identity, dying life is transformed into a living death that can be ended only by the boon of actual bodily death, whether that is understood as extinction or a passage to a better life.

On the other hand, for those whose quotidian personal identities are distortedly defined either by satisfying commonly shared criteria of excellence in socially shared practices or by sheer self-assertion against all proximate contexts, death becomes the symbol of all threats to their reality and value. They trust in fellow creatures to ground their reality and value; death will inevitably undercut each such ground. Death becomes the enemy most important to ward off as long as possible, either by action to secure one's own immortality or by psychological denial of the reality of death. Then dying life is transformed into a living death because it is invested wholly in a lifelong, and inevitably losing, struggle against death.

The living death of bondage in distorted personal identities, and of the existential hows that manifest personal bodies' faithlessness to God relating to them creatively, is an obscuring of personal bodies as the glory of God. It does not negate them as the glory of God. They are that solely by God's free and creative relating to them. But it obscures personal bodies' splendor as God's glory so that fellow human creatures do not see it. They become unable to respond to one another with faith's wonder, perseverance, and, above all, delight. They become unable to look on one another with joy.

PART 2

Consummated: Living on Borrowed Time

Preface

The root question for this theological anthropology is, what does the specifically Christian conviction that God actively relates to us imply about what and who we are and how we are to be? The structure of the overall answer is made complex by the intersection of two specifically Christian background beliefs: that God is best understood in a triune way, and that the triune God actively relates to us in three interrelated but distinct ways—as One who creates, grounding our reality and its flourishing; as One who promises us an eschatological consummation and draws us to it; and as One who reconciles us in our multiple estrangements. In part 1, I elaborated some anthropological remarks rooted in the background belief that the triune God relates to us creatively. In effect, part 2 starts over from the beginning to elaborate anthropological remarks rooted in a second aspect of our ultimate and proximate contexts—namely, remarks rooted in the background belief that the triune God relates to us to draw us to eschatological consummation. Chapter 12 sketches our ultimate context as the blessing of the eschatological Spirit "sent by the Father with the Son." Chapter 13 then develops an account of our proximate contexts as borrowed time. Against the background of these two chapters, I explore their implications for a second aspect of human flourishing, flourishing in hope (in contradistinction to flourishing in faith). These implications directly address the question, "How are we to be?" (chap. 14) and indirectly address the questions, What are we?" and "Who are we?" (chap. 15). Correlated with this is chapter 16's account of sins in the plural as distortions of human flourishing in hope, and chapter 17's account of sin in the singular as a distortion of hopeful personal identity.

CHAPTER **12A**

Our Ultimate Context:
The Spirit Sent
by the Father with the Son

The ultimate context into which we are born is not constituted solely by the triune God relating to us creatively; it is also constituted, in a second aspect, by God drawing all creation, and with it humankind, to the blessing of a final consummation. Scriptural accounts of this second mode of divine relating echo accounts of God creating, but use a distinctive rhetoric. The tropes they use for this summing up, notably "kingdom of God" or "God's kingly reign," are often referred to in theological shorthand as images of the end time or *eschaton* (Gk.: "furthest"). According to this narrative, the consummation to which God draws us is eschatological. The correlative theological claim is that being drawn to eschatological consummation characterizes one aspect of our ultimate context.

This way in which the triune God actively relates to all that is not God is distinct from God relating creatively. It constitutes a distinct aspect of our ultimate context. Where God relating creatively promises the blessing of creaturely well-being through the cycles of the generations, the triune God relating in this second way promises an eschatological consummation that goes beyond anything implied in creaturely blessing. It is the blessing of a new creation, a new age of justice and communion with God. If the claim that God relates to draw us to eschatological consummation is nonnegotiable for Christian faith, its bearing on theological anthropology must be examined on its own terms and not as though it were merely an alternative description of God relating to us creatively (or merely an alternative description of God relating to us to reconcile us when we are estranged from God).

When God is understood in a Trinitarian way, this claim may be reformulated in the following fashion: it is the three "persons" of the triune God who, perichoretically, but in a certain pattern, draw us to eschatological consummation. The Trinitarian claim is conventionally framed in a technical theological formula: the "Spirit sent by the Father with the Son" draws us to eschatological consummation. For personal bodies, this consummation consists in nothing less than a creaturely participation as adopted children in the relationships that constitute the very life of the triune God. The formulation "Spirit sent by the Father with the Son" introduces a certain pattern in the way the three "persons" perichoretically draw humankind to eschatological consummation. This pattern signals the key differences between this mode of divine relating and God relating to create or God relating to reconcile us when we are estranged.

The Circumambient Spirit: Living on Borrowed Time
In the New Testament, the Spirit relating to humankind is a sign that the divinely promised eschatological kingdom of God is just over the horizon or has in fact broken into history. It makes a difference whether the end time is just dawning or has in fact invaded (as is discussed in the next two chapters). But in either case, the significance of the Spirit's presence is thoroughly eschatological. As R. P. C. Hanson puts it, in the New Testament the Holy Spirit is "the form in which, or in whom, God appears to reign over his people at the Last Time" (1973, 121).

Although they express it in many and various ways, New Testament texts generally suggest that the Spirit's role is to draw human creatures into the eschatological life made possible by God's raising the crucified Jesus from the dead. The way in which the Spirit relates to us in order to do that is characterized in canonical Christian Holy Scripture quite differently from either its characterization of Jesus' relation to us as one *among* us or its characterizations of the Creator's creative relation *to* us. I suggest that the Spirit's relation is perhaps best expressed by the adjective *circumambient*.

In John, a major image for the eschatological Spirit is wind. The Spirit is as circumambient as the air, and as dynamic as the atmosphere. Drawing creatures to eschatological consummation, it, like air, is an aspect of creatures' most embracing and most necessary context. It is the condition of human life, independent of human creatures' thoughts and fantasies. The Spirit's circumambience is public and not confined to the privacy of human creatures' interiorities, commonly shared but not owned or controlled by them.

Accordingly, when the claim that the triune God relates to all that is not God to draw it to eschatological consummation is reformulated as "the Spirit, sent by the Father with the Son," the point is not only to stress that this relating has an eschatological goal ("Spirit" signaling "end time"), but more particularly that drawing us to that goal involves a distinctive mode of divine relating to us—namely, circumambiently. The circumambience of the Spirit is an aspect of human creatures' ultimate context. It has implications for accounts of their proximate contexts, for a theocentric picture of human flourishing, and, correlatively, for understanding sinful distortions of that flourishing.

Granted, it is not self-evident that "circumambience" is the most apt representation of New Testament characterizations of the Spirit's way of relating to human persons. A brief rationale is in order. New Testament texts, both by the structure of their narratives and by the metaphors they employ, characterize the Spirit's way of relating to human persons in a wide and not entirely consistent variety of ways. However, a certain bipolar pattern is consistent. The Spirit is regularly characterized both as persons' environing context always already there and enveloping them, and as intimately interior to them. The images of intimate interiority have, perhaps, had the most powerful impact on the language of popular piety and on the more formal language of liturgy. It is commonplace to speak mostly of the Spirit's being "within" us.

However, not only is it one-sided to ignore the Spirit's environing relation around about us; to do so subverts the way in which New Testament accounts of the Spirit ground its intimate relation to human persons' interiorities in its always already being there as those persons' environing context, and not the reverse.

In the Synoptic Gospels and Acts, the Spirit that empowered Jesus' proclamation of the imminence of the end time empowers the disciples' proclamation, on behalf of the community, of the eschatological significance of Jesus' ministry, crucifixion, and resurrection. In John, the risen Jesus breathes the Spirit on the community of disciples to empower their new eschatological life in love. For Paul, the Spirit works in and through the common life of the community of faith, and especially through the proclamation of the gospel, to incorporate persons into the new and eschatological creation that has invaded history in the resurrection of the crucified Jesus.

But these summaries put the matter too abstractly. For the Synoptic Gospels and Acts, the Spirit works in, through, and under a network of practices—socially established cooperative human activity that is complex and internally coherent, is subject to standards of excellence that partly define it, and is done to some end but does not necessarily have a product. In Acts, the church's mission involves practices of witnessing to God's saving act in Jesus, healing, feeding the community and caring for the needy, prayer, Scripture interpretation, regulating the economics and administration of their common life, holding one another accountable to standards of excellence that partly define the practices that make up their common life. In John, the Spirit works in and through the common life of communities of faith to empower the proclaiming and hearing of the gospel. Central to the common life of such communities are such public and bodily acts as foot washing and meals. Their common life is marked by a love that imitates and replicates in bodily action toward one another Jesus' relation with the One he called Father. For Paul, the Spirit works in and through the ways in which people act toward one another in the common life of the community, and especially through acts of proclamation of the gospel, to draw persons ever more deeply into life "in Christ"—that is, into the life of the new eschatological creation inaugurated by the resurrection of the crucified Jesus.

These are all complex practices, socially established. Though they may have "products" in the sense of new members for the community and deeply changed personal identities, they are done as the appropriate response to what God has done for humankind in the death and resurrection of Jesus Christ. These practices are the always-already-there social context of the personal bodies in the community who cooperatively enact such practices in their own intentional bodily actions. The eschatological Spirit is present as the always-already-there context of the community's common life, and hence is itself the ultimate context of the lives of personal bodies who are members of such communities, precisely in, through, and under the communities' enactments of such practices.

Learning to be part of the common life of such community means learning to cooperate in one's own way in such practices. Such learning is existentially shaping. It gives new determinate definition to one's personal identity. It capacitates one to act in ways one would not otherwise act. Indeed, such learning is itself one more of the practices making up the community's common life.

As the eschatological Spirit is present in and through enactments of the practices constituting the church's common life, including practices of learning to engage in such practices, it empowers personal bodies. That is, in and through their learning new ways to be oriented to the world and to act in it, their personal identities undergo change. Thus, as the Spirit works in and through the practices that constitute the enveloping always-already-there context of personal bodies' lives, it is for that reason also intimately present to such persons' most interior changes. The Spirit is both environing and intimately interior, and is the latter because it is the former. It is within us just insofar as we are in it. This is signaled by the consensus judgment that the Greek of Luke 17:21 is better translated as "The kingdom of God is among you" than as "The kingdom of God is within you." "Circumambience" expresses the basic way in which the eschatological Spirit relates to us more aptly than does "within."

If we ascribe what the New Testament says of the Spirit (which it does not, of course, conceive in Nicene Trinitarian terms) to the triune God, we may say that in drawing us to eschatological consummation, the triune God relates to us circumambiently as our ultimate context, albeit it in a *taxis* that focuses on the Spirit.

There is a conceptual theological advantage to characterizing the triune God's relating to us as "circumambience." It cuts against a conceptual assumption of much Trinitarian doctrinal discussion of the Spirit and its roles in human life—namely, assumption of the validity and appropriateness of contrastive use in anthropology of such pairs of metaphors as "inside" and "outside," "within" and "without," "interior" and "exterior." Used contrastively, the two terms of each pair are construed as mutually exclusive relations. Each is used as a metaphor for the Spirit's relation to human persons drawn from possible relation between three-dimensional physical bodies: the dog is outside the house; the cat is in the hat, and so on. Pictures of human persons as autonomous subjects or autonomous centers of consciousness tend to assume contrastive use of such metaphors.

The assumption surfaces as an apparent dilemma about the Spirit: if it is "outside," "without," or "exterior" to human persons, then stories about its "entering" persons can only be seen as the violation of their freely self-determining subjectivity. It negates them precisely as autonomous subjects. A Spirit relating that way could only mean the death of a subject, not new eschatological life. On the other hand, if it is "inside," "within," or "interior," then accounts of the Spirit's bearing on persons' lives tend to be individualized, subjectivized, and privatized. It is difficult to see how the Spirit within subjects constituted by their autonomous self-determinations could also be within a community, except that "within the community" is shorthand for "aggregate of individuals each with the Spirit within her or him." It is difficult to see what the Spirit changes in persons except interior states of consciousness expressible only in a subjective rhetoric that may always more or less objectivize and distort those states of consciousness. Furthermore, it is difficult to see how anyone other than the person undergoing those changes could come to know them; they are ineffably private. One overall consequence of locating the Spirit within in contrast to without is a difficulty showing how the Spirit's subjective, individual, and private relating to human persons can really entail any radical change in the public realm, despite Paul's tying it to a new creation.

"The eschatological Spirit, sent by the Father with the Son" is the triune God relating to humankind now in the way in which God has promised to relate to all that is not God at the last time. That is the point of calling it the "eschatological" Spirit. As the form in which God reigns in the last time, the Spirit is lord of the time of the eschaton. If, "sent by the Father," the Spirit invades our history "with the Son," it is the eschaton that invades our time. Hence, as the "Spirit sent by the Father with the Son" draws us into eschatological consummation, it draws us into the time of which the Spirit is Lord. It is not our own time. It is the end time, the last time, the time of the triune God's eschatological kingly rule come circumambiently in our history. When this is our ultimate context, we live on borrowed time.

By the Father: Freely Blessing

To say that it is the "Spirit sent by the Father" who draws humankind to eschatological consummation is to stress that this mode of the triune God's relating to us is the utterly free gift of a promised eschatological blessing by the same triune God who relates in creative blessing to all that is not God.

The ontological identity of the God who draws to eschatological consummation with the God who creates secures the identity and singleness of our ultimate context. The distinguishable ways in which the triune God relates to us mean that our ultimate context is complex, but it is one ultimate context. God relating to all that is not God to draw it to eschatological consummation does not succeed, displace, or conflict with God relating to create.

This God is consistent. The triune God's active relating in each of three modes is consistently marked by freedom, love, and creativity. Each of God's ways of relating to us is giftlike or gracious, for gifts are given freely in love and create new relationships or new moments in established relationships.

The irruption into history of the end time and the circumambience of the Spirit are a blessing on creation from the God who also relates to create. That is part of the force of the technical theological formula that it is "the Father" who "sends" the Spirit. As Claus Westermann has pointed out (1972; 1974; 1978), "blessing" is understood in two distinctive ways in Scripture.

First, God's blessings are distinct from God's mighty deeds of deliverance. In such deeds, God relates punctiliarly to persons and communities in particular events to deliver them, usually from bondage. By contrast, in blessing God relates continuously and creatively. So God's relating in blessing is not conceptually tied to the concept of God's mighty deeds of deliverance. God's deeds of deliverance, however, presuppose God's creative blessing as their necessary context. It is only as there is something continuingly "there" that anything could require deliverance and any proximate contexts for acts of deliverance.

Second, although many deeds of divine deliverance occur in history, there are two abiding conditions of history: creation as the blessing expressed by stories of a primal time, and consummation expressed by stories of the blessing of the end time. Both are universal in scope, God relating to all that is not God. Considered in abstraction from their being related to by God, humankind's proximate contexts are too ambiguous, I suggest, to allow us to discover either of these conditions of history. To the extent that signs of these conditions can be read in features of the ecology of our biological and social proximate contexts or in patterns of long-range historical events, it is only when those contexts and histories are understood in terms of God's relating to them, respectively, in creative and eschatological blessing—that is, only as they are understood as creatively and eschatologically blessed.

A theological claim that is fundamental to the network of Christian beliefs is that the first ("Be fruitful and multiply") is the blessing that makes for the well-being of all living creatures across cycles of seed-time and harvest and across the generations, and makes for change and development in human culture. In it, God creatively sustains reality other than God in being in and through repeated cycles of birth and death. Such blessing is the condition of the possibility of continuity in history, which a string of punctiliar events does not provide. As I argued in part 1, this blessing entails no *telos* for creatures other than their own well-being.

Another theological claim that is fundamental to the network of Christian beliefs is that the second blessing brings exactly that *telos*. Already hinted at in Genesis 2:3, it "is the eternal rest which has been suggested in the rest of the seventh day" (Westermann 1974, 65). It is the consummation of creatures. This blessing is the condition of the possibility that otherwise profoundly ambiguous history can be viewed teleologically: "The course of history . . . set in motion by the conclusion of Creation by the sanctification of the seventh day [in Gen. 2:2] is no longer a monotonous succession in the monotonous rhythm of life; it runs to its goal just like the days of the week . . ." (65).

Eschatological blessing is different from the primal blessing of creation in one especially important way. Like a number of God's blessings on particular persons and peoples in history, eschatological blessing comes to be understood in a historically tensed way. Once given by God, it is actually in effect; on the other hand, even when actually bestowed, it may not yet be fully actualized.

In the New Testament, it is understood to have been promised long before Jesus, but fulfillment of that promise is only inaugurated through the resurrection of Jesus. The historically tensed character of such blessing surfaces here too. For both Acts 3 (Peter's sermon in Solomon's portico) and Galatians 3:9 ("those who believe [in Christ] are blessed with Abraham who believed," and to whom, as Paul reads the story, the eschatological promise was first made), Jesus simply is God's eschatological blessing already present in history; and for Galatians 3:13–14 the fulfilled promise of the Spirit is also identified with God's promised eschatological blessing. Here God's blessing is linked with God's mighty deed of deliverance in Jesus Christ, though the blessing and deliverance are not identical. On the other hand, other New Testament texts use "blessing" in a future-oriented way as the promised outworking of God's past saving act in Christ (e.g., 1 Pet. 3:9; Heb. 12:17). Ephesians 1:3–14 holds the two sides of the tension together:

> Blessed be the God and Father of our Lord Jesus Christ, who has blessed us in Christ with every spiritual blessing in the heavenly places, just as he chose us in Christ before the foundation of the world to be holy and blameless before

him in love [blessing as primordial as creation]. . . . In him we have redemp-tion through his blood, the forgiveness of our trespasses. . . . With all wisdom and insight he has made known to us the mystery of his will . . . as a plan for the fullness of time, to gather up all things in him, things in heaven and things on earth. . . . In him you also, when you had heard the word of truth . . . . and had believed in him, were marked with the seal of the promised Holy Spirit [Blessing of the promised Holy Spirit as God's future-oriented way of working out God's past saving act in Christ]. (Eph. 1:3, 4, 7, 8b–9a, 10, 13a, 13c)

Either way, the identification of God's inauguration of eschatological blessing with the resurrection of the crucified Jesus gives more deter-minate content to eschatological blessing: eschatological consummation consists in being drawn as adopted, newborn children into the same rela-tion that Jesus has with the One he calls "Father." According to the way in which various canonical New Testament texts plot the narratives they tell of God relating to draw creatures to eschatological consummation, given that estrangement from God is the condition of human creatures, the way of the cross is de facto the concrete way in which the same triune God who blesses by creating also goes about blessing by drawing all creation into eschatological consummation.

Finally, to say that it is "the Spirit, sent by the Father with the Son" who draws all that is not God, including humankind, to eschatological consummation stresses in particular the freedom of this divine relating. The Spirit, Jesus tells Nicodemus, is like the wind that "blows where it chooses, and you hear the sound of it, but you do not know where it comes from or where it goes" (John 3:8). What I seek to outline here is a theo-logically important part of the narrative logic of canonical New Testament stories of God relating to bless creation eschatologically, because theologi-cal proposals about anthropological implications of God relating to draw creatures to eschatological consummation ought to be held accountable to those narratives. Their respective narrative logics suggest that (a) God's relating in creative blessing and God's promise to relate in eschatologi-cal blessing are equi-primordial and (b) a very long time indeed separates God's actualizing creative blessing and God's inauguration of actualization of the promise of eschatological blessing. This raises the question, natu-rally enough, why God "waits" so long. So far as I can see, the canonical narratives to which secondary theology is accountable do not offer any clear answer. That leaves the door open for theologically informed pro-posals, coherent with other proposals in the web of interrelated propos-als made in practice of secondary theology, warranted by some of them, but not accountable to any particular feature of canonical narratives of God's ways of relating to all that is not God. There is no reason in prin-ciple that such proposals ought not to be advanced. It is equally the case that it is not obvious that the project of Christian secondary theology needs to offer proposals in answer to the question. If comprehensive systematization of theological proposals is not a standard of excellence in the practice of secondary theology, there is room for some questions to be left dangling.

Eschatological blessing is given freely by God. It is not the outcome of human effort. Nor is it a reward for human goodness. To the contrary, God commits Godself to it concurrently with creating, logically before there is anyone either to achieve or to earn it. That is the import, on one hand, of the hint at this eschatological blessing in Genesis 2:3 and, on the other hand, of the remark in Ephesians that this is a blessing for which God "chose us in Christ before the foundation of the world" (1:4).

Nor is God logically or morally committed to give this blessing by virtue of a continuing self-commitment to all that to which God relates creatively. God's relating to create is self-involving, but what it involves God in is commitment to the well-being of finite creatures for their own sakes and on their own creaturely terms. It does not logically or morally involve commitment by God to actualize any *telos* for human creatures other than the sustaining of their finite lives as long as they last and the quotidian goods proper to them. If God is also self-committed to a logically distinct *telos* whose actualization lies beyond creatures' finite capacities, such as eschatological blessing, then that is a logically and morally distinct commitment. God's self-determination to draw creatures to consummation is the utterly free gift of eschatological blessing.

The freedom of the Spirit's circumambience rules out any simple correlation of God drawing us to eschatological consummation with divine immanence, in contrast, say, to a correlation of God as creating with divine transcendence. I contended in part 1 that in connection with the triune God's creative relating, "immanence" and "transcendence" need not be understood contrastively as mutually exclusive characterizations of divine relating. In the context of a Christian theological understanding of the triune God's creating, immanence and transcendence may be understood to be dialectically related, each entailing the other. So, too, in regard to the triune God's relating to draw all that is not God to eschatological consummation. The triune God as "Spirit sent by the Father with the Son" relates circumambiently to draw creatures to eschatological consummation. In that relating, the triune God is utterly intimate to creatures—that is, immanent to them such that, by virtue of a self-involving commitment to them, relating to creatures in this way makes a difference to who God is. In the very same relating, the triune God relates intimately in a way that is utterly free of them both singly and as some sort of vast, interconnected whole. That is, in relating to creatures in this fashion, God is transcendent of them one and all, both in being and in self-involving commitment to them.

With the Son: Advent of Promise

To say that it is the Spirit "with the Son" who draws humankind to eschatological consummation is to stress that the triune God relates to us in this mode in a particular, peculiar, concrete way as the advent of the fulfillment of an open-ended promise by God to all that is not God.

In the New Testament the Spirit's circumambience in history is tied closely to the concrete particularity of Jesus' life, ministry, crucifixion, and resurrection from the dead. According to Mark, no sooner has John baptized Jesus than he promises that Jesus will "baptize you with the Holy Spirit" (1:8). In John, Jesus breathes the Spirit on his disciples (20:22). Paul identifies the Spirit so closely with the presence of the risen Christ that they sometimes seem to be alternate names for the same reality (e.g., 2 Cor. 3:17–18). In these texts, the Spirit's relation to Jesus has a logical priority to its relation to human persons in community. The Spirit's presence on persons in community depends on Jesus, whereas its presence on Jesus in no way depends on its circumambient presence in communities of disciples.

"The Spirit with the Son" stresses that the freedom of the triune God's circumambient relating is not the freedom of arbitrariness. Of course, it is not arbitrary whether God will continue to relate in this way. The relation is a blessing continuous across time, not a momentary event of deliverance. In giving the promise of eschatological blessing, God is self-committed to actualize the promise. In addition, the triune God is not arbitrary in regard to the concrete ways in which God goes about actualizing this blessing. It is not arbitrary in that it is always consistent with the concrete particularity of Jesus Christ. "Son" norms the radical freedom of "Spirit." That is part of the point of formulating the Trinitarian claim in this pattern: the "Spirit sent by the Father with the Son" draws us to eschatological consummation.

In particular, three features of the concrete, unsubstitutable identity of Jesus Christ norm this mode of the triune God's relating to all that is not God.

1. God's resurrection of the crucified Jesus simply is the inauguration of God's long-promised blessing of eschatological rule. The one resurrected has just this particular and unsubstitutable personal identity: as rendered narratively by the several Gospels, it is an identity constituted at once by Jesus' own intentional actions in ministry that led to his undergoing suffering and crucifixion, and by God's action in and through what Jesus did and underwent that led to his resurrection as the first sign of the general resurrection marking the end time. As Hans Frei has suggested in a striking way (1975), Jesus' resurrection is integral to his identity as that is rendered narratively in the Synoptic Gospels. If the resurrection of Jesus in his unsubstitutable personal identity is the inauguration of eschatological blessing, then it is Jesus' identity that defines the character of God's eschatological rule. (We return to this theme in more detail in part 3.)

In particular, Jesus' identity defines glory and power in God's eschatological kingly rule. Given that God inaugurates the long-promised blessing of eschatological consummation among human creatures who are estranged from God, God's glory is disclosed in the suffering and weakness of crucifixion (John 3:13–14) and God's power is manifested in apparent weakness rather than in violent force. The triune God, Spirit sent with the Son by the Father, is utterly free in drawing us to eschatological consummation but is always free in ways normed by the specific and concrete manner in which the eschatological kingdom is in fact inaugurated in history in Jesus Christ under the circumstances of human creatures' estrangement from God.

2. The inauguration of the promised eschatological blessing in Jesus' resurrection relates the future to the present in a distinctly odd way. Eschatological blessing is a promised future that brings creation's history to an end and inaugurates something new. What is inaugurated is discontinuous with the continuities of life, growth, and development across generations that are God's creative blessing. The discontinuity is brought out most forcefully by the rhetoric of apocalyptic texts in the Old Testament and subsequently used and echoed by New Testament writers, most especially Paul. Apocalyptic rhetoric stresses that the eschatological future is not the future of any particular present and past. The eschatological future is not a future that is rooted in and grows out of possibilities provided by any given present on the basis of its roots, in turn, in its past. Rather, the eschatological future is often depicted by apocalyptic rhetoric as not only the judgment and termination of creation's history, but as a new creation. Where expectation of such a future is given voice in the Old Testament, it tends to be spoken of in a linear way as the discontinuous successor to the history of what God has hitherto related to creatively.

New Testament writers, however, construe the significance of Jesus' resurrection as the inauguration of just that eschatological future in history. In that case, rather than succeeding creaturely history, the long-promised blessing of the eschatological future overlaps the history of changes, growth, and development that constitutes creatures' own futures as creatures. It is present proleptically—that is, ahead of time. However, it only overlaps with creaturely history and its future; the two are not identical. In consequence of its inauguration, the promised eschatological future is actually present. Further, as God's blessing, in contrast to one of God's deeds of deliverance, it is constantly actually present across time following its inauguration. But it is not yet fully actualized.

As a result, human creatures have two futures concurrently: the future that develops out of possibilities inherent in their particular creaturely presents and pasts, sometimes called *futuram* in the theological literature; and the eschatological future, sometimes called *adventus*, actually present but still awaiting its future actualization (see Moltmann 1967; on Moltmann, see also Morse 1979; cf. W. Pannenberg 1968, esp. chap. 3; 1969, esp. chaps. 1 and 4). The blessing of the eschatological rule of God is called *adventus* because it comes or arrives (Lat. *advenire*) from God's future as opposed to growing out of creatures' past. In apocalyptic rhetoric, its arrival is an invasion of or an irruption into the present. In virtue of the fact that God has actually inaugurated the eschatological time in the resurrection of Jesus during the course of history—the eschatological future invading (*adventus*) the creaturely future (*futuram*)—the resurrection of Jesus is characterized as the inauguration of eschatological time proleptically present, the eschaton present ahead of time.

The *adventus* character of eschatological blessing has important implications for a description of the relation between two aspects of our ultimate contexts: the triune God relating to create all that is not God, and the triune God relating to draw all that is not God to eschatological consummation. The *adventus* character of eschatological blessing rules out use of metaphors of human creaturely action to build or co-create the eschatological kingdom of God. It also rules out use of metaphors of a cosmic physical or spiritual evolution into the eschatological kingdom. All such metaphors trade on a picture of eschatological blessing as *futuram*, a future developed by human effort or developing by the logic of some cosmic dynamic out of the resources of the present. God relating to create and God relating to draw to eschatological consummation are certainly related to each other in positive ways, but not in these positive ways. I return to this topic at the end of the chapter.

3. The temporally tensed character of eschatological blessing gives it the force of a promise. It is actually inaugurated, so that eschatological blessing is an aspect of our ultimate context and helps define what and who we are and how we are to be. And, although promised, it is not yet fully actualized, which means that what and who we are, and how we are to be, are in part defined by the tension between "now actual" and "not yet actualized." The tension has the character of promise. The actual inauguration of eschatological blessing in the person of Jesus, especially in his resurrection, is itself the fulfillment of a promise; the fact that it is a blessing not yet fully actualized entails a promise that it will be actualized, for God's eschatological blessing is continuous across time and not an episodic divine act. God giving an eschatological blessing is also God making a promise of the full actualization of the blessing already inaugurated. Thus, in one aspect, our ultimate context has the character of a promise.

Moltmann (1967) and Pannenberg (1968) have made it impossible to ignore the radical character of the distinction between future as *futuram* and future as *adventus*. They have shown the enormously rich theological implications of the latter as promise. This part of this book is devoted to teasing out some of its anthropological implications. Crucial to doing so is attention to the logic of promise.

A promise is an utterance, a speech-act using ordinary language. The logic of such utterances has been analyzed by philosopher J. L. Austin (1962). His work fructified helpful analyses by Donald Evans (1963), Christopher Morse (1979), and Nicholas Wolterstorff (1995) of theological talk of God "speaking" and, especially, of God making promises. The analyses make plain that the utterance of a promise does not describe or report the interior state of the promiser. Rather, the utterance of a promise does something: make a promise. It is a performative utterance. If I promise to pay the costs of repairing your car after I crashed my car into it, my saying so just makes the promise.

An act of promise making has three types of force at once. It has commissive force. In making a promise to cover your auto repair costs, I am thereby committed to keeping the promise. Making a promise is thus self-involving on the part of the promiser. Second, making a promise has a type of causal force. My promising to pay your car repair bills creates a personal and social bond between us. It creates a social context within which you then live, a context in which it is appropriate for you to hope for that which was promised. The personal bond and social context created by the making of a promise presuppose conventions ruling the use of ordinary language that are shared by promiser and promisee(s) within a common society and its culture. However, the hope that is appropriate to the context created by my promise to pay your expenses in getting your car back in running order is not made appropriate by any feature of your context apart from my promise. My promise creates a genuinely new social context in which alone is your hope appropriate. Third, my promise making plainly has the force of stating a certain content: "I will pay the costs of fixing your car."

When the triune God is said to promise humankind eschatological consummation, the same logic of promise is invoked. The premise, of course, is that some utterance or utterances by some human being in some ordinary language may intelligibly be taken as also being God's utterance of a promise. That premise is not defended here; however, it is defensible, as Nicholas Wolterstorff has argued (1995). In the Christian tradition, promises made by prophets in ancient Israel function in that way. The Christian claim is that God begins to keep that promise in the resurrection of the crucified Jesus. That claim makes sense only within a tradition that hands on accounts of God's promising eschatological blessing, framed in the rhetoric of apocalyptic. As the first instance of the general resurrection marking the end time, Jesus' resurrection is a sign that the end time, the promised blessing of the eschaton, is actually already present. Of course, it no more has that significance self-evidently as a factoid in atomic isolation from other facts than does any single event considered in isolation. Events have meaning in the contexts of traditions of interpretation and explanation. Indeed, an event can be defined and recognized as "such-and-so an event" only in such contexts. The appearances of the risen Jesus to some of his disciples following his crucifixion were recognized by early Christians as his "resurrection," rather than, say, his ghost, his resuscitated body, or his emergence from hiding after escape from his trial, precisely because they were experienced in the context of traditions, especially ones couched in apocalyptic rhetoric, expectant of God's keeping the promise of eschatological blessing, of which a general resurrection was one sign and the pouring of the Spirit of prophecy on the entire community was another.

At the same time it is clear that the resurrection of Jesus does not keep all of God's promise. As promised, eschatological blessing was to be marked by God's triumph over all injustice, conflict, death, and suffering, but those features of ambiguous quotidian life continue. However, God's promising has commissive force. In making this promise, God is self-committed to keeping it. So that which is actually present by the inauguration of eschatological blessing itself inherently promises later full actualization of the blessing.

This promise making is implicit and not explicit. It is implicit in the very act of God inaugurating the keeping of God's original promise, which made through some human person's ordinary language utterances, say, a prophet's utterances. The promise implicit in the resurrection of Jesus is commissive also. God is self-involved in making it, committed to keeping it. Further, like all promises, it creates a new social context for those to whom the promise is made. Given the resurrection of the crucified Jesus, understood against the background of Old Testament prophetic promises construed in apocalyptic rhetoric, we now live in a context in which hope for the full actualization of God's promise to draw us to eschatological blessing is appropriate. Nothing else about our social context makes such hope appropriate.

Moreover, this implied promise has content. Where many promises have determinate content ("I will pay to repair your car, whatever the costs"), this implied promise is open-ended. It does not at all specify when or how it will be kept. It does not much specify what counts as keeping it. It is as though I had promised after our accident, "I'll make it all up to you." I'm free to decide what counts as "making it up to you," as well as when and how to do so. It is an open-ended promise.

To say that the Spirit "with the Son" draws us to eschatological consummation is to stress that our ultimate context is in this aspect a promise implied in eschatological blessing's advent quite concretely in the resurrection of the crucified Jesus, whose personal identity norms the ways in which the triune God goes about keeping that promise under the conditions of human creatures' estrangement from God.

Two Aspects of Our Ultimate Context

Part 1 characterized our ultimate context as the triune God, "Father through the Son in the power of the Spirit," relating creatively to all that is not God.

Part 2 characterizes our ultimate context as the triune God, "Spirit sent by the Father with the Son," relating to all that is not God to draw it into eschatological consummation. They are different ways in which the triune God actively relates, they have a definite relationship to each other, and they are ways in which one God relates to all that is not God.

These are different modes of relating that require different conceptual schemes. God relating to create is a relation in being, a metaphysical relation. The distinction and relation between God and all that is not God can be clarified by drawing ontological distinctions. A modest description of "Father through Son in power of Spirit" as one term of this relation can be offered with judicious, ad hoc, and highly qualified use of metaphysical categories.

God relating to draw to eschatological consummation, on the other hand, is a social and historical relation. Here the distinction and relation between God and all that is not God can be clarified mostly in terms of analyses of social roles using the social and cultural conventions of ordinary language. The clarification will be limited at best because it is close to impossible to develop a description of "Spirit sent by the Father with the Son" as one of the two terms of the relation. This follows from the privileging of New Testament metaphors for the Spirit. These metaphors keep the Holy Spirit obscure because, as Hanson puts it, the Spirit "is immediately concerned with our own intimate subjective apprehension of God, and we find it impossible to regard with complete objectivity a phenomenon which involves ourselves as subjects. But he is obscure much more because, as an eschatological force, his work is not yet completed. He is sovereign over history and cannot be completely understood by us because we are in history and because, unlike him, we cannot see the end of history, its completion, its consummation" (1973, 137).

In their differences, these two modes of God's relating are related to each other in a definite pattern. God relating to draw us to eschatological consummation presupposes God relating creatively. Accounts of God drawing us to eschatological consummation logically and ontologically presuppose accounts of God relating to us creatively. Accounts of eschatological consummation are unintelligible unless they presuppose accounts of something to be brought to eschatological consummation. Ontologically speaking, without God relating creatively, there is no reality "there" to be drawn to eschatological consummation. Furthermore, God drawing us to eschatological consummation is God giving us something radically new. The "new" that God gives in eschatological blessing must be consistent with what God gives in creative blessing, or it would be a violation of the creature. However, God relating in eschatological blessing is not a subset of God relating in creative blessing. The giving cannot be reduced to the actualizing in creatures of *teloi* that reside as potentialities in creatures simply by virtue of God relating to them creatively.

On the other hand, God relating to create does not in any way presuppose God's relating to draw to eschatological consummation. Accounts of God relating creatively are perfectly intelligible without accounts of God drawing what God creates to eschatological consummation. Furthermore, accounts of God creating do not imply God drawing what God creates to eschatological consummation. If God does draw to eschatological consummation, that is both logically and ontologically independent of, although consistent with, God's logically and ontologically prior relating to create that which is drawn to consummation.

In their complex interrelations, these are two modes of one triune God relating to all that is not God. In both modes of relating, that triune God is at once immanent to and transcendent of all that is not God. God is immanent in both creating and drawing to eschatological consummation in that in so relating God is utterly intimate to each and all reality other than God, in one case ontologically and in the other sociohistorically. But God's intimacy is always free intimacy, a relating that neither constitutes God as God nor is entailed by what God is as God, and a relating that cannot be exacted or manipulated by any creature. God is free to be intimately related, and as intimately relating God is always free of the control of the term of the relation. Together these two are two aspects of our one ultimate context.

The Unity of Canonical Holy Scripture and the Structure of Secondary Theology

Part 2 has, in effect, begun this project in Christian theological anthropology all over again. Where the anthropological proposals promoted in part 1 were held accountable to canonical Christian Holy Scripture's narrative of God relating creatively to all that is not God and were derived from the more basic theological claim that God relates creatively, part 2 promotes an analogous set of anthropological proposals that are held accountable to canonical Christian Holy Scripture's narrative of God relating to all that is not God to draw it to eschatological consummation and are derived from the more basic theological claim that God relates to consummate eschatologically. Some explanation of this procedure is in order.

An explanation is offered in this chapter on two levels. The first level has to do with the sense in which the canonical Christian Holy Scripture to which secondary theology's proposals are held accountable is some kind of whole. The second level of the explanation of this project's systematically unsystematic procedure has to do with the way the overall conceptual structure of secondary theology's proposals abstractly reflects the kind of wholeness that is ascribed to Christian Holy Scripture when it is acknowledged to be canonical.

Chapter 3B explained the sense in which this project construes biblical texts as the canonical Holy Scripture to which the practice of secondary theology is accountable. It concluded with the claim that, in conventional practice of secondary theology, acknowledgment of the texts making up Christian Holy Scripture as a canon implies that they form some kind of whole having some kind of unity, but that acknowledgment does not by itself imply any particular kind of wholeness or unity. That left open the question of just what kind of wholeness to attribute to it. This chapter builds on chapter 3B to characterize and critique the kind of wholeness that is conventionally ascribed to canonical Holy Scripture, to argue that that wholeness is reflected in an abstract way in the conventional and unstable, bipolar, overall structure of secondary theology, and to propose a modification of the conventional kind of wholeness ascribed to canonical Holy Scripture that would be reflected abstractly in a more stable overall structure for secondary theology.

The Conventional Wholeness of Canonical Holy Scripture

To review: the practice of secondary theology centrally addresses the questions, "In what ways does God relate to all that is not God? Who is the God who relates? How are realities other than God to be understood in their God-relatedness? In present circumstances, what are the best ways in which to respond appropriately to God's ways of relating?" One of the standards of excellence internal to the practice of secondary theology is that its proposals be held accountable to canonical Holy Scripture. The four questions to which the practice of secondary theology is centrally addressed express the theological interests that govern the practice's study of canonical Holy Scripture.

This has involved secondary theology in making two types of imaginative construals of the kind of wholeness canonical Holy Scripture has to which its theological proposals are held accountable.

It is particularly the first question that has governed the ways in which secondary theology has conventionally construed the kind of wholeness that canonical Holy Scripture has. Secondary theology's proposals in answer to the question, "In what ways does God relate to all that is not God?" have conventionally been held accountable to stories throughout canonical Holy Scripture of a multitude of ways in which God relates to all else. Each of those stories has been classified as a variant telling of one or another of an array of types of ways in which God relates to all else.

Distinguishing these types of ways in which God is said to relate to all else turns on the distinctive plot and outcome of each type of canonical story of God's relating to all else. Differences among types of ways in which God relates to which I want to draw attention do not lie in different attitudes or dispositions that are ascribed to God. The types of stories I want to distinguish do not consist, for example, of stories of God relating lovingly, stories of God relating judgmentally, stories of God relating angrily, stories of God relating sorrowfully, and so on, although it is certainly possible to organize canonical stories of God relating in that fashion. Nor are the differences I have in mind in "the ways God relates" that distinguish one type of story from another differences in the type of metaphysical explanation of "relating" that each suggests. The stories doubtless raise metaphysical questions about the nature of God's causal effectiveness in bringing about the outcomes told in the stories. And they may suggest interesting speculative metaphysical proposals about that causality. However, canonical stories of the types of ways in which God relates to all else are not themselves metaphysical explanations, nor do they imply any one systematic metaphysical theory about causality in general or divine causality in particular. Rather, I suggest, canonical stories of God relating have conventionally been construed as instances of stories of creation, or providential governance, or moral injunction, or covenant making, or judgment, or reconciliation, or eschatological consummation, and so on.

The act of classifying canonical stories of God relating to all else as stories of distinct types of ways in which God relates is grounded in an act of imaginative judgment. It is the first of the two types of imaginative judgment that are made in the practice of secondary theology about the kind of wholeness that unifies the canonical Holy Scripture to which its theological proposals are accountable. This judgment formulates paradigmatic images of the constitutive patterns (see chap. 3B) of the plot of canonical stories of each distinct way in which God relates to all that is not God. Thus, for example, the plot of the creation stories in Genesis 1 and 2 has conventionally served as the paradigmatic pattern of canonical stories of God relating to create; the plot of the story in Genesis 3 of Adam and Eve's "disobedience" has conventionally served as the paradigmatic pattern of canonical stories of human sin; the plot of the story in Exodus 19ff. of God creating a covenant with the children of Israel at Mount Sinai has conventionally served as the paradigmatic pattern of canonical stories of God entering into covenant with human beings; the plot of the narratives in 1 and 2 Kings and 1 and 2 Chronicles of divine blessing for obedience to God's law, and punishment for disobedience, on the kings and people of ancient Israel and Judah has conventionally served as the paradigmatic pattern of canonical stories of God's providential governance of historical events; the plot of the Joseph story in Genesis 37–45 has conventionally served as the paradigmatic pattern of canonical stories of God's particular providence in individual persons' lives; the plot of the Synoptic Gospels' passion stories has served as the paradigmatic pattern of canonical stories of God relating to reconcile estranged human beings; the plot of Jesus' parable of the Last Judgment (Matt. 25:31–46) and Revelation's vision of the last things have served as the paradigmatic patterns of canonical stories of God relating to draw creation to eschatological consummation; and so forth. Such acts of imaginative judgment, of course, can always be contested by appealing to details in the stories that arguably do not cohere with the judgment. They are always underdetermined interpretations of the canonical stories.

That first act of imaginative judgment organizes canonical stories of God relating to all that is not God into a limited array of types of ways in which God relates. In a second act of imaginative judgment, the practice of secondary theology has conventionally formulated a paradigmatic image of the constitutive pattern (see chap. 3B) of a single narrative plot capable of incorporating as subplots all the various types of canonical stories of different ways in which God relates, whose respective constitutive patterns were formulated in the first act of imaginative judgment. The overall narrative is constituted as one unified narrative by its constitutive pattern or narrative logic that makes it possible to follow it as a single sustained intelligible whole. The unity of that overall narrative makes a certain kind of whole of canonical Holy Scripture. Just what kind of whole it makes of canonical Holy Scripture depends, of course, on what is judged to be the appropriate paradigmatic image for the canon-unifying narrative's constitutive pattern. At least since Irenaeus in the early second century (see von Campenhausen's [1972] review and amendment of the scholarly discussion, and Barton's [1997] revisions of von Campenhausen), it has been conventional, at least in secondary theology practiced in the West, to construe these types of stories of God relating to all else as a sustained narrative whose movement is plotted in such a way that it can accommodate this variety of stories of different types of ways in which God relates to all else. It is the unity of this overall narrative that is conventionally taken to make a whole of canonical Holy Scripture.

It cannot be stressed enough that this narrative is not found as such in any text in canonical Holy Scripture. Fragments of such a narrative are explicit or implicit in canonical texts that tell stories of one type or another of ways in which God relates to all else. Every version of the canon-unifying narrative is based on an act of paradigmatic imagination. It is the act by which the constitutive pattern of some such fragmentary narrative is identified and used as the paradigmatic image that illumines the complex whole of the overall narrative of God's ways of relating to all that is not God.

The history of ecclesial secondary theology exhibits several quite different ways of imagining the constitutive pattern of the plot of a canon-unifying narrative. They all share certain features. They also differ profoundly in other respects. Consider the differences among the way it is construed, whether explicitly or implicitly, in Irenaeus's *Against Heresies*, Origen's *On First Principles*, Pelagius (or Augustine's version of Pelagius!), Augustine's *The City of God* and anti-Pelagian writings, Schleiermacher's *The Christian Faith*, and to move to the relatively more recent practice of secondary theology, Barth's *Church Dogmatics*, II/2, III/1, and III/2; Rahner's *Foundations of Christian Faith*; and Pannenberg's *Systematic Theology*.

All of these ways of imagining the plot of the canon-unifying narrative are alike in that they share several judgments about the overall movement of the narrative. They share the judgment that the narrative opens with a story of God relating creatively to all else, is interrupted by a story of a calamity that deforms all that is not God and threatens its ultimate disintegration, and then resumes with stories of God relating in two additional ways—namely, to save all that is not God from the consequences of the calamity and to draw all else to an eschatological consummation that, beyond merely restoring creation following the calamity, enhances it.

Different ways of imagining the plot of the canon-unifying story share, second, the judgment that God relates to save creation from the consequences of its calamity in all that Jesus does and undergoes, and that God relates to draw creation to an eschatological consummation through Jesus' resurrection and his coming at the end time as judge of the living and the dead. Jesus is the central figure in Christian canonical Holy Scriptures' stories of God relating to save and to consummate eschatologically.

They share, finally, the judgment that stories of God relating to save in what Jesus does and undergoes are themselves part of, and must be understood in the context of, an extended story of earlier ways in which God relates to save through what God's covenant people Israel do and undergo, from the story of Abram's call through stories of God liberating Israel from bondage in Egypt, creating covenant with her and giving her the Law, to stories of Israel's return from exile in Babylon. Thus, in all versions of the canon-unifying narrative, stories of God relating creatively, on one hand, and stories of God relating to save and to consummate creation, on the other, are always asymmetrically related in the narrative order. Stories of God relating to save and to consummate presuppose a story of God relating creatively, or there is nothing to save or consummate; but a story of God relating creatively does not require prior stories of God relating to save or consummate in order to make narrative sense.

Hence, stories of God relating to save and consummate are understood as stories of God's free grace relative both to God's relating creatively and to the consequences of the calamity that befell what God creates.

However, versions of the canon-unifying narrative differ profoundly about important features of the plot that drives the movement of the canon-unifying narrative as a whole. The points on which these versions differ intersect and overlap in complex ways that I do not attempt to chart here. My more modest aim is to illustrate how the conventional broad agreement about the overall movement of the canon-unifying narrative opens space for a great deal of disagreement about important particulars of the plot that drives the narrative.

In general, the differences arise from different theological judgments about at least two interrelated questions:

1.0 *How deeply disruptive of the narrative is the calamity?* Conventional construals of the canon-unifying narrative are divided into two broad groups because they turn on differing answers to this question:

1.1 The calamity is unforeseeable given the plot of stories of God relating creatively, and it threatens to disrupt the narrative's continuity radically because its effects threaten reality other than God with ultimate annihilation so that there is nothing there to which God could relate.

1.2 The calamity is a foreseeable function of the plot of stories of God relating to create. It is a contingent and regrettable swerve in the narrative line, but the stories of God relating to create can be plotted in a way that accommodates stories of the calamity without any break in the narrative line.

2.0 *What drives the movement of the overall canon-unifying narrative?* Conventional construals of the canon-unifying narrative are divided into several broad groups because they turn on differing answers to this question. At one level, of course, the answer is clear: since it is a narrative about God's ways of relating to all else, God's purposes drive the movement of the narrative. However, the three broad types of canonical stories of God relating to all else offer different ways of characterizing those purposes. Each of them has been influential:

2.1.0 What drives the movement of the canon-unifying narrative is God's commitment to the flourishing of creation in the face of the calamity that has befallen it. Stories about God relating to create physical, finite, good creatures specify the nature of that flourishing. At least two versions exist of this way of plotting the movement of the overall narrative:

2.1.1 When the calamity is related to stories of God relating creatively in the manner of 1.1, above, stories of God relating to save are construed as stories of the restoration of creation by its radical re-creation through God's relating to it by incarnation. Usually they plot the stories of Jesus' passion and crucifixion as the dramatic center of the narrative in which the drama of God's relating to save creatures from the consequences of the calamity is played out. Stories of God relating in this way to save are plotted, not as additional moments in stories of God relating creatively, but as stories of a new and distinct way in which God relates to all else in response to the calamity in order to re-recreate and restore it.

Because this way in which God relates is contingent on and subsequent to the calamity, they usually are known as "infralapsarian" ("after the fall") versions of the overall narrative. Stories of God relating to consummate eschatologically are not construed as yet another way in which God relates to all else. Rather, they are absorbed into stories of God relating to save as their final moment, telling of the ultimate outcome of God relating to save (e.g., some broadly Augustinian, especially Anselmian, versions of the narrative).

2.1.2 When the calamity is related to stories of God relating creatively in the manner of 1.2 (above), stories of God relating to save are construed as stories of God helping creatures exercise the powers given them by God's creative relating to resist and overcome the effects of the calamity. This help takes the form of innate human knowledge of their moral duty, explicit moral instruction, the moral and spiritual example of Jesus' life, and freedom by God's forgiveness from bondage to guilt. In this version of the narrative also, stories of God relating to consummate eschatologically are not construed as a different way in which God relates to all else. They are absorbed into stories of God relating to save as their final moment, telling of the ultimate outcome of God relating to save. This version of the canon-unifying narrative also has an infralapsarian plot, but in it stories of God relating to save simply are additional moments in a story of God relating creatively, specifically under the conditions of the calamity. In this type of version of the overall narrative, stories of God relating to save and to consummate are effectively absorbed into stories of God relating creatively (e.g., broadly Pelagian versions of the narrative).

2.2.0 What drives the movement of the overall narrative is God's commitment fully to actualize creatures' eschatological consummation. Canonical stories about God promising eschatological consummation and stories about God actualizing the promised eschatological consummation specify the nature of that consummation. At least two influential variations on this way of plotting the canon-unifying narrative result from different ways in which God relating to consummate eschatologically is related to God relating creatively:

2.2.1 Eschatological consummation is the full actualization of God relating creatively, and is not realized without God's own involvement in the process of actualization. Actualization of fully consummated reality other than God is inherently a process that involves the struggle of self-conflict. If self-conflict is either the basis of the calamity or its principal consequence, and if it is a necessary moment in the process of actualizing reality other than God, then it would appear that this version of the canon-unifying narrative adopts the view (1.2, above) that the calamity does not threaten the continuity of the overall narrative. On the contrary, it is necessary to the narrative's continuity. God's involvement in the process also involves God in the struggle of self-conflict. It is God's own internal struggle. Hence, if the canon-unifying narrative is just the narrative of God relating to all else to draw it to eschatological consummation, then the narrative's movement is driven by God's own struggle to overcome self-conflict. Plotted in this way, the canon-unifying narrative absorbs canonical stories of God relating creatively into a larger story of God relating to consummate eschatologically, not as stories of a distinct and different way in which God relates to all else, but as initial moments in the larger story of God relating to consummate eschatologically. Stories of God relating creatively are construed as stories about God relating to establish the mere possibility of fully actualized reality, not to establish its actuality. And stories of God relating to save by way of Incarnation are absorbed into the larger story of God relating to consummate eschatologically, not as stories of yet another distinct and different way in which God relates to all else, but as symbolic expressions of the struggle of self-conflict that lies at the heart of the inner dynamic or logic that drives both the process of full actualization of reality other than God and this version of the canon-unifying narrative (e.g., broadly Hegelian versions).

2.2.2 Canonical stories of God promising eschatological consummation and of God relating to fulfill those promises by drawing all that is not God to eschatological consummation move the overall canon-unifying narrative, but they tell of a different and distinct way in which God relates than the one told by stories of God relating creatively. Stories of God relating creatively do not require stories of God relating to consummate eschatologically in order to make narrative sense. The promise and subsequent fulfillment of the promise of eschatological consummation is a blessing by God on creatures constituted by God's creative relating. The promise is as primal as God relating creatively, and God relating to fulfill that promise by actually drawing all else to eschatological consummation is concurrent with God relating creatively. Nonetheless, God relating to draw all reality other than God to eschatological consummation is a different way of relating than God's relating creatively. It is a blessing on creation, a free and superadded gift. God relating creatively is the condition of its possibility, for without it there is no reality other than God to be drawn to consummation. However, while God's creative relating is reliably the same at every moment in the narrative, it does not itself move the narrative along. God relating to fulfill and actualize the promise of eschatological consummation is what moves the narrative. What gives the narrative dramatic tension in this way of plotting its movement is the calamity that threatens its eschatological extinction. Canonical stories of God relating to save serve to tell the concrete way—that is, the incarnation—in which God goes about actually fulfilling the promise of consummation in response to the calamity. Canonical stories of Jesus' passion, crucifixion, and resurrection are told as stories of the concrete way God struggles with and overcomes the consequences of the calamity. The climax of the entire narrative lies in particular in stories of Jesus' resurrection, because his resurrection is the concrete way in which God inaugurates the actual fulfillment of God's long-promised eschatological consummation of creation. Clearly, in this way of plotting the movement of the canon-unifying narrative, the calamity is judged to be a radical threat to the continuity of the narrative (1.1, above) and God's decision to fulfill the eschatological promise in the particular and concrete way of incarnation is infralapsarian (2.1, above). It is also clear that in this version of the way the canon-unifying narrative is plotted, canonical stories of God relating to save by way of the incarnation are absorbed into a more basic story of God relating to draw all else to eschatological consummation. Stories of God relating to save are not so much stories of a distinct and different way in which God relates to all else as they are instrumental moments in stories of God relating to consummate that specify how God goes about it (e.g., Orthodox and some broadly Augustinian versions of the narrative).

2.3.0 What drives the movement of the canon-unifying narrative of ways in which God relates to all else is God's commitment to enter, as God incarnate, into communion with human creatures capable of such fellowship with God. By relating to human beings in just that way—that is, as one of them and among them—God could draw them on their own terms into a community bound together by the kind of love that constitutes God's own life. What moves the overall narrative, then, is neither God relating creatively or God relating to draw all else to eschatological consummation, nor even God relating to save, but God preparing the conditions that incarnation will require: becoming incarnate, struggling with consequences of incarnation given the calamity (rejection, betrayal, estrangement, death), and triumphing as incarnate over those consequences (resurrection). In this way of plotting the movement of the overall narrative, stories of God relating to create tell of God preparing the preconditions for incarnation: in order for God to enter into communion with carnal human creatures, they must exist as bodied creatures, and that in turn requires the larger physical and social content in which they are sustained in life. Stories of God relating to consummate eschatologically are told as stories about the outcome of that way of relating: in the eschaton, what is inappropriate to such communion with God is brought to light and purged (judgment), and the full actualization of such communion is enjoyed (glorification). In this way of plotting the movement of the overall narrative, stories of God relating to all else by way of the incarnation clearly are told in a supralapsarian fashion. One consequence is that God's relating to all else by way of incarnation is not inherently and necessarily a relating to save. Rather, God relates by way of the incarnation anyway, whether there is a calamity from which all else needs to be saved. Hence, canonical stories of God relating to save are absorbed into stories of God relating by way of the incarnation as stories of the effect of that way of relating on the consequences of the calamity, effects that are, so to speak, contingent side effects of the incarnation rather than its fundamental purpose. There are at least two influential versions of this way of plotting the overall narrative, depending on whether the calamity is told as a foreseeable function of creatures' finitude (as in 1.2, above) or as a story of a radical threat to the narrative's continuity and integrity (as in 1.1, above):

2.3.1 The opening moments of an overall, incarnation-oriented narrative that prepare the necessary preconditions for the incarnation (i.e., moments told in canonical stories of God relating creatively) may be construed as stories of a maturational and pedagogical process focused on the promise of an eschatological outcome that consists in sharing the communion that the incarnate one has with God. They are absorbed into stories of God relating by way of incarnation. What God's creative relating creates are human beings who are intended for communion with God incarnately present as one among them, but because they are inexperienced and immature emotionally, morally, and spiritually, they are as yet incapable of such communion. They are promised that if they allow themselves to be taught by God they will mature properly—that is, they will develop the emotional, moral, and spiritual capacities (the virtues) they need in order to enter into an everlasting participation in the promised communion with God. However, given their inexperience and immaturity, it is almost inevitable that human beings' process of maturation will be distorted by their decisions to shape their own education rather than allowing themselves to be taught by God. In consequence, they experience the calamity that shapes the maturation and education of subsequent generations in the same distorting ways (as in 1.2, above). Such a calamity does not radically threaten the continuity and intelligibility of the canon-unifying narrative, however. Canonical stories of God educating human beings by instructing Adam and Eve, Noah, the patriarchs, and the Hebrew people at Sinai in the giving of Torah, are not construed as stories of a different and distinct way God relates (namely, to save), but rather are absorbed into this narrative of incarnation as stories of God continuing the educative process preparatory to the incarnation. This narrative line culminates in stories that tell of God relating to realize the goal of the entire narrative, the incarnation. It is "incarnation" constituted not just by Jesus' birth, but by the entire story of his life of perfect obedience to God, his ministry, passion, crucifixion, and resurrection. Stories of God relating to all else to consummate it eschatologically are absorbed into this narrative, not as stories of a distinct and different way in which God relates, but as stories of the final moment of God relating by way of incarnation. They tell of its outcome for human beings that suffer the consequences of their calamity, the actualization of the promised final outcome of their process of maturation under God's pedagogy in the gift of everlasting participation in community with God (e.g., broadly Irenaeian and Schleiermacherian versions of the narrative).

2.3.2 Canonical stories of God relating creatively may be told as stories of God relating to establish the necessary preconditions for God's entering into communion with creaturely companions by way of incarnation, but nonetheless construe them as stories of a distinct way in which God relates to all else that is different from God relating by incarnation. Stories of God's relating creatively are construed as stories with a fundamentally different plot than stories of God relating by incarnation. Nonetheless, stories of God relating creatively are construed as necessitated by logically prior stories of God relating by incarnation: incarnation necessarily presupposes a created world within which, and a community of bodied human beings among whom, to be incarnated. Hence, this version of the canon-unifying narrative has two plot lines moving concurrently, one consisting of stories of God relating creatively, and the other of stories of God relating by incarnation. However, since the overall narrative is incarnation oriented, the plot of stories of God relating creatively is decidedly a subplot in which not much happens. This opens up the possibility of telling stories of God relating creatively in ways that entail nothing materially about the dynamics and structures of creation, enhancing the possibility of their compatibility with other, nonscriptural stories about the dynamics and structures of creatures told by the several sciences. So, too, it means that canonical stories of God relating creatively need not necessarily be plotted as inherently maturational and pedagogical stories concerning the psychological, moral, and spiritual education of the race (as in 2.3.1, above), even when they are plotted as developmental stories in line, say, with evolutionary thinking. In this way of plotting the canon-unifying narrative, stories of the calamity that befalls human beings are set in the context of the stories about God relating to create, not in the narrative context of God relating by incarnation. They are construed as posing a radical threat to the continuity and narrative intelligibility of stories about God relating creatively (as in 1.1, above). The major point at which the two concurrent plot lines intersect in this overall narrative concerns the effect of stories of God's relating by way of incarnation on the radically threatening consequences of the calamity on the stories of God relating creatively. This is the point at which the narrative's dramatic tension reaches its climax. It consists of the stories of Jesus' ministry, conflict with civil and religious authorities, betrayal, passion, crucifixion, and resurrection appearances that tell of God's actualizing the goal toward which the entire narrative has been moving—incarnation—and at the same time tell of God's redemption and transformation of creation from the annihilation threatened by the calamity it has undergone. In this version of the canon-unifying narrative, canonical stories of God relating to draw all else to eschatological consummation are not construed as stories of a different way in which God relates, distinct from the way God relates by incarnation. Rather, they are absorbed into stories about God relating by way of the incarnation as stories of its final moments (e.g., broadly Barthian and Rahnerian versions of the narrative).

This typology of various ways in which the movement of the canon-unifying narrative can be plotted is in no way exhaustive. It serves to show that while the wholeness that acknowledgment of canonical Holy Scripture ascribes to Holy Scripture may be construed as the unity of a single extended narrative, such acknowledgment only creates a space in which a large number of different versions of that narrative can be imagined and warranted by appeal to the constitutive patterns of simpler canonical stories taken to be paradigmatic of the more complex overall narrative.

The typology shows two other things about these variations of the canon-unifying narrative that are fateful for the practice of secondary theology insofar as it holds itself accountable to canonical Holy Scripture.

First, each of the variations on the overall narrative tends to absorb stories of other types of ways in which God relates to all that is not God into the set of stories that tell of some one type of way in which God relates to all else, as though they were not stories of distinct types of ways in which God relates that are different from the one into which they are absorbed.

When it addresses the question, "In what ways does God relate to all that is not God?" in a way that is accountable to canonical Holy Scripture, secondary theology has an important theological interest in resisting such absorption of canonical stories of God relating to all else in one way into canonical stories of God relating in a distinct and different way. Such absorption allows an all-too-easy harmonization of the canonical accounts to which it is supposed to be held accountable. It may serve to simplify the task of secondary theology when addressing questions about how God bears on us and our creaturely contexts. But it does so at the peril of domesticating in dangerously misleading ways the complexity, ambiguity, and fierceness of God.

Second, the versions that plot the movement of the canon-unifying narrative in a way that does preserve the distinction between two distinct sets of stories as stories of two different ways in which God relates to all else (variations 2.1.1, 2.2.2, and 2.3.2, above) consistently recognize that difference between, on one side, stories of God relating creatively and, on the other, stories of God relating in the person of Jesus, either to save, or to draw to eschatological consummation, or to be an incarnate companion of human beings in communion (but usually not more than one of these). In the next section, I explore the consequences of this second feature of many influential versions of the canon-unifying narrative for the practice of ecclesial secondary theology when it seeks to satisfy its internal standard of excellence by holding itself accountable to canonical Holy Scripture.

The Conventional Binary Structure of Secondary Theology

Let us shift focus now from the question of the kind of wholeness that canonical Holy Scripture has, and its basis in a canon-unifying narrative, to the structure of ecclesial secondary theologies that hold themselves accountable to canonical Holy Scripture. We have just noted that the movement of some widely adopted versions of the canon-unifying narrative (variations 2.1.1, 2.2.2, and 2.3.2, above) are plotted in a way that preserves the distinction between two sets of stories of genuinely different ways in which God relates to all else: (1) stories of God relating creatively and (2) stories of God relating in the person of Jesus (to save, or to draw to eschatological consummation, or to be an incarnate companion of human beings in communion, but usually not more than one of these).

Each of these types of stories has a different plot. Hence, the movement of these versions of the overall canon-unifying narrative is doubly plotted. That is, it is plotted in such a way that the overall narrative can accommodate the second set of stories as a subplot. The first type of story has a certain narrative priority: if God does not relate creatively, there is nothing there for God to relate to by way of the person of Jesus. One sign that the second story tells of a way in which God relates to all else that is fundamentally different from the first is that it is told as a gift super-added to that which is constituted by God relating creatively. Nevertheless, as we saw in the typology in the previous section, the plot of the movement of either set of stories may serve as the plot of the overall narrative, with the plot of the movement of the other set serving as the subplot. The overall narrative may be plotted as a story of God relating creatively, with stories of God relating in the person of Jesus serving as its subplot, or the overall narrative may be plotted as a story of God relating in the person of Jesus, with stories of God relating creatively serving as its subplot.

That double plotting of the movement of these widely influential variants of the canon-unifying narrative is reflected abstractly in the binary overall conceptual structure of conventional secondary theologies about the ways in which God relates. I suggest that these binary overall conceptual structures tend to make conventional ecclesial secondary theologies structurally unstable in ways that are particularly dangerous for theological anthropology.

This conventional binary scheme is usually organized around a contrast between two major theological themes: usually either nature and grace, or law and gospel. In these structures, nature and law have tended to be theological rubrics under which fall theological questions about the implications of the affirmation that God relates to create, nurture, and providentially govern all that is not God, and grace and gospel have tended to be theological rubrics under which fall theological questions about the implications of the affirmations that God relates to draw all else to eschatological consummation and relates to save, reconcile, and redeem creatures threatened by the consequences of estrangement from God as a gift "super-added" to nature or above and beyond the law. Theological proposals that address questions that fall under the rubrics of nature and law, respectively, tend to be held accountable to canonical Holy Scripture that tells of God relating creatively. Theological proposals that address questions that fall under the rubrics of grace and gospel, respectively, tend to be held accountable to stories in canonical Holy Scripture that tell of God relating in the person of Jesus (whether to save, or to draw to eschatological consummation, or to be an incarnate companion of human beings in communion).

It must be kept in mind that these two sets of types of stories do *not* correlate with the distinction between Old Testament and New Testament texts. Some New Testament texts, read as Christian Holy Scripture, can be construed as telling or assuming stories of God relating creatively; and some Old Testament texts, read as Christian Holy Scripture, can be construed as telling or assuming parts of long stories of God relating in complex ways that culminate in the person of Jesus, whether to save, or to draw to eschatological consummation, or to be an incarnate companion of human beings in communion.

The ideal is that the two broad poles of these binary structures, in which theological proposals about the ways in which God relates to all that is not God, are organized and related to each other in a reciprocal dialectic. The proposals that are grouped in each pole of the binary are supposed to be related to each other and interrelated with the proposals grouped in the other pole in an enormously complex web of conceptual relations in which they modify and nuance one another. No one of them can be explicated in isolation from explication of the others without seriously distorting its meaning. Consequently, it should not be possible to explicate adequately theological proposals about questions that fall under the rubrics, respectively, of nature or law apart from reference to related proposals about questions that fall under the rubrics, respectively, of grace or gospel, and vice versa. Secondary theology cannot help being systematic in the specific sense of requiring attention to these interconnections and their systematic consequences as it formulates its proposals.

Indeed, one major reason to attend to the systematic relation among theological proposals in the practice of secondary theology is to be sure that theological formulations of one way in which canonical stories tell of God relating to all else not be conflated into formulations of a quite different way in which canonical stories tell of God relating to all else. When they are conflated, the cumulative theological account of ways in which God relates will misleadingly harmonize very different claims about God, oversimplifying and domesticating the rough edges and wildness of the One with whom we have to do and to whom we seek to respond appropriately.

However, precisely this attention to the complex systematic relations among theological proposals about the different ways in which God relates to all else also has the effect of encouraging secondary theology to construct single systematic conceptual schemes in which to organize its proposals in a single comprehensive, internally coherent system. When that is done, the two poles of the conventional binary structures of secondary theology are no longer reciprocally related to each other dialectically. Instead they are related in some overarching systematic structure in which theological proposals addressing questions that fall under one rubric (whether nature or grace, law or gospel) are logically ordered to and conceptually subordinated to proposals addressing topics that fall under the other rubric.

There are several ways in which to achieve such overall systematization of secondary theology's proposals. Two are particularly common in modern Western practice of secondary theology. In one, a philosophical conceptual scheme, most frequently that of a comprehensive speculative metaphysics or of an existential phenomenology, is adopted to provide a technical conceptuality in which to articulate theological proposals.

In another, secondary theology is practiced in a way that explicitly rejects the first strategy of adopting a systematic philosophical conceptual scheme. It argues that doing so collapses the different ways in which God relates into interchangeable instances of the one way that can be explicated in terms provided by the philosophical scheme (e.g., Barth's reasons for not relying on philosophy to make theology systematic). Instead, this second way of practicing secondary theology turns back to the canon-unifying narrative that tells of genuinely different ways in which God relates to all else. It seeks the systematic basis for the unity of the narrative in different ways in which God relates to all else in the logical relations *among* God's basic decisions or decrees that are enacted in God's various ways of relating to all else. They are logical rather than temporal relations because there can be no temporal intervals between God's eternal decisions. The decision to create may be deemed God's logically primary decision, with the decision to become incarnate and draw creation to eschatological consummation a logically secondary decision contingent on the calamity, which God does not cause but eternally foreknows. Or God's decision to enter into the type of communion with reality other than God that marks eschatological glory may be deemed logically primary, which implies as secondary and logically derivative a decision to create and, since God foresees the calamity, a decision to become incarnate in order to overcome the consequences of the calamity that make creatures incapable of eschatological glorification. Or God's decision to enter into community with creatures by becoming one among them in the person of Jesus may be deemed God's logically primary decision, which implies as secondary and logically derivative a decision to create a community of creatures capable of such community and the larger creaturely context required for the creatures' life and flourishing.

Such proposals about the logical relations among God's eternal decisions or decrees are often warranted by appeal to a precious few, very fragmentary canonical stories that may or may not be telling about God's decision making in general. Such judgments about how God's eternal decisions are related to one another are astonishing acts of creative theological speculation in their own right. However, it is difficult to show that they are acts of paradigmatic imagination that could yield an image of the constitutive pattern of a canon-unifying narrative, whose narrative structure might then be reflected abstractly in the conceptual structure of secondary theology, because it is difficult to identify relevant paradigmatic canonical stories—that is, stories exhibiting the logical structure of God's fundamental decisions.

Clearly, these diverse ways of grounding the overall structure of theological proposals in the logical structure of God's eternal decisions reflect different ways we have seen the movement of the canon-unifying narrative plotted. Earlier, we saw ways of doubly plotting the movement of the canon-unifying narrative such that stories of one way in which God relates to all else (whether it is to create, to consummate eschatologically, to save) serves the narrative's central plot, and a second type of story of a way in which God relates is absorbed into a third type of story of a way in which God relates, as though the two were variants on a second distinct way in which God relates and serves as the narrative's subplot.

We also saw that the impetus for plotting the movement of the canon-unifying narrative in one way or another does not lie in the judgment that the canon has the kind of wholeness of an extended narrative. I suggest that the impetus to plot the canon-unifying narrative in a way that absorbs one or even two of the types of canonical stories of different ways in which God relates to all else into another type of canonical story of a way in which God relates lies in secondary theology's responsibility, and hence interest, to attend constantly to the systematic interrelations among its many proposals. More exactly, it lies in a dangerous choice of strategy to satisfy the pressure of that interest. The strategy is to guarantee adequate attention to the systematic interrelations among theological proposals by showing how they fit together in a comprehensively systematic conceptual structure.

Under the pressure of that interest, I suggest, the conventional binary overall structure of secondary theology's proposals about ways in which God relates to all that is not God is unstable. It is extremely vulnerable to the collapse of quite different types of claims about ways in which God relates to all else into some one type of such a claim, as though they were at bottom merely variations of a claim about a single way in which God relates whose differences are merely verbal. The practice of ecclesial secondary theology has a responsibility for, and therefore a strong interest in, attending to the systematic interconnections among the topics on which it makes proposals. However, under the pressure of that interest, the binary structure of conventional secondary theology provides no conceptual resources to help conventionally organized secondary theology resist the temptation to satisfy that responsibility by systematizing its entire array of theological proposals in one, comprehensive, internally coherent conceptual structure that orders the proposals falling under one of its two organizing rubrics (nature or grace; law or gospel) to the proposals falling under the other rubric.

One sign of the vulnerability of the binary structure of most secondary theology to that temptation is the interminable and, apparently, irresolvable methodological debates in Roman Catholic and Protestant theology whether theological topics falling, *mutatis mutandis*, under the rubrics of nature or law are logically prior to or secondary to topics falling under the rubrics of grace or gospel. Should grace, and all theological proposals about grace, be conceived only by reference to and in terms of nature on the grounds that nature is the logically prior theological concept because stories of God relating creatively are more basic to the canon-unifying narrative than stories of God relating in the person of Jesus, as though nature could be adequately conceptualized theologically without reference to grace? Should gospel, and all theological proposals about gospel, be conceived only by reference to and in terms of law on the grounds that law is the logically prior theological concept because stories of God's relating creatively are more basic to the canon-unifying narrative than stories of God relating in the person of Jesus, as though law could be adequately conceptualized theologically without reference to gospel? Or, in each case, is the converse the case? When secondary theology's proposals are structured around two poles, and there is a theological interest that exerts pressure to order them into a single systematic structure, it is easy to resolve the problem by systematically subordinating one pole to the other. The conventional binary structure of secondary theological proposals does not itself clearly imply either logically subordinating proposals about grace or gospel to proposals about nature or law, or the converse. When they are made, those decisions evidently must be made on other grounds. My points here are (a) that that binary structure is inherently unstable and can yield to either move, and (b) that in its instability it is inherently vulnerable to the pressure that is properly internal to the practice of secondary theology that some such move is necessary.

Systematization of the proposals of secondary theology about the ways in which God relates to all else into a single, comprehensive, systematic conceptual structure should be considered a temptation because of its consequences. When it happens, the reciprocal dialectic between the two poles of the binary structure of conventional secondary theology collapses into a monolithic conceptual order. The result is that theological proposals about all the different ways in which canonical Holy Scripture tells of God relating to all else are conflated as though they were all instances of one, or at most two, ways in which God relates (whether it be to create, to be human creatures' incarnate companion, to draw to eschatological consummation, or to save). Or, when they are construed as proposals about two genuinely different ways in which God relates to all that is not God (nature and grace, law and gospel), they are ordered to each other in a nonreciprocal way that effectively subordinates one way in which God is said to relate to the other way, theologically marginalizing the way of relating that is made subordinate. The theological inadequacy of such subordination eventually prompts theological protest and a proposed revision of the systematic structure of theological proposals about the ways in which God relates to all that is not God that reverses the order of subordination. The reversal's theological inadequacy, in turn, prompts another protest and the proposal of a fresh reversal that amounts to a new version of the first order of subordination of theological accounts of one way in which God relates to accounts of a second way in which God relates.

Its instability and its vulnerability to misplaced systematization of theological proposals makes the binary structure of conventional secondary theology's proposals dangerous, especially to theological anthropology. I have urged that the binary structure's conflation of different ways in which God relates to all else is dangerous to secondary theology's proposals about the ways in which God relates to all else because it domesticates God by oversimplifying the complexity and apparent inconsistency of canonical stories of different ways in which God relates. There is a correlative danger to anthropological proposals.

For example, when the canon-unifying narrative is primarily a narrative about God relating to create, and canonical stories of God relating to consummate creatures eschatologically and relating to save them from the consequences of the calamity are absorbed into that narrative, then theological proposals about actual human creatures insofar as they are *also* either (or both) eschatologically consummated and saved cannot consistently characterize them under the aspect of redeemed in theological proposals framed in terms of a super-added gift—that is, in terms of grace as radically new, free gift above and beyond the gift of creatureliness. That is a theologically unacceptable consequence for anthropology.

Or, when the canon-unifying narrative is primarily a narrative about God relating to consummate creatures eschatologically, and canonical stories of God relating to create are absorbed into that narrative, then theological proposals about actual (not potential or possible) human beings as creatures cannot be framed as proposals about fully actual human creatures until the process of eschatological consummation is completed. Apparently their lives before then can only count as somehow preparatory, subhuman (or, depending on the technical meaning ascribed to "person," subpersonal), and consequently lacking the dignity and value of the actual human beings (or persons) that they will become. That is a theologically unacceptable consequence for anthropology.

Or, when the canon-unifying narrative is primarily a narrative about God relating by way of incarnation either (or both) to save creatures from the consequences of the calamity or/and to consummate them eschatologically by incorporating them into Christ, and stories of God relating creatively are absorbed into that narrative, then it would appear that theological proposals about actual (not potential or possible) human beings can only be framed as proposals about those who are in Christ—that is, liturgically speaking, the baptized. But then the unbaptized would appear to lack the dignity and value of human beings (or persons) properly speaking. That is a theologically unacceptable consequence for anthropology.

Or, finally, when the canon-unifying narrative is doubly plotted as both (a) a narrative about God relating to create that has one plot and (b) a narrative about God relating to creatures in the person of Jesus that has a second, different plot according to which it is primarily a narrative about God relating by way of incarnation to draw creatures to an eschatological consummation into which stories of God relating to save are absorbed as mere variations of the same plot, then theological proposals about actual (not merely potential or possible) human creatures under the aspect of reconciliation (by God's relating to them in Jesus Christ) can only be framed as proposals about their condition at the end of the process of eschatological consummation and cannot be framed as characterizations of their actual condition here and now before the eschaton. On the other hand, when the canon-unifying narrative's subplot is primarily a narrative about God relating by way of incarnation to save creatures here and now from the consequences of the calamity, into which stories of God relating to consummate them eschatologically are absorbed as mere variations on the same plot of a story of God relating to save here and now in a "realized eschatology," then theological proposals about actual (not merely potential or possible) human creatures under the aspect of eschatologtical consummation by God's relating to them in Jesus Christ can only be framed as proposals about their condition here and now and cannot be framed as characterizations of their condition under the aspect of destined for eschatological consummation. Those are theologically unacceptable consequences for anthropology.

Each of these consequences for theological anthropology of conventional ways of grounding the structure of secondary theology's proposals in a different way of plotting the movement of narrative that unifies the canon of Holy Scriptures to which the proposals are accountable needs to be warded off systematically (!) because it underwrites dangerous beliefs, attitudes, and policies regarding our human companions and ourselves.

A Counterproposal

On one side, this project in theological anthropology relies on an alternative to the conventional way of plotting the movement of the canon-unifying narrative and, on the other, it relies on an alternative to the conventional binary way of structuring secondary theology's anthropological proposals so as to maximize attention to their systematic interrelations. The inadequacies identified above in conventional variations on ways of plotting the movement of the canon-unifying narrative, the instability of the conventional binary structure of secondary theology's proposals in general, and the dangerous consequences of that instability both for theological proposals about ways in which God relates to all else and for theological anthropology, provide strong reasons to find such an alternative. Whether the alternative adopted here is itself finally any more satisfactory than the reigning theological conventions can only be decided when it shapes an actual set of secondary theological proposals. This project offers such a set of proposals in the theological *locus* "anthropology."

The two interrelated alternatives can be stated briefly.

1. *Concerning the way the movement of the canon-unifying narrative is plotted*: A standard of excellence internal to the practice of secondary theology is that its anthropological proposals about humankind as related to by God and about God as relating to humankind should be held accountable to canonical Holy Scripture's stories of different ways in which God relates to all else. Differences in the ways in which God relates are conveyed in differences in the ways stories of God relating are plotted. Canonical stories about ways in which God relates may be classified as different types of stories on the basis of differences in the "constitutive patterns" of their plots. As I noted earlier, judgments about the type of story to which any one canonical story belongs are based on acts of paradigmatic imagination that heuristically employ an image of the constitutive pattern of the plot of a paradigmatic instance of stories of the type in question to help identify other stories exhibiting the same pattern.

Genuine differences among the ways in which God relates to all that is not God, including humankind, may have consequences for the content of theological proposals about what and who human beings are and how they ought to be set in their proximate and ultimate contexts. A major thesis of this project is that, indeed, they have very important consequences. Consequently, canonical stories about God relating to all else in different ways ought not to be absorbed into one another as though they were interchangeable instances of stories of some way in which God relates.

This project explores the consequences for theological anthropology of the proposal that, contrary to conventional construals, canonical stories about God relating to all else, including humankind, exhibit not two, but three different plots and so fall into three, not two, basic types of stories: stories of God relating creatively, stories of God relating to draw all else to eschatological consummation, and stories of God relating to all else to reconcile it when it has become estranged from God.

This proposal agrees with conventional construals of Christian Holy Scripture as some kind of canonical whole that inasmuch as these three types of stories of God relating are all canonical stories, they are parts of an overall, canon-unifying narrative. However, since the differences among these three types of stories of God relating to all else ought not to be occluded by absorbing any two of them into the third (as though they were merely further instances of that type of story), the plot of the movement of the overall canon-unifying narrative cannot be identified, as some theological conventions do, with the plot of just one type of story. Nor, for the same reason, will it do to doubly plot the movement of the overall canon-unifying narrative, as some theological conventions do, such that one type of story provides the major plot of overall narrative and the plot of a second type, into which the third type has simply been absorbed (as though it merely provides additional instances of the same way God relates), serves as the narrative's subplot.

Instead, this project proceeds on the basis of a construal of the movement of the canon-unifying narrative as plotted by three distinct but complexly and inseparably interrelated plots of stories of, respectively, God relating creatively, to draw to eschatological consummation, and to reconcile. The interrelations among the three can be imaged as a triple helix: stories of God relating to consummate eschatologically and to reconcile are distinct from each other and cannot be absorbed into each other, but because in Christian canonical Holy Scripture both sets of stories have Jesus of Nazareth as their central figure, they are inseparably wound around each other like a helix. In addition, the pair of them is wound helixlike around a story of God relating creatively, from which they are inseparable because they necessarily presuppose it, but into which they cannot be absorbed. The logic of the relations among these three plots, each with a distinctive narrative logic that cannot be absorbed into or conflated with that of either of the other two, makes it impossible to relate them to one another in a simple linear fashion, as a sequence of different stories of three different ways in which God successively relates to all that is not God. It is to canonical Holy Scripture whose wholeness is grounded in a narrative complexly plotted in just this concurrently triple way that this theological project's anthropological proposals are held accountable.

2. *Concerning the overall structure of ecclesial secondary theology's proposals*: A standard of excellence internal to the practice of secondary theology is that it attend carefully to the complex web of systematic relations that obtains among its theological proposals regarding many different *loci*. In order to do that, enactments of the practice of secondary theology conventionally organize their proposals in some overall conceptual structure. As we saw earlier, that structure is conventionally a binary overall structure, organizing theological proposals around either of two poles (e.g., nature and grace; law and gospel).

In addition, enactments of the practice of secondary theology conventionally attempt to attend to the systematic interconnections among their theological proposals by systematizing the proposals in some comprehensive, systematically coherent conceptual scheme, often provided by either a philosophical conceptual scheme or a structure of God's decisions or decrees. I have urged that systematizing theological proposals in these ways has the theological drawback of tending to conflate proposals in quite different theological *loci* with proposals in some theological *locus* that is, at least implicitly, treated as though it were logically "basic." Proposals regarding eschatology or reconciliation become subtopics in proposals about creation, or proposals regarding creation or reconciliation become subtopics in proposals about eschatology, or proposals about creation or eschatology become subtopics in proposals about reconciliation.

We also saw earlier that the binary overall structure of conventional secondary theology is inherently unstable and vulnerable to the temptation to satisfy the standard of excellence that demands attention to the systematic interrelations among theological proposals by adopting a scheme that systematizes them by collapsing them into one systematic conceptual structure.

This project explores the consequences for theological anthropology of the proposal that secondary theology's proposals be organized in a triplex way rather than in the conventionally binary way. The instability and vulnerability we noted above in binary ways of organizing secondary theology's proposals are reasons for adopting this alternative. This project organizes its anthropological proposals around the poles of three, not two, logically more basic theological claims about God: God relating to create, God relating to consummate eschatologically, and God relating to reconcile. This triplex structure mirrors at the abstract level of theological analysis the triple plot of the movement of the canon-unifying narrative, to whose stories of different concrete ways in which God relates secondary theology's anthropological proposals are held accountable.

The three poles of the proposed overall conceptual structure of secondary theology are interrelated in complex and definite ways that can be charted. This triplex structure requires that proposals belonging with any one pole be explicitly formulated in ways that make clear what its systematic relations are, not only to those belonging to the same pole, but also to those belonging to each of the other two poles. Finally, organizing theological proposals around three poles rather than two makes the overall structure of the proposals a three-legged stool that is less unstable than the conventional binary structure. It is less vulnerable than the binary structure to the temptation to guarantee attention to the proposals' place in the web of systematic relations among them by simply subordinating one to the other, formulating all the proposals around one pole in a way that orders them to the proposals around the other pole. In that way, it wards off the undesirable consequences for theological anthropology that we noted earlier of just that kind of conflation.

The meaning and merit of methodological proposals like these only come clear when they are actually followed and inscripted (embodied?) in some exercise of the practice of secondary theology. This project in theological anthropology offers just that.

CHAPTER 13

Our Proximate Context: Living on Borrowed Time

Perhaps the most important anthropological question about our proximate social contexts is whether historical change—social, cultural, political, and economic—is meaningful. Given the ontological and moral ambiguities of creaturely finitude and the moral ambiguities of sinfully distorted creatureliness, historical change over time is usually conflictual, often violent, and, when it is radical change, always traumatic. It generates enormous waste of human life and inestimable suffering. Do such changes amount to a movement toward any goal of such transcendent value that it redeems the suffering and loss? Or is unrelenting historical change finally sheer "sound and fury, signifying nothing"? These are anthropologically important questions because they are questions about one dimension of humankind's proximate contexts. If the historical and social contexts of our lives have meaningful purpose, perhaps our lives themselves have a larger meaning. If, on the other hand, history is not ordered toward any meaningful goal, does that imply that our lives are finally meaningless?

In regard to this question, I explore some implications of the claim developed in chapter 12 about one aspect of our ultimate context—namely, that the triune God draws creation toward the consummation of eschatological blessing, for which the preeminent biblical image is the kingdom of God. In particular, I focus on the import of New Testament use of apocalyptic rhetoric to characterize eschatological blessing as a new creation marked by cosmic struggle. The theological importance of doing this has been clear ever since Ernst Käsemann published two groundbreaking essays (1969, 82–107, 108–37) arguing that apocalyptic is the "mother of theology," beginning with Paul's theology.

I suggest that affirmation of the triune God's eschatological blessing, especially as it is couched by Paul in apocalyptic rhetoric, allows a positive answer to questions about the meaning of history, but only a highly quali-fied positive answer. In virtue of this aspect of our ultimate context, our proximate contexts are marked by a teleological, future-oriented move-ment, although it is conflict-ridden and anything but linear. Moreover, what gives our proximate contexts meaning, and hence gives our common and personal lives meaning, is not a goal to be actualized by us but rather God drawing us to that goal.

The account of our ultimate context in chapter 12 warrants stress on six features of our proximate contexts: (1) In them, we live on borrowed time. (2) In them, the triune God engages us in our public life. (3) They are ambiguous contexts. (4) They are doubly tensed contexts. (5) They are promising contexts. (6) Their own values are thoroughly relativized. These are salient features of our proximate, historically extended social and cul-tural contexts insofar as the triune God relates to them in eschatological blessing, in addition to relating to them in creative blessing. When these features of our proximate contexts are stressed, an account of the mean-ingfulness of history cannot but be highly qualified.

Living on Borrowed Time

If one aspect of our ultimate context is "the Father with the Son in the power of the Spirit" relating creatively, then, or so I argued in part 1, one aspect of our proximate contexts is their finitude in which we live on bor-rowed breath. If another aspect of our ultimate context is "the Spirit sent by the Father with the Son" drawing us to eschatological consummation, then another aspect of our proximate contexts is that they are the objects of the triune God's mission, the *missio Dei*, to draw them, and us with them, to just that consummation. To live in such proximate contexts is to live in the coincidence of two ways in which the triune God actively relates to all that is not God, including us. Reflection on the relation between these two aspects of our proximate contexts suggests that our life in them is lived on borrowed time.

The goal of the eschatological *missio Dei* is a divine blessing not included in God's blessing on creatures. Understood in ways guided by canonical Wisdom literature's creation theology, creaturely human his-tory as such has no overall teleological order. To be sure, over time crea-tures in their kinds do change and amazing developments take place. In all of these changes and developments, creatures are radically dependent for their reality and value on the triune God who delights in them. God's creative relating to creatures is a creative blessing in the midst of their ambiguities, nurturing them across the generations in the endlessly pro-liferating richness and the terrible beauty of their varieties. However, God does not create them for any end beyond being creatures that precisely in their quotidian lives mirror the inexhaustibly rich and complex beauty of God's glory. So I argued in part 1.

God relating to all that is not God to draw it into eschatological consummation takes place in a quite different way: the promised eschatological blessing, creation's promised future, appears in history ahead of time—proleptically, in the resurrection of the crucified Jesus. The future-oriented teleological movement God inaugurates in humankind's proximate context is not rooted in, nor does God draw it out of, any resources or dynamics inherent in personal bodies or in their proximate contexts. Nor does its inauguration violate the integrity of creaturely personal bodies in community. Nor is it a process of divine correction of a faulty or inadequate creation; finite personal bodies in community are exactly what God creates and declares "good." It is a logically and ontologically distinct mode of God's relating, a fresh blessing above and beyond the blessing of creation. The goods of the blessing of eschatological consummation are different from the goods of God's creative blessing, yet neither type of good is mutually exclusive of the other.

To live in proximate contexts marked by the coincidence of the cyclical movement of God's creative blessing and the goal-oriented movement of the blessing that accompanies God's drawing creation to eschatological consummation is to live on borrowed time. In colloquial English we speak in different ways of persons living on borrowed time. A criminal who receives a stay of execution while the governor of the state reviews a petition for pardon is said to be living on borrowed time. He is living on time to which he had not been legally entitled. A person who walks away unscratched from a terrible automobile accident is said to be living on borrowed time. She is living on time that she had no statistical probability of calling her own. A person who recovers from the bodily damage caused by an unbroken fall from an extraordinary height is said to be living on borrowed time. Medically speaking, her "time was up." She is living on time that biologically speaking could not have been expected to be hers. To understand oneself to be living on borrowed time is to understand oneself to have a radically new gift of unanticipated, unearned, and unplanned possibilities. It is to understand one's world as the context for a new start, a new life.

By analogy, as spatio-temporal personal bodies, human creatures both have and are their own time and space. In creating them, God gives them time and space that is their own and for the use of which they are accountable. God calls them to be wise in their stewardship of their own time and space for the well-being of their proximate contexts, including themselves. On the other hand, inasmuch as it is none other than personal bodies in community who are caught up in the circumambient triune God's mission to draw creation to eschatological consummation, they also concurrently live on borrowed time. It is the time of the triune God's mission in and through changes in creaturely cultures and societies to actualize eschatological blessing. It is the proleptically present time of God's future for creation, not time that is the creatures' own just because they are creatures. It is the time of a radically new start and a new life. It is a time of unearned, unanticipated, unimaginable possibilities, "far more than all we can ask or imagine" (Eph. 3:20).

Living concurrently on their own time and on borrowed time, personal bodies defy a single, comprehensive, conceptually integrated account, a truly systematic theological anthropology. This, and nothing more portentous, is the point of the remark that, theologically speaking, human persons are inexhaustibly mysterious.

However, the coincidence of creaturely and eschatological aspects in personal bodies' proximate contexts is radicalized into a living contradiction when their creatureliness is distorted in sin by inappropriate response to either or both of these two of God's ways of actively relating to them. When that happens, personal bodies' ways of living on their own time contradict what and who they are and how they are to be by virtue of God's ways of relating to them. Their proximate contexts become self-contradictory, defined simultaneously by the triune God's ways of relating to them and by the distorted human practices that constitute those proximate contexts. It is just such self-contradiction in our proximate contexts that is signaled by New Testament references to the "world" as hostile to God's eschatological blessing or references to God's creatures "in bondage" to the power of evil.

Under those circumstances, the theological remark that personal bodies live on borrowed time acquires an ominous edge. Eschatological blessing then means that they concurrently live under judgment for the way they live on their own time, and live in the time of God's mercy in the midst of judgment until the ways in which they live on their own time are transformed. To say that they live on borrowed time is to say that they live concurrently according to the flesh in this world subject to God's rejection and according to the Spirit sent by the Father with the Son in a new creation.

This is a living contradiction. It makes human persons mysteries in a second sense. They are mysterious not because of the unsystematizable richness of what and who they are and how they are to be by virtue of God's ways of relating to them, but, in this second sense, because of their rationally inexplicable self-contradictoriness, which, in its opacity to human inquiry, "makes no sense."

A Public *Missio Dei*

The Trinitarian God's eschatological mission, the mission of the "Spirit sent by the Father with the Son," takes place in public and shapes all humankind's public proximate contexts, social and cultural. The content of the eschatological blessing actualized by the *missio Dei* is characterized biblically by interpersonal and social imagery as God's "kingly rule," an unending and inviolable communion among creatures and God marked by justice, love, and peace. That is, it is characterized by images having to do with the way in which social, political, economic, and cultural powers are optimally arranged. This type of imagery emphasizes that eschatological blessing engages the social and cultural dimensions of personal bodies' lives quite as much as it does the privacy of their subjective interiorities and the networks of their more psychologically intimate interpersonal relationships.

How could it be otherwise if in relating to living human personal bodies in communities as their eschatological consummator God genuinely engages them as creaturely personal bodies? In part 1, following patterns of thought in canonical Wisdom literature, and borrowing from Paul Ricoeur, I used the phrase "personal bodies" to characterize our creatureliness in order to avoid conventional contrastive use of such pairs of concepts as body/soul, subjectivity/objectivity, individual/social, and historical/natural. Anthropological use of these concept-pairs as contrasting terms in ways that privilege one term in each pair tends to lead to dichotomizing descriptions of human persons. If "individual," "soul," "subjectivity," and "historicity" are not to be privileged over "social," "body," "objectivity," and "natural," to name the defining characteristics of human personhood, then neither can the private sphere be privileged over the public sphere. The point stressed by using the phrase "personal bodies" is that, theologically speaking, while these are all properly abstractable features of personal bodies, no one of them or one subset of them is definitive of creaturely human personal bodies. What human creatures are is personal bodies having a complex array of capacities for exercising various types of power. To be sure, for purposes of convenience and clarity in exposition, each of these aspects of personal bodies may be abstracted from the full complexity of actual, concrete personal bodies. But when that is done, what we are discussing is, precisely, an abstraction from human personal bodies.

The triune God engages actual, concrete personal bodies in community; God does not engage abstracted aspects of human persons. The interplay in our proximate context between God's creative blessing in relating to us as our creator and God's eschatological blessing in relating to us as our eschatological consummator is itself played out in the entire range of human capacities, as much in capacities for public human action as in capacities for a private interior life.

Nor is the *missio Dei* limited to the more or less intimate, intersubjective community of the church. It may be that the defining mission of the church is to follow at a distance the *missio Dei* in the world. That is a question for a doctrine of the church. Granted, the Spirit is sent upon the church. The story in Acts 2:1–36 of the Spirit's bestowal on the church at Pentecost is a sign that the promised eschatological blessing has indeed been inaugurated. It does not follow, however, that the eschatological blessing of the Spirit is limited to the public called "the church." It does not even follow that the Spirit is primarily located in the church and is only in the wider world by derivation from the church. That is, it does not follow that the blessing of the Spirit marks our public social and cultural context only because it first marks the community of the church, which is a public in its own right, and on that basis spills out onto the larger public aspects of our common life. Rather, God's eschatological blessing marks our proximate contexts as such because the eschatological *missio Dei* takes place in the public aspect of our common life, which includes, no doubt in a special way, the common life of the smaller public called "church."

This is the profoundly important theological intuition that has been worked out in such different ways and on such different theological bases in liberal Protestant social gospel theology; classic and modern Roman Catholic social teachings; Reinhold Niebuhr's neo-orthodox theological realism; various Latin American, African American, and feminist liberationist theologies; the political theologies of Jürgen Moltmann and Johannes Metz; and arguably in Karl Barth's thought (see Hunsinger 1976). Whatever the final assessment may be of the theological cogency of the way each of these has been argued, they at least rightly stress that interiorized, privatized, spiritualized interpretations of biblical stories of the advent of the eschatological kingdom of God are distorted in ways that are dangerous for Christians' understanding of their vocation and mission in the world. They are perhaps even more dangerous for the people in the wider world among which Christians enact their vocation and mission.

Doubly Ambiguous Proximate Contexts

The eschatological *missio Dei* takes place in proximate social and cultural contexts that are ambiguous in their own right. Quotidian human societies and their cultures are integral aspects of God's human creatures, integral aspects of what God affirms as "good." At the same time, while remaining God's good creatures, and in addition to the ontological and moral ambiguity that correlates with their finitude as creatures, they are also so profoundly and systemically distorted in consequence of humankind's inappropriate responses to God relating creatively as to be social and cultural living deaths. Chapters 10 and 11 developed that claim. Hence they are ambiguous contexts, in one way good, in others distorted. Neither the distortions nor the ambiguity they introduce into our proximate contexts are functions of God relating to them creatively. They are "adventitious." As I argued in part 1, the ambiguity is not merely the result of the complicated distribution and combination of individually morally good and wicked people in our proximate contexts, morally good and evil individual actions in individual persons' lives, or morally good and bad discrete social and cultural movements in history. More than that, this ambiguity is a function of the subtle and complex interweaving of moral good and evil within even the most morally admirable as well as the most despicable, in the most God-oriented as well as the least God-oriented persons, actions, and movements.

God's promise of eschatological blessing to creatures is as such an absolute promise, but given the moral ambiguity of our proximate contexts, it also implies a contingent promise. If, independent of and coincident with God relating creatively to all that is not God, God also relates to draw all that is not God to eschatological blessing, then God's relating in eschatological blessing is as absolute as God's relating in creative blessing. Neither is contingent on any action, accomplishment, or desire of the ones blessed. However, God drawing our proximate contexts, and us with them, to eschatological consummation implicitly promises that their distortions and ours will undergo transformation. This implicit promise is contingent on the fact that those contexts, and we in them, are distorted and in need of transformation. God is not said to draw all that is not God to eschatological consummation in order to transform creatures' distortions. That is part of the point of saying that God's promise of eschatological blessing is absolute. It is not contingent on creatures being distorted in sin and horrendous evil. Furthermore, were they not distorted in sin and horrendous evil, actualization of their promised eschatological consummation would involve some kind of largely unimaginable transformation of their quotidian creatureliness. Given that they are distorted, however, God's actually keeping God's absolute promise also contingently implies the promise of transformation of that distortion and its consequences.

Although it brings an implied promise for transformation of the sinful distortions of our proximate contexts, the eschatological *missio Dei* does not warrant the theological view that historical change moves in the direction of actualizing an overall incremental moral improvement in our social and cultural proximate contexts. Instead, precisely because it takes place in the midst of such ambiguity, what the *missio Dei* actually does is introduce a second type of ambiguity into our proximate contexts. It is an ambiguity in every historical change that is apparently a change for the better. The ambiguity is brought out by the apocalyptic rhetoric used in some, especially Pauline, New Testament accounts of God drawing us to eschatological consummation. Such rhetoric relies heavily on images of struggle and conflict. Because the proximate contexts into which the end time has proleptically come in the resurrection of the crucified Jesus are already morally ambiguous, the proximate contexts and their eschatological blessing are in conflict with each other. Not only are creaturely situations, persons, and human actions in our proximate contexts morally and theologically ambiguous, but all apparent moral improvements in them across time that might be claimed as anticipations of eschatological blessing, signs of the triune God drawing them into the eschatological kingdom, are themselves inherently conflictual and ambiguous.

This second type of ambiguity in our proximate contexts is brought out by the implicit narrative logic of New Testament texts using apocalyptic imagery. That logic challenges the conceptual adequacy of construing good and evil as qualities inversely related to each other on a sliding scale in social and cultural changes across time, as though an increase in goodness, justice, or freedom in certain aspects of a particular proximate context necessarily entails an overall decline in evil, injustice, or oppression in that proximate context. It suggests to the contrary that good and evil both increase correlatively in the same social and cultural changes across time in a given proximate context. Apocalyptic rhetoric seems to stress that not only are persons, human acts, and social movements ambiguous mixtures of good and evil, but that—one and the same—social and cultural change over time moves simultaneously in the direction of new and (in comparison to earlier social and cultural situations) sometimes clearly superior goods and in the direction of new and sometimes obviously horrendous evils. Accordingly, the moral and theological ambiguity of the overall direction in which those changes are moving simply intensifies.

Thus, the notion that social and cultural changes can be characterized as moving in some overall direction incrementally "for the better, overall" is undercut by apocalyptic rhetoric. Such rhetoric warrants instead the picture that social and cultural change may indeed eliminate an older social or personal evil, introduce a new social or personal good, and introduce unprecedented new social or personal evils all at once.

Consider one very complex and well-worn illustration. The abolition of the institution of chattel slavery in the United States eliminated an old, horrendous moral evil. The emancipation of slaves introduced a new social good in that proximate context. It is unquestionably a moral improvement over the previous social situation. The Reconstruction of the South under the control of the Northern victors following the American Civil War created a situation marked by unprecedented and powerful racist evils, only partially symbolized by Jim Crow laws (see, e.g, Woodward 1957). Arguably all of these goods and evils characterize one self-same, large-scale social and cultural change in the United States. The fact that this proximate context came to be marked by new and powerful evils in no way invalidates the judgment that this proximate context was also marked by an important and powerful new (for the United States) moral good. Nor does it invalidate the judgment that the social and cultural changes wrought by the Civil War brought to an end a horrendous evil. However, it is at least misleading, and perhaps meaningless, to ask whether as a result of these changes American society and its culture had become morally better or worse *overall* than it had been before. "Good" and "evil" are properly used to express moral judgment on these changes. However, they cannot be added up and subtracted to arrive at a bottom-line calculation of overall increase or decrease in social, cultural, or personal goodness.

So, too, in a framework shaped by New Testament apocalyptic, it is theologically unintelligible to cite the abolition of slavery and the emancipation of slaves, along with, for example, the national requirement of universal free education, extension of voting rights to women, the rise of acknowledged social responsibility for the welfare of citizens most vulnerable to homelessness and hunger, and so on, as indices that by God's grace American society and culture are historically moving through overall increased good and decreased evil toward actualization of the kingdom of God. Even if these changes in Americans' proximate contexts were not themselves ambiguous, it would be arbitrary to lift them out of their larger social and cultural contexts as somehow more indicative of an alleged direction of overall social moral improvement in American society than are other major social changes.

It would be theologically arbitrary, that is, unless there were theological grounds for claiming that God, actively relating to Americans and their proximate contexts as their eschatological consummator, is peculiarly identified with the social and cultural dynamics that moved American society and culture toward these changes. Such grounds would necessarily include the judgment that the triumph in them of good over evil would be the criterion by which to distinguish the events in which God is actively relating to us as our eschatological consummator from the events in which God is not so relating to us. That in turn would require some theological consensus about the definition of what counts as "good," "evil," and "triumph."

However, it is precisely reliance on such broadly held consensus, especially any theologically validated consensus, that is ruled out by the way in which New Testament eschatological stories are told when they use apocalyptic rhetoric. They make it clear that the appropriate criteria do not lie in theologically warranted abstract concepts of good and its triumph over evil. Rather, they lie in the very odd way in which God concretely inaugurates the fulfillment of long-promised eschatological blessing. The stories tell of a concrete particular personal body and what he did and underwent. For the New Testament writers, it is the concrete person Jesus, and not patterns abstracted from human moral experience, that provide theological criteria by which to discern God actively relating to draw us and our proximate contexts to eschatological consummation. Moreover, the criterion is not self-evident in Jesus' explicit teachings. The upshot of the Gospels' narrative rendering of Jesus' identity is that God inaugurates the long-promised eschatological consummation through this one whose personal identity is constituted by his being the crucified One whom God raised from the dead. The inauguration of God's kingdom is not manifested in the powerful triumph of the good. Rather it is hidden by God in the weakness of the crucifixion.

The particular plot of this story of the resurrection of the crucified Jesus serves to rule out theological efforts to clarify the moral and theological ambiguity of our proximate context by attempting to identify unambiguous signs of the overall direction of historical changes. The triune God actively relating to creatures as their eschatological consummator is hidden in that ambiguity, not just metaphysically, but christologically. God actively relating to us as our eschatological consummator is hidden in Jesus' weakness before the ambiguities of our proximate contexts.

The choice of prepositions in theological formulations is critically important. God's enactment of the promise to bring creation to eschatological consummation is not best characterized theologically as a process somehow driving history from within, a process in which potentialities latent in our contexting societies and their cultures are actualized. Nor is it best characterized theologically as one type of event among others that occur in history, not even the Enlightenment's favorite type of event, "liberating" events. Rather, the *missio Dei* moves in God's own very peculiar way sometimes with, sometimes directly against, and sometimes obliquely at cross-grain to the various trajectories of change that we can discern in our social and cultural contexts. In this way, the triune God engaging our proximate contexts to draw them, and us with them, to eschatological consummation just complexifies the moral and theological ambiguity that already marks them.

Relativized Social Structures

Not only does the mission of "the Spirit sent from the Father with the Son" to draw us to eschatological consummation double the ambiguity of our proximate contexts, it also defines them in a doubly tensed way. One tension is a structural tension between two overlapping "worlds," an old creation and a new creation, in both of which every proximate context always participates simultaneously. I explore in this section some of the anthropologically relevant implications of this tension. The other is a historical tension inherent in the new-creation pole of the old-creation/new-creation tension. It marks every proximate context with a tension between the now actually inaugurated eschatological blessing and the not-yet-full actualization of that blessing. I explore in the next section some anthropologically relevant implications of that tension.

The apostle Paul tells the story of God inaugurating the long-promised eschatological blessing as the story of the "turn of the ages," a time of transition from one era to another in which two "worlds" overlap. Paul tells the Corinthians, "So if anyone is in Christ, there is a new creation: everything old has passed away; see, everything has become new!" (2 Cor. 5:17). So, too, Paul brings his argument in Galatians to a close with the words: "May I never boast of anything except the cross of our Lord Jesus Christ, by which the world [cosmos] has been crucified to me, and I to the world [cosmos]. For neither circumcision nor uncircumcision is anything; but a new creation is everything!" (6:14–15). According to this story, through the crucifixion of Jesus, God is inaugurating a new creation marked by a communal life in the power of the Spirit in which human persons are drawn as adopted children into Jesus' own relationship with the One he called "Father." However, Paul makes it clear to some in the Corinthian church that they are wrong to conclude that therefore they already live in the fully actualized new cosmos. The *missio Dei* to displace the old creation with the new is not yet complete. Paul saw himself and humankind universally standing at the juncture and overlap of these two worlds.

For Paul, this overlap between two worlds is a time marked by conflict between God and forces that hold humankind in bondage. In Galatians he twice identifies these forces as "elements of the cosmos" (*ta stoicheia tou kosmou*, 4:3, 9). The new creation is a world freed from bondage to these forces. In one way, the battle has already been won by God through the resurrection of the crucified Jesus. In another way, the struggle continues. In Paul's view, the Galatian Christians are at risk of resubmitting to the bondage to elements of the cosmos from which they had been freed (Gal. 4:8, 9).

The conjoining of imagery of "new creation," "elements of the cosmos," and "cosmic struggle" is distinctively apocalyptic rhetoric. Such rhetoric is used in both biblical and extrabiblical texts to tell of a disclosure (Gk. *apokalypsis*) of the mystery—that is, the secret—of God's overall purpose for history, the stages through which and, perhaps, the timetable on which, God will actualize that purpose. It often employs lurid imagery to identify signs of God actually beginning to actualize God's plan: calamitous wars, meteorological disasters, astronomical catastrophes. These literary tropes are mythological, and not coded historical predictions. Paul is not much interested in the details or timetable of God's plan. As Paul uses it, such rhetoric points to an aspect of our proximate contexts that results from God's inauguration of eschatological blessing. Every proximate context is marked by the overlap of two worlds in both of which it participates simultaneously, and by the structural tension of the struggle between them. Our proximate contexts are tensed through and through.

For the modern Christian, such apocalyptic tropes seem thoroughly mythological. As J. Louis Martyn says in particular of the passage that culminates in Galatians 6:13–15 (quoted above), "These statements are of a kind to make the head swim. One might even wonder whether they do not constitute flight from reality" (1997, 114). The symbolic character of such imagery is clear. It is also clear that Paul's use of such imagery is misread if it is taken as a coded description of the stages of God's plan or as a timetable of things to come. The question remains just how theological reflection today is to respond to it.

Mid-twentieth-century theology by and large construed Paul's apocalyptic eschatology as an implicit theology of history. In that case, its indirect bearing on theological anthropology was clear. A theology of history is the natural theological home of a discussion of what makes history, and therewith human lives, meaningful. Hence this construal of Paul's apocalyptic theology had clear, if indirect, anthropological consequences.

At least two different types of theology of history were derived from Paul's use of apocalyptic rhetoric when discussing the end time. Both interpreted apocalyptic imagery by drawing analogies to Allied military experiences in World War II. Both are instructive for theological anthropology.

One version of this, represented by the work of Oscar Cullmann (1950), was drawn from World War II in Europe in December 1944. Arguably, the crucial campaign was the Battle of the Bulge in which counterattacking German forces pushed a large bulge in the Allies' line in the Ardennes region of Belgium and Luxembourg. When the Allies won that battle, the war itself was in effect already won. The decisive battle had been fought. However, the enemy did not quit fighting, nor could the Allies. The end was coming. The Allies looked in hope for it without knowing precisely when it would be. In the meantime, the fighting raged ever more fiercely. By analogy, what apocalyptic symbolism expresses, on this interpretation, is a conflict between God and evil in which God has, in Jesus Christ, already won the decisive battle and therewith won the conflict, but the enemy has not yet ceased resisting and so God cannot cease either. Hence, our proximate contexts are marked by the tension between the "now already" of God's victory in principle, bringing in a time of liberation from bondage to forces of evil, and the "not yet" of forces of evil ceasing to resist God. Thus, every proximate context is a time between times, marked by ever more intense conflict between God and evil.

A second version of this type of analogy is drawn from the war in the Pacific (see Forman 1957). There were islands in the Pacific where fighting continued long after Japan had surrendered, the war had officially ended, and peace had been declared. Japanese troops on those islands either had not heard the news of peace or disbelieved what they heard, convinced that it was an American ruse to undermine their morale. By analogy, apocalyptic symbolism expresses a situation in which God has definitively conquered evil but those who resist God do not yet know it. Hence, our proximate contexts are marked by a tension between the objective reality that God's eschatological kingly rule has been established and the subjective reality that some people do not yet know it and therefore keep on resisting God.

These two interpretations of Pauline apocalyptic eschatology have theologically interesting differences. The first version stresses that ongoing conflict between God and forces of evil is simply an objective fact, and therewith makes God's victory "already" a matter of mere victory "in principle" (as opposed, perhaps, to "in operative fact"). The second version stresses that God's victory over resistance to God is fully accomplished, and not just "in principle" (the war in the Pacific was definitively over), but therewith makes continued conflict result from a cognitive and emotional problem. It results from the ignorance or distrust of those who resist God.

What the two versions of this type of analogy share is the assumption that apocalyptic symbolism expresses a view of our historical proximate contexts. What the analogies seek to illuminate is this: From the time of the resurrection of the crucified Jesus, human history has been marked by a tension between the objective fact of God's victory already over forces of evil and the not-yet-actualized consequences of that victory, a tension manifested in increasing and utterly needless conflict that is at bottom a conflict between God and forces of evil.

However, what these analogies share is what finally makes them inadequate analogies for the eschatological story Paul tells using apocalyptic rhetoric. As J. Louis Martyn has shown (1997), apocalyptic imagery concerns the structure of the cosmos, not the logic of history. Certainly, it is true that much apocalyptic literature tells of a disclosure of the mystery of God's overall purpose for history. However, as we have seen, Paul does not use apocalyptic rhetoric for that purpose. He uses it to describe a radical change in the structure of the world, a shift from an old creation to a new creation.

Martyn implies another type of analogy to illuminate Paul's apocalyptic rhetoric. The relation between the old creation and the new may be likened to the relation between two radically different, socially constructed lived worlds, one of which deconstructs the other, but which may, nevertheless, overlap in one society so that people in that society concurrently live in both. The proximate contexts of such people are marked by the intense tensions of the struggle between the two lived worlds, both of which they inhabit.

Focusing on Galatians, Martyn asks what the cosmos is that Paul says has been crucified to him and he to it (6:14). A clue to the answer, he suggests, lies in Paul's two earlier references to "elements of the cosmos" (4:3, 9) in relation to which there are two periods. Before the advent of Christ, all humankind was in bondage to these elements. After Christ's crucifixion, all have been liberated. (For the next three paragraphs, see Martyn 1997, 125–41 and 111–25.)

What are these "elements of the cosmos"? In several Hellenistic syncretistic religious movements, such elements are identified either as "elementary spirits" or, in more gnostic contexts, as "elements of learning." Sometimes Paul's use of the phrase has been interpreted analogously with these explanations. However, because the sources for such interpretations are later than Paul, this line of interpretation is dubious. Lexio-graphical observations favor interpreting the phrase to mean "elemental substances"—earth, water, air, and fire—the basic elements from which everything in the natural world is made according to ancient cosmologies.

The effort of the ancients to identify the elemental substances of the cosmos was oriented to practical ends. Centuries of cosmological speculation in the ancient world had reflected on relations among the four elemental substances in order to discover how changes in their relationships explained changes in human beings, their circumstances, and their conduct.

It was commonplace for thinkers in the ancient world to draw up tables of pairs of opposite cosmological principles. For example, Paul's great contemporary, the Hellenistic Jewish thinker Philo, relying on Pythagorean precedents, develops such a list in discussing God's act of creation. Besides Philo, a "number of thinkers close to Paul's time, including both Sirach and the author of Wisdom, would have readily agreed with the traditional statement: The elements of the cosmos are pairs of opposites" (1997, 138). The two poles of each pair can be understood to be in dynamic conflict with each other, or, as tends to be the case in late, extracanonical Wisdom literature, they can be seen as complementary. These pairs are the elemental substances of the cosmos in that the cosmos is structured by them; it is constituted a cosmos and preserved from being a chaos by these pairs. Given the fundamentally practical interest driving such cosmological speculation, the cosmos is, in effect, humankind's lived world. The whole point of identifying these elemental substances is to understand better what causes the changes that occur in human life and its proximate contexts.

Against this background, Martyn urges, we are to interpret Paul's remark "neither circumcision nor uncircumcision is anything," with which Paul prefaces his remark, "but a new creation is everything" (Gal. 6:15). Apparently the pair circumcision/uncircumcision is one of the elemental substances of the cosmos that he has just claimed was crucified to him and he to it in "the cross of our Lord Jesus Christ" (6:14).

Moreover, it is against this background that we are to interpret Galatians 3:28. Given their baptism into Christ, Paul tells the Galatians, "There is no longer Jew or Greek, there is no longer slave or free, there is no longer male or female; for all of you are one in Christ Jesus." These pairs are further elemental substances constituting the cosmos whose center no longer holds after God's act in the crucified Jesus.

They are an interestingly diverse set of pairs because they apparently have quite different grounds. Male/female would be grounded for Paul in the structure of created reality. Jew/Greek would be grounded in God's election of Israel for covenant relationship with God. It has two variants in Galatians, circumcision/uncircumcision, and law/no law. Both male/female and Jew/Greek are objectively grounded, the first ontologically by God's creative fiat, the second by God's electing will. By contrast, slave/free would seem even for Paul to be grounded in the conventions of contemporary societies. It appears to be an elemental substance of a socially constructed cosmos, a human creation.

Paul, however, is indifferent to these distinctions. His point is descriptive (perhaps we should say phenomenological). All Gentiles and Jews have in fact lived in a cosmos structured by these pairs, and for them all it has been a life in bondage. It is a life of bondage because it is a life based on worship of elemental substances rather than of God. To structure one's lived world on the bases of these contrasts is to trust one's life to realities that are not God but creatures. Such trust constitutes worship, and to worship creatures is to live in bondage. Precisely such a lived cosmos, Paul claims, has been brought to an end in the crucifixion of Jesus Christ.

The new creation is structured and constituted by Jesus Christ himself, in whom "all of you are one" (Gal. 3:28c). It has as its elemental substance a quite new pair: flesh/Spirit. Flesh and Spirit do not designate alternative forms of life, either of which we are free to appropriate. Rather, they designate two powers whose ongoing struggle shapes our proximate context.

The point may be generalized by analogy. All human societies provide a lived cosmos structured by fundamental principles that tend to be binary. These principles are variations on such pairs as us/them, insider/outsider, kinfolk/alien, powerful/powerless, female/male, well-born/low-born, rich/poor, dark skin/light skin, clean/unclean, edible/inedible, sacred/profane, and so on. Often the paired terms are understood to be inherently conflictual so that the socially constructed lived cosmos is understood to be inherently conflictual.

It does not matter whether any given variant of these pairs can be shown to be warranted by the structure of reality. Creaturely reality is extraordinarily rich in binary patterns because of the remarkable structural symmetry disclosed in experience ranging from the most abstruse branches of physics, from cosmology at one end to subatomic physics at the other, to everyday experience of up/down, left/right, tall/short, before/after, powerful/powerless, rich/poor, male/female, skillful/unskilled, adept/inept, and so on. The question is not whether reality exhibits binary structures. The question is why certain terms of certain pairs should be privileged as organizing principles in the social construction of a lived cosmos.

We have been exploring the anthropological significance of Paul's use of apocalyptic rhetoric for understanding his picture of two overlapping worlds, an old creation and a new creation, in both of which every proximate context always participates simultaneously, marking it with a structural tension between the two. Paul uses apocalyptic rhetoric, not as a mythological theology of history, but as a way to make a point about the implications of Jesus' resurrection for the structure of our lived worlds. The theological upshot of Paul's use of apocalyptic conventions in telling of God's inauguration of the eschaton in the resurrection of the crucified Jesus is that all such principles used to constitute a socially constructed lived cosmos are relativized. They do not have absolute or reality-defining importance. The lived world they constitute has been crucified to us and we to it. We cannot help but continue to live in proximate contexts deeply shaped by those socially constructed worlds and the values and principles that fund them. However, such values and principles have no privileged objective grounding, either in the structure of created reality or the will of God. Thus, the principles and values by which our received and distorted social and cultural contexts are ordered are radically relativized by the inauguration of God's promised eschatological blessing in the resurrection of Jesus. In drawing us to eschatological consummation in that way, God draws us into a new creation whose elemental principle is Spirit rather than flesh. This new creation is a lived world constituted by living in the time of and by the power of the eschatological Spirit. It is in conflict with the old, but still obtaining, world constituted by living in the time of socially constructed worlds grounded in faith in the power of finite creatures—that is, according to the "flesh."

This entails, it should be noted, the relativization of the values and principles basic to socially constructed proximate contexts, values, and principles by which the overall moral improvement over time of any social and cultural proximate context might be measured. The only fair way to assess any given proximate context's moral development over time is according to the standard of excellence internal to its own life. Such values are standards of excellence internal to the practices that constitute any lived world. They may or may not be the values and principles that actually preside over the social construction of their particular lived world, but they are the values and principles explicitly celebrated in that world as its "highest" goals. But it is just such "highest and best" values and principles that are relativized in the new creation that overlaps our ambiguous proximate contexts when the triune God inaugurates eschatological blessing. They are relativized in regard to their own lived worlds. That is, they are relativized as criteria by which to assess overall incremental moral development and improvement in the history of the lived worlds to whose practices they are integral.

The values and principles constituting our proximate contexts, our lived worlds, have been relativized, but not indiscriminately invalidated. For Paul, life in the Spirit is, by baptism in the power of the Spirit, life in the crucified and risen Christ. It is participation as adopted children in the risen Jesus' filial relationship with God. Given the sinful distortions of our responses to God relating to us both to create and to draw us to eschatological consummation, this participation has a very concrete form: it is new life lived in the way of the cross. In the practices constituting that "way" lie the criteria by which to assess the relative adequacy or inadequacy of the principles and values that structure the proximate contexts that are our lived worlds.

Promising Proximate Contexts

The eschatological *missio Dei* taking place in our proximate contexts defines those contexts with a second, historical tension. It is a tension inherent in the new-creation pole of the first tension between two creations (see previous section). The new creation simply is the eschatological blessing inaugurated in the resurrection of the crucified Jesus. As I noted above, given the moral ambiguity of our proximate contexts, the inauguration of eschatological blessing implicitly promises transformation of our contexts. The way in which the New Testament speaks about the transforming effect of the triune God drawing creatures to eschatological consummation makes it clear that it promises they will undergo real change. De-formations are promised to undergo re-formation, beginning now; dis-tortions are promised to undergo ex-tortion in its full Latinate sense (*ex torquere* [Lat.], to twist out), beginning now.

However, such divine transforming defines our proximate contexts with a temporally extended tension. The tension is inherent in the concrete way in which God inaugurates the new creation. It is especially important at this juncture to keep clear the difference between the promise of an eschatological blessing, on one side, and the promise inherent in New Testament narratives of the proleptic inauguration of that eschatological blessing, on the other.

Canonical Scripture's narratives about God drawing creation into an eschatological consummation include stories of prophets uttering oracles in which God promises such consummation to Israel. By those promises, God self-involvingly and performatively constituted a covenantal context that embraced God and Israel. Such promise is not itself part of the actualized eschatological consummation, precisely because it is a promise of something not at all actual yet.

By contrast, many New Testament texts implicitly or explicitly tell the story of God's resurrection of Jesus from the dead as the story of the inauguration of the fulfillment of just that long-promised eschatological consummation. It is the proleptic presence of eschatological blessing that is promised full actualization in the future. The New Testament name for that future is Parousia, an immanent arrival. What is promised here is not eschatological consummation; that has already actually been inaugurated. Rather, this promise is itself ingredient in the eschatological consummation that has already been inaugurated in the resurrection of Jesus. It is a promissory dimension implicit in the concrete way in which God fulfills a promise to which God has been self-committed coincident with creating. This implicit promise is itself performative and self-involving. In raising Jesus from the dead, God at once makes a promise that performatively constitutes a new, objectively actual, covenantal context embracing God and all creation, and is self-involvingly committed in that covenant to actualize what has been inaugurated.

In short, understood within the context of the long traditioning of Israel's witness to God's promise of eschatological blessing, the story of God raising Jesus from the dead signifies four things. First, the peculiarly intimate relationship Jesus has with God has a future. Second, especially within the conventions of apocalyptic expressions of God's promised eschatological blessing, Jesus' resurrection signifies that God has begun to fulfill a blessing for which all creation is destined. Jesus' resurrection is only the "first fruits" (1 Cor. 15:20, 23) of that eschatological blessing. Third, it promises to humankind generally communal participation as adopted children in Jesus' relation with God. Furthermore, fourth, Jesus' resurrection signifies that God's inauguration of universal eschatological blessing does not involve escape from or the abolition of creatureliness. Rather, it is a blessing precisely on creatures in their creatureliness. It is a blessing on humankind that begins in each of their proximate contexts now. In themselves, their social and cultural contexts across time are far from promising anything radically new; given the resurrection of the crucified Jesus, these contexts are blessed with promise.

The way these canonical stories are told, Jesus in his own person quite concretely is the promissory dimension of the triune God's drawing our proximate contexts to eschatological consummation, *adventus* ingressing from "God's future," not just the "disclosure" of a promissory dimension already latent in our creaturely proximate contexts but previously unrecognized or undiscovered. It is not that Jesus and his resurrection somehow illustrate, express, or symbolize some promising capacity for self-transformation and self-transcendence toward ideally perfect human life that already is and always has been universally latent in creaturely reality, perhaps by divine creation, infusion, or inspiration. In order to make any such claim, we would need to know about that latent capacity independently of the story of Jesus and his resurrection so that we could then recognize Jesus as its illustration or symbol when viewed against the background of our knowledge of that latent capacity. A skeptical question mark has to be placed opposite every independent effort to identify such promising latencies in the human spirit or its history, on the theological grounds that it likely will turn out to be a piece of complacent human self-congratulation. Instead, the pattern of theological thought needs to go in the other direction, not from widespread evidence of promising potentialities generally present in our proximate contexts to Jesus as most adequate symbol for them, but from the presence of the risen Christ in our proximate contexts to the claim that therefore those contexts are in some way promising. His presence concretely is the promise of the triune God which is implicit in the very way in which God goes about keeping God's promise of eschatological blessing.

To see the force of this remark, consider again the logic of utterances by which promises are made. To make a promise is not usually to offer a possibility that may or may not be appropriated and actualized. Rather, to make a promise is to constitute an objective social actuality. Promising is a performative and self-involving act. To make a promise is to constitute an objective context that embraces the one who promised and those to whom the promise was made. It is a social context in which the promiser and those to whom the promise is made are bound in a covenant unilaterally constituted by the promiser. This context is "objective" in that its actuality does not depend on whether those to whom the promise was made believe that it was made, or whether they trust it even if they do believe that it was made. Neither the recipients' belief nor their trust can be said to actualize a possibility offered by the promise. Rather, simply to make the promise performatively constitutes a covenant that embraces promiser and promisees. At the same time, to make the promise self-involves the promiser in this covenant relationship. Leaving aside questions of motives and preceding conditions, both the self-involving and the constituting of the covenantal context are unilateral acts by the promiser. The recipients of the promise do nothing and contribute nothing to constituting the objectively actual social context in which they find themselves.

Thus, in the resurrection of the crucified Jesus Christ, God not only keeps the promise of eschatological blessing, but in so doing God unilaterally constitutes a new social reality, a new lived world, an objectively new creation, that embraces humankind with God as adopted children sharing in Jesus' relation with God, a community to whose flourishing God is self-committed by the very act of making the promise. Further, the specific way in which God kept the promise of eschatological blessing in the resurrection of the crucified Jesus involves a historical tension between the actual inaugurating of promise keeping and its full actualization. That tension is an implicit promise in fact to bring what is inaugurated to full actualization. Moreover, Jesus himself is concretely at once God's way of keeping the promise of eschatological blessing in our proximate contexts and is God's promise of full actualization of that blessing for our proximate contexts. What he did and underwent—that is, the way of the cross—is the way by which that implied promise is kept for us in our proximate contexts. The way of the cross is the way in which we experience the tension in the history of our proximate contexts between the now-actual and the not-yet-fully actualized poles of eschatological blessing. It is in just this tensed way that our proximate contexts may be said to be promising by virtue of their ultimate context in the triune God relating to draw them to eschatological consummation.

Given this tension, our proximate contexts' promise is at once God's graciousness and God's judgment. The promise is gracious, or like God's grace. It is not strictly speaking what New Testament writers generally mean by God's grace, for it is not given despite our estrangement from God in order to overcome that estrangement. On the contrary, God's commitment to draw creation into this eschatological blessing is as primordial as is God's commitment to creation itself, conceptually prior to there being any reality "there" to bless, let alone to reconcile if alienated. Nonetheless, the promising character of our proximate context is gracelike in being the gift of God's love at God's free initiative. It is not merely that God's inauguration of eschatological blessing in the resurrection of Jesus is motivated by love, though that would not be wrong to say. Rather, the content of eschatological blessing now inaugurated simply is the triune God's own experience of love. Its content is the distinctive relationship with God that Jesus enjoys. The content of the triune God's eschatological blessing specifically on human personal bodies—that is, their participation in Jesus' relationship with the One he calls "Father"—is an undistorted relationship in which personal bodies share undistorted communion with God and with one another. It is finite creatures' participation in the communion the persons of the triune God enjoy with one another, the love that is the triune God's own life. In fully actualized eschatological blessing, this communion is freely shared by finite creatures *in their own finite and creaturely ways*, unexacted and unearned from God.

As God's love freely given, it is gracelike.

"Gracelike" qualifies promising. Our proximate contexts are promising, but in a distinctive way defined by the free loving of the One who promises. We are not celebrating some abstract pattern exhibited by our social and cultural context, but something utterly singular: God's own free loving. God's promise of eschatological blessing is itself unconstrained, unexacted, and unearned from God. Given that God has made such a promise, God is self-committed to fulfill it and, correlatively, human personal bodies are entitled to expect its fulfillment. Indeed, expectation and hope are the heart of appropriate human response to the triune God relating in this way. However, as noted in chapter 12A, God's promise of eschatological blessing is an open-ended promise, largely nonspecific about the contents of eschatological blessing. Consequently, while the appropriate human response to God relating in this way is expectation, the expectation cannot include any particular claims on God for the actualization of any specific promises. By making this promise, God is self-involved and self-committed to the fulfillment of the promise, but God remains unconstrained regarding the way in which it is to be concretely fulfilled—through the crucifixion and resurrection of Jesus with whom God was self-identified. And God remains unconstrained regarding the specific content of that fulfillment in the actualization of human personal bodies' communion with God and with one another. In these respects God's promising is gracelike.

Accordingly, God's promise, for example, does not establish a legal relationship between God and creatures that constrains God and gives creatures any particular rightful claims as a kind of leverage on God. The promise confers no independent rights on creatures in relation to God's concrete ways of relating to them. Furthermore, neither the promise itself nor the way its fulfillment is inaugurated in God's resurrection of Jesus provides any basis on which to project a curriculum of stages through which God's actualization of eschatological blessing will pass. Nor do they provide criteria by which to identify unambiguously which new social and cultural situations across time are absolutely closer than others to full actualization of the promised communion. To believe in the triune God who promises is to trust the promiser; it is not to have entered into a contract with God that constrains God.

The promising character of our proximate context is not only gracious; it is also ultimate and final judgment on our proximate contexts. It discloses how radically inadequate our social and cultural contexts in fact are for the full well-being of personal bodies in community, given their distortions by humankind's inappropriate responses to God's ways of relating to them. Not only does it make undeniably clear the failures and distortions of our proximate context. It also brings into question all that our social and cultural contexts assume is morally best and most profound about themselves.

Our social and cultural contexts across time do, of course, bring relative judgment on themselves. Their power arrangements are internally complex and conflictual. Those arrangements unjustly deprive some groups of persons of full respect, adequate food, shelter, health, work, play, or education. They universally and systemically deprive persons of the social and cultural goods that are necessary for the well-being of quotidian creaturely life. At least those who suffer from these injustices need know nothing of the promising character of our proximate context to recognize such injustice, to protest it passionately, and to seek vigorously to correct it.

However, human projects for the correction of creaturely injustices tend themselves to be distorted by an idolatry of our proximate context. We tend to justify the concrete realities of the fundamental arrangements of social, economic, political, and cultural power in our proximate contexts by a set of values rooted in assumed pictures of what makes for the truly good human life. These values are tacitly assumed to be of ultimate importance. We tend to assume further that a profoundly improved version of our proximate context that overcame perceived injustices and was brought to an ideal perfection, as measured by those uncriticized pictures of the good life, would constitute the ultimately good proximate context for humankind.

However, all of humankind's most admirable pictures of the truly good life are themselves the fruit of temporally extended human traditions. They are shaped by and are relative to thoroughly finite histories of social thought and practice. To rely on them as the basis of ultimate and absolute judgment on our proximate context is to engage in idolatry, confusing finite, relative, and preliminary values with what is of ultimate significance.

The demonic aspects of cultural arrogance, communal and ethnic bigotry, and chauvinist nationalism manifest such idolatry in the crudest, clearest, and most destructive way.

The promissory character of our proximate context brings into judgment all relative pictures of the truly good life. It does not do so because of their contingency and relativity. Their contingency and relativity are simply a function of their creatureliness, which God declares to be good. Rather, the inauguration of God's eschatological blessing brings into judgment our idolatrous reliance on culturally relative values to generate such blessing on their own, were they only practiced in undistorted and whole-hearted ways, thus grounding the truly "good" society.

In summary: The triune God, "Spirit sent by the Father with the Son," relating to all that is not God to draw it to eschatological blessing, gives a certain goal-oriented overall direction to changes across time in our social and cultural proximate contexts. The goal is not inherent in, nor implied by, the structure and dynamics that our proximate contexts have by virtue of God relating to them creatively. It is a function of a second way in which God actively relates to them that is distinct from God relating to them to create them. This goal is not the future of our proximate contexts— that is, not a future latent in their potentialities by virtue of God's creative blessing. It is a future promised to them by God as eschatological blessing and inaugurated proleptically in the resurrection of the crucified Jesus. This inauguration of the actualization of the promise of eschatological blessing is the basis for the theological claim that our proximate contexts are indeed meaningful because they are truly promising.

However, the way in which this goal is made present in our proximate contexts requires a radical theological qualification of this claim. The triune God's mission to keep the promise of eschatological blessing takes place in our public proximate contexts, which are already thoroughly ambiguous morally. It is hidden in that ambiguity, and its course there cannot be traced, deduced, or predicted. Its presence in those public contexts defines them as tensed in two ways. They are defined by an abiding structural tension between an old cosmos—that is, lived worlds distorted by personal bodies' inappropriate responses to the ways in which the triune God relates to them—and a new cosmos: re-formed, trans-formed lived worlds. In consequence of that structural tension, ostensible historical "development" or "progress" in our proximate contexts is always inherently ambiguous, marked not by a correlative decline in evil and increase in good, but by ever-increasing tension between increasingly potentiated good and evil in the same historical changes. The triune God's transformative movement in our contexts to draw us to eschatological consummation is hidden in that tension. By virtue of the way the eschatological *missio Dei* is present in them, our proximate contexts are also defined by a second historical tension within the new-creation side of the first tension defining our proximate contexts because of the coincidence in them of old creation and new creation. This second tension is a tension between the now-already actual inauguration of eschatological blessing of a new creation and its not-yet full actualization. The way in which this tension is concretely present, defining our proximate contexts, is the person of Jesus Christ, whose personal identity is rendered in the story of his ministry, crucifixion, and resurrection. The triune God's transformative movement in our proximate contexts to draw us to eschatological consummation is hidden in the way of the cross.

Because it is hidden in these ways, God's relating to draw us to eschatological consummation, which is the ground for affirming an overall direction to historical changes, cannot be the basis for any theological theory about the nature, dynamics, and direction of history which could, in turn, provide the framework within which to identify evidence of a purpose to history that gives it meaning, despite its massive wastefulness and incalculable sufferings. God's drawing humankind to eschatological consummation does not imply that what has been wasted has been recovered or that suffering was somehow an inappropriate, "faithless" response to experienced loss and horrific pain. No, many possibilities for enriched lives enriching others' lives in shared proximate contexts have been permanently lost. Suffering because of those losses is a fully appropriate response. Nor does the *missio Dei* entail that all this waste and suffering are the unavoidable costs of the actualization of the goal to which God has destined all that is not God. However, God drawing humankind to eschatological consummation does entail that, by the creativity of God's free love, what has been distorted will be transformed, the threat of meaninglessness overcome, and living deaths liberated into true life.

To understand our proximate context this way is rich with implications in answer to the anthropological question, "How ought we to be?" We turn to them in chapter 14.

*Faith tells us only that God is. Love tells us
that God is good. But hope tells us that God
will work God's will. And hope has two lovely
daughters: anger and courage. Anger so that
what cannot be, may not be. And courage, so
that what must be, will be.*

ST. AUGUSTINE

CHAPTER **14**

Hope: Flourishing
on Borrowed Time

The triune God, drawing all that is
not God to eschatological consummation, makes our ultimate context a
promise; the circumambient triune God makes our lived worlds promising proximate contexts in which we live on borrowed time. Personal bodies
flourish in appropriate response to God relating to them. The appropriate
response to God relating to them in this mode is hope.

Eccentric Hope

Hope is the appropriate response to "the Spirit sent by the Father with the
Son," drawing our proximate contexts, and us with them, to eschatological
blessing,

A. "*Hope in the Spirit . . . with the Son*" stresses that hope is the response
to one aspect of our ultimate context, the singular *way* in which the triune God goes about drawing us to eschatological blessing. God keeps the
promise to draw all that is not God to eschatological consummation by
proleptically intruding the end time and its new creation into the lived
worlds of the old creation. The triune God does this quite concretely in the
resurrection of the crucified Son whose filial relation in the power of the
Spirit to the One he calls "Father" simply is the eschatological community
into which the rest of humankind is drawn by the circumambient Spirit.
The identity of the Spirit is defined by the identity of the Son; it is the
Spirit of Christ. That singular way is expressed by the formula that it is "the
Spirit sent . . . with the Son" who relates to humankind to draw them to
eschatological consummation.

As appropriate response to this singular way, hope, like faith (see chap.
8), is best construed as personal bodies' attitude in which they are oriented
toward their ultimate and proximate contexts. It is an attitude of expectancy that a good and desired transformation of our quotidian contexts,

now actually begun, will be fully actualized. However, because it is a response to the resurrection of One who was crucified in and by just such a proximate context, it is an expectancy that is especially sensitive to the bondage to oppression and suffering that marks just those lived worlds about which it is expectant. It is not expectant because it supposes that Jesus' resurrection eliminated the oppression that crucified him, but because Jesus' resurrection inaugurates the end time in the midst of such oppression. As the appropriate response to just that concrete way in which the triune God has gone about beginning to keep the promise of eschatological blessing, such expectancy is not mutually exclusive of suffering on account of oppressive injustice and horrendous evil. On the contrary, this expectancy is an attitude of personal bodies who acknowledge the present reality of such suffering and evil and are actively engaged in resisting it as much as possible. This in particular is what is brought out by the formula, "hope in the Spirit . . . *with* the Son."

Let us call this attitude of personal bodies a "joyous hopefulness." It is an attitude that, along with doxological gratitude, orients them in and to their ultimate and proximate contexts. As the previous paragraph indicates, the "joy" in "joyous hopefulness" is specified by the nature of the ground of the hope—that is, the inauguration of God's eschatological promise in the resurrection of the crucified Jesus. Used in this theocentric way, "joy" names a certain glad hopefulness but not a gleeful hopefulness, a happy hope but not a euphoric hope, hope's cheerful confidence that is anything but complacency.

Because joyous hopefulness is an orientation of whole personal bodies who are, by God's creative relating to them, centers of finite power, they necessarily enact their hopefulness in public spaces and times. Therefore, joyous hopefulness may not be described in a privatizing way. For example, it may not be construed as primarily an interior state of consciousness, a mode of subjective inwardness. Of course, one aspect of it is an interior mode of consciousness. However, joyous hopefulness is not constituted by a mode of interiority that could be defined without reference to a personal body's public enactments of certain practices. Consequently, it ought not to be defined in terms of modes of consciousness that are, by definition, wholly interior and private.

If hope is construed as a mode of subjective inwardness, it becomes difficult if not conceptually impossible to show that joyous hopefulness is a disposition to enact certain types of practices publicly. Some human actions might be construed to be expressive of hopefulness or manifestations of hope, but that is different from enacting hope. Hope is not an affective state that might color an indeterminately wide array of actions as does, say, a mood (as in, "He does everything euphorically"). There is no necessary connection between such an affective state and the actions that express or manifest it. All the same actions might be done, but colored by a different mood—say, depression. Nor is it apt to construe hope as an inner efficient cause that drives or motors (motivates?) certain human actions. Where effects must be definable without reference to their alleged cause, or else the alleged causal explanation is viciously circular, enactments of eschatological hope cannot be defined without reference to the hope they enact. As appropriate response to the public eschatological *missio Dei*, eschatological hope is best defined as a personal bodies' orientation that disposes them for enactments of certain practices in public proximate contexts.

Joyous hopefulness is a settled and long-lasting attitude. It orients personal bodies in their quotidian contexts as agents, disposing them across extended periods of time to engage in certain types of socially established cooperative human action. In that regard it has similarities to good *habitus* or virtues. However, where virtues form particular human powers in determinate ways, joyous hopefulness is an attitude that orients personal bodies in their entireties in their contexts. Personal bodies are agents, exercisers of a rich and complex array of creaturely powers. Accordingly, joyous hopefulness concretely orients practices in quotidian contexts that may engage any or all of the powers of personal bodies. Such practices may be enacted by personal bodies in a multitude of ways, each of which is some personal body's existential how at the moment of enactment.

Joyous hopefulness is a complex, responsive attitude. This follows from the complexity of that to which it is a response. The triune God does not keep God's promise of eschatological blessing simply by unambiguously terminating the quotidian in an eschatological blessing. Rather, God keeps this promise by proleptically introducing eschatological blessing into all quotidian public contexts in the resurrection of the crucified Jesus. Hence, hope is necessarily an attitude responsive at once to our ultimate context (God relating to all else in a promise of eschatological blessing) and toward the consequent character of our proximate public contexts (they are, in an odd, doubly stressed way, promising; see chap. 13).

Hence, like faith, hope involves a commitment to an array of diverse practices in public. They are practices celebratory of the quotidian's eschatological flourishing; they are, after all, joyously hopeful practices. They include practices of forming and enacting intentions. They include practices expressive of certain emotions, passions, and feelings. And, because both cooperative human actions and human feelings are conceptually formed, some of them are practices of learning relevant concepts and ways in which to think. In short, they are practices that engage the full range of personal bodies' powers.

For all of its complexity, joyous hopefulness is nonetheless unified as one attitude. What unifies it is that it is a response of personal bodies in their integral entirety to the singular way in which God keeps God's promise of eschatological blessing on all that to which God also relates creatively.

The overall pattern of God's concrete way of drawing us to eschatological consummation gives a distinctive and unifying shape to the response of joyous hopefulness.

Personal bodies concretely express joyous hopefulness in their existential hows that enact certain practices. As in chapter 9, concerning faith's hows, so here the phrase "existential how" is borrowed from its home in philosophical existentialism and used in modified ways. The phrase is used in ways shaped by the picture of human creatures as personal bodies, to stress (1) that existential hows are enactments of practices that may engage any of the entire array of personal bodies' powers and not merely their interior subjectivity; (2) that existential hows are conceptually formed; and (3) that God relating to personal bodies is the eccentric condition, not only of their reality, but also of their activity, including the existential hows that express human persons' fundamental orientation to their proximate contexts.

B. *"Hope in the Spirit sent by the Father . . ."* stresses that, just as what hope responds to is a blessing sent, so joyous hopefulness is itself a gift given. It is hope "by the power of the Spirit sent by the Father. . . ." Hope is grounded and defined eccentrically, from outside itself.

The ground for hope is eccentric to each and all living human personal bodies. Theocentrically understood, joyous hopefulness is neither a psychological competency whose mastery is a necessary stage in the curriculum of psychological maturation as outlined, for example, by Erik Erikson (1963). Nor is it grounded in the logic of the dynamic driving the historical-cosmic process as analyzed, for example, by Hegel. Nor is it rooted in the dynamics of history as analyzed by revisionist Marxist theoreticians such as Ernst Bloch (1986), an analysis that arguably remains conceptually determinative in "theologies of hope" like Jürgen Moltmann's (1967; see Morse, 1979). Rather, the possibility of such hope lies solely in the actuality of God keeping God's promise.

Grounded outside itself, joyous hopefulness is defined from outside itself. It is given definition by the distinctive shape of the promissory story to which it is the appropriate response. It is hope in the promise inherent in our living on borrowed eschatological time inaugurated in our proximate contexts through the resurrection of a crucified man. Hence, it is hope in the midst of both dying life and living death. It is not hope as an evasion or denial of death. Nor is it hope that can somehow build on persons' deaths as a part of the conditions of soul making, the price of social and cultural progress, or the cost of revolution that transcends death in a utopian future. Indeed, the hopefulness of this orientation is most evident in circumstances that appear devoid of possibility for anything approximating God's eschatological rule. It is a disposition to act hopefully in chaotic circumstances when extreme social and cultural disorder appear to hold few possibilities for well-being in community. And it is a disposition to act hopefully in tyrannical and oppressive circumstances of excessive social and cultural control that appear to offer little possibility for individual human well-being.

However, such hope ought not to be defined as the negation of negations, simply as resistance to chaos or oppression. Grounded in the promise intrinsic to God's actual inauguration of the eschatological kingdom, hope is response to that promise. Hence, eschatological hope is not in the first instance hope despite sin and evil. The disposition to act hopefully is a disposition to act in creaturely quotidian circumstances in ways hopeful of their flourishing in eschatological blessing even when the quotidian happens to be neither especially chaotic nor especially oppressive, even were it, contrary to fact, not at all distorted by sin and bound in evil.

Grounded and defined eccentrically, hope in God is not an existential how that personal bodies devise for themselves free-hand, self-constituting themselves as hopeful by actualizing their own emotional and imaginative potentialities. To be sure, God relating to us circumambiently as our eschatological consummator engages whole personal bodies. Therefore, when a person responds to the triune God in hope, many if not all of her creaturely powers are engaged that are open to further definition. This includes shaping a generic human hopefulness, if there be such (see Erikson 1963), to be the response specifically appropriate to the concrete way in which God engages us. Such shaping gives human powers a theocentric definition. Nonetheless, joyous hopefulness is not acquired or achieved *de novo* through rigorous reflection or spiritual self-discipline independent of the way in which God keeps God's eschatological promise.

Hope as a gift has been characterized throughout as the appropriate response by personal bodies to the concrete way in which the triune God inaugurates the actualization of God's promise to draw all that is not God to eschatological consummation. However, use of the word "response" needs to be carefully nuanced. The relation into which the triune God enters with all that is not God in drawing it to eschatological consummation was characterized in chapter 13 as "circumambience," in contradistinction to the relation into which God enters in creating, which was characterized in part 1 as God's relation to our proximate contexts and us with them. It was pointed out that the radical and dynamic freedom of this circumambience calls for emphasis on the elusiveness of the triune God relating in this way. As was the case with human creatures relating responsively to the creative triune God, so here, the character of the responding cannot be understood on analogy with a responsive relating of an entity to another discrete, identifiable, and locateable entity within a common field of reference.

The triune God and creature are no more on the same ontological level or plane when God relates to draw creatures to eschatological blessing than when God relates in creative blessing. This was expressed by the observation that unlike the way in which the triune God, "Son sent by the Father in the power of the Spirit," relates quite concretely to reconcile estranged creatures incarnately in the person of Jesus, the way in which the triune God, "Spirit sent by the Father with the Son," relates to draw to eschatological consummation has no human face. The circumambient One, although radically other than we, is no identifiable thou and cannot be identified with any particular other. It is no accident that the dominant biblical rhetoric for the Holy Spirit's relating to human beings plays off against each other, on one side, images of the Spirit as radically free— "other" grasping and seizing human beings quite "impersonally"—and, on the other side, images of the Spirit relating to human beings so intimately as to deepen and enrich, rather than violate, their integrities such that it is more interior to them than they are to themselves, not to say more interior to them than any other human being could or should be.

Hence personal bodies' response to the triune God drawing them to eschatological consummation cannot be understood on analogy with I-Thou relations. Being given the gift of hope and responding to God in joyous hopefulness is not analogous to any familiar human interpersonal relation. So far as ordinary English usage is concerned, I suggest, it would be misleading to call it a "personal relation."

Hope for Glory

It would be odd to talk about hopefulness without saying just what it is that hope expects. As a response to the triune God drawing us to eschatological blessing, hope is the expectant attitude that eschatological blessing will be fully actualized in and upon our proximate contexts, and therewith in and on ourselves. That expectation is expressed biblically in images of transformation for which the traditional theological term is "glorification." Chapter 7 stressed that as God relates to us creatively, we are at once (1) living bodies who, in our creaturely way, simply are God's glory, and (2) ones to whom living bodies have been given so that we are accountable for having our creaturely actions glorify God. However, as God relates to draw us to eschatological blessing, we and our proximate contexts are promised glory in a different sense of the term. We are promised participation in God's own glory. Call it creatures' "eschatological glory."

Because God's promise is open-ended (see chap. 12), it is impossible to say exactly what the content of "eschatological glory" is. Accordingly, joyous hopefulness is itself open-ended. It is the expectant attitude that God will actualize eschatological blessing on our proximate contexts and on us, and that we will know it when it comes, without being able ahead of time to say much about what it will be like and nothing at all about when it will be.

It is not possible to say much, but it is possible to say a very little. This can be done by way of rhetorical gestures in certain directions and not in others. There are two types of biblical imagery for fully actualized eschatological blessing that suggest a certain range of ways of imagining eschatological glory and rule out others. One type is imagery for the risen Jesus and our relationship with him; the other is cosmic imagery.

In divergent ways, the Gospels image the risen Jesus as an identifiable individual human person by virtue of his bodily agency. In all the canonical resurrection appearance stories, the risen Jesus is (eventually) recognized. The Gospel writers stress that it is his bodiliness, however transformed in resurrection, that makes him identifiable. More precisely, according to the stories, it is familiar intentional bodily actions that were characteristically and peculiarly his that enable his disciples to identify him as the friend who had been crucified, had died, and was buried. At the same time, the resurrection appearance stories stress that, perhaps because he is transformed, the risen Jesus is mysterious and not always easily recognizable. When Paul attempts to make this point about the risen Jesus' genuine yet somehow transfigured bodiliness, he uses commonplace imagery from current Jewish eschatological speculation, contrasting a "physical body" to the "spiritual body" in which he was raised (see 1 Cor. 15). By analogy, for Paul, so shall we all be transformed in glory.

A second type of biblical image for actualized eschatological blessing is cosmic. Both Old and New Testaments provide metaphors that image the end time in universal, cosmic terms. They are images of judgment and destruction on an old creation, and images of a new creation marked by peace, free of predation, suffering, and grief.

The two kinds of image are combined in apocalyptic rhetoric introduced into the canon in late Old Testament texts and employed in the Synoptic Gospels, Paul's letters, and Revelation. The images in apocalyptic rhetoric at once radicalize and qualify images of transformation. Images for the risen Jesus and the resurrected body as transformations or transfigurations of physical bodies are radicalized by images of the destruction of an old creation, including living physical bodies, and by the image of a new creation. At the same time, images of both radical re-creation of human creatures and of their participation in the risen Jesus' relationship in the power of the Spirit with the One he called "Father" are clearly qualified. Whatever follows any one personal body's death and whatever follows cosmic destruction is, by God's eschatological blessing, still finite and creaturely. Whatever its content may be and no matter how great a transformation it involves, eschatological consummation does not bring transformation out of the status of creature. The resurrected personal body may be a new creation, but it's still a creature. Participation in the communion that constitutes the life of the triune God does not turn human creatures into something ontologically other than creatures. Theirs is strictly a creaturely participation in God's life.

And if still creatures, then still finite. Finite, first, in their radical dependence on God for reality and value. By God's gracious support, they will not cease to be. Death as a sign of finitude may be gone, but transfigured human creatures nonetheless remain finite in their ongoing radical dependency on God's creativity.

The imagery suggests, second, that eschatologically glorified creatures remain finite in their interdependence with, and hence mutual limitation by, other personal bodies in community in shared proximate contexts. In fully actualized eschatological blessing, the proximate contexts may be a "new" heaven and earth, but personal bodies nonetheless are still inherently related to such creaturely proximate contexts. They cannot be without fellow creatures, and they cannot be without proximate creaturely contexts.

Furthermore, in such contexts, they remain inherently social creatures whose personal identities are constituted by their interrelations with others in community. Their communion with one another in eschatological community is a communion normed by "the Spirit sent by the Father with the Son." Such communion is the kingdom of God, the community whose time is subject to the triune God's circumambient eschatological sovereign rule. The common life of such community is marked, as Paul says in his only reference to the kingdom of God, by "righteousness and peace and joy in the Holy Spirit" (Rom. 14:17). "Righteousness" is radically just mutual love that honors the otherness of the beloved, supports the beloved with all they need, and nurtures them in all their growing, without violation of their integrities, so that peace among them is unbroken and joy in one another unrestricted.

We may suppose that eschatologically transformed personal bodies remain finite in a third way. We noted in part 1 that it is inherent to the finitude of living bodies to grow and develop. Following Gregory of Nyssa, we may suppose that even as eschatologically transformed, they continue to grow and develop at least in the depth and richness of their creaturely participation in the communion which is the divine life. Perhaps Jesus' remark that "in the resurrection they neither marry nor are given in marriage" (Matt. 22:30; see Mark 12:25; Luke 20:35) may be generalized to say that eschatologically transformed personal bodies have no specially close and ever-deepening relationships with particular others whose claims take precedence over the claims of all other relations. If their radical transformation means that they do not have physical bodies of the sort we know, they obviously would not grow physically. Correlatively, whatever it takes to sustain "spiritual bodies," they need not kill in order to get it (cf. Isa. 11:9; 65:25). Nor, lacking physical bodies, would they be subject to physical suffering. "Mourning and crying and pain will be no more" (Rev. 21:4b). However, none of that implies that they would not be both capable of and in need of growth in other respects in regard to the richness of their creaturely participation together in the communion that is God's triune life.

The fourth Gospel's imagery of new birth and Paul's own use of apocalyptic rhetoric both warrant one further qualification of the rhetorical trajectory set by biblical metaphors for eschatological glory. The use in John of the image of radically new birth (3:1–10) and the use by Paul of the apocalyptic image of radically new creation (2 Cor. 5:17) both stress that eschatological transformation does not wait to begin until after the destruction of an old life or an old world. Rather, it already begins in the midst of the old world. It is inaugurated in our ambiguous quotidian contexts in an odd way that implicitly promises its full actualization in the transformation of those very contexts. This promise, too, is open-ended. It is impossible to say concretely when God will go about keeping it, or how, except that it brings liberation from the old lived world's bondage to its elemental principles. Nonetheless, as the appropriate response to this implicit promise, hope is personal bodies' fundamental orientation to their proximate contexts, expectant that God is keeping that promise, not only for their shared public space and time, but in it now.

It would be easy to contrast these two types of image for eschatologically glorified life as, respectively, individualistic and communal. Where apocalyptic images of a new creation seem to construe us as members of the human community and the society of creatures, images of the eschatological transformation of the individual Jesus seem to be analogous to our transformations only as we are considered one by one. Traditional Christian theological eschatology has tended to privilege the latter type of image of transformation interpreted individualistically. Consequently, the content of traditional eschatology has focused almost exclusively on the question of which individuals, if any, will survive death and, if they do, what their destinies will be.

However, the contrast is misplaced from the outset. Whatever images may be used to express it, the fundamental theological ground for confident hope of eschatologically glorified life is the conviction Paul affirmed to the Roman Christians that nothing whatever can "separate us [plural!] from the love of God in Christ Jesus our Lord'" (Rom. 8:39). The absolutely persistent character of God's love for humankind is disclosed in the resurrection of the crucified Jesus. For Paul, the "us" that cannot be separated from that love is usually imaged not as an aggregate of individuals but as a single living body, a communal new creation. Hence the central content of hope, even hope for personal "life everlasting," is communal and cosmic in character.

Both types of image make clear that eschatological transformation of personal bodies in and with transformation of their communal lived worlds is at once an unconditional gift of love to them and an irreversible judgment upon them. Since the content of the full actualization of God's promise is a community marked by righteousness and love, the "yes" this gift says to quotidian reality brings with it the "no" of judgment on the quotidian. This is vividly clear in apocalyptic rhetoric's images of the judgment and destruction of the old creation that is inherent in the unpredictable and unconditional arrival of the new creation. So, too, the Synoptic Gospels' imagery of the coming of the Son of Man on the last day is heavy with imagery of judgment, of disclosure of (im)moral reality obscured by the moral and theological ambiguity that distorts the quotidian in consequence of personal bodies' inappropriate responses to the ways in which the triune God relates to them. Even the imagery of judgment is communal imagery. Each personal body is judged for him or herself, to be sure. But each is judged in the presence of the community. Further, each is judged in regard to how she or he has been in relation to brother and sister personal bodies in community: On that day the righteous will say, "When did we see you hungry and feed you, thirsty and give you drink, naked and clothe you, stranger and welcome you, sick or imprisoned and visit you? And he will reply, 'Truly I tell you, just as you did it to one of the least of these who are members of my family, you did it to me'"(Matt. 25:40). They are the ones who "inherit the kingdom prepared for [them] from the foundation of the world" (25:34). It is those whose action is for the neighbor in hopefulness of the neighbors' flourishing who will participate in the communion constituting God's own life.

In order to be an appropriate response to the actualization of what God has promised, joyous hopefulness has to be understood primarily as hope for a distinctive type of communal life (proximate context) in communion with God (ultimate context). Only in those contexts can it be hope for a distinctive type of individual life. What is important and desirable about personal eternal life is not that it defeats death and lasts without end, nor even that it is personal life with God. Rather, what is important and desirable is that it is a peculiar type of communion in community—that is, a creaturely participation in the very quality of God's own life which, consistent with God's hospitable generosity in creating, is eschatologically shared with neighbors, most of whom have hitherto been strangers and some of whom have been enemies.

Thus, while there is not very much to say about the content of the open-ended divine promise to which hope is the fitting response, there is a little that can be said. It is hope for the full actualization of an eschatological blessing already actually inaugurated now, involving radically transformed creaturely life in transformed proximate contexts, lived in community that participates in the triune God's own life and is marked by righteousness, peace, and joy.

Flourishing in Joyous Hopefulness

As human creaturely flourishing lies in faithful response—that is, trust and loyalty—to the triune God relating to us creatively, so human eschatological flourishing lies in joyously hopeful response to the triune God drawing us to eschatological consummation.

Discussion of creaturely faithfulness to the triune God in chapter 8 involved a theological account of human flourishing that relied on a sharp distinction between human well-being and maximal good health, on one side, and human flourishing theocentrically conceived on the other. Where the health and well-being of human living bodies, societies, and cultures are properly understood in functional and self-referencing terms, human flourishing was understood theocentrically in terms of personal bodies' relating to the triune God in response to God's prior relating to them. Faith—that is, trust in God as the ground of our reality and value and as loyalty to God's own creative project—is the appropriate response of personal bodies to God relating to them creatively. Because God's creative relating constitutes us at once as living human personal bodies and as ones who have borrowed living bodies for whose dispositions in the world we are accountable, our creaturely flourishing in faith has two aspects. In one way, flourishing human life is life that blossoms to manifest God's glory in the beauty and richness of the powers it has by virtue of God relating to it creatively. In another way, it is human life that thrives, in the sense of "having itself in hand" in such a way that its response in appropriate doxological gratitude to the concrete way in which God creatively relates to it also manifests the glory of God. Such flourishing assumed, we saw, a certain answer to the perennial anthropological question about what we are, and implied answers to perennial questions about who we are and how we are to be.

In joyous hopefulness, personal bodies flourish in the same theocentric sense of "flourish." Furthermore, because God drawing us to eschatological consummation places our proximate contexts, and us with them, in borrowed time tensed between eschatological blessing now actually inaugurated and its full actualization later, our flourishing in hope also has two aspects. In one way, eschatologically flourishing human life is life that blossoms to manifest the eschatological glory of the not yet promised by what is now actually the case with our proximate contexts. In another way, it is human life that thrives, in the sense of "having itself in hand" so that its responses in hope to the now of its proximate contexts are appropriate to those contexts' eschatological not yet. Such flourishing implies, above all, answers to the question "How are we to be?" It also incidentally implies further answers to the questions, "Who are we?" and "What are we?" To develop the idea of human flourishing in joyous hopefulness, I take up here its implied answer to the question, "How are we to be?" The answers it implies to the other two questions are taken up in the next chapter.

Flourishing in Hope: How We Are to Be in Borrowed Time

Joyous hopefulness, we said above, is personal bodies' orientation to their proximate contexts that disposes them to enact certain types of cooperative practices in and for their quotidian worlds. Each enactment is an existential how of a personal body living according to the Spirit. Such enactments are expressions of existential hopefulness. The traditional theological name for shaping and disciplining personal bodies' powers in order to capacitate them for such enactments of joyous hopefulness is "sanctification." Inasmuch as hope is itself a gift of the triune God, the disciplining and shaping of human creatures' powers that constitute sanctification are themselves God's gift.

The number and variety of existential hows—that is, of concrete enactments of such practices—is indefinitely large. This is partly because personal bodies are constantly orienting to new contexts as their quotidian worlds change over time. Hence, they must express their hopeful orientation in changing ways as the concrete contexts about which they are hopeful change. Their hopeful orientation may need to be expressed in the exercise of different sets of powers in different contexts.

However, although the number of existential hows expressive of joyous hopefulness is inestimable, there are types of the practices which they enact that can be identified. Chapter 9 developed the theme that, in faithful response to God creatively relating to them, personal bodies' practices of doxological gratitude seek the well-being of their quotidian worlds; here, on the other hand, we must say that in response to God relating to draw them to eschatological consummation, personal bodies' practices of joyous hopefulness consist of socially established cooperative actions of personal bodies in community that exemplify, however incompletely, the quality of common life that constitutes personal bodies' eschatological glory.

Practices that exemplify such life certainly include practices that seek out signs of the eschatological flourishing of their quotidian worlds in order to celebrate them. Such celebratory practices may include practices that actively contribute to social, cultural, economic, and political changes in the quotidian, changes that exemplify here and now the peculiar liberty brought by eschatological blessing in the midst of the quotidian world's bondage to oppressive powers.

Such practices are enacted in the old creation, but enacted in the old creation as invaded by the eschatological time of the new creation. They are enacted in the moral and ontological ambiguity of the quotidian, but on time borrowed from the new. The promise implicit in the now actual inauguration of new creation in the old creation of our quotidian worlds is that God will fully actualize that new creation; accordingly, practices of joyous hopefulness seek to be responsive both to the actual now of not-yet-fully actualized borrowed time and to the not-yet of borrowed time in which it lives now.

1. *Practicing joyous hopefulness in the "now" of not-yet-fully actualized borrowed time.* Because they are responses to the triune God's inauguration of eschatological blessing in the here and now, eschatologically hopeful practices are enacted in our proximate contexts, not so much to

enhance their well-being as to participate in and witness to their eschatological flourishing. They are practices that seek to be true to the *missio Dei* active in personal bodies' quotidian lived worlds. Such practices express hope's faithfulness to the triune God drawing our proximate contexts, and us with them, to eschatological blessing actually inaugurated but not fully actualized here and now.

The hallmark of such flourishing is the liberation of socially constructed proximate contexts from bondage to their own functional analogues of Paul's elemental substances. For several decades, liberation and political theologies have made the systemic reality of such social and cultural bondage, and the necessity of practices of critique and resistance to them, an undeniable and urgent focus of theological reflection.

Schematically outlined, their analyses have tended to have the following form: The social construction of our lived worlds classifies and locates each of us in some structure of social, cultural, economic, and political powers. The classification and location of personal bodies in such structures is governed by certain ordering principles relating to such factors as gender, lineage, wealth, race, religion, ethnicity, sexual orientation, and so on. Often these factors can be formulated in binary ways: male/female, noble/common, rich/poor, white/black, believers/infidels, straight/gay, and so forth. One pole of each pair is privileged as a principle, ruling the distribution of various kinds of power. Whoever is located in the part of the structure of power defined by the privileged pole is advantaged over whoever is located in a part defined by other factors. Bondage in oppression is systemic in such structures because their social construction systematically arranges and distributes social, economic, political, and cultural power in such a way that entire groups of persons, defined by gender, lineage, race, and so forth, are unjustly denied certain kinds of power. Such persons are systematically vulnerable to oppression by those groups to whom the power is more generously distributed. The systemic bondage such analysis describes can be identified as the very thing from which the eschatological *missio Dei* liberates humankind in a new creation.

From this analysis a theological conclusion follows about what we may call "hope's faith." Hope, as an appropriate response to the triune God relating to draw humankind to eschatological consummation, involves a certain faithfulness to the triune God. It consists of a disposition to participate actively in liberating movements of social change in which the triune *missio Dei* may also be at work. Practices of participation in such liberating movements are practices of theological, and not just a socioeconomic/political, critique of our distorted proximate contexts. Such theological analysis provides theological warrant for practices that not only make for resistance to, but make for radical change of, systemically oppressive socially constructed lived worlds.

Such analyses can find functional analogies in Paul's use of apocalyptic imagery to explain the liberation brought by the eschatological *missio Dei*. Particularly analogous to liberationist and political theological analyses is the way in which Paul's appropriation of apocalyptic rhetoric undercuts the otherworldly dualism of much apocalyptic literature. What the apocalypse marks is not, for Paul, a sheer succession and discontinuity between an old creation and a new, but the irruption of the new into the old, marking quotidian lived worlds with a double tension: one between the new creation and the old with which it overlaps, and the other between the actual inauguration of the "new" now and its full actualization later.

Furthermore, the privileged socioeconomic markers (gender, race, lineage, ethnicity, etc.) according to which our proximate contexts are socially constructed are functionally analogous to the elementary substances by which, according to Paul, the old creation was structured. In both cases, the elementary substances are finite creatures given the power to order and govern human life as though they were gods. To grant them the power to rule—that is, to trust them to order our lived world—is to worship them. Worship of only relatively valuable creatures as though they were the absolute ground of value is idolatry. It is the root of a profound communal bondage. Liberation from such bondage necessarily involves transformation of the lived worlds that have been structured by such idolatry, a transformation so radical as to constitute a new creation.

The practices fostered by the analyses offered by liberation and political theologies in many respects count as eschatologically hopeful practices that are appropriate response to the triune God's inauguration of eschatological blessing. In the first place, such practices are quite clearly understood in many of these theologies to be responses to the *missio Dei*, and not themselves to be identical with the *missio Dei*. Gustavo Gutiérrez, for example, was quite clear a generation ago that those who seek to live in appropriate response to God do not themselves "build" the eschatological kingdom (1973). Moreover, since the eschatological *missio Dei* takes place publicly in our deeply ambiguous proximate contexts, the practices of social critique and engagement in radical social change fostered by political and liberation theologies are also enacted here and now in the public realm.

Such practices can effect genuinely liberating changes in our lived worlds only when they are utterly realistic about those quotidian worlds. Hence it is obvious that eschatologically hopeful practices must be shaped by two types of knowledge about the now in which the triune God has actually inaugurated eschatological blessing.

First, as Latin American liberationist writers in particular have insisted (see Boff 1987, part 1), these practices must be shaped by a clear grasp of the dynamics of the various kinds of power structuring the proximate contexts in which they are enacted. In particular, they must be shaped by as much clarity as possible about the distinction between the realities of the distribution and interrelations of such powers, on the one hand, and societies' capacities to obscure and deny these realities, on the other. The latter is the theologically profound truth in Reinhold Niebuhr's Christian realism.

Second, as Asian liberationist writers in particular have insisted (see Song 1996), practices of liberation must be shaped by realism about the modes of suffering caused here and now by our social worlds' bondage to oppressive structures of power. Such consciousness is necessary, not only to energize participation in liberating practices through outrage at unjust human suffering, but also to keep enactments of such practices as concrete as possible. They are to be enactments of liberating practices in just this concrete circumstance here and now involving just this specific range of suffering by just these particular persons. When liberating practices are not shaped by consciousness of the specific suffering that is part of their proximate context, they risk becoming abstract and in their own right oppressive by reason of their inhuman iciness.

The entire array of personal bodies' powers needs to be formed in distinctive ways for them to enact eschatologically hopeful practices. Such formation is personal bodies' sanctification, or "being made holy." Understood this way, holiness clearly involves a great deal more than ritual and moral purity—that is, acting in ways that avoid the stain of guilt. Rather, holiness is the eschatological flourishing of entire personal bodies, in community in their shared lived worlds. It is collectively the full range of existential hows of living human personal bodies who respond appropriately to the fact that their proximate contexts are being drawn to eschatological transformation by the triune God. Such lives are lived in a new creation socially constructed by the dynamics of a giving and a receiving: A new and liberating elemental substance—namely, the eschatological "Spirit sent by the Father with the Son" giving itself proleptically to draw them to eschatological consummation—and they, in turn, responding in joyous hopefulness. Since holiness engages the whole of personal bodies, becoming holy, or sanctification, involves shaping and disciplining the whole range of their powers in certain ways, not simply disciplining their volitional capacities so as always and only to act guiltlessly.

Enacting eschatologically hopeful practices also involves cultivating the intellectual disciplines required for analysis of the structure and dynamics of social, cultural, economic, and political power in particular lived worlds across time. Specifically, it involves cultivation of the discipline of thinking historically. This involves acquiring the intellectual capacities to identify those historically formed assumptions about reality that always deeply form personal bodies' proximate contexts, and to question those assumptions critically. Such discipline does not consist in the mastery of some body of critical theory. All bodies of critical theory are rightly contested. Some may be disallowed on theological grounds. None, however, is theologically privileged. The intellectual disciplines in question are rather the discipline of the intellectual and imaginative capacities required for critical assessment of every body of theory purporting to illumine the dynamics of power in any given proximate context, combined with the discipline of related capacities to use a body of theory to help understand any given proximate context. Acquiring such capacities is part of the existential hows of personal bodies seriously engaged in concrete enactments of eschatologically hopeful practices in particular proximate contexts.

Learning to enact such practices also involves the cultivation and discipline of the affections. For example, it involves discipline of certain emotions. Emotions are affections that have particular objects. Whereas moods such as depression and euphoria are free-floating, fear and rejoicing are defined by particular determinate objects—namely, respectively, a threat (a brown bear is approaching your campsite) or a success (your favorite hockey team wins the championship game). Unlike moods, however, emotions are relatively short-lived. Once the bear turns aside from your campsite, your fear fades, to be replaced perhaps by the emotion of relief; once the hockey season is over, your rejoicing fades.

One emotion required by joyously hopeful practices in the quotidian is compassion—that is, suffering with those who suffer oppression. Learning compassion involves such emotional disciplines as learning to identify and set aside one's own psychological defenses against experiencing others' suffering; recognizing and setting aside one's own overriding need to get others to acknowledge one's own suffering; and recognizing and setting aside one's easy assimilation of suffering persons to convenient abstract stereotypes of sufferers rather than entering into their suffering in its concrete particularity.

Another emotion required in joyously hopeful practices in proximate contexts marked by the inauguration now of eschatological blessing is what William Lynch calls "absolute wishing." In proximate contexts marked by actually inaugurated eschatological blessing, joyously hopeful practices involve an absolute wishing specifically for the ultimate full actualization of the blessing that has been inaugurated. Joyous hopefulness includes wishing for very concrete things, events, or states of affairs that would reflect the promised actualization of eschatological blessing for particular people in their specific proximate contexts—for example, wishing for removal of particular injustices, liberation from particular bondages, healing of particular brokenness in relationships, reforming of particular distortions of community.

Using William Lynch's important distinction, these are wished absolutely but not as absolutes (1965, 86–108, 122–36). To wish some particular creaturely thing, event, or circumstance as absolute is idolatry. It is to wish that thing, event, or circumstance as though by itself it somehow provided the consummation of human life. To wish it as absolute is to wish it as though in its creaturely finitude it were itself the fully actualized eschatological kingdom. By contrast, to wish something absolutely is just to wish it wholeheartedly.

Because joyous hopefulness, as a response now to the gift of eschatological blessing, is itself a gift received, enactment of eschatologically hopeful practices also involves learning to be open to receiving the gift of help in such enactments. It is not as though once God has inaugurated eschatological blessing in our proximate contexts, it is then up to us to respond on our own out of our own resources. Rather, the triune God relating in, with, and through our proximate contexts to draw us to eschatological consummation continually sustains us in our responding. Accordingly, learning to enact appropriate response involves learning to receive the gift of help. It involves learning to be open to receive help from God.

Moreover, since God relates to us in and through our proximate contexts to draw us to eschatological consummation, learning to enact appropriate response also involves learning to receive help from companion personal bodies. Some of them may be sisters and brothers in a community whose common life seeks to be an appropriate response to the triune God. Others may be fellow human creatures who, for whatever reason and without any concern to respond to God, also actively seek to engage in practices that help liberate our common lived world from its bondage to oppression. There is no theological reason not to be open to God's help through them quite as much as through those who join in trying to respond appropriately to God. "Hope," William F. Lynch pointed out, "cannot be achieved alone. It must in some way or other be an act of community, whether the community of the church or a nation or just two people struggling together to produce liberation in each other" (1965, 19).

Finally, sanctification—learning to enact appropriate responses to the triune God drawing humankind to eschatological consummation—also requires discipline of personal bodies' imaginative powers. It requires personal bodies' imaginative powers to be so formed and disciplined, perhaps above all by Jesus' parables of the eschatological "kingdom of God," that they are capacitated to discern when and where changes over time in their lived worlds might, for all of their ambiguity, count as additional ad hoc parables of God drawing those contexts to eschatological blessing.

All these ways of shaping personal bodies' intellectual, emotional, and imaginative powers are aspects of their sanctification. They are ascetical disciplines of human intellectual, affective, imaginative, and moral powers. Such ascetical disciplines are inherent in the existential hows of lives lived according to the Spirit in joyous hopefulness. Such discipline of their creaturely powers strengthens the faithfulness of personal bodies' hopeful response to God drawing them in their proximate contexts to eschatological blessing.

2. *Practicing joyous hopefulness in the "not yet" of the "now" of borrowed time.* Hopeful practices are enacted in the here and now of quotidian lived worlds bound in oppression. In such proximate contexts they are eschatologically hopeful because they are responses, not to creative or progressive possibilities discerned in the old creation, but to the triune God's inauguration of the eschatological new creation in just that old creation. Enacted as an appropriate response to the new creation but in the context of the old creation, such practices may cooperate with liberating practices. They may do so by discerning, drawing attention to, and engaging in social, economic, political, and cultural changes already going on in their quotidian contexts that make for the liberation of those contexts from some aspect of their previous bondage. Such liberating changes may serve as parables of God's eschatological transformation of the quotidian, and eschatologically hopeful engagement in them is an appropriate way in which to respond to the triune God drawing humankind to eschatological blessing. All this is the burden of the previous subsection.

At the same time it must be insisted that joyously hopeful practices are not defined as practices to liberate our quotidian lived worlds from bondage to oppression and the suffering it causes. They are not practices defined by an orientation to any such goal. What makes them specifically eschatologically hopeful practices is not that they aim to achieve liberation. This is the point of insisting that, unlike doxologically grateful practices, they are not defined as practices in the service of the well-being of the quotidian. Liberation from bondage makes for the well-being of proximate contexts, and liberative practices are oriented to that well-being. By contrast, joyously hopeful practices are celebratory of the quotidian's eschatological flourishing. They celebrate it by seeking to be communal practices that are exemplary of such flourishing. By the same token, they seek also to be a living ongoing critique of their proximate contexts insofar as those contexts are not exemplary of that flourishing. Such practices may contribute to the quotidian's well-being. However, it is an indirect contribution that is a secondary effect of practices that intend to be exemplary of eschatologically flourishing lived worlds.

Joyously hopeful practices are not defined by the goal of transforming our lived worlds precisely because they are a response to God already having inaugurated the actualization of God's own promised goal—namely, eschatological blessing. God's self-commitment to bless eschatologically all that is not God is as primordial as God's self-commitment to bless all that is not God creatively. Because it is God's primordial self-commitment to a blessing given only at the end time, it has the form of promise. This promise of eschatological blessing is not contingent on creatures being in bondage to oppression. If, hypothetically and contrary to fact, creatures were not in bondage to their lived worlds' "elemental substances," the Christian witness is that God would still be self-committed to keep the promise of eschatological blessing. But in those circumstances doing so would not entail the creatures' liberation, for there would be no bondage from which to be liberated. Presumably, creatures would simply be drawn to their promised eschatological glorification. However, given that creatures have adventitiously fallen into bondage to oppressive distortions, then God's keeping the promise of eschatological glorification means, contingently, that they are also liberated from such oppression. Thus, what makes hopeful practices appropriate responses to the triune God relating to draw us to eschatological consummation is not that they are liberating practices, although they are in fact also that, given the absurd fact of creaturely bondage to self-distortions.

Rather, practices are defined as joyously hopeful when they are appropriate to the odd way God does keep the promise of eschatological blessing. They are eschatological practices in that they are enacted on borrowed time, responsive not to possibilities and actualities inherent in the quotidian as creaturely, but to the actuality of the eschatological end time proleptically present. They are joyous practices in that they are celebratory of the proleptic presence of the end time. However, they are hopeful practices in that they are oriented, not to the present condition of their proximate contexts, but to the later full realization of eschatological glorification that is promised in its inauguration in these practices' proximate contexts now.

Such practices are not only expectant of full actualization of eschatological blessing, but passionately yearn for it. Thus, such practices express hope's love for God's promised eschatological consummation.

In that passion, they may include practices that identify and participate in particular social and cultural changes that are liberating of at least some personal bodies from bondage to particular systemically oppressive social, cultural, economic, or political powers. Such liberating changes may be celebrated as ad hoc parables of the arrival of God's promised future. Accordingly, appropriate response to God drawing humankind to eschatological consummation may properly include ad hoc participation in and celebration of such parables.

Such celebratory practices are practices exemplary of eschatologically blessed communal life. They are socially established cooperative actions that make up the common life of intentional communities that seek to be signs within the old creation of the eschatologically transformed life of the new creation. These practices make up the common life of communities marked by mutuality, justice, and reconciliation of those estranged by unjust distribution of power and its concurrent oppression.

Such practices are celebratory of all signs of the inbreaking of eschatological glory into our quotidian worlds, of the new creation into the old. Since the triune God draws us to eschatological consummation by circumambiently engaging us in our proximate contexts, appropriately responsive celebratory practices must be enacted in public, in our shared quotidian contexts here and now. They are not spiritual practices in contradistinction to worldly practices. They are thoroughly engaged in this everyday world and must be enacted in ways for which we can be held accountable.

Nonetheless, they are, in a very broad sense of the term, eucharistic practices. That is, centered in eucharistic or thankful celebration of the inauguration of eschatological blessing in the resurrection of the crucified Jesus, they are practices that constitute a communal common life that reflects, however dimly, the righteous communion of the triune God's own life. Such practices are not restricted to what the community does when gathered, however. They are the community's practices, and they are enacted communally, but they may just as authentically be enacted by society that is host to the community.

Such practices are marked by struggle because of the tension generated in their proximate contexts by God drawing those contexts to eschatological consummation. Because the new creation overlaps the old, the latter is the context of practices exemplary of the former. Inasmuch as the new creation is in tension with the old, the practices making up communal life exemplary of eschatological blessing are continually in deep tension with the practices constituting quotidian life insofar as it is bound in distortion and oppression. It is correct to say that they are in many ways countercultural practices, even though they are practices that make for the culture's well-being. In these practices, personal bodies share in the whole creation's "groaning in labor pains" (Rom. 8:22) for full actualization of the promised eschatological blessing when it will be set free from bondage to decay and will obtain the "freedom of the glory of the children of God" (Rom. 8:21). Since such practices are a continual struggle, personal bodies may not enact them in triumphalist ways, as though they already lived in the time of fully actualized eschatological glory instead of living on time borrowed from fully actualized eschatological blessing.

Enactments of both the exemplary and the critical versions of eschatologically hopeful practices require capacities for spiritual discernment—that is, for discerning concrete occasions of the circumambient triune God relating to quotidian lived worlds to draw them to eschatological glory. This calls for the nurture and discipline of certain human affective powers and powers to master certain ranges of concepts. Consider conceptual mastery first.

For example, discernment of ad hoc occasions of "the Spirit sent by the Father with the Son" drawing certain human creatures toward their eschatological consummation involves a grasp of the ways in which the terms "Spirit" and "Holy Spirit" are used in biblical stories of God drawing humankind to eschatological consummation. It involves a grasp of related concepts, such as "holiness," "sanctification," "liberation," and "new creation" as they are used in the common life of communities of hope seeking to respond appropriately to God relating to us in eschatological blessing.

Capacities for spiritual discernment require learning such concepts in such a way that learning the concepts is existentially forming, shaping the fundamental way in which the learners are oriented to their proximate contexts.

Inseparable from such conceptual formation, capacities for spiritual discernment require formation of personal bodies' affections. Such formation turns on the discipline, that is, the shaping of the relevant affections. In large part, that is a conceptual matter. For example, capacities for spiritual discernment of signs of the inbreaking now of eschatological blessing involve such object-specific emotions as expectancy of signs and anticipations of eschatological blessing in one's quotidian contexts, rejoicing in such signs, and righteous anger on account of particular persons' particular oppression by distortions of their proximate contexts. These emotions are specific to God's gift of eschatological new creation and its tensions with the old creation with which it overlaps. Such affections are conceptually shaped. That is, they are made the specific emotions that they are by mastery of concepts of what they are affections about—in this case, various aspects of the inbreaking of the triune God's long-promised eschatological blessing.

Righteous anger is a particularly important example of the need for discipline of affections required by hope's spiritual discernment. It is a form of anger. Anger is a very complex emotion. It is an annihilating emotion, albeit patient of many degrees of intensity. It is one thing, however, to feel annihilating anger about a person, and quite another to feel it at an action, event, or circumstance. Moreover, it is one thing to feel anger on one's own behalf and another to feel it on behalf of another. Jesus is represented as condemning anger as a sinful emotion: "But I say to you that if you are angry with a brother or sister, you will be liable to judgment" (Matt. 5:22). However, in context this saying about anger is related to murder. Perhaps what is condemned is anger as annihilating murderous rage, whether on one's own behalf or that of another. Ephesians 4:26, on the other hand, advises: "Be angry but do not sin; do not let the sun go down on your anger." The context is reflection on how we are all members of one another in eschatological life, and the sin we are warned against is not anger but protracted unreconciled estrangement generated by anger. Anger in the form of righteous indignation, however, may have an unjust and oppressive action, event, or circumstance as its object, rather than a person. Especially in response to God's inauguration of eschatological blessing, it is an appropriate response on behalf of others to unjust actions, oppressive events, and circumstances to which they are subject. "Righteous anger" need not be a self-contradiction.

However, no sooner is that recognized than the very possibility of a virtuous anger opens the door to an emotional, sinful self-righteousness in which we delude ourselves that our annihilating anger at other persons on our own behalf occurs because our own projects have been frustrated. Personal bodies' enactments of existential hows expressive of joyous hopefulness involve disciplining their emotions, such as anger, to be appropriate responses to the triune God drawing them to eschatological consummation, and that involves learning to discriminate among feelings easily confused with one another.

Above all, however, capacities for spiritual discernment involve discipline of personal bodies' passions. It involves their learning to focus their powers on the triune God's gift of eschatological blessing so that seeking "first the kingdom of God" (see Matt. 6:33) becomes the basic and stable passion of their lives. Such passion is hope's love.

Søren Kierkegaard described hope as a passion for the possible. However, the "possible" in this case is grounded in an actuality—namely, the already inaugurated eschatological kingdom. Hence, we should say more exactly that joyous hopefulness is personal bodies' passionate orientation within their proximate contexts to seek in their midst examples and parables of the kingdom of God and its righteousness.

Because "passion" is used in several ways in everyday English, we need to clarify the term. "Passion" is sometimes used, especially in religious contexts, as a name for suffering, as in "the passion according to St. Matthew." Often the term is used as a name for romantic infatuation, a distinct type of suffering, as in "Romeo developed a passion for Juliet." It can also be used broadly to indicate high intensity of feeling, as in, "She is passionate about civil rights." Even more vaguely, "passion" is used to refer to inchoate, intense, largely ineffable, inner emotional turmoil. Each of these suggests that passion is a private state of subjective inwardness that is in some degree diffuse, inarticulate, even ineffable.

In contrast to all of these uses of the term, "passion" is also used to name a way of being related to and engaged with a public world. This sense of the term overlaps with other senses in that it names an intense desire for something. However, that "something" is something definite in the public world and defines the passion as something definite. Hence, such a passion is conceptually formed—that is, formed by a concept of that for which it is a passion. The concept forming a passion may ordinarily be expressed linguistically, but it need not be. It may be expressed in other media, especially in one of the arts. Or it may be expressed in the pattern of an impassioned personal body's actions in community.

In this sense of the term, a passion is stable and long-lasting. The intensity and persistence of the passion's desire structures a personal body's basic relations to its proximate context. It structures them as an intensely active engagement with one's proximate context, and not simply one's mere presence in it. It organizes one's time and energies about the object of the passion. Indeed, the object of the passion so profoundly shapes one's life that it is said one is "in the grip" of the passion.

Both the intensity and the persistence of a desire are essential to a passion. The intensity of desire may vary in degree, of course, but its presence is what distinguishes a passion from a continuing bland interest in an object. The desire's persistence across time and through many vicissitudes is what distinguishes a passion from an emotional outburst or episode. Neither the intensity nor the persistence of a passion need be self-conscious, though of course they often are. A person may have a passion even when extended periods of time pass during which she is not conscious of the passion. Indeed, a person may never be self-aware about her passion. An observer may be in a position to point out that she is living in the grip of a passion even when the impassioned person does not herself know to say that.

In short, a passion is a conceptually formed, intense, and persisting desire for some thing or some state of affairs in the public space of a shared lived world such that it organizes a personal body's energies and time and constitutes one way in which she is engaged in that world. It is in this sense of "passion" that we may say, following Kierkegaard at a distance, that hope is a passion "for the possible" in the sense of a passion for the eschatological flourishing of our proximate contexts that is possible precisely because, and only because, God has already actually inaugurated such flourishing in our lived worlds.

Since its object is eschatological community in communion with the triune God, which God has already inaugurated in our proximate contexts, this passion takes the form of an intense and persistent search to find, live in, and nurture quotidian communities that, however ambiguously, reflect the justice and love that constitute the righteousness of God's kingdom.

Such passion entails intense resistance to all that opposes and undercuts such justice and community. Hope's passion is the passion against all unjust community and for the establishment of genuinely just community. It may be that hope's concepts of justice and community differ from the concepts of justice and community that go with other, especially nontheocentric, ways of being set in our common proximate contexts. Nonetheless, it is often possible to identify conceptual overlaps and coherences with other ways of being set in our shared proximate contexts. Thus, it is often possible for hope's search for community marked by the justice and love of God's kingdom to join with others in the project of identifying and attacking the roots of injustice and of oppressive community and to search jointly for new structures of justice and authentic community.

Finally, hope's passion is a courageous love for God's promised eschatological blessing. Just as the practice of perseverance is fundamental to doxological gratitude, so too the practice of courage is fundamental to joyous hopefulness in the "not yet" of fully actualized eschatological blessing. Courage is required because of the double tension with which borrowed time marks our proximate contexts. Because the inauguration of new creation take place in the old creation, with its continuing suffering and bondage to oppression, eschatologically hopeful practices require courage. And because they are enacted in full knowledge that although actually inaugurated, eschatological blessing is not yet fully actualized, eschatologically hopeful practices must courageously face the indisputable evidence challenging their hopefulness. Thus, all the existential hows that consist in enactments of existential hopefulness entail the moral discipline that capacitates personal bodies to be courageous.

All of these ways of shaping human persons' intellectual and emotional powers in order to capacitate them for spiritual discernment in their proximate contexts—that is, discernment of places in their lived worlds where "the Spirit sent by the Father with the Son" is drawing those worlds to eschatological flourishing—are aspects of personal bodies' sanctification. They are ascetical disciplines that are inherent in the existential hows of lives lived according to the Spirit in joyous hopefulness.

As the appropriate response to the "Spirit sent by the Father with the Son" drawing us to eschatological consummation, hope also implies some answers to the perennial anthropological questions "Who are we?" and "What are we?" We turn to them in the next chapter.

To be raised up into the new creation,
we don't need to be good, holy, smart,
accountable, or even faithful: We only
need to be dead.
ROBERT FARRAR CAPON

CHAPTER **15A**

Who and What We Are as Eschatologically Consummated Creatures

Personal bodies flourish in joyous hopefulness, which is their appropriate response to the triune God relating to personal bodies to draw them to eschatological consummation. This hope is expressed in a distinctive set of practices, each of which may be enacted in myriad ways. The actual ways in which any given community of personal bodies does enact joyful hopefulness constitute a range of existential hows in which personal bodies are concretely oriented to their proximate contexts in the particular times and spaces of those enactments. Thus, as we saw in chapter 14, joyous hopefulness directly entails a set of answers to the perennial anthropological question, "How are we to be?" It also suggests answers to the questions, "Who are we?" and "What are we?" We consider them now.

Who We Are on Borrowed Time

The attitude of joyous hopefulness brings with it answers to the question of what constitutes our basic unsubstitutable personal identities in the sense of identity introduced in chapter 9.

In the context of the triune God relating to us creatively, the "who?" question was answered in terms of a vocation. In the context of the triune God relating to them creatively, human creatures' vocation requires a twofold description because the creative address by God that constitutes them as personal bodies is at once direct and indirect. Inasmuch as God addresses them directly, constituting us as personal bodies with an array of finite powers, the answer is, "We are finite creatures empowered by God's call to be and to act, to give and to receive in our own places and times." Inasmuch as God addresses personal bodies indirectly through the medium of their proximate contexts, the answer is, "We are finite creatures called by God to be wise for the well-being of the quotidian, including ourselves." In the first case, a human creature's personal identity is appropriately reflected in her response to God in trust. In the second case, her personal identity is appropriately reflected in her response to God in loyalty to God's own loyalty to the quotidian and its flourishing.

In the context of God relating to draw our proximate contexts to eschatological consummation, however, the answer to the "Who?" question must be articulated in a different, although still double, way. The character of the triune God's creative relating to all that is not God is such as to give human creatures considerable epistemic distance from God. I urged in chapter 4A that part of the point of characterizing the triune God's creative relating as a relation *to* all that is not God is to underscore that epistemic distance. Furthermore, the epistemic over-againstness that comes with such epistemic distance helps make the analogy of "address" appropriate for God's relating to human creatures. However, this epistemic distance is so great that "address" must be used in a very extended sense if it is to serve as an analogy for this relation.

In contrast to that, the character of the triune God's relating to draw all that is not God to eschatological consummation allows minimal epistemic distance. That, I argued in chapter 12, is part of the point of characterizing God's relating to draw to eschatological blessing as God "circumambient." Relating in that manner, the triune God is closer to us as experiencers and knowers than we are to ourselves. Relating in that manner, God has next to no epistemic over-againstness in relation to us. That is part of what makes it impossible to give an identity description of God the Holy Spirit or of the triune God relating to humankind in the pattern "Spirit sent by the Father with the Son." Accordingly, an answer to the "Who?" question implied by this mode of God's relating to humankind cannot be articulated using the analogy of address. If the relation cannot be characterized as a being "addressed," who the addressees are cannot be characterized as "ones called" or "ones having a vocation."

Instead, in the context of God relating to draw our proximate contexts to eschatological consummation, the answer to the "Who?" question must be expressed by analogies implied by the ways in which the metaphors "drawn" and "being drawn" are employed in this way of telling the story of God relating. In chapter 12, we noted that the triune God's drawing our proximate contexts, and us with them, to eschatological blessing is grace-like. This "drawing" is like grace in being a free and loving creative gift by God. Since God's self-commitment to draw us to such blessing is as primordial as God's creative relating, it is not God's response to the distortions of humankind grounded in their inappropriate responses to God's creative relating to them. It is not a response to anything. Nor is God's gift given despite humankind's alienation from God in order to overcome it. Hence it is not strictly speaking what New Testament writers generally mean by God's "grace" which is given to humankind despite their sin. However, it is also the case that in actual and inexplicable fact, all that God draws to eschatological blessing is distorted and alienated from God. Under those circumstances, God's gracious gift of actually inaugurating this drawing in their proximate contexts helps bring to light just how alienated personal bodies are from God and from the existential hows to which they are called by God's creative relating to them.

Eschatological blessing on all that is constituted by God's creative relating implies no negative judgment on the finite reality thus constituted. Creaturely reality's finite reality, undistorted by sin, is no doubt different in important respects from its reality in fully actualized eschatological consummation, even though it remains creaturely and finite when eschatologically consummated; but the differences in its consummated state imply no negative judgment on its creatureliness. However, insofar as human creatures and their proximate contexts are distorted, human personal bodies are incapable of accurately assessing from their perspective within their proximate contexts the extent, complexity, and depth of those distortions. However, the canonical narrative of God's proleptic inauguration of eschatological consummation in the resurrection of the crucified Jesus does disclose how radically distorted their orientations to their proximate contexts really are. Such disclosure is a final and definitive judgment that God's gracious gift brings on our proximate contexts as they are, and us with them. This is not to claim that God's judgment on creatures' sinful self-distortion is confined to God's relating to draw creation to eschatological consummation. Canonical Holy Scripture contains innumerable stories of God's relating in judgment to humankind as an aspect of God's relating to them creatively. However, the judgment that comes with God's relating to draw to eschatological consummation is decisive and final precisely because it is an aspect of God relating to draw creation to an eschatological—that is, final—consummation. Given our lived worlds' *de facto* condition of sinful distortion and consequent moral ambiguity, God's gracious eschatological "Yes" to all that is constituted by God's creativity includes a final "No." Accordingly, the "Spirit sent by the Father with the Son" drawing us to eschatological consummation implies a double answer to the question, "Who are we?"

As a gracious gift given in love and radical freedom, the triune God's inauguration of eschatological blessing implies that the answer to the "Who?" question is: *We are those who have been elected for eschatological consummation.* At the same time, as final judgment on the sinful distortion of our proximate contexts, and of us in them, the triune God's inauguration of eschatological blessing implies that the answer to the "Who?" question is: *We are those to whom the catastrophe of final judgment is happening.* The second answer obviously presupposes both the first answer and the inexplicable reality of sinful distortions of who we are and how we are to be. Our personal identities as personal bodies drawn by the triune

God to eschatological consummation can be described adequately only by telling stories about us that render us as ones at once chosen and rejected, affirmed and judged. More needs to be said about each description of our personal identities as personal bodies drawn to eschatological consummation.

Those Elected

"We are those who have been elected for eschatological consummation." In traditional theological terminology, "elected" is interchangeable with "chosen." In the present context "election" means very specifically, "elected for the blessing of eschatological glory."

That is not always the force of "elected," "predestined," or "chosen" in the New Testament. It seems clear that such terms are used in two rather different ways.

Sometimes "elected," "chosen," and their cognates are used in relation to God's selection of a human person or persons for a particular mission, not for a special status. In these cases it is clear that "election" or "chosenness" is meant contrastively: This one (or, these ones) chosen out of all other logically possible candidates. For Paul, Israel remained a people chosen by God out of all the nations (Rom. 11:28), and from time to time certain persons were elected by God out of all of Israel—in contrast to their fellow Israelites, as those through whom, although not necessarily in whom, God would fulfill God's promise to Abraham (Rom. 9:6–13; 11:5, 7). First Peter understands Jesus to be one chosen for his mission (2:6). Out of all the people he encounters, Jesus chooses twelve to be his apostles (e.g., John 15:19). In such cases, New Testament writers continue the most frequent type of use of such terms in Old Testament texts. There God chooses kings and prophets. Of all nations on earth, Israel is chosen (e.g., Deut. 7:6, 7; see also 14:2) to be a light to the Gentiles (Isa. 42:6). In all these cases "x's election" is x's being chosen *in contrast* to other possible candidates.

In contradistinction to such uses, "elected," "chosen," and "predestined" are sometimes used in the New Testament in regard to human persons' being "in Christ" or "in Christ Jesus" and thereby saved in the eschatological judgment from the consequences of sinful distortion and alienation from God. This is election to a particular relation with God, rather than election to a particular rôle or task. It is election to participation in Jesus' own relation to God.

Because Christian stories, respectively, of God drawing us to eschatological consummation and of God reconciling us when we are alienated from God are so closely intertwined, this second type of use of "chosen," "elected," and "predestined" (election to a particular relation with God rather than election to a particular mission or role) can have either of two sorts of force. Stress may fall on estranged personal bodies' reconciliation now that comes with God's inauguration of eschatological blessing, or stress may fall on personal bodies being drawn to a not-yet-actualized eschatological glory.

Thus, sometimes these terms are used in the New Testament with the force elected to benefit from the work of Christ which makes fellowship with God possible for the sinfully distorted. First Peter 1:2, for instance, addresses its readers as those "who have been chosen and destined by God the Father and sanctified by the Spirit to be obedient to Jesus Christ and to be sprinkled with his blood." "Sprinkled" probably alludes either to the blood of the covenant (Exod. 24:3–8) or to water sprinkled for purification (Num. 19:9–21). Because of human creatures' sin, such election is the precondition of fulfillment of their destiny to be with "the Father." In 1 Corinthians, having made the point that in his apparent weakness and foolishness Christ crucified defines "the power of God and the wisdom of God" (1:24), Paul goes on to remind his readers that in electing them God also "chose what is foolish in the world [namely, people like you] to shame the wise; God chose what is weak in the world to shame the strong; God chose what is low and despised in the world, things that are not, to reduce to nothing things that are" (1:27, 28). "Reduce to nothing" echoes apocalyptic rhetoric for what the inauguration of new creation does to the old creation, intimating that through God's choosing of Corinthian Christians, eschatological blessing is inaugurated for them. Then Paul nails down the concrete ground of their new eschatological life: because of their sinfulness it is a "life" that they can enter only as they are "in Christ Jesus, who became for us wisdom from God, and righteousness and sanctification and redemption" (1:30).

Mark and Matthew use "elect" and similar terms, not in reference to human persons' relation to Christ, but in reference to those who will in the judgment day be in God's company and not estranged from it. These texts use these terms exclusively in explicitly apocalyptic contexts (Mark 13 and Matt. 24, respectively). For both texts the Lord has cut short the catastrophes leading up to the last day "for the sake of the elect" (Mark 13:20; Matt. 24:22), in the last time false messiahs will try to "lead astray, if possible, the elect" (Mark 13:22; Matt. 24:24), but on the last day God "will gather his elect" (Mark 13:27; Matt. 24:31) into fellowship with God. While the apocalyptic contexts of these uses of "elect" signal a catastrophic event of cosmic proportions, the term "elect" is used in regard to otherwise sinful human persons' survival of the catastrophes in God's company.

Sometimes, however, "elected," "chosen," and "predestined" are used with the sense of "elected for eschatological glory" without reference to anyone's distortion in sin. For example, the literary context of Romans 8:29–30 is a discussion of eschatological glory (18–27). Verses 29–30 are focused on election to glory as such and the odd way in which God inaugurates that eschatological blessing: "For those whom [God] foreknew he also predestined to be conformed to the image of his Son, in order that he might be the firstborn within a large family. And those whom he predestined he also called; and those whom he called he also justified; and those whom he justified he also glorified." The *telos* of this chain of divine actions is the point of the passage—namely, eschatological glorification. It is acknowledged in passing that those brought to glory also need to be "justified," but that is not the main point of the passage. In Colossians a passage about the quality of life of those who have "died to the elemental spirits of the universe" (2:20) leads to a series of exhortations including, "As God's chosen ones, holy and beloved, clothe yourselves with compassion, kindness, humility, meekness, and patience" (3:12). What they are chosen for is life in the new creation liberated from the elemental substances that order and rule the old creation. Here election is election to or for eschatologically blessed life.

The election text with this force that has had the greatest historical influence in secondary theology is undoubtedly the doxological blessing with which Ephesians begins (1:3–14). The theme of election for eschatological glory is precisely that for which God is blessed and praised in this text: "Blessed by the God and Father of our Lord Jesus Christ, who has blessed us in Christ with every spiritual blessing in the heavenly places, just as he chose us in Christ before the foundation of the world to be holy and blameless before him in love" (vv. 3–4). "Before the foundation of the world" affirms that God's self-commitment to give eschatological consummation is as primordial as God's self-commitment to give creative blessing. The "choosing" here is logically prior to and independent of the question of whether the chosen are also, however absurdly, distorted and alienated from God and in need of reconciliation.

In the next verse, Christ's role is that of the concrete way in which God keeps God's self-commitment to give eschatological glory: "[God] destined us for adoption as his children through Jesus Christ, according to the good pleasure of his will, to the praise of his glorious grace that he freely bestowed on us in the Beloved" (vv. 5–6). There follows, as a secondary theme, acknowledgment that those elected for eschatological glory also stand in need of justification: "In him we have redemption through his blood, the forgiveness of our trespasses" (vv. 7–8a). Then the text returns to the major theme: personal bodies' election to eschatological glory. That election is part of the "mystery" (v. 9) of God's will, God's hitherto secret "plan for the fullness of time, to gather up all things in him [Christ], things in heaven and things on earth" (v. 10) in an eschatological consummation. This mystery is precisely what is disclosed in Christ (v. 9). Echoing apocalyptic rhetoric's effort to express the event of *apokalypsis*—that is, the disclosure of God's secret plan for all that is not God—these verses identify Christ in his unsubstitutable personal identity as at once the way in which eschatological blessing is inaugurated and the disclosure of the content of that blessing. The text then explicitly grounds human persons' participation in eschatological blessing—reconciliation quite aside—in their election to be "in Christ": "In Christ we have also obtained an inheritance, having been destined according to the purpose of him [God] who accomplishes all things according to his counsel and will" (v. 11).

"Elected" in the specific sense of "elected for the blessing of eschatological glory": It is only in this sense that the term is used in the identity description, "We are those who have been chosen for eschatological consummation."

There are four important entailments of the use of "election," in this sense, in a personal identity description. It entails, first, confirmation of the theme of the last chapter, claimed there and warranted here: Joy is indeed the pervasive mood most appropriate to personal bodies responding in hope to the triune God relating to them to draw them to eschatological consummation. It is a specifically eschatological joy. Such joy at the gift of a personal identity defined by election to glory is neither euphoric nor in denial of evil. As eschatological blessing is inaugurated in the midst of horrendous evil, oppression, and suffering, so eschatological joy at its inauguration is joy in the midst of anguished and angry realism about the quotidian's bondage to evil, intense awareness of one's own bondage to evil and one's complicity in others' bondage under oppression, and compassion for others' suffering. Such joy is characterized by what Dietrich Bonhoeffer called *hilaritas*, "a high-spirited self-confidence," a "boldness and defiance of the world and of popular opinion" in the "steadfast certainty" that those who exhibit it are "showing the world something *good* (even if the world doesn't like it)" (1972, 229; emphasis in the original).

However, joy is a more egalitarian and generalized mood than what Bonhoeffer describes. Where for Bonhoeffer, *hilaritas* characterizes only a few extraordinarily creative people (Rubens, Lessing, Luther, Barth, and in a certain way, Michelangelo and Rembrandt; 1972, 229), and only characterizes their mood about their creative projects, eschatological joy is a mood all personal bodies are invited and permitted to have simply in the living of their quotidian lives. If who they are is "ones elect for eschatological consummation," why should they not live their lives in high-spirited self-confidence in the midst of eschatologically celebratory, realistic, and liberative engagement in their proximate contexts' moral ambiguities and sinful distortions?

Second, this use of "elected" entails that God's electing of human persons for eschatological glory is logically prior, not only to anything they may do, but to their very existence. It is in this sense that it is appropriate to say that this electing is a pre-destinating of people for eschatological blessing. Election is logically prior to human existence and action because it is rooted in a self-commitment by God to give eschatological blessing, which is as primordial as God's self-commitment to bless creatively, and both divine self-commitments are logically prior to God actually relating in either way to all that is not God.

Use of "elect" with this distinctive force entails, third, that all creation is, in some way, elect for eschatological blessing. Election for mission connotes selection from a larger population. Not everyone is elected to be king, prophet, apostle, or even church member. But election for eschatological glory has no such connotation. We have seen that the cosmic scope of God's eschatological blessing surfaces in canonical Christian Holy Scripture in many ways, most vividly in the apocalyptic rhetoric employed at least as the background, and often explicitly in the foreground, in most New Testament and many Old Testament eschatological texts. Inasmuch as God is self-committed to give eschatological blessing to all that is not God, the election of personal bodies for eschatological consummation must be construed all-inclusively. Accordingly, "We are those who have been chosen for eschatological consummation" is an identity description of all human personal bodies.

Finally, used in this way, "elected" and "predestined" and "chosen" do not mean "fate." Personal identity does not determine any particular fate. The ways in which personal bodies are oriented in their proximate contexts, their concrete existential hows, may be coherent with their basic personal identities, or they may, in varying degrees, be incoherent with their identities. Personal bodies' complex array of finite powers makes them quite capable of enacting hows that are in some degree at cross-grain to who they are. They can be to themselves untrue. Accordingly, personal bodies may in fact enact lives at cross-grain to their particular identity as ones whose personal identities are defined by their election for eschatological consummation. The claim that part of their personal identity description is, "We are those who have been elected for eschatological consummation," does not imply, "We are those who are destined, whether we acknowledge it or not, whether we believe it or not, whether we choose it or not, to lead lives that are appropriate responses to God relating to consummate us eschatologically."

Not even use of the expression "predestined" by itself warrants inferences to the contrary. To be destined for eschatological glory is to have glory as the destination for which God chooses or elects personal bodies. To say that we have such identities is to say that we are all primordially meant by God for eschatological consummation. In chapter 16 I discuss distortions of personal bodies' identities grounded in distorted responses to "the Spirit sent by the Father with the Son." The point that needs to be made here is that in living at cross-grain to their identity, such persons do not thereby lose their identity as ones elected by God for eschatological consummation. Rather, they have distorted versions of that identity and participate in eschatological blessing precisely as personal bodies with distorted versions of their own identities.

This naturally raises the question of whether it is possible that some personal body's existential hows might never cohere with his personal identity as one elected to eschatological glory—even though God chooses him for that destiny. Whatever transformation is signified by "the resurrection of the dead," would it mean that someone who had lived until her death at cross-grain to her own personal identity as one elect for eschatological glory would then be transformed by her resurrection from the dead into someone whose eschatological existential hows thereafter do cohere with her identity? Or, whatever the transformation she undergoes in resurrection, might she nonetheless continue to enact a response to her ultimate context that is inappropriate to the triune God's relating to give eschatological blessing, and thus contradictory of her personal identity as one elect for such blessing?

This is an instance of a kind of theological question about which I say more in chapter 15B. Here it is enough to observe that the question is undecideable on the basis of the theological remarks developed thus far in this book. It is only decideable in the context of a far more systematically integrated and comprehensive structure of argument than can be provided by the methodological commitments of this project (see chaps. 1B, 2B, 3B, and 12B). Whether such highly systematized conceptual structure is a good thing in secondary theology depends on whether one judges that it is more Christianly appropriate to keep theological reflection systematically unsystematic, as I aim to do here, or judges that it is more Christianly appropriate to seek as much closure as possible of such questions by developing a rigorously and systematically argued structure of theological claims.

Those Judged

In the context of proximate contexts doubly tensed by the triune God's proleptic inauguration of the long-promised eschatological blessing in the resurrection of the crucified Jesus, the second part of the answer to the question "Who are we?" is "We are those to whom the catastrophe of final judgment is happening." This judgment is the "no" to human creatures that is inherent in the triune God's electing "yes" to them when the distortions of who and how they are estrange them from God. Thus, personal bodies' identity as ones undergoing judgment presupposes their identity as creatures elected by God, and presupposes that those elected creatures' identities are also distorted.

This judgment takes the form of disclosure. It is a disclosure revealing unambiguously the real condition of personal bodies in their quotidian communities shaped by sinfully distorted personal identities. No doubt, personal bodies in their quotidian lived worlds simply as creatures know well enough their appalling moral and ontological ambiguity. They do not require the inauguration of eschatological blessing to know that. Nonetheless, it is hardly more than the sheer fact of the moral ambiguity of their proximate contexts that they know. Their creativity in underestimating and obscuring the depth and systemic complexity of the distortions of their proximate contexts, including themselves, is inexhaustible. The disclosure brought by eschatological blessing is not judgment in the sense of a decision a judge must make on the basis of the particularities of some possibly ambiguous evidence, on one side, and the generalities of the law on the other. Rather, the triune God's inauguration of eschatological blessing simply places the distortions of human creatures' quotidian lived worlds and of the creatures in those contexts in clear, bright light where their depth and systemic interconnections are clearly disclosed.

This judgment is final so far as the old creation is concerned. As a disclosure inherent in the inauguration of the eschatological new creation, it constitutes the terminal catastrophe of the old creation. The old creation's catastrophe is expressed in apocalyptic rhetoric by vivid images of cosmic calamities (the sun and moon darkened and the stars falling from heaven "and the powers of heaven" shaken; e.g. Mark 13:29; Matt. 24:29), and in images of human creatures' calamitous eternal punishment in eternal fire (e.g., Matt. 25:41). Cosmic imagery of a darkening sun and moon and falling stars, on one side, and judicial imagery of eternal punishment in eternal fire are conventional tropes in apocalyptic rhetoric expressive of the absolute finality of eschatological judgment as the old creation's terminal catastrophe: No more cosmic or personal time for making changes for the better in our shared proximate contexts or for amendment of life personally that could reverse the distorting consequences of human personal bodies' inappropriate responses to the ways in which God relates to them. Eschatological transformation brings something new, but only by bringing something else to an end. According to Jesus' parable of the final judge as a shepherd separating sheep from goats (Matt. 25:31–46), only those who, in response to God's ways of relating to them, relate back to God in appropriate forms of response will avoid this terminal catastrophe.

Understood in the context of the triune God's primordial self-commitment to give eschatological blessing to all that is not God, the "no" of this judgment does not invalidate the "yes" of God's election of all personal bodies to eschatological glory. Rather, it discloses that those whose personal identity is that they are elect for eschatological blessing are also those whose identity is this: they are those whose relating to God in response to God relating to them is profoundly distorted. This too is who they finally are. Consequently, in the context of proximate contexts in which God's promise of eschatological consummation is actually inaugurated but not yet fully actualized, their personal identities must be characterized as self-contradictory. They are at once constituted by God's electing "yes" to personal bodies in community in drawing them to eschatological consummation by the resurrection of the crucified Jesus, and by their own enactments in community of concrete existential hows that are disclosed by the resurrection of the crucified Jesus, the "no" of God's judgment, to be at cross-grain to just that eccentrically grounded personal identity.

Such judgment is final in the sense that it discloses the self-contradictoriness of who and how personal bodies are in fact, beyond or below which there is no other modifying or extenuating truth about who they are and how they are set into their proximate contexts. There are other truths about who and how they are, but none more fundamental. Hence, God's judgment on this state of affairs in personal bodies' proximate contexts this side of full actualization of eschatological blessing is definitive of their personal identities insofar as that judgment is inherent in God's election of them for eschatological glory.

However, that judgment, that "no," presupposes the "yes," presupposes that in relating to consummate all else eschatologically God elects humankind for eschatological blessing. The order between the "yes" and the "no" is not dialectical and is irreversible. The "yes" is fundamental; the "no" is derivative, contingent on the absurd fact of sin. The "no" is not a separate and distinct type of way in which God relates to personal bodies. It is rather the way in which God's electing "yes" bears on personal bodies whose personal identities are distorted in bondage to inappropriate responses to God's ways of relating to them.

Those whose personal identities are defined by their being judged by God live on borrowed time. A parable for living in this way on borrowed time in the wake of catastrophe appears in the work of photographer Diane Arbus. At one point, Arbus had an exhibit of portraits of physically abnormal people. They were unusually short, tall, heavy, or thin, capable of rare physical contortions. Many of them were employed in circus sideshows and as clowns. A frequently noted feature of the portraits was their subjects' extraordinarily unguarded presence. Neither ingratiating nor indifferent, shrinking nor self-assertive, wary nor in any other way self-protective, they were just confidently, stunningly there. According to her biographer, Arbus explained this to writer Joseph Mitchell, saying, "Most people go through life dreading they'll have a traumatic experience. Freaks were born with their trauma. They've passed their test in life. They're aristocrats" (Bosworth 1984, 207). So, too, for those who are being judged by God; the worst has happened. There is nothing more terrible left to fear in their lived worlds, nothing worse to protect themselves against, to disguise, or to deny.

The time of quotidian life, in its moral ambiguity, is measured, ordered, and spent in practices of self-protection. Those judged by the inauguration of eschatological blessing are freed of all that and have permission to live on time borrowed from an eschatological new creation that begins on the other side of divine judgment, although it is inaugurated now. To live on borrowed time is to have both invitation and permission to live in ways colored by an eschatological joy that is not only characterized by high-spirited self-confidence, but is also calmly secure and un-self-protective.

These reflections on the answers implied to the "Who?" question by God relating to humankind to draw it to eschatological consummation imply in turn a qualification of the answer it implies to the question "How are we to be?" The general answer to the latter, I suggested, is "joyously hopeful." Hopefulness is the appropriate response to God relating to draw us to eschatological blessing. It is best understood, I suggested, not as a feeling but an attitude that orients personal bodies in and to their ultimate and proximate contexts. Reflection on the question "Who are we?" qualifies that characterization by showing that the joy that modifies hopefulness is best understood as a feeling that colors all enactments of eschatological hopefulness. Such joy is more like a mood than an emotion or a passion. Unlike emotions and passions, it has no particular object, although it always has some occasion. Unlike a fleeting emotion and like a passion, joy is relatively long-lived. And like all of them, it is conceptually formed. It is a moodlike feeling specifically shaped by that to which it is a response: the "Spirit sent by the Father with the Son" to draw us all, with our proximate contexts, to eschatological glory.

What We Are on Borrowed Time

Eschatological consummation may re-create and transform all that is constituted by God relating creatively, but what is eschatologically consummated is identical with what is constituted by God relating creatively. In the case of human creatures, what are eschatologically blessed are creaturely living human personal bodies in community. God relating to human creatures to bless them eschatologically may bring them radical changes, globally signaled by such words as "re-created" and "transformed," but it does not constitute the creation of a new kind of creature different from humankind. The theological claim that the triune God who relates creatively also relates to bless eschatologically entails a strong continuity between that which is constituted by God relating creatively and that which is glorified by God relating to consummate eschatologically. That continuity lies in the constancy of what it is to be a living human personal body.

According to the narrative logic of canonical Holy Scripture's stories of God relating to draw creation to eschatological consummation, God concretely inaugurates actualization of the promise of eschatological blessing proleptically in the person of Jesus. Accordingly, in relating to humankind in eschatological blessing, God relates initially to untransformed living human personal physical bodies in their ontologically and morally ambiguous proximate contexts to draw them to eschatological consummation—relates to them as physical bodies and not as some other kind of body. Consequently, the answer to the question, "What are human beings as those living on borrowed time by virtue of the triune God relating to them in eschatological blessing?" is "Precisely what they are by virtue of God relating to them creatively."

Part 1 outlined salient features of that "what" (see chap. 6): living human personal bodies in community, centers of energy constantly dependent for their reality and value on God creatively relating to them directly in their having been born as living human bodies set within creaturely proximate contexts, and creatively relating to them indirectly in their being given living human bodies for whose responses to God's creative relating within their proximate contexts they are responsible and accountable. Here "living bodies" is understood to have a number of dimensions: a biological dimension, whose nature is explained by the relevant physical sciences, classified as human by its DNA; a body that is a precondition of a rich and complex range of affective, cognitive, rational, self-regulative, and expressive powers capable of being strengthened, focused, and conceptually formed, whose exercise constitutes additional social, moral, creative, and cultural dimensions of human living bodies; bodies with these multiple dimensions constituted as personal by God's delight in them, valuing them as good, and calling them through their proximate contexts to act wisely for the well-being of their proximate contexts; and in all their dimensions, creaturely personal bodies that are finite centers of energy, limited, both internally in respect to the range and energy of their powers and externally in respect to the way they are impinged on by other creatures and impinge on them in turn, inherently vulnerable to damage, violation, disintegration, and death. All this constitutes what God relates to when God draws human creatures into borrowed time by relating proleptically to them in eschatological blessing in the resurrection of the crucified Jesus in the midst of their ambiguous and distorted proximate contexts.

The claim that God actively relates to human creatures in eschatological blessing does not imply that God thereby violates their creaturely integrity. Since being related to creatively by God is inherent in human creatures' "what," there need be no anthropological conceptual problem generated by the affirmation that God also relates to personal bodies to draw them to eschatological consummation. Being related to by God is inherent in what it is to be a human personal body; it is not a violation or change of it.

How is it possible for the triune God to relate to uniquely free human creatures in this way without violating their freedom? Do we not need to exhibit some particular feature of what human creatures are that is the point of contact, the condition of the possibility of God relating to such creatures to draw them to eschatological consummation in a way that does not violate or restrict their freedom? To the contrary, I suggest that the possibility of the triune God relating to personal bodies in this way, and of their relating to God in appropriate response, follows excellently from its actuality, and hardly from anything else. Because it is to whole personal bodies in their entirety that the "Spirit sent by the Father with the Son" circumambiently relates to draw to eschatological consummation, it is not necessary to postulate some one God-specific, much less Holy Spirit–specific, human capacity or openness, whether given to them in their creation or given as a new capacity along with eschatological blessing, that is the condition of the possibility of the triune God in the *taxis* "Spirit sent by the Father with the Son" relating to them in a nonviolating way. Conversely, and for the same reason, it is not necessary to postulate some special God-specific, much less Holy Spirit–specific, human creaturely spiritual power to respond appropriately to the triune God's circumambient relating to draw humankind to glory, whether inherent in their creatureliness or freshly given with eschatological blessing. It is the same God who is radically intimate to human creatures both in relating to them creatively and in relating circumambiently to them to give eschatological blessing. The intimacy of God's creative relating constitutes personal bodies in their specific modes of freedom and liberty. It is to that same kind of creature in its wholeness that the triune God relates to draw it to eschatological consummation. As the triune God relates to human creatures in their wholeness, so they respond as whole personal bodies. Their response engages the entire array of their creaturely powers. They require no additional specifically spiritual dimension above and beyond the range of powers they are given in their having been born in order to respond appropriately to the Holy Spirit.

According to the narrative logic of canonical Holy Scripture's stories of God relating to draw creation to eschatological consummation, God concretely inaugurates actualization of the promise of eschatological blessing proleptically in the person of Jesus, but that is only the inauguration of the actualization of that promise. It is not yet fully actualized. God's active drawing of creatures to eschatological consummation is ongoing. Because the inauguration of the actualization of the promise occurs proleptically in the midst of creaturely proximate contexts, God's drawing human creatures and their proximate contexts to eschatological consummation initially engages living physical human personal bodies. Because the inauguration of the actualization of the promise occurs in proximate contexts profoundly distorted by human creatures' inappropriate responses to the triune God relating to them, God's ongoing drawing of human creatures (but not only human creatures) to eschatological consummation occurs on borrowed time only obscurely, occluded by the way the overlap of old creation and new creation tenses the proximate contexts in which the drawing occurs. Because the inauguration of the actualization of the promise also tenses human creatures' proximate contexts between the actuality now of the inauguration of eschatological blessing and the not-yet full actualization of eschatological consummation, God's ongoing drawing of human creatures is headed somewhere, leading to profound changes, not in what human creatures are, but in the modes in which they will be what human creatures are in fully actualized eschatological consummation.

Since those "modes" are not yet actualized, except in the resurrection of the crucified Jesus, they are hardly intelligible or describable. As we noted

in chapter 14, the imagery of canonical accounts of eschatological—resurrected—human life characterize it as communion in human community
participating in creaturely fashion in the quality of the communion that
constitutes the life of the triune God. The claim that eschatological life is a
participation in the life of God in creaturely fashion entails that, no matter how radically the mode may change in which they live what they are
by God's creative relating, eschatologically consummated human creatures
will nonetheless remain creatures, radically dependent on God for their
reality and value. Being-related-to-by-God will still be intrinsic to what
they are. They will still be finite, limited not only by their inability to be the
ground of their own reality and value, but also by internal limits intrinsic
to their creaturely powers, and by external limits imposed by their interdependence on other creatures in networks of relationships that constitute
their shared proximate contexts.

At a high level of abstraction, it is fair to characterize fully actualized
eschatological human creatures as finite centers of energy that have an array
of affective, cognitive, rational, self-regulative, and expressive powers by
whose exercise they are interrelated in a community constituted by mutual
love that is richly expressive of love, joy, and gratitude to God in which
they reflect God's glory. Such community-in-communion would seem to
presuppose capacities for mutual recognition, which in turn would seem
to presuppose powers of memory, cognition, and concept formation.

We also noted in chapter 14 that imagery in canonical Christian Holy
Scripture suggests that the major change in the mode in which human
creatures are what they are when their being drawn by God to eschatological consummation is fully realized is that their bodiliness is no longer
physical. The *locus classicus* is Paul's notoriously tangled rumination in
1 Corinthians 15 on the difference between physical and spiritual bodies. Whatever else a spiritual body may be, it is a not-physical body. It is
nevertheless a creaturely and finite living body of some sort, for which
our nearest vague approximation is "finite center of energy." Other important changes in the mode in which human creatures live what they are as
creatures follow from this change in the mode in which they are bodied.
Not-physical bodies are imaged as not vulnerable to death of the body
or to physical damage and disintegration and suffering. For such bodies,
predation ceases because they do not require nourishment by the physical
bodies of other creatures.

One narrower point may be made: There is no warrant for supposing
that eschatologically transfigured or glorified nonphysical bodies are perfect bodies in which the imperfections and disabilities that were among
the factors constituting their concrete particularity as pre-mortem physical bodies have been removed, healed, or corrected. Such a claim cannot be said to follow any trajectory of thought rooted in the narrative
logic of accounts in canonical Christian Holy Scripture of God drawing

humankind to eschatological consummation (see chapter 15B). Nor is such a claim required by the logic of the relations between proposals in secondary theology about the implications for the anthropological "What?" question of canonical narratives of God relating creatively and proposals about the implications of narratives of God relating to draw humankind to eschatological consummation. The proposals addressing the anthropological "What?" question made in part 1 on the basis of canonical narratives of God relating to all else creatively set aside the traditional claim that God creates absolutely perfect living human bodies on the grounds that the concept of absolutely perfect human bodies is incapable of coherent explanation and exposition.

What is theologically at stake here, of course, is the status of imperfections (e.g., wounds) and "disabilities" as properties constitutive of the concrete particularity of eschatologically glorified human bodies. Is the concept of an eschatologically glorified human body inconsistent with the ascription to it of bodily imperfections and disabilities that could serve as some of the properties by which it is recognized in its concrete particularity as continuous with a pre-mortem human living body one had known? I urge that it is not. I suggest that there are no theological grounds for rejecting the proposal that eschatologically glorified bodies, spiritual bodies in Paul's sense, continue in their concrete particularity to have the imperfections and disabilities that were properties constitutive of their concrete particularities before death.

These are almost entirely negative characterizations of the mode in which human beings are what they are as God's creatures when their eschatological consummation is fully actualized. The major challenge to the formulation of positive characterizations lies in explicating the kind of body (e.g., Paul's notion of a "spiritual body") that an eschatologically consummated living human personal body would be and have. It is exegetically difficult to warrant a clear account of what the phrase would have meant in Paul's context to his contemporaries that might suggest an analogous account of resurrected human bodies that would be intelligible to our contemporaries. Beyond that is another sort of challenge. It is increasingly clear from research in neurology, evolutionary neurology, and neuropsychology that human powers of sensation, feeling, emotion, awareness, self-awareness, cognition, memory, reasoning, language, and consciousness (if that be something in its own right, say, one more human power, over and above complex relations among some or all of the aforementioned) presuppose an organic basis in the human physical brain and nervous system.

That does not necessarily imply that this array of mental powers is nothing but an epiphenomenal by-product of the chemistry and biology of the brain and nervous system. It is at least clear that what is meant by conventional references to and claims about mental acts, events, and processes is not what is meant by scientific claims about the neurology of sense experience, cognition, emotions, awareness, and so on. The question of the ontological status of mental acts, events, and processes and their metaphysical relation to physical bodily processes does not need to be settled here. No matter how it is settled, it appears that the maxim must be honored: no physical brain and nervous-system processes, no mental acts, events, or processes (see N. Murphy 2006). Consequently it needs to be acknowledged that theological claims about the human bodily powers of eschatologically consummated human creatures, where the body in question is not the kind of organic physical body we are and have by God creating us in our having been born, face serious conceptual challenges in explaining how such creatures can have just those powers in the absence of organic physical bodies.

This challenge invites a variety of thought experiments that may be considered exercises in a (new) literary genre: theological science fantasy. For example, one might develop such an experiment by postulating that fully eschatologically consummated—that is, resurrected—human creatures in community are finite centers of energy whose various powers are analogous to coherent, integrated artificial intelligence programs that do not need a physical basis, either organic or inorganic, are interrelated in networks of reciprocal exchange of information (i.e., communal proximate contexts) that require no physical basis, and are all powered by a kind of energy unknown to us in the cosmos to which we have cognitive access (say, by so-called dark energy?). The point of devising such myths, like Plato's point in devising his myths, might be to tell a likely story that prompts the skeptic's or critic's imagination to look at the conceptual issues from a fresh perspective from which the initial conceptual difficulties seem less daunting and the notion of nonphysical personal bodies more plausible. The consequence of devising such myths, however, is perhaps as likely to be the generation of fresh objections that are more an artifact of the exercise in theological science fantasy than they are a function of the original theological proposal. I incline to the view that the invitation to play this game ought to be declined in secondary theology. At the notion that eschatologically consummated human bodies are not-physical, spiritual bodies, we have probably reached that of which nothing more can be said concerning what human beings are as eschatologically consummated, wherefore one should be silent. Given its defining task in the common life of communities of Christian faith, the practice of secondary theology is under no obligation to pursue every question generated by its theological proposals. In some cases like this one, I suggest, a certain pious agnosticism is both faithful and appropriate.

Against the background of this chapter and its predecessor, we move back to the topic of sin. In this case it is sin as distortion of hope, distortion of appropriate response to the "Spirit sent by the Father with the Son" to draw humankind to eschatological consummation. Indeed, it is only against the background of a discussion of how we are to be and who and what we are in light of the graciousness and judgment of the triune God drawing us to eschatological glory that the character and depth of sin come into view. I turn to that in chapter 16. However, before doing that, it is necessary to acknowledge and justify the growing number of loose ends in these theological remarks. I take up that matter in the next backup chapter.

Resurrected Bodies and Theological Loose Ends

The account offered at the end of chapter 15A of what actual living human personal bodies in community are in fully actualized eschatological consummation requires further backing. It is offered here, opening up into a broader discussion of this project's deliberate practice of leaving obvious theological loose ends dangling at the end of each part.

Broadly speaking, chapter 15A ended by proposing that what it is to be a human creature whose eschatological consummation is fully actualized can be most adequately expressed by appropriating the traditional trope "the resurrection of the body," interpreted in ways guided by the apostle Paul's distinction between "physical" and "spiritual" "bodies" (1 Cor. 15:44). Backing for that proposal is developed here in three steps. First, I focus in this section on paradigmatic patterns in canonical biblical narratives of encounters with the risen Jesus, interpreted as canonical Christian Holy Scripture. In the next section, I focus on the relation between Jesus' resurrection and his proximate context as one "bodily" risen. I focus in the following section on his ultimate context as one raised from death in his humanity. A fourth section outlines implications of this analysis for address to the anthropological "What?" question. The fifth section reflects on how the proposals made here relate to other types of theological address to the *locus* "eschatology." The final section opens up more broadly to methodological questions raised by the growing number of loose ends in this set of theological anthropological proposals.

Jesus' Resurrected Body: Discontinuity in Continuity

Canonical biblical narratives of encounters with the risen Jesus, interpreted as canonical Christian Holy Scripture, exhibit a complex pattern of continuity and discontinuity between Jesus' pre-Easter and post-Easter "bodies." That pattern is also exhibited in canonical New Testament texts, especially by Paul, that reflect on accounts of encounter with the risen Jesus. Put abstractly, it is a pattern of discontinuity-in-continuity between the post-Easter Jesus and the pre-Easter Jesus. The way in which encounters with the risen Jesus are narrated in the canonical Gospels, the continuity is fundamental to the personal identity of the figure they render, but the discontinuity is instrumentally essential both to cognitive access to that continuity and to specifying the concrete character of the continuity.

The discontinuities between the post-Easter and pre-Easter Jesus, as described by the narrative accounts of encounters with the risen Jesus in the canonical Gospels, are familiar and easily summarized. The same stories in Luke and John, for example, that stress the tangibility of the body encountered post-Easter also stress its difference from physical bodies: having walked with them on the road to Emmaus and broken bread with two disciples in Luke, Jesus abruptly vanishes (24:31); Jesus abruptly appears in the room on the occasion when he eats broiled fish with disciples in Jerusalem and invites them to touch him, and afterward when they went out to Bethany "he withdrew from them and was carried up into heaven" (Luke 24:51); in John, Jesus abruptly "came and stood among" disciples even though the door was locked (20:19–20) and a week later "came and stood among them" and invited Thomas to touch his hands and side even though the doors were shut (20:26–27). These are not movements in space of which physical living bodies are capable.

Paul's commentary on such descriptions of the resurrected human body in 1 Corinthians 15 famously marks the discontinuity-in-continuity between pre- and postmortem living human personal bodies by distinguishing between the "physical" body that dies and the "spiritual" body that is raised (v. 44). The continuity between the two lies in their being one and the same body. The discontinuity between the two seems to turn for the apostle on the distinction between the physical body's weakness and perishability and the spiritual body's power and imperishability (vv. 42, 43b).

Indeed, as Michael Welker points out (2000, 38), canonical narratives of encounters with the risen Christ generally use the term "body" to "indicate the continuity between the pre-Easter and the post-Easter Christ." Peter Lampe notes (2002, 104) that "whenever traditional Jews said 'body,' they meant not just the tangible, physical parts but rather the entire person." Thus, in the canonical stories of the Greek New Testament, *soma* (usually translated as "body") means the whole of what part 1 characterizes as an "actual living human personal body." Canonical stories of palpable bodily acts by Jesus, especially eating and inviting direct physical touch, convey that the one encountered post-Easter truly is "one body" with the pre-Easter Jesus. In Matthew 28:9, Jesus meets Mary Magdalene and the other Mary "and they came to him, took hold of his feet, and worshiped him"; in Luke 24:30, he takes bread, blesses and breaks it, and gives it to Cleopas and his companion; in Luke 24:36–43, he invites a group of disciples in Jerusalem to touch him "for a ghost does not have flesh and bones as you see that I have," and he eats a piece of broiled fish; in John 20:24–29, he invites Thomas to touch his wounded hand and side, and in 21:9–13, by the Sea of Tiberias in Galilee, Jesus cooks and serves breakfast to some of his disciples.

However, "continuity" needs to be parsed carefully in relation to the use of "body" in canonical accounts of encounters with the risen Jesus. Affirmation of Jesus' bodily resurrection in these narratives indicates continuity of his numerical identity; it does not indicate that the basis of that continuity of identity lies in the continuity of the matter, or the formed matter, that constitutes the pre-Easter Jesus' body. The tangible body that, according to the canonical narratives, the disciples encounter post-Easter is the self-same tangible body as the one they had encountered for several years pre-Easter, a body they knew had been killed. It is the risen body of the crucified Jesus. However, precisely that mark of continuity also marks the most decisive discontinuity between the pre- and post-Easter bodied Jesus. The report that, as rendered by the canonical Gospel narratives, Jesus is encountered as bodily resurrected may make the point that he is one and the same as the pre-Easter Jesus, but it does not imply that his pre-Easter bodiliness is the principle of continuity that metaphysically explains the continuity of the post- and pre-Easter Jesus. On the contrary, the canonical narratives of encounters with the risen Christ use the term "body" to indicate continuity between the pre-Easter and the post-Easter Jesus despite the way that same "body" indicates the most radical discontinuity to the matter of his pre-Easter body—namely, its discontinuity in consequence of its death by crucifixion. It is a bodily continuity despite, we may say, the not-so-slow disintegration of his carbon-based material body.

One conceptual consequence of this analysis is that if "body" is used in primary and secondary Christian theology as it is in canonical accounts of encounters with the resurrected Jesus to indicate the continuity between the post- and pre-Easter Jesus, it must be explained in a way that can include the biochemistry with which we are acquainted, but does not make it essential to the concept of a living human body.

The discontinuities between the post- and pre-Easter Jesus that canonical narratives build into their accounts of encounters with the risen Jesus are necessary for at least two reasons. One has to do with the significance of encounters with the risen crucified Jesus. The larger narrative context of the canonical Gospels' accounts of encounters with the risen Jesus are narratives of Jesus' mission proclaiming the imminent in-breaking of God's eschatological reign, coming with both blessing and judgment. Their accounts of Jesus' proclamation of this message often employ the rhetoric of already well-known apocalyptic writings. Jesus is presented as assuming that the rhetoric and themes of apocalyptic are familiar to his listeners. Theological differences among the canonically edited Gospels themselves may derive, in part, from their different construals of apocalyptic themes, especially in regard to how the in-breaking of God's eschatological reign relates to the time in which the Gospels are written. The Gospels nonetheless seem tacitly to assume themes from apocalyptic as background beliefs that shape the logics of the movement of their narratives. Among those themes is the belief that resurrection from the dead is a sign that the long-promised eschatological reign of God is in fact beginning to break into a world bound by evil powers. Against that background, encounters with the risen Jesus have a cosmic significance. Jesus' bodily resurrection is not merely significant as a sign of God's approval and vindication of Jesus in particular. Nor is the significance of Jesus' bodily resurrection limited to its being a sign that God's eschatological reign is about to break in very, very soon. Beyond all that, the canonical narratives render who Jesus is. The significance of the bodily resurrection of the crucified Jesus is that it is the particular and concrete way in which God goes about actually inaugurating then and there the fulfillment of the long-promised eschatological blessing of the in-breaking of God's eschatological reign, without therein fully actualizing it. Part 2 has argued that the Gospels' narrative identity-descriptions of Jesus are plotted in such a way that the movement of their narrative renders Jesus in just this way.

Accordingly, canonical narratives of encounters with the risen Jesus are plotted in such a way that their movement renders Jesus as risen bodily, but in a way discontinuous with the mode of bodiliness he is and has pre-Easter. As Hans-Joachim Eckstein points out, for example, Luke's way of indicating the discontinuity between Jesus' pre-Easter bodiliness and his post-Easter bodiliness fits the way that discontinuity is drawn in the other canonical stories of encounters with the risen Christ: "the Risen One no longer suffers, is not mortal, and is not subject to transience; he is not restricted to [physical] space and time, and he is not rooted in this world; rather he is depicted as living in the [eschatological] heavenly world" (2002, 119). The canonical narratives generally are so framed as to make clear that the living human personal body, identical with the pre-Easter Jesus, who is encountered post-Easter is a transfigured or glorified body that is in important ways discontinuous with the pre-Easter Jesus' body. Indeed, stress on the discontinuity between Jesus' pre-Easter and post-Easter bodiliness is directly, rather than inversely, related to stress on their continuity. This coheres with Paul's reason for contrasting "spiritual body" to "physical body": "flesh and blood cannot inherit the kingdom of God, nor does the perishable inherit the imperishable" (1 Cor. 15:50). Only an eschatologically glorified body can "inherit the kingdom of God" or "inherit the imperishable." As the proleptic intrusion of the eschatological reign of God into human creatures' quotidian proximate contexts, Jesus is not raised back into his old physical nature, tied to quotidian space, time, and matter, but rather into the borrowed time of God's eschatological future.

Two theological anthropological consequences follow from this. First, Jesus' "resurrected body" must not be confused conceptually with a resuscitated body. Canonical narratives of Jesus' ministry proclaiming the imminent in-breaking of God's eschatological rule include stories of healings, some of which extend to restoring to life those who had recently died—for example, Jairus's daughter (Mark 5:21–43; Luke 8:41–50); the widow's son in Nain (Luke 7:11–17); Lazarus (John 11:1–44). These may serve as signs that the in-breaking is near, or as signs that Jesus has the authority to proclaim that it is near. However, they are resuscitations, not resurrections of eschatologically transfigured or glorified bodies. They do not have the significance of being the concrete way in which God inaugurates fulfillment of eschatological blessing (without fully actualizing it).

A second theological point follows. If fulfillment of God's promise of eschatological blessing has actually been inaugurated in the bodily resurrection of Jesus, then Jesus' adopted human brothers and sisters are now being drawn by the triune God into the same eschatological consummation. Bodily resurrection as eschatologically transfigured or glorified bodies is social and communal.

Future full actualization of that consummation entails their bodily resurrection also as eschatologically transfigured or glorified bodies in community-in-communion in the same relation to God that Jesus has—that is, their finite participation in the life of the triune God. Canonical Christian Holy scriptural texts do not suggest that Jesus' bodily resurrection "causes" others' bodily resurrection. Rather, Paul in particular characterizes Jesus' bodily resurrection as the "first fruits" of, as it were, the eschatological harvest. He is the first, but he is not bodily resurrected alone. He is resurrected in and with community.

In addition to their necessity in regard to the significance of Jesus' bodily resurrection, the discontinuities between the post- and pre-Easter Jesus that canonical narratives build into their accounts of encounters with the bodily risen Jesus are necessary for recognition of the one who is encountered. This point needs to be developed in two steps. The first step in making this point is to note that there is no one kind of experience of an appearance of this resurrected glorified body that is the basis or ground of belief in Jesus' resurrection. In the canonical accounts, encounters with this body take many different forms, ranging "from visions of light to the appearance of a person with all the impressions of palpability" (Welker 2002, 37). Furthermore, Frank Crusemann argues, the pattern in Luke, exemplified by the story of two disciples' encounter with the risen Jesus on the road to Emmaus (24:13–35), shows that "no faith [in the resurrection of Jesus] is evoked by the experience of the resurrection without the mediation of Scripture" (2002, 93). He contends that this pattern is continued in the account in Acts of Saul's encounter with the risen Christ, and is consistent with Paul's own principle (e.g., in 1 Cor. 4:6) that nothing to which he testifies (including, presumably, his own experience) goes beyond what is already in Scripture (i.e., Torah and the Prophets). The conviction that the bodily risen Christ is "with us" comes, not from some kind of "experience of the risen Christ," but from a variety of kinds of appearance that are mediated by and shaped by Scripture (see Welker 2002, 37).

The second step in showing that discontinuities between the post- and pre-Easter bodied Jesus are necessary for recognition of the one who is encountered is to show the function of a dialectic between continuities and discontinuities in the movement of canonical narratives of encounter with the risen Jesus. Luke provides an especially clear example. In Luke 24:39, the risen Jesus shows the scars on his hands and feet so that they recognize him as their crucified Lord: "Look at my hands and my feet; see that it is I myself." In Luke 24:30–31 the disciples on the road to Emmaus identify Jesus at the moment when he repeats a physical action they have often seen before, breaking bread with a blessing and sharing it with them. In these cases the risen Jesus' disciples recognize him on the basis of continuities between the post-Easter resurrected Jesus' bodily features or action and those of the pre-Easter bodily crucified Jesus, and in the case of the disciples on the Emmaus road, their recognition of him explicitly comes against the background of Jesus' "opening the scriptures" to them.

Hans-Joachim Eckstein suggests, however, that bodily features continuous with those of the pre-Easter Jesus are not sufficient basis for the disciples' recognition of the one they encounter as the resurrected—that is, eschatologically transfigured or glorified—Jesus. Eckstein urges that in Luke's narrative it is simultaneously the case that in order for the disciples to recognize that the one they encounter is the bodily resurrected Jesus, it is necessary that discontinuities between the post- and pre-Easter Jesus also be stressed in the narrative. Against the background of "the Old Testament—Jewish—and there specifically apocalyptic—tradition" (2002, 121), Luke's narrative includes details that render an eschatologically transfigured or glorified body that can do things physical bodies cannot do, showing Jesus as one who has "already been raised into eschatological reality out of the grave on the third day. This is why the angels can reproach the women who in Easter morning search in vain for 'the *soma* [body] of the Lord Jesus' in the empty grave . . . (Luke 24:3; cf. 24:34): 'Why do you look for the living among the dead?' . . . "He is not here, but risen" . . . (Luke 24:5–6)." "The new reality of this resurrection implies such a fundamental transformation that the disciples do not [at first] recognize their Lord after the resurrection as the one they have known; instead, they identify him first of all and for the first time as the Risen One" and only after seeing his wounds as the same as Jesus the crucified one. Therefore the identity of the risen Lord cannot be grasped without recognizing the *discontinuity* of his physical existence" (2002, 119–20; emphasis in original).

In their diversity, canonical New Testament characterizations of encounters with the risen Jesus generally tell stories that move back and forth between accounts that seem to stress continuity between the risen postcrucifixion Jesus and the precrucifixion Jesus and accounts that stress discontinuity. Furthermore, both the continuities and the discontinuities are located precisely in Jesus' human body as crucified and as raised, given an adequately broad concept of "human body." I suggest that Eckstein's characterization of this dialectical use of narratives about Jesus' body in Luke's stories of encounters with the risen Jesus fit, *mutatis mutandis*, other such canonical stories of encounters with the risen Jesus, and with Paul's theological reflection on them, especially in 1 Corinthians 15. The larger theological anthropological import of this observation is that any account of what it is to be a fully actualized eschatologically consummated human creature should exhibit the same pattern and narrative logic.

It should be noted that there is disagreement in the tradition about whether the eschatological glorification or transfiguration of Jesus' body, which marks the discontinuity between the post-Easter Jesus and the pre-Easter Jesus that makes it difficult for the disciples to recognize Jesus, restores his body to a perfection that eliminates his wounds. It can be argued, for example, that the canonical narrative is so plotted that Jesus' body is not eschatologically glorified until he ascends to the Father. At that point, his wounded body is returned to its precrucifixion bodily completeness or perfection. Consequently, the risen crucified Jesus encountered post-Easter, who has not yet ascended, still has and can show his bodily wounds that make him recognizable as the one the disciples knew to have been crucified to death. The wounds are subsequently removed when he ascends to the Father.

The argument for this reading would be more persuasive, however, if the canonical Gospels' narratives shared the same narrative logic at this point in the narrative. But they do not. It is clear that the narrative of passion week,

Easter, and Pentecost in Luke–Acts is plotted as a sequence of three numerically distinct moments: trial and crucifixion, resurrection, ascension. One narrative strand in John seems to equate Jesus' being "lifted up" with his being put up on the cross rather than as a separate moment of his ascending to the Father (John 3:14; so, too, 12:32?); on the other hand, in John 20:17, the risen Jesus tells Mary Magdalene in their post-Easter encounter, "Do not hold on to me, because I have not yet ascended to the Father. But go to my brothers and say to them, 'I am ascending to my Father and your Father, to my God and your God,'" which obviously suggests a distinction between Jesus' resurrection and his ascension. However, it is not clearly entailed that Jesus' eschatological transfiguration comes only following his ascension. Mark's minimal narrative of Easter suggests no distinction between Jesus' resurrection and ascension. Matthew's slightly longer narrative of the disciples' post-Easter encounters with the risen Jesus makes no reference to an ascension in addition to Jesus' resurrection. It seems both exegetically and theologically dubious to harmonize these narratives by conflating them all into the narrative logic of Luke's account. Absent such harmonization, the narrative logics of canonical descriptions of Jesus' personal identity do not seem to warrant the claim that part of what he is as an eschatologically glorified living human body is grammatically paradigmatic of accounts of perfect—that is, absolutely complete—human bodies lacking all bodily imperfections.

The Proximate Context of Bodily Resurrected Jesus

In their larger narrative contexts in the canonical Gospels' accounts of "who" Jesus is, the significance of his resurrection is cosmic. The resurrection of the crucified Jesus is narrated as the concrete way in which God goes about actually inaugurating in the quotidian the fulfillment of God's long-promised eschatological consummation. Hence, Jesus' bodily resurrection is in itself *in concreto* the proleptic intrusion into the quotidian of the "new creation" of God's eschatological reign. It is its actual inauguration; it is not yet its full actualization. However, as the canonical stories tell it, Jesus' own bodily resurrection is the full actualization of his eschatological consummation in his glorified body already accomplished now, the sign of hope that the full actualization of the eschatological new creation as his and our proximate context, and the full actualization of our own eschatological consummation in the glorification of our own living bodies in community, will be realized. Thus, the bodily resurrected Jesus at once inaugurates and lives within his, and our, eschatological proximate context, a new creation, a new heaven and earth.

Canonical New Testament narratives of encounters with the risen crucified Jesus, and canonical theological reflection, mostly Pauline, on those narratives, make it clear that Jesus' resurrected bodily life, in virtue of God relating to him in eschatological blessing, is somehow more than his pre-Easter bodily life in virtue of God relating to him in creative blessing, even though God has not ceased also to relate to him in creative blessing. Inasmuch as Jesus' resurrection is not merely God's singular eschatological blessing on him, but is God's concrete particular way of inaugurating the actualization in and for creaturely quotidian proximate contexts of God's promise to draw them to eschatological consummation, this "more" may be generalized. John Polkinghorne captures well the point that must be made by such generalization when he observes that theological accounts of the "new heaven and earth" of God's eschatological reign, and of the resurrection of human creatures that is part of it, must express "sufficient discontinuity [from theological accounts of the creatureliness of human bodily life and its quotidian proximate contexts] to ensure that the new creation is not just a redundant repetition of the old" (2002, 50).

Part of that "more" lies in the character of the new creation of God's eschatological reign. God's relating to humankind in eschatological blessing locates them in a new heaven and earth where they live as glorified human bodies in a proximate context constituted by networks of interrelationships with fellow creatures. That new heaven and earth is as ontologically other than God as is the quotidian world constituted by God relating to it creatively. It, too, is a creaturely reality that is finite, radically contingent for its reality on God relating to it, in its finitude vulnerable to disintegration absent God's relating to it. It is also other than the creaturely quotidian world into which human creatures are born as God relates to them creatively. The new creation's otherness vis à vis the quotidian creaturely world is marked by the way in which it is "more." The way in which it is more than human creatures' morally ambiguous quotidian proximate contexts is marked by the justice, peace, and love that characterize the community-in-intimate-communion that constitutes the life of the triune God.

At the same time, the movement of canonical narratives of encounters with the risen crucified Jesus, as the "grammatical" paradigm of humanity in the "new creation," supports Polkinghorne's generalization (2002, 50) that the "new creation arises *ex vetere*, as the redeemed transformation of the old creation, and not as a second, totally new, creation *ex nihilo*." This coheres with the contention of this entire anthropological project that the logic of the relations among Christian beliefs entails that the triune God relating in eschatological blessing necessarily presupposes beliefs about the triune God relating in creative blessing, whereas beliefs about God relating in creative blessing do not necessarily entail beliefs about God relating in eschatological blessing. The triune God's faithful and trustworthy self-consistency in relating freely in wise and creative love entails that God's relating in eschatological blessing respects the creaturely integrity of that to which God is relating. If God does indeed relate in eschatological blessing, that is an added gift to that to which God also relates in creative blessing. In one sense of the term, it is grace. That is why the new creation that characterizes actualization of God's eschatological reign is not strictly speaking *creatio ex nihilo* but rather *creatio ex vetere*. The continuity-within-discontinuity that marks the relation between Jesus' post-Easter and pre-Easter human bodiliness is itself located within the embracing continuity of the triune God's faithful self-consistency in the significantly different, freely loving ways in which God relates.

Consequently, the triune God's relating to draw all that is not God to eschatological consummation presupposes and takes place within terms set by God's relating creatively to all that is not God, and not the other way around. What is eschatologically consummated is what is created, in this case, living human personal bodies interacting both with one another in community and with their proximate contexts. In relating to them in eschatological blessing, the triune God engages the whole of each living human creaturely body in community as created. God does not engage some particular God-specific, or Holy Spirit–specific, human capacity to relate to God. Nor does the triune God relating to human creatures in eschatological blessing require as a precondition the gift of such a capacity from God. In relating in eschatological blessing, the triune God just gives itself in a complex threefold way. What God relates to in eschatological blessing is what is constituted by God relating creatively.

The Ultimate Context of Bodily Resurrected Jesus

The ultimate context of the risen human Jesus, and of all human beings whose eschatological consummation is fully actualized in glorified bodies within the proximate context of the new creation of God's eschatological reign, is the triune God relating to him and to them in eschatological blessing. The dialectic between God relating to them in creative blessing and God relating in eschatological blessing is misunderstood if it is considered in abstraction from the context of a theocentric continuity that embraces the dialectic. That continuity is constituted by the fact that it is the self-same triune God that relates to Jesus in his "physical" bodily humanity in his quotidian proximate contexts in creative blessing and to Jesus in eschatological blessing in his glorified bodily humanity in the proximate context of the new creation. It is the self-same triune God who relates to all human beings both as physical living human personal bodies in their quotidian proximate contexts and as physical living human bodies being drawn to eschatological consummation that is eventually fully actualized in their eschatological consummation as glorified bodies in the proximate context of the fully actualized new creation of God's eschatological reign.

Part of the force of the claim that the triune God relating in eschatological blessing as well as in creative blessing is the ultimate context in which Jesus lives as an eschatologically glorified or, in Paul's term, "spiritual," body is that the triune God relating to him is the ultimate basis of the continuity between the post-Easter Jesus and the pre-Easter Jesus. It was noted above that, although canonical New Testament texts use the term "body" to mark this continuity, that does not imply that Jesus' body is the principle of continuity that explains his continuity-through-radical-discontinuity or, to turn it around, the continuity that embraces the discontinuity, between Good Friday and Easter. Part 1 of this project urged that God relating creatively to what is other than God such that it is constitutive of the actual reality of that which is other than God is a relation internal to the concrete actual reality of the creature. For that reason, it is urged, proposals about ways in which the triune God relates to all else do not entail proposals of ways in which God necessarily violates the ontological integrity of that to which God relates. On the contrary, properly understood, God's faithfulness to God's self-commitment to creatures' well-being entails that in God's ways of relating to that which is not God constitutes their actual being rather than threatening their ontological integrity. In the order of being, then, the ultimate explanation of the continuity of the post-Easter Jesus with the pre-Easter Jesus is the identity, the faithfulness of the self-same triune God who relates to Jesus in both creative and eschatological blessing. This claim does not yet amount to the proposal of a systematic metaphysical theory explaining how God's unbroken relating to Jesus in his creaturely bodily humanity secures the continuity of that body through the discontinuity marked by his death and by the eschatological transfiguration or glorification of his body. The claim is limited to identifying the theological theme that is centrally important because it must frame any such metaphysical proposal: ultimately that continuity is based on the continuity of the faithful constancy of the one self-same triune God in relating to all else in both creative and eschatological blessing.

To propose that canonical narratives of encounters with the risen crucified Jesus are grammatically paradigmatic for secondary theological remarks about human creatures' fully actualized eschatological consummation generally, and about their eschatological proximate context, is to suggest that the same theological theme should frame theological remarks about the continuities between the post- and preresurrection living human personal bodies generally, and between their proximate context in the eschatological new creation and their creaturely quotidian proximate contexts. Ultimately, the basis of these continuities lies in the faithfulness of the self-same God relating to them in both creative and eschatological blessing. So, too, just as human creatures' continued actual existence as creatures in their creaturely quotidian proximate contexts ultimately is based on God relating to them creatively, the theological claim that resurrected bodies are imperishable is grounded in the theological claim that the triune God is faithful in sustaining human creatures, in and with their proximate contexts, in community-in-communion with God. It is grounded, that is, in a claim about humankind's ultimate context.

Actual Living Human Personal Bodies Whose Eschatological Consummation is Fully Actualized

Any secondary theological effort to tease out the anthropological implications of the claim that the triune God relates to all that is not God to draw it to eschatological consummation walks a knife edge between vacuity and self-indulgent fantasy. The resurrection of the crucified Jesus of Nazareth in his humanity—that is, raised bodily, understood in ways guided by the canonical Gospels' narratives of encounters with the risen Jesus that identify his resurrection as the concrete way in which God inaugurates the fulfillment of promised eschatological blessing—is the principal ground for hope for the full eschatological consummation of all humankind. Explication of the anthropological implications of that hope is vacuous if no coherent conceptual content can be provided. The challenge at this point is not to persuade that claims about Jesus' resurrection or about humankind's being drawn to eschatological consummation are true. More basically, the challenge is to show that such claims have any articulable, coherent content.

On the other hand, there are virtually no grounds on which to warrant proposals that characterize eschatologically transfigured or glorified human personal bodily life and its proximate context in any determinate way. Efforts to do so are usually guided by imagery and symbolism used in canonical Christian

Holy Scripture. However, the literary and historical contexts of this imagery decisively show that they are to be read at most as metaphors and rhetorical tropes that are simply misinterpreted if construed as providing conceptual framing for claims about eschatological existence and its context. More often than not, focus on that imagery in theology has sponsored fantasy pictures of resurrection life in the new heaven and earth that may be engaging and even admirable for their imaginative originality, but too often tend to promote forms of piety, consolation, and pastoral care whose faithfulness to the canonical narratives of God's ways of relating to all else are dubious, and whose psychological consequences are too often hurtful. If there are relatively clear proposals that can be made about the Christian concept of the fully actualized eschatological consummation of human personal bodies in community, they would go some way both toward showing that the concept is not vacuous and toward outlining the internal logic or grammar of Christian beliefs that should steer imaginative speculation away from the more misleading and dangerous fantasies.

I suggest that some such relatively clear proposals about the fully actualized eschatological consummation of human personal bodies in community can be formulated at an extremely abstract, formal level and only in analogical discourse. They can be formulated by focusing on the intersection among (1) the features of what it is to be an actual living human personal body in community that are outlined in chapter 6 and (2) some aspects of current evolutionary biology's account of the bare minimal conditions that must be met for something to be called "life," as that is also outlined in chapter 6; and (3) by remarks made above about the logic of relations among some of the relevant, more basic, theological claims, when (4) the "intersecting" of these three is guided by the dialectic between the continuity and the discontinuity of post-Easter Jesus and pre-Easter Jesus in canonical accounts of encounters with the risen Jesus, as outlined above. Canonical accounts of encounters with the risen Jesus are privileged inasmuch as the One they identify is grammatically paradigmatic for theological accounts of fully actualized eschatological consummation of humankind generally.

That is the procedure followed in the proposals sketched in chapter 15A and again in the three codas of this work. It cannot be stressed too often that the resulting outline of what eschatologically fully consummated living human personal bodies are is highly formal. It has no empirical content. Indeed, it is difficult to know what would count as empirical content in regard to living bodies that are not physical. Its key concepts—for example, "energy," "homeostasis," "entropy"—are used in analogical ways. It neither offers nor implies any particular metaphysical explanations of how eschatologically glorified living human bodies are continuous with their pre-mortem quotidian physical mode, nor how they act and interact, nor how they communicate, know, recognize one another, experience emotions and passions such as love and joy, and so on. What it does seek to show is that an internally coherent conceptual scheme can be formulated that can be used, making allowances for the fact that many of its key concepts are used analogically, to make certain theological claims about fully consummated eschatological bodily life in ways that make sense—that are intelligible, given certain coherent assumptions, and are not vacuous:

1. It is possible to conceive coherently an integral, relatively self-regulating and self-directing set of energy systems having the functions and organization essential to life, that is the resurrection of one and the same human quotidian body that had died, but is continuous with it only through the discontinuities of having a non-carbon-based biochemistry and of no longer being subject to evolution. Central to the relatively self-regulating and self-directing set of energy systems having the functions and organization essential to life is the double process of (1) self-regulating its intake and outflow of energy to resist entropic forces and maintain the homeostasis of its specific function and organization and of (2) teleonomic self-directing activity seeking both sources of energy in its proximate context and knowledge about its proximate context and its energy resources.

2. It is possible to conceive coherently that, continuous with the way quotidian physical living bodies are internally related to the proximate contexts within which they find sources for the energy they require to overcome entropic forces, eschatologically glorified bodies also are internally related to the proximate contexts within which they find sources for the energy they require to overcome entropic forces. The canonical scriptural metaphors for the eschatologically consummated proximate context are "new creation" and "new heaven and earth." God relating to eschatologically glorified bodies in their proximate context is their ultimate context, ultimately the source on which they depend for their life in their creaturely finitude.

3. It is possible to conceive coherently that, if resurrected human bodies are said to be "living" in an analogous sense of "life," they must be conceived to be dependent in part on relationships with other creatures that are their sources of the kinds of energy they need, and to be capable of knowing what they need and recognizing such sources when they encounter them. It is within the eschatological proximate context of the new heaven and earth of God's eschatological reign that resurrected human bodies find those sources outside themselves of the energies they require. What the positive character of creaturely energy sources might be in a new heaven and earth can only be a field for speculation, and hardly a fruitful one. What may be said negatively, however, is that the source of energy for the sets of energy systems that constitute eschatologically consummated living human personal bodies as finite centers of power will not lie in the carbon-based biochemistry of the evolving living matter we know and on which our bodily lives depend in all the complexity of their life.

4. It is possible to conceive coherently that, continuous with human creatures' quotidian proximate contexts, the new creation, the proximate context of which an eschatologically glorified body is a part, is finite in the way all creatures are in the ultimate context of the triune God relating to them in a threefold way, and is radically dependent on that divine relating for its reality and value.

5. It is possible to conceive coherently that, in consequence of the creaturely finitude of its proximate context (the new creation), an eschatologically glorified body's dependence on creaturely sources of energy outside itself entails (in continuity with like quotidian bodily life) that it is inherently mortal. As a mode of life, it is marked by a tension between entropic forces, on one side, and

energy to resist those forces on the other. It must be understood that entropy, which is a concept that gets its meaning in its use in physical theory, must be used analogically here because, discontinuous with quotidian physical living bodies, eschatologically glorified bodies do not depend on a carbon-based physical energy system. Nonetheless, in continuity with quotidian physical living bodies, eschatologically glorified bodies are creatures that are inherently mortal in the sense of being inherently vulnerable to disintegration. If disintegration is a kind of death, then the possibility of their death is as essential to what an eschatologically glorified body is as it is essential to what a quotidian physical body is. Eschatologically glorified living bodies are as fully finite creatures as are quotidian physical living bodies.

6. It is possible to conceive coherently that, in continuity with quotidian physical living bodies, eschatologically glorified living bodies are finite in a second way. They are conditioned, and in that sense limited or hemmed in, by the fact that they are inherently relational, interacting with fellow human resurrected creatures in community-in-communion through which they give and receive energy, not only being enlivened but having their concretely particular lives growing in degrees of intensity, richness, and depth of community-in-communion.

7. It is possible to conceive coherently that, in discontinuity with a living physical body, and by virtue of God continuously relating to it in eschatological blessing in addition to relating to it in creative blessing, an eschatologically consummated living human personal body is, in the apostle Paul's terms, "imperishable" and "powerful" in the sense that it is an integral set of energy systems that does not in fact disintegrate or die, although in its finitude it is nonetheless vulnerable to disintegration and death. Thus, the claim that resurrected bodies are "imperishable" is grounded in a claim about the triune God's faithfulness in sustaining human creatures, in and with their proximate contexts, in community-in-communion with God. It is grounded, that is, in a claim about humankind's ultimate context.

8. It is possible to conceive coherently that, discontinuous with pre-mortem quotidian living physical bodies, lacking physical energy systems, and in particular carbon-based ones, eschatologically consummated human bodies do not depend on predation for their energy source. This coheres with such canonical scriptural tropes as, "The wolf shall live with the lamb, the leopard shall lie down with the kid, and the calf and the lion and the fatling together, and a little child shall lead them" (Isa. 11:6), and "The wolf and the lamb shall feed together, the lion shall eat straw like the ox" (Isa. 65:25). Correlatively, no other living bodies, from microbes to lions, need to depend on them or their kind for their own sources of energy.

9. It is possible to conceive coherently that, discontinuous with pre-mortem quotidian living physical bodies, eschatologically glorified living bodies that lack carbon-based physical energy systems would have no occasion for physical pain because they do not have the biochemical basis for it. This coheres with the canonical scriptural trope, "Death will be no more; mourning and crying and pain will be no more, for the first things have passed away" (Rev. 21:4b; cf. Isa. 25:8; 35:10). Nor would they have occasion for mourning and grief because

no one dies in the proximate context constituted by the eschatological new heaven and earth, in which, having some other (unknown to us) creaturely source of the energies they need, neither resurrected human living bodies nor any other kind of living bodies would depend on other living bodies for their sources of energy.

10. It is possible to conceive coherently that, continuous with the range of kinds of energy systems that constitute quotidian living physical bodies, the set of energy systems that need to be self-governed and self-directed to constitute a life as complex as that of living human bodies includes not only bodily, but also mental, social, cultural, and expressive systems of energy.

11. It is possible to conceive coherently that, continuous with quotidian physical living bodies, what such eschatologically glorified living bodies are as God-related bodies, whether pre- or postresurrection, empowers both them and the others for the sociality of community-in-communion. It empowers them to be recognizable, not merely as individual instances of a kind ("human"), but as the unsubstitutable personal bodies they are, whose unconditional dignity and worth in virtue of God's relation to them is to be unqualifiedly respected.

12. It is possible to conceive coherently that, in continuity with quotidian physical living bodies, each eschatologically glorified living body has its own singular personal identity that is defined by what it has done and undergone in the past. Its personal identity in its concrete particularity and singularity is best described in narratives that render the interplay between its interactions and its circumstances. Although discontinuous with quotidian physical living bodies, it has no DNA by which to classify it as human, it is an essential feature of its personal identity that the physical living personal body of which it is the eschatologically glorified mode did have the DNA of *Homo sapiens*. Similarly, although biological gender has no physical role to play in a proximate context in which there is no need for propagation in order to continue humankind across time (see Matt. 22:30, "For in the resurrection they neither marry nor are given in marriage, but are like angels in heaven," read in light of the interpretation of Gen. 1:27–28 that understands God's creation of humankind as male and female in relation to God's command to be fruitful and multiply), it is an essential feature of its personal identity that the premortem physical living personal body, of which it is the eschatologically glorified mode, did have some biological gender.

13. It is possible to conceive coherently that, continuous with quotidian physical living bodies, despite major discontinuities, the set of energy systems includes not only bodily, but also mental, social, cultural, and expressive systems of energy that empower eschatologically glorified living bodies to be capable of being so formed by what they have done and undergone, and how they have responded to what they have undergone, that their concrete ways of interrelating are determined by the particular unsubstitutable personal identities they have come to be.

14. It is possible to conceive coherently that, continuous with quotidian physical living bodies, the set of energy systems includes not only bodily, but also mental, social, cultural, and expressive systems of energy that empower eschatologically glorified living bodies to be capable of relating to other resurrected

living human bodies in ways that are specifically appropriate to the others' concrete, particular, unsubstitutable personal identities. In that regard, while their relations to one another in their community-in-communion are all equally and unqualifiedly just, they need not be uniform. In being appropriate to the other's concrete particularity, their relating is differentiated according to that particularity, so that it is justly fit to the others' particular capacities and needs.

15. It is possible to conceive coherently that, discontinuous with quotidian physical living bodies, what eschatologically glorified bodies are empowers them, as Gregory of Nyssa suggested, endlessly to change, grow, and deepen in their creaturely participation in the communion-in-community that constitutes the life of the triune God. This coheres with the canonical scriptural trope, "And all of us, with unveiled faces, seeing the glory of the Lord as though reflected in a mirror, are being transformed into the same image [i.e., Christ] from one degree of glory to another; for this comes from the Lord, the Spirit" (2 Cor. 3:18).

16. Finally, it is possible to conceive coherently that the continuity that embraces the discontinuities between eschatologically glorified living bodies and the quotidian physical living bodies of which they are the eschatological mode is grounded in the fact that both are located within three more ontologically basic and embracing continuities that are entailed by the three ways in which they are related to by the triune God. In a theocentric theological anthropololgy, being related to by God in a threefold way is an inherent property of specifically human being, whether in the quotidian or the glorified mode. The complex way in which the triune God relates to actual living human personal bodies entails that, whether they are material bodies or spiritual bodies, they are always and unconditionally (a) on a par with all realities other than God in regard to the unqualified immediacy and freedom of God's relating, (b) are delighted in and deemed "good" by God, and are (c) freely given gifts, to whose well-being God is faithfully self-committed. These three features of what human beings are—that is, three aspects of their property of being actively related to by God—undergird the features that are discontinuous in a continuity of resurrected living human bodies with created living human bodies.

Realistic Eschatology?

It has been conventional to classify theological eschatologies as "realized eschatologies" or as "realistic futurist eschatologies." The categories are ambiguous, and in any case the proposals promoted here about the anthropological implications of the Christian claim that God relates in eschatological blessing to all that is not God do not fit easily in either one. If the contrast between "realized" and "realistic futurist" is understood in strictly temporal terms (with the stress on "futurist"), these proposals do not fall into either category. The proposals advanced here are guided by the tension, which drives the narrative movement of canonical New Testament narratives of God relating to draw all else to eschatological consummation, between the actual inauguration now of God's fulfillment of the promise of eschatological blessing, on one side, and the full actualization of that promise that is not yet, on the other. The inauguration is "realized," but the full actualization is "future."

However, the contrast between "realized" and "realistic future," with the stress on "realistic," may be understood in an experiential way. In that case, a realized eschatology is an eschatology that proposes that the eschatological new creation, and with it glorified eschatological life, may be experienced here and now. That, in turn, may be understood in an objectivist, ontologically realist, way as a transformation of humankind's proximate context that they may or may not experience, but obtains objectively whether they are conscious of it or not. Or it may be understood as an existential transformation that human creatures may experience now, a transformation into genuinely authentic existence marked by true freedom, that marks the end (eschaton) of bondage in inauthentic, unfree existence. In that case, the new creation obtains just insofar as one undergoes it existentially in a transformation of one's subjectivity. Alternatively, a realistic futurist eschatology is an eschatology that proposes that the eschatological new creation, and with it glorified eschatological life, can be experienced only at some point in the future and as a state of affairs that is real, independently of one's consciousness of it. However, "realistic" turns out to be ambiguous here. It may be used formally, without implying anything either about what it is like to experience the new creation or the nature of what is experienced. Or "realistic" may signify that what is experienced empirically conforms to selected images from canonical scriptural eschatological texts. In the latter case, to characterize a set of theological eschatological proposals as "realistic futurist" often amounts to charging them with being biblically literalist.

On their not-yet side, the proposals promoted here about the implications of Christian claims about humankind's fully actualized eschatological consummation for the anthropological "What?" question imply futurist claims that are ontologically realist. However, while these proposals' dialectical relation to their now really inaugurated side commits them to being framed in ways consistent with what human beings are by virtue of God's logically prior active relating to them creatively, they remain formal and abstract proposals. They imply no particular theses about either the character of experience of fully actualized eschatological consummation or the nature of what is experienced.

Theological Loose Ends

Theological reflection in chapter 15A on who we are and what we are ends well before all of its lines of thought have been woven neatly and tightly together. In particular, it leaves lines of thought at loose ends concerning two major issues. They are two examples (a third from part 1 will be mentioned briefly below as well) of a large class of theological loose ends in this book. Some rationale needs to be offered for not even trying to tie them up.

The Freedom of the Resurrected

The first example of theological loose ends concerns the freedom of resurrected personal bodies. This set of loose ends generates the following question. Given that prior to their resurrection personal bodies exhibit the power to enact, as their concrete existential hows, orientations to their proximate contexts that are contrary to their basic personal identities as ones elect by

God for eschatological glory, should we affirm that having been transformed by their resurrection they continue to have this power? As raised bodily from the dead, could their existential hows nonetheless continue, in effect, to reject and contradict their who?

The question has its importance. One topic that is at stake in this question is the nature of the freedom or freedoms that are inherent in the "what" of personal bodies' finite creatureliness.

Nonetheless, the question was left open on the grounds that the theological commitments explored in this part of the book do not lead to any one answer. Instead, they provide a set of theological claims that any proposed answer must take into account and with which it must be coherent in order to be acceptable. These theological desiderata for an acceptable answer include the following:

— The triune God relates to finite creaturely personal bodies in community to draw them and their proximate contexts to eschatological consummation. "Finite creaturely personal bodies" designates what it is that God draws to this consummation.

— As related to by the triune God drawing them to eschatological glory, human creatures' personal identities are, in part, "ones elect by God for eschatological community in a shared participation in the communion that constitutes the triune God's life." That is, in part, their "who."

— Personal bodies orient themselves in and to their proximate contexts by an array of practices in which they engage in those contexts. Particular enactments of those practices are personal bodies' existential hows.

— Personal bodies exhibit the power to enact practices in their proximate contexts that are at cross-grain to their personal identities as related to by God. Doing so constitutes them as radically distorted personal bodies— that is, as sinners sinning.

— The power to be self-distorting in this way is inherent in what personal bodies are by virtue of the triune God's creative relating to them.

— Full actualization of personal bodies' eschatological consummation, which is now actually inaugurated but not yet actualized, involves their radical transformation, expressed by "bodily resurrection."

The open question, basically, is whether, when the sixth bullet point obtains, the fifth must not continue to obtain also, implying the possibility that when the sixth obtains, the fourth might also obtain.

This set of theological proposals does not imply any one answer to this question. Building on this set of theological proposals, proposed answers would probably have to rely on additional, probably metaphysical, claims whose warrants lie outside the convictions by which this set of theological proposals are warranted in the first place—namely, that the triune God actively relates to all that is not God in a peculiar threefold way.

Relying on such additional claims is not in itself theologically objectionable. However, the set of theological proposals in this list is, for theological purposes, negatively normative. Any proposed answer that set aside or necessarily contradicted any of these theological proposals would be unacceptable. On the other hand, this set of theological proposals may not be positively definitive. That is, it may not by itself provide sufficient basis on which to decide which of all possible answers that are coherent with it is theologically preferable. That may be decideable on other grounds, but not on the grounds provided by this set of theological remarks.

Continuity in Discontinuity

The last section of the previous chapter gives a second example of loose ends in these theological anthropological remarks. God's promised eschatological blessing involves a transformation of personal bodies in their proximate contexts so radical as to be called a new creation and a new birth. This suggests discontinuity between the old and the new. Yet the claim that God gives this blessing to precisely creaturely personal bodies implies a strong continuity between the creatures constituted by God's creative blessing and the creatures transformed by God's eschatological blessing. How is continuity to be reconciled with discontinuity? Let us call this the "eschatological continuity question."

The question has its theological importance. One topic that is at stake in the answer accepted to this question is personal bodies' accountability before God for the way their existential hows orient them in their proximate and ultimate contexts. If an eschatologically transfigured personal body is simply discontinuous with its pretransfigured distorted condition, then it is difficult to see how it is the same personal body transfigured, in contradistinction to an ontologically altogether distinct personal body. And if it is not strictly speaking the same personal body, it is difficult to see how it is accountable for another personal body's orientations.

Nonetheless, the question was left open on the grounds that the theological commitments explored in this part of the book do not lead to any one answer. Instead, they provide a set of theological claims that any proposed answer must take into account and with which it must be coherent in order to be acceptable. These theological desiderata of an acceptable answer include:

— The eschatological transformation that personal bodies undergo involves at least the following discontinuities from their preresurrection condition: They are not vulnerable to separation from God's love; they are not subject to violation of any sort, especially grievous loss, suffering, and death.

— What is continuous is personal identity. It is the same basic personal identity in the new creation that it was in the old. The one who is eschatologically glorified must be the same who as is called, in being created, to be wise in action for the well-being of its proximate contexts, who is elected for eschatological consummation and therewith also subject to a decisive and final judgment, and as one whose sinful distortions and estrangements have been reconciled.

— The eschatologically transformed personal body must be the same "what" as the creaturely personal body. Because of the logical priority of God creating to God eschatologically consummating, the basis of the continuity must have something to do with personal bodies' creaturely "what." However, just what it is about personal bodies' "what" that is the basis of continuity through the discontinuity of eschatological transformation is far from clear.

— Because that which is eschatologically blessed is the "same" as that which is created, whatever discontinuity eschatological transformation brings, the transformed ones must remain finite even as it is eschtologically glorified—that is, must remain radically dependent on God as the ground of their reality and value and interdependent with fellow creatures in common proximate contexts. Furthermore, that which is the basis of the creatures' continuity in transformation must itself be creaturely (i.e., it is not a divine principle somehow resident in the creature).

— Because what are transformed are personal bodies in their proximate contexts, as transformed they must in some sense be bodied, as they are bodied as created. This is the force of traditional Christian witness to the resurrection of the body. It does not necessarily imply that the body is the basis of continuity through eschatological transformation. It does necessarily have implications for the nature of the discontinuity involved here. It does imply that there is no relevant transformation of personal bodies unless, as transformed, they are still in some sense bodied.

— Because eschatologically transformed personal bodies are a community in communion, and because the love that constitutes that communion is by definition love for particular identifiable and recognizable other personal bodies, they must in their transformed state be just as capable of communicating with one another and of recognizing and identifying one another as human creatures are who have not been thus transformed.

— Because what is transformed are living personal bodies, the major sign of whose finitude is their mortality, their eschatological transformation cannot be construed to involve a denial that they had truly died or a denial that, as resurrected creatures, they continue to be subject to the logical and ontological possibility of ceasing to be. However, this remark does not clarify what happens to a personal body in its dying and death precisely in its relating to God and being related to by God.

Given the first point, the open question, basically, is what is it in the second and third points that is the basis for the final four?

Like the first case, here too the set of theological claims does not imply any one answer to the question. Building on this set of theological claims, proposed answers would probably have to rely on additional, probably metaphysical, claims whose warrants lie outside the convictions by which the set of theological claims are warranted—namely, that the triune God actively relates to all that is not God in a peculiar threefold way. Here too, reliance on such additional claims is not in itself theologically problematic.

However, the set of theological claims here serves to rule out some possible answers. Any proposed answer that sets aside or necessarily contradicts any of the theological claims would be unacceptable. On the other hand, this set of theological claims may not by itself provide sufficient basis on which to decide which of all possible answers that are coherent with it is theologically preferable. While that may be decideable on other grounds, it is not on grounds provided by this set of theological remarks.

Interconnected Loose Ends

The loose ends left by keeping these two questions open may well be interconnected in such a way that an answer to one question would have a bearing on the answer to the other. Indeed, they may be interconnected in ways that connect them also to the loose ends that generate a third question left open in chapter 14.

Suppose, for example, that there were strong reasons to affirm that eschatologically transformed personal bodies do retain the power to orient themselves to their new eschatological proximate context in ways that are inappropriate responses to the triune God drawing them to eschatological glory, and therefore retain the power to live in contradiction to, at cross-grain with, their basic personal identities as ones elected for eschatological glory. In short, suppose that there were strong reasons to affirm that while personal bodies are universally elected by God for eschatological glory, some when resurrected may in fact continue to damn themselves—that is, may continue to estrange themselves from God, from themselves, and from their neighbors. In that case, whatever is accepted in answer to the second question about the basis of personal bodies' continuity through the discontinuities of eschatological transformation must at least have the character of preserving their power to continue to respond inappropriately to God. This is one way in which the first set of loose ends may be interconnected with the second.

Conversely, suppose that there are good reasons to adopt the following answer to the question about the basis of personal bodies' continuity through the discontinuities of eschatological transformation: The self-same self-aware consciousness persists throughout the transformation. A personal body's physical body, including the brain, dies and is replaced with something different but analogous (St. Paul's "spiritual body"; the specifics of the difference need not concern us at this point), while the person's self-aware consciousness remains the same throughout. Of course, what counts as "sameness" of consciousness would have to be specified, but, again, it need not be specified for our purposes here. If arguments for such an answer were deemed persuasive, and if it were by virtue of its self-aware consciousness that a personal body had the power or powers to respond to God inappropriately before death, then it would retain those powers when eschatologically transformed. In that case, the second set of loose ends would be interconnected with the first set in that an answer accepted to the second question implies an answer to the first.

Answers to the two questions would be similarly interconnected were an acceptable answer to the second question cast in terms of a substantial soul. The body may die, but the self-same soul, though changed in many of its accidental properties, continues substantially unchanged. If a personal body's power or powers to respond to God inappropriately were seated in and essential to its substantial soul, then it would retain those powers in eschatological glory. In that case, also, an answer to the first question is implied in the answer accepted to the second.

Clearly, these observations about possible interconnectedness among the loose ends left dangling by two questions left open in the previous chapter suggest that they may also be interconnected with additional loose ends left by questions kept open in part 1.

For example, the question was left open whether it is appropriate to use some version of a metaphysical distinction between body and soul to articulate Christian theological remarks about human creatures as living bodies. My contention was that the theological commitments that generate an understanding of human beings as bodied creatures do not necessarily entail such a body/soul distinction, but that there may be other considerations that amply warrant use of such a distinction in theological anthropology. Philosophically impressive arguments in support of the importance of just that distinction in theological anthropology have been proposed by John W. Cooper (1989) and Stephen T. Davis (1993). These arguments quite properly rely on largely metaphysical considerations that are not grounded in or limited to the theologically basic claims about the triune God's three ways of relating to humankind, claims that are the basis of the anthropological remarks promoted in this project. Clearly, if there are strong arguments for a metaphysics of human persons that entails a distinction between a human body and a human substantial soul, the same arguments may also warrant appealing to the soul as the basis of human persons' continuity through the discontinuities of eschatological transformation. In this way, the types of loose ends left by all three of the open questions identified here would turn out to be interconnected.

The relations among these sets of loose ends are even more complex. They are left by open questions that may be interconnected with a nest of questions about God that were left open in chapters 2 and 3A.

To see how this might be, suppose that arguments in support of yet another type of answer were deemed persuasive in regard to the question about personal bodies' continuity through eschatological transformation. Suppose the following is proposed: Personal bodies' continuity through eschatological transformation depends solely on the triune God ongoingly relating to them creatively. If God relates in creative love to each reality other than God in its particularity, and if God is self-committed to both the creaturely well-being and the eschatological flourishing of each creature, and if nothing can separate us from the love of God (Rom. 8:39b), then God's sustaining each creature in its particularity is all that is needed to account for its continuity through eschatological transformation. In the case of personal bodies, no basis for that continuity needs to be found within their creaturely "what" because it lies eccentrically in the triune God's active creative relating to them.

What would such a proposal imply in answer to the other question we first considered—that is, the question whether eschatologically transformed creatures retain the power to respond inappropriately to God relating to them? As it stands, it is unclear that it implies any answer to that question, which is to say, it is unclear whether such a proposal connects the loose ends left by these two questions. The answer would depend in part on whether God can self-consistently deprive eschatologically transforming personal bodies of such powers.

However, a decision about whether God can self-consistently deprive transformed personal bodies of such powers must be based on answers to a nest of questions about God that were left open by the discussion of the triunity of God in chapters 2 and 3A. In particular, it seems to me, whether God can self-consistently deprive transformed personal bodies of such powers depends on how God's causal efficacy in relation to all that is not God is explained. Such an explanation of God's causal actions probably entails an explanation of the relation between God's "intellect" and "will" in God's causal actions. Is there a difference in reality between God's intellect and God's will? If there is a real difference, is one more basic than the other? Is it coherent, for example, to hold both (a) that God knows that eschatologically transformed personal bodies' full flourishing lies in responding appropriately to God, which is their greatest good, and (b) that God wills to transform personal bodies eschatologically in such a way that they retain their powers to refuse to respond to God appropriately—that is, so that they may not realize their greatest good? Is it coherent, for another example, to hold both (a) that God can will that every eschatologically transformed personal body respond appropriately to God, and (b) that nonetheless God knows that certain eschatologically transformed personal bodies will exercise their power to refuse to respond appropriately to God? Arguments for proposed answers to such questions properly rely on metaphysical theses that are not derived from the claims about the triune God's three modes of relating to all that is not God, Christian theological claims that are the basis of these anthropological remarks. None of these and related questions were addressed in chapters 2 and 3A. Leaving them open left a lot of loose ends in the discussion of God that are interconnected with the loose ends left by keeping open the three questions noted above insofar as God's causal efficacy is involved in their answers.

Justifying Open Questions and Loose Ends

These types of loose ends (and doubtless many others) have been left by questions kept open by the anthropological remarks proposed in this book. Having such loose ends in a theological discussion can be justified only by a justification for keeping certain legitimate theological questions open while arguing the correctness of certain proposed answers to others.

The justification lies in the nature of the enterprise. The overall aim of this project is to identify what, if any, anthropological claims are in some sense nonnegotiable for Christian secondary theology in its ongoing effort to bring Christian faith to articulate understanding in its proximate context, that is, in its current cultural and social setting. The point of the project is, in part, to show that there is in fact plenty of conceptual space for ongoing intellectual negotiations with atheological anthropological wisdom, and in part to identify Christian procedural or regulative theological commitments that govern the use of such atheological wisdom that is appropriated by Christian theological anthropology.

Certain anthropological claims are nonnegotiable for Christian theology, I have urged, if they are part of a set of claims that are essential to the identity of communities of Christian faith. The effort to bring faith to articulate understanding necessarily takes place in some proximate context shaped by its culture and employing its common language. Hence, doing theological anthropology unavoidably involves continuous conversation with the atheological anthropological wisdom inherent in the culture of its proximate context. Across time, earlier formulations of Christian anthropological remarks have been reformulated, modified, and amplified by the appropriation and incorporation of more recent cultural wisdom about human being. Some older claims, such as the historicity of Adam and Eve, are widely deemed not to be essential to the identity of the community of Christian faith and are abandoned. All this quite properly involves intellectual negotiation between Christian theological anthropological claims and atheological anthropological claims prominent in the culture. Through such negotiation the appropriation and incorporation of atheological wisdom must be selective, and what is borrowed must often be reformulated, bent by its use in a new context made up of a network of interrelated Christian claims on many topics. The nonnegotiable anthropological claims warrant the principles of selection and provide the conceptual pressures under which appropriated atheological wisdom is bent.

Such nonnegotiable anthropological claims do not exhaust what may properly be said by faith seeking understanding about human being. Within Christian discourse about anthropological questions, such nonnegotiable claims serve, in Robert Calhoun's lovely image, "like buoys that mark the channels of the deep" (Morse 1994, 78). The buoys themselves are interconnected in certain definite patterns that outline the identity of Christian communities' common life as it flows through the channels marked by the buoys. The aim of this book is to trace some of those patterns. However, between such channel markers there is a great deal of conceptual space. It provides plenty of room in which to explore additional questions about patterns of relationship among some or all of the buoys and other features of the context, on or beneath the surface. Some such additional questions are raised by loose ends left by discussion of the anthropological buoys that declines to attempt to bring all questions to closure.

Theological proposals to tie up loose ends like the ones left in chapters 13 and 14, and elsewhere in this book, must be supported by arguments that rightly rely in part, often in large part, on warrants drawn from atheological cultural wisdom. They require such warrants precisely because the questions they seek to address are questions about how nonnegotiable theological anthropological claims are compatible with atheological anthropological claims that are generally accepted as well established in their shared culture as much by persons who identify with communities of Christian faith as by those who do not. Some such warrants will need to be drawn from the sciences that study relevant features of human beings and their social and physical proximate contexts. Other such warrants, as was noted above several times, will be derived from systematic philosophical accounts of the metaphysics of human being in its proximate contexts.

My practice of leaving the loose ends loose in this book is not predicated on systematic methodological rejection of reliance on scientific or philosophical arguments as warrants in Christian theological argument. In particular, it is not based on rejection of use of such warrants on the grounds that they turn the arguments using them into exercises in apologetics. Whether apologetic arguments are acceptable in Christian theology depends, it seems to me, entirely on the ways in which the arguments are framed and not on the nature and goals of apologetics as such.

It is important on Christian theological grounds, I believe, to resist use in theology of systematic philosophical strategies that construe Christian practices and thought as instances that illustrate general philosophical theories about the essence of religion-as-such, the nature of religious-practices-as-such, and the nature of religious-language-as-such. Precisely because such essentializing theory abstracts at a very high level from the particularities of Christian practices and thought (and from the particularities of all other religious traditions), the internal logic of any such systematic philosophy of religion tends to warp the account it gives of the inner logic of specifically Christian practices and thought, and the logic of Christian anthropological claims in particular.

However, I see no Christian theological grounds on which to resist use of philosophical arguments in the effort to tie up loose ends left by questions kept open by an exercise in dogmatic theology. In particular, I see no a priori grounds on which to resist use in theological anthropology of philosophical arguments about the metaphysics of human being. Such use of philosophy in theology has long-standing precedent and is in any case, it seems to me, inescapable. Many of the key questions in anthropology are metaphysical questions. In contrast to philosophy of religion, in the sense of philosophical theory about the essence of "the religious" or "the sacred," let us call such philosophy in theology "philosophical theology." What must be required on theological grounds, however, is that the philosophical arguments used in theological anthropology cohere with the theological claims deemed nonnegotiable and that, where the philosophical arguments may imply claims incoherent with nonnegotiable theological claims, the latter trump the former. With those provisos it may be cheerfully acknowledged that by knowing when its job is done, declining to close certain questions, and leaving intellectual loose ends hanging, dogmatic theology provides work for philosophical theology to do.

CHAPTER 16

Sins as Distortions of Hopeful Existential "Hows"

If distortions of faith—that is, personal bodies' inappropriate responses to the triune God relating to them creatively—constitute one type of sin (chaps. 10 and 11), then distortions of hope—that is, personal bodies' inappropriate responses to the triune God drawing them to eschatological consummation—constitute a second type of sin. There are, of course, many ways in which to respond in distortions of joyous hopefulness; not responding at all to God relating in this way is the limit case of inappropriate response.

Sin turns personal bodies' lives in community into a living death. It is a violation of who they are and how they are to be as ones related to by God. Following the distinction between evil and sin introduced in chapter 10, let evil be defined by reference to creatures (it is some sort of violation of them), and let sin be defined only by reference to God (it is an inappropriate response to God). Accordingly, as violation of personal bodies, a living death is an evil, whereas the distorted response to God that leads to living death is sin.

In chapter 10, sin is defined by reference to God in two ways. The entire class of sins in the plural are distorted existential hows, that is, enactments of practices that express distorted responses to the triune God. Sin in the singular, on the other hand, is a personal identity defined by distorted response to God.

Sin in the Plural: Distorted Hopeful Existential Hows

Just as personal bodies' inappropriate response to the triune God relating to them creatively involves distortions of faith, both as loyalty to God's creaturely project and as trust in God to ground their reality and value, so, too, inappropriate response to God drawing them to eschatological consummation generates distorted versions of joyous hopefulness grounded in both the not yet of eschatological blessing now actually inaugurated and in the now of not-yet-fully actualized eschatological blessing.

Chapter 12 promoted the theme that the appropriate response to the triune God drawing personal bodies to eschatological consummation is joyous hopefulness, a distinctive orientation to their ultimate and proximate contexts. This posture is expressed in a set of practices—that is, socially established cooperative human actions enacted by living human personal bodies in their quotidian lived worlds. There is an indefinitely large number of possible enactments of such practices. Each enactment constitutes a personal body's existential how—that is, the concrete way in which she is set into her lived world at the time and place of the enactment. Although such existential hows are indefinitely large in number, two types of the practices they enact were identified. Practices of joyful hopefulness seek to be appropriately responsive both to the not-yet of borrowed time in which it lives and to the "now" of not-yet-fully actualized borrowed time.

Correspondingly, sins as enactments of distorted versions of joyous hopefulness also make up an indefinitely large number of existential hows enacting practices that are expressive of personal bodies' inappropriate responses to one aspect of their ultimate context—namely, God drawing them to eschatological blessing. On this understanding of sin in the plural, sins need not be consciously inappropriate responses. Hence the Psalmist's prayer, "Clear me from hidden [KJV: secret] faults" (19:12). Some inappropriate responses may be conscious. However, as we shall see in part 3, personal bodies' distorted practices of self-justification and their attendant practices of denial and self-deception tend to have the psychological effect of rendering personal bodies unaware of the distorted inappropriateness of their orientations to their ultimate and proximate contexts.

What makes existential hows sinful is not their conscious intent but a formal or structural distortion that manifests the inappropriateness of the response they express to their ultimate context. The attitude of hope, as well as the moodlike joy which may color it, are both made specific by the determinate character of their object—that is, that on account of which and for which they are joyful. Joyous hope is distorted when the ground of the hope and occasion for the joy is something other than the quotidian as actively related to in eschatological blessing by the triune God, related to precisely in the peculiar, proleptic way in which, in the resurrection of the crucified Jesus, God concretely makes good on the promise of eschatological blessing. That peculiar way has this formal structure: actually inaugurated now, but not yet fully actualized. When personal bodies' attitude to their proximate context is not given definition by that Christianly specific conceptualization of their ultimate context, then the practices that express their orientation to their proximate contexts are distorted versions of joyfully hopeful practices. Consequently, theocentrically speaking, enactments of those practices are distorted, deformed, counterfeit versions of hopeful existential hows. That is, they are sins.

Although there is an indefinitely large number of such sins, two broad types of them can be distinguished. Some are enactments of practices expressive of distorted response to the not-yet of now actually inaugurated eschatological blessing. Others are enactments of practices expressive of distorted response to the now of not-yet-fully actualized eschatological blessing.

Distorted Hopeful Practices Based on the Not-Yet of Eschatological Blessing

Distorted versions of joyfully hopeful practices arise when personal bodies' hopefulness is grounded in a not-yet that may arguably be the future of the present state of their proximate contexts, but is not God's eschatological future, which now already proleptically overlaps the present state of their creaturely proximate contexts. Such distortedly hopeful practices are enacted on the time of their creaturely proximate contexts, not on time borrowed from God's promised eschatological future which has now actually been inaugurated. In varying degrees, hopeful practices distorted in this way tend to distort hope's joy in its enactments in the quotidian and to be disconnected from faith's loyalty to and love for the quotidian.

Among hopeful practices distorted in this way, we may distinguish between (a) personal bodies' practices that are active expressions of inappropriate responses, and (b) practices that are passive expressions of inappropriate response to the triune God drawing them to the not-yet of eschatological consummation. These distortions of hopeful practices are formal and structural, not subjective. That is, their distortions do not necessarily lie in their affective tone or in their conscious purposes but in that which gives them definition—namely, that to which they respond.

Active distorted hopeful practices are hopeful in a certain way. They hope to overcome particular injustices in their lived worlds and to liberate them from particular kinds of oppression. Personal bodies enact such practices for the well-being of their companions in the quotidian. They enact such practices in order to transform their proximate contexts so radically that they eliminate once and for all the oppressive social and cultural structures and dynamics in those contexts that undercut personal bodies' dignity. However, they do so in a way that confuses human flourishing with human well-being.

Chapter 7 stressed a distinction between human flourishing and human well-being. According to that distinction, personal bodies' flourishing is defined by reference to the triune God relating creatively. In chapter 14 the distinction was developed further in connection with God relating to personal bodies to draw them to eschatological blessing. In both settings, human flourishing was explicated in terms of human glory. Personal bodies' flourishing simply is their creaturely and eschatological glory—that is, their expressing the glory of the triune God by virtue of God's absolute self-commitment to relate to them creatively and to draw them to eschatological consummation. That glory is the ground of their intrinsic dignity and value. Human well-being, on the other hand, was defined by reference to what personal bodies are. Relative to that "what," human well-being is measured in degrees along several different but complexly interrelated axes (physical, psychological, social, cultural, etc.).

When personal bodies' flourishing is identified with their well-being, as one type of distorted active practice does, human flourishing generally is identified with the highest degree of human well-being. If human dignity and value are grounded in personal bodies' well-being, as the same type of distorted practices assumes, then anything less than the highest degree of well-being is a diminution of their dignity and value. When personal bodies suffer somewhat less than maximal well-being, their humanity (read: "dignity and value") is said to be undercut. If theirs is a significantly lower degree of human well-being, they are said to be "dehumanized." It is precisely in order to resist and correct such loss of personal bodies' dignity through diminution of well-being that distorted actively hopeful practices are enacted to increase, sustain, and ensure human well-being.

It is morally imperative to resist and correct unjust diminution of human well-being. Enactment of such practices is inherent in faithful response to God relating to humankind creatively. However, enactments of faithful practices seek, among other things, to further human well-being, not to further human creaturely flourishing. Nor do they aim at an eschatologically radical transformation of their proximate contexts. On the other hand, while joyously hopeful practices are enacted with the aim of exemplifying eschatological flourishing in their proximate contexts, and with the aim of celebrating signs of such flourishing, they do not necessarily aim at furthering the quotidian's well-being. The distortions of active practices of distorted eschatological hope are manifested in their confusion of expectancy of the latter with expectancy of the former. Enactments of such practices hope to bring about changes for the well-being of proximate contexts by effecting a transformation of them that is so radical as to be an eschatological transformation. The distortion lies in the hope and its object (human well-being), not in the hope's joyousness. Practices of distorted hope may well be enacted in ways colored by joy's *hilaritas*, by a cheerful, high-spirited self-confidence and boldness in the certainty that the practices being enacted will show the world something good.

What distorts such actively hopeful practices is that their hope is based in a not-yet that has the status of a wholly ideal future possibility for their proximate contexts, the present's inherent *futuram*. Such a not-yet is literally a utopia, a "no place." Hence, practices expressive of a joyful hopefulness distorted in this way may be called "utopian practices." They are hopeful responses to utopian ideal possibilities.

Many utopian practices express personal bodies' orientation to their proximate contexts that are inappropriate responses to God, in the sense that they decline to be theocentric at all. That to which they respond is conceptually formed a-theistically. Rather than express response to God, such practices express a positive response to an ideal possibility for just and free social, political, economic, and cultural proximate contexts. Personal bodies' enactments of such practices orient them in their proximate contexts in idealistic existential hows.

By a utopian picture of an ideal possibility for one's lived world, I have in mind pictures promoted by a class of writings specified by F. E. and F. P. Manuel in their magisterial intellectual history, *Utopian Thought in the Western World*. "Utopia is a hybrid plant, born of the crossing of a paradisiacal, other-worldly belief of Judeo-Christian religion with the Hellenic myth of an ideal city on earth." Western utopia is "a creation of the world of the Renaissance and the Reformation" (1979, 15) whose intellectual history has two parts. Initially utopias, epitomized by Thomas More's publication of *Utopia* in 1516, tended to be "a dramatic narrative portrayal of a way of life that was so essentially good and fulfills so many profound longings that it wins immediate, almost instinctive, approbation" (2). In a second period, from the seventeenth century to their final demise, which the Manuels seem to think has perhaps happened by the mid-twentieth century (810–903), the hallmark of utopias has been that, in addition to portraying an ideally good way of life, they "embrace as well the underlying principles of an optimum society . . . Utopias also came to denote general programs and platforms for ideal societies, codes, and constitutions that dispensed with the fictional apparatus altogether" (2). I use "utopia" here broadly in this second sense.

The Manuels point out that such utopias are of a different order from scientific futurology's "immediate problem solving" by virtue of the utopias' "leap into a new state of being in which contemporary values in at least one area—the critical one for the utopian—are totally transformed or turned upside down" (1979, 8). If actualized in a society, such turning upside down would amount to a transformation of eschatological dimensions. At the same time, "the great utopians have been great realists. They have an extraordinary comprehension of the time and place in which they are writing" (28). Indeed, for all of their turning their lived worlds' values upside down, "When the imaginary world [of a utopia] is cut off from all relationship with reality, it becomes a vaporous fairy tale, formless and pointless" (29).

Many actively hopeful practices express an orientation to their proximate contexts that personal bodies adopt as a positive response to a utopian account of an ideal possibility for just and free proximate contexts. Generated by a body of social theory that provides analyses of unjust and oppressive social, political, and economic dynamics in the quotidian, such utopias suggest how to bring about morally desirable changes in those dynamics. In response to such a utopian picture and the changes it promises, personal bodies may orient themselves expectantly in their lived worlds. They express that expectancy in practices that seek to transform their proximate contexts radically. Nonetheless, the existential hows that enact such practices are sinful distortions of joyous hopefulness.

What is distorted about them is certainly not their intent to make their lived worlds more just and free proximate contexts. Faithful response to the triune God relating to the quotidian creatively that is loyal to God's creative project is enacted to the same end. Nor are they distorted by expressing a positive response to a utopian ideal possibility for their proximate contexts. Such utopian pictures really can inspire and guide efforts to promote the social, economic, political, and cultural well-being of the quotidian. There is nothing inherently sinful about being inspired in that way to act for the liberation and justice of one's proximate contexts. Nor is what is distorted about them the fact that subjectively they are not personal bodies' intentional responses to the triune God actively relating to them. Rather, from a theocentric perspective, they are distorted structurally. Their distortion lies in their enacting practices that are given definition by wholly future utopian ideal possibilities to which they are responses, and are not defined by a future (*adventus*) grounded in God *already* inaugurating radical transformation of personal bodies' proximate contexts here and now.

This distortion surfaces in the conjunction of utopian practices' ambition radically to transform their proximate contexts and the ambivalence of their realism about whether their proximate contexts provide the resources required for such total transformation. If, in their bold self-confidence, they are insufficiently realistic about the ambiguities of their proximate contexts, such practices drive toward inevitable disillusionment. Eventually confronting the complexity of the interlocking systemic evils characterizing their proximate contexts, optimistic enactments of such practices surrender utopian expectations for participation in the quotidian's ambiguous business-as-usual practices. Moving toward disillusion, insufficiently realistic utopian practices may express a certain loyalty to and love for the quotidian's current well-being, but their optimistic expectancy is surrendered and their *hilaritas* squelched.

On the other hand, if utopian practices are utterly realistic about the finitude and moral ambiguities of the resources their proximate contexts make available for radical transformation, they have no recourse in their passion for their utopian ideal but cynically to use all available means to achieve utopian ends. In their passion to actualize a utopian ideal possibility for their lived worlds, such cynically realistical practices are both disloyal and unloving toward their creaturely contexts' well-being here and now.

The limiting cases of such distortion of actively utopian practices are Promethean practices. In full awareness that there is little or no dynamic inherent within the quotidian moving it toward radical transformation of its oppressions and injustices, enactments of Promethean practices are attempted by sheer heroic, indeed titanic, self-assertion. Such limited resources as their proximate contexts do provide, including human resources, are used as instruments in the service of realization of the utopian dream. Such enactments exhibit a parody of joy's *hilaritas*, a grim glee at the overthrow of perceived causes of oppression and injustice. Furthermore, in their radical indifference to the current well-being of their proximate contexts, they are neither loyal to nor loving of those contexts, including their human companions. In such practices, a certain kind of hope is enacted in ways completely divorced from enactments of faith's loyalty to the quotidian. The brutal inhumanity of numerous such strong-man utopian regimes in the last two-thirds of the twentieth century, whether of the left or the right, is too horrifyingly familiar to require elaboration.

Utopianly distorted, actively hopeful practices are not necessarily nontheocentric, however. Some utopian practices express personal bodies' explicit efforts to respond to the triune God relating to them with the promise of eschatological blessing. Such practices are utopian when they express a response to God drawing them to an eschatological consummation construed as a wholly future promise. Understood in this way, God's promise presents one more utopian picture of what an eschatologically blessed lived world would be like were it ever realized. Such a picture highlights the injustice and oppression of the quotidian. Hope in God's entirely future promise inspires the personal bodies who respond to God in this way to enact morally admirable practices to correct particular injustices in their proximate contexts and to liberate them from particular oppressions.

Nonetheless, enactments of such practices are, theocentrically speaking, distorted existential hows. They are enactments of practices expressive of hopeful response to God's promise of future eschatological blessing on their proximate contexts, but not hopeful in response to God's actual inauguration now of not-yet-fully actualized eschatological blessing. While they look forward to the end time, personal bodies engaged in such practices assume that that time lies solely in the future, successive to and perhaps discontinuous with the time and space God gives them in relating to them creatively. Hence, they enact such practices on the time of the quotidian, not on time borrowed from eschatological blessing now actually inaugurated in the quotidian.

Enactments of such practices ought not to be defined as generically "spiritual" sins that have been endemic in many of the great religions, such as "spiritual pride," "fanaticism," and "antinomianism." They are sinful existential hows given specific shape and power by the peculiarly Christian conceptualities that (de)form them. In their passion to transform their lived worlds radically by building the eschatological kingdom, personal bodies' enactments of theocentrically utopian active practices are dangerous for the well-being of their proximate contexts, and for their neighbors in particular. In their power, such Christian-specific sins exemplify the danger of responding to God relating to us. Human flourishing lies in appropriate response to the triune God, but distorted response simply potentiates violation of human life.

Passive distorted hopeful practices express another type of inappropriate response to the triune God drawing personal bodies with their proximate contexts to the not-yet of eschatological consummation. As distorted versions of eschatological hopefulness, such responses are expressed in practices that are in some way expectant of something that will make all the difference and transform their proximate contexts. However, such practices do not seek actively to help bring about such transformation, nor do they respond in any other active way to either divine or secular promises of societal transformation. Rather, they are practices of awaiting some future radical change. It is their posture of waiting that marks them as passive practices.

Passive distortions of theocentrically hopeful practices are expressive of personal bodies' response to God's promise when it is understood as a promise of an entirely future eschatological blessing for which they can only wait. On this understanding of it, eschatological blessing is in no way actually now inaugurated and does not overlap with the quotidian whose transformation it promises. Such practices are genuinely expectant of God's future fulfillment of promised eschatological blessing. They may even be joyous practices, colored by *hilaritas*'s boldness grounded in the confidence that God will make good on the promised eschatological blessing. However, such practices focus exclusively on personal bodies' preparation for their eventual reception of eschatological blessing when God does finally grant it. They typically focus on having whatever experiences, or doing whatever believing, or undergoing whatever spiritual discipline they need in order to be saved at the last, and wholly future, day. Personal bodies' enactments of such practices are the way in which they wait in their proximate contexts for God to give the promised blessing. While they wait, they do not seek actively either to further the quotidian's well-being or to exemplify and celebrate signs in it of its eschatological flourishing.

Waiting marks personal bodies' enactments of such practices as sinfully distorted, but what is sinful about their enactments is not that they are marked by waiting. In enactments of faith's loyalty to the well-being of God's creaturely project, waiting can often be an appropriate strategy. There are plenty of situations in which temporary strategic waiting may be the best thing to do for the quotidian's well-being. Waiting is also inherent in eschatological hopefulness. One can only be hopeful or hopeless as one awaits something. When one no longer needs to await it because one has it, one can no longer hope (or lack hope) for it. What is sinful about enactments of passive theocentrically hopeful practices is structural: they express a response to the not-yet of the triune God's full actualization of the promise of eschatological consummation, but not any response to that consummation's now actual inauguration in the quotidian. Personal bodies' enactments of practices expressive of such distorted response to God are existential hows that are concrete distortions of eschatological hopefulness in which they are sinfully set into and oriented toward their proximate contexts.

That distortion makes enactments of these passive practices dangerous. At their most extreme, such passive practices express an inappropriate response to God relating in eschatological blessing that is completely disjoined from any response to God relating creatively. In their passion to prepare themselves for their future eschatological transformation, personal bodies' enactments of such passive theocentric distortions of joyous hopefulness are at risk of becoming indifferent to the well-being of their proximate contexts. Such a world-ignoring, if not world-rejecting, orientation to the quotidian is dangerous to the well-being of their proximate contexts, including their companions in those contexts. Here, too, Christian-specific sins are all the more powerfully dangerous for being expressive of distortions of that appropriate response to God in which human eschatological flourishing truly lies.

Passive distortions of joyous hopefulness need not be theocentric, of course. There are many practices in which personal bodies express a vaguely expectant orientation toward their proximate contexts. Their orientation is not a response to a utopian ideal possibility for such change. Nonetheless they are oriented to their contexts in a low-intensity expectancy that maybe "something will happen" or "something come along" to transform the quotidian. Practices expressive of this orientation are practices of sheer waiting.

Such practices are crystallized in Samuel Beckett's play *Waiting for Godot*, "a tragicomedy in two acts" (1954). Beckett characterizes Estragon and Vladimir, the two central characters, by using the music hall and vaudeville conventions of quick verbal exchange and wordplay between two tramps. Beckett is brilliantly funny in his use of these conventions, and much of the power of the play lies in the tension between this humor and the bleak world it depicts. The two spend the play on a sparse set, a country road near a tree and a low mound, where they await Godot. Their lived world is rendered cumulatively through their interchanges. The play is considered a classic expression of the meaningless lived world, a quotidian realm of undeserved and unredeemed sufferings in which nothing really changes and from which there is no escape. In each act Estragon and

Vladimir encounter two characters, Pozzo and Lucky, who come along the road enacting, in effect, a parody of Hegel's analysis of the dynamics of the master-slave relation with its endless cycle of victimization and counter-victimization. Almost at the end of the play, Pozzo has a line that epitomizes their lived world: "They give birth astride a grave, the light gleams an instant, then it's night once more" (57).

Such a world is a living death. The opening line of the play, repeated frequently with variations, is, "Nothing to be done." To be sure, although they constantly squabble and threaten to part, Estragon and Vladimir regularly reconcile and comfort each other in their miseries, often quite tenderly. Beckett undercuts sentimentality here. The two are not unambiguously altruistic. Each clearly fears being alone and needs the other. Yet there remain traces of humanist values in this world, such as empathy, compassion, and friendship. Such values, however, do not make this world meaningful. Nothing can be done from within it, not even acts of compassion, to change its meaninglessness.

This has an important consequence for the experience of time in the play. The characters constantly complain about time. They cannot remember the past very confidently. The end of the day seems never to come. In the present, time seems to have stopped. Time lies heavy on their hands because, if nothing can be really changed, then no period of time is more significant than any other, no moment has more meaning than any other. Time is experienced as undifferentiated and stagnant.

The play is an astringent rendering of a meaningless lived world; it is also a meditation on the persistence of expectancy in such a world and on a type of waiting that is inherent in that expectancy. Estragon and Vladimir understandably yearn to be saved from their lived world. The theme is struck right off in the play in an exchange about Christ's crucifixion between two thieves, one of whom repented and was saved. Vladimir thinks one out of two is pretty good odds and perhaps they, too, ought to try repenting in order to be saved. Estragon asks what they need to be saved from, and Vladimir first answers "Hell" (in the second act Estragon cries, "I'm in hell" [Beckett 1954, 47]) and then, to Estragon's confusion, answers "Death." The scene ends in farce as they prove physically incompetent even at trying to hang themselves. Indeed, it is far from clear they are serious about the effort. As usual in this play, it is a scene of more talk than action. Throughout, they never completely lose heart, expecting that what they yearn for might happen. Something will turn up, someone come along, who will save them. Such expectancy is doubtless absurd. It has no ground either in any assessment of their lived world's resources or in any acknowledged divine promise. It may be simply one more dim trace of humanist value in the otherwise nihilistic lived world rendered by the play.

Estragon and Vladimir attach their expectancy of salvation somehow to Godot for whom they wait, although they acknowledge that they have never seen him and would not recognize him were he to appear. They cannot remember how they learned that he would meet them. Nor do they seem to have any idea what he would do for them were he to arrive. Yet they are, they acknowledge, tied to him by their expectation of him. They cannot leave the lived world they inhabit, not even by suicide. Each act ends with the line, "Yes, let's go," followed by the stage directions, *They do not move.*

The object of their expectancy is, to say the least, vague, and it is deferred. In the first moments of the play, Estragon complains, "You always wait until the last moment," and Vladimir responds, "'The last moment' . . . Hope deferred maketh the something sick, who said that?" (Beckett 1954, 8). An eschatological allusion is joined to Proverbs 13:12, "Hope deferred maketh the heart sick" (KJV). The first act ends as a boy arrives to bring a message of deferral, a message from Godot that he could not come that day but will come the next. The boy returns in the penultimate scene of the second act with the same message.

Thus, the waiting in this play is a particular type of waiting. It is a waiting in the interim between, on one hand, every present empty, meaningless, and unchangeable time and, on the other hand, such time as Godot comes and the expected transformation of the quotidian, however vaguely imagined, in fact happens. Such waiting is inherent in an expectancy whose object is somehow eschatological but is at once vague and deferred.

Almost all of the interactions between Estragon and Vladimir can be read as enactments of practices of this sort of waiting. In a world where time is experienced as undifferentiated and stagnant, these practices aim mainly to fill the time, to move the time along more quickly, to kill the time. Beckett devises an extraordinarily large number of routines between Estragon and Vladimir, parodies of exchanges between music-hall comedians. Sometimes they involve a bit of stage business; more often they are like verbal versions of very short riffs in jazz. They tell stories, make conversation about nothing, have hilariously absurd arguments, quiz each other, play at being Pozzo and Lucky, get into a name-calling contest, do their exercises. They either begin these exchanges with the formulaic remark, "That's the idea, let's . . . [have a conversation, contradict each other, abuse each other, etc.]" or end them with remarks like, "It'll pass the time" (Beckett 1954, 9); "That wasn't such a bad little canter" (42); "How time flies when one has fun" (49).

Particularly telling is an exchange they have after Vladimir suggests they try to put Estragon's boots back on his hurting feet, which involves a bit of stage business. They agree that doing so would be an occupation, a relaxation, a recreation. Recreations, relaxations, and occupations are all familiar quotidian practices. Were they expressive of an attitude of loyalty to their proximate contexts, some such practices might be enacted in ways that make for the quotidian's well-being. A few of them might even be enacted in ways that exemplify the quotidian's eschatological flourishing. However, when these familiar practices express an attitude to their proximate contexts as utterly meaningless unless and until changed from the outside, they can only be enacted as ways to sustain one's own existence in the meantime by killing time. After a series of these exchanges, Estragon says to Vladimir, "We always find something, eh Didi, to give us the impression we exist?" (Beckett 1954, 44).

Such practices are exemplary of a wide variety of nontheocentric passively hopeful practices—occupations, recreations, relaxations—that express a vague attitude of expectancy toward their proximate contexts. They are hopeful in their expectancy, however vague and deferred, that something will come along radically to transform their proximate contexts. They are passive in that, rather than aiming to change their proximate contexts, they are ways of waiting in the meanwhile until what is expected actually happens. They are the practices that make up the common life of a consumerist culture of entertainment. The existential hows constituted by enactment of such practices are sinful distortions of enactments of joyous hopefulness. They are distortions because, while they enact practices expressive of a sort of "hope," it is an expectancy grounded in a vague and deferred possibility of an eschatological transformation of the quotidian that is wholly future and in no way actually inaugurated now. They are done, not to exemplify and celebrate eschatological flourishing, but to reassure ourselves while waiting in suspended animation that we really exist.

Distorted Hopeful Practices Based on the Now of Eschatological Blessing
There is a second type of distorted version of joyfully hopeful practices. Instead of being expressions of responses to a not-yet that would in the future, if actualized, radically transform the quotidian but does not in any way already actually overlap the quotidian's now, they express a response solely to some feature of the quotidian's now without reference to its not-yet. Like the first type, this second type of distorted hopeful practice is enacted on the time of its creaturely proximate context and not on time borrowed from God's promised eschatological future which, having been inaugurated, overlaps creaturely time and space. In varying degrees, hopeful practices distorted in this way tend to be conflated with practices of faith's loyalty to and love for the quotidian. Furthermore, like the first type of distorted hopeful practices, the energy behind this type of distorted practice is grounded in the assumption that human persons' dignity and value are diminished when their well-being is diminished. Assuming that oppression and injustice inherently dehumanize human persons, it is obvious that practices aiming at liberating human persons from oppression and injustice are of paramount urgency. By contrast, I have urged that if it is the case that God relates to humankind in both creative blessing

and in eschatological blessing, then the dignity and value of living human personal bodies is not tied to their well-being but to their flourishing, to their glory, in virtue of being related to by God creatively and to draw to eschatological blessing. The well-being of living human personal bodies is important, and acting wisely for its preservation and enhancement is central to faith's loyalty to God's creative project. However, the well-being of human personal bodies does not ground their dignity and value, and diminution of their well-being does not threaten their dignity and value nor threaten to make them any the less either human or personal (see part 1).

Some hopeful practices distorted in this way actively express inappropriate responses, and some passively express inappropriate responses to the triune God drawing them to the not-yet of eschatological consummation.

Active hopeful practices distorted in this way may nonetheless be theocentric practices. They may be personal bodies' practices that express a response to God in which response to God's eschatological blessing on the quotidian is conflated with response to God's creative blessing of the quotidian. In that case they also conflate practices celebratory of the quotidian's eschatological flourishing with practices making for the quotidian's well-being. They substitute the latter for the former as though they were the same set of practices.

Practices expressive of such distorted theocentric response are hopeful in the mode of optimism—that is, expecting the best (Lat. *optimus*) to happen. But that is to say that they are distortions of eschatological hope. Optimism is a quite different attitude toward proximate contexts than joyous hopefulness. Optimism is at least implicitly rooted in an assessment of proximate contexts' resources now. Such optimism is a distortion of joyful hopefulness which is properly grounded, not in creaturely resources constituted by God's creative blessing, but in God's actual *proleptic* inauguration now of God's future (*adventus*) eschatological blessing that is not yet fully actualized. Hence, optimistic practices express personal bodies' response to God that is a distortion of appropriate response to God's inauguration now of a not-yet-fully actualized eschatological blessing.

Optimistic theocentric practices seek the well-being of their proximate contexts and expect to realize it. They understand themselves to be practices inspired by God's promise of eschatological blessing to make their proximate contexts more just and to liberate them from various types of bondage.

The most commonly condemned versions of this are moralistic. They are practices enacted on the assumption that not only is what God wills to be changed in our proximate contexts for their moral improvement absolutely clear, but also just how to go about changing it is unambiguously clear, brooking no qualification or compromise. A standard illustration is the successful movement in the United States to prohibit the alcohol trade by amendment of the Constitution. Such moralistic practices are commonly condemned for their blindness to the complexity of social and cultural change and the power of unexpected and unintended evil consequences of simplistic, repressive, and regressive social and cultural change.

However, socially and culturally progressive practices may also be optimistic theocentric practices. They may assume, as do some social gospel versions of Christian hopefulness, that properly planned and implemented cooperative liberating human actions for more just and peaceful proximate contexts simply are building God's eschatological kingdom in the quotidian—as though God had not already actually inaugurated eschatological blessing and will bring it to full actualization in God's own unanticipatable and peculiar way. They may well do so in ways colored by joy's cheerful, high-spirited, self-confident boldness. Expressive of trust in and loyalty to God, these practices are optimistic that, as God relates to them creatively, they are capable of furthering the quotidian's well-being. However, enactments of such practices in effect conflate response to God's eschatological blessing on the quotidian with response to God's creative blessing of the quotidian. Therewith, they also confuse practices celebratory of the quotidian's eschatological flourishing with practices making for the quotidian's well-being. They substitute the latter for the former as though they were two versions of the same set of practices.

Enactments of such actively hopeful practices constitute existential hows that are distortions of joyously hopeful hows. Despite being enactments of theocentric practices, they are nonetheless sins. They are specifically Christian sins. That is, they are enactments of practices shaped by specifically Christian concepts of God and of God's eschatological kingdom. To the extent that their Christian specificness shapes, focuses, and intensifies the energies with which they are enacted, such sins are made, not milder, but rather more potent for evil by their Christianness.

Active distorted hopeful practices, of course, need not be theocentric to be optimistic. They may be enacted in morally admirable nontheocentric public action that seeks radical, virtually eschatological, social, cultural, political, and economic transformation making for greater justice and freedom. They are enacted in their proximate contexts without reference to God's commitment to either creative or eschatological blessings. On the basis of analysis of resources empowering radical transformation found in the quotidian, they are optimistic about realizing that well-being. Such optimism, however, is qualitatively different from eschatological hopefulness. Such optimistic practices are structurally distortions of practices of joyous hopefulness.

Because the optimism of active practices rests on assessment of resources for radical transformation that are provided by their proximate context, it is urgent that those assessments be realistic. From a theocentric point of view, the moral and ontological ambiguity of personal bodies' quotidian proximate contexts means that the urgency of such realism makes the optimism of such practices inherently unstable.

To the extent that optimistically active practices do rigorously seek to be governed by the most acute and rigorous analyses of their lived worlds' most pressing moral problems, the social and cultural dynamics that generate those problems, and the resources in the quotidian that might be drawn on to help correct those problems, they tend to give way to pessimism. They tend to become practices expecting the worst (Lat. *pessimus*). Seeking to be realistic, what they learn is the quotidian's moral and ontological ambiguity. Their enactments' effort to correct their lived worlds' moral problems can, at best, be only guardedly hopeful. They are rightly pessimistic about the possibility, not only of changes that would fundamentally transform the quotidian, but of lasting correction of particular injustices and liberation from particular oppressions in their proximate contexts.

In their realistic pessimism, such practices tend to become self-protective and exclusionary. Their enactments are constrained by the recognition that their proximate contexts provide them only limited resources with which to resist and correct the ways in which some personal bodies' well-being, and therewith (given the assumptions that fuel optimistic practices) their dignity, are diminished. The enactments of such practices are guided by this self-protective calculus: if there are not the resources to liberate all personal bodies from socially systemic oppression and injustice, there may be sufficient resources to protect us and our group from oppression.

The obverse of self-protection is exclusion. In contrast to the hospitable openness of practices expressive of undistorted joyous hopefulness, realistic recognition by hitherto optimistic active practices of the limits of their resources leads to a construal of efforts to transform the quotidian as a zero-sum game. Every improvement in the degree of the well-being, and therewith (on the assumptions of optimistic practices) the dignity of one group of personal bodies in their shared social and cultural proximate contexts, is understood necessarily to entail a loss in degree of well-being, and therewith of dignity, of other groups of personal bodies. What is understood to be at stake is not just the relative degrees of well-being of different groups of human personal bodies, but their dignity. Decisions about whom to privilege among groups of persons are viewed as tragic choices that are unavoidable. Consequently, enactments of pessimistically active practices aiming to increase justice and human dignity in their proximate contexts tend to become increasingly exclusionary. The limited resources provided by finite proximate contexts requires the exclusion of certain groups of personal bodies from the population targeted for liberation from dehumanization and oppression to injustice.

In these ways, optimistic active practices tend to shift unstably from optimism to pessimism. This instability is a function of the way in which they are distorted versions of joyously hopeful practices. Because undistorted eschatological hope is based in the actual inauguration now of the triune God's eschatological blessing for whose not-yet-full actualization of transformation of the quotidian it hopes, and is not based in realistic assessment of resources provided by the quotidian with which to transform it, its realism about the resources of its proximate context does not undercut the ground of its hopefulness and make it pessimistic. However, optimistic active practices can be based only on assessment of resources provided by the quotidian now, and not on God's inauguration of God's promised eschatological rule; the moral and ontological ambiguities of the quotidian can only move such practices toward pessimism.

Enactments of unstably optimistic practices constitute existential hows that are distortions of joyously hopeful hows. They are sins. However, it must be kept clear that what qualifies such hows as sins is not that they are either optimistic or pessimistic. There are plenty of particular projects, episodes, and situations in our finite and ambiguous proximate contexts about which either optimism or pessimism may be the only appropriate attitude. Furthermore, in regard to pessimism in particular, there is nothing inherently faithless or hopeless about realistically assessing the quotidian to be ambiguous. On the contrary, such assessment is a necessary moment in appropriate response to God. It was a key element of the account in part 1 of our quotidian proximate contexts precisely as God relates to them creatively. Rather, what is in view in classifying personal bodies' optimistic and pessimistic existential hows as sins are certain overall orientations which those hows express. They are orientations that are distorted versions of eschatological hope, expressed in distorted versions of joyously hopeful practices and enacted in distorted existential hows.

Passive hopeful practices distorted in this way may also be either theocentric or nontheocentric.

Practices expressive of a nontheocentric response to the quotidian's now without reference to its not-yet become sentimental if their assessment of the quotidian's resources making for radical change are unrealistic. They are sentimental practices in that they are enacted in denial of, or in willful ignorance of, the complexity and power of the systemic evils they seek to transform. In their unrealism, the sentimentality of such practices is a distorted version of eschatological hope's joy, which rejoices in the inauguration of the eschatological flourishing of the quotidian precisely in the midst of its very real ambiguities. Such sentimentality about the quotidian's well-being is also a distorted version of faith's love for the quotidian, which is only genuinely love insofar as it is realistic about the concrete particularities of that which it loves.

Such sentimental practices are passive practices in that they do not seek deep changes in their proximate contexts. Rather, in their unrealism about the quotidian, they sentimentally suppose that the changes it needs are not radical changes.

Enactments of sentimental practices are inherently dangerous to the well-being of their proximate contexts. Such practices are complacent about their proximate contexts. Failing to acknowledge, let alone address, the social, economic, political, and cultural dynamics that cause the injustice and oppression they seek to overcome, sentimental enactments risk compounding the evil they seek to overcome. Furthermore, such practices are complacent about themselves. Sentimental practices' blindness to their own moral ambiguity simply intensifies the ways in which they compound the evil they seek to transform.

Their sentimentality and complacency may make enactments of such nontheocentric practices dangerous as causes of evils, but that does not make them sins. What makes such enactments sins is that they constitute existential hows that are structural distortions of those hows that are enactments of practices expressive of appropriate response to the triune God drawing creatures to eschatological consummation.

By contrast to the sentimentality of passive nontheocentrically hopeful practices, passive theocentrically hopeful practices are triumphalist. They are explicitly expressive of personal bodies' response to God drawing them to eschatological consummation, but as though that consummation were now already fully actualized so that there is no longer any not-yet. They construe their proximate contexts in some way to be the eschatological kingdom actualized by God. They are passive practices in that they do not seek any further radical change of their proximate contexts. What is to be hoped for is only that what is now actual will continue to be the way it is, perhaps with modest and minor modifications. Such practices are, of course, inherently conservative. If the proximate context's status quo basically is God's eschatological blessing, not only does it not require radical change, it must be conserved, preserved from any significant alteration.

Broadly speaking, there tend to be two versions of passive theocentric practices. They differ in the scope of the proximate context which is construed as the triumph of God's eschatological kingdom.

One version identifies the practices' proximate context with a particular type of community of faith. That type of community just is the eschatologically transformed quotidian. In the community's common life, eschatological blessing triumphs over the ambiguities of creaturely proximate contexts. Such communities are utopian sectarian churches. They are sectarian in that they distance themselves from their larger social and cultural contexts. The latter are understood to be excluded from eschatological blessing altogether. Utopian sectarian churches constitute radically alternative social and cultural proximate contexts. Personal bodies whose lived worlds are the former can participate in eschatological blessing only by leaving their host proximate contexts entirely and entering the alternative lived world of the utopian sect. Personal bodies whose proximate context becomes that of the utopian sect confine their lives to the alternative lived world of the sect—that is, to the fully actualized eschatological world. They cannot consistently do that and also be actively engaged in a broader social and cultural proximate context, neither to act for its well-being nor to celebrate signs in it of the inauguration of eschatological blessing.

Use of the adjective "utopian" here is important and yet could be misplaced. It is important because not all sectarian understandings of the church are utopian. Not all claim that in them eschatological blessing has triumphed and that no moral ambiguities remain. Only some sectarian understandings of the church are utopian. The term "utopian" is misplaced, however, if it suggests that such churches are constituted as a response to a utopian picture of an ideally possible society. They are not. They are constituted as a response to what is taken to be God's full actualization of eschatological blessing in their midst.

The second type of such passive theocentric practices identifies the practices' proximate context with their broader social and cultural context. Whether or not it is fair to the historical Hegel, this identification is frequently illustrated by Hegel's apparent view that the culture and society of the Prussia of his day simply was the concrete expression of full actualization of Absolute Spirit. Hegel aside, variations on such identification of practices responsive to the triumph in history of God's eschatological kingdom with the practices constituting the common life of some particular social and cultural proximate context undergird theological claims about a Christian America or South Africa or Chile (see Cavanaugh 1998).

Enactments of both types of passive theocentric practices constitute distorted existential hows. Such hows are sins inasmuch as they are distorted versions of those hows that are personal bodies' enactments of practices expressive of appropriate response to the full complexity of the way in which the triune God is drawing them to eschatological consummation.

Desperate Practices

Enactments of practices expressive of despair are the limiting case of existential hows enacting distorted response to the "Spirit sent by the Father with the Son" to draw personal bodies to eschatological consummation. Despair (Lat. *de* [without]-*sparare* [to hope]) is an orientation that personal bodies have to their proximate and ultimate contexts that is wholly without hope in their ultimate context and without hope for their proximate contexts. As an overall orientation to personal bodies' contexts, despair is so complete a distortion of hopefulness as to be, not just its absence, but its opposite.

Such despair is expressed in desperate practices that are often, and understandably, colored by the overall mood that is the opposite of joyfulness—namely, depression. Despair and depression are sometimes taken to be similar moods. People are sometimes said to feel desperate because they feel depressed or, conversely, to be psychologically depressed because they feel desperate. However, to use the terms in this way seems to me to be a conceptual mistake. Depression is a psychological mood that may have more than one cause, but seems clearly at least to have an organic basis in brain chemistry. As recent descriptions have shown, perhaps most notably by novelist William Styron in his searing account of his own struggles with it (1992), depression at its most severe is so intense a suffering that like physical torture it utterly enervates and isolates its victims, entirely constricting their consciousness to a tight focus on their psychic pain. By contrast, despair names a certain pattern or structure in personal bodies' orientation to and engagement with their proximate contexts. It is best described formally, objectively, and phenomenologically, not in the evocative rhetoric of subjectivity. As Kierkegaard took pains to show (1954), personal bodies (he would not have used such a phrase!) may not even be conscious of being in despair. Hence, they might express their despair in practices that are colored, not by depression, but by a certain a certain emotional blandness or even by a mood of can-do self-assertiveness.

Desperate practices may be both theocentric and nontheocentric. If theocentric, they are practices in which personal bodies respond to a God whom they understand to be at least indifferent and perhaps hostile, not only to their eschatological consummation, but to their creaturely well-being as well. Hence, theocentric desperate practices may take the active form of practices that aim, whether as acts of rebellion against this God, to preserve as long as possible human creatures' well-being on their own in the face of hostile ultimate and proximate contexts. Or, they may take the passive form of practices of resignation in the face of hostile ultimate and proximate contexts. Or, whether active or passive, they may simply take the form of distraction from the reality of their despair. In distractive practices, personal bodies express no expectancy. In these cases, practices of killing time have shifted from being a way of waiting to being a way of avoiding the truth about one's fundamental orientation to one's proximate contexts.

Enactments of desperate practices are sinful existential hows. They contrast more clearly than do other distorted versions with enactments of practices of joyous hopefulness. However, they cannot be said to be necessarily more seriously sinful than other distorted versions of enactment of joyous hopefulness just because they stand in stronger contrast to enactments of undistorted practices of joyous hopefulness. When sins are defined theocentrically as existential hows that enact inappropriate responses to the constitutive pattern of the triune God's way of relating to humankind in eschatological blessing, they are defined structurally and not as either violations of God's commands or as modes of human subjectivity. Either an existential how enacts a practice that is a response to God's way of relating that appropriately reflects that constitutive pattern or it does not. There are many types of ways in which it may not, but they are all equally sins. It does not follow that some of them may be deemed more serious than others, and there may be various theological criteria by which to assess that. Obviousness of distortion, however, would not seem to be a particularly compelling criterion in that regard. In some ways, less obviously distorted existential hows are arguably more serious sins because their deceptiveness makes them the more dangerous.

In any case, even sinful enactments of desperate practices, theocentric or not, are complex. On one side, they are enactments of practices that express an inappropriate response to the triune God drawing personal bodies to eschatological consummation. On the other side, insofar as they are personal bodies' enactments of active practices aiming at preserving the well-being of their proximate contexts, they express a certain loyalty to those contexts that is formally consonant with appropriate response to God relating to them creatively. Hence, the intense ambiguity of some enactments of desperate practices: they may simultaneously conform to enactments of faithful practices and be profoundly distorted versions of enactments of eschatologically hopeful practices.

We have been reviewing sinful concrete existential hows constituted by enactments of distorted versions of joyously hopeful practices—that is, socially established cooperative human actions that have a goal but not necessarily a product. Although such sins are innumerable, they can be classified as enactments of types of practices that seek, whether actively or passively, radically to change their proximate contexts either by responding to a not-yet (conceived either theocentrically or nontheocentrically) that is in no way already actual in the now of their proximate contexts, or by responding to the now of their proximate contexts which is conceived (either theocentrically or nontheocentrically) without reference to its not-yet. Or they may be enactments of a type of desperate practices, practices that express absolute lack of hope. In each case, these types of practices express a response to their ultimate and proximate contexts that is a distorted version of joyful hopefulness in the triune God's inauguration of the promised eschatological consummation that is not-yet-fully actualized. Particular enactments of these types of practices are just how some personal body is set in his or her quotidian proximate context as someone whose overall orientation is a distorted version of joyous hopefulness. Such hows are sins.

This class of sinful human actions has one important feature in common. They are not enacted on borrowed time. Rather than expressing hopeful response to the triune God's distinctive and very odd way of drawing creatures to eschatological transformation by the resurrection of the crucified Jesus, sinful actions in this class seek to actualize on their own an eschatologically radical transformation of their proximate contexts; or they seek to preserve what they conceive to be an already fully actualized, eschatologically radical alteration of their quotidian; or they seek to survive in proximate contexts of whose radical transformation they despair. Thus, whereas joyously hopeful practices are enacted in their proximate contexts in response to the proleptic inbreaking of eschatological blessing on time borrowed from God's eschatological future, all practices of distorted versions of joyously hopeful practices are enacted in space and time given by creative blessing and distorted by inappropriate human personal bodies' response to God's relating to them in both creative and eschatological blessing.

The Theological Concept of Sin in the Plural

Considered in conjunction with the typology of sinful enactments of distorted versions of faithful practices developed in chapter 10, the typology developed here of sinful enactments of distorted versions of hopeful practices draws attention to two features of a general concept of sins (in the plural).

First, it underscores the point made in chapter 10 that there is no single root sin, such as pride or selfishness, that underlies all sins. Because they are in part defined by the particularities of their proximate contexts, individual concrete sinful enactments of distorted versions of faithful and hopeful practices are innumerable and irreducibly diverse. I have suggested that they can be characterized by rough typologies. However, enactments of distorted versions of joyously hopeful practices can no more be explained by a single root distortion of hope than can distorted versions of faithful practices be explained by a single root distortion of faithfulness. Moreover, there is no single distortion of personal bodies' responses to the triune God that underlies distortions of both hopeful and faithful practices.

The typology also underscores a difference between ordinary concepts of immoral acts and the Christian theological concept of sinful acts. "Immoral" and "sinful" are often used interchangeably to characterize the same human actions, attitudes, and affections. Murder, pride, and contempt are conventionally called both immoral and sinful. However, it seems to me that such usage is theologically misleading.

Some attitudes, actions, and affections of personal bodies are judged to be sinful (sin in the plural) by reference to God: A sinful how is a personal body's en-act-ment of a practice that is a distorted version of a practice expressive of an appropriate response to the triune God actively relating to humankind. Such practices, however, also express an attitude that orients a personal body to her proximate contexts in a fashion that is a distorted version of orientations that are appropriate responses to the way in which God relates to her. Furthermore, the emotions, feelings, and passions that a human personal body has in such a distorted orientation are distorted versions of the affections appropriate as responses to God's relating to her.

Personal bodies' actions are judged to be immoral, on the other hand, in the first instance by reference to fellow creatures: An immoral act is a personal body's enactment of a practice that causes evil—that is, it is an act that directly or indirectly violates the personal bodies who enact them, or violates other personal bodies, or violates their shared proximate contexts, including the fabric of mutual trust and obligation that is the minimal condition for human community. Immoral attitudes, such as pride, and affections, such as hatred and contempt of other people, denigrate the dignity of fellow human beings and corrupt the one who has them, voluntarily or involuntarily. They are inherently immoral.

The immorality of such acts, attitudes, and affections could be explained theocentrically simply by saying that God has revealed that God considers them to be immoral and forbids them. However, their immorality may also be explained by various philosophical ethical theories. For instance, their immorality could be theorized as violation of rationally discoverable rights inherent in fellow creatures considered as rational autonomous agents; or as violation of natural moral norms or laws discoverable by reason in the metaphysical structure of personal bodies and their proximate contexts; or as violation of a rationally discoverable a priori unconditional imperative, and the duties it imposes on us; or as violations of a moral responsibility for their well-being that other personal bodies lay on us by their sheer presence to us; or as violation of the rationally discoverable moral rule that the morally best action is the one that makes for the greatest happiness of the greatest number of human persons; and so on. There are plenty of versions of each of these moral theories that logically require no direct reference to God actively relating to personal bodies. Each of them may also be formulated in ways compatible with affirmation of God relating creatively to personal bodies. All of this might suggest that certain human actions, attitudes, and affections may equally well be characterized interchangeably as "immoral" or as "sinful."

Theologically speaking, this apparent equivalence may hold within the context of reflection on the ethical implications of the claim that the triune God relates creatively to all that is not God and that the appropriate response by personal bodies is faithfulness to God. However, when we shift to the context of reflection on the implications of the claim that the triune God relates to all that is not God to draw it to eschatological consummation and that the appropriate response is hope, some human actions, attitudes, and affections must be judged to be sinful even when they would not normally be judged to be immoral. Such actions are sinful because they are enactments of practices expressive of attitudes that are distorted forms of hopefulness and of affects that are distorted versions of, or substitutes for, joy. (I shall argue that there are analogous consequences when we shift focus from reflection, not only on the anthropological implications of God relating creatively, but also from reflection on the anthropological implications of God relating to draw to eschatological consummation, to anthropological implications of the triune God relating to all that is not God to reconcile creatures that are estranged from God, to which the appropriate response is love to God and fellow creatures. Examined in that context also, some human actions, attitudes, and affections must be judged to be sinful even when they would not normally be judged to be immoral.)

Although, as we have seen in this chapter, some of these actions, attitudes, and affections must also be judged to be immoral because they do end up causing evil, we also saw that some such actions, attitudes, and affections, far from violating fellow creatures and their proximate contexts, make for their well-being. By most ordinary standards, such human actions count as morally good actions, attitudes, and affections. Nonetheless, theocentrically considered, despite their being morally good, they are also sins. In general, then, all immoral acts, attitudes, and affections are also sinful, in one way (i.e., enactments of practices expressive of distorted versions of faithful attitudes and affections), but some actions, attitudes, and affections that constitute another type of sinful existential hows (e.g., some enactments of practices expressive of distorted versions of joyous hopefulness) may not count as immoral. Although they overlap significantly, immoral human actions, attitudes, and affections and sinful human actions, attitudes, and affections are not, as it were, isomorphic classes.

CHAPTER 17

Living Death: Sin as Distortion of Hope

Where sins (in the plural) are personal bodies' concrete existential hows constituted by enactments of practices expressive of inappropriate responses to the triune God relating to them, sin (in the singular) is distortion of their basic personal identities.

This claim about sin in the singular hangs on a distinction between basic personal identities and quotidian personal identities. Our quotidian identities are defined by how we respond to our proximate contexts. More exactly, they are determined by what we implicitly or explicitly acknowledge in our responses to our proximate contexts as the ground of the reality and value of our lives. The theological proposals I am promoting in chapters on both the flourishing of personal bodies' lives and on their sin in the singular are (1) that human personal bodies' quotidian personal identities may be distorted into living deaths, and (2) that the norm by which such distortion may be identified is the basic personal identity, which they do not constitute by their responses to their proximate contexts but rather are given by the ways in which the triune God relates to them. Their basic personal identities are defined eccentrically. Theocentrically speaking, while my basic personal identity is most definitely my own identity that only I can live, it is finally not defined by me but is defined eccentrically by God relating to me. It is defined by its "related-to-by-God-ness"—that is, by its orientation to the triune God—not by my particular mode of self-relating—that is, by its orientation to me. Its only adequate description takes narrative form. But I finally am not the narrative's hero, in the classical sense of "hero." The narrative identity-description of my basic identity is not purely, or even primarily, about me; it is about God relating to me in community and only on that basis about me in community relating in some way back to God.

The distinction between one's basic and one's quotidian personal identity makes the living deaths of sin in the singular possible. Just as personal bodies have basic, albeit eccentrically grounded, personal identities, it is also the case that they may actually live at cross-grain to those identities, losing their identities, or being untrue to them, or being inauthentic in respect to them. And human persons actually do live distorted versions of their actual identities. I suggested in chapter 11 that such distorted identities are a bondage in some type of living death. Doctrines of original sin, insofar as they offer descriptions of human predicaments and not causal explanations of their origin, are analyses of just such bondage.

Chapter 9 promoted the proposal that although personal bodies' basic identities are eccentrically and objectively grounded in the ways in which the triune God relates to them, they are nonetheless shaped by their subjective ways of acknowledging God relating to them. Personal bodies' identities are not constituted by God apart from their own subjective involvement. Acknowledging is a performative act. It is performed through an indefinitely large set of ordinary, everyday human actions that are always concretely located in some society and its culture. Hence, acknowledging the ground of one's personal identity always occurs in concrete and particular ways.

If personal bodies' identities are shaped by their particular, concretely located acknowledgment of the ground of their identities, then their identities are shaped by at least implicit construals of just what it is that they are acknowledging. Those construals may be misconstruals. Therein lies a possibility of their living at cross-grain to their actual identities. Such misconstruing happens when personal bodies' concrete acknowledgment of the ground of their identities is inappropriate to just that ground— that is, to the way in which the triune God actually relates to them. That is the possibility of personal bodies' bondage to the living death of self-contradictory identities.

We have already explored in chapter 11 forms of living death to which personal bodies are in bondage as creatures when their identities are defined by acknowledgment of the quotidian as that which alone is worth trusting to ground their creaturely reality and value; or acknowledgment of God alone as worthy of their loyalty, but without loyalty to God's creative project; or acknowledgment of themselves as worthy of the trust and loyalty appropriate to the ground of their reality and value. Here we explore a second aspect of the living death of distorted personal identity: the bondage incurred by personal bodies' inappropriate acknowledgments of their election for and judgment by eschatologically radical transformation.

Election and judgment, I urged in chapter 15, define personal bodies' basic identities inasmuch as the triune God in the *taxis* "the Spirit sent with the Son by the Father" draws them to eschatological consummation.

Because they are defined by the triune God's eschatological blessing, personal bodies' basic personal identities are eschatologically hopeful identities. Given that one aspect of personal bodies' ultimate context is the triune God drawing them and their proximate contexts to eschatological consummation, the answer to the perennial anthropological question, "Who are we?" is both, "We all are those chosen for eschatological consummation," and "We all are those to whom the catastrophe of final judgment is happening."

Left at that, "election" and "judgment" are too abstract. According to the canonical stories that elicit and form Christian understanding of God, and of all else in relation to God, the triune God relates to personal bodies to elect and to judge in very particular, concrete, and peculiar ways: God elects all human creatures for eschatological transformation and, given that they are self-alienated from God, judges them in the person of a first-century crucified Jew raised from the dead, whose own identity is constituted at once by his own actions and by God's action, in a peculiar coinherence of the two. Acknowledgment of election and judgment, and therewith the personal identities shaped by such acknowledgment, are distorted when what is acknowledged is, however implicitly and unselfconsciously, construed otherwise. In this case, what may be acknowledged in misconstrued ways is not merely the election and judgment that partly define personal bodies' basic personal identities, but the particularities of the very odd way in which, according to relevant canonical narratives, the triune God does about electing and judging quite concretely in the life, ministry, passion, crucifixion, and resurrection of Jesus of Nazareth.

Personal identities may be distorted in this regard in three broad ways: election may be acknowledged, but not as election by God and without acknowledgment of final judgment; judgment may be acknowledged, but not as judgment by God and not in the context of election; election may be acknowledged precisely as election for terminal judgment, but not for consummation. Throughout it needs to be kept in mind that the distortions of personal identity in view here are distortions of personal identities inasmuch as they are joyfully hopeful responses to God relating in eschatological blessing.

Bound in a Distorted Identity: Acknowledging Election without Judgment

Personal bodies' identities are distorted when they are defined by an acknowledgment of election for a social role or function that is necessary for the well-being of their proximate contexts. It may be acknowledgment of a conservative role to protect proximate contexts from radical change through deterioration. Or it may be a liberal role to promote radical reformation for the better. It does not matter whether the acknowledgment of election to such roles is conscious and explicit or unconscious and implicit in personal bodies' actions. Either way, such acknowledgment defines the personal identities of those whose lives are invested in roles in their societies that, in however minor a way, save the societies, either by helping to protect them from perceived inner and outer enemies or by participating in social movements to improve them socially and morally. Such acknowledgment conflates election for eschatological consummation with election for a social role. Insofar as personal bodies' basic identities are in fact defined by and given to them by the triune God drawing them to eschatological consummation, identities formed in these ways are distorted identities.

The personal identity of a personal body distorted in these ways is bound in and bound by some social role or function. Inasmuch as his identity is formed by his acknowledgment of his election to some task for the well-being of his proximate context, his answer to the question, "Who am I?" is "I am town office holder, or community organizer, or middle manager, or entrepreneur and employer, or community service organization leader, or spouse, or parent, or teacher, or religious leader, etc. That is who I am."

When such a role defines one's personal identity, one's identity is in bondage to that role. That role is who one is. If one fails to fill the role, one has at least been untrue to one's identity, and has perhaps lost it entirely. One can then no longer say who one is.

This is a doubly constricting bondage. The roles and functions that define such personal identities are pre-formed by the society and are prior to any given personal body. Hence, the range of types of personal identity a personal body may have is constricted by the particular ways in which their proximate contexts have predefined the social roles or functions that may define their identities. If one's personal identity is defined by the socially predefined role one plays in one's proximate context—even if, indeed, especially if it is a role ordered to a proposed moral improvement of that context—then one's identity cannot be defined in a way that transcends society's predefinition of such roles. One's identity is constrained by the limits of the society's creativity regarding the roles within it that contribute to its moral improvement. "Who we are" and "who I am" are then no more than products of our proximate contexts.

Identities bound in this fashion are constricted in a second way. Every personal body in fact fills a multitude of social roles and functions. Different roles usually engage different subsets of personal bodies' powers. When one's personal identity is defined by just one of those roles, no matter how important it is for the quotidian's well-being or how personally rewarding it is, only those powers engaged by the role are acknowledged as part of who one is. By contrast, when one's personal identity is formed by acknowledgment of election for eschatological consummation, all of the social roles and functions one fills and the entirety of one's powers are acknowledged as parts of one's identity, but none are acknowledged as definitive of, or the basis of, one's identity. Therefore, one is free to leave off roles and take on new ones without being untrue to who one basically is, or risking loss of personal identity altogether.

These theological remarks about distorted personal identities resonate with well-known analysis of emotional problems created by self-images defined by particular social roles ("Who am I? I'm only a housewife; or, I'm only an office drone"; or "I am the founder of a highly successful enterprise"). Acute and searching analyses of emotional problems created by poor or restricted self-images have played powerfully helpful roles in psychological therapy, for which one can only give thanks. However, the theological remarks made here about distorted personal identities involve a different type of claim about personal bodies' identities—namely, there is an objective dimension to human personal bodies' personal identities that is who they basically are, independent of their pictures of themselves and how they feel about themselves. Even a distorted personal identity is who she is objectively. It is not reducible to how she feels about herself or how she images herself.

In the perspective of a theocentric anthropology, the first-person answer to the question, "Who am I/who are we?" is, "This is who I have been called and elected to be by God, regardless of how I may feel about it. This is who I basically am. This is just the way it is so far as my personal identity is concerned." Such an answer is an acknowledgment of one's objective basic personal identity. As a self-involving act of acknowledgment, it at the same time constitutes a quotidian personal identity that is congruent with one's basic personal identity because in it one defines one's quotidian identity as grounded in the triune God's ways of relating to one. To this first-person description is conjoined the third-person theocentric remark, "And personal identities shaped by the types of acknowledgments that, however implicitly, ground certain of these identities elsewhere than in God relating to them are, in fact, distorted identities."

Distorted hopeful personal identities acknowledge an election that comes without judgment. As we saw in chapter 15, personal bodies' undistorted personal identity is formed by acknowledgment of their election for eschatological consummation that, given the distortions of their existential hows, their bondage in living deaths, and the moral ambiguities of their distorted proximate contexts, is also necessarily a final and decisive judgment on them. Indeed, that is part of what makes such election liberating: those who have been elected have therewith also undergone the worst possible crisis; there is no more ultimate calamity left to fear. By contrast, election to a social role or function that makes for deep social or cultural change in the quotidian is not an election that brings judgment with it. Such election comes without judgment, and to acknowledge election to such a role does not involve acknowledgment of one's having already been judged.

Rather, it sets the elect up for a wholly future judgment on their faithfulness and success in filling the role to which they have been elected and which defines their personal identities. Personal identities distorted in this way are identities that are hostage to the outcomes of their exercise of the social functions to which they acknowledge being elected. Where undistorted hopeful personal identities are the identities of personal bodies living on borrowed eschatological time, distorted personal identities are lived in bondage to the moral ambiguities of outcomes of projects making for social improvement in the quotidian's own future.

Personal identities distorted in these ways may be defined by acknowledgment of either of at least two types of election. Personal bodies' identities will be bound in such distortion if they are formed by acknowledgment of an election by society to particular social roles. Many societies exert more or less subtle pressures on the young to prepare for and take up particular social roles that are necessary for the society's enhanced well-being. When those pressures come to bear on someone largely by virtue of accidents of gender or of birth into a particular family or social class whose members have traditionally filled those roles, such election may be experienced as a kind of fate.

Personal bodies' identities may also be bound in such distortion if they are formed by acknowledgment of their election, in effect, by themselves to fill particular roles in their social proximate contexts. In some societies, personal bodies are relatively free to assess their own interests and talents and, on that basis, select one of the roles or functions their society has already defined. This freedom is, of course, a value especially prized in emancipated, liberal, post-Enlightenment societies' myths about themselves. To the extent that such freedom is socially actualized, it is arguably a morally desirable achievement. Nonetheless, societies that celebrate such freedom thereby also generate considerable social pressure on the personal bodies shaped by them to elect themselves, in effect, for some social role that will make for the moral and material improvement of their social and cultural proximate contexts as though that were election for the eschatological transformation of those contexts and of themselves. From a theocentric perspective, that is their society's invitation to—indeed, social pressure on—personal bodies to distort their personal identities.

It does not matter whether they were elected by society or by themselves for tasks making for the quotidian's well-being. In neither case do personal bodies with such identities acknowledge an election by that which is eccentric to them in the peculiar way in which the triune God is eccentric to personal bodies in electing them for eschatological consummation. The consequence in either case is the same structural distortion of their personal identities.

Given that, precisely as personal, personal bodies are inherently social bodies, personal identities formed in either of these ways will be instances of the characterization of sin (in the singular) as *incurvatus a se*, being turned in on oneself. *Incurvatus a se* is a structural, but not necessarily a psychological, description of such distorted personal identities. That is, such identities are not necessarily marked by the psychological dynamics of conscious or unconscious self-preoccupation which is so closed in on itself that it is incapable of self-forgetfulness in concern for another. The limiting case of such psychological dynamics is, perhaps, the narcissistic personality. However, whether psychologically self-preoccupied or not, personal identities distorted in this way do all have the following structure: they are identities turned in on themselves in that they are identities formed by acknowledgment of election from within their proximate contexts to a role that makes for their proximate contexts' well-being, a role that is predefined by their proximate contexts, binding them into their proximate contexts in ways they cannot escape without losing just those identities.

Human personal bodies' personal identities are also distorted in a bondage to social role or function when they are shaped by acknowledgment of election by God to a role for the well-being of the quotidian as though it were election to a role in a project to bringing eschatological—radical—transformation. As we saw in chapter 11, such conflation of eschatologically radical change of the quotidian and massive improvement in the quotidian's well-being grounded in its inherent resources also characterizes one type of personal identity distorted by distorted faithfulness to God relating to it creatively. In such cases, a personal identity's distortion in distorted hope coincides with its distortion in distorted faithfulness.

Personal identities distorted in this way do not necessarily exhibit the structure of *incurvatus a se*. They are formed by acknowledgment of an election by One who *is* genuinely eccentric to them. However, they are formed by an acknowledgment that confuses election by God to a social role making for the quotidian's well-being with election by God for the radical transformation that comes by eschatological consummation. Despite being shaped by acknowledgment of God's election, they are nonetheless distorted personal identities.

Whether formed by acknowledgment of election by society, by themselves, or by God, all such hopeful personal identities are sinful because they are distortions of personal bodies' basic identities as ones elect by the triune God for eschatological consummation. They are identities bound in sin in the singular. "Sinful" marks who they are, not just how they are. All hopeful personal identities whatever are formed by personal bodies' acknowledgment of election, acknowledgment that they are destined to participate in something that makes a change for the better for their proximate contexts, including themselves. However, acknowledgment of election specifically by the triune God's eschatological consummation of them grounds a hopeful personal identity that is radically free of definition by the quotidian. It is free of definition by the quotidian because it has already passed through final judgment and is in no way subject as a personal identity to evaluation according to criteria of excellence inherent in the practices constituted by social roles predefined in their proximate contexts.

As creaturely personal bodies in community in shared proximate contexts, they continue, of course, to fill many social roles and social status. Inherent in the socially constructed practices by which they fill those roles and status are standards of excellence by which their enactments of those practices will be assessed. In those regards, they will be deemed relative successes or failures. However, because their basic personal identity is defined by God's election of them as among those drawn to eschatological consummation and by the final and definitive judgment they have already undergone by the concrete inauguration of that consummation in the midst of the distortions of their quotidian proximate contexts, existential hows, and bondage in living death, none of those assessments of success and failure in filling their roles and status in their quotidian proximate contexts defines who they basically are.

Distorted versions of hopeful identities, on the other hand, are lived at cross-grain to their basic identities. They are lived bound in and bound to the quotidian's predefined roles and subject to the judgments passed on the outcomes of the practices of the personal bodies who fill those roles. It makes no difference whether that judgment is expected to come from God in a wholly future end time, or is expected to come simply out of the quotidian's own future ("what our successors will say"). In particular, the ground and measure of the value of their lives is their success in radically (eschatologically) transforming their proximate contexts for the better through the social roles and functions to which they understand themselves to be elected; hence, failure to achieve such transformation by definition undercuts the value of their lives.

Such bondage in distorted personal identities is a living death. Distorted identities are distortions of personal identities of living personal bodies. But as distortions untrue to their real, God-given identities, they are identities that bind personal bodies in ways that constrict their eschatological freedom vis à vis their proximate contexts and constrict their exercise of their rich array of powers within their proximate contexts. Who such personal bodies are is a kind of entombment in the quotidian.

Bound in Distorted Identities: Acknowledging Final Judgment without Election

Personal bodies' hopeful identities are distorted in a second way if they are defined by acknowledgment of a fundamentally positive judgment on them, but without any acknowledgment of election by God to eschatological consummation. The identity descriptions they give in answer to the questions "Who are we?" and "Who am I?" take the form of stories whose plots are optimistic rather than eschatologically hopeful.

598 | CONSUMMATED: LIVING ON BORROWED TIME

I urged in chapter 16 that optimism is a distortion of eschatological hopefulness. The very structure of optimistic narrative identity descriptions expresses acknowledgment of a positive final judgment that will be warranted by the final outcome of a progressive developmental dynamic inherent in the quotidian. It is a dynamic that inexorably works across time for the increased well-being and, when necessary, radical social and cultural change, of personal bodies' proximate contexts. Thus, optimism is a type of hope—namely, hope that history will pass a positive judgment on our proximate contexts, and therewith on us, because the dynamic at work within our quotidians will in time make them radically more just and good societies. Such a hope for final positive judgment is based on a human society's own assessment of its proximate creaturely context's resources and dynamics, rather than being the judgment that comes with the triune God's election of personal bodies for an eschatological blessing, whose dynamic is not inherent in God's creative blessing. When personal identities are formed by acknowledgment of such a future positive judgment, those identities are appropriately described in optimistic stories rather than in eschatologically hopeful stories. What is rendered in such stories are distorted hopeful identities.

A hallmark of such personal identities is the absence of acknowledgment of any type of election. Since they are not formed by acknowledgment of the triune God's final judgment on them, they also are not formed by acknowledgment of the divine election for eschatological transformation, that necessarily also brings judgment if the transformation is concretely inaugurated in the context of distorted quotidian proximate contexts, personal bodies' distorted existential hows, and bondage in living deaths. Neither are they formed by personal bodies' acknowledgment of election, whether by society, themselves, or God, to any social role or function that makes for radical moral change in their proximate contexts. If there is a dynamic inherent in the very structure of their proximate contexts that, across time, moves change in those contexts in the direction of radical social and cultural improvement, then the concept of the election to a particular destiny has no place. From this perspective, fundamental to the very nature of the entire context of personal bodies' lives, and therewith to their lives as well, is a dynamic inherent in their proximate context moving them and their lived worlds to a final culminating state, a final destiny. Personal bodies may be actively, perhaps inevitably, engaged in practices whose governing purposes acknowledge that dynamic and are coherent with its goal. But in such a context it would be odd to say they were "elected" to engage in such practices.

Inasmuch as they are formed by acknowledgment of a future final judgment that they and their proximate contexts have become radically better in the future, personal identities distorted in this fashion are bound to precisely that judgment. In that case, they are also bound to the assessment that inherent in their proximate contexts are both a dynamic making for radical social and moral improvement, and the resources needed to achieve that improvement. That is to put the point too abstractly. In concrete actuality, personal identities distorted in this way are in bondage to some ideology. That is, they are identities in bondage to some theory about the dynamics of social and moral progress in history.

Such bondage to ideology may indicate that this sort of distorted identity is peculiar to the modern period. Certainly, modernity has been awash with explicit, formal, systematic, critical theories about history's progressive dynamics. Some have been transcendentally ontological theories (e.g., sundry Hegelianisms); some have been economic theory (from classic capitalism, through various versions of socialism and Marxism, back more recently to free-market, transnational capitalism); some have been psychosexual theory; some have attempted to synthesize economic and psychosexual theory. Some such view, perhaps vaguely absorbed from the culture, may equally well be held implicitly, informally, unsystematically, and uncritically as the basis of an optimistic judgment about the quotidian's future. To the extent that a personal body's identity is formed by acknowledgment of such a positive future and final judgment on the basis of such ideology, it is in bondage to such ideology.

Personal bodies whose identities are in bondage to some such ideology live a specific type of living death because they are lived at cross-grain to creaturely finitude. They live as ones whose identities are shaped by acknowledgment of a finally positive judgment grounded in historical dynamics that are said to be inherent in the quotidian and make for long-term moral improvement. However, from a theocentric perspective guided by canonical Wisdom literature's creation theology, the creaturely quotidian has no inherent overriding dynamic moving proximate contexts across time toward radical social and moral improvement. Ecclesiastes, we noted, presses against conventional Wisdom theology to test its compatibility with just such a nonoptimistic theological judgment. The hopefulness of personal bodies' undistorted identities is grounded in the triune God's drawing them with their proximate contexts to an eschatological blessing that is logically and conceptually distinct from God's creative blessing; what promises radical transformation of the quotidian is precisely not a dynamic inherent in the deep structure of God's gift of creatureliness. Such is the character of personal bodies' contexts, ultimate and proximate.

Personal identities defined optimistically are perpetually at risk of invalidation by random and arbitrary conflicts in the interactions of finite creaturely centers of power. Such identities preserve themselves from disillusion in the face of this risk by a certain rigidity of thought, emotion, and imagination. The rigidity is required in order to deny evidence that they live at cross-grain to their contexts. To live such an identity is a living death.

Bound in Distorted Identities: Acknowledging Election
for Negative Final Judgment Only

Insofar as they are future oriented, personal bodies' identities are distorted in a third way when they are formed by acknowledgment of election for a finally negative judgment on them and their proximate contexts. The identity descriptions they give in answer to the questions, "Who are we?" and "Who am I?" have the form of stories whose plots are pessimistic rather than eschatologically hopeful.

The structure of pessimistic narrative identity descriptions expresses acknowledgment of the negative judgment that there are no sure grounds on which to expect the long-term well-being of personal bodies and their proximate contexts. The hallmark of such narrative identity descriptions, however, is the fated character of this negative judgment. They are stories that say, in effect, "Who we are is this: Those elected, whether by blind fate or by God's wrath, to live in finite, conflictual proximate contexts no aspects of which that promises future transformation."

There are two versions of personal identities distorted in this way. One is simply pessimistic; the other is the limiting case of pessimistic personal identities, the despairing personal identity.

When personal bodies' identities are formed by an acknowledgment of a negative judgment on their prospects for radical transformation, based on a negative assessment of the dynamics and resources for radical change inherent in their proximate contexts, they are formed as pessimistic identities in the proper sense of the term. Such identities may be minimally hopeful in the sense that they are open to the possibility that unforeseen changes might generate possibilities and resources for radical change in the quotidian. They may be open to such possibilities; they do not expect them. Pessimistic identities count as distorted versions of joyfully hopeful personal identities for the obvious reason that hopefulness is nearly extinguished in pessimistic personal identities.

What makes pessimism a distortion of eschatologically hopeful personal identity is not that it expects no radical change of the quotidian on the strength of its own resources. Given the combination of the limits of creaturely quotidian proximate contexts' powers and resources and the profundity of their distortions in consequence of personal bodies' inappropriate responses to the triune God's ways of relating to them, it is realistic not to expect radical changes of the quotidian on the strength of its own resources.

As a deformity of eschatological hopefulness, pessimism is simply the obverse of optimism. Both are grounded in assessment of the dynamics and resources for radical social and moral change that are inherent in the quotidian. What makes pessimism a distortion of eschatological hopeful identity is what makes optimism a distortion: both are structural distortions of identities defined, not by assessment of the dynamics and resources inherent in creaturely quotidian proximate contexts, but by the triune God's concrete inauguration of fully actualized eschatological consummation in the resurrection of the crucified Jesus.

On the other hand, when personal bodies' identities are formed by acknowledgment of a negative judgment about their prospects for radical transformation, not on the basis of an assessment of the quotidian's resources, but on the basis of God's election of them for just that judgment, then they are formed as desperate identities in the proper sense of the word. Their self-identity description is, "We are those judged negatively by God and condemned to life in evil and fundamentally untransformable quotidian contexts." Such despair is the total absence of hope, closed even to the bare possibility of unimagined transformation. Desperate personal identities are the limiting case of distortions of hopeful personal identities.

Personal bodies whose future-oriented personal identities are distorted in these ways live in bondage to the living death of perpetual victimhood. The stories by which they render their personal identities all say, in effect, "Who we are is this: Those who either were fated by the limited resources afforded by their proximate contexts or who were condemned by God to lives that cannot radically change." To have one's personal identity defined as one who is a victim of x (the possible variables are innumerable) without hope of transformation of x, is to be bound in a living death.

I urged in chapter 7 that insofar as personal identities are present-oriented, they are appropriately defined by faithful trust in God and loyalty to God's creative project as something to be delighted in and given thanks for in itself, and not because of a future state of affairs that will develop out of it. I urged in chapter 14 that insofar as personal identities are future-oriented, they are appropriately defined by hope in God's promise of eschatological blessing, a promise proleptically inaugurated in the quotidian by God's resurrection of the crucified Jesus but not yet fully actualized. Future-oriented personal identities distorted in the ways that are in view in this chapter are in bondage to the living death of pessimistic victimhood because they are defined, not by acknowledgment of God's eschatological promise, but by the reality of the moral and ontological ambiguity of the creaturely here and now. Or they are in bondage to the living death of despairing victimhood because they are personal identities defined by acknowledgment of God's election, but rather than acknowledging election to an eschatological blessing that is not inherent in creaturely blessing, they acknowledge election to a creaturehood whose finitude amounts to victimization because it promises no transformed future. In either case, future-oriented personal identities that are basically defined by the distorted quotidian here and now are thereby in bondage to living death.

Bound Identities and Obscured Eschatological Glory

Sin in the singular is distortion of personal bodies' identities that places them in bondage. To be in sin is to be in bondage. What I argued in chapter 11 in connection with distortion of personal identities insofar as they are present-oriented also applies to this discussion of distortion of personal identities insofar as they are future-oriented: Personal bodies' bondage in sin in the singular is part of what the tradition calls "original sin."

Traditional doctrines of original sin give both a descriptive account of a condition in which human persons find themselves and a genetic account of how that condition afflicts them. The account given here of sin in the singular brackets any effort to give a genetic account of this condition and reformulates central features of traditional descriptions of the condition of original sin: that sin in the singular is not essential to what personal bodies are; that it entails personal bodies' loss of a specific freedom; that it is universal; that it is in a certain way culpable; and that it gives to death a power over human life it otherwise would not have. The arguments advanced in chapter 11 to demonstrate the isomorphism between my account of bondage in sin in the singular and the descriptive aspect of classical original sin doctrine applies *mutatis mutandi* to the analysis in this chapter of distorted future-oriented personal identities and need not be repeated with relevant variations here.

The living death of bondage in distorted future-oriented personal identities obscures the reflection of God's eschatological glory in personal bodies. It does not necessarily wholly annul that reflection. Nonetheless, bondage in living death does obscure that reflection so that personal bodies become unable to respond to one another with hope's eccentric, temporally tensed, passionate joy. They become unable to look on one another with joy.